# The Complete England FC 1872-2020

Dirk Karsdorp

British Library Cataloguing in Publication Data
A catalogue record for this book is available from the British Library

ISBN 978-1-86223-441-3

Copyright © 2020, SOCCER BOOKS LIMITED. (01472 696226)
72 St. Peter's Avenue, Cleethorpes, N.E. Lincolnshire, DN35 8HU, England

All rights are reserved. No part of this publication may be reproduced, stored in a retrieval system or transmitted, in any form or by any means, electronic, mechanical, photocopying, recording, or otherwise, without the prior written permission of Soccer Books Limited.

**Printed in the UK by Severn**

# FOREWORD

Three years ago we published a book covering the international games played by England from the very first international match against Scotland in 1872 through to 2017. This new edition brings these statistics right up to date to the end of 2020 and, as before, lists full team line-ups and goalscorers for both England and their opponents.

Only officially-recognised full international games are included in this book and other titles updated to 2020 in this series are also available for Scotland, Wales, Northern Ireland and the Republic of Ireland. We have also published new books containing complete statistics for the international matches of Belgium, Italy and the Netherlands.

Although we have endeavoured to include statistics which are as complete as possible, inevitably there are omissions with one or two small pieces of information missing for a handful of games. Most notably, the times at which goals were scored were not recorded for a number of the earliest games although the goalscorers themselves are known. In such cases, the following symbol has been used to indicate that the time of the goal is not known: "#".

1.   30.11.1872
**SCOTLAND v ENGLAND  0-0**
*West of Scotland Cricket Ground, Glasgow*
Referee: William Keay (Scotland)    Attendance: 3,000
**SCOTLAND**: Robert Gardner (Cap), Joseph Taylor, William Ker, James Thomson, James Smith, William Muir MacKinnon, James Begg Weir, Robert Leckie, David N. Wotherspoon, Robert Smith, Alexander Rhind.
**ENGLAND**: Robert Barker, Ernest Harwood Greenhalgh, Reginald de Courtenay Welch, Frederick Maddison, William John Maynard, John Brockbank, John Charles Clegg, Arnold Kirke Smith, Cuthbert John Ottaway (Cap), Charles John Chenery, Charles John Morice.


2.   08.03.1873
**ENGLAND v SCOTLAND  4-2**  (2-0)
*Kennington Oval, London*
Referee:  T. Lloyd (England)    Attendance: 3,000
**ENGLAND**: Alexander Morton (Cap), Ernest Harwood Greenhalgh, Leonard Sidgwick Howell, Alfred George Goodwyn, Robert Walpole Sealy Vidal, Pelham George Von Donop, Charles John Chenery, William Edwin Clegg, Alexander George Bonsor, William Kenyon-Slaney, George Hubert Hugh Heron.
**SCOTLAND**:  Robert W. Gardner (Cap), Joseph Taylor, William Ker, James J. Thomson, Robert Smith, William Muir MacKinnon, Henry Waugh Renny-Tailyour, Arthur Fitzgerald Kinnaird, John Edward Blackburn, William Gibb, David N. Wotherspoon.
**Goals**:  William Kenyon-Slaney (1, 75), Alexander George Bonsor (10), Charles John Chenery (85) / Henry Waugh Renny-Tailyour (#), William Gibb (70)


3.  07.03.1874
**SCOTLAND v ENGLAND  2-1**  (1-1)
*West of Scotland Cricket Ground, Glasgow*
Referee:  Rae (Scotland)    Attendance: 7,000
**SCOTLAND**:  Robert W. Gardner, John Hunter, Joseph Taylor, Charles Campbell, James J. Thomson (Cap), James Begg Weir, John Ferguson, Henry McNeil, William Muir MacKinnon, Angus McKinnon, Frederick Anderson.
**ENGLAND**:  Reginald de Courtenay Welch, Robert Andrew Muter MacIndoe Ogilvie, Alfred Hugh Stratford, Cuthbert John Ottaway (Cap), Francis Hornby Birley, Charles Henry Reynolds Wollaston, Robert Kennett Kingsford, John Hawley Edwards, Charles John Chenery, George Hubert Hugh Heron, John Robert Blayney Owen.
**Goal**:  Frederick Anderson (42), Angus McKinnon (47) / Robert Kennett Kingsford (28)


4.   06.03.1875
**ENGLAND v SCOTLAND  2-2**  (1-1)
*Kennington Oval, London*
Referee: Marindin (England)    Attendance: 2,000
**ENGLAND**: William Henry Carr, Edward Brownlow Haygarth, William Stepney Rawson, Francis Hornby Birley, Pelham George Von Donop, Charles Henry Reynolds Wollaston, Charles William Alcock (Cap), Herbert Edward Rawson, Alexander George Bonsor, George Hubert Hugh Heron, Richard Lyon Geaves.
**SCOTLAND**:  Robert W. Gardner, John Hunter, Joseph Taylor (Cap), Alexander Kennedy, Alexander McLintock, James Begg Weir, William Muir MacKinnon, Henry McNeil, Thomas Cochrane Highet, Peter Andrews, John McPherson.
**Goals**:  Charles Henry Reynolds Wollaston (5), Charles William Alcock (70) / Henry McNeil (#), Peter Andrews (75)


5.   04.03.1876
**SCOTLAND v ENGLAND  3-0**  (3-0)
*West of Scotland Cricket Ground, Glasgow*
Referee: Mitchell (Scotland)    Attendance: 16,000
**SCOTLAND**: Alexander McGeoch, Joseph Taylor (Cap), John Hunter, Alexander McLintock, Alexander Kennedy, Henry McNeil, William Muir MacKinnon, Thomas Cochrane Highet, William Miller, John Ferguson, John Campbell Baird.
**ENGLAND**:  Arthur Henry Patrick Savage, Thomas Frederick Green, Edgar Field, Ernest Henry Bambridge, Beaumont Griffith Jarrett, George Hubert Hugh Heron, Arthur William Cursham, Charles Francis William Heron (Cap), Charles Eastlake Smith, Walter Scott Buchanan, William John Maynard.
**Goals**:  William Muir MacKinnon (8), Henry McNeil (12), Thomas Cochrane Highet (16)


6.  03.03.1877
**ENGLAND v SCOTLAND  1-3**  (0-1)
*Kennington Oval, London*
Referee:  Robert Ogilvie (England)    Attendance: 1,200
**ENGLAND**:  Morton Peto Betts, William Lindsay, Lindsay Bury, William Stepney Rawson (Cap), Beaumont Griffith Jarrett, Charles Henry Reynolds Wollaston, Arthur William Cursham, Alfred Lyttelton, Cecil-Vernon Wingfield-Stratford, John Bain, William Mosforth.
**SCOTLAND**:  Alexander McGeoch, Robert W. Neill, Thomas C. Vallance, Charles Campbell (Cap), James Phillips, James Tassie Richmond, William Muir MacKinnon, John C. McGregor, John McDougall, John Smith, John Ferguson.
**Goal**:  Alfred Lyttelton (55) /
John Ferguson (#, 86), James Tassie Richmond (48)

7.  02.03.1878

**SCOTLAND v ENGLAND  7-2**  (4-0)

*First Hampden Park, Glasgow*

Referee: Dick (Scotland)    Attendance: 15,000

**SCOTLAND**: Robert W. Gardner, Andrew McIntyre, Thomas C. Vallance, Charles Campbell (Cap), Alexander Kennedy, James Tassie Richmond, John C. McGregor, John McDougall, Thomas Cochrane Highet, William Muir MacKinnon, Henry McNeil.

**ENGLAND**: Conrad Warner, Edward Lyttelton, John Hunter, Norman Coles Bailey, Beaumont Griffith Jarrett, Arthur William Cursham (Cap), Percy Fairclough, Henry Wace, John George Wylie, George Hubert Hugh Heron, William Mosforth.

**Goals**: John McDougall (7, 41, 46), John C. McGregor (32), Henry McNeil (39, 70), William Muir MacKinnon (62) / John George Wylie (65), Arthur William Cursham (75)

8.  18.01.1879

**ENGLAND v WALES  2-1**  (2-0)

*Kennington Oval, London*

Referee: Richard Segal Bastard (England)    Att: 2,000

**ENGLAND**: Rupert Darnley Anderson, Lindsay Bury, Claude William Wilson, Norman Coles Bailey, William Edwin Clegg, Edward Hagarty Parry, Thomas H. Sorby, Arthur W. Cursham (Cap), Henry Wace, William Mosforth, Herbert Whitfeld.

**WALES**: George William Glascodine, Samuel Llewelyn Kenrick, George Garnet Higham, William Williams, Thomas Owen, William Henry Davies, Watkin William Shone, Dennis Heywood, John Henry Price, William Digby Owen, William Roberts I.

**Goals**: Herbert Whitfeld (8), Thomas Heathcote Sorby (20) / William Henry Davies (45)

Due to very poor weather conditions, two halves of 30 minutes each were played in this game.

9.  05.04.1879

**ENGLAND v SCOTLAND  5-4**  (1-4)

*Kennington Oval, London*

Referee: Wollaston (England)    Attendance: 4,500

**ENGLAND**: Reginald Halsey Birkett, Harold Morse, Edward Christian, Norman Coles Bailey, James Frederick McLeod Prinsep, Arnold Frank Hills, Arthur Copeland Goodyer, Henry Wace (Cap), Francis John Sparks, Edward Charles Bambridge, William Mosforth.

**SCOTLAND**: Robert Parlane, William S. Somers, Henry McNeil, Thomas C. Vallance, Charles Campbell (Cap), John Campbell McLeod McPherson, Robert Paton, William Wightman Beveridge, John Smith, John McDougall, William Muir MacKinnon.

**Goals**: William Mosforth (5), Edward C. Bambridge (48, 83) Arthur Goodyer (60), Norman Coles Bailey (75) / William Muir MacKinnon (15, 41), John McDougall (23), John Smith (26)

10.  13.03.1880

**SCOTLAND v ENGLAND  5-4**  (3-2)

*First Hampden Park, Glasgow*

Referee: Donald Hamilton (Scotland)    Attendance: 10,000

**SCOTLAND**: Archibald Rowan, Alexander McLintock, Robert W. Neill (Cap), Charles Campbell, John Campbell McLeod McPherson, John Smith, Moses McLay McNeil, George Ker, John C. McGregor, John Campbell Baird, John Leck Kay.

**ENGLAND**: Harry Albemarle Swepstone, Thomas Brindle, Edwin Luntley, Norman Coles Bailey, John Hunter, Charles Henry Reynolds Wollaston (Cap), Richard Segal Bastard, Francis John Sparks, Samuel Weller Widdowson, William Mosforth, Edward Charles Bambridge.

**Goals**: George Ker (5, 44, 48), John Campbell Baird (39), John Leck Kay (67) / William Mosforth (8), Edward Charles Bambridge (42, 87), Francis John Sparks (89)

11.  15.03.1880

**WALES v ENGLAND  2-3**  (0-0)

*Racecourse Ground, Wrexham*

Referee: Robert Lythgoe (England)    Attendance: 3,000

**WALES**: Harold Hibbott, John Richard Morgan, John Powell, Henry Valentine Edwards, William Williams, William Pierce Owen, William Henry Davies, Thomas Boden, John Henry Price, John Roberts, William Roberts.

**ENGLAND**: John Sands, Edwin Luntley, Thomas Brindle, John Hunter, Frederick William Hargreaves, Thomas Marshall, Henry Alfred Cursham, Francis John Sparks (Cap), Clement Mitchell, Edward Johnson, William Mosforth.

**Goals**: John Roberts (#), William Roberts (#) / Francis John Sparks (50, 70), Thomas Brindle (55)

12.  26.02.1881

**ENGLAND v WALES  0-1**  (0-0)

*Alexandra Meadows, Blackburn*

Referee: Richard Segal Bastard (England)    Att: 3,000

**ENGLAND**: John Purvis Hawtrey, Alfred Harvey, Arthur Leopold Bambridge, John Hunter (Cap), Frederick William Hargreaves, Thomas Marshall, Tot Rostron, James Brown, George Tait, John Hargreaves, William Mosforth.

**WALES**: Robert McMillan, John Richard Morgan, Samuel Llewelyn Kenrick, William Stafford Bell, William Williams, William Pierce Owen, Thomas Lewis, Knyvett Crosse, John Henry Price, Uriah Goodwin, John Vaughan.

**Goal**: John Vaughan (34)

### 13.  12.03.1881
**ENGLAND v SCOTLAND 1-6** (0-1)

*Kennington Oval, London*

Referee: Marindin (England)    Attendance: 8,500

**ENGLAND**: John Purvis Hawtrey, Edgar Field, Claude William Wilson, Norman Coles Bailey (Cap), John Hunter, George Holden, Tot Rostron, Reginald Heber Macauley, Clement Mitchell, Edward Charles Bambridge, John Hargreaves.

**SCOTLAND**: George Gillespie, Andrew Watson, Thomas C. Vallance, Charles Campbell (Cap), David Davidson, David Hill, William McGuire, George Ker, Joseph Lindsay, Henry McNeil, John Smith.

**Goal**: Edward Charles Bambridge (64) /
John Smith (10, 69, 79), David Hill (53), George Ker (74, 89)

### 14.  18.02.1882
**IRELAND v ENGLAND 0-13** (0-5)

*Bloomfield Park, Belfast*

Referee: Robert Kennedy (Ireland)    Attendance: 2,500

**IRELAND**: James Hamilton, John McRedy McAlery, Donald Rattray, David Martin, John Hastings, James Buckle, William McWha, Dr. John Robert Davison, John Sinclair, Alick H. Dill, D. McCaw.

**ENGLAND**: John Frederick P. Rawlinson, Alfred Thomas Carrick Dobson, Doctor Haydock Greenwood, Frederick William Hargreaves, Robert Stuart King, Edward Charles Bambridge (Cap), Horace Hutton Barnet, Arthur Brown, James Brown, Oliver Howard Vaughton, Henry Alfred Cursham.

**Goals**: Oliver H. Vaughton (5 goals), Arthur Brown (4 goals), James Brown (#, #), Henry Alfred Cursham (#), Edward Charles Bambridge (#)

The times at which the goals were scored not recorded.

### 15.  11.03.1882
**SCOTLAND v ENGLAND 5-1** (2-1)

*First Hampden Park, Glasgow*

Referee: Wallace (Scotland)    Attendance: 10,000

**SCOTLAND**: George Gillespie, Andrew Watson, Andrew McIntyre, Charles Campbell (Cap), Peter Miller, Malcolm James Eadie Fraser, William Anderson, George Ker, William Harrower, John Leck Kay, Robert McPherson.

**ENGLAND**: Harry Albemarle Swepstone, Doctor Haydock Greenwood, Alfred Jones, Norman Coles Bailey (Cap), John Hunter, Henry Alfred Cursham, Edward Hagarty Parry, Arthur Brown, Oliver Howard Vaughton, William Mosforth, Edward Charles Bambridge.

**Goal**: William Harrower (15), George Ker (43, 70) Robert McPherson (46), John Leck Kay (85) /
Oliver Howard Vaughton (35)

### 16.  13.03.1882
**WALES v ENGLAND 5-3** (1-3)

*Racecourse Ground, Wrexham*

Referee: Morgan Roberts (England)    Attendance: 5,000

**WALES**: Harry Adams, John Richard Morgan, John Powell, Henry Valentine Edwards, Frederick William Hughes, William Williams, William Pierce Owen, Walter Hugh Roberts, John Henry Price, John Roberts, John Vaughan.

**ENGLAND**: Harry Albemarle Swepstone, John Hunter, Alfred Jones, Norman Coles Bailey (Cap), Edward Charles Bambridge, Edward Hagarty Parry, Henry Alfred Cursham, Percival Chase Parr, Arthur Brown, Oliver Howard Vaughton, William Mosforth.

**Goals**: William Pierce Owen (#, #), John Richard Morgan (#), Alfred Jones (# og), John Vaughan (#) /
William Mosforth (30), Edward Hagarty Parry (35), Henry Alfred Cursham (48)

### 17.  03.02.1883
**ENGLAND v WALES 5-0** (2-0)

*Kennington Oval, London*

Referee: Donald Hamilton (Scotland)    Attendance: 2,000

**ENGLAND**: Harry Albemarle Swepstone, Percy John de Paravincini, Bruce Bremner Russell, Norman Coles Bailey (Cap), Stuart Macrae, Arthur William Cursham, Arthur Leopold Bambridge, Clement Mitchell, Harry Chester Goodhart, Henry Alfred Cursham, Edward Charles Bambridge.

**WALES**: Harry Adams, John Richard Morgan, John Powell, Thomas Burke, Frederick William Hughes, Walter Hugh Roberts, William Pierce Owen, John Price Davies, William Roberts, John Roberts, John Vaughan.

**Goals**: Clement Mitchell (16, 70, 90), Edward C. Bambridge (43), Arthur William Cursham (65)

### 18.  24.02.1883
**ENGLAND v IRELAND 7-0** (4-0)

*Aigburth Cricket Ground, Liverpool*

Referee: John McDowall (Scotland)    Attendance: 2,500

**ENGLAND**: Harry Albemarle Swepstone, Percy John de Paravincini, Henry Thomas Moore, John Hudson (Cap), Stuart Macrae, Oliver Whateley, Francis William Pawson, Harry Chester Goodhart, Arthur Tempest Blakiston Dunn, William Nevill Cobbold, Henry Alfred Cursham.

**IRELAND**: James Rankine, James Watson, Donald Rattray, Thomas Bryson Molyneux, David C. Martin, William J. Morrow, Renwick M.C. Potts, William McWha, Dr. John Robert Davison, John Reid, E. Arthur Spiller.

**Goals**: Oliver Whateley (15, 47), William N. Cobbold (17, 19), Arthur Tempest Blakiston Dunn (43, 80), Francis William Pawson (88)

19. 10.03.1883
**ENGLAND v SCOTLAND 2-3** (2-2)

*Bramall Lane, Sheffield*

Referee: John Sinclair (Ireland)   Attendance: 7,000

**ENGLAND**: Harry Albemarle Swepstone, Percy John de Paravincini, Alfred Jones, Norman Coles Bailey (Cap), Stuart Macrae, Arthur William Cursham, William Nevill Cobbold, Clement Mitchell, Harry Chester Goodhart, Henry Alfred Cursham, Oliver Whateley.

**SCOTLAND**: James McAulay, Andrew Hair Holm (Cap), Michael Paton, Peter Miller, John Campbell McLeod McPherson, Malcolm James Eadie Fraser, William Anderson, John Smith, John Inglis, John Leck Kay, William Neilson McKinnon.

**Goals**: Clement Mitchell (24), William Nevill Cobbold (43) / John Smith (22, 39), Malcolm James Eadie Fraser (86)

20. 23.02.1884   Home Championship
**IRELAND v ENGLAND 1-8** (0-4)

*Ballynafeigh Park, Belfast*

Referee: Thomas Lawrie (Scotland)   Attendance: 3,000

**IRELAND**: Robert John Hunter, Matt Wilson, William Crone, John Hastings, Thomas Bryson Molyneux, Alick H. Dill, E. Arthur Spiller, William McWha, Samuel Johnston, Dr. John Robert Davison, Arthur W. Gaussen.

**ENGLAND**: William Crispin Rose, Alfred Thomas Carrick Dobson, Joseph Beverley, Norman Coles Bailey (Cap), Stuart Macrae, Edward Johnson, George Holden, Arthur Leopold Bambridge, Arthur Tempest Blakiston Dunn, Edward Charles Bambridge, Henry Alfred Cursham.

**Goals**: William McWha (88) / Edward Johnson (#, 15), Edward Bambridge (#, #), Henry Alfred Cursham (#, #, #), Arthur Leopold Bambridge (76)

The times at which the goals were scored is not recorded.

21. 15.03.1884   Home Championship
**SCOTLAND v ENGLAND 1-0** (1-0)

*Cathkin Park, Glasgow*

Referee: John Sinclair (Ireland)   Attendance: 10,000

**SCOTLAND**: James McAulay, Walter Arnott, John Forbes, Charles Campbell (Cap), John Campbell McLeod McPherson, William Anderson, Francis Watson Shaw, John Smith, Joseph Lindsay, Robert Main Christie, William Neilson McKinnon.

**ENGLAND**: William Crispin Rose, Alfred Thomas Carrick Dobson, Joseph Beverley, Norman Coles Bailey (Cap), Stuart Macrae, Charles Plumpton Wilson, William Bromley-Davenport, William Gunn, Edward Charles Bambridge, Oliver Howard Vaughton, George Holden.

**Goal**: John Smith (7)

22. 17.03.1884   Home Championship
**WALES v ENGLAND 0-4** (0-1)

*Racecourse Ground, Wrexham*

Referee: Sydney Broadfoot (Scotland)   Attendance: 4,500

**WALES**: Elias Owen, John Powell, Charles Conde, Maurice John Evans, Peter Griffiths, Joseph Henry Williams, William Pierce Owen, John Arthur Eyton-Jones, William Owen, John Vaughan, Robert Albert Jones.

**ENGLAND**: William Crispin Rose, Alfred Thomas Carrick Dobson, Joseph Beverley, Norman Coles Bailey (Cap), James Henry Forrest, Charles Plumpton Wilson, George Holden, Oliver Howard Vaughton, William Bromley-Davenport, William Gunn, Edward Charles Bambridge.

**Goals**: William Bromley-Davenport (7, 85), Norman Coles Bailey (75), William Gunn (90)

23. 28.02.1885   Home Championship
**ENGLAND v IRELAND 4-0** (1-0)

*Whelley Range, Manchester*

Referee: James McKillop (Scotland)   Attendance: 6,000

**ENGLAND**: William John Herbert Arthur, Percy Melmoth Walters, Arthur Melmoth Walters, Norman Coles Bailey (Cap), James Henry Forrest, Joseph Morris Lofthouse, Benjamin Ward Spilsbury, James Brown, Francis William Pawson, William Nevill Cobbold, Edward Charles Bambridge.

**IRELAND**: Anthony W. Henderson, George Hewison, Frederick William Moorehead, Thomas Bryson Molyneux, William John Houston, William L'Estrange Eames, William McWha, Dr. John Robert Davison, John T. Gibb, George McGee, Alick H. Dill.

**Goals**: Edward Charles Bambridge (43), James Brown (#), Benjamin Ward Spilsbury (75), Joseph Morris Lofthouse (77)

24. 14.03.1885   Home Championship
**ENGLAND v WALES 1-1** (1-1)

*Leamington Road, Blackburn*

Referee: Alexander Stuart (Scotland)   Attendance: 7,500

**ENGLAND**: William John Herbert Arthur, Henry Thomas Moore, James Thomas Ward, Norman Coles Bailey (Cap), James Henry Forrest, Joseph Morris Lofthouse, James Kenneth Davenport, James Brown, Clement Mitchell, John Augur Dixon, Edward Charles Bambridge.

**WALES**: Robert Herbert Mills-Roberts, Frederick Robert Jones, George Thomas, Robert Davies, Humphrey Jones, Thomas Burke, John Edward Davies, Thomas Vaughan, George Farmer, William Lewis, Job Wilding.

**Goal**: Clement Mitchell (35) / Job Wilding (37)

**25. 21.03.1885   Home Championship**
**ENGLAND v SCOTLAND  1-1**  (0-1)

*Kennington Oval, London*

Referee: John Sinclair (Ireland)   Attendance: 8,000

**ENGLAND**: William John Herbert Arthur, Percy Melmoth Walters, Arthur Melmoth Walters, Norman Coles Bailey (Cap), James Henry Forrest, Andrew Amos, James Brown, Joseph Morris Lofthouse, Thomas Danks, Edward Charles Bambridge, William Nevill Cobbold.

**SCOTLAND**: James McAulay, Walter Arnott, Michael Paton, Charles Campbell (Cap), John James Gow, William Anderson, Alexander Hamilton, William Sellar, Joseph Lindsay, David Steel Allan, Robert Calderwood.

**Goal**: Edward Charles Bambridge (57) / Joseph Lindsay (20)


**26. 13.03.1886   Home Championship**
**IRELAND v ENGLAND  1-6**  (1-2)

*Ballynafeigh Park, Belfast*

Referee: James McKillop (Scotland)   Attendance: 4,500

**IRELAND**: Shaw Gillespie, James Watson, Oliver Devine, Thomas Bryson Molyneux, William Crone, John Hastings, William Turner, John Condy, Samuel Johnston, John McClatchey, James Williams.

**ENGLAND**: William Crispin Rose, Percy Melmoth Walters (Cap), Richard Baugh, George Shutt, Ralph Tyndall Squire, Charles Frederick Dobson, John Edward Leighton, Frederick Dewhurst, Tinsley Lindley, Benjamin Ward Spilsbury, Thelwell Mather Pike.

**Goals**: James Williams (15) / Benjamin Spilsbury (4 goals), Frederick Dewhurst (#), Tinsley Lindley (#)

The times at which the goals were scored is not recorded.


**27. 27.03.1886   Home Championship**
**SCOTLAND v ENGLAND  1-1**  (0-1)

*First Hampden Park, Glasgow*

Referee: Hunter (Wales)   Attendance: 11,000

**SCOTLAND**: James McAulay, Walter Arnott (Cap), Michael Paton, Charles Campbell, John MacDonald, Alexander Hamilton, William Sellar, George Somerville, Joseph Lindsay, Woodville Gray, Ralph Allan Aitken.

**ENGLAND**: William John Herbert Arthur, Arthur Melmoth Walters, Percy Melmoth Walters, Norman Coles Bailey (Cap), Ralph Tyndall Squire, James Henry Forrest, William Nevill Cobbold, Edward Charles Bambridge, Tinsley Lindley, Benjamin Ward Spilsbury, George Brann.

**Goal**: George Somerville (80) / Tinsley Lindley (35)


**28. 29.03.1886   Home Championship**
**WALES v ENGLAND  1-3**  (1-0)

*Racecourse Ground, Wrexham*

Referee: Stewart Lawrie (Scotland)   Attendance: 5,000

**WALES**: Dr. Robert Herbert Mills-Roberts, Dr. Alfred Owen Davies, Seth Powell, John Owen Vaughan, William Stafford Bell, Humphrey Jones, Job Wilding, William Roberts, Thomas Davies, Thomas Bryan, William Lewis.

**ENGLAND**: William John Herbert Arthur, Ralph Tyndall Squire, Percy Melmoth Walters, Norman Coles Bailey (Cap), Andrew Amos, James Henry Forrest, Frederick Dewhurst, George Brann, Tinsley Lindley, William Nevill Cobbold, Edward Charles Bambridge.

**Goals**: William Lewis (43) / Frederick Dewhurst (70), Tinsley Lindley (74), Edward Charles Bambridge (#)


**29. 05.02.1887   Home Championship**
**ENGLAND v IRELAND  7-0**  (4-0)

*Bramall Lane, Sheffield*

Referee: Alexander Hunter (Wales)   Attendance: 6,000

**ENGLAND**: William John Herbert Arthur, Robert Henry Howarth, Charles Mason, George Haworth, Edward Brayshaw, James Henry Forrest, James Sayer, Frederick Dewhurst, Tinsley Lindley, William Nevill Cobbold, Edward Charles Bambridge (Cap).

**IRELAND**: Shaw Gillespie, Frederick Browne, William Fox, Archibald Rosbotham, William Leslie, William Crone, Jim Allen, John T. Gibb, Olphert M. Stanfield, James Small, W. Nathaniel Brown.

**Goals**: Frederick Dewhurst (2, 87), William Cobbold (25, 49), Tinsley Lindley (27, 43, 52)


**30. 26.02.1887   Home Championship**
**ENGLAND v WALES  4-0**  (1-0)

*Kennington Oval, London*

Referee: Thomas Devlin (Scotland)   Attendance: 4,500

**ENGLAND**: William John Herbert Arthur, Percy Melmoth Walters, Arthur Melmoth Walters, George Haworth, Norman Coles Bailey (Cap), James Henry Forrest, Joseph Morris Lofthouse, Frederick Dewhurst, Tinsley Lindley, William Nevill Cobbold, Edward Charles Bambridge.

**WALES**: Dr. Robert Herbert Mills-Roberts, Dr. Alfred Owen Davies, John Powell, Thomas Burke, Humphrey Jones, Edward Clement Evelyn, William Owen, John Bonamy Challen, Job Wilding, William Haighton Turner, William Lewis.

**Goals**: William Nevill Cobbold (14, 75), Tinsley Lindley (55, 80)

31. 19.03.1887   Home Championship
**ENGLAND v SCOTLAND  2-3**  (1-1)

*Leamington Road, Blackburn*

Referee: John Sinclair (Ireland)   Attendance: 12,000

**ENGLAND**: Robert John Roberts, Arthur Melmoth Walters, Percy Melmoth Walters, Norman Coles Bailey (Cap), George Haworth, James Henry Forrest, Edward Charles Bambridge, William Nevill Cobbold, Joseph Morris Lofthouse, Frederick Dewhurst, Tinsley Lindley.

**SCOTLAND**: James McAulay (Cap), Walter Arnott, John Forbes, Robert Robinson Kelso, John Robertson Auld, Leitch Keir, John Marshall, William Robertson, William Sellar, James McCall, James Allan.

**Goals**: Tinsley Lindley (32), Frederick Dewhurst (69) / James McCall (30), Leitch Keir (68), James Allan (70).


32. 04.02.1888   Home Championship
**ENGLAND v WALES  5-1**  (1-1)

*Nantwich Road, Crewe*

Referee: John Sinclair (Ireland)   Attendance: 6,000

**ENGLAND**: William Robert Moon, Robert Henry Howarth, Charles Mason, Frank Etheridge Saunders, Henry Allen, Charles Henry Holden-White, George Woodhall, John Goodall, Tinsley Lindley (Cap), Frederick Dewhurst, Dennis Hodgetts.

**WALES**: Dr. Robert Herbert Mills-Roberts, Dr. Alfred Owen Davies, John Powell, Robert Roberts, Peter Griffiths, Joseph Davies, William Ernest Pryce-Jones, John Bonamy Challen, John Doughty, William Lewis, William Owen.

**Goals**: Frederick Dewhurst (15, 65), George Woodhall (70), Tinsley Lindley (75), John Goodall (88) / John Doughty (17).


33. 17.03.1888   Home Championship
**SCOTLAND v ENGLAND  0-5**  (0-4)

*First Hampden Park, Glasgow*

Referee: John Sinclair (Ireland)   Attendance: 10,000

**SCOTLAND**: John Lindsay, Walter Arnott, Donald Robertson Gow (Cap), James Kelly, Leitch Keir, Robert Robinson Kelso, Alexander Hamilton, William Hall Berry, William Sellar, James McCall, John Alexander Lambie.

**ENGLAND**: William Robert Moon, Robert Henry Howarth, Percy Melmoth Walters, Henry Allen, George Haworth, Charles Henry Holden-White, George Woodhall, John Goodall, Tinsley Lindley (Cap), Dennis Hodgetts, Frederick Dewhurst.

**Goals**: Tinsley Lindley (32), Dennis Hodgetts (34), Frederick Dewhurst (40, 49), John Goodall (43).


34. 07.04.1888   Home Championship
**IRELAND v ENGLAND  1-5**  (1-3)

*Ballynafeigh, Belfast*

Referee: James McKillop (Scotland)   Attendance: 7,000

**IRELAND**: Ralph Lawther, Madesto Silo, Frederick Browne, James Forsythe, Archibald Rosbotham, William Crone, Arthur W. Gaussen, Olphert M. Stanfield, John McVicker, James M. Wilton, John Peden.

**ENGLAND**: Robert John Roberts, Alfred James Aldridge, Percy Melmoth Walters, Robert Holmes, Henry Allen, Charles Shelton, William Isaiah Bassett, Frederick Dewhurst, Tinsley Lindley (Cap), Albert Allen, Dennis Hodgetts.

**Goals**: William Crone (32) / Frederick Dewhurst (10), Albert Allen (14, 39, 60), Tinsley Lindley (#).


35. 23.02.1889   Home Championship
**ENGLAND v WALES  4-1**  (1-1)

*Victoria Ground, Stoke*

Referee: Campbell (Scotland)   Attendance: 6,000

**ENGLAND**: William Robert Moon, Arthur Melmoth Walters (Cap), Percy Melmoth Walters, Albert Thomas Fletcher, Arthur Lowder, William Betts, William Isaiah Bassett, John Goodall, John Southworth, Frederick Dewhurst, William John Townley.

**WALES**: James Trainer, William P. Jones, David Jones, Ernest Percival Whitley Hughes, Humphrey Jones, Robert Roberts, John Hallam, Richard Owen Jones, William Lewis, Arthur Lea, William Owen.

**Goals**: John Goodall (#), William Isaiah Bassett (57), Frederick Dewhurst (#), John Southworth (#) / William Owen (14).


36. 02.03.1889   Home Championship
**ENGLAND v IRELAND  6-1**  (3-1)

*Anfield Road, Liverpool*

Referee: Alfred Owen Davies (Wales)   Attendance: 6,000

**ENGLAND**: William Rowley, Thomas Clare, Alfred James Aldridge, Charles Wreford-Brown, David Weir, Alfred Shelton, Joseph Morris Lofthouse, Frank Ernest Burton, James Brant Brodie (Cap), Henry Butler Daft, John Yates.

**IRELAND**: John Clugston, Manliffe Fraser Goodbody, James Watson, Alexander Crawford, Archibald Rosbotham, Samuel Cooke, Arthur W. Gaussen, Olphert M. Stanfield, John Barry, James M. Wilton, John Peden.

**Goals**: David Weir (#), John Yates (#, #, 35), James Brant Brodie (#), Joseph Morris Lofthouse (#) / James M. Wilton (10).

37.　13.04.1889　Home Championship
**ENGLAND v SCOTLAND  2-3**  (2-0)
*Kennington Oval, London*
Referee: John Sinclair (Ireland)　Attendance: 10,000
**ENGLAND**: William Robert Moon, Arthur Melmoth Walters (Cap), Percy Melmoth Walters, Henry Edward Denison Hammond, Henry Allen, James Henry Forrest, James Brant Brodie, John Goodall, William Isaiah Bassett, David Weir, Tinsley Lindley.
**SCOTLAND**: James Wilson, Robert Smellie (Cap), Walter Arnott, James Kelly, George Dewar, James McLaren, James Oswald, William Hall Berry, Alexander Latta, John McPherson, Neil Munro.
**Goals**: William Isaiah Bassett (15), David Weir (17) / Neil Munro (55), James Oswald (82), John McPherson (90)

38.　15.03.1890　Home Championship
**WALES v ENGLAND  1-3**  (1-0)
*Racecourse Ground, Wrexham*
Referee: James Walker (Scotland)　Attendance: 5,000
**WALES**: Samuel Gladstone Gillam, Dr. Alfred Owen Davies, David Jones, Joseph Davies, Humphrey Jones, Walter Gwynne Evans, John Bonamy Challen, Richard Owen Jones, John Doughty, Edmund Gwynne Howell, William Lewis.
**ENGLAND**: William Robert Moon, Arthur Melmoth Walters (Cap), Percy Melmoth Walters, Albert Thomas Fletcher, John Holt, Alfred Shelton, William Isaiah Bassett, Edward Samuel Currey, Tinsley Lindley, Henry Butler Daft, Harry Wood.
**Goals**: William Lewis (38) / Edward Samuel Currey (#, 49), Tinsley Lindley (#)

39.　15.03.1890　Home Championship
**IRELAND v ENGLAND  1-9**  (0-3)
*Ballynafeigh Park, Belfast*
Referee: James McKillop (Scotland)　Attendance: 6,000
**IRELAND**: John Clugston, Robert Stewart, Robert Crone, James Williamson, Samuel Spencer, Samuel Cooke, Allan Elleman, Olphert Stanfield, James Wilton, Robert McIlvenny, John Reynolds.
**ENGLAND**: Robert John Roberts, Richard Baugh, Charles Mason, John Barton, Charles Perry, James Henry Forrest (Cap), Joseph Morris Lofthouse, James Kenneth Davenport, Fred Geary, Nathaniel Walton, William John Townley.
**Goals**: John Reynolds (70) / Fred Geary (15, 60, 80), William John Townley (16, 84), Joseph Morris Lofthouse (40), James Kenneth Davenport (46, 75), John Barton (88)

40.　05.04.1890　Home Championship
**SCOTLAND v ENGLAND  1-1**  (1-1)
*Hampden Park, Glasgow*
Referee: Reid (Ireland)　Attendance: 26,379
**SCOTLAND**: James Wilson, Walter Arnott, Thomas Michael McKeown, Thomas Robertson, James Kelly, James McLaren (Cap), William Groves, William Hall Berry, William Johnstone, John McPherson, James McCall.
**ENGLAND**: William Robert Moon, Arthur Melmoth Walters, Percy Melmoth Walters (Cap), George Haworth, Henry Allen, Alfred Shelton, William Isaiah Bassett, Edward Samuel Currey, Tinsley Lindley, Harry Wood, Henry Butler Daft.
**Goal**: John McPherson (37) / Harry Wood (17)

41.　07.03.1891　Home Championship
**ENGLAND v WALES  4-1**  (4-0)
*Newcastle Road, Sunderland*
Referee: Thomas Park (Scotland)　Attendance: 15,000
**ENGLAND**: Leonard Rodwell Wilkinson, Thomas Stoddard Porteous, Elphinstone Jackson, Albert Smith, John Holt, Alfred Shelton, George Brann, John Goodall (Cap), John Southworth, Alfred Weatherell Milward, Edgar Wallace Chadwick.
**WALES**: Richard Turner, Walter Gwynne Evans, Seth Powell, William Hughes, Humphrey Jones, Charles Frederick Parry, Joseph Davies, William Owen, William Haighton Turner, Edmund Gwynne Howell, William Lewis.
**Goals**: John Goodall (30), John Southworth (30), Edgar Wallace Chadwick (40), Alfred Weatherell Milward (43) / Edmund Gwynne Howell (84)

42.　07.03.1891　Home Championship
**ENGLAND v IRELAND  6-1**  (3-0)
*Molineux, Wolverhampton*
Referee: Richard Thomas Gough (Wales)　Att: 15,231
**ENGLAND**: William Crispin Rose, Joseph Thomas Marsden, Alfred Underwood, Albert Edward James Matthias Bayliss, Charles Perry, James Brant Brodie, William Isaiah Bassett, George Huth Cotterill, Tinsley Lindley (Cap), Arthur George Henfrey, Henry Butler Daft.
**IRELAND**: John Clugston, George Forbes, Robert Morrison, Alexander Crawford, John Reynolds, Richard Moore, Thomas Whiteside, Olphert M. Stanfield, William McCabe, Robert McIlvenny, John Peden.
**Goals**: George Huth Cotterill (15), Arthur G. Henfrey (17), Henry Butler Daft (35), Tinsley Lindley (#, #), William Isaiah Bassett (#) / Thomas Whiteside (#)

**43.  04.04.1891    Home Championship**
**ENGLAND v SCOTLAND  2-1**  (2-0)

*Ewood Park, Blackburn*

Referee: Morrow (Ireland)    Attendance: 31,000

**ENGLAND**: William Robert Moon (Cap), Robert Henry Howarth, Robert Holmes, Albert Smith, John Holt, Alfred Shelton, William Isaiah Bassett, John Goodall, Fred Geary, Edgar Wallace Chadwick, Alfred Weatherell Milward.

**SCOTLAND**: James Wilson, Walter Arnott (Cap), Robert Smellie, Isaac Begbie, John McPherson, John Hill, Gilbert Rankin, Francis Watt, William Sellar, William Hall Berry, David Baird.

**Goals**: John Goodall (20), Edgar Wallace Chadwick (30) / Francis Watt (85)

**44.  05.03.1892    Home Championship**
**WALES v ENGLAND  0-2**  (0-1)

*Racecourse Ground, Wrexham*

Referee: James Robertson (Scotland)    Attendance: 4,500

**WALES**: Dr. Robert Herbert Mills-Roberts, Walter Gwynne Evans, Seth Powell, Joseph Davies, Caesar August Llewelyn Jenkyns, John Owen, William Owen, Joseph Hudson Turner, Benjamin Lewis, Robert Davies, William Lewis.

**ENGLAND**: George Toone, Arthur Tempest Blakiston Dunn (Cap), Harry Edward Lilley, Anthony Henry Hossack, William Norman Winckworth, George Kinsey, Robert Cunliffe Gosling, George Huth Cotterill, Arthur George Henfrey, Joseph Alfred Schofield, Rupert Renorden Sandilands.

**Goals**: Arthur George Henfrey (15), Rupert Renorden Sandilands (87)

**45.  05.03.1892    Home Championship**
**IRELAND v ENGLAND  0-2**  (0-1)

*Solitude, Belfast*

Referee: Robert Harrison (Scotland)    Attendance: 7,000

**IRELAND**: John Clugston, William Gordon, Robert K. Stewart, Nathaniel McKeown, Samuel Spencer, William Cunningham, William Dalton, George Gaffikin, Olphert M. Stanfield, Samuel Torrans, John Peden.

**ENGLAND**: William Rowley, Alfred Underwood, Thomas Clare, John Davies Cox, John Holt, Michael Whitham, William Charles Athersmith, John Hargreaves Pearson, John Henry George Devey, Henry Butler Daft (Cap), Dennis Hodgetts.

**Goals**: Henry Butler Daft (44, 47)

**46.  02.04.1892    Home Championship**
**SCOTLAND v ENGLAND  1-4**  (0-4)

*Ibrox Park, Glasgow*

Referee: Smith (Scotland)    Attendance: 21,000

**SCOTLAND**: John McLeod, Daniel Doyle, Walter Arnott, James Kelly, William Sellar (Cap), David Mitchell, Donald Currie Sillars, William Taylor, Thomas Smith Waddell, Alexander McMahon, John Bell.

**ENGLAND**: George Toone, Arthur Tempest Blakiston Dunn (Cap), Robert Holmes, John Holt, John Reynolds, Alfred Shelton, William Isaiah Bassett, John Goodall, John Southworth, Dennis Hodgetts, Edgar Wallace Chadwick.

**Goals**: John Bell (80) / Edgar Wallace Chadwick (1), John Goodall (20, 26), John Southworth (25)

**47.  25.02.1893    Home Championship**
**ENGLAND v IRELAND  6-1**  (4-1)

*Perry Barr, Birmingham*

Referee: Thomas Park (Scotland)    Attendance: 10,000

**ENGLAND**: Charles Christopher Charsley, Alban Hugh Harrison, Frederick Raymond Pelly, Albert Smith, William Norman Winckworth, Norman Charles Cooper, Robert Topham, Gilbert Oswald Smith, George Huth Cotterill (Cap), Walter Evelyn Gilliat, Rupert Renorden Sandilands.

**IRELAND**: John Clugston, William Gordon, Robert K. Stewart, Alexander Crawford, Samuel Spencer, William Cunningham, James Small, George Gaffikin, Olphert M. Stanfield, Samuel Torrans, John Peden.

**Goals**: Walter E. Gilliat (10, 18, 30), Gilbert O. Smith (43), William Norman Winckworth (60), Rupert Renorden Sandilands (75) / George Gaffikin (12)

**48.  13.03.1893    Home Championship**
**ENGLAND v WALES  6-0**  (2-0)

*Victoria Ground, Stoke*

Referee: Campbell (Scotland)    Attendance: 10,000

**ENGLAND**: John William Sutcliffe, Thomas Clare, Robert Holmes (Cap), John Reynolds, Charles Perry, James Albert Turner, William Isaiah Bassett, James Whitehead, John Goodall, Joseph Alfred Schofield, Frederick Spiksley.

**WALES**: James Trainer, David Jones, Charles Frederick Parry, Edwin Hugh Williams, Joseph Davies, Edward Morris, John Butler, James Vaughan, Edwin James, Benjamin Lewis, Robert Roberts II.

**Goals**: Frederick Spiksley (25, 43), William I. Bassett (47), John Goodall (49), John Reynolds (75), Joseph Alfred Schofield (88)

**49. 01.04.1893   Home Championship**
**ENGLAND v SCOTLAND  5-2  (1-1)**
*Richmond Athletic, London*

Referee: Clegg (England)   Attendance: 16,000

**ENGLAND:** Leslie Hewitt Gay, Alban Hugh Harrison, Robert Holmes, John Reynolds, John Holt, George Kinsey, William Isaiah Bassett, Robert Cunliffe Gosling, George Huth Cotterill (Cap), Edgar Wallace Chadwick, Frederick Spiksley.

**SCOTLAND:** John Lindsay, Walter Arnott, Robert Smellie, William Maley, James Kelly (Cap), David Mitchell, William Sellar, Thomas Smith Waddell, James Hamilton, Alexander McMahon, John Campbell.

**Goals:** Robert Cunliffe Gosling (15), George Cotterill (65), Frederick Spiksley (75, 80), John Reynolds (86) / William Sellar (20, 47)


**50. 03.03.1894   Home Championship**
**IRELAND v ENGLAND  2-2  (1-0)**
*Solitude, Belfast*

Referee: Thomas Park (Scotland)   Attendance: 8,000

**IRELAND:** Thomas Scott, Robert Stewart, Samuel Torrans, Samuel Johnston, John Burnett, Robert Milne, William Dalton, George Gaffikin, Olphert Stanfield, William Kennedy Gibson, James Barron.

**ENGLAND:** Joseph Reader, Robert Henry Howarth, Robert Holmes (Cap), John Reynolds, John Holt, James William Crabtree, Harry Chippendale, James Whitehead, John Henry George Devey, Dennis Hodgetts, Frederick Spiksley.

**Goals:** Olphert M. Stanfield (#), William Kennedy Gibson (#)/ John Henry George Devey (43), Frederick Spiksley (55)


**51. 12.03.1894   Home Championship**
**WALES v ENGLAND  1-5  (1-2)**
*Racecourse Ground, Wrexham*

Referee: Thomas Park (Scotland)   Attendance: 5,500

**WALES:** James Trainer, Charles Frederick Parry, David Jones, John Evans, Thomas Chapman, Abel Hughes, Edwin James, Benjamin Lewis, William Lewis, John Charles Rea, John Charles Henry Bowdler.

**ENGLAND:** Leslie Hewitt Gay, Lewis Vaughn Lodge, Frederick Raymond Pelly, Anthony Henry Hossack, Charles Wreford-Brown (Cap), Arthur George Topham, Robert Topham, Robert Cunliffe Gosling, Gilbert Oswald Smith, John Gould Veitch, Rupert Renorden Sandilands.

**Goals:** John Charles Henry Bowdler (10) / John Gould Veitch (30, 55, 80), Charles F. Parry (44 og), Robert Cunliffe Gosling (85)


**52. 07.04.1894   Home Championship**
**SCOTLAND v ENGLAND  2-2  (1-1)**
*Parkhead, Glasgow*

Referee: Reid (Ireland)   Attendance: 45,107

**SCOTLAND:** David Haddow, Donald Currie Sillars, Daniel Doyle (Cap), Isaac Begbie, Andrew McCreadie, David Mitchell, William Gulliland, James Blessington, Alexander McMahon, John McPherson, William Allan Lambie.

**ENGLAND:** Leslie Hewitt Gay, Thomas Clare, Frederick Raymond Pelly, John Reynolds, John Holt, Ernest Needham, William Isaiah Bassett, Gilbert Oswald Smith, John Goodall (Cap), Edgar Wallace Chadwick, Frederick Spiksley.

**Goals:** William Allan Lambie (7), Alexander McMahon (75) / John Goodall (35), John Reynolds (85)


**53. 09.03.1895   Home Championship**
**ENGLAND v IRELAND  9-0  (5-0)**
*County Cricket Club, Derby*

Referee: James Robertson (Scotland)   Attendance: 8,000

**ENGLAND:** John William Sutcliffe, James William Crabtree, Robert Holmes (Cap), Rabbi Howell, Thomas Henry Crawshaw, James Albert Turner, William Isaiah Bassett, Stephen Bloomer, John Goodall, Francis Becton, Joseph Alfred Schofield.

**IRELAND:** Thomas Gordon, Hugh Gordon, Samuel Torrans, Hymie McKie, Robert Milne, John Burnett, Thomas Morrison, George Gaffikin, Olphert Stanfield, William Sherrard, Thomas Jordan.

**Goals:** Samuel Torrans (3 og), Stephen Bloomer (4, 58), Francis Becton (15, 60), William Isaiah Bassett (30), Rabbi Howell (36), John Goodall (65, 87)


**54. 18.03.1895   Home Championship**
**ENGLAND v WALES  1-1  (0-0)**
*Queen's Club, London*

Referee: Thomas Park (Scotland)   Attendance: 13,000

**ENGLAND:** George Berkeley Raikes, Lewis Vaughn Lodge, William John Oakley, Arthur George Henfrey, Charles Wreford-Brown (Cap), Robert Raine Barker, Morris Hugh Stanbrough, Gerald Powys Dewhurst, Gilbert Oswald Smith, Robert Cunliffe Gosling, Rupert Renorden Sandilands.

**WALES:** James Trainer, Charles Frederick Parry, David Jones, George Williams, Caesar August Llewelyn Jenkyns, John Leonard Jones, William Henry Meredith, Joseph Davies, Harry Trainer, Albert Westhead Pryce-Jones, William Lewis.

**Goal:** Gilbert Oswald Smith (74) / William Lewis (69)

**55.   06.04.1895   Home Championship**
**ENGLAND v SCOTLAND   3-0   (3-0)**

*Goodison Park, Liverpool*

Referee: Reid (Ireland)   Attendance: 42,500

**ENGLAND**: John William Sutcliffe, James William Crabtree, Lewis Vaughn Lodge, Ernest Needham, John Holt, John Reynolds, Robert Cunliffe Gosling, Stephen Smith, John Goodall (Cap), William Isaiah Bassett, Stephen Bloomer.

**SCOTLAND**: Daniel McArthur, John Drummond, Daniel Doyle, David Kennedy Russell, James Simpson, Neil Gibson, William Allan Lambie, John McPherson, James Oswald (Cap), Thomas Smith Waddell, William Gulliland.

**Goals**: Stephen Bloomer (30), Neil Gibson (35 og), Stephen Smith (44)


**56.   07.03.1896   Home Championship**
**IRELAND v ENGLAND   0-2   (0-1)**

*Solitude, Belfast*

Referee: James Robertson (Scotland)   Attendance: 12,000

**IRELAND**: Thomas Scott, Joseph Ponsonby, Samuel Torrans, James Fitzpatrick, Robert Milne, Hugh Gordon, Giddy Baird, James Kelly, Olphert M. Stanfield, Edward Turner, John Peden.

**ENGLAND**: George Berkeley Raikes, Lewis Vaughn Lodge, William John Oakley, James William Crabtree, Thomas Henry Crawshaw, George Kinsey, William Isaiah Bassett, Stephen Bloomer, Gilbert Oswald Smith (Cap), Edgar Wallace Chadwick, Frederick Spiksley.

**Goals**: Gilbert Oswald Smith (40), Stephen Bloomer (75)


**57.   16.03.1896   Home Championship**
**WALES v ENGLAND   1-9   (0-5)**

*Arms Park, Cardiff*

Referee: Thomas Robertson (Scotland)   Attendance: 10,000

**WALES**: Samuel Jones, Charles Frederick Parry, Smart Arridge, Joseph Rogers, Thomas Chapman, John Leonard Jones, William Henry Meredith, Joseph Davies, Arthur Grenville Morris, Hugh Morris, William Lewis.

**ENGLAND**: George Berkeley Raikes, William John Oakley, James William Crabtree, Arthur George Henfrey, Thomas Henry Crawshaw, George Kinsey, William Isaiah Bassett, Stephen Bloomer, Gilbert Oswald Smith (Cap), John Goodall, Rupert Renorden Sandilands.

**Goals**: Thomas Chapman (65 pen) / Gilbert O. Smith (15, 44), Stephen Bloomer (25, 40, 60, 83, 89), William Isaiah Bassett (33), John Goodall (80)


**58.   04.04.1896   Home Championship**
**SCOTLAND v ENGLAND   2-1   (2-0)**

*Parkhead, Glasgow*

Referee: Jones (Wales)   Attendance: 57,000

**SCOTLAND**: John Edward Doig, John Drummond (Cap), Thomas Brandon, George Hogg, James Cowan, Neil Gibson, Alexander King, William Allan Lambie, Thomas Hyslop, James Blessington, John Bell.

**ENGLAND**: George Berkeley Raikes, Lewis Vaughn Lodge, William John Oakley, James William Crabtree, Thomas Henry Crawshaw, Arthur George Henfrey, John Goodall, William Isaiah Bassett, Gilbert Oswald Smith (Cap), Harry Wood, Cuthbert James Burnup.

**Goal**: William Allan Lambie (22), John Bell (33) / William Isaiah Bassett (80)


**59.   20.02.1897   Home Championship**
**ENGLAND v IRELAND   6-0   (3-0)**

*Trent Bridge, Nottingham*

Referee: Thomas Robertson (Scotland)   Attendance: 14,000

**ENGLAND**: John William Robinson, William John Oakley, William Williams, Bernard Middleditch, Thomas Henry Crawshaw, Ernest Needham, William Charles Athersmith, Stephen Bloomer, Gilbert Oswald Smith (Cap), George Frederick Wheldon, Thomas Henry Bradshaw.

**IRELAND**: Thomas Scott, Joseph Ponsonby, Samuel Torrans, John Pyper, Robert Milne, George McMaster, James Campbell, George Hall, Olphert M. Stanfield, John Darling, James Barron.

**Goals**: Stephen Bloomer (19, 85), George Frederick Wheldon (30, 33, 55), William Charles Athersmith (75)


**60.   29.03.1897   Home Championship**
**ENGLAND v WALES   4-0   (2-0)**

*Bramall Lane, Sheffield*

Referee: Thomas Robertson (Scotland)   Attendance: 5,000

**ENGLAND**: William Foulke, William John Oakley, Howard Spencer, John Reynolds, Thomas Henry Crawshaw, Ernest Needham, William Charles Athersmith, Stephen Bloomer, Gilbert Oswald Smith (Cap), Francis Becton, Alfred Weatherell Milward.

**WALES**: James Trainer, John Samuel Matthias, James Alfred Edwards, Thomas Chapman, John Mates, John Leonard Jones, William Henry Meredith, Joseph Davies, Arthur Grenville Morris, Hugh Morris, William Lewis.

**Goals**: Ernest Needham (23), Stephen Bloomer (44), Alfred Weatherell Milward (62, 64)

**61.  03.04.1897   Home Championship**
**ENGLAND v SCOTLAND  1-2**  (1-1)
*Crystal Palace, London*
Referee: Gough (Wales)   Attendance: 37,000
**ENGLAND**: John William Robinson, William John Oakley, Howard Spencer, John Reynolds, Thomas Henry Crawshaw, Ernest Needham, William Charles Athersmith, Stephen Bloomer, Gilbert Oswald Smith (Cap), Edgar Wallace Chadwick, Alfred Weatherell Milward.
**SCOTLAND**: John Patrick, Nicol Smith, Daniel Doyle, Neil Gibson, James Cowan, Hugh Wilson, John Bell, James Millar, George Horsburgh Allan, Thomas Hyslop, William Allan Lambie (Cap).
**Goal**: Stephen Bloomer (19) /
Thomas Hyslop (27), James Millar (83)


**62.  05.03.1898   Home Championship**
**IRELAND v ENGLAND  2-3**  (1-2)
*Solitude, Belfast*
Referee: Thomas Robertson (Scotland)   Attendance: 12,000
**IRELAND**: Thomas Scott, William Kennedy Gibson, Samuel Torrans, William Anderson, Robert Milne, Michael Cochrane, James Campbell, John Thompson Mercer, James Pyper, John Peden, Joseph McAllen.
**ENGLAND**: John William Robinson, William John Oakley, William Williams, Frank Forman, Thomas Morren, James Albert Turner, William Charles Athersmith, Charles Henry Richards, Gilbert Oswald Smith (Cap), Benjamin Walter Garfield, George Frederick Wheldon.
**Goals**: James Pyper (18), John Thompson Mercer (70) /
Gilbert Oswald Smith (37), William Charles Athersmith (40), Thomas Morren (50)


**63.  28.03.1898   Home Championship**
**WALES v ENGLAND  0-3**  (0-1)
*Racecourse Ground, Wrexham*
Referee: Thomas Robertson (Scotland)   Attendance: 4,000
**WALES**: James Trainer, Charles Frederick Parry, Smart Arridge, John Taylor, Caesar August Llewelyn Jenkyns, John Leonard Jones, William Henry Meredith, Thomas Bartley, Morgan Maddox Morgan-Owen, Alfred Ernest Watkins, Edwin James.
**ENGLAND**: John William Robinson, William John Oakley, William Williams, Thomas Perry, Thomas Edward Booth, Ernest Needham, William Charles Athersmith, John Goodall, Gilbert Oswald Smith (Cap), George Frederick Wheldon, Frederick Spiksley.
**Goals**: Gilbert Oswald Smith (9), George F. Wheldon (75, 88)


**64.  02.04.1898   Home Championship**
**SCOTLAND v ENGLAND  1-3**  (0-2)
*Parkhead, Glasgow*
Referee: Thomas Robertson (Scotland)   Attendance: 40,000
**SCOTLAND**: Kenneth Anderson, John Drummond, Daniel Doyle, Neil Gibson, James Cowan (Cap), John Tait Robertson, John Bell, John Campbell, William Sturrock Maxwell, James Millar, Alexander Smith.
**ENGLAND**: John William Robinson, William Williams, William John Oakley, Ernest Needham, Charles Wreford-Brown, Frank Forman, Frederick Spiksley, George Frederick Wheldon, Gilbert Oswald Smith (Cap), Stephen Bloomer, William Charles Athersmith.
**Goals**: James Millar (48) /
George Frederick Wheldon (3), Stephen Bloomer (23, 72)


**65.  18.02.1899   Home Championship**
**ENGLAND v IRELAND  13-2**  (5-0)
*Roker Park, Sunderland*
Referee: Donald Hamilton (Scotland)   Attendance: 13,000
**ENGLAND**: John Hillman, Philip Bach, William Williams, Frank Forman, James William Crabtree, Ernest Needham, William Charles Athersmith, Stephen Bloomer, Gilbert Oswald Smith (Cap), James Settle, Frederick Ralph Forman.
**IRELAND**: James Lewis, John S. Pyper, Samuel Torrans, Joseph Ponsonby, Robert Milne, Michael Cochrane, James Campbell, John Thompson Mercer, John Waring, John Wattie, Joseph McAllen.
**Goals**: Frank Forman (15), Frederick Ralph Forman (20, 52), William Athersmith (25), Gilbert O. Smith (32, 59, 60, 63), Stephen Bloomer (40, 89), James Settle (53, 55, 80) /
James Campbell (88), Joseph McAllen (# penalty)


**66.  20.03.1899   Home Championship**
**ENGLAND v WALES  4-0**  (2-0)
*Ashton Gate, Bristol*
Referee: Thomas Robertson (Scotland)   Attendance: 10,000
**ENGLAND**: John William Robinson, Henry Thickett, William Williams, Ernest Needham, James William Crabtree, Frank Forman, William Charles Athersmith, Stephen Bloomer, Gilbert Oswald Smith (Cap), James Settle, Frederick Ralph Forman.
**WALES**: Samuel Jones, Horace Elford Blew, Smart Arridge, George Richards, Thomas John Buckland, William Clare Harrison, James Vaughan, William Henry Meredith, Trevor Owen, Arthur Grenville Morris, Robert Atherton.
**Goals**: Ernest Needham (30), Stephen Bloomer (44, 86), Frederick Ralph Forman (60)

**67. 08.04.1899   Home Championship**
**ENGLAND v SCOTLAND  2-1  (2-0)**
*Villa Park, Birmingham*

Referee: James Torrans (Ireland)   Attendance: 25,590

**ENGLAND**: John William Robinson, Henry Thickett, James William Crabtree, Frank Forman, Rabbi Howell, Ernest Needham, William Charles Athersmith, Stephen Bloomer, Gilbert Oswald Smith (Cap), James Settle, Frederick Ralph Forman.

**SCOTLAND**: John Edward Doig, Nicol Smith (Cap), David Storrier, Neil Gibson, Alexander John Christie, John Tait Robertson, John Campbell, Robert Cumming Hamilton, Robert Smyth McColl, Hugh Morgan, John Bell.

**Goals**: Gilbert Oswald Smith (25), James Settle (40) / Robert Cumming Hamilton (52)

**68. 17.03.1900   Home Championship**
**IRELAND v ENGLAND  0-2  (0-2)**
*Lansdowne Road, Dublin*

Referee: John Marshall (Scotland)   Attendance: 8,000

**IRELAND**: Matthew Michael Reilly, John S. Pyper, Michael Cochrane, John McShane, Archibald Goodall, Hugh Maginnis, George Sheehan, James Campbell, James Pyper, Joseph McAllen, Alfred Kearns.

**ENGLAND**: John William Robinson, William John Oakley, James William Crabtree, William Harold Johnson, John Holt, Ernest Needham, Arthur John Turner, Daniel Cunliffe, Gilbert Oswald Smith (Cap), Charles Sagar, Alfred Ernest Priest.

**Goals**: William Harold Johnson (22), Charles Sagar (26)

**69. 26.03.1900   Home Championship**
**WALES v ENGLAND  1-1  (0-1)**
*Arms Park, Cardiff*

Referee: Roberts (Scotland)   Attendance: 20,000

**WALES**: Frederick John Griffiths, David Jones, Charles Richard Morris, Samuel James Brookes, Robert Morris, William Clare Harrison, William Henry Meredith, Joseph Davies, Hugh Morgan-Owen, Alfred Ernest Watkins, Thomas David Parry.

**ENGLAND**: John William Robinson, Howard Spencer, William John Oakley, William Harold Johnson, Arthur Chadwick, James William Crabtree, William Charles Athersmith, Reginald Erskine Foster, Gilbert Oswald Smith (Cap), George Plumpton Wilson, William Alfred Spouncer.

**Goal**: William Henry Meredith (55) / George Plumpton Wilson (3)

**70. 07.04.1900   Home Championship**
**SCOTLAND v ENGLAND  4-1  (4-1)**
*Parkhead, Glasgow*

Referee: James Torrans (Ireland)   Attendance: 64,000

**SCOTLAND**: Henry George Rennie, Nicol Smith, John Drummond, Neil Gibson, Alexander Galloway Raisbeck, John Tait Robertson (Cap), John Bell, Robert Walker, Robert Smyth McColl, John Campbell, Alexander Smith.

**ENGLAND**: John William Robinson, William John Oakley, James William Crabtree, William Harold Johnson, Arthur Chadwick, Ernest Needham, William Charles Athersmith, Stephen Bloomer, Gilbert Oswald Smith (Cap), George Plumpton Wilson, John Plant.

**Goal**: Robert Smyth McColl (1, 25, 44), John Bell (6) / Stephen Bloomer (35)

**71. 09.03.1901   Home Championship**
**ENGLAND v IRELAND  3-0  (1-0)**
*The Dell, Southampton*

Referee: Thomas Robertson (Scotland)   Attendance: 8,000

**ENGLAND**: John William Robinson, Charles Burgess Fry, William John Oakley (Cap), William Jones, Thomas Henry Crawshaw, Ernest Needham, Arthur John Turner, Reginald Erskine Foster, George Albert Hedley, Herbert Ernest Banks, John Cox.

**IRELAND**: James V. Nolan-Whelan, William Kennedy Gibson, Peter Boyle, James Connor, Archibald Goodall, Joseph Burnison, Thomas Black, Robert Rea, John Mansfield, Isaac Doherty, Robert Clarke.

**Goals**: Thomas Henry Crawshaw (9), Reginald Erskine Foster (81, 83)

**72. 18.03.1901   Home Championship**
**ENGLAND v WALES  6-0  (1-0)**
*St.JamesPark, Newcastle*

Referee: Thomas Robertson (Scotland)   Attendance: 11,000

**ENGLAND**: Matthew Kingsley, James William Crabtree, William John Oakley, Albert Wilkes, William Bannister, Ernest Needham (Cap), Walter Bennett, Stephen Bloomer, William Edwin Beats, Reginald Erskine Foster, Bertram Oswald Corbett.

**WALES**: Leigh Richmond Roose, Samuel Meredith, Charles Richard Morris, Maurice Pryce Parry, William James Jones, Edward Hughes, William Henry Meredith, David Henry Pugh, Morgan Maddox Morgan-Owen, Thomas David Parry, Ephraim Williams.

**Goals**: Stephen Bloomer (38, 60, 71, 74), Ernest Needham (51 pen), Reginald Erskine Foster (72)

73.  30.03.1901   Home Championship
**ENGLAND v SCOTLAND  2-2**  (1-0)

*Crystal Palace, London*

Referee: James Torrans (Ireland)   Attendance: 35,000

**ENGLAND**: John William Sutcliffe, James Iremonger, William John Oakley, Albert Wilkes, Frank Forman, Ernest Needham, Walter Bennett, Stephen Bloomer, Gilbert Oswald Smith (Cap), Reginald Erskine Foster, Frederick Blackburn.

**SCOTLAND**: Henry George Rennie, Bernard Battles, John Drummond, Andrew Aitken, Alexander Galloway Raisbeck, John Tait Robertson (Cap), Robert Walker, John Campbell, Robert Smyth McColl, Robert Cumming Hamilton, Alexander Smith.

**Goals**: Frederick Blackburn (36), Stephen Bloomer (80) / John Campbell (48), Robert Cumming Hamilton (75)

05.04.1902   Home Championship
**SCOTLAND v ENGLAND  1-1**  (1-1)

*Ibrox Park, Glasgow*

Referee: James Torrans (Ireland)   Attendance: 80,500

**SCOTLAND**: John Edward Doig, Nicol Smith, John Drummond, Andrew Aitken (Cap), Alexander Raisbeck, John Tait Robertson, Robert Bryson Templeton, Robert Walker, Alexander Brown, George Turner Livingstone, Alexander Smith.

**ENGLAND**: William George, Robert Crompton, George Molyneux, Albert Wilkes, Frank Forman, Albert Edward Houlker, William Hogg, Stephen Bloomer (Cap), William Edwin Beats, James Settle, John Cox.

**Goal**: James Settle (44)

This match was abandoned in the 51st minute and is not considered a full international by either the English or Scottish Football Associations.

74.  03.03.1902   Home Championship
**WALES v ENGLAND  0-0**

*Racecourse Ground, Wrexham*

Referee: Thomas Robertson (Scotland)   Attendance: 8,000

**WALES**: Leigh Richmond Roose, Samuel Meredith, Charles Richard Morris, Maurice Pryce Parry, John Leonard Jones, William James Jones, William Henry Meredith, Walter Martin Watkins, Thomas David Parry, Ephraim Williams, Richard Morris.

**ENGLAND**: William George, Robert Crompton, James William Crabtree, Albert Wilkes, Walter Abbott, Ernest Needham, William Hogg, Stephen Bloomer, Charles Sagar, Reginald Erskine Foster (Cap), Herbert Broughall Lipsham.

76.  03.05.1902   Home Championship
**ENGLAND v SCOTLAND  2-2**  (0-2)

*Villa Park, Birmingham*

Referee: James Torrans (Ireland)   Attendance: 15,000

**ENGLAND**: William George, Robert Crompton, George Molyneux, Albert Wilkes, Frank Forman, Albert Edward Houlker, William Hogg, Stephen Bloomer (Cap), William Edwin Beats, James Settle, John Cox.

**SCOTLAND**: Henry George Rennie, Nicol Smith, John Drummond, Andrew Aitken (Cap), Alexander Galloway Raisbeck, John Tait Robertson, Robert Bryson Templeton, Robert Walker, Robert Smyth McColl, Ronald Orr, Alexander Smith.

**Goals**: James Settle (65), Albert Wilkes (67) / Robert Bryson Templeton (3), Ronald Orr (28)

75.  22.03.1902   Home Championship
**IRELAND v ENGLAND  0-1**  (0-0)

*Balmoral Showgrounds, Belfast*

Referee: Thomas Robertson (Scotland)   Attendance: 16,000

**IRELAND**: Matthew Michael Reilly, William McCracken, Peter Boyle, John Darling, Robert Milne, Harold Nicholl, John Thompson Mercer, Thomas Morrison, Andrew Gara, Alfred Kearns, John Henry Kirwan.

**ENGLAND**: William George, Robert Crompton, James Iremonger, Albert Wilkes, William Bannister, Frank Forman (Cap), William Hogg, Stephen Bloomer, John Calvey, James Settle, Frederick Blackburn.

**Goal**: James Settle (86)

77.  14.02.1903   Home Championship
**ENGLAND v IRELAND  4-0**  (1-0)

*Molineux, Wolverhampton*

Referee: William Nunnerley (Wales)   Attendance: 24,240

**ENGLAND**: Thomas Baddeley, Howard Spencer (Cap), George Molyneux, William Harold Johnson, Thomas Holford, Harry Hadley, Harry Davis, John Sharp, Vivian John Woodward, James Settle, Arthur Lockett.

**IRELAND**: William Scott, William R. McCracken, George McMillan, John Darling, Robert Milne, Archibald Goodall, James Campbell, James Maxwell, James Sheridan, Harold Alexander Sloan, John Henry Kirwan.

**Goals**: Vivian John Woodward (19, 52), John Sharp (63), Harry Davis (87)

**78.  02.03.1903    Home Championship**
**ENGLAND v WALES   2-1  (1-0)**
*Fratton Park, Portsmouth*

Referee: Thomas Robertson (Scotland)    Attendance: 4,000

**ENGLAND**: John William Sutcliffe, Robert Crompton (Cap), George Molyneux, William Harold Johnson, Frank Forman, Albert Edward Houlker, Harry Davis, William Garraty, Vivian John Woodward, Joseph William Bache, Reginald Corbett.

**WALES**: Robert Owen Evans, Horace Elford Blew, Charles Richard Morris, Maurice Pryce Parry, Robert Morris, Thomas Davies, William Henry Meredith, Walter Martin Watkins, Arthur William Green, Arthur Grenville Morris, Robert Atherton.

**Goals**: Joseph William Bache (12), Vivian J. Woodward (78) / Walter Martin Watkins (54)


**79.  04.04.1903    Home Championship**
**ENGLAND v SCOTLAND   1-2  (1-0)**
*Bramall Lane, Sheffield*

Referee: William Nunnerley (Wales)    Attendance: 36,000

**ENGLAND**: Thomas Baddeley, Robert Crompton (Cap), George Molyneux, William Harold Johnson, Thomas Edward Booth, Albert Edward Houlker, Harry Davis, Percy Humphreys, Vivian John Woodward, Arthur John Capes, John Cox.

**SCOTLAND**: John Edward Doig, Andrew McCombie, James Watson, Andrew Aitken, Alexander Galloway Raisbeck (Cap), John Tait Robertson, Robert Bryson Templeton, Robert Walker, Robert Cumming Hamilton, Finlay Ballantyne Speedie, Alexander Smith.

**Goal**: Vivian John Woodward (10) / Finlay Ballantyne Speedie (57), Robert Walker (59)


**80.  29.02.1904    Home Championship**
**WALES v ENGLAND   2-2  (1-0)**
*Racecourse Ground, Wrexham*

Referee: Thomas Robertson (Scotland)    Attendance: 9,000

**WALES**: Leigh Richmond Roose, Samuel Meredith, Horace Elford Blew, Richard Morris, Maurice Pryce Parry, Edward Hughes, John Leonard Jones, William Henry Meredith, Walter Martin Watkins, Lloyd Davies, Robert Atherton.

**ENGLAND**: Thomas Baddeley, Robert Crompton (Cap), Herbert Burgess, Ernest Albert Lee, Thomas Henry Crawshaw, Herod Ruddlesdin, William Frederick Brawn, Alfred Common, Arthur Samuel Brown, Joseph William Bache, George Henry Davis

**Goals**: Walter Martin Watkins (15), Lloyd Davies (85) / Alfred Common (77), Joseph William Bache (77)


**81.  12.03.1904    Home Championship**
**IRELAND v ENGLAND   1-3  (0-2)**
*Solitude, Belfast*

Referee: Thomas Robertson (Scotland)    Attendance: 15,000

**IRELAND**: William Scott, William McCracken, Peter Boyle, Robert Milne, Archibald Goodall, Hugh Maginnis, John Thompson Mercer, James Sheridan, Maurice Joseph Connor, John Henry Kirwan, Henry Redmond Buckle.

**ENGLAND**: Thomas Baddeley, Robert Crompton (Cap), Herbert Burgess, Herod Ruddlesdin, Thomas Henry Crawshaw, Alexander Leake, William Frederick Brawn, Alfred Common, Vivian John Woodward, Joseph William Bache, George Henry Davis.

**Goals**: John Henry Kirwan (#) / Joseph William Bache (12), Alfred Common (16), George Henry Davis (65)


**82.  09.04.1904    Home Championship**
**SCOTLAND v ENGLAND   0-1  (0-0)**
*Parkhead, Glasgow*

Referee: William Nunnerley (Wales)    Attendance: 40,000

**SCOTLAND**: Peter McBride, Thomas Alexander Skinner Jackson, James Watson, Andrew Aitken, Alexander Galloway Raisbeck, John Tait Robertson (Cap), Thomas Bruce Niblo, Robert Walker, Alexander Brown, Ronald Orr, Robert Bryson Templeton.

**ENGLAND**: Thomas Baddeley, Robert Crompton (Cap), Herbert Burgess, Samuel Wolstenholme, Bernard Wilkinson, Alexander Leake, John Rutherford, Stephen Bloomer, Vivian John Woodward, Stanley Schute Harris, Frederick Blackburn.

**Goal**: Stephen Bloomer (64)


**83.  25.02.1905    Home Championship**
**ENGLAND v IRELAND   1-1  (0-0)**
*Ayresome Park, Middlesbrough*

Referee: Thomas Robertson (Scotland)    Attendance: 21,700

**ENGLAND**: Reginald Garnet Williamson, William Balmer, John Carr, Samuel Wolstenholme, Charles Roberts, Alexander Leake, Richard Bond, Stephen Bloomer, Vivian John Woodward, Stanley Schute Harris (Cap), Frank Booth.

**IRELAND**: William Scott, William R. McCracken, Alexander McCartney, John Darling, James Connor, Harold Nicholl, Harold Alexander Sloan, James Sheridan, Neill Murphy, Thomas Shanks, John Henry Kirwan.

**Goal**: Stephen Bloomer (50) / Reginald G. Williamson (48 og)

**84.  27.03.1905   Home Championship**
**ENGLAND v WALES  3-1  (0-0)**

*Anfield Road, Liverpool*

Referee: Thomas Robertson (Scotland)   Attendance: 16,100

**ENGLAND:** James Henry Linacre, Howard Spencer (Cap), Herbert Smith, Samuel Wolstenholme, Charles Roberts, Alexander Leake, Richard Bond, Stephen Bloomer, Vivian John Woodward, Stanley Schute Harris, Harold Payne Hardman.

**WALES:** Leigh Richmond Roose, Albert Thomas Jones, Charles Richard Morris, George Latham, Edward Hughes, John Hughes, William Henry Meredith, William Jones, Walter Martin Watkins, Arthur Grenville Morris, Alfred Oliver.

**Goals:** Vivian Woodward (55, 88), Stanley Schute Harris (80)


**85.  01.04.1905   Home Championship**
**ENGLAND v SCOTLAND  1-0  (0-0)**

*Crystal Palace, London*

Referee: William Nunnerley (Wales)   Attendance: 27,559

**ENGLAND:** James Henry Linacre, Howard Spencer (Cap), Herbert Smith, Herod Ruddlesdin, Charles Roberts, Alexander Leake, John Sharp, Stephen Bloomer, Vivian John Woodward, Joseph William Bache, George Arthur Bridgett.

**SCOTLAND:** John Lyall, Andrew McCombie, James Watson, Andrew Aitken, Charles Bellany Thomson (Cap), Peter McWilliam, Robert Walker, James Howie, Alexander Simpson Young, Peter Somers, George W. Wilson.

**Goal:** Joseph William Bache (80)


**86.  17.02.1906   Home Championship**
**IRELAND v ENGLAND  0-5  (0-2)**

*Solitude, Belfast*

Referee: Thomas Robertson (Scotland)   Attendance: 16,000

**IRELAND:** James Sherry, John Darling, Hugh McIlroy, John Wright, Robert Milne, James English McConnell, Andrew Hunter, Thomas Stephen Mulholland, Valentine Harris, Charles O'Hagan, John Henry Kirwan.

**ENGLAND:** James Ashcroft, Robert Crompton, Herbert Smith, Benjamin Warren, Colin Campbell McKechnie Veitch, Albert Edward Houlker, Richard Bond, Samuel Hulme Day, Arthur Samuel Brown, Stanley Schute Harris (Cap), Albert Arthur Gosnell.

**Goals:** Richard Bond (26, 89), Arthur Samuel Brown (32), Stanley Schute Harris (56), Samuel Hulme Day (70)


**87.  19.03.1906   Home Championship**
**WALES v ENGLAND  0-1  (0-0)**

*Arms Park, Cardiff*

Referee: Gough (Wales)   Attendance: 15,000

**WALES:** Leigh Richmond Roose, Albert Thomas Jones, Horace Elford Blew, Maurice Pryce Parry, Morgan Maddox Morgan-Owen, Edward Hughes, William Jones, Hugh Morgan-Owen, Arthur William Green, John Richard Lewis, Robert Ernest Evans.

**ENGLAND:** James Ashcroft, Robert Crompton, Herbert Smith, Benjamin Warren, Colin Campbell McKechnie Veitch, Albert Edward Houlker, Richard Bond, Samuel Hulme Day, Alfred Common, Stanley Schute Harris (Cap), Edward Gordon Dundas Wright.

**Goal:** Samuel Hulme Day (86)


**88.  07.04.1906   Home Championship**
**SCOTLAND v ENGLAND  2-1  (1-0)**

*Hampden Park, Glasgow*

Referee: William Nunnerley (Wales)   Attendance: 102,741

**SCOTLAND:** Peter McBride, Donald McLeod, William T. Dunlop, Andrew Aitken, Alexander Galloway Raisbeck (Cap), Peter McWilliam, George Stewart, James Howie, Alexander William Menzies, George Turner Livingstone, Alexander Smith.

**ENGLAND:** James Ashcroft, Robert Crompton, Herbert Burgess, Benjamin Warren, Colin Campbell McKechnie Veitch, Joseph William Harry Makepeace, Richard Bond, Samuel Hulme Day, Albert Shepherd, Stanley Schute Harris (Cap), James Conlin.

**Goal:** James Howie (40, 55) / Albert Shepherd (81)


**89.  16.02.1907   Home Championship**
**ENGLAND v IRELAND  1-0  (0-0)**

*Goodison Park, Liverpool*

Referee: Thomas Robertson (Scotland)   Attendance: 22,235

**ENGLAND:** Samuel Hardy, Robert Crompton (Cap), John Carr, Benjamin Warren, William John Wedlock, Robert Murray Hawkes, John Rutherford, John George Coleman, George Richard Hilsdon, Joseph William Bache, Harold Payne Hardman.

**IRELAND:** William Scott, William R. McCracken, Alexander McCartney, John Wright, James Connor, James English McConnell, John Blair, Valentine Harris, Harold Alexander Sloan, Charles O'Hagan, Samuel Young.

**Goal:** Harold Payne Hardman (53)

90.  18.03.1907   Home Championship
**ENGLAND v WALES  1-1**  (0-1)
*Craven Cottage, London*

Referee: Robert Murray (Scotland)     Attendance: 25,000

**ENGLAND**: Samuel Hardy, Robert Crompton (Cap), Jesse Pennington, Benjamin Warren, William John Wedlock, Colin Campbell McKechnie Veitch, John Rutherford, Stephen Bloomer, Irvine Thornley, James Stewart, George Wall.

**WALES**: Leigh Richmond Roose, Lloyd Davies, Samuel Meredith, George Latham, Morgan Maddox Morgan-Owen, Edward Hughes, William Henry Meredith, William L. Jones, Arthur William Green, Arthur Grenville Morris, Robert Ernest Evans.

**Goal**: James Stewart (62) / William Jones (25)


91.  06.04.1907   Home Championship
**ENGLAND v SCOTLAND  1-1**  (1-1)
*St. James' Park, Newcastle*

Referee: Thomas Robertson (Scotland)     Attendance: 35,829

**ENGLAND**: Samuel Hardy, Robert Crompton (Cap), Jesse Pennington, Benjamin Warren, William John Wedlock, Colin Campbell McKechnie Veitch, John Rutherford, Stephen Bloomer, Vivian John Woodward, James Stewart, Harold Payne Hardman.

**SCOTLAND**: Peter McBride, Charles Bellany Thomson, James Sharp, Andrew Aitken, Alexander Galloway Raisbeck (Cap), Peter McWilliam, George Stewart, Robert Walker, Andrew Wilson, Walter White, George Wilson.

**Goal**: Stephen Bloomer (42) / Robert Crompton (2 og)


92.  15.02.1908   Home Championship
**IRELAND v ENGLAND  1-3**  (1-1)
*Solitude, Belfast*

Referee: Thomas Robertson (Scotland)     Attendance: 22,600

**IRELAND**: William Scott, Alexander Craig, Alexander McCartney, Valentine Harris, James Connor, George McClure, John Blair, Denis J. Hannon, Harold Victor Aitken Mercer, Samuel Burnison, Samuel Young.

**ENGLAND**: Harry Mart Maskery, Robert Crompton, Jesse Pennington, Benjamin Warren, William John Wedlock, Evelyn Henry Lintott, John Rutherford, Vivian John Woodward (Cap), George Richard Hilsdon, James Edward Windridge, George Wall.

**Goals**: Denis J. Hannon (13) /
George R. Hilsdon (7, 83), Vivian John Woodward (80)


93.  16.03.1908   Home Championship
**WALES v ENGLAND  1-7**  (0-4)
*Racecourse Ground, Wrexham*

Referee: David Phillips (Scotland)     Attendance: 8,000

**WALES**: Leigh Richmond Roose (46 David Davies), Charles Richard Morris, Horace Elford Blew, Maurice Pryce Parry, Edwin Hughes, George Latham, William Henry Meredith, William Henry Matthews, William Davies, Arthur Grenville Morris, Robert Ernest Evans.

**ENGLAND**: Horace Peter Bailey, Robert Crompton, Jesse Pennington, Benjamin Warren, William John Wedlock, Evelyn Henry Lintott, John Rutherford, Vivian John Woodward (Cap), George Richard Hilsdon, James Edward Windridge, Harold Payne Hardman.

**Goals**: William Davies (90) / Vivian J. Woodward (18, 70, 80), James Edward Windridge (25), William John Wedlock (30), George Richard Hilsdon (40, 63)


94.  04.04.1908   Home Championship
**SCOTLAND v ENGLAND  1-1**  (1-0)
*Hampden Park, Glasgow*

Referee: James Mason (England)     Attendance: 121,452

**SCOTLAND**: Peter McBride, Alexander McNair, James Sharp, Andrew Aitken, Charles Bellany Thomson (Cap), John May, James Howie, Robert Walker, Andrew Wilson, Walter White, James Quinn.

**ENGLAND**: Samuel Hardy, Robert Crompton, Jesse Pennington, Benjamin Warren, William John Wedlock, Evelyn Henry Lintott, John Rutherford, Vivian John Woodward (Cap), George Richard Hilsdon, James Edward Windridge, George Arthur Bridgett.

**Goal**: Andrew Wilson (27) / James Edward Windridge (75)


95.  06.06.1908
**AUSTRIA v ENGLAND  1-6**  (0-3)
*Cricketer Platz, Wien*

Referee: Christiaan Jacobus Groothoff (Holland)     Attendance: 3,500

**AUSTRIA**: Josef Prager, Wilhelm Weihrauch, Rudolf Smolek, Robert Cimera, Dr. Paul Fischl, Arthur Wackenreuther, Wilhelm Schmieger, Robert Merz, Engelbert König, Friedrich Hirschl, Ernst Thurm.

**ENGLAND**: Horace Peter Bailey, Robert Crompton, Walter Samuel Corbett, Benjamin Warren, William John Wedlock, Robert Murray Hawkes, John Rutherford, Vivian John Woodward (Cap), George Richard Hilsdon, James Edward Windridge, George Arthur Bridgett.

**Goals**: Wilhelm Schmieger (#) / James E. Windridge (21, 38), Vivian John Woodward (40), George Richard Hilsdon (57, 70), George Arthur Bridgett (85)

96.  08.06.1908
**AUSTRIA v ENGLAND  1-11**  (0-5)

*Hohe Warte, Wien*

Referee: Ede Herczog (Hungary)    Attendance: 5,000

**AUSTRIA**: Rudolf Donhardt, Johann Schwarz, Rudolf Smolek, Karl Jech, Dr. Paul Fischl, Arthur Wackenreuther, Ludwig Hussak, Robert Merz, Engelbert König, Friedrich Hirschl, Ernst Thurm.

**ENGLAND**: Horace Peter Bailey, Robert Crompton, Jesse Pennington, Benjamin Warren, William John Wedlock, Robert Murray Hawkes, John Rutherford, Vivian John Woodward (Cap), Frank Bradshaw, James Edward Windridge, George Arthur Bridgett.

**Goals**: Friedrich Hirschl (#) / Vivian J. Woodward (4, 43, #, #), James Edward Windridge (6), John Rutherford (15), Frank Bradshaw (18, #, #), Benjamin Warren (#), George Arthur Bridgett (#)


97.  10.06.1908
**HUNGARY v ENGLAND  0-7**  (0-4)

*Millenáris-pálya, Budapest*

Referee: Hugo Meisl (Austria)    Attendance: 7,000

**HUNGARY**: László Domonkos, Gyula Rumbold, Ferenc Csüdör, Péter Ficzere, Sándor Bródy, Ferenc Simon, Zoltán Rónay, Ferenc Weisz, Károly Koródy, Imre Schlosser, Gáspár Borbás.   Trainer: Ferenc Stobbe

**ENGLAND**: Horace Peter Bailey, Robert Crompton, Walter Samuel Corbett, Benjamin Warren, William John Wedlock, Robert Murray Hawkes, John Rutherford, Vivian John Woodward (Cap), George Richard Hilsdon, James Edward Windridge, George Arthur Bridgett.

**Goals**: Vivian John Woodward (13), George Richard Hilsdon (28, 48, 71, 88), James Edward Windridge (30), John Rutherford (38)


98.  13.06.1908
**BOHEMIA v ENGLAND  0-4**  (0-1)

*Sparta, Praha*

Referee: Lewis (England)    Attendance: 12,000

**BOHEMIA**: Miroslav Jeník, Rudolf Krummer, Richard Veselý, Emanuel Benda, Karel Kotouč, Jan Jirkovský, Široký, Josef Bělka, Jan Starý, C. Malyy, Miloslav Macoun.

**ENGLAND**: Horace Peter Bailey, Robert Crompton, Walter Samuel Corbett, Benjamin Warren, William John Wedlock, Robert Murray Hawkes, John Rutherford, Vivian John Woodward (Cap), George Richard Hilsdon, James Edward Windridge, George Arthur Bridgett.

**Goals**: George Richard Hilsdon (24, 50 pen), James Edward Windridge (55), John Rutherford (83)


99.  13.02.1909    Home Championship
**ENGLAND v IRELAND  4-0**  (0-0)

*Valley Parade, Bradford*

Referee: James Stark (Scotland)    Attendance: 28,000

**ENGLAND**: Samuel Hardy, Robert Crompton, Joseph Richard Cottle, Benjamin Warren, William John Wedlock, Evelyn Henry Lintott, Arthur Berry, Vivian John Woodward (Cap), George Richard Hilsdon, James Edward Windridge, George Arthur Bridgett.

**IRELAND**: William Scott, James Balfe, Alexander McCartney, Valentine Harris, John Darling, George McClure, Andrew Hunter, William Lacey, William Greer, Charles O'Hagan, Samuel Young.

**Goals**: George Richard Hilsdon (50, 87 pen), Vivian John Woodward (60, 80)


100.  15.03.1909    Home Championship
**ENGLAND v WALES  2-0**  (2-0)

*City Ground, Nottingham*

Referee: David Phillips (Scotland)    Attendance: 11,500

**ENGLAND**: Samuel Hardy, Robert Crompton (Cap), Jesse Pennington, Benjamin Warren, William John Wedlock, Colin Campbell McKechnie Veitch, Frederick Beaconsfield Pentland, Vivian John Woodward, Bertram Clewley Freeman, George Henry Holley, George Arthur Bridgett.

**WALES**: Leigh Richmond Roose, Charles Richard Morris, Horace Elford Blew, Maurice Pryce Parry, Ernest Peake, Ioan Haydn Price, William Henry Meredith, George Arthur Wynn, William Davies, William Jones, William Charles Davies.

**Goals**: George H. Holley (15), Bertram Clewley Freeman (42)


101.  03.04.1909    Home Championship
**ENGLAND v SCOTLAND  2-0**  (2-0)

*Crystal Palace, London*

Referee: James Stark (Scotland)    Attendance: 27,000

**ENGLAND**: Samuel Hardy, Robert Crompton (Cap), Jesse Pennington, Benjamin Warren, William John Wedlock, Evelyn Henry Lintott, Frederick Beaconsfield Pentland, Harold John Fleming, Bertram Clewley Freeman, George Henry Holley, George Wall.

**SCOTLAND**: James Brownlie, John Cameron, James Watson, Alexander McNair, James Stark (Cap), Peter McWilliam, Alexander Bennett, Robert Walker, James Quinn, George W. Wilson, Harold McDonald Paul.

**Goals**: George Wall (3, 10)

102. 29.05.1909
**HUNGARY v ENGLAND  2-4**  (1-3)

*Millenáris-pálya, Budapest*

Referee:  Christiaan Jacobus Groothoff (Holland)    Attendance:  10,000

**HUNGARY**:  Ferenc Bihari, Ferenc Manglitz, Béla Révész, János Weinber, Jenő Károly, Lipót Kanyaurek, Ferenc Weisz, István Nyilas, Ákos Késmárky, István Tóth-Potya, József Grósz.
Trainer:  Frigyes Minder

**ENGLAND**:  Samuel Hardy, Robert Crompton, Jesse Pennington, Benjamin Warren, William John Wedlock, Evelyn Henry Lintott, Frederick Beaconsfield Pentland, Harold John Fleming, Vivian John Woodward (Cap), George Henry Holley, George Arthur Bridgett.

**Goals**:  Ákos Késmárky (44), József Grósz (72) / George Arthur Bridgett (5), Vivian John Woodward (39, 79), Harold John Fleming (42)

103. 31.05.1909
**HUNGARY v ENGLAND  2-8**  (0-5)

*Millenáris-pálya, Budapest*

Referee:  Hugo Meisl (Austria)    Attendance:  13,000

**HUNGARY**:  Ferenc Bihari, Gyula Rumbold, Oszkár Szendrő, Gyula Bíró, Jenő Károly, Antal Vágó, Gyula Feketeházy, Ferenc Weisz, Imre Schlosser, Árpád Mészáros, Gáspár Borbás.
Trainer:  Frigyes Minder

**ENGLAND**:  Samuel Hardy, Robert Crompton, Jesse Pennington, Benjamin Warren, William John Wedlock, Evelyn Henry Lintott, Frederick Beaconsfield Pentland, Harold John Fleming, Vivian John Woodward (Cap), George Henry Holley, George Arthur Bridgett.

**Goals**:  Imre Schlosser (47), Árpád Mészáros (78) / Harold John Fleming (4, 44), Vivian Woodward (12, 36, 55, 58), George Henry Holley (17, 89)

104. 01.06.1909
**AUSTRIA v ENGLAND  1-8**  (0-2)

*Hohe Warte, Wien*

Referee:  Ferenc Schubert (Hungary)    Attendance:  3,000

**AUSTRIA**:  Josef Prager, Karl Gross, Heinrich Retschury, Viktor Löwenfeld, Arthur Preiss, Heinrich Lenczewsky, Ludwig Hussak, Josef Schediwy, Karl Schrenk, Leopold Neubauer, Franz Scheu.

**ENGLAND**:  Samuel Hardy, Robert Crompton, Jesse Pennington, Benjamin Warren, William John Wedlock, George Henry Richards, Frederick Beaconsfield Pentland, Harold James Halse, Vivian John Woodward (Cap), George Henry Holley, George Arthur Bridgett.

**Goals**:  Leopold Neubauer (#) / Vivian Woodward (#, #, #), Harold James Halse (#. #), George Henry Holley (#, #), Benjamin Warren (#)

The times at which the goals were scored is not recorded.

105. 12.02.1910    Home Championship
**IRELAND v ENGLAND  1-1**  (1-0)

*Solitude, Belfast*

Referee:  Alexander Jackson (Scotland)    Attendance:  8,000

**IRELAND**:  William Scott, Samuel Burnison, Patrick McCann, Valentine Harris, James English McConnell, John Darling, William Thomas James Renneville, William Lacey, James M. Murray, John Murphy, Frank Thompson.

**ENGLAND**:  Samuel Hardy, Herbert Morley, Arthur Cowell, Andrew Ducat, William John Wedlock, William Bradshaw, Richard Bond, Harold John Fleming, Vivian John Woodward (Cap), Joseph William Bache, Albert Edward Hall.

**Goal**:  Frank W. Thompson (43) / Harold John Fleming (51)

106. 14.03.1910    Home Championship
**WALES v ENGLAND  0-1**  (0-0)

*Arms Park, Cardiff*

Referee:  James Stark (Scotland)    Attendance:  20,000

**WALES**:  Leigh Richmond Roose, Horace Elford Blew, Charles Richard Morris, Edwin Hughes, George Latham, Llewelyn Davies, William Henry Meredith, George Arthur Wynn, William Jones, Arthur Grenville Morris, Robert Ernest Evans.

**ENGLAND**:  Samuel Hardy, Robert Crompton (Cap), Jesse Pennington, Andrew Ducat, William John Wedlock, William Bradshaw, Richard Bond, Harold John Fleming, John Parkinson, George Henry Holley, George Wall.

**Goal**:  Andrew Ducat (66)

107. 02.04.1910    Home Championship
**SCOTLAND v ENGLAND  2-0**  (2-0)

*Hampden Park, Glasgow*

Referee:  James Mason (England)    Attendance:  106,205

**SCOTLAND**:  James Brownlie, George Law, James Hay, Andrew Aitken, Charles Bellany Thomson (Cap), Peter McWilliam, Alexander Bennett, James McMenemy, James Quinn, Alexander Higgins, Robert Bryson Templeton.

**ENGLAND**:  Samuel Hardy, Robert Crompton (Cap), Jesse Pennington, Andrew Ducat, William John Wedlock, Joseph William Harry Makepeace, Richard Bond, William Hibbert, John Parkinson, Harold Thomas Walter Hardinge, George Wall.

**Goals**:  James McMenemy (20), James Quinn (32)

**108. 11.02.1911   Home Championship**
**ENGLAND v IRELAND  2-1  (1-0)**
*Baseball Ground, Derby*

Referee: David Phillips (Scotland)   Attendance: 20,000

**ENGLAND:** Reginald Garnet Williamson, Robert Crompton (Cap), Jesse Pennington, Benjamin Warren, William John Wedlock, Albert Sturgess, John Simpson, Harold John Fleming, Albert Shepherd, George Woodger, Robert Ernest Evans.

**IRELAND:** William Scott, Samuel Burnison, Patrick McCann, Valentine Harris, James Connor, Henry Vernon Hampton, William Lacey, Denis J. Hannon, John McDonnell, James Lowry Macauley, Frank W. Thompson.

**Goals:** Albert Shepherd (18), Robert Ernest Evans (87) / James Lowry Macauley (88)


**109. 13.03.1911   Home Championship**
**ENGLAND v WALES  3-0  (0-0)**
*The Den, Millwall, London*

Referee: James Stark (Scotland)   Attendance: 22,000

**ENGLAND:** Reginald Garnet Williamson, Robert Crompton (Cap), Jesse Pennington, Benjamin Warren, William John Wedlock, Kenneth Reginald Gunnery Hunt, John Simpson, Harold John Fleming, George William Webb, Vivian John Woodward, Robert Ernest Evans.

**WALES:** Robert Owen Evans, Charles Richard Morris, Thomas John Hewitt, Edwin Hughes, Lloyd Davies, William Jones, William Henry Meredith, Evan Jones, William Davies, Arthur Grenville Morris, Edward Thomas Vizard.

**Goals:** Vivian Woodward (65, 83), George William Webb (67)


**110. 01.04.1911   Home Championship**
**ENGLAND v SCOTLAND  1-1  (1-0)**
*Goodison Park, Liverpool*

Referee: William Nunnerley (Wales)   Attendance: 38,000

**ENGLAND:** Reginald Garnet Williamson, Robert Crompton (Cap), Jesse Pennington, Benjamin Warren, William John Wedlock, Kenneth Reginald Gunnery Hunt, John Simpson, James Stewart, George William Webb, Joseph William Bache, Robert Ernest Evans.

**SCOTLAND:** James Lawrence, Donald Cameron Colman, John Walker, Andrew Aitken, Wilfrid Lawson Low, James Hay (Cap), Alexander Bennett, James McMenemy, William Reid, Alexander Higgins, Alexander Smith.

**Goal:** James Stewart (20) / Alexander Higgins (88)


**111. 10.02.1912   Home Championship**
**IRELAND v ENGLAND  1-6  (1-3)**
*Dalymount Park, Dublin*

Referee: Alexander Jackson (Scotland)   Attendance: 15,000

**IRELAND:** William Scott, Samuel Burnison, Patrick McCann, Valentine Harris, Patrick O'Connell, Henry Vernon Hampton, William Lacey, Michael Hamill, William Halligan, James Lowry Macauley, Frank W. Thompson.

**ENGLAND:** Samuel Hardy, Robert Crompton (Cap), Jesse Pennington, James Thomas Brittleton, William John Wedlock, William Bradshaw, John Simpson, Harold John Fleming, Bertram Clewley Freeman, George Henry Holley, John Mordue.

**Goals:** Michael Hamill (35) / Harold J. Fleming (12, 40, 64), George Henry Holley (17), Bertram Clewley Freeman (50), John Simpson (85)


**112. 11.03.1912   Home Championship**
**WALES v ENGLAND  0-2  (0-2)**
*Racecourse Ground, Wrexham*

Referee: Thomas Dougray (Scotland)   Attendance: 14,000

**WALES:** Robert Owen Evans, Llewelyn Davies, Lloyd Davies, Edwin Hughes, Ernest Peake, Joseph Thomas Jones, William Henry Meredith, George Arthur Wynn, Evan Jones, Arthur Grenville Morris, Edward Thomas Vizard.

**ENGLAND:** Reginald Garnet Williamson, Robert Crompton (Cap), Jesse Pennington, James Thomas Brittleton, William John Wedlock, Joseph William Harry Makepeace, John Simpson, Frank Jefferis, Bertram Clewley Freeman, George Henry Holley, Robert Ernest Evans.

**Goals:** George H. Holley (2), Bertram Clewley Freeman (41)


**113. 23.03.1912   Home Championship**
**SCOTLAND v ENGLAND  1-1  (1-1)**
*Hampden Park, Glasgow*

Referee: James Mason (England)   Attendance: 127,307

**SCOTLAND:** James Brownlie, Alexander McNair (Cap), John Walker, James Eadie Gordon, Charles Bellany Thomson, James Hay, Robert Bryson Templeton, Robert Walker, David Prophet McLean, Andrew Wilson, James Quinn.

**ENGLAND:** Reginald Garnet Williamson, Robert Crompton (Cap), Jesse Pennington, James Thomas Brittleton, William John Wedlock, Joseph William Harry Makepeace, John Simpson, Frank Jefferis, Bertram Clewley Freeman, George Henry Holley, George Wall.

**Goal:** Andrew Wilson (7) / George Henry Holley (13)

**114. 15.02.1913   Home Championship**
**IRELAND v ENGLAND   2-1  (1-1)**
*Windsor Park, Belfast*

Referee: Alexander Jackson (Scotland)   Attendance: 20,000

**IRELAND**: William Scott, William George McConnell, Peter Warren, Henry Vernon Hampton, Valentine Harris, William Andrews, John Houston, Denis Hannon, William Gillespie, James Lowry Macauley, Frank W. Thompson.

**ENGLAND**: Reginald Garnet Williamson, Robert Crompton (Cap), Robert William Benson, Francis Cuggy, Thomas Wilkinson Boyle, George Utley, John Mordue, Charles Murray Buchan, George Washington Elliott, Joseph Smith, George Wall.

**Goal**: William Gillespie (43, 60) / Charles M. Buchan (10)

**115. 17.03.1913   Home Championship**
**ENGLAND v WALES   4-3  (3-1)**
*Ashton Gate, Bristol*

Referee: Alexander Jackson (Scotland)   Attendance: 8,000

**ENGLAND**: Ernald Oak Scattergood, Robert Crompton (Cap), Jesse Pennington, Hugh Moffat, Joseph McCall, William Bradshaw, Charles William Wallace, Harold John Fleming, Joseph Harold Hampton, Edwin Gladstone Latheron, Joseph Charles Hodkinson.

**WALES**: William Ellis Bailiff, Llewelyn Davies, Lloyd Davies, Thomas John Hewitt, Edwin Hughes, Ernest Peake, Joseph Thomas Jones, William Henry Meredith, George Arthur Wynn, Walter Otto Davis, William Jones.

**Goals**: Harold John Fleming (15), Edwin G. Latheron (25), Joseph McCall (35), Joseph Harold Hampton (55) / Walter Otto Davis (10), William Henry Meredith (52), Ernest Peake (70)

**116. 05.04.1913   Home Championship**
**ENGLAND v SCOTLAND   1-0  (1-0)**
*Stamford Bridge, London*

Referee: Alexander Jackson (Scotland)   Attendance: 52,500

**ENGLAND**: Samuel Hardy, Robert Crompton (Cap), Jesse Pennington, James Thomas Brittleton, Joseph McCall, William Watson, John Simpson, Harold John Fleming, Joseph Harold Hampton, George Henry Holley, Joseph Charles Hodkinson.

**SCOTLAND**: James Brownlie, Alexander McNair, John Walker, James Eadie Gordon, Charles Bellany Thomson (Cap), David Wilson, Joseph Donnachie, Robert Walker, William Reid, Andrew Wilson, George Robertson.

**Goal**: Joseph Harold Hampton (37)

**117. 14.02.1914   Home Championship**
**ENGLAND v IRELAND   0-3  (0-2)**
*Ayresome Park, Middlesbrough*

Referee: Alexander Jackson (Scotland)   Attendance: 25,000

**ENGLAND**: Samuel Hardy, Robert Crompton (Cap), Jesse Pennington, Francis Cuggy, Franklin Charles Buckley, William Watson, Charles William Wallace, Daniel Shea, George Washington Elliott, Edwin Gladstone Latheron, Henry Martin.

**IRELAND**: Frederick W. McKee, William George McConnell, Alexander Craig, Henry Vernon Hampton, Patrick O'Connell, Michael Hamill, David Rollo, Samuel Young, William Gillespie, William Lacey, Frank W. Thompson.

**Goals**: William Lacey (6, 80), William Gillespie (36)

**118. 16.03.1914   Home Championship**
**WALES v ENGLAND   0-2  (0-0)**
*Ninian Park, Cardiff*

Referee: James Mason (England)   Attendance: 17,000

**WALES**: Edward John Peers, Moses Richard Russell, Thomas James Matthias, Thomas John Hewitt, Lloyd Davies, William Jennings, William Henry Meredith, George Arthur Wynn, Alfred Stanley Rowlands, William Charles Davies, Edward Thomas Vizard.

**ENGLAND**: Samuel Hardy, Robert Crompton (Cap), Henry Colclough, James Thomas Brittleton, William John Wedlock, Robert McNeal, John Simpson, Daniel Shea, Joseph Harold Hampton, Joseph Smith, Edwin Mosscrop.

**Goals**: Joseph Smith (50), William John Wedlock (70)

**119. 04.04.1914   Home Championship**
**SCOTLAND v ENGLAND   3-1  (1-1)**
*Hampden Park, Glasgow*

Referee: Bamlett (England)   Attendance: 105,000

**SCOTLAND**: James Brownlie, Alexander McNair, Joseph Dodds, James Eadie Gordon (Cap), Charles Bellany Thomson, James Hay, Alexander Pollock Donaldson, James McMenemy, William Reid, James Anderson Croal, Joseph Donnachie.

**ENGLAND**: Samuel Hardy, Robert Crompton (Cap), Jesse Pennington, Albert Sturgess, Joseph McCall, Robert McNeal, Frederick Ingram Walden, Harold John Fleming, Joseph Harold Hampton, Joseph Smith, Edwin Mosscrop.

**Goal**: Charles Bellany Thomson (2), James McMenemy (50), William Reid (67) / Harold John Fleming (15)

**120. 25.10.1919    Home Championship**
**IRELAND v ENGLAND  1-1  (0-1)**
*Windsor Park, Belfast*

Referee: Thomas Dougray (Scotland)    Attendance: 30,000

**IRELAND**: William O'Hagan, William McCandless, William McCracken, William Emerson, Michael Hamill, William Lacey, James Ferris, Alfred Snape, Joseph Gowdy, Patrick Gallagher, David Lyner.

**ENGLAND**: Samuel Hardy, Joseph Smith, Arthur Egerton Knight (Cap), John James Bagshaw, Sidney Bowser, William Watson, Robert Joseph Turnbull, Jack Carr, John Gilbert Cock, Joseph Smith, Joseph Charles Hodkinson.

**Goal**: James Ferris (70) / John Gilbert Cock (1)


**121. 15.03.1920    Home Championship**
**ENGLAND v WALES  1-2  (1-2)**
*Highbury, London*

Referee: Alexander Jackson (Scotland)    Attendance: 21,110

**ENGLAND**: Samuel Hardy, Thomas Clay, Jesse Pennington (Cap), Andrew Ducat, Frank Barson, Arthur Grimsdell, Samuel Chedgzoy, Charles Murray Buchan, George Washington Elliott, Joseph Smith, Alfred Edward Quantrill.

**WALES**: Edward John Peers, Harold Millership, Moses Richard Russell, Thomas James Matthias, Joseph Thomas Jones, Frederick Charles Keenor, William Henry Meredith, William Jones, Stanley Charles Davies, Richard William Richards, Edward Thomas Vizard.

**Goal**: Charles Murray Buchan (7) / Stanley C. Davies (14 pen), Richard William Richards (35)


**122. 10.04.1920    Home Championship**
**ENGLAND v SCOTLAND  5-4  (2-4)**
*Hillsborough, Sheffield*

Referee: Thomas Dougray (Scotland)    Attendance: 35,000

**ENGLAND**: Samuel Hardy, Ephraim Longworth, Jesse Pennington (Cap), Andrew Ducat, Joseph McCall, Arthur Grimsdell, Charles William Wallace, Robert Kelly, John Gilbert Cock, Frederick Morris, Alfred Edward Quantrill.

**SCOTLAND**: Kenneth Campbell, Alexander McNair (Cap), James Blair, James Bowie, Wilfrid Lawson Low, James Eadie Gordon, Alexander Pollock Donaldson, Thomas Miller, Andrew Nesbit Wilson, John Paterson, Alexander Troup.

**Goals**: John G. Cock (9), Alfred Edward Quantrill (15), Robert Kelly (57, 73), Frederick Morris (67) / Thomas Miller (13), Andrew Nesbit Wilson (21), Alexander Pollock Donaldson (31), Thomas Miller (40)


**123. 23.10.1920    Home Championship**
**ENGLAND v IRELAND  2-0  (1-0)**
*Roker Park, Sunderland*

Referee: Alexander Jackson (Scotland)    Attendance: 22,000

**ENGLAND**: John William Mew, Richard Downs, Frederick Edwin Bullock, Andrew Ducat, Joseph McCall (Cap), Arthur Grimsdell, Samuel Chedgzoy, Robert Kelly, William Henry Walker, Frederick Morris, Alfred Edward Quantrill.

**IRELAND**: Elisha Scott, David Rollo, William McCandless, Robert McCracken, William Lacey, William Emerson, Patrick Kelly, James Ferris, John Francis Doran, William Gillespie, John McCandless.

**Goals**: Robert Kelly (10), William Henry Walker (47)


**124. 14.03.1921    Home Championship**
**WALES v ENGLAND  0-0**
*Ninian Park, Cardiff*

Referee: Alexander Jackson (Scotland)    Attendance: 12,000

**WALES**: Edward John Peers, Harold Millership, Moses Richard Russell, Frederick Charles Keenor, Joseph Thomas Jones, Thomas James Matthias, David Rees Williams, Ivor Jones, Francis Thomas Hoddinott, Stanley Charles Davies, Edward Thomas Vizard.

**ENGLAND**: Ernest Herbert Coleman, Warneford Cresswell, John Silcock, John Bamber, George Wilson, Thomas George Bromilow, Samuel Chedgzoy, Robert Kelly, Charles Murray Buchan (Cap), Henry Chambers, Alfred Edward Quantrill.


**125. 09.04.1921    Home Championship**
**SCOTLAND v ENGLAND  3-0  (1-0)**
*Hampden Park, Glasgow*

Referee: Arthur Ward (England)    Attendance: 85,000

**SCOTLAND**: John Ewart, John Marshall (Cap), James Blair, Stewart Davidson, George Brewster, James McMullan, Alexander McNab, Thomas Miller, Andrew Nesbit Wilson, Andrew Cunningham, Alan Lauder Morton.

**ENGLAND**: Harold Gough, Thomas Smart, John Silcock, Bertram Smith, George Wilson, Arthur Grimsdell (Cap), Samuel Chedgzoy, Robert Kelly, Henry Chambers, Herbert Bliss, James Henry Dimmock.

**Goals**: Andrew Nesbit Wilson (20), Alan Lauder Morton (46), Andrew Cunningham (57)

**126. 21.05.1921**
**BELGIUM v ENGLAND 0-2** (0-1)

*Sint-Jans Molenbeek, Bruxelles*

Referee: Johannes Mutters (Holland)    Attendance: 25,000

**BELGIUM**: Jean De Bie, Armand Swartenbroeks, Oscar Verbeeck, Joseph Musch (Cap), André Fierens, Guillaume Vanden Houten, Louis Van Hege, Robert Coppée, Frans Dogaer, Henri Larnoe, Georges Michel.
Trainer: William Sturrock Maxwell

**ENGLAND**: Benjamin Howard Baker, John Fort, Ephraim Longworth (Cap), Albert Read, George Wilson, Percival Henry Barton, Archibald Rawlings, James Marshall Seed, Charles Murray Buchan, Henry Chambers, George Harrison.

**Goals**: Charles Murray Buchan (33), Henry Chambers (76)


**127. 22.10.1921    Home Championship**
**IRELAND v ENGLAND 1-1** (1-1)

*Windsor Park, Belfast*

Referee: Alexander Jackson (Scotland)    Attendance: 30,000

**IRELAND**: Elisha Scott, William R. McCracken, David Rollo, Robert McCracken, Michael Scraggs, William Emerson, William Lacey, William Gillespie, John Francis Doran, Allan Mathieson, Louis Bookman.

**ENGLAND**: Jeremiah Dawson, Thomas Clay, Thomas Lucas, Frank Moss, George Wilson (Cap), Percival Henry Barton, Samuel Chedgzoy, William John Kirton, Ernest Simms, William Henry Walker, George Harrison.

**Goal**: William Gillespie / William Kirton (35)


**128. 13.03.1922    Home Championship**
**ENGLAND v WALES 1-0** (1-0)

*Anfield Road, Liverpool*

Referee: Forshaw (England)    Attendance: 30,000

**ENGLAND**: John Edward Davison, Thomas Clay, Frederick Titmuss, Bertram Smith, Maxwell Woosnam (Cap), Thomas George Bromilow, Frederick Ingram Walden, Robert Kelly, William Ernest Rawlings, William Henry Walker, William Henry Smith.

**WALES**: Edward John Peers, Moses Richard Russell, James Henry Evans, Herbert Price Evans, Joseph Thomas Jones, Thomas James Matthias, William James Hole, Stanley Charles Davies, Leonard Stephen Davies, Richard William Richards, Edward Thomas Vizard.

**Goal**: Robert Kelly (3)


**129. 08.04.1922    Home Championship**
**ENGLAND v SCOTLAND 0-1** (0-0)

*Villa Park, Birmingham*

Referee: Thomas Dougray (Scotland)    Attendance: 33,646

**ENGLAND**: Jeremiah Dawson, Thomas Clay, Samuel John Wadsworth, Frank Moss, George Wilson (Cap), Thomas George Bromilow, Richard Ernest York, Robert Kelly, William Ernest Rawlings, William Henry Walker, William Henry Smith.

**SCOTLAND**: Kenneth Campbell, John Marshall, James Blair (Cap), John Wotherspoon Gilchrist, William Cringan, Neil McBain, Alexander Archibald, John Anderson Crosbie, Andrew Nesbit Wilson, Thomas Cairns, Alan Lauder Morton.

**Goal**: Andrew Nesbit Wilson (63)


**130. 21.10.1922    Home Championship**
**ENGLAND v NORTHERN IRELAND 2-0** (0-0)

*The Hawthorns, West Bromwich*

Referee: Alexander Jackson (Scotland)    Attendance: 20,173

**ENGLAND**: Edward Hallows Taylor, Joseph Smith, Jack Harry Harrow, Frank Moss, George Wilson, Arthur Grimsdell (Cap), David William Mercer, James Marshall Seed, Frank Raymond Osborne, Henry Chambers, Owen Williams.

**NORTHERN IRELAND**: Alfred Ireland Harland, David Rollo, John Joseph Curran, William Emerson, Ernest Edwin Smith, Francis Gerald Morgan, David R. Lyner, Robert William Irvine, Patrick Nelis, William Gillespie, James Burns.

**Goals**: Henry Chambers (66, 85)


**131. 05.03.1923    Home Championship**
**ENGLAND v WALES 2-2** (1-1)

*Ninian Park, Cardiff*

Referee: Bryan (England)    Attendance: 15,000

**ENGLAND**: Edward Hallows Taylor, Ephraim Longworth, Frederick Titmuss, Thomas Patrick Magee, George Wilson, Arthur Grimsdell (Cap), Jack Carr, James Marshall Seed, Victor Martin Watson, Henry Chambers, Owen Williams.

**WALES**: Edward John Peers, Edward Parry, Moses Richard Russell, Frederick Charles Keenor, Robert William Matthews, William Jennings, William James Hole, Ivor Jones, Leonard Stephen Davies, Edward Thomas Vizard, John Hugh Evans.

**Goals**: Henry Chambers (36), Victor Martin Watson (48) / Frederick Charles Keenor (17), Ivor Jones (86)

132. 19.03.1923
**ENGLAND v BELGIUM 6-1** (2-1)

*Highbury, London*

Referee: George Noel Watson (England)    Att: 14,052

**ENGLAND:** Edward Hallows Taylor, Ephraim Longworth, Samuel John Wadsworth, Frederick William Kean, George Wilson (Cap), Thomas George Bromilow, David William Mercer, James Marshall Seed, Norman Bullock, Henry Chambers, Kenneth Edward Hegan.

**BELGIUM:** Jean De Bie, Armand Swartenbroeks (Cap), Oscar Verbeeck, André Fierens, Florimond Van Halme, Achille Schelstraete, Louis Bessems, Honoré Vlamynck, Henri Larnoe, Maurice Gillis, Désiré Bastin.
Trainer: William Sturrock Maxwell

**Goals:** Kenneth E. Hegan (5, 40), David William Mercer (55), Henry Chambers (59), James Marshall Seed (60), Norman Bullock (70) / Honoré Vlamynck (16)

133. 14.04.1923    Home Championship
**SCOTLAND v ENGLAND 2-2** (1-2)

*Hampden Park, Glasgow*

Referee: Arthur Ward (England)    Attendance: 71,000

**SCOTLAND:** William Harper, John Hutton, James Blair, David Morton Steele, William Cringan (Cap), Thomas Allan Muirhead, Denis Lawson, Andrew Cunningham, Andrew Nesbit Wilson, Thomas Cairns, Alan Lauder Morton.

**ENGLAND:** Edward Hallows Taylor, Ephraim Longworth, Samuel John Wadsworth, Frederick William Kean, George Wilson (Cap), John Tresadern, Samuel Chedgzoy, Robert Kelly, Victor Martin Watson, Henry Chambers, Frederick Edward Tunstall.

**Goals:** Andrew Cunningham (28), Andrew N. Wilson (55) / Robert Kelly (31), Victor Martin Watson (42)

134. 10.05.1923
**FRANCE v ENGLAND 1-4** (0-2)

*Pershing, Paris*

Referee: Barette (Belgium)    Attendance: 30,000

**FRANCE:** Pierre Chayrigues, Pierre Mony, Lucien Gamblin (Cap), Louis Mistral, François Hugues, Philippe Bonnardel, Jules Dewaquez, Louis Darques, Marcel Dangles, Henri Bard, Raymond Dubly.

**ENGLAND:** John Thomas Alderson, Warneford Cresswell, Harry Jones, Seth Lewis Plum, James Seddon, Percival Henry Barton, Frank Raymond Osborne, Charles Murray Buchan (Cap), Frederick Norman Smith Creek, Frederick Hartley, Kenneth Edward Hegan.

**Goals:** Jules Dewaquez (89) / Kenneth Edward Hegan (9, 84), Charles M. Buchan (35), Frederick Norman Smith Creek (55)

135. 21.05.1923
**SWEDEN v ENGLAND 2-4** (1-3)

*Råsunda, Solna*

Referee: Hugo Meisl (Austria)    Attendance: 14,500

**SWEDEN:** Sigfrid Lindberg, Valdus Lund, Henning Svensson, Hjalmar Andersson, Sven Friberg (Cap), Ivar Klingström, Gunnar Olsson, Harry Dahl, Otto Malm, Erik Hjelm, Rudolf Kock.   Trainer: John Pettersson

**ENGLAND:** Ernest C. Williamson, William Ashurst, Jack Harry Harrow, Basil Patchitt (Cap), James Seddon, John Tresadern, George Thornewell, James Moore, Henry Bedford, William Henry Walker, Thomas Urwin.

**Goals:** Harry Dahl (33, 83) / William Henry Walker (22, 75), George Thornewell (25), James Moore (40)

136. 24.05.1923
**SWEDEN v ENGLAND 1-3** (1-1)

Råsunda, Solna, Att: 12,000

**SWEDEN:** Sigfred Lindberg, Albert Andersson, Gosta Wihlborg, Sven Lindqvist, John Persson, Ivar Klingstrom, Rune Bergstrom, Harry Dahl, Gunnar Olsson, Albin Dahl, Rudolf Kock.

**ENGLAND:** Ernest Williamson, William Ashurst, John Silcock, Thomas Patrick Magee, James Seddon, Basil Patchitt (Cap), George Thornewell, William Gray Moore, William Henry Walker, Harold Sidney Miller, Thomas Urwin.

**Goals:** Harry Dahl (41) /
William Gray Moore (32, 78), Harold Sidney Miller (59)

137. 20.10.1923    Home Championship
**NORTHERN IRELAND v ENGLAND 2-1** (1-1)

*Windsor Park, Belfast*

Referee: Alexander Jackson (Scotland)    Attendance: 23,000

**NORTHERN IRELAND:** Thomas J. Farquharson, Andrew McCluggage, John Joseph Curran, Samuel Johnstone Irving, Ernest Edwin Smith, William Emerson, John Brown, Thomas Croft, Robert William Irvine, William Gillespie, Joseph Toner.

**ENGLAND:** Edward Hallows Taylor, Alfred George Bower, Samuel John Wadsworth, Harry Harold Pantling, George Wilson (Cap), Thomas Meehan, Kenneth Edward Hegan, Robert Kelly, Joseph Bradford, Henry Chambers, Frederick Edward Tunstall.

**Goal:** William Gillespie (16), Thomas Croft (70) / Joseph Bradford (11)

138. 01.11.1923
**BELGIUM v ENGLAND 2-2 (1-1)**
*Bosuil, Antwerpen*

Referee: Johannes Mutters (Holland)   Attendance: 40,000

**BELGIUM**: Jean De Bie, Armand Swartenbroeks (Cap), Oscar Verbeeck, André Fierens, Florimond Van Halme, Achille Schelstraete, Hector Goetinck, Maurice Gillis, Henri Larnoe, Ivan Thys, Désiré Bastin.   Trainer: William Sturrock Maxwell

**ENGLAND**: Arthur Edward Hufton, Warneford Cresswell, Alfred George Bower, Frank Moss, James Seddon, Percival Henry Barton, Kenneth Edward Hegan, William Brown, William Thomas Roberts, Alexander William Doggart (Cap), Thomas Urwin.

**Goals**: Henri Larnoe (7), Achille Schelstraete (75 pen) / William Brown (32), William Thomas Roberts (80)

139. 03.03.1924   Home Championship
**ENGLAND v WALES 1-2 (0-0)**
*Ewood Park, Blackburn*

Referee: George Noel Watson (England)   Att: 30,000

**ENGLAND**: William Ronald Sewell, Thomas Smart, Thomas Mort, Frederick William Kean, George Wilson (Cap), Percival Henry Barton, Samuel Chedgzoy, David Bone Nightingale Jack, William Thomas Roberts, Clement Stephenson, Frederick Edward Tunstall.

**WALES**: Albert Gray, Moses Richard Russell, John Jenkins, Herbert Price Evans, Frederick Charles Keenor, William Jennings, William Davies, John Barry Nicholls, Leonard Stephen Davies, Richard William Richards, Edward Thomas Vizard.

**Goal**: William Thomas Roberts (55) / William Davies (59), Edward Thomas Vizard (62)

140. 12.04.1924   Home Championship
**ENGLAND v SCOTLAND 1-1 (0-1)**
*Wembley, London*

Referee: Thomas Dougray (Scotland)   Attendance: 37,250

**ENGLAND**: Edward Hallows Taylor, Thomas Smart, Samuel John Wadsworth, Frank Moss (Cap), Charles William Spencer, Percival Henry Barton, William Butler, David Bone Nightingale Jack, Charles Murray Buchan, William Henry Walker, Frederick Edward Tunstall.

**SCOTLAND**: William Harper, John Smith, Philip McCloy, William Clunas, David Morris, James McMullan (Cap), Alexander Archibald, William Duncan Cowan, Neil L. Harris, Andrew Cunningham, Alan Lauder Morton.

**Goal**: William H. Walker (60) / William Duncan Cowan (40)

141. 17.05.1924
**FRANCE v ENGLAND 1-3 (0-2)**
*Pershing, Paris*

Referee: Eymers (Holland)   Attendance: 20,000

**FRANCE**: Pierre Chayrigues, Edouard Baumann, Ernest Gravier, Marcel Domergue, Antoine Parachini, Philippe Bonnardel, Jules Dewaquez, Jean Boyer, Paul Nicolas, Ernest Gross, Raymond Dubly (Cap).

**ENGLAND**: Edward Hallows Taylor, Thomas Lucas, Thomas Mort, Frederick Harold Ewer, George Wilson (Cap), George Frederick Blackburn, George Thornewell, Stanley George James Earle, William Vivian Gibbins, Harry Storer, Frederick Edward Tunstall.

**Goals**: Jules Dewaquez (58) / William Vivian Gibbins (25), Harry Storer (40), Edouard Baumann (83 og)

142. 22.10.1924   Home Championship
**ENGLAND v NORTHERN IRELAND 3-1 (1-0)**
*Goodison Park, Liverpool*

Referee: Craigmoyle (Scotland)   Attendance: 25,000

**ENGLAND**: James Frederick Mitchell, Warneford Cresswell, Samuel John Wadsworth (Cap), Frederick William Kean, Henry Healless, Percival Henry Barton, Samuel Chedgzoy, Robert Kelly, Henry Bedford, William Henry Walker, Frederick Edward Tunstall.

**NORTHERN IRELAND**: Thomas J. Farquarharson, Robert B. Manderson, Andrew L. Kennedy, James H.A. Chatton, Michael Terence O'Brien, Samuel Johnstone Irving, William Lacey, Patrick Gallagher, Robert William Irvine, William Gillespie, Joseph Toner.

**Goals**: Robert Kelly (15), Henry Bedford (60), William Henry Walker (70) / William Gillespie (77)

143. 08.12.1924
**ENGLAND v BELGIUM 4-0 (1-0)**
*The Hawthorns, West Bromwich*

Referee: James Robert Mac Farlane (Scotland), Att:15,405

**ENGLAND**: Henry Hardy, William Ashurst, Alfred George Bower (Cap), Thomas Patrick Magee, John Dennis Butler, Frederick Harold Ewer, Frank Raymond Osborne, Frank Roberts, Joseph Bradford, William Henry Walker, Arthur Reginald Dorrell.

**BELGIUM**: Jean De Bie, Armand Swartenbroeks (Cap), Louis Baes, Julien Cnudde, Joseph Augustus, Pierre Braine, Leópold Dries, Maurice Gillis, Ferdinand Adams, Laurent Grimmonprez, Désiré Bastin.
Trainer: William Sturrock Maxwell

**Goals**: Joseph Bradford (17, 61), William H. Walker (59, 66)

144. 28.02.1925   Home Championship
**WALES v ENGLAND   1-2**  (1-2)

*Vetch Field, Swansea*

Referee: Cahill (Northern Ireland)   Attendance: 8,000

**WALES**: Albert Gray, Ernest James Morley, Moses Richard Russell, Edwin Samuel Jenkins, Frederick Charles Keenor, Daniel Edgar Thomas, William Davies, John Barry Nicholls, John Fowler, George Beadles, Frederick Cook.

**ENGLAND**: Richard Henry Pym, William Ashurst, Alfred George Bower (Cap), John Henry Hill, Charles William Spencer, Leonard Graham, Robert Kelly, Frank Roberts, Thomas Edwin Reed Cook, William Henry Walker, Arthur Reginald Dorrell.

**Goals**: Frederick C. Keenor (35) / Frank Roberts (11, 15)


145. 04.04.1925   Home Championship
**SCOTLAND v ENGLAND   2-0**  (1-0)

*Hampden Park, Glasgow*

Referee: Arthur Ward (England)   Attendance: 92,000

**SCOTLAND**: William Harper, William McStay, Philip McCloy, David Ditchburn Meiklejohn, David Morris (Cap), James McMullan, Alexander Skinner Jackson, William Fraser Russell, Hugh Kilpatrick Gallacher, Thomas Cairns, Alan Lauder Morton.

**ENGLAND**: Richard Henry Pym, William Ashurst, Samuel John Wadsworth (Cap), Thomas Patrick Magee, John Edward Townrow, Leonard Graham, Robert Kelly, James Marshall Seed, Frank Roberts, William Henry Walker, Frederick Edward Tunstall.

**Goals**: Hugh Kilpatrick Gallacher (36, 86)


146. 21.05.1925
**FRANCE v ENGLAND   2-3**  (0-1)

*Stade Olympique, Colombes, Paris*

Referee: van Zwieteren (Holland)   Attendance: 35,000

**FRANCE**: Pierre Chayrigues, Marcel Vignoli, Marcel Domergue, Philippe Bonnardel, François Hugues, Robert Dauphin, Raymond Dubly, Jean Boyer, Paul Nicolas (Cap), Guillaume Lieb, Jules Dewaquez.

**ENGLAND**: Frederick Samuel Fox, Thomas Robert Parker, William Felton, Thomas Patrick Magee, William Ingram Bryant, George Henry Green, George Thornewell, Frank Roberts, William Vivian Gibbins, William Henry Walker (Cap), Arthur Reginald Dorrell.

**Goals**: Jean Boyer (62), Jules Dewaquez (75) / William Vivian Gibbins (23), Philippe Bonnardel (46 og), Arthur Reginald Dorrell (50)


147. 24.10.1925   Home Championship
**NORTHERN IRELAND v ENGLAND   0-0**

*Windsor Park, Belfast*

Referee: William Nunnerley (Wales)   Attendance: 35,000

**NORTHERN IRELAND**: Elisha Scott, David Rollo, William Henry McConnell, Joseph Gowdy, James Chatton, Thomas Sloan, Andrew Bothwell, Robert William Irvine, Hugh H. Davey, James Hopkins, David McMullan.

**ENGLAND**: Benjamin Howard Baker, Thomas Smart, Francis Carr Hudspeth, Frederick William Kean, George Henry Armitage, Thomas George Bromilow, Sidney William Austin, Sydney Charles Puddefoot, Claude Thesiger Ashton (Cap), William Henry Walker, Arthur Reginald Dorrell.


148. 01.03.1926   Home Championship
**ENGLAND v WALES   1-3**  (0-1)

*Selhurst Park, London*

Referee: William Russell (England)   Attendance: 23,000

**ENGLAND**: Richard Henry Pym, Warneford Cresswell, Samuel John Wadsworth (Cap), Willis Edwards, John Edward Townrow, George Henry Green, Thomas Urwin, Robert Kelly, Norman Bullock, William Henry Walker, James Henry Dimmock.

**WALES**: Albert Gray, Moses Richard Russell, John Jenkins, Stanley Charles Davies, William John Pullen, Robert Frederick John, William Davies, Leonard Stephen Davies, John Fowler, Charles Jones, Edward Thomas Vizard.

**Goal**: William Henry Walker (47) / John Fowler (43, 57), William Davies (56)


149. 17.04.1926   Home Championship
**ENGLAND v SCOTLAND   0-1**  (0-1)

*Old Trafford, Manchester*

Referee: Thomas Dougray (Scotland)   Attendance: 49,000

**ENGLAND**: Edward Hallows Taylor, Frederick Roy Goodall, Thomas Mort, Willis Edwards, John Henry Hill, George Henry Green, Richard Ernest York, Sydney Charles Puddefoot, Edward Cashfield Harper, William Henry Walker (Cap), James William Ruffel.

**SCOTLAND**: William Harper, John Hutton, William McStay (Cap), James Davidson Gibson, William Summers, James McMullan, Alexander Skinner Jackson, Alexander Thomson, Hugh Kilpatrick Gallacher, Andrew Cunningham, Alexander Troup.

**Goal**: Alexander Skinner Jackson (37)

150. 24.05.1926
**BELGIUM v ENGLAND 3-5** (1-1)

*Olympisch, Antwerpen*

Referee: Heinrich Retschury (Austria)    Attendance: 33,000

**BELGIUM:** Jean Caudron, Armand Swartenbroeks (Cap), François Demol, Georges Ditzler, Florimond Van Halme, Pierre Braine, Maurice Gillis, Ferdinand Adams, Raymond Braine, Ivan Thys, Jan Diddens.
Trainer: William Sturrock Maxwell

**ENGLAND:** George Samuel Austin Ashmore, Thomas Lucas (Cap), Richard Henry Hill, Frederick William Kean, Samuel Cowan, George Henry Green, Joseph Walter Spence, Joseph Henry Carter, Frank Raymond Osborne, Thomas Clark Fisher Johnson, James Henry Dimmock.

**Goals:** Ivan Thys (17), Raymond Braine (51, 58) / Frank R. Osborne (15, 78, 86), Thomas C.F. Johnson (52), Joseph Henry Carter (88)


151. 20.10.1926    Home Championship
**ENGLAND v NORTHERN IRELAND 3-3** (1-2)

*Anfield Road, Liverpool*

Referee: Sambrooke (Wales)    Attendance: 20,000

**ENGLAND:** Albert McInroy, Warneford Cresswell, Samuel John Wadsworth (Cap), Willis Edwards, John Henry Hill, George Henry Green, Joseph Walter Spence, George Brown, Norman Bullock, William Henry Walker, James William Ruffel.

**NORTHERN IRELAND:** Elisha Scott, David Rollo, William Henry McConnell, Joseph Gowdy, Francis Gerald Morgan, Samuel Johnstone Irving, Andrew Bothwell, Robert William Irvine, Hugh H. Davey, William Gillespie, Joseph Toner.

**Goals:** George Brown (8), Joseph Walter Spence (47), Norman Bullock (80) / William Gillespie (5), Hugh H. Davey (44), Robert William Irvine (51)


152. 12.02.1927    Home Championship
**WALES v ENGLAND 3-3** (2-2)

*Racecourse Ground, Wrexham*

Referee: Albert Edward Fogg (England)    Att: 16,101

**WALES:** Daniel Lewis, Thomas Jones, Robert Frederick John, Frederick Charles Keenor, Thomas Percival Griffiths, David Evans, David Rees Williams, Wilfred Leslie Lewis, Leonard Stephen Davies, David Sidney Nicholas, Henry Thomas.

**ENGLAND:** John Henry Brown, Alfred George Bower (Cap), George Smith Waterfield, Willis Edwards, James Seddon, George Henry Green, William Harold Pease, George Brown, William Ralph Dean, William Henry Walker, Louis Antonia Page.

**Goals:** Leonard Davies (13, 36 pen), Wilfred L. Lewis (60) / William Ralph Dean (10, 58), William Henry Walker (20)


153. 02.04.1927    Home Championship
**SCOTLAND v ENGLAND 1-2** (0-0)

*Hampden Park, Glasgow*

Referee: Arthur Ward (England)    Attendance: 111,214

**SCOTLAND:** John Diamond Harkness, William McStay (Cap), Robert Thomson, Thomas Morrison, James Davidson Gibson, James McMullan, Adam McLean, Andrew Cunningham, Hugh Kilpatrick Gallacher, Robert Low McPhail, Alan Lauder Morton.

**ENGLAND:** John Henry Brown, Frederick Roy Goodall, Herbert Jones, Willis Edwards, John Henry Hill (Cap), Sidney Macdonald Bishop, Joseph Harold Anthony Hulme, George Brown, William Ralph Dean, Arthur Rigby, Louis Antonia Page.

**Goals:** Alan Lauder Morton (53) / William R. Dean (69, 88)


154. 11.05.1927
**BELGIUM v ENGLAND 1-9** (0-5)

*Sint-Jans, Molenbeek, Bruxelles*

Referee: Johannes Mutters (Holland)    Attendance: 35,000

**BELGIUM:** Jean Caudron, Armand Swartenbroeks (Cap), François Demol, Pierre Braine, Florimond Van Halme, Henri Van Averbeke, Ferdinand Adams, Raymond Braine, Georges De Spae, Henri Bierna, Michel Vanderbauwhede.
Trainer: William Sturrock Maxwell

**ENGLAND:** John Henry Brown, Frederick Roy Goodall, Herbert Jones, Willis Edwards, John Henry Hill (Cap), Sidney Macdonald Bishop, Joseph Harold Anthony Hulme, George Brown, William Ralph Dean, Arthur Rigby, Louis Antonia Page.

**Goals:** Florimond Van Halme (80) / George Brown (11, 34), Joseph Harold Anthony Hulme (17), Arthur Rigby (29, 53), William Ralph Dean (36, 47, 70), Louis Antonia Page (63)


155. 21.05.1927
**LUXEMBOURG v ENGLAND 2-5** (2-2)

*Stade de la Frontière, Esch-sur-Alzette*

Referee: Paul Putz (Belgium)    Attendance: 5,000

**LUXEMBOURG:** Henri Scharry, Nicolas Kirsch (Cap), Emile Kolb, Joseph Fischer, Joseph Koetz, Pierre Kremer, Adolphe Hubert, Mathias Becker, Joseph Kirpes, Jean-Pierre Weisgerber, Léon Lefèvre.

**ENGLAND:** John Henry Brown, Frederick Roy Goodall, Herbert Jones, Willis Edwards, Frederick William Kean (Cap), Sidney Macdonald Bishop, Robert Kelly, George Brown, William Ralph Dean, Arthur Rigby, Louis Antonia Page.

**Goals:** Adolphe Hubert (#), Léon Lefèvre (12) / William Ralph Dean (18, 65, 72), Robert Kelly (35), Sidney Macdonald Bishop (86)

156. 26.05.1927
**FRANCE v ENGLAND  0-6**  (0-2)
*Stade Olympique, Colombes, Paris*
Referee: Maeck (Belgium)   Attendance: 25,000
**FRANCE**: Alexis Thépot, Urbain Wallet, André Rollet, Robert Dauphin, François Hugues (Cap), Jacques Wild, Marcel Langiller, Guillaume Lieb, Julien Sottiault, Georges Taisne, Maurice Gallay.
**ENGLAND**: John Henry Brown, Frederick Roy Goodall, Herbert Jones, Willis Edwards, John Henry Hill (Cap), Sidney Macdonald Bishop, Joseph Harold Anthony Hulme, George Brown, William Ralph Dean, Arthur Rigby, Louis Antonia Page.
**Goals**: George Brown (4, 50), William Ralph Dean (24, 75), André Rollet (55 og), Arthur Rigby (87)


157. 22.10.1927   Home Championship
**NORTHERN IRELAND v ENGLAND  2-0**  (1-0)
*Windsor Park, Belfast*
Referee: Thomas Dougray (Scotland)   Attendance: 30,000
**NORTHERN IRELAND**: Elisha Scott, Andrew McCluggage, William Henry McConnell, Samuel Johnstone Irving, Francis Gerald Morgan, Thomas Sloan, Robert James Chambers, Robert William Irvine, Hugh H. Davey, William Gillespie, John Mahood.
**ENGLAND**: Arthur Edward Hufton, Thomas Cooper, Herbert Jones, Henry Nuttall, John Henry Hill (Cap), Harry Storer, Joseph Harold Anthony Hulme, Stanley George James Earle, William Ralph Dean, John Ball, Louis Antonia Page.
**Goals**: Herbert Jones (36 og), John Mahood (72)


158. 28.11.1927   Home Championship
**ENGLAND v WALES  1-2**  (0-2)
*Turf Moor, Burnley*
Referee: Bell (Scotland)   Attendance: 32,089
**ENGLAND**: Richard Daniel Tremelling, Frederick Roy Goodall, Reginald Osborne, Alfred Baker, John Henry Hill (Cap), Henry Nuttall, Joseph Harold Anthony Hulme, George Brown, William Ralph Dean, Arthur Rigby, Louis Antonia Page.
**WALES**: Albert Gray, Benjamin David Williams, Thomas John Evans, Samuel Bennion, Frederick Charles Keenor, Robert Frederick John, William James Hole, Leonard Stephen Davies, Wilfred Leslie Lewis, Charles Jones, Frederick Cook.
**Goal**: Frederick Keenor (79 og) / Wilfred Leslie Lewis (22), John Henry Hill (40 og)


159. 31.03.1928   Home Championship
**ENGLAND v SCOTLAND  1-5**  (0-2)
*Wembley, London*
Referee: Bell (Scotland)   Attendance: 80,868
**ENGLAND**: Arthur Edward Hufton, Frederick Roy Goodall (Cap), Herbert Jones, Willis Edwards, Thomas Wilson, Henry Healless, Joseph Harold Anthony Hulme, Robert Kelly, William Ralph Dean, Joseph Bradford, William Henry Smith.
**SCOTLAND**: John Diamond Harkness, James Nelson, Thomas Law, James Davidson Gibson, Thomas Bradshaw, James McMullan (Cap), Alexander Skinner Jackson, James Dunn, Hugh Kilpatrick Gallacher, Alexander Wilson James, Alan Lauder Morton.
**Goal**: Robert Kelly (89) / Alexander S. Jackson (3, 65, 85), Alexander W. James (44, 66)


160. 17.05.1928
**FRANCE v ENGLAND  1-5**  (1-3)
*Stade Olympique, Colombes, Paris*
Referee: Adolf Miesz (Austria)   Attendance: 40,000
**FRANCE**: Alexis Thépot, Urbain Wallet, Jacques Canthelou, Robert Dauphin, Marcel Domergue (Cap), Alexandre Villaplane, Jules Monsallier, Juste Brouzes, Charles Bardot, Henri Pavillard, Marcel Langiller.
**ENGLAND**: Benjamin Albert Olney, Frederick Roy Goodall (Cap), Ernest Blenkinsop, Willis Edwards, Vincent Matthews, George Henry Green, John Bruton, David Bone Nightingale Jack, William Ralph Dean, George Ternant Stephenson, Leonard James Barry.
**Goals**: Marcel Langiller (2) / George T. Stephenson (21, 80), David Bone Nightingale Jack (23), William R. Dean (27, 64)


161. 19.05.1928
**BELGIUM v ENGLAND  1-3**  (1-1)
*Olympisch, Antwerpen*
Referee: Heinrich Retschury (Austria)   Attendance: 25,000
**BELGIUM**: Jean De Bie, Jules Lavigne, Nikolaas Hoydonckx, Pierre Braine, Florimond Van Halme (Cap), Gustave Boesman, Bernard Voorhoof, Gérard Devos, Raymond Braine, Jacques Moeschal, Jan Diddens.   Trainer: William Sturrock Maxwell
**ENGLAND**: Benjamin Albert Olney, Frederick Roy Goodall (Cap), Ernest Blenkinsop, Willis Edwards, Vincent Matthews, George Henry Green, John Bruton, David Bone Nightingale Jack, William Ralph Dean, George Ternant Stephenson, Leonard James Barry.
**Goals**: Jacques Moeschal (25) / William Ralph Dean (25, 64), Vincent Matthews (66)

**162. 22.10.1928    Home Championship**
**ENGLAND v NORTHERN IRELAND  2-1**  (1-1)
*Goodison Park, Liverpool*

Referee: Sambrooke (Wales)    Attendance: 34,000

**ENGLAND**: John Hacking, Thomas Cooper, Ernest Blenkinsop, Willis Edwards (Cap), John William Barrett, Austin Fenwick Campbell, Joseph Harold Anthony Hulme, Ernest William Hine, William Ralph Dean, Joseph Bradford, James William Ruffel.

**NORTHERN IRELAND**: Elisha Scott, Andrew McCluggage, Robert Hamilton, Samuel Johnstone Irving, Thomas Sloan, Francis Gerald Morgan, Robert James Chambers, Robert William Irvine, Joseph Bambrick, William Gillespie John Mahood.

**Goals**: Joseph Harold Anthony Hulme (26), William Ralph Dean (77) / Joseph Bambrick

**163. 17.11.1928    Home Championship**
**WALES v ENGLAND  2-3**  (0-2)
*Vetch Field, Swansea*

Referee: Bell (Scotland)    Attendance: 22,000

**WALES**: Albert Gray, Ernest James Morley, Moses Richard Russell, Thomas Percival Griffiths, Frederick Charles Keenor, Samuel Bennion, William James Hole, William Davies, John Fowler, Leonard Stephen Davies, David Rees Williams.

**ENGLAND**: John Hacking, Thomas Cooper, Ernest Blenkinsop, Willis Edwards (Cap), Ernest Arthur Hart, Austin Fenwick Campbell, Joseph Harold Anthony Hulme, Ernest William Hine, William Ralph Dean, Joseph Bradford, James William Ruffel.

**Goals**: John Fowler (#), Frederick Charles Keenor (#) / Joseph Harold Anthony Hulme (11, 25), Ernest W. Hine (86)

**164. 13.04.1929    Home Championship**
**SCOTLAND v ENGLAND  1-0**  (0-0)
*Hampden Park, Glasgow*

Referee: Joseph (England)    Attendance: 110,512

**SCOTLAND**: John Diamond Harkness, James Sermagour Crapnell, Joseph Nibloe, John Buchanan, David Ditchburn Meiklejohn, James McMullan (Cap), Alexander Skinner Jackson, Alexander George Cheyne, Hugh Kilpatrick Gallacher, Alexander Wilson James, Alan Lauder Morton.

**ENGLAND**: John Hacking, Thomas Cooper, Ernest Blenkinsop, Willis Edwards (Cap), James Seddon, Henry Nuttall, John Bruton, George Brown, William Ralph Dean, William Russell Wainscoat, James William Ruffel.

**Goal**: Alexander George Cheyne (90)

**165. 09.05.1929**
**FRANCE v ENGLAND  1-4**  (0-1)
*Stade Olympique, Colombes, Paris*

Referee: Louis Baert (Belgium)    Attendance: 35,000

**FRANCE**: Alexis Thépot, Manuel Anatol, Marcel Bertrand, Yvon Segalen, Robert Dauphin, Alexandre Villaplane, Jules Dewaquez, André Cheuva, Paul Nicolas (Cap), Edmond Delfour, Maurice Gallay.

**ENGLAND**: Arthur Edward Hufton, Ernest Blenkinsop, Thomas Cooper, Frederick William Kean, John Henry Hill (Cap), John Joseph Peacock, Hugh Adcock, Edgar Isaac Lewis Kail, George Henry Camsell, Joseph Bradford, Leonard James Barry.

**Goals**: Jules Dewaquez (54) / Edgar Isaac Lewis Kail (35, 68), George Henry Camsell (59, 86)

**166. 11.05.1929**
**BELGIUM v ENGLAND  1-5**  (0-3)
*Parc Duden, Bruxelles*

Referee: Achille da Gama Malcher (Italia)    Att: 35,000

**BELGIUM**: Jean De Bie, Theodoor Nouwens, Nikolaas Hoydonckx, Henri Van Averbeke, Florimond Van Halme (Cap), Gustave Boesman, Pierre Braine, Michel Vanderbauwhede, Raymond Braine, Jacques Moeschal, Jan Diddens.
Trainer: Viktor Löwenfeld

**ENGLAND**: Arthur Edward Hufton, Thomas Cooper, Ernest Blenkinsop, Leonard Frederick Oliver, John Henry Hill (Cap), John Joseph Peacock, Hugh Adcock, Edgar Isaac Lewis Kail, George Henry Camsell, Joseph Henry Carter, Leonard James Barry.

**Goals**: George H. Camsell (32, 34, 37, 60), Joseph Carter (64)

**167. 15.05.1929**
**SPAIN v ENGLAND  4-3**  (2-2)
*Metropolitano, Madrid*

Referee: John Langenus (Belgium)    Attendance: 50,000

**SPAIN**: Ricardo Zamora (Cap), Félix Quesada, Jacinto Fernández Quincoces, Francisco Prats, Martín Marculeta, Anacleto Peña, Jaime Lazcano, Severino Goiburu, Gaspar Rubio, José Padrón, Mariano Yurrita.
Trainer: José María Mateos Larrucea

**ENGLAND**: Arthur Edward Hufton, Thomas Cooper, Ernest Blenkinsop, Frederick William Kean, John Henry Hill (Cap), John Joseph Peacock, Hugh Adcock, Edgar Isaac Lewis Kail, Joseph Bradford, Joseph Henry Carter, Leonard James Barry.

**Goals**: Gaspar Rubio (35), Jaime Lazcano (39), Gaspar Rubio (79), Severino Goiburu (82) / Joseph Henry Carter (13, 20), Joseph Bradford (50)

168.  19.10.1929    Home Championship
**NORTHERN IRELAND v ENGLAND  0-3**  (0-2)

*Windsor Park, Belfast*

Referee: Thomas Small (Scotland)    Attendance: 40,000

**NORTHERN IRELAND**: Elisha Scott, Samuel Russell, Robert Hamilton, Joseph Miller, James Elwood, William McCleery, Harold Anthony Duggan, Richard William Morris Rowley, Joseph Bambrick, Lawrence Cumming, Peter Kavanagh.

**ENGLAND**: John Henry Brown, Warneford Cresswell, Ernest Blenkinsop, Willis Edwards (Cap), Ernest Arthur Hart, Albert Frank Barrett, Hugh Adcock, Ernest William Hine, George Henry Camsell, Joseph Bradford, Eric Frederick George Brook.

**Goals**: George H. Camsell (37 pen, 42), Ernest W. Hine (80)


169.  20.11.1929    Home Championship
**ENGLAND v WALES  6-0**  (2-0)

*Stamford Bridge, London*

Referee: William McLean (Northern Ireland)    Att: 32,945

**ENGLAND**: Henry Edward Hibbs, Thomas Smart, Ernest Blenkinsop, Willis Edwards (Cap), Ernest Arthur Hart, William Marsden, Hugh Adcock, Ernest William Hine, George Henry Camsell, Thomas Clark Fisher Johnson, James William Ruffel.

**WALES**: Daniel Lewis, Benjamin David Williams, Arthur Albert Lumberg, Frederick Charles Keenor, Thomas Percival Griffiths, Robert Frederick John, William Davies, Leonard Stephen Davies, Wilfred Leslie Lewis, Charles Jones, Frederick Cook.

**Goals**: Thomas Clark Fisher Johnson (12, 65), George Henry Camsell (16, 61, 75), Hugh Adcock (70)


170.  05.04.1930    Home Championship
**ENGLAND v SCOTLAND  5-2**  (4-0)

*Wembley, London*

Referee: William McLean (Northern Ireland)    Att: 87,375

**ENGLAND**: Henry Edward Hibbs, Frederick Roy Goodall, Ernest Blenkinsop, Alfred Henry Strange, Maurice Webster, William Marsden, Samuel Dickinson Crooks, David Bone Nightingale Jack (Cap), Victor Martin Watson, Joseph Bradford, Ellis James Rimmer.

**SCOTLAND**: John Diamond Harkness, Douglas Herbert Gray, Thomas Law, John Buchanan, David Ditchburn Meiklejohn (Cap), Thomas Craig, Alexander Skinner Jackson, Alexander Wilson James, James William Fleming, George Stevenson, Alan Lauder Morton.

**Goals**: Victor Martin Watson (12, 28), Ellis J. Rimmer (30, 54), David Bone Nightingale Jack (33) / James W. Fleming (48, 62)


171.  10.05.1930
**GERMANY v ENGLAND  3-3**  (1-2)

*Grünewald, Berlin*

Referee: Johannes Mutters (Holland)    Attendance: 50,000

**GERMANY**: Willibald Kreß, Franz Schütz, Hans Stubb, Conrad Heidkamp, Ludwig Leinberger, Hugo Mantel, Josef Bergmaier, Josef Pöttinger, Ernst Kuzorra, Richard Hofmann, Ludwig Hofmann (Cap).    Trainer: Otto Nerz

**ENGLAND**: Henry Edward Hibbs, Frederick Roy Goodall (Cap), Ernest Blenkinsop, Alfred Henry Strange, Maurice Webster, William Marsden, Samuel Dickinson Crooks, David Bone Nightingale Jack, Victor Martin Watson, Joseph Bradford, Ellis James Rimmer.

**Goals**: Richard Hofmann (21, 49, 60) / Joseph Bradford (8, 31), David Bone Nightingale Jack (83)


172.  14.05.1930
**AUSTRIA v ENGLAND  0-0**

*Hohe Warte, Wien*

Referee: Johannes Mutters (Holland)    Attendance: 61,000

**AUSTRIA**: Rudolf Hiden, Karl Rainer, Johann Tandler, Johann Klima, Leopold Hofmann, Johann Luef, Ignaz Siegl, Walter Nausch, Friedrich Gschweidl, Johann Horvath, Ferdinand Wessely.    Trainer: Hugo Meisl

**ENGLAND**: Henry Edward Hibbs, Frederick Roy Goodall (Cap), Ernest Blenkinsop, Alfred Henry Strange, Maurice Webster, Samuel Cowan, Samuel Dickinson Crooks, David Bone Nightingale Jack, Victor Martin Watson, Joseph Bradford, Ellis James Rimmer.


173.  20.10.1930    Home Championship
**ENGLAND v NORTHERN IRELAND  5-1**  (0-0)

*Bramall Lane, Sheffield*

Referee: Thomson (Scotland)    Attendance: 35,000

**ENGLAND**: Henry Edward Hibbs, Frederick Roy Goodall (Cap), Ernest Blenkinsop, Alfred Henry Strange, Thoms Leach, Austin Fenwick Campbell, Samuel Dickinson Crooks, Gordon Hodgson, James Hampson, Harry Burgess, William Eric Houghton.

**NORTHERN IRELAND**: Elisha Scott, Andrew McCluggage, Robert P. Fulton, John Jones, Willie Reid, William McCleery, Harold Anthony Duggan, Robert William Irvine, James Dunne, William Gillespie, J. Harold McCaw.

**Goals**: Harry Burgess (15, 35), James Hampson (25), Samuel Dickinson Crooks (30), William Eric Houghton (40) / James Dunne (80)

174. 22.11.1930   Home Championship
**WALES v ENGLAND  0-4**  (0-2)
*Racecourse Ground, Wrexham*

Referee:  Hugh Watson (Scotland)   Attendance: 11,282

**WALES**:  Sidney John Vivian Leonard Evans, Frederick Dewey, Wynne Crompton, William Rogers, Frederick Charles Keenor, Emrys Ellis, Albert Leslie Williams, John Edward Neal, Thomas Bamford, Walter William Robbins, William Rees Thomas.

**ENGLAND**:  Henry Edward Hibbs, Frederick Roy Goodall (Cap), Ernest Blenkinsop, Alfred Henry Strange, Thomes Leach, Austin Fenwick Campbell, Samuel Dickinson Crooks, Gordon Hodgson, James Hampson, Joseph Bradford, William Eric Houghton.

**Goals**:  James Hampson (12, 70), Gordon Hodgson (35), Joseph Bradford (72)


175. 28.03.1931   Home Championship
**SCOTLAND v ENGLAND  2-0**  (0-0)
*Hampden Park, Glasgow*

Referee:  Atwood (Wales)   Attendance: 129,810

**SCOTLAND**:  John Thomson, Daniel Blair, Joseph Nibloe, Colin Duncan McNab, David Ditchburn Meiklejohn (Cap), John Miller, Alexander Archibald, George Stevenson, James Edward McGrory, Robert Low McPhail, Alan Lauder Morton.

**ENGLAND**:  Henry Edward Hibbs, Frederick Roy Goodall (Cap), Ernest Blenkinsop, Alfred Henry Strange, Herbert Roberts, Austin Fenwick Campbell, Samuel Dickinson Crooks, Gordon Hodgson, William Ralph Dean, Harry Burgess, John Forsyth Crawford.

**Goals**:  George Stevenson (60), James Edward McGrory (62)


176. 14.05.1931
**FRANCE v ENGLAND  5-2**  (3-1)
*Stade Olympique, Colombes, Paris*

Referee:  John Langenus (Belgium)   Attendance: 35,000

**FRANCE**:  Alexis Thépot (Cap), Étienne Mattler, Marcel Capelle, Louis Finot, Joseph Kaucsar, Pierre Hornus, Ernest Liberati, Edmond Delfour, Robert Mercier, Lucien Laurent, Marcel Langiller.

**ENGLAND**:  Hugh Turner, Thomas Cooper, Ernest Blenkinsop, Alfred Henry Strange (Cap), Thomas Graham, Joseph Thomas Tate, Samuel Dickinson Crooks, George Ternant Stephenson, Thomas Waring, Harry Burgess, William Eric Houghton.

**Goals**:  Lucien Laurent (15), Robert Mercier (18), Marcel Langiller (29), Edmond Delfour (57), Robert Mercier (76) / Samuel Dickinson Crooks (10), Thomas Waring (71)


177. 16.05.1931
**BELGIUM v ENGLAND  1-4**  (1-1)
*Sint-Jans Molenbeek, Bruxelles*

Referee:  Peco Bauwens (Germany)   Attendance: 30,000

**BELGIUM**:  Arnold Badjou, Theodoor Nouwens, Constant Joacim, Charles Simons, August Hellemans, Jacques Moeschal (Cap), Louis Versijp, Bernard Voorhoof, Jean Capelle, Jozef Van Beeck, Stanley Vanden Eynde.   Trainer: Hector Goetinck

**ENGLAND**:  Hugh Turner, Frederick Roy Goodall, Ernest Blenkinsop, Alfred Henry Strange (Cap), Samuel Cowan, Joseph Thomas Tate, Samuel Dickinson Crooks, Henry Roberts, Thomas Waring, Harry Burgess, William Eric Houghton.

**Goals**:  Jean Capelle (36) / William Eric Houghton (42 pen), Harry Burgess (65, 76), Henry Roberts (80)


178. 17.10.1931   Home Championship
**NORTHERN IRELAND v ENGLAND  2-6**  (1-3)
*Windsor Park, Belfast*

Referee:  Hugh Watson (Scotland)   Attendance: 40,000

**NORTHERN IRELAND**:  Alfred Gardiner, Samuel Russell, Robert Fulton, Robert McDonald, John Jones, William Mitchell, Robert James Chambers, Patrick McConnell, James Dunne, James McCambridge, James Kelly.

**ENGLAND**:  Henry Edward Hibbs, Frederick Roy Goodall (Cap), Ernest Blenkinsop, Alfred Henry Strange, Thomas Graham, Austin Fenwick Campbell, Samuel Dickinson Crooks, John William Smith, Thomas Waring, Ernest William Hine, William Eric Houghton.

**Goals**:  James Dunne (40), James Kelly (89) / John William Smith (10), Thomas Waring (12, 50), Ernest William Hine (30), William Eric Houghton (60, 85)


179. 18.11.1931   Home Championship
**ENGLAND v WALES  3-1**  (1-1)
*Anfield Road, Liverpool*

Referee:  Bunnell (England)   Attendance: 15,000

**ENGLAND**:  Henry Edward Hibbs, Thomas Cooper, Ernest Blenkinsop, Alfred Henry Strange (Cap), Charles William Gee, Austin Fenwick Campbell, Samuel Dickinson Crooks, John William Smith, Thomas Waring, Ernest William Hine, Clifford Sydney Bastin.

**WALES**:  Albert Gray, Benjamin David Williams, Benjamin Ellis, Charles Jones, Thomas Percival Griffiths, Robert Frederick John, Cuthbert Phillips, Eugene O'Callaghan, David Astley, Walter William Robbins, Frederick Cook.

**Goals**:  John W. Smith (25), Samuel Dickinson Crooks (50), Ernest William Hine (65) / Walter William Robbins (30)

180.  09.12.1931
**ENGLAND v SPAIN  7-1**  (3-0)

*Highbury, London*

Referee: Peco Bauwens (Germany)   Attendance: 55,000

**ENGLAND**: Henry Edward Hibbs, Thomas Cooper, Ernest Blenkinsop (Cap), Alfred Henry Strange, Charles William Gee, Austin Fenwick Campbell, Samuel Dickinson Crooks, John William Smith, William Ralph Dean, Thomas Clark Fisher Johnson, Ellis James Rimmer.

**SPAIN**: Ricardo Zamora (Cap), Ramón Zabalo, Jacinto Fernández Quincoces, Leonardo Cilaurren, Francisco Gamborena, Roberto Etxebarría, Martín Ventolrà, Ángel León "Leoncito", José "Pepe" Samitier, Juan Marrero "Hilario", Guillermo Gorostiza.   Trainer: José María Mateos Larrucea

**Goals**: John William Smith (2, 44), Thomas Clark Fisher Johnson (3, 70), Samuel Dickinson Crooks (50, 85), William Ralph Dean (60) / Guillermo Gorostiza (87)


181.  09.04.1932    Home Championship
**ENGLAND v SCOTLAND  3-0**  (1-0)

*Wembley, London*

Referee: Samuel Thompson (Northern Ireland)   Att: 92,180

**ENGLAND**: Harold Frederick Pearson, George Edward Shaw, Ernest Blenkinsop (Cap), Alfred Henry Strange, James Peter O'Dowd, Samuel Weaver, Samuel Dickinson Crooks, Robert Barclay, Thomas Waring, Thomas Clark Fisher Johnson, William Eric Houghton.

**SCOTLAND**: Thomas Hamilton, James Sermagour Crapnell (Cap), Joseph Nibloe, Colin Duncan McNab, Allan Craig, George Clark Phillips Brown, Alexander Archibald, Dr. James Marshall, Neil Hamilton Dewar, Charles Edward Napier, Alan Lauder Morton.

**Goals**: Thomas Waring (36), Robert Barclay (79), Samuel Dickinson Crooks (88)


182.  17.10.1932    Home Championship
**ENGLAND v NORTHERN IRELAND  1-0**  (1-0)

*Bloomfield Road, Blackpool*

Referee: Hugh Watson (Scotland)   Attendance: 23,000

**ENGLAND**: Henry Edward Hibbs, Frederick Roy Goodall, Ernest Blenkinsop (Cap), Alfred Henry Strange, James Peter O'Dowd, Samuel Weaver, Samuel Dickinson Crooks, Robert Barclay, William Ralph Dean, Thomas Clark Fisher Johnson, Arthur Cunliffe.

**NORTHERN IRELAND**: Elisha Scott, William Cook, Robert P. Fulton, William Mitchell, John Jones, William McCleery, Harold Anthony Duggan, Patrick Moore, James Dunne, James Doherty, James Kelly.

**Goal**: Robert Barclay (30)


183.  16.11.1932    Home Championship
**WALES v ENGLAND  0-0**

*Racecourse Ground, Wrexham*

Referee: Samuel Thompson (Northern Ireland)   Att: 25,250

**WALES**: William Ronald John, Benjamin David Williams, Benjamin Ellis, James Patrick Murphy, Thomas Percival Griffiths, David Thomas Richards, Frederick Windsor Warren, Eugene O'Callaghan, David Astley, Walter William Robbins, David Jenkin Lewis.

**ENGLAND**: Henry Edward Hibbs, Frederick Roy Goodall, Ernest Blenkinsop, Lewis Stoker, Alfred Young, Joseph Thomas Tate, Samuel Dickinson Crooks, David Bone Nightingale Jack (Cap), George Brown, Edward Sandford, Arthur Cunliffe.


184.  07.12.1932
**ENGLAND v AUSTRIA  4-3**  (2-0)

*Stamford Bridge, London*

Referee: John Langenus (Belgium)   Attendance: 42,000

**ENGLAND**: Henry Edward Hibbs, Frederick Roy Goodall, Ernest Blenkinsop, Alfred Henry Strange, Ernest Arthur Hart, Errington Ridley Liddell Keen, Samuel Dickinson Crooks, David Bone Nightingale Jack, James Hampson, William Henry Walker (Cap), William Eric Houghton.

**AUSTRIA**: Rudolf Hiden, Karl Rainer, Karl Sesta, Karl Gall, Josef Smistik, Walter Nausch, Karl Zischek, Friedrich Gschweidl, Matthias Sindelar, Anton Schall, Adolf Vogel. Trainer: Hugo Meisl

**Goals**: Samuel D. Crooks (5), James Hampson (27, 82), William Eric Houghton (77) / Karl Zischek (58, 87), Matthias Sindelar (80)


185.  01.04.1933    Home Championship
**SCOTLAND v ENGLAND  2-1**  (1-1)

*Hampden Park, Glasgow*

Referee: Samuel Thompson (Northern Ireland)   Att: 134,170

**SCOTLAND**: John Jackson, Andrew Anderson, Peter McGonagle, Peter Wilson, Robert Gillespie (Cap), George Clark Phillips Brown, James Crawford, Dr. James Marshall, James Edward McGrory, Robert Low McPhail, Douglas Duncan.

**ENGLAND**: Henry Edward Hibbs, Thomas Cooper, Ernest Blenkinsop (Cap), Alfred Henry Strange, Ernest Arthur Hart, Samuel Weaver, Joseph Harold Anthony Hulme, Ronald William Starling, George Samuel Hunt, John Pickering, John Arnold.

**Goal**: James Edward McGrory (4, 81) / George Samuel Hunt (30)

186. 13.05.1933
**ITALY v ENGLAND  1-1**  (1-1)

*Stadio Nazionale del Partito Nazianale Fascisto, Roma*

Referee:  Peco Bauwens (Germany)     Attendance:  50,000

**ITALY**:  Gianpiero Combi, Virginio Rosetta, Umberto Caligaris (Cap), Mario Pizziolo, Luisito Monti, Luigi Bertolini, Raffaele Costantino, Giuseppe Meazza, Angelo Schiavio, Giovanni Ferrari, Raimondo Orsi.   Trainer:  Vittorio Pozzo

**ENGLAND**:  Henry Edward Hibbs, Frederick Roy Goodall (Cap), Edris Albert Hapgood, Alfred Henry Strange, Thomas Angus White, Wilfred Copping, Albert Geldard, James Robert Richardson, George Samuel Hunt, William Isaac Furness, Clifford Sydney Bastin.   Manager:  Herbert Chapman

**Goal**:  Giovanni Ferrari (4) / Clifford Sydney Bastin (24)


187. 20.05.1933
**SWITZERLAND v ENGLAND  0-4**  (0-1)

*Neufeld, Bern*

Referee:  Peco Bauwens (Germany)     Attendance:  26,000

**SWITZERLAND**:  Frank Séchehaye, Severino Minelli, Karl Bielser, Gabriele Gilardoni, Otto Imhof, Ernst Hufschmid, Willy von Känel, André Abegglen, Raymond Passello, Max Abegglen, Alfred Jaeck.

**ENGLAND**:  Henry Edward Hibbs, Frederick Roy Goodall (Cap), Edris Albert Hapgood, Alfred Henry Strange, James Peter O'Dowd, Wilfred Copping, Albert Geldard, James Robert Richardson, George Samuel Hunt, Clifford Sydney Bastin, Eric Frederick George Brook.

**Goals**:  Clifford Sydney Bastin (15, 75), James Robert Richardson (71, 77)


188. 14.10.1933    Home Championship
**NORTHERN IRELAND v ENGLAND  0-3**  (0-1)

*Windsor Park, Belfast*

Referee:  Hugh Watson (Scotland)     Attendance:  40,000

**NORTHERN IRELAND**:  Elisha Scott, Sydney Edward Reid, Robert Fulton, Walter McMillen, John Jones, Samuel Jones, Harold Anthony Duggan, Alexander Ernest Stevenson, David Kirker Martin, John Coulter, Thomas Priestley.

**ENGLAND**:  Henry Edward Hibbs, Frederick Roy Goodall (Cap), Edris Albert Hapgood, Alfred Henry Strange, James Phillips Allen, Wilfred Copping, Samuel Dickinson Crooks, Albert Thomas Grosvenor, John William Anslow Bowers, Clifford Sydney Bastin, Eric Frederick George Brook.

**Goals**:  Eric Frederick George Brook (30), Albert Thomas Grosvenor (51), John William Anslow Bowers (60)


189. 15.11.1933    Home Championship
**ENGLAND v WALES  1-2**  (0-1)

*St.James' Park, Newcastle*

Referee:  Samuel Thompson (Northern Ireland)    Att:  15,000

**ENGLAND**:  Henry Edward Hibbs, Frederick Roy Goodall (Cap), Edris Albert Hapgood, Alfred Henry Strange, James Phillips Allen, Wilfred Copping, Samuel Dickinson Crooks, Albert Thomas Grosvenor, John William Anslow Bowers, Clifford Sydney Bastin, Eric Frederick George Brook.

**WALES**:  William Ronald John, Sidney Wilfred Lawrence, David Owen Jones, James Patrick Murphy, Thomas Percival Griffiths, David Thomas Richards, Cuthbert Phillips, Eugene O'Callaghan, David Astley, Thomas James Mills, William Evans.

**Goal**:  Eric Frederick George Brook (59) / Thomas James Mills (22), David Astley (82)


190. 06.12.1933
**ENGLAND v FRANCE  4-1**  (3-0)

*White Hart Lane, London*

Referee:  John Langenus (Belgium)     Attendance:  17,097

**ENGLAND**:  Henry Edward Hibbs, Frederick Roy Goodall (Cap), David Liddle Fairhurst, Alfred Henry Strange, Arthur Sydney Rowe, Wilfred Copping, Samuel Dickinson Crooks, Albert Thomas Grosvenor, George Henry Camsell, George William Hall, Eric Frederick George Brook.

**FRANCE**:  Robert Défossé, Jules Vandooren, Étienne Mattler, Célestine Delmer, Maurice Banide, Edmond Delfour (Cap), Roger Courtois, René Gérard, Jean Nicolas, Roger Rio, Emile Veinante.

**Goals**:  George Henry Camsell (14, 41), Eric F.G. Brook (21), Albert Thomas Grosvenor (53) / Emile Veinante (78)


191. 14.04.1934    Home Championship
**ENGLAND v SCOTLAND  3-0**  (1-0)

*Wembley, London*

Referee:  Samuel Thompson (Northern Ireland)    Att:  92,363

**ENGLAND**:  Frank Moss, Thomas Cooper (Cap), Edris Albert Hapgood, Lewis Stoker, Ernest Arthur Hart, Wilfred Copping, Samuel Dickinson Crooks, Horatio Stratton Carter, John William Anslow Bowers, Clifford Sydney Bastin, Eric Frederick George Brook.

**SCOTLAND**:  John Jackson, Andrew Anderson, Peter McGonagle, Alexander Massie (Cap), Thomas M. Smith, John Miller, William Lawrence Cook, Dr. James Marshall, Hugh Kilpatrick Gallacher, George Stevenson, James Connor.

**Goals**:  Clifford Sydney Bastin (43), Eric F.G. Brook (80), John William Anslow Bowers (88)

192. 10.05.1934
**HUNGARY v ENGLAND 2-1** (0-0)
*Üllői út, Budapest*
Referee: Rinaldo Barlassina (Italy)   Attendance: 35,000
**HUNGARY**: József Háda, József Vágó, László Sternberg, Antal Szalay, György Szűcs, Gyula Lázár, Ede Rökk, István Avar, György Sárosi, Géza Toldi, Tibor Kemény. Trainer: Ödön Nádas
**ENGLAND**: Frank Moss, Thomas Cooper (Cap), Edris Albert Hapgood, Lewis Stoker, Ernest Arthur Hart, Horace Burrows, Samuel Dickinson Crooks, Horatio Stratton Carter, Samuel Frederick Tilson, Clifford Sydney Bastin, Eric Frederick George Brook.
**Goal**: István Avar (56), György Sárosi (69) / Samuel Frederick Tilson (81)

193. 16.05.1934
**CZECHOSLOVAKIA v ENGLAND 2-1** (1-1)
*Sparta, Praha*
Referee: John Langenus (Belgium)   Attendance: 35,000
**CZECHOSLOVAKIA**: František Plánička (Cap), Ladislav Ženíšek, Josef Čtyřoký, Josef Košťálek, Štefan Čambal, Rudolf Krčil, František Junek, Josef Silný, Jiří Sobotka, Oldřich Nejedlý, Antonín Puč.   Trainer: Karel Petrů
**ENGLAND**: Frank Moss, Thomas Cooper (Cap), Edris Albert Hapgood, Thomas Gardner, Ernest Arthur Hart, Horace Burrows, Samuel Dickinson Crooks, Joseph Beresford, Samuel Frederick Tilson, Clifford Sydney Bastin, Eric Frederick George Brook.
**Goal**: Oldřich Nejedlý (42), Antonín Puč (62) / Samuel Frederick Tilson (20)

194. 29.09.1934   Home Championship
**WALES v ENGLAND 0-4** (0-2)
*Ninian Park, Cardiff*
Referee: Samuel Thompson (Northern Ireland)   Attendance: 51,000
**WALES**: William Ronald John, Sidney Wilfred Lawrence, David Owen Jones, James Patrick Murphy, Thomas Percival Griffiths, David Thomas Richards, Cuthbert Phillips, Eugene O'Callaghan, Ronald Williams, Thomas James Mills, William Evans.
**ENGLAND**: Henry Edward Hibbs, Thomas Cooper (Cap), Edris Albert Hapgood, Clifford Samuel Britton, John William Barker, John Bray, Stanley Matthews, Edwin Raymond Bowden, Samuel Frederick Tilson, Raymond William Westwood, Eric Frederick George Brook.
**Goals**: Samuel Frederick Tilson (10, 85), Eric Frederick George Brook (30), Stanley Matthews (84)

195. 14.11.1934
**ENGLAND v ITALY 3-2** (3-0)
*Highbury, London*
Referee: Otto Olsson (Sweden)   Attendance: 56,044
**ENGLAND**: Frank Moss, Charles George Male, Edris Albert Hapgood (Cap), Clifford Samuel Britton, John William Barker, Wilfred Copping, Stanley Matthews, Edwin Raymond Bowden, Edward Joseph Drake, Clifford Sydney Bastin, Eric Frederick George Brook.
**ITALY**: Carlo Ceresoli, Eraldo Monzeglio, Luigi Allemandi, Attilio Ferraris IV (Cap), Luisito Monti, Luigi Bertolini, Enrico Guaita, Pietro Serantoni, Giuseppe Meazza, Giovanni Ferrari, Raimondo Orsi.   Trainer: Vittorio Pozzo
**Goals**: Eric Frederick George Brook (3, 10), Edward Joseph Drake (12) / Giuseppe Meazza (58, 62)

196. 06.02.1935   Home Championship
**ENGLAND v NORTHERN IRELAND 2-1** (2-1)
*Goodison Park, Liverpool*
Referee: Willie Webb (Scotland)   Attendance: 32,000
**ENGLAND**: Henry Edward Hibbs, Charles George Male, Edris Albert Hapgood (Cap), Clifford Samuel Britton, John William Barker, Wilfred Copping, Samuel Dickinson Crooks, John Gilbert Bestall, Edward Joseph Drake, Clifford Sydney Bastin, Eric Frederick George Brook.
**NORTHERN IRELAND**: Thomas Breen, William Cook, Robert P. Fulton, William Alexander Gowdy, John Jones, William Mitchell, John Brown, Peter Dermont Doherty, David Kirker Martin, Alexander Ernest Stevenson, John Coulter.
**Goals**: Clifford Sydney Bastin (18, 70) / Alexander Ernest Stevenson (50)

197. 06.04.1935   Home Championship
**SCOTLAND v ENGLAND 2-0** (1-0)
*Hampden Park, Glasgow*
Referee: Samuel Thompson (Northern Ireland)   Att: 129,693
**SCOTLAND**: John Jackson, Andrew Anderson, George Wilfred Cummings, Alexander Massie, James McMillan Simpson (Cap), George Clark Phillips Brown, Charles Edward Napier, Thomas Walker, Hugh Kilpatrick Gallacher, Robert Low McPhail, Douglas Duncan.
**ENGLAND**: Henry Edward Hibbs, Charles George Male, Edris Albert Hapgood (Cap), Clifford Samuel Britton, John William Barker, Walter John Alsford, Albert Geldard, Clifford Sydney Bastin, Robert Gurney, Raymond William Westwood, Eric Frederick George Brook.
**Goals**: Douglas Duncan (43, 50)

198. 18.05.1935
**HOLLAND v ENGLAND  0-1**  (0-0)

*Olympic, Amsterdam*

Referee: Peco Bauwens (Germany)   Attendance: 33,000

**HOLLAND:** Leo Halle, Bertus Caldenhove, Sjef van Run, Bas Paauwe, Wim Anderiesen, Gerrit 'Puck' van Heel (Cap), Frank Wels, Daaf Drok, Beb Bakhuys, Jaap Smit, Kees Mijnders. Trainer: Bob Glendenning

**ENGLAND:** Henry Edward Hibbs, Charles George Male, Edris Albert Hapgood (Cap), Thomas Gardner, John William Barker, Horace Burrows, Frederic Worrall, George Richard Eastham, William Ginger Richardson, Raymond William Westwood, Walter Edward Boyes.

**Goal:** Frederic Worrall (46)

199. 19.10.1935   Home Championship
**NORTHERN IRELAND v ENGLAND  1-3**  (1-0)

*Windsor Park, Belfast*

Referee: Willie Webb (Scotland)   Attendance: 28,000

**NORTHERN IRELAND:** Elisha Scott, Sydney Edward Reid, Cecil Allan, William Mitchell, John Jones, Robert James Browne, John Brown II, Keiller McCullough, Joseph Bambrick, Peter Dermot Doherty, James Kelly.

**ENGLAND:** Edward Sagar, Charles George Male, Edris Albert Hapgood (Cap), Septimus Charles Smith, John William Barker, John Bray, Ralph James Evans Birkett, Edwin Raymond Bowden, Samuel Frederick Tilson, Raymond William Westwood, Eric Frederick George Brook.

**Goals:** John Brown II (16) / Samuel Frederick Tilson (66, 69), Eric Frederick George Brook (85)

200. 04.12.1935
**ENGLAND v GERMANY  3-0**  (1-0)

*White Hart Lane, London*

Referee: Otto Olsson (Sweden)   Attendance: 54,164

**ENGLAND:** Henry Edward Hibbs, Charles George Male, Edris Albert Hapgood (Cap), William John Crayston, John William Barker, John Bray, Stanley Matthews, Horatio Stratton Carter, George Henry Camsell, Raymond William Westwood, Clifford Sydney Bastin.

**GERMANY:** Hans Jakob, Sigmund Haringer, Reinhold Münzenberg, Paul Janes, Ludwig Goldbrunner, Rudolf Gramlich, Ernst Lehner, Fritz Szepan (Cap), Karl Hohmann, Josef Rasselnberg, Josef Fath.   Trainer: Otto Nerz

**Goals:** George H. Camsell (35, 50), Clifford S. Bastin (68)

201. 05.02.1936   Home Championship
**ENGLAND v WALES  1-2**  (1-0)

*Molineux, Wolverhampton*

Referee: Willie Webb (Scotland)   Attendance: 22,613

**ENGLAND:** Henry Edward Hibbs, Charles George Male, Edris Albert Hapgood (Cap), William John Crayston, John William Barker, John Bray, Samuel Dickinson Crooks, Edwin Raymond Bowden, Edward Joseph Drake, Clifford Sydney Bastin, Eric Frederick George Brook.

**WALES:** William Ronald John, David Owen Jones, Benjamin Ellis, James Patrick Murphy, Harry Hanford, David Thomas Richards, Idris Morgan Hopkins, Cuthbert Phillips, David Astley, Brynmor Jones, William Evans.

**Goal:** Edwin Raymond Bowden (38) / David Astley (47), Brynmor Jones (66)

202. 04.04.1936   Home Championship
**ENGLAND v SCOTLAND  1-1**  (1-0)

*Wembley, London*

Referee: William Hamilton (Northern Ireland)   Att: 93,267

**ENGLAND:** Edward Sagar, Charles George Male, Edris Albert Hapgood (Cap), William John Crayston, John William Barker, John Bray, Samuel Dickinson Crooks, Robert Barclay, George Henry Camsell, Clifford Sydney Bastin, Eric Frederick George Brook.

**SCOTLAND:** James Dawson, Andrew Anderson, George Wilfred Cummings, Alexander Massie, James McMillan Simpson (Cap), George Clark Phillips Brown, John Crum, Thomas Walker, David McCulloch, Alexander Venters, Douglas Duncan.

**Goal:** George Henry Camsell (30) / Thomas Walker (77 pen)

203. 06.05.1936
**AUSTRIA v ENGLAND  2-1**  (2-0)

*Prater, Wien*

Referee: John Langenus (Belgium)   Attendance: 60,000

**AUSTRIA:** Peter Platzer, Karl Sesta, Willibald Schmaus, Johann Urbanek, Johann Mock, Walter Nausch, Rudolf Geiter, Josef Stroh, Matthias Sindelar, Josef Bican, Rudolf Viertl. Trainer: Hugo Meisl

**ENGLAND:** Edward Sagar, Charles George Male, Edris Albert Hapgood (Cap), William John Crayston, John William Barker, Wilfred Copping, Richard Spence, Edwin Raymond Bowden, George Henry Camsell, Clifford Sydney Bastin, Harold Henry Frank Hobbis.

**Goals:** Rudolf Viertl (12), Rudolf Geiter (17) / George Henry Camsell (54)

204. 09.05.1936
**BELGIUM v ENGLAND  3-2**  (0-1)

*Heizel, Bruxelles*

Referee: Johannes Franciscus van Moorsel (Holland)     Attendance: 40,000

**BELGIUM**: Arnold Badjou, Robert Paverick, Constant Joacim, Pierre Dalem, Emile Stijnen (Cap), Alfons De Winter, Jean Fiévez, Robert Lamoot, Jean Capelle, Hendrik Isemborghs, Antoon Franckx.    Trainer: John Dennis Buttler

**ENGLAND**: Edward Sagar, Charles George Male, Edris Albert Hapgood (Cap), William John Crayston, Bernard Joy, Wilfred Copping, Richard Spence, Samuel Barkas, George Henry Camsell, James Nathaniel Cunliffe, Harold Henry Frank Hobbis.

**Goals**: Hendrik Isemborghs (62, 82), Jean Fiévez (84) / George Henry Camsell (56), Harold Henry Frank Hobbis (88)


205. 17.10.1936    Home Championship
**WALES v ENGLAND  2-1**  (0-1)

*Ninian Park, Cardiff*

Referee: William McLean (Northern Ireland)    Att: 44,729

**WALES**: Albert Gray, Herbert Gwyn Turner, Robert Frederick John, John Warner, Thomas Percival Griffiths, David Thomas Richards, Idris Morgan Hopkins, Brynmor Jones, Ernest Matthew Glover, Leslie Jenkin Jones, Seymour Morris.

**ENGLAND**: George Henry Holdcroft, Bert Sproston, Arthur Edward Catlin, Tom Smalley, John William Barker (Cap), Errington Ridley Liddell Keen, Samuel Dickinson Crooks, William Reed Scott, Frederick Charles Steele, Raymond William Westwood, Clifford Sydney Bastin.

**Goal**: Seymour Morris (64), Ernest Matthew Glover (66) / Clifford Sydney Bastin (44)


206. 18.11.1936    Home Championship
**ENGLAND v NORTHERN IRELAND  3-1**  (1-1)

*Victoria Ground, Stoke*

Referee: Willie Webb (Scotland)    Attendance: 47,882

**ENGLAND**: George Henry Holdcroft, Charles George Male (Cap), Arthur Edward Catlin, Clifford Samuel Britton, Charles William Gee, Errington Ridley Liddell Keen, Frederic Worrall, Horatio Stratton Carter, Frederick Charles Steele, Clifford Sydney Bastin, Joseph Arthur Johnson.

**NORTHERN IRELAND**: Thomas Breen, William Cook, Robert P. Fulton, Keiller McCullough, John Jones, William Mitchell, John Brown, Alexander Ernest Stevenson, Thomas Lawrence Davis, Peter Dermont Doherty, James Kelly.

**Goals**: Horatio Stratton Carter (30), Clifford S. Bastin (67), Frederic Worrall (75)


207. 02.12.1936
**ENGLAND v HUNGARY  6-2**  (3-1)

*Highbury, London*

Referee: Lucien Leclerq (France)    Attendance: 36,000

**ENGLAND**: George Jacob Tweedy, Charles George Male (Cap), Arthur Edward Catlin, Clifford Samuel Britton, Alfred Young, Errington Ridley Liddell Keen, Samuel Dickinson Crooks, Edwin Raymond Bowden, Edward Joseph Drake, Horatio Stratton Carter, Eric Frederick George Brook.

**HUNGARY**: Antal Szabó, József Vágó, Sándor Bíró, Gyula Lázár, György Sárosi dr., János Dudás, Ferenc Sas, Jenő Vincze, László Cseh, Gyula Zsengellér, Pál Titkos.
Trainer: Károly Dietz

**Goals**: Eric F.G. Brook (25), Edward Joseph Drake (32, 43, 80), Clifford Samuel Britton (52), Horatio Stratton Carter (87) / László Cseh II (26), Jenő Vincze (50)


208. 17.04.1937    Home Championship
**SCOTLAND v ENGLAND  3-1**  (0-1)

*Hampden Park, Glasgow*

Referee: William McLean (Northern Ireland)    Att: 149,547

**SCOTLAND**: James Dawson, Andrew Anderson, Andrew Beattie, Alexander Massie, James McMillan Simpson (Cap), George Clark Phillips Brown, James Delaney, Thomas Walker, Francis O'Donnell, Robert Low McPhail, Douglas Duncan.

**ENGLAND**: Victor Robert Woodley, Charles George Male (Cap), Samuel Barkas, Clifford Samuel Britton, Alfred Young, John Bray, Stanley Matthews, Horatio Stratton Carter, Frederick Charles Steele, Ronald William Starling, Joseph Arthur Johnson.

**Goal**: Francis O'Donnell (47), Robert Low McPhail (80, 88) / Frederick Charles Steele (40)


209. 14.05.1937
**NORWAY v ENGLAND  0-6**  (0-4)

*Ullevaal, Oslo*

Referee: Ejner Ullrich (Denmark)    Attendance: 20,000

**NORWAY**: Henry Johansen, Nils Eriksen, Øivind Holmsen, Frithjof Ulleberg, Jørgen Juve, Rolf Holmberg, Odd Frantzen, Reidar Kvammen, Alf Martinsen, Magnar Isaksen, Arne Brustad.    Trainer: Asbjørn Halvorsen

**ENGLAND**: Victor Robert Woodley, Charles George Male (Cap), Arthur Edward Catlin, Clifford Samuel Britton, Alfred Young, Wilfred Copping, Alfred John Kirchen, Thomas Galley, Frederick Charles Steele, Leonard Arthur Goulden, Joseph Arthur Johnson.

**Goals**: Alfred John Kirchen (18), Oyvind Holmsen (26 og), Thomas Galley (40), Frederick Charles Steele (43, 61), Leonard Arthur Goulden (85)

210. 17.05.1937
**SWEDEN v ENGLAND 0-4** (0-4)
*Råsunda, Solna*
Referee: John Langenus (Belgium)   Attendance: 34,119
**SWEDEN:** Gustav Sjöberg, Nils Axelsson, Walter Sköld, Fritz Berg, Sven Andersson (Cap), Ernst Andersson, Gustaf Josefsson, Erik Persson, Sven Jonasson, Karl-Erik Grahn, Axel Nilsson.  Trainer: Carl Linde
**ENGLAND:** Victor Robert Woodley, Charles George Male (Cap), Arthur Edward Catlin, Clifford Samuel Britton, Alfred Young, Wilfred Copping, Alfred John Kirchen, Thomas Galley, Frederick Charles Steele, Leonard Arthur Goulden, Joseph Arthur Johnson.
**Goals:** Frederick Charles Steele (7, 13, 37), Joseph Arthur Johnson (34)

211. 20.05.1937
**FINLAND v ENGLAND 0-8** (0-4)
*Pallokentta, Helsinki*
Referee: Eklöw (Sweden)   Attendance: 9,533
**FINLAND:** Paavo Salminen, Frans Karjagin, Kaarlo Oksanen (Cap), Eino Lahti, Armas Pyy, Antero Rinne, Paavo Virtanen, Kurt Weckström, Aatos Lehtonen, Pentti Larvo, Yrjö Kylmälä. Trainer: Ferdinand Fabra
**ENGLAND:** Victor Robert Woodley, Charles George Male (Cap), Edris Albert Hapgood, Charles Kenneth Willingham, Harry Betmead, Wilfred Copping, Alfred John Kirchen, John Robinson, Joseph Payne, Frederick Charles Steele, Joseph Arthur Johnson.
**Goals:** Alfred John Kirchen (6), Joseph Payne (27, 56), Frederick Charles Steele (36, 52), Joseph Arthur Johnson (44), Charles Kenneth Willingham (75), John Robinson (87)

212. 23.10.1937   Home Championship
**NORTHERN IRELAND v ENGLAND 1-5** (0-2)
*Windsor Park, Belfast*
Referee: Willie Webb (Scotland)   Attendance: 36,000
**NORTHERN IRELAND:** Thomas Breen, William Edward Hayes, William Cook, William Mitchell, John Jones, Robert James Browne, Noel Kernaghan, Alexander Ernest Stevenson, David Kirker Martin, Peter Dermont Doherty, Owen Madden.
**ENGLAND:** Victor Robert Woodley, Bert Sproston, Samuel Barkas (Cap), William John Crayston, Stanley Cullis, Wilfred Copping, Albert Geldard, George William Hall, George Robert Mills, Leonard Arthur Goulden, Eric Frederick George Brook.
**Goals:** Alexander Ernest Stevenson (#) / George Robert Mills (10, 20, 55), George William Hall (58), Eric Frederick George Brook (75)

213. 17.11.1937   Home Championship
**ENGLAND v WALES 2-1** (1-1)
*Ayresome Park, Middlesbrough*
Referee: Willie Webb (Scotland)   Attendance: 30,608
**ENGLAND:** Victor Robert Woodley, Bert Sproston, Samuel Barkas (Cap), William John Crayston, Stanley Cullis, Wilfred Copping, Stanley Matthews, George William Hall, George Robert Mills, Leonard Arthur Goulden, Eric Frederick George Brook.
**WALES:** Albert Gray, Herbert Gwyn Turner, William Marshall Hughes, James Patrick Murphy, Harry Hanford, David Thomas Richards, Idris Morgan Hopkins, Leslie Jenkin Jones, Edwin Perry, Brynmor Jones, Seymour Morris.
**Goals:** Stanley Matthews (28), George William Hall (59) / Edwin Perry (18)

214. 01.12.1937
**ENGLAND v CZECHOSLOVAKIA 5-4** (3-2)
*White Hart Lane, London*
Referee: John Langenus (Belgium)   Attendance: 45,879
**ENGLAND:** Victor Robert Woodley, Bert Sproston, Samuel Barkas (Cap), William John Crayston, Stanley Cullis, Wilfred Copping, Stanley Matthews, George William Hall, George Robert Mills, Leonard Arthur Goulden, John Morton.
**CZECHOSLOVAKIA:** František Plánička (Cap), Josef Košťálek, Ferdinand Daučik, Antonín Vodička, Jaroslav Bouček, Karel Kolský, Jan Říha, František Kloz, Josef Zeman, Oldřich Nejedlý, Antonín Puč.  Trainer: Josef Tesař
**Goals:** William John Crayston (5), John Morton (19), Stanley Matthews (28, 55, 75) / Antonín Puč (12), Josef Zeman (45), Oldřich Nejedlý (60, 75)

215. 09.04.1938   Home Championship
**ENGLAND v SCOTLAND 0-1** (0-1)
*Wembley, London*
Referee: William Hamilton (Northern Ireland)   Att: 93,267
**ENGLAND:** Victor Robert Woodley, Bert Sproston, Edris Albert Hapgood (Cap), Charles Kenneth Willingham, Stanley Cullis, Wilfred Copping, Stanley Matthews, George William Hall, Michael Fenton, Joseph Eric Stephenson, Clifford Sydney Bastin.
**SCOTLAND:** David Scott Cumming, Andrew Anderson, Andrew Beattie, William Shankly, Thomas M. Smith, George Clark Phillips Brown (Cap), John Vance Milne, Thomas Walker, Francis O'Donnell, George Mutch, Robert Reid.
**Goal:** Thomas Walker (6)

216.  14.05.1938
**GERMANY v ENGLAND  3-6**  (2-4)

*Olympia, Berlin*

Referee: John Langenus (Belgium)    Attendance: 120,000

**GERMANY**: Hans Jakob, Paul Janes, Reinhold Münzenberg, Andreas Kupfer, Ludwig Goldbrunner, Albin Kitzinger, Ernst Lehner, Rudolf Gellesch, Josef Gauchel, Fritz Szepan (Cap), Hans Pesser.    Trainer: Josef Herberger

**ENGLAND**: Victor Robert Woodley, Bert Sproston, Edris Albert Hapgood (Cap), Charles Kenneth Willingham, Alfred Young, Donald Welsh, Stanley Matthews, John Robinson, Frank Henry Broome, Leonard Arthur Goulden, Clifford Sydney Bastin.

**Goals**: Rudolf Gellesch (20), Josef Gauchel (44), Hans Pesser (77) / Clifford Sydney Bastin (16), John Robinson (26, 49), Frank Henry Broome (28), Stanley Matthews (42), Leonard Arthur Goulden (80)


217.  21.05.1938
**SWITZERLAND v ENGLAND  2-1**  (1-1)

*Hardturm, Zürich*

Referee: Peco Bauwens (Germany)    Attendance: 25,000

**SWITZERLAND**: Willy Huber, Severino Minelli, August Lehmann, Hermann Springer, Sirio Vernati, Ernest Lörtscher, Lauro Amadò, Eugène Walaschek, Alfred Bickel, André Abegglen, Georges Aeby.    Trainer: Karl Rappan

**ENGLAND**: Victor Robert Woodley, Bert Sproston, Edris Albert Hapgood (Cap), Charles Kenneth Willingham, Alfred Young, Donald Welsh, Stanley Matthews, John Robinson, Frank Henry Broome, Leonard Arthur Goulden, Clifford Sydney Bastin.

**Goal**: Georges Aeby (25), André Abegglen III (73 pen) / Clifford Sydney Bastin (33 pen)


218.  26.05.1938
**FRANCE v ENGLAND  2-4**  (2-3)

*Yves du Manoir, Colombes, Paris*

Referee: Louis Baert (Belgium)    Attendance: 46,920

**FRANCE**: Laurent Di Lorto, Hector Cazenave, Étienne Mattler (Cap), François Bourbotte, Auguste Jordan, Raoul Diagne, Roger Courtois, Michel Brusseaux, Jean Nicolas, Oscar Heisserer, Alfred Aston.

**ENGLAND**: Victor Robert Woodley, Bert Sproston, Edris Albert Hapgood (Cap), Charles Kenneth Willingham, Alfred Young, Stanley Cullis, Frank Henry Broome, Stanley Matthews, Edward Joseph Drake, Leonard Arthur Goulden, Clifford Sydney Bastin.

**Goals**: Auguste Jordan (32), Jean Nicolas (36) / Frank Henry Broome (6), Edward Joseph Drake (34, 40), Clifford Sydney Bastin (85 pen)


219.  22.10.1938    Home Championship
**WALES v ENGLAND  4-2**  (2-2)

*Ninian Park, Cardiff*

Referee: William Hamilton (Northern Ireland)    Att: 55,000

**WALES**: William Ronald John, William John Whatley, William Marshall Hughes, George Henry Green, Thomas George Jones, David Thomas Richards, Idris Morgan Hopkins, Leslie Jenkin Jones, David Astley, Brynmor Jones, Reginald Horace Cumner.

**ENGLAND**: Victor Robert Woodley, Bert Sproston, Edris Albert Hapgood (Cap), Charles Kenneth Willingham, Alfred Young, Wilfred Copping, Stanley Matthews, John Robinson, Thomas Lawton, Leonard Arthur Goulden, Walter Edward Boyes.

**Goals**: David Astley (5, #), Idris Morgan Hopkins (33), Brynmor Jones (61) /
Thomas Lawton (27 pen), Stanley Matthews (35)


220.  26.10.1938
**ENGLAND v F.I.F.A. XI  3-0**  (2-0)

*Highbury, London*

Referee: Arthur James Jewell (England)    Attendance: 40,185

**ENGLAND**: Victor Robert Woodley, Bert Sproston, Edris Albert Hapgood (Cap), Charles Kenneth Willingham, Stanley Cullis, Wilfred Copping, Stanley Matthews, George William Hall, Thomas Lawton, Leonard Arthur Goulden, Walter Edward Boyes.

**FIFA**: Aldo Olivieri, Alfredo Foni, Pietri Rava, Andreas Kupfer, Michele Andreolo, Albin Kitzinger, Alfred Aston, Raimond Braine (Cap), Silvio Piola, Gyula Zsengeller, Arne Brustad.    Trainer: Vittorio Pozzo

**Goals**: George William Hall (20), Thomas Lawton (39), Leonard Goulden (73)


221.  09.11.1938
**ENGLAND v NORWAY  4-0**  (4-0)

*St. James' Park, Newcastle*

Referee: James Martin (Scotland)    Attendance: 39,887

**ENGLAND**: Victor Robert Woodley, Bert Sproston, Edris Albert Hapgood (Cap), Charles Kenneth Willingham, Stanley Cullis, John Douglas Wright, Stanley Matthews, Frank Henry Broome, Thomas Lawton, Ronald William Dix, James Christopher Reginald Smith.

**NORWAY**: Henry Johansen, Lars Marthinsen, Øivind Holmsen, Kristian Henriksen, Nils Eriksen, Rolf Holmberg, Knut Brynildsen, Reidar Kvammen, Alf Martinsen, Magnar Isaksen, Arne Brustad.    Trainer: Asbjørn Halvorsen

**Goals**: James Christopher Reginald Smith (13, 40), Ronald William Dix (20), Thomas Lawton (35)

**222. 16.11.1938    Home Championship**
**ENGLAND v NORTHERN IRELAND  7-0**  (4-0)

*Old Trafford, Manchester*

Referee: Craigmoyle (Scotland)    Attendance: 40,386

**ENGLAND**: Victor Robert Woodley, William Walker Morris, Edris Albert Hapgood (Cap), Charles Kenneth Willingham, Stanley Cullis, Joseph Mercer, Stanley Matthews, George William Hall, Thomas Lawton, Joseph Eric Stephenson, James Christopher Reginald Smith.

**NORTHERN IRELAND**: James Franus Twoomey, William Edward Hayes, William Cook, Thomas Henry Brolly, Walter S. McMillen, Robert James Browne, David Cochrane, Alexander Ernest Stevenson, Henry C. Baird, Peter Dermont Doherty, John Brown.

**Goals**: Thomas Lawton (8), George W. Hall (36, 38, 40, 55, 65), Stanley Matthews (75)

**223. 15.04.1939    Home Championship**
**SCOTLAND v ENGLAND  1-2**  (1-0)

*Hampden Park, Glasgow*

Referee: William Hamilton (Northern Ireland)    Att: 149,269

**SCOTLAND**: James Dawson, James Carabine, George Wilfred Cummings, William Shankly, Robert Denholm Baxter, Alexander McNab, Alexander McSpadyen, Thomas Walker, James Dougall (Cap), Alexander Venters, John Vance Milne.

**ENGLAND**: Victor Robert Woodley, William Walker Morris, Edris Albert Hapgood (Cap), Charles Kenneth Willingham, Stanley Cullis, Joseph Mercer, Stanley Matthews, George William Hall, Thomas Lawton, Leonard Arthur Goulden, Albert Beasley.

**Goals**: James Dougall (21) /
Albert Beasley (66), Thomas Lawton (88)

**224. 13.05.1939**
**ITALY v ENGLAND  2-2**  (0-1)

*San Siro, Milano*

Referee: Peco Bauwens (Germany)    Attendance: 60,000

**ITALY**: Aldo Olivieri, Alfredo Foni, Pietro Rava, Teobaldo Depetrini, Michele Andreolo, Ugo Locatelli, Amedeo Biavati, Pietro Serantoni, Silvio Piola, Giuseppe Meazza (Cap), Gino Colaussi.    Trainer: Vittorio Pozzo

**ENGLAND**: Victor Robert Woodley, Charles George Male, Edris Albert Hapgood (Cap), Charles Kenneth Willingham, Stanley Cullis, Joseph Mercer, Stanley Matthews, George William Hall, Thomas Lawton, Leonard Arthur Goulden, Frank Henry Broome.    Manager: Thomas Whittacker

**Goals**: Amedeo Biavati (49), Silvio Piola (64) /
Thomas Lawton (19), George William Hall (77)

**225. 18.05.1939**
**YUGOSLAVIA v ENGLAND  2-1**  (1-0)

*BSK, Beograd*

Referee: Georges Capdeville (France)    Attendance: 35,000

**YUGOSLAVIA**: Ljubomir Lovrić, Zvonimir Požega, Ernest Dubac, Peter Manola, Prvoslav Dragićević, Gustav Lehner, Svetislav Glišović, Đorđe Vujadinović (Cap), Aleksandar Petrović, Frane Matošić, Nikola Perlić.
Trainer: Boško Simonović

**ENGLAND**: Victor Robert Woodley, Charles George Male, Edris Albert Hapgood (Cap), Charles Kenneth Willingham, Stanley Cullis, Joseph Mercer, Stanley Matthews, George William Hall, Thomas Lawton, Leonard Arthur Goulden, Frank Henry Broome.    Manager: Thomas Whittacker

**Goals**: Svetislav Glišović (15), Nikola Perlić (62) /
Frank Henry Broome (21)

**226. 24.05.1939**
**ROMANIA v ENGLAND  0-2**  (0-1)

*ANEF, București*

Referee: John Langenus (Belgium)    Attendance: 40,000

**ROMANIA**: Dumitru Pavlovici, Rudolf Bürger, Lazăr Sfera, Vintilă Cossini, Augustin Juhász, Rudolf Demetrovicz, Cornel Orza, Silviu Ploeșteanu, Nicolae Reuter, Iuliu Bodola (Cap), Ștefan Dobay.    Manager: Liviu Iuga

**ENGLAND**: Victor Robert Woodley, Charles George Male, William Walker Morris, Joseph Mercer, Stanley Cullis (Cap), Wilfred Copping, Frank Henry Broome, Leonard Arthur Goulden, Thomas Lawton, Donald Welsh, Leslie George Frederick Smith.    Manager: Thomas Whittacker

**Goals**: Leonard Arthur Goulden (10), Donald Welsh (52)

**227. 28.09.1946    Home Championship**
**NORTHERN IRELAND v ENGLAND  2-7**  (0-3)

*Windsor Park, Belfast*

Referee: Willie Webb (Scotland)    Attendance: 57,111

**NORTHERN IRELAND**: Alex Russell, William Charles Gorman, Thomas Aherne, John James Carey, John Joseph Vernon, James P. Douglas, David Cochrane, James McAlinden, Edward James McMorran, Peter Dermont Doherty, Norman Lockhart.

**ENGLAND**: Frank Victor Swift, Lawrence Scott, George Francis Moutry Hardwick (Cap), William Ambrose Wright, Cornelius "Neil" Franklin, Henry Cockburn, Thomas Finney, Horatio Stratton Carter, Thomas Lawton, Wilfred Mannion, Robert Langton.    Manager: Walter Winterbottom

**Goals**: Norman Lockhart (#, #) / Horatio S. Carter (1), Wilfred Mannion (7, 28, 61), Thomas Finney (60), Thomas Lawton (82), Robert Langton (83)

228. 30.09.1946
**REPUBLIC OF IRELAND v ENGLAND  0-1**  (0-0)
*Dalymount Park, Dublin*

Referee:  Willie Webb (Scotland)     Attendance:  32,000

**IRELAND**:  Thomas Breen, William Charles Gorman, William Edward Hayes, John James Carey (Cap), Cornelius Joseph Martin, William Walsh, Kevin Patrick O'Flanagan, Patrick Coad, Michael O'Flanagan, Alexander Ernest Stevenson, Thomas Joseph Eglington.

**ENGLAND**:  Frank Victor Swift, Lawrence Scott, George Francis Moutry Hardwick (Cap), William Ambrose Wright, Cornelius "Neil" Franklin, Henry Cockburn, Thomas Finney, Horatio Stratton Carter, Thomas Lawton, Wilfred Mannion, Robert Langton.     Manager:  Walter Winterbottom

**Goal**:  Thomas Finney (81)


229.  13.11.1946     Home Championship
**ENGLAND v WALES  3-0**  (2-0)
*Maine Road, Manchester*

Referee:  Willie Webb (Scotland)     Attendance:  59,121

**ENGLAND**:  Frank Victor Swift, Lawrence Scott, George Francis Moutry Hardwick (Cap), William Ambrose Wright, Cornelius "Neil" Franklin, Henry Cockburn, Thomas Finney, Horatio Stratton Carter, Thomas Lawton, Wilfred Mannion, Robert Langton.     Manager:  Walter Winterbottom

**WALES**:  Cyril Sidlow, Alfred Thomas Sherwood, William Marshall Hughes, Douglas Frederick Witcomb, Thomas George Jones, William Arthur Ronald Burgess, William Ernest Arthur Jones, Aubrey Powell, Stanley Verdun Richards, Ivor Verdun Powell, George Edwards.

**Goals**:  Wilfred Mannion (8, 16), Thomas Lawton (40)


230.  27.11.1946
**ENGLAND v HOLLAND  8-2**  (6-1)
*Leeds Road, Huddersfield*

Referee:  James Martin (Scotland)     Attendance:  32,435

**ENGLAND**:  Frank Victor Swift, Lawrence Scott, George Francis Moutry Hardwick (Cap), William Ambrose Wright, Cornelius "Neil" Franklin, Harry Johnstonon, Thomas Finney, Horatio Stratton Carter, Thomas Lawton, Wilfred Mannion, Robert Langton.     Manager:  Walter Winterbottom

**HOLLAND**:  Piet Kraak, Jan Potharst, Henk van der Linden, Bas Paauwe (Cap), Arie Vermeer, Arie de Vroet, Guus Dräger, Faas Wilkes, Wim Roosen, Jaap Smit, Co Bergman.   Trainer:  Karel Kaufman & Otto Bonsema

**Goals**:  Thomas Lawton (20, 24, 35, 78), Horatio Stratton Carter (30, 71), Wilfred Mannion (34), Thomas Finney (44) / Co Bergman (42), Jaap Smit (83)


231.  12.04.1947     Home Championship
**ENGLAND v SCOTLAND  1-1**  (0-1)
*Wembley, London*

Referee:  Charles Delasalle (France)     Attendance:  98,200

**SCOTLAND**:  William Miller, George Lewis Young, John Shaw (Cap), Archibald Renwick MacAuley, William Alexander Woodburn, Alexander Rooney Forbes, Gordon Smith, Andrew McLaren, James Delaney, William Steel, Thomas Usher Pearson.

**ENGLAND**:  Frank Victor Swift, Lawrence Scott, George Francis Moutry Hardwick (Cap), William Ambrose Wright, Cornelius "Neil" Franklin, Harry Johnstonon, Stanley Matthews, Horatio Stratton Carter, Thomas Lawton, Wilfred Mannion, James Mullen.     Manager:  Walter Winterbottom

**Goal**:  Andrew McLaren (16) / Horatio Stratton Carter (56)


232.  03.05.1947
**ENGLAND v FRANCE  3-0**  (0-0)
*Highbury, London*

Referee:  Louis Baert (Belgium)     Attendance:  54,389

**ENGLAND**:  Frank Victor Swift, Lawrence Scott, George Francis Moutry Hardwick (Cap), William Ambrose Wright, Cornelius "Neil" Franklin, Edmund Lowe, Thomas Finney, Horatio Stratton Carter, Thomas Lawton, Wilfred Mannion, Robert Langton.     Manager:  Walter Winterbottom

**FRANCE**:  Julien Darui, Jean Swiatek, Jean Grégoire, Roger Marche, Antoine Cuissard, Jean Prouff, Boleslav Tempowski, Oscar Heisserer (Cap), Ernest Vaast, Emile Bongiorni, Jean Lechantre.

**Goals**:  Thomas Finney (50), Wilfred Mannion (64), Horatio Stratton Carter (77)


233.  18.05.1947
**SWITZERLAND v ENGLAND  1-0**  (1-0)
*Hardturm, Zürich*

Referee:  Sdez (France)     Attendance:  34,000

**SWITZERLAND**:  Erwin Ballabio, Rudolf Gyger, Willy Steffen, André Belli, Oliver Eggimann, Roger Bocquet, Jean Tamini, Walter Fink, Alfred Bickel, Lauro Amadò, Jacques Fatton.   Trainer:  Karl Rappan

**ENGLAND**:  Frank Victor Swift, Lawrence Scott, George Francis Moutry Hardwick (Cap), William Ambrose Wright, Cornelius "Neil" Franklin, Edmund Lowe, Stanley Matthews, Horatio Stratton Carter, Thomas Lawton, Wilfred Mannion, Robert Langton.     Manager:  Walter Winterbottom

**Goal**:  Jacques Fatton (27)

234. 25.05.1947
**PORTUGAL v ENGLAND 0-10** (0-5)
*National, Lisboa*

Referee: Charles Delasalle (France)    Attendance: 65,000

**PORTUGAL**: João Mendonça Azevedo (26 Manuel Maria Nogueira Capela), Alvaro Cardoso da Silva (Cap) (29 VASCO de Jesus Oliveira), Francisco Ferreira, Mariano Rodrigues Amaro, António Feliciano, Francisco Moreira, António Jesus Correia, António de Araújo, Fernando Baptista Peyroteo, José António Barreto Travaços, ROGÉRIO Lantres de Carvalho. Trainer: Tavares da Silva

**ENGLAND**: Frank Victor Swift, Lawrence Scott, George Francis Moutry Hardwick (Cap), William Ambrose Wright, Cornelius "Neil" Franklin, Edmund Lowe, Stanley Matthews, Stanley Harding Mortensen, Thomas Lawton, Wilfred Mannion, Thomas Finney.    Manager: Walter Winterbottom

**Goals**: Thomas Lawton (2, 20, 40, 50), Stanley Harding Mortensen (1, 55, 60, 62), Thomas Finney (30), Stanley Matthews (80)


235. 21.09.1947
**BELGIUM v ENGLAND 2-5** (1-3)
*Heysel, Bruxelles*

Referee: James Martin (Scotland)    Attendance: 54,326

**BELGIUM**: François Daenen, Léon Aernaudts, Joseph Pannaye, Henri Coppens, Jules Henriet, Fernand Massay, Victor Lemberechts, Joseph Mermans, Albert De Cleyn (Cap), Léopold Anoul, René Thirifays.    Trainer: William Gormlie

**ENGLAND**: Frank Victor Swift, Lawrence Scott, George Francis Moutry Hardwick (Cap), Timothy Victor Ward, Cornelius "Neil" Franklin, William Ambrose Wright, Stanley Matthews, Stanley Harding Mortensen, Thomas Lawton, Wilfred Mannion, Thomas Finney.
Manager: Walter Winterbottom

**Goals**: Joseph Mermans (34), Albert De Cleyn (53) / Thomas Lawton (1, 63), Stanley Harding Mortensen (15), Thomas Finney (22, 60)


236. 18.10.1947    Home Championship
**WALES v ENGLAND 0-3** (0-3)
*Ninian Park, Cardiff*

Referee: James Martin (Scotland)    Attendance: 55,000

**WALES**: Cyril Sidlow, Raymond Lambert, Walley Barnes, Ivor Verdun Powell, Thomas George Jones, William Arthur Ronald Burgess, David Sidney Thomas, Aubrey Powell, George Lowrie, Brynmor Jones, George Edwards.

**ENGLAND**: Frank Victor Swift, Lawrence Scott, George Francis Moutry Hardwick (Cap), Philip Henry Taylor, Cornelius "Neil" Franklin, William Ambrose Wright, Stanley Matthews, Stanley Harding Mortensen, Thomas Lawton, Wilfred Mannion, Thomas Finney.
Manager: Walter Winterbottom

**Goals**: Thomas Finney (6), Stanley Harding Mortensen (11), Thomas Lawton (25)


237. 05.11.1947    Home Championship
**ENGLAND v NORTHERN IRELAND 2-2** (0-0)
*Goodison Park, Liverpool*

Referee: P. Fitzpatrick (Scotland)    Attendance: 67,980

**ENGLAND**: Frank Victor Swift, Lawrence Scott, George Francis Moutry Hardwick (Cap), Philip Henry Taylor, Cornelius "Neil" Franklin, William Ambrose Wright, Stanley Matthews, Stanley Harding Mortensen, Wilfred Mannion, Thomas Lawton, Thomas Finney.
Manager: Walter Winterbottom

**NORTHERN IRELAND**: Edward Hinton, Cornelius Joseph Martin, John James Carey, William Walsh, John Joseph Vernon, Peter Desmond Farrell, David Cochrane, Samuel Smyth, David John Walsh, Peter Dermont Doherty, Thomas Joseph Eglington.

**Goals**: Wilfred Mannion (84), Thomas Lawton (86) / David John Walsh (54), Peter Dermont Doherty (89)


238. 19.11.1947
**ENGLAND v SWEDEN 4-2** (3-1)
*Highbury, London*

Referee: Willie Webb (Scotland)    Attendance: 44,282

**ENGLAND**: Frank Victor Swift, Lawrence Scott, George Francis Moutry Hardwick (Cap), Philip Henry Taylor, Cornelius "Neil" Franklin, William Ambrose Wright, Thomas Finney, Stanley Harding Mortensen, Thomas Lawton, Wilfred Mannion, Robert Langton.    Manager: Walter Winterbottom

**SWEDEN**: Torsten Lindberg, Knut Nordahl, Erik Nilsson (Cap), Sune Andersson, Bertil Nordahl, Rune Emanuelsson, Malte Mårtensson, Gunnar Gren, Gunnar Nordahl, Nils Liedholm, Stellan Nilsson.    Trainer: Rudolf Kock

**Goals**: Stanley Harding Mortensen (15, 80, 87), Thomas Lawton (18 pen) / Gunnar Nordahl (22), Gunnar Gren (68 pen)

239. 10.04.1948  Home Championship
**SCOTLAND v ENGLAND  0-2**  (0-1)
*Hampden Park, Glasgow*
Referee: David Maxwell (Northern Ireland)  Att: 135,376
**SCOTLAND**: Ian Henderson Black, John Govan, David Shaw, William Bowie Campbell, George Lewis Young (Cap), Archibald Renwick MacAuley, James Delaney, James Robert Combe, William Thornton, William Steel, William Beveridge Liddell.
**ENGLAND**: Frank Victor Swift, Lawrence Scott, George Francis Moutry Hardwick (Cap), William Ambrose Wright, Cornelius "Neil" Franklin, Henry Cockburn, Stanley Matthews, Stanley Harding Mortensen, Thomas Lawton, Stanley Clare Pearson, Thomas Finney.  Manager: Walter Winterbottom
**Goals**: Thomas Finney (44), Stanley Harding Mortensen (62)

240. 16.05.1948
**ITALY v ENGLAND  0-4**  (0-2)
*Comunale, Torino*
Referee: Escartin (Spain)  Attendance: 50,000
**ITALY**: Valerio Bacigalupo, Aldo Ballarin, Alberto Eliani, Carlo Annovazzi, Carlo Parola, Giuseppe Grezar, Romeo Menti, Ezio Loik, Guglielmo Gabetto, Valentino Mazzola (Cap), Riccardo Carapellese.  Trainer: Vittorio Pozzo
**ENGLAND**: Frank Victor Swift (Cap), Lawrence Scott, John Robert Howe, William Ambrose Wright, Cornelius "Neil" Franklin, Henry Cockburn, Stanley Matthews, Stanley Harding Mortensen, Thomas Lawton, Wilfred Mannion, Thomas Finney.  Manager: Walter Winterbottom
**Goals**: Stanley Harding Mortensen (4), Thomas Lawton (23), Thomas Finney (70, 72)

241. 26.09.1948
**DENMARK v ENGLAND  0-0**
*Idraetsparken, København*
Referee: Karel van der Meer (Holland)  Attendance: 41,000
**DENMARK**: Eigil Nielsen, Poul Petersen, Viggo Jensen, Axel Pilmark, Dion Ørnvold, Ivan Jensen, Johannes Pløger, Karl Aage Hansen (Cap), Carl Aage Præst, John Hansen, Holger Seebach.
**ENGLAND**: Frank Victor Swift (Cap), Lawrence Scott, John Aston, William Ambrose Wright, Cornelius "Neil" Franklin, Henry Cockburn, Stanley Matthews, James Hagan, Thomas Lawton, Leonard Francis Shackleton, Robert Langton.  Manager: Walter Winterbottom

242. 09.10.1948  Home Championship
**NORTHERN IRELAND v ENGLAND  2-6**  (0-1)
*Windsor Park, Belfast*
Referee: Willie Webb (Scotland)  Attendance: 53,629
**NORTHERN IRELAND**: William Smyth, John James Carey, Cornelius Joseph Martin, William Walsh, John Joseph Vernon, Peter Desmond Farrell, John Francis O'Driscoll, James McAlinden, David John Walsh, Charles Tully, Thomas Joseph Eglington.
**ENGLAND**: Frank Victor Swift, Lawrence Scott, John Robert Howe, William Ambrose Wright (Cap), Cornelius "Neil" Franklin, Henry Cockburn, Stanley Matthews, Stanley Harding Mortensen, John Edward Thompson Milburn, Stanley Clare Pearson, Thomas Finney.  Manager: Walter Winterbottom
**Goals**: David John Walsh (50, 89) / Stanley Matthews (27), John Milburn (52), Stanley Harding Mortensen (55, 60, 80), Stanley Clare Pearson (83)

243. 10.11.1948  Home Championship
**ENGLAND v WALES  1-0**  (1-0)
*Villa Park, Birmingham*
Referee: John Alexander Mowatt (Scotland)  Att: 67,770
**ENGLAND**: Frank Victor Swift, Lawrence Scott, John Aston, Timothy Victor Ward, Cornelius "Neil" Franklin, William Ambrose Wright (Cap), Stanley Matthews, Stanley Harding Mortensen, John Edward Thompson Milburn, Leonard Francis Shackleton, Thomas Finney.  Manager: Walter Winterbottom
**WALES**: William Arthur Hughes, Alfred Thomas Sherwood, Walley Barnes, Roy Paul, Thomas George Jones, William Arthur Ronald Burgess, William Ernest Arthur Jones, Aubrey Powell, Trevor Ford, William Morris, Royston James Clarke.
**Goal**: Thomas Finney (39)

244. 02.12.1948
**ENGLAND v SWITZERLAND  6-0**  (3-0)
*Highbury, London*
Referee: Karel van der Meer (Holland)  Attendance: 48,000
**ENGLAND**: Edwin George Ditchburn, Alfred Ernest Ramsey, John Aston, William Ambrose Wright (Cap), Cornelius "Neil" Franklin, Henry Cockburn, Stanley Matthews, John Frederick Rowley, John Edward Thompson Milburn, John Thomas William Haines, John Hancocks.
Manager: Walter Winterbottom
**SWITZERLAND**: Eugenio Corrodi, Rudolf Gyger, Roger Bocquet, Bernard Lanz, Oliver Eggimann, Gerhard Lusenti, Alfred Bickel, Lauro Amadò, Jean Tamini, René Bader, Jacques Fatton.  Trainer: Karl Rappan
**Goals**: John Haines (5, 26), John Hancocks (25, 70), John Milburn (52), John Frederick Rowley (60)

245. 09.04.1949   Home Championship
**ENGLAND v SCOTLAND  1-3** (0-1)

*Wembley, London*

Referee: Mervyn Griffiths (Wales)   Attendance: 98,188

SCOTLAND: James Clews Cowan, George Lewis Young (Cap), Samuel Richmond Cox, Robert Evans, William Alexander Woodburn, George Graham Aitken, William Waddell, James Mason, William Houliston, William Steel, Lawrence Reilly.

ENGLAND: Frank Victor Swift, John Aston, John Robert Howe, William Ambrose Wright (Cap), Cornelius "Neil" Franklin, Henry Cockburn, Stanley Matthews, Stanley Harding Mortensen, John Edward Thompson Milburn, Stanley Clare Pearson, Thomas Finney.   Manager: Walter Winterbottom

**Goal**: John Milburn (75) /
James Mason (28), William Steel (52), Lawrence Reilly (61)


246. 13.05.1949
**SWEDEN v ENGLAND  3-1** (3-0)

*Råsunda, Solna*

Referee: Giovanni Galeatti (Italy)   Attendance: 37,500

SWEDEN: Karl Svensson, Knut Nordahl, Erik Nilsson (Cap), Kjell Rosén, Börje Leander, Sune Andersson, Egon Johnsson, Gunnar Gren, Hans Jeppson, Henry Carlsson, Bertil Bäckvall.   Trainer: Rudolf Kock

ENGLAND: Edwin George Ditchburn, Edmund Shimwell, John Aston, William Ambrose Wright (Cap), Cornelius "Neil" Franklin, Henry Cockburn, Thomas Finney, Stanley Harding Mortensen, Roy Thomas Frank Bentley, John Frederick Rowley, Robert Langton.   Manager: Walter Winterbottom

**Goal**: Henry Carlsson (3), Hans Jeppson (36), Egon Johnsson (39) / Thomas Finney (67)


247. 18.05.1949
**NORWAY v ENGLAND  1-4** (0-2)

*Ullevaal, Oslo*

Referee: Andersson (Sweden)   Attendance: 36,000

NORWAY: Torgeir Torgersen, Bjørn Spydevold, Harry Boye Karlsen, Knut Andersen, Thorbjørn Svenssen, Odd Andersen, Trygve Arnesen, Gunnar Thoresen, Willy Andresen, Hans Nordahl, Gunnar Dahlen.

ENGLAND: Frank Victor Swift, William Ellerington, John Aston, William Ambrose Wright (Cap), Cornelius "Neil" Franklin, James William Dickinson, Thomas Finney, John Morris, Stanley Harding Mortensen, Wilfred Mannion, James Mullen.   Manager: Walter Winterbottom

**Goals**: Willy Andresen (50) / James Mullen (6), Thomas Finney (38), B. Spydevold (60 og), John Morris (70)


248. 22.05.1949
**FRANCE v ENGLAND  1-3** (1-2)

*Stade Olympique, Colombes, Paris*

Referee: Karel van der Meer (Holland)   Attendance: 61,308

FRANCE: René Vignal, André Grillon, Roger Mindonnet, Marcel Salva, Robert Jonquet, Louis Hon, Antoine Cuissard, Albert Batteux (Cap), Roger Gabet, Roger Quenolle, Georges Moreel.

ENGLAND: Bert Frederick Williams, William Ellerington, John Aston, William Ambrose Wright (Cap), Cornelius "Neil" Franklin, James William Dickinson, Thomas Finney, John Morris, John Frederick Rowley, Wilfred Mannion, James Mullen.   Manager: Walter Winterbottom

**Goals**: Georges Moreel (1) /
John Morris (8, 86), William Ambrose Wright (24)


249. 21.09.1949
**ENGLAND v REPUBLIC OF IRELAND  0-2** (0-1)

*Goodison Park, Liverpool*

Referee: John Mowatt (Scotland)   Attendance: 51,487

ENGLAND: Bert Frederick Williams, Bertram Mozley, John Aston, William Ambrose Wright (Cap), Cornelius "Neil" Franklin, James William Dickinson, Peter Philip Harris, John Morris, Jesse Pye, Wilfred Mannion, Thomas Finney.   Manager: Walter Winterbottom

IRELAND: Thomas Fergus Godwin, Cornelius Joseph Martin, Thomas Aherne, Thomas Moroney, David John Walsh, Peter Joseph Corr, Thomas O'Connor, John James Carey (Cap), Peter Desmond, Peter Desmond Farrell, William Walsh.

**Goals**: Cornelius Joseph Martin (33 pen), Peter Desmond Farrell (85)


250. 15.10.1949   4th World Cup Qualifiers, Home Championship
**WALES v ENGLAND  1-4** (0-3)

*Ninian Park, Cardiff*

Referee: John Mowatt (Scotland)   Attendance: 61,079

WALES: Cyril Sidlow, Walley Barnes, Alfred Thomas Sherwood, Roy Paul, Thomas George Jones, William Arthur Ronald Burgess, William Maldwyn Griffiths, William Henry Lucas, Trevor Ford, Francis Henry Scrine, George Edwards.

ENGLAND: Bert Frederick Williams, Bertram Mozley, John Aston, William Ambrose Wright (Cap), Cornelius "Neil" Franklin, James William Dickinson, Thomas Finney, Stanley Harding Mortensen, John Edward Thompson Milburn, Leonard Francis Shackleton, John Hancocks.   Manager: Walter Winterbottom

**Goals**: William Maldwyn Griffiths (80) /
Stanley Harding Mortensen (22), John Milburn (29, 34, 66)

251. 16.11.1949    4th World Cup Qualifiers, Home Championship
**ENGLAND v NORTHERN IRELAND  9-2**  (4-0)
*Maine Road, Manchester*

Referee: Mervyn Griffiths (Wales)    Attendance: 69,762

**ENGLAND**: Bernard Reginald Streten, Bertram Mozley, John Aston, William Watson, Cornelius "Neil" Franklin, William Ambrose Wright (Cap), Thomas Finney, Stanley Harding Mortensen, John Frederick Rowley, Stanley Clare Pearson, Jack Froggatt.    Manager: Walter Winterbottom

**NORTHERN IRELAND**: Hugh Redmond Kelly, James McBurney Feeney, Alfred McMichael, Gerard Columba Bowler, John Joseph Vernon, James Joseph McCabe, David Cochrane, Samuel Smyth, Robert Anderson Brennan, Charles P. Tully, John McKenna.

**Goals**: John F. Rowley (6, 47, 56, 58), Jack Froggatt (25), Stanley Clare Pearson (33, 68), Stanley Mortensen (35, 50) / Samuel Smyth (52), Robert Anderson Brennan (85)


252. 30.11.1949
**ENGLAND v ITALY  2-0**  (0-0)
*White Hart Lane, London*

Referee: John Mowatt (Scotland)    Attendance: 71,797

**ENGLAND**: Bert Frederick Williams, Alfred Ernest Ramsey, John Aston, William Watson, Cornelius "Neil" Franklin, William Ambrose Wright (Cap), Thomas Finney, Stanley Harding Mortensen, John Frederick Rowley, Stanley Clare Pearson, Jack Froggatt.    Manager: Walter Winterbottom

**ITALY**: Giuseppe Moro, Alberto Bertuccelli, Attilio Giovannini, Carlo Annovazzi, Carlo Parola, Alberto Piccinini, Giampiero Boniperti, Benito Lorenzi, Amedeo Amadei, Rinaldo Martino, Riccardo Carapellese (Cap). Technical commission president: F. Novo

**Goals**: John Frederick Rowley (75), William Wright (79)


253. 15.04.1950    4th World Cup Qualifiers, Home Championship
**SCOTLAND v ENGLAND  0-1**  (0-0)
*Hampden Park, Glasgow*

Referee: Reginald Leafe (England)    Attendance: 133,300

**SCOTLAND**: James Clews Cowan, George Lewis Young (Cap), Samuel Richmond Cox, John Miller McColl, William Alexander Woodburn, Alexander Rooney Forbes, William Waddell, William Moir, William Russell Logan Bauld, William Steel, William Beveridge Liddell.

**ENGLAND**: Bert Frederick Williams, Alfred Ernest Ramsey, John Aston, William Ambrose Wright (Cap), Cornelius "Neil" Franklin, James William Dickinson, Thomas Finney, Wilfred Mannion, Stanley Harding Mortensen, Roy Thomas Frank Bentley, Robert Langton.    Manager: Walter Winterbottom

**Goals**: Roy Thomas Frank Bentley (64)


254. 14.05.1950
**PORTUGAL v ENGLAND  3-5**  (0-3)
*Nacional, Lisboa*

Referee: Giuseppe Carpani (Italy)    Attendance: 65,000

**PORTUGAL**: ERNESTO Nogueira de Oliveira, VIRGÍLIO Marques Mendes (31 Octávio dos Santos Barrosa), Angelo Ferreira Carvalho, Serafim Pereira Baptista, FÉLIX Assunção Antunes, Francisco Ferreira (Cap) (26 Carlos Augusto Ribeiro Canário), ROGÉRIO Lantres de Carvalho, Manuel Vasques, Henrique Ben David, José António Barreto Travaços, ALBANO Narciso Pereira.    Trainer: Salvador do Carmo

**ENGLAND**: Bert Frederick Williams, Alfred Ernest Ramsey, John Aston, William Ambrose Wright (Cap), William Henry Jones, James William Dickinson, John Edward Thompson Milburn, Stanley Harding Mortensen, Roy Thomas Frank Bentley, Wilfred Mannion, Thomas Finney.    Manager: Walter Winterbottom

**Goals**: Ben David (47, 59), Vasques (70) / Thomas Finney (5 pen, 25, 55, 77 pen), Stan Mortensen (15)


255. 18.05.1950
**BELGIUM v ENGLAND  1-4**  (1-0)
*Heizel, Bruxelles*

Referee: Raymond Vincenti (France)    Attendance: 55,854

**BELGIUM**: Henri Meert, Arsène Vaillant, Léopold Anoul, Jan Van der Auwera, Louis Carré, Victor Mees, Jozef Van Looy, Frédéric Chavès D'Aguilar (Cap), Joseph Mermans, Albert De Hert, Georges Mordant.    Trainer: William Gormlie

**ENGLAND**: Bert Frederick Williams, Alfred Ernest Ramsey, John Aston, William Ambrose Wright (Cap), William Henry Jones, James William Dickinson, John Edward Thompson Milburn (11 James Mullen), Stanley Harding Mortensen, Roy Thomas Frank Bentley, Wilfred Mannion, Thomas Finney.    Manager: Walter Winterbottom

**Goals**: Joseph Mermans (43) / James Mullen (46), Stanley Harding Mortensen (65), Wilfred Mannion (68), Roy Thomas Frank Bentley (86)


256. 25.06.1950    4th World Cup, 1st Round
**ENGLAND v CHILE  2-0**  (1-0)
*Maracana, Rio de Janeiro*

Referee: Karel van der Meer (Holland)    Attendance: 29,703

**ENGLAND**: Bert Frederick Williams, Alfred Ernest Ramsey, John Aston, William Ambrose Wright (Cap), Lawrence Hughes, James William Dickinson, Thomas Finney, Wilfred Mannion, Roy Thomas Frank Bentley, Stanley Harding Mortensen, James Mullen.    Manager: Walter Winterbottom

**CHILE**: Sergio Roberto Livingstone, Arturo Farías, Fernando Roldán, Manuel Alvarez, Miguel Busquets, Hernán Carvallo Castro, Luis Lindorfo Mayanés, Atilio Cremaschi, Jorge Robledo, Manuel Muñoz, Guillermo Díaz Zambrano.    Trainer: Alberto Buccicardi

**Goals**: Stanley Mortensen (27), Wilfred Mannion (51)

257. 29.06.1950   4th World Cup, 1st Round
**U.S.A. v ENGLAND  1-0**  (1-0)

*Mineiro, Belo Horizonte*

Referee: Generoso Dattilo (Italy)   Attendance: 10,151

**U.S.A.:** Frank Borghi, Harry Joseph Keough, Joseph Maca, Edward John McIlvenny (Cap), Charles Martin Colombo, Walter Alfred Bahr, Frank Wallace, Gino Pariani, Joseph Edouard Gaetjens, John Benevides Souza, Edward Netto Souza.   Trainer: William Jeffrey

**ENGLAND:** Bert Frederick Williams, Alfred Ernest Ramsey, John Aston, William Ambrose Wright (Cap), Lawrence Hughes, James William Dickinson, Thomas Finney, Stanley Harding Mortensen, Roy Thomas Frank Bentley, Wilfred Mannion, James Mullen.   Manager: Walter Winterbottom

**Goal:** Joseph Edouard Gaetjens (38)


258. 02.07.1950   4th World Cup, 1st Round
**SPAIN v ENGLAND  1-0**  (0-0)

*Maracana, Rio de Janeiro*

Referee: Giovanni Galeatti (Italy)   Attendance: 74,462

**SPAIN:** Antonio Ramallets, Gabriel Alonso, José Parra, Mariano Gonzalvo, José Gonzalvo, Antonio Puchades, Estanislao Basora, Silvestre Igoa, Telmo Zarraonandía "Zarra", José Luis Panizo, Agustin Gaínza (Cap).
Trainer: Guillermo Eizaguirre Olmos

**ENGLAND:** Bert Frederick Williams, Alfred Ernest Ramsey, William Eckersley, William Ambrose Wright (Cap), Lawrence Hughes, James William Dickinson, Stanley Matthews, Stanley Harding Mortensen, John Edward Thompson Milburn, Edward Francis Baily, Thomas Finney.
Manager: Walter Winterbottom

**Goal:** Zarra (49)


259. 07.10.1950   Home Championship
**NORTHERN IRELAND v ENGLAND  1-4**  (0-1)

*Windsor Park, Belfast*

Referee: Thomas Mitchell (Northern Ireland)   Att: 50,000

**NORTHERN IRELAND:** Hugh Redmond Kelly, Charles Gallogly, Alfred McMichael, Robert Denis Blanchflower, John Joseph Vernon, Wilbur W. Cush, John Peter Campbell, Edward Crossan, Edward James McMorran, Robert Anderson Brennan, John McKenna.

**ENGLAND:** Bert Frederick Williams, Alfred Ernest Ramsey, John Aston, William Ambrose Wright (Cap), Allenby Chilton, James William Dickinson, Stanley Matthews, Wilfred Mannion, John Lee, Edward Francis Baily, Robert Langton.   Manager: Walter Winterbottom

**Goals:** Edward James McMorran (70) /
Edward F. Baily (43, 86), John Lee (64), William Wright (85)


260. 15.11.1950   Home Championship
**ENGLAND v WALES  4-2**  (2-0)

*Roker Park, Sunderland*

Referee: John Alexander Mowatt (Scotland)   Att: 59,137

**ENGLAND:** Bert Frederick Williams, Alfred Ernest Ramsey (Cap), Lionel Smith, William Watson, Leslie Harry Compton, James William Dickinson, Thomas Finney, Wilfred Mannion, John Edward Thompson Milburn, Edward Francis Baily, Leslie Dennis Medley.   Manager: Walter Winterbottom

**WALES:** Iorwerth Hughes, Walley Barnes, Alfred Thomas Sherwood, Roy Paul, William Raymond Daniel, William Henry Lucas, William Maldwyn Griffiths, Brynley William Allen, Trevor Ford, Ivor John Allchurch, Royston James Clarke.

**Goals:** Edward Francis Baily (31, 40), Wilfred Mannion (66), John Edward Thompson Milburn (89) / Trevor Ford (59, 74)


261. 22.11.1950
**ENGLAND v YUGOSLAVIA  2-2**  (2-1)

*Highbury, London*

Referee: Karel van der Meer (Holland)   Attendance: 61,454

**ENGLAND:** Bert Frederick Williams, Alfred Ernest Ramsey (Cap), William Eckersley, William Watson, Leslie Harry Compton, James William Dickinson, John Hancocks, Wilfred Mannion, Nathaniel Lofthouse, Edward Francis Baily, Leslie Dennis Medley.   Manager: Walter Winterbottom

**YUGOSLAVIA:** Vladimir Beara, Branko Stanković, Ratko Čolić, Zlatko Čajkovski, Ivan Horvat, Predrag Đajić, Tihomir Ognjanov, Rajko Mitić (Cap), Todor Živanović, Stjepan Bobek, Bernard Vukas.   Trainer: Milorad Arsenijević

**Goals:** Nathaniel Lofthouse (29, 34) /
Leslie Harry Compton (41 og), Todor Živanović (78)


262. 14.04.1951   Home Championship
**ENGLAND v SCOTLAND  2-3**  (1-1)

*Wembley, London*

Referee: George Mitchell (Scotland)   Attendance: 98,000

**ENGLAND:** Bert Frederick Williams, Alfred Ernest Ramsey, William Eckersley, Harry Johnstonon, Jack Froggatt, William Ambrose Wright (Cap), Stanley Matthews, Wilfred Mannion, Stanley Harding Mortensen, Harold William Hassall, Thomas Finney.   Manager: Walter Winterbottom

**SCOTLAND:** James Clews Cowan, George Lewis Young (Cap), Samuel Richmond Cox, Robert Evans, William Alexander Woodburn, William Yates Redpath, William Waddell, Robert Johnstone, Lawrence Reilly, William Steel, William Beveridge Liddell.

**Goals:** Harold William Hassall (26), Thomas Finney (63) / Robert Johnstone (33), Lawrence Reilly (47), Billy Liddell (53)

263. 09.05.1951
**ENGLAND v ARGENTINA 2-1** (0-1)
*Wembley, London*
Referee: Mervyn Griffiths (Wales)   Attendance: 60,000
**ENGLAND**: Bert Frederick Williams, Alfred Ernest Ramsey, William Eckersley, William Ambrose Wright (Cap), James Guy Taylor, Henry Cockburn, Thomas Finney, Stanley Harding Mortensen, John Edward Thompson Milburn, Harold William Hassall, Victor Metcalfe.   Manager: Walter Winterbottom
**ARGENTINA**: Miguel Ángel Rugilo, Juan Carlos Colman (36 Ángel Natalio Allegri), Juan Manuel Filgueiras, Norberto Antonio Yácono (Cap), Ubaldo Faina, Natalio Agustín Pescia, Mario Emilio Heriberto Boyé, Norberto Doroteo Méndez, Rubén Norberto Bravo, Ángel Amadeo Labruna, Félix Loustau.   Trainer: Guillermo Stábile
**Goals**: John Thompson Milburn (79), Stanley Mortensen (86) / Mario Emilio Heriberto Boyé (18)

264. 19.05.1951
**ENGLAND v PORTUGAL 5-2** (2-1)
*Goodison Park, Liverpool*
Referee: Louis Baert (Belgium)   Attendance: 52,686
**ENGLAND**: Bert Frederick Williams, Alfred Ernest Ramsey (Cap), William Eckersley, William Edward Nicholson, James Guy Taylor, Henry Cockburn, Thomas Finney, Stanley Clare Pearson, John Edward Thompson Milburn, Harold William Hassall, Victor Metcalfe.   Manager: Walter Winterbottom
**PORTUGAL**: ERNESTO Nogueira de Oliveira, VIRGÍLIO Marques Mendes, SERAFIM das Neves, Carlos Augusto Ribeiro Canário, FÉLIX Assunção Antunes, Francisco Ferreira (Cap), Domingos Carrilho Demétrio "Patalino" (36 Carlos Martinho Gomes "Martinho"), José António Barreto Travaços, Henrique Ben David, Fernando Augusto Amoral Caiado, ALBANO Narciso Pereira.   Trainer: Tavares da Silva
**Goals**: William Nicholson (1), John Milburn (12, 80), Thomas Finney (76), Harold William Hassall (83) / Patalino (2), Albano (48)

265. 03.10.1951
**ENGLAND v FRANCE 2-2** (2-2)
*Highbury, London*
Referee: John Mowatt (Scotland)   Attendance: 57,603
**ENGLAND**: Bert Frederick Williams, Alfred Ernest Ramsey, Arthur Willis, William Ambrose Wright (Cap), Allenby Chilton, Henry Cockburn, Thomas Finney, Wilfred Mannion, John Edward Thompson Milburn, Harold William Hassall, Leslie Dennis Medley.   Manager: Walter Winterbottom
**FRANCE**: René Vignal, André Grillon, Robert Jonquet, Marcel Salva, Abdelkader Firoud, Antoine Bonifaci, Jean Baratte (Cap), Pierre Flamion, René Alpsteg, Jean Grumellon, André Doye.
**Goals**: Abdelkader Firoud (4 og), Leslie Dennis Medley (32) / André Doye (18), René Alpsteg (19)

266. 20.10.1951   Home Championship
**WALES v ENGLAND 1-1** (1-1)
*Ninian Park, Cardiff*
Referee: G. Gerrard (Scotland)   Attendance: 60,000
**WALES**: William Warren Shortt, Walley Barnes, Alfred Thomas Sherwood, Roy Paul, William Raymond Daniel, William Arthur Ronald Burgess, William Isaiah Foulkes, Noel Kinsey, Trevor Ford, Ivor John Allchurch, Royston James Clarke.
**ENGLAND**: Bert Frederick Williams, Alfred Ernest Ramsey, Lionel Smith, William Ambrose Wright (Cap), Malcolm Williamson Barrass, James William Dickinson, Thomas Finney, Thomas Thompson, Nathaniel Lofthouse, Edward Francis Baily, Leslie Dennis Medley.
Manager: Walter Winterbottom
**Goal**: William Isaiah Foulkes (3) / Edward Francis Baily (6)

267. 14.11.1951   Home Championship
**ENGLAND v NORTHERN IRELAND 2-0** (1-0)
*Villa Park, Birmingham*
Referee: Mervyn Griffiths (Wales)   Attendance: 57,889
**ENGLAND**: Gilbert Harold Merrick, Alfred Ernest Ramsey, Lionel Smith, William Ambrose Wright (Cap), Malcolm Williamson Barrass, James William Dickinson, Thomas Finney, John Sewell, Nathaniel Lofthouse, Leonard Horace Phillips, Leslie Dennis Medley.
Manager: Walter Winterbottom
**NORTHERN IRELAND**: William Uprichard, William George Leonard Graham, Alfred McMichael, William Dickson, John Joseph Vernon, Francis Joseph McCourt, William Bingham, Samuel Smyth, Edward James McMorran, James McIlroy, John McKenna.
**Goal**: Nathaniel Lofthouse (40, 83)

268. 28.11.1951
**ENGLAND v AUSTRIA 2-2** (0-0)
*Wembley, London*
Referee: John Mowatt (Scotland)   Attendance: 100,000
**ENGLAND**: Gilbert Harold Merrick, Alfred Ernest Ramsey, William Eckersley, William Ambrose Wright (Cap), Jack Froggatt, James William Dickinson, Clement Arthur Milton, Ivan Arthur Broadis, Nathaniel Lofthouse, Edward Francis Baily, Leslie Dennis Medley.   Manager: Walter Winterbottom
**AUSTRIA**: Walter Zeman, Rudolf Röckl, Ernst Happel, Gerhard Hanappi, Ernst Ocwirk, Theodor Brinek, Ernst Melchior, Leopold Gernhardt, Adolf Huber, Ernst Stojaspal, Alfred Körner II.   Trainer: Walter Nausch
**Goals**: Alfred Ernest Ramsey (68), Nathaniel Lofthouse (75) / Ernst Melchior (47), Ernst Stojaspal (77 pen)

269.  05.04.1952   Home Championship
**SCOTLAND v ENGLAND  1-2**  (0-1)
*Hampden Park, Glasgow*

Referee: Patrick Morris (Northern Ireland)   Att: 133,991

SCOTLAND: Robert Brown, George Lewis Young (Cap), William McNaught, James Scoular, William Alexander Woodburn, William Yates Redpath, Gordon Smith, Robert Johnstone, Lawrence Reilly, John Livingstone McMillan, William Beveridge Liddell.

ENGLAND: Gilbert Harold Merrick, Alfred Ernest Ramsey, Thomas Garrett, William Ambrose Wright (Cap), Jack Froggatt, James William Dickinson, Thomas Finney, Ivan Arthur Broadis, Nathaniel Lofthouse, Stanley Clare Pearson, John Frederick Rowley.   Manager: Walter Winterbottom

Goals: Lawrence Reilly (77) / Stanley Clare Pearson (9, 44)

270.  18.05.1952
**ITALY v ENGLAND  1-1**  (0-1)
*Comunale, Firenze*

Referee: Alois Beranek (Austria)   Attendance: 60,000

ITALY: Giuseppe Moro, Attilio Giovannini, Sergio Manente, Giacomo Mari, Rino Ferrario, Alberto Piccinini, Giampiero Boniperti, Egisto Pandolfini, Silvio Piola (Cap), Amedeo Amadei, Gino Cappello IV.   Trainer: Giuseppe Meazza

ENGLAND: Gilbert Harold Merrick, Alfred Ernest Ramsey, Thomas Garrett, William Ambrose Wright (Cap), Jack Froggatt, James William Dickinson, Thomas Finney, Ivan Arthur Broadis, Nathaniel Lofthouse, Stanley Clare Pearson, William Henry Elliott.   Manager: Walter Winterbottom

Goal: Amedeo Amadei (58) / Ivan Arthur Broadis (4)

271.  25.05.1952
**AUSTRIA v ENGLAND  2-3**  (2-2)
*Prater, Wien*

Referee: Giuseppe Carpani (Italia)   Attendance: 65,000

AUSTRIA: Josef Musil, Rudolf Röckl, Ernst Happel, Dr. Walter Schleger, Ernst Ocwirk, Theodor Brinek, Ernst Melchior, Gerhard Hanappi, Robert Dienst, Adolf Huber, Walter Haummer.   Trainer: Walter Nausch

ENGLAND: Gilbert Harold Merrick, Alfred Ernest Ramsey, William Eckersley, William Ambrose Wright (Cap), Jack Froggatt, James William Dickinson, Thomas Finney, John Sewell, Nathaniel Lofthouse, Edward Francis Baily, William Henry Elliott.   Manager: Walter Winterbottom

Goals: Adolf Huber (27 pen), Robert Dienst (42) / Nathaniel Lofthouse (25, 83), John Sewell (28)

272.  28.05.1952
**SWITZERLAND v ENGLAND  0-3**  (0-1)
*Hardturm, Zürich*

Referee: Louis Baert (Belgium)   Attendance: 33,000

SWITZERLAND: Thomas Preiss, Willy Kernen, Roger Bocquet, Hannes Schmidhauser, Oliver Eggimann, Willy Neukom, Robert Ballaman, Josef Hügi, René Bader, Lucien Pasteur, Jacques Fatton.   Selection Commitee: William Baumgartner, Gaston Tschirren, Leopold Kielholz

ENGLAND: Gilbert Harold Merrick, Alfred Ernest Ramsey, William Eckersley, William Ambrose Wright (Cap), Jack Froggatt, James William Dickinson, Ronald Allen, John Sewell, Nathaniel Lofthouse, Edward Francis Baily, Thomas Finney.   Manager: Walter Winterbottom

Goals: John Sewell (13), Nathaniel Lofthouse (51, 87)

273.  04.10.1952   Home Championship
**NORTHERN IRELAND v ENGLAND  2-2**  (1-1)
*Windsor Park, Belfast*

Referee: D. Gerrard (Scotland)   Attendance: 58,000

NORTHERN IRELAND: William Uprichard, William Edward Cunningham, Alfred McMichael, Robert Denis Blanchflower, William Dickson, Francis Joseph McCourt, William Bingham, Samuel Donal D'Arcy, Edward James McMorran, James McIlroy, Charles Tully.

ENGLAND: Gilbert Harold Merrick, Alfred Ernest Ramsey, William Eckersley, William Ambrose Wright (Cap), Jack Froggatt, James William Dickinson, Thomas Finney, John Sewell, Nathaniel Lofthouse, Edward Francis Baily, William Henry Elliott.   Manager: Walter Winterbottom

Goals: Charles P. Tully (15, 46) / Nathaniel Lofthouse (2), William Henry Elliott (87)

274.  12.11.1952   Home Championship
**ENGLAND v WALES  5-2**  (2-1)
*Wembley, London*

Referee: D. Gerrard (Scotland)   Attendance: 94,094

ENGLAND: Gilbert Harold Merrick, Alfred Ernest Ramsey, Lionel Smith, William Ambrose Wright (Cap), Jack Froggatt, James William Dickinson, Thomas Finney, Redfern Froggatt, Nathaniel Lofthouse, Roy Thomas Frank Bentley, William Henry Elliott.   Manager: Walter Winterbottom

WALES: William Warren Shortt, Roland Frederick Stitfall, Alfred Thomas Sherwood, Roy Paul, William Raymond Daniel, William Arthur Ronald Burgess, William Isaiah Foulkes, Ellis Reginald Davies, Trevor Ford, Ivor John Allchurch, Royston James Clarke.

Goals: Thomas Finney (8), Nathaniel Lofthouse (10, 75), Jack Froggatt (44), Roy Thomas Frank Bentley (47) / Trevor Ford (15, 49)

275. 26.11.1952
**ENGLAND v BELGIUM  5-0**  (2-0)
*Wembley, London*

Referee:  Leopold Sylvain Horn (Holland)     Att: 68,333

**ENGLAND**:  Gilbert Harold Merrick, Alfred Ernest Ramsey, Lionel Smith, William Ambrose Wright (Cap), Jack Froggatt, James William Dickinson, Thomas Finney, Roy Thomas Frank Bentley, Nathaniel Lofthouse, Redfern Froggatt, William Henry Elliott.    Manager:  Walter Winterbottom

**BELGIUM**:  Ferdinand Boogaerts, Henri Dirickx, Alfons Van Brandt, Victor Mees, Louis Carré, Robert Maertens, Victor Lemberechts, Jan Van der Auwera, Joseph Mermans (Cap), Rik Coppens, Jean Straetmans.    Trainer:  William Gormlie

**Goals**:  William H. Elliott (4, 48), Nathaniel Lofthouse (42, 86), Redfern Froggatt (60)


276. 18.04.1953    Home Championship
**ENGLAND v SCOTLAND  2-2**  (1-0)
*Wembley, London*

Referee:  Thomas Mitchell (Northern Ireland)     Att: 97,000

**ENGLAND**:  Gilbert Harold Merrick, Alfred Ernest Ramsey, Lionel Smith, William Ambrose Wright (Cap), Malcolm Williamson Barrass, James William Dickinson, Thomas Finney, Ivan Arthur Broadis, Nathaniel Lofthouse, Redfern Froggatt, Jack Froggatt.    Manager:  Walter Winterbottom

**SCOTLAND**:  George Neil Farm, George Lewis Young (Cap), Samuel Richmond Cox, Thomas Henderson Docherty, Francis Brennan, Douglas Cowie, Thomas Wright, Robert Johnstone, Lawrence Reilly, William Steel, William Beveridge Liddell.

**Goals**:  Ivan Arthur Broadis (18, 70) / Lawrence Reilly (54, 89)


277. 17.05.1953
**ARGENTINA v ENGLAND  0-0**
*Monumental de Nuñez, Buenos Aires*

Referee:  Arthur Edward Ellis (England)     Att: 80,000

**ARGENTINA**:  Julio Elías Musimessi, Pedro Rodolfo Dellacha, José M. García Pérez, Juan Francisco Lombardo, Eliseo Víctor Mouriño (Cap), Ernesto Gutiérrez, Rodolfo Joaquín Micheli, Carlos José Cecconato, Carlos Lacasia, Ernesto Grillo, Osvaldo Héctor Cruz.
Trainer:  Guillermo Stábile

**ENGLAND**:  Gilbert Harold Merrick, Alfred Ernest Ramsey, William Eckersley, William Ambrose Wright (Cap), Harry Johnstonon, James William Dickinson, Thomas Finney, Ivan Arthur Broadis, Nathaniel Lofthouse, Thomas Taylor, John Reginald Berry.    Manager:  Walter Winterbottom

The match was abandoned after 21 minutes due to heavy rain.


278. 24.05.1953
**CHILE v ENGLAND  1-2**  (0-0)
*Nacional, Santiago*

Referee:  Arthur Edward Ellis (England)     Att: 56,398

**CHILE**:  Sergio Roberto Livingstone, Manuel Alvarez, Arturo Farías, Rogelio Núñez, Carlos Rodolfo Rojas, Ramiro Cortés, Sergio Alvarez, Atilio Cremaschi, René Meléndez, Manuel Muñoz, Guillermo Díaz Carmona.    Trainer:  Luis Tirado

**ENGLAND**:  Gilbert Harold Merrick, Alfred Ernest Ramsey, William Eckersley, William Ambrose Wright (Cap), Harry Johnstonon, James William Dickinson, Thomas Finney, Ivan Arthur Broadis, Nathaniel Lofthouse, Thomas Taylor, John Reginald Berry.    Manager:  Walter Winterbottom

**Goals**:  Alfred Ernest Ramsey (86 og) /
Thomas Taylor (48), Nathaniel Lofthouse (68)


279. 31.05.1953
**URUGUAY v ENGLAND  2-1**  (1-0)
*Centenario, Montevideo*

Referee:  Arthur Edward Ellis (England)     Att: 66,072

**URUGUAY**:  Roque Gastón Máspoli, Matías González, William Ruben Martínez, Víctor Pablo Rodríguez Andrade, Néstor Carballo, Luis Alberto Cruz, Julio César Abbadie, Julio Gervasio Pérez, Oscar Omar Míguez, Juan Alberto Schiaffino, Juan Carlos Cabrera.    Trainer:  Juan López

**ENGLAND**:  Gilbert Harold Merrick, Alfred Ernest Ramsey, William Eckersley, William Ambrose Wright (Cap), Harry Johnstonon, James William Dickinson, Thomas Finney, Ivan Arthur Broadis, Nathaniel Lofthouse, Thomas Taylor, John Reginald Berry.    Manager:  Walter Winterbottom

**Goals**:  Julio César Abbadie (27), Oscar Omar Míguez (70) /
Thomas Taylor (89)


280. 08.06.1953
**U.S.A. v ENGLAND  3-6**  (0-1)
*Yankee Stadium, New York*

Referee:  S. Gallin (USA)     Attendance: 7,271

**U.S.A.**:  Cecil Moore, Harry Joseph Keough, Raymond Milne, Terrence Springthorpe, Rolf Decker, Walter Alfred Bahr (Cap), Thomas Schultz (46 Otto Decker), William Connelly, Bernard McLaughlin, George Atheneos, Efraim Chachurian.    Trainer:  Ernő Schwartz

**ENGLAND**:  Edwin George Ditchburn, Alfred Ernest Ramsey, William Eckersley, William Ambrose Wright (Cap), Harry Johnstonon, James William Dickinson, Thomas Finney, Ivan Arthur Broadis, Nathaniel Lofthouse, Redfern Froggatt, Jack Froggatt.    Manager:  Walter Winterbottom

**Goals**:  Otto Decker (64, 65), George Atheneos (70 pen) /
Ivan Arthur Broadis (43), Thomas Finney (50, 73), Nathaniel Lofthouse (48, 62), Redfern Froggatt (80)

**281.  10.10.1953   5th World Cup Qualifiers, Home Championship**
**WALES v ENGLAND  1-4**  (1-1)
*Ninian Park, Cardiff*

Referee:  Charles Edward Faultless (Scotland)   Att: 61,000

**WALES**:  Ronald Gilbert Howells, Walley Barnes, Alfred Thomas Sherwood, Roy Paul, William Raymond Daniel, William Arthur Ronald Burgess, William Isaiah Foulkes, Ellis Reginald Davies, William John Charles, Ivor John Allchurch, Royston James Clarke.

**ENGLAND**:  Gilbert Harold Merrick, Thomas Garrett, William Eckersley, William Ambrose Wright (Cap), Harry Johnstonon, James William Dickinson, Thomas Finney, Albert Quixall, Nathaniel Lofthouse, Dennis James Wilshaw, James Mullen.   Manager: Walter Winterbottom

**Goals**:  Ivor John Allchurch (22) / Dennis James Wilshaw (45, 48), Nathaniel Lofthouse (50, 51)


**282.  21.10.1953**
**ENGLAND v REST OF EUROPE XI  4-4**  (2-3)
*Wembley, London*

Referee:  Mervyn Griffiths (Wales)   Attendance: 96,000

**ENGLAND**:  Gilbert Harold Merrick, Alfred Ernest Ramsey, William Eckersley, William Ambrose Wright (Cap), Derek Gilbert Ufton, James William Dickinson, Stanley Matthews, Stanley Harding Mortensen, Nathaniel Lofthouse, Albert Quixall, James Mullen.   Manager: Walter Winterbottom

**EUROPE**:  Walter Zemen (46 Vladimir Beara), Joaquin Navarro, Gerhardt Hannappi, Zlatko Cajkovski, Josef Posipal, Ernst Ocwirk, Giampiero Boniperti, Ladislav Kubala, Gunnar Nordahl, Bernard Vukas, Branko Zebec.

**Goals**:  Stanley Harding Mortensen (7), James Mullen (42, 48), Alfred Ernest Ramsey (89 pen)


**283.  11.11.1953   5th World Cup Qualifiers, Home Championship**
**ENGLAND v NORTHERN IRELAND  3-1**  (1-0)
*Goodison Park, Liverpool*

Referee:  R. Smith (Wales)   Attendance: 70,000

**ENGLAND**:  Gilbert Harold Merrick, Stanley Rickaby, William Eckersley, William Ambrose Wright (Cap), Harry Johnstonon, James William Dickinson, Stanley Matthews, Albert Quixall, Nathaniel Lofthouse, Harold William Hassall, James Mullen.   Manager: Walter Winterbottom

**NORTHERN IRELAND**:  William Smyth, William George Leonard Graham, Alfred McMichael, Robert Denis Blanchflower, William Dickson, Wilbur Cush, William Bingham, James McIlroy, William J. Simpson, Edward James McMorran, Norman Lockhart.

**Goals**:  Harold Hassall (1, 57), Nathaniel Lofthouse (74) / Edward James McMorran (54)


**284.  25.11.1953**
**ENGLAND v HUNGARY  3-6**  (2-4)
*Wembley, London*

Referee:  Leopold Sylvain Horn (Holland)   Att: 100,000

**ENGLAND**:  Gilbert Harold Merrick, Alfred Ernest Ramsey, William Eckersley, William Ambrose Wright (Cap), Harry Johnstonon, James William Dickinson, Stanley Matthews, Ernest Taylor, Stanley Harding Mortensen, John Sewell, George Robb.   Manager: Walter Winterbottom

**HUNGARY**:  Gyula Grosics (78 Sándor Gellér), Jenő Buzánszky, Gyula Lóránt, Mihály Lantos, József Bozsik, József Zakariás, László Budai, Sándor Kocsis, Nándor Hidegkuti, Ferenc Puskás, Zoltán Czibor.   Trainer: Gusztáv Sebes

**Goals**:  John Sewell (14), Stanley Harding Mortensen (38), Alfred Ernest Ramsey (57 pen) / Nándor Hidegkuti (1, 22, 53), Ferenc Puskás (25, 29), József Bozsik (50)


**285.  03.04.1954   5th World Cup Qualifiers, Home Championship**
**SCOTLAND v ENGLAND  2-4**  (1-1)
*Hampden Park, Glasgow*

Referee:  Thomas Mitchell (Northern Ireland)   Att: 134,544

**SCOTLAND**:  George Neil Farm, Michael Haughney, Samuel Richmond Cox (Cap), Robert Evans, Francis Brennan, George Graham Aitken, John Archibald MacKenzie, Robert Johnstone, John Gillespie Henderson, Allan Duncan Brown, William Esplin Ormond.   Manager: Andrew Beattie

**ENGLAND**:  Gilbert Harold Merrick, Ronald Staniforth, Roger William Byrne, William Ambrose Wright (Cap), Henry Alfred Clarke, James William Dickinson, Thomas Finney, Ivan Arthur Broadis, Ronald Allen, John Nicholls, James Mullen.   Manager: Walter Winterbottom

**Goals**:  Allan Duncan Brown (7), William Esplin Ormond (89) / Ivan Arthur Broadis (14), John Nicholls (51), Ronald Allen (68), James Mullen (83)


**286.  16.05.1954**
**YUGOSLAVIA v ENGLAND  1-0**  (0-0)
*JNA, Beograd*

Referee:  Carl Erich Steiner (Austria)   Attendance: 60,000

**YUGOSLAVIA**:  Vladimir Beara, Branko Stanković (Cap), Tomislav Crnković, Zlatko Čajkovski, Sima Milovanov, Vujadin Boškov, Miloš Milutinović, Rajko Mitić, Bernard Vukas, Stjepan Bobek, Dionizie Dvornić (46 Branko Zebec). Team selection committee:  Branko Pešić, Aleksandar Tirnanić, Leo Lemešić, Franjo Völfl and Milovan Ćirić

**ENGLAND**:  Gilbert Harold Merrick, Ronald Staniforth, Roger William Byrne, William Ambrose Wright (Cap), Sidney William Owen, James William Dickinson, Thomas Finney, Ivan Arthur Broadis, Ronald Allen, John Nicholls, James Mullen.   Manager: Walter Winterbottom

**Goal**:  Rajko Mitić (88)

287.  23.05.1954
**HUNGARY v ENGLAND  7-1**  (3-0)
*Népstadion, Budapest*

Referee:  Giorgio Bernardi (Italy)     Attendance:  92,000

**HUNGARY**:  Gyula Grosics (77 Sándor Gellér), Jenő Buzánszky, Gyula Lóránt, Mihály Lantos, József Bozsik, József Zakariás, József Tóth, Sándor Kocsis, Nándor Hidegkuti, Ferenc Puskás, Zoltán Czibor.    Trainer:  Gusztáv Sebes

**ENGLAND**:  Gilbert Harold Merrick, Ronald Staniforth, Roger William Byrne, William Ambrose Wright (Cap), Sidney William Owen, James William Dickinson, Peter Philip Harris, John Sewell, Bedford Alfred George Jezzard, Ivan Arthur Broadis, Thomas Finney.    Manager:  Walter Winterbottom

**Goal**:  Mihály Lantos (8), Ferenc Puskás (21, 73), Sándor Kocsis (31, 56), József Tóth II (60), Nándor Hidegkuti (62) / Ivan Arthur Broadis (68)


288.  17.06.1954     5th World Cup, 1st Round
**ENGLAND v BELGIUM  4-4**  (2-1, 3-3)  (AET)
*Sankt Jakob, Basel*

Referee:  Emil Schmetzer (West Germany)     Att:  14,000

**ENGLAND**:  Gilbert Harold Merrick, Ronald Staniforth, Roger William Byrne, William Ambrose Wright (Cap), Sidney William Owen, James William Dickinson, Stanley Matthews, Ivan Arthur Broadis, Nathaniel Lofthouse, Thomas Taylor, Thomas Finney.    Manager:  Walter Winterbottom

**BELGIUM**:  Leopold Gernaey, Marcel Dries, Alfons Van Brandt, Constant Huysmans, Louis Carré, Victor Mees, Joseph Mermans (Cap), Léopold Anoul, Rik Coppens, Denis Houf, Pierre Vanden Bosch.    Trainer:  Dougall Livingstone

**Goals**:  Ivan Broadis (25, 62), Nathaniel Lofthouse (37, 91) / Léopold Anoul (5, 74), Rik Coppens (77), J. Dickinson (93 og)


289.  20.06.1954     5th World Cup, 1st Round
**SWITZERLAND v ENGLAND  0-2**  (0-1)
*Wankdorf, Bern*

Referee:  István Zsolt (Hungary)     Attendance:  30,000

**SWITZERLAND**:  Eugène Parlier, André Neury, Roger Bocquet, Willy Kernen, Oliver Eggimann, Heinz Bigler, Charles Antenen, Roger Vonlanthen, Eugen Meier, Robert Ballaman, Jacques Fatton.    Trainer:  Karl Rappan

**ENGLAND**:  Gilbert Harold Merrick, Ronald Staniforth, Roger William Byrne, William Harry McGarry, William Ambrose Wright (Cap), James William Dickinson, Thomas Finney, Ivan Arthur Broadis, Thomas Taylor, Dennis James Wilshaw, James Mullen.    Manager:  Walter Winterbottom

**Goals**:  James Mullen (43), Dennis James Wilshaw (69)


290.  26.06.1954     5th World Cup, 1st Round
**URUGUAY v ENGLAND  4-2**  (2-1)
*St. Jakob, Basel*

Referee:  Carl Erich Steiner (Austria)     Attendance:  35,000

**URUGUAY**:  Roque Gastón Máspoli, José Emilio Santamaría, William Ruben Martínez, Víctor Pablo Rodríguez Andrade, Obdulio Jacinto Varela (Cap), Luis Alberto Cruz, Julio César Abbadie, Javier Ambrois, Oscar Omar Míguez, Juan Alberto Schiaffino, Carlos Ariel Borges.    Trainer:  Juan López

**ENGLAND**:  Gilbert Harold Merrick, Ronald Staniforth, Roger William Byrne, William Harry McGarry, William Ambrose Wright (Cap), James William Dickinson, Stanley Matthews, Ivan Arthur Broadis, Nathaniel Lofthouse, Dennis James Wilshaw, Thomas Finney.    Manager:  Walter Winterbottom

**Goals**:  Carlos Ariel Borges (5), Obdulio Jacinto Varela (44), Juan Alberto Schiaffino (47), Javier Ambrois (78) / Nathaniel Lofthouse (16), Thomas Finney (67)


291.  02.10.1954     Home Championship
**NORTHERN IRELAND v ENGLAND  0-2**  (0-0)
*Windsor Park, Belfast*

Referee:  Charles Edward Faultless (Scotland)     Att:  59,000

**NORTHERN IRELAND**:  William Uprichard, Frank J. Montgomery, Alfred McMichael, Robert Denis Blanchflower, William Dickson, Robert Peacock, William Bingham, John Blanchflower, William J. Simpson, James McIlroy, Peter James McParland.

**ENGLAND**:  Raymond Ernest Wood, William Anthony Foulkes, Roger William Byrne, John Edward Wheeler, William Ambrose Wright (Cap), Raymond John Barlow, Stanley Matthews, Donald George Revie, Nathaniel Lofthouse, John Norman Haynes, Brian Pilkington.    Manager:  Walter Winterbottom

**Goals**:  John Norman Haynes (75), Donald George Revie (77)


292.  10.11.1954     Home Championship
**ENGLAND v WALES  3-2**  (0-1)
*Wembley, London*

Referee:  Charles Edward Faultless (Scotland)     Att:  89,789

**ENGLAND**:  Raymond Ernest Wood, Ronald Staniforth, Roger William Byrne, Leonard Horace Phillips, William Ambrose Wright (Cap), William John Slater, Stanley Matthews, Roy Thomas Frank Bentley, Ronald Allen, Leonard Francis Shackleton, Frank Blunstone.    Manager:  Walter Winterbottom

**WALES**:  John King, Stuart Grenville Williams, Alfred Thomas Sherwood, Roy Paul, William Raymond Daniel, Derrick Sullivan, Derek Robert Tapscott, Trevor Ford, William John Charles, Ivor John Allchurch, Royston James Clarke.

**Goals**:  Roy Thomas Frank Bentley (70, 74, 88) / William John Charles (36, 74)

293. 01.12.1954
**ENGLAND v WEST GERMANY 3-1** (1-0)
*Wembley, London*

Referee: Vicenzo Orlandini (Italy)    Attendance: 100,000

**ENGLAND**: Bert Frederick Williams, Ronald Staniforth, Roger William Byrne, Leonard Horace Phillips, William Ambrose Wright (Cap), William John Slater, Stanley Matthews, Roy Thomas Frank Bentley, Ronald Allen, Leonard Francis Shackleton, Thomas Finney.    Manager: Walter Winterbottom

**WEST GERMANY**: Fritz Herkenrath, Josef Posipal (Cap), Werner Kohlmeyer, Herbert Erhardt, Werner Liebrich, Gerhard Harpers, Gerhard Kaufhold, Michael Pfeiffer, Uwe Seeler, Josef Derwall, Alfred Beck.    Trainer: Josef Herberger

**Goals**: Roy Thomas Frank Bentley (28), Ronald Allen (48), Leonard Francis Shackleton (79) / Alfred Beck (77)


294. 02.04.1955    Home Championship
**ENGLAND v SCOTLAND 7-2** (4-1)
*Wembley, London*

Referee: Mervyn Griffiths (Wales)    Attendance: 96,847

**ENGLAND**: Bert Frederick Williams, James Meadows, Roger William Byrne, Kenneth Armstrong, William Ambrose Wright (Cap), Duncan Edwards, Stanley Matthews, Donald George Revie, Nathaniel Lofthouse, Dennis James Wilshaw, Frank Blunstone.    Manager: Walter Winterbottom

**SCOTLAND**: Frederick Martin, William Carruthers Cunningham (Cap), Harold Haddock, Thomas Henderson Docherty, James Anderson Davidson, John Cumming, John Archibald MacKenzie, Robert Johnstone, Lawrence Reilly, John Livingstone McMillan, Thomas Ring.

**Goals**: Dennis James Wilshaw (1, 70, 73, 80), Nathaniel Lofthouse (7, 27), Donald George Revie (25) / Lawrence Reilly (15), Thomas Henderson Docherty (85)


295. 15.05.1955
**FRANCE v ENGLAND 1-0** (1-0)
*Stade Olympique, Colombes, Paris*

Referee: Emil Schmetzer (West Germany)    Att: 54,696

**FRANCE**: François Remetter, Guilhem Bieganski, Robert Jonquet, Roger Marche (Cap), Armand Penverne, Xercès Louis, Léon Glovacki, René Bliard, Joseph Ujlaki, Raymond Kopa, Jean Vincent.    Trainer: Albert Batteux

**ENGLAND**: Bert Frederick Williams, Richard Peter Tudor Sillett, Roger William Byrne, Ronald Flowers, William Ambrose Wright (Cap), Duncan Edwards, Stanley Matthews, Donald George Revie, Nathaniel Lofthouse, Dennis James Wilshaw, Frank Blunstone.    Manager: Walter Winterbottom

**Goal**: Raymond Kopa (37 pen)


296. 18.05.1955
**SPAIN v ENGLAND 1-1** (0-1)
*Chamartin, Madrid*

Referee: Ricardo Pieri (Italy)    Attendance: 125,000

**SPAIN**: Antonio Ramallets (Cap), Román Matito, Jesús Garay, Marcelino Vaquero González "Campanal", Mauricio Ugartemendia "Mauri", José María Zárraga, Daniel Mañó, José Luis Pérez Payá, Ladislao Kubala, José Héctor Rial, Francisco Gento.    Trainer: Ramón Melcón

**ENGLAND**: Bert Frederick Williams, Richard Peter Tudor Sillett, Roger William Byrne, James William Dickinson, William Ambrose Wright (Cap), Duncan Edwards, Stanley Matthews, Roy Thomas Frank Bentley, Nathaniel Lofthouse, Albert Quixall, Dennis James Wilshaw.
Manager: Walter Winterbottom

**Goal**: Rial (65) / Roy Thomas Frank Bentley (39)


297. 22.05.1955
**PORTUGAL v ENGLAND 3-1** (1-1)
*das Antas, Porto*

Referee: Giorgio Bernardi (Italy)    Attendance: 52,000

**PORTUGAL**: Alberto Costa Pereira, Manuel António Caldeira, Angelo Ferreira Carvalho, José Maria Carvalho Pedroto, Manuel Passos (Cap), Júlio Cernades Pereira "Juca", José Romão Dimas, Lucas Sebastião da Fonseca "Matateu", JOSÉ Carvalho Santos Pinto ÁGUAS, José António Barreto Travaços, JOSÉ PEDRO Biléu (35 João Baptista Martins).
Trainer: Tavares da Silva

**ENGLAND**: Bert Frederick Williams, Richard Peter Tudor Sillett, Roger William Byrne, James William Dickinson, William Ambrose Wright (Cap), Duncan Edwards, Stanley Matthews, Roy Thomas Frank Bentley, Nathaniel Lofthouse (39 Albert Quixall), Dennis James Wilshaw, Frank Blunstone.
Manager: Walter Winterbottom

**Goal**: José Águas (24), Matateu (79), José Águas (83) / Roy Thomas Frank Bentley (19)


298. 02.10.1955
**DENMARK v ENGLAND 1-5** (0-3)
*Idraetsparken, København*

Referee: Giorgio Bernardi (Italy)    Attendance: 53,000

**DENMARK**: Per Henriksen, Paul Andersen, Verner Nielsen, Erik Pondal Jensen, Christen Brøgger (28 John Jørgensen), Jørgen Olesen, Jørgen Hansen, Jørgen Jacobsen, Ove Andersen, Knud Lundberg (Cap), Poul Pedersen.

**ENGLAND**: Ronald Leslie Baynham, Jeffrey James Hall, Roger William Byrne, William Harry McGarry, William Ambrose Wright (Cap), James William Dickinson, John Edward Thompson Milburn, Donald George Revie, Nathaniel Lofthouse, Geoffrey Reginald William Bradford, Thomas Finney.    Manager: Walter Winterbottom

**Goals**: Knud Lundberg (62) / Donald Revie (26 pen, 53), Nathaniel Lofthouse (31, 41), Geoffrey Bradford (80)

299. 22.10.1955   Home Championship
**WALES v ENGLAND  2-1**  (2-0)
*Ninian Park, Cardiff*
Referee: Thomas Mitchell (Northern Ireland)    Att: 60,000

**WALES**: Alfred John Kelsey, Stuart Grenville Williams, Alfred Thomas Sherwood, Melvyn Charles, William John Charles, Roy Paul, Derek Robert Tapscott, Noel Kinsey, Trevor Ford, Ivor John Allchurch, Clifford William Jones.
Trainer: Walley Barnes

**ENGLAND**: Bert Frederick Williams, Jeffrey James Hall, Roger William Byrne, William Harry McGarry, William Ambrose Wright (Cap), James William Dickinson, Stanley Matthews, Donald George Revie, Nathaniel Lofthouse, Dennis James Wilshaw, Thomas Finney.
Manager: Walter Winterbottom

**Goal**: Derek Robert Tapscott (41), Clifford Jones (43) / William John Charles (51 og)

300. 02.11.1955   Home Championship
**ENGLAND v NORTHERN IRELAND  3-0**  (0-0)
*Wembley, London*
Referee: Mervyn Griffiths (Wales)    Attendance: 60,000

**ENGLAND**: Ronald Leslie Baynham, Jeffrey James Hall, Roger William Byrne, Ronald Clayton, William Ambrose Wright (Cap), James William Dickinson, Thomas Finney, John Norman Haynes, Bedford Alfred George Jezzard, Dennis James Wilshaw, William Perry.
Manager: Walter Winterbottom

**NORTHERN IRELAND**: William Uprichard, William Edward Cunningham, William George Leonard Graham, Robert Denis Blanchflower, William Terence McCavana, Robert Peacock, William Bingham, James McIlroy, Francis Coyle, Charles Tully, Peter James McParland.

**Goals**: Dennis James Wilshaw (50, 52), Thomas Finney (88)

301. 30.11.1955
**ENGLAND v SPAIN  4-1**  (2-0)
*Wembley, London*
Referee: Maurice Guigue (France)    Attendance: 95,550

**ENGLAND**: Ronald Leslie Baynham, Jeffrey James Hall, Roger William Byrne, Ronald Clayton, William Ambrose Wright (Cap), James William Dickinson, Thomas Finney, Peter John Walter Atyeo, Nathaniel Lofthouse, John Norman Haynes, William Perry.    Manager: Walter Winterbottom

**SPAIN**: Carmelo Cedrún, Joan Segarra (Cap), Jesús Garay, Marcelino Vaquero González "Campanal", Mauricio Ugartemendia "Mauri", José María Maguregui, MIGUEL González, José Luis Pérez Payá, Ignacio Arieta, Manuel Doménech, Enrique Collar.
Trainer: Guillermo Eizaguirre Olmos

**Goals**: Peter John Walter Atyeo (12), William Perry (13, 60), Thomas Finney (59) / Ignacio Arieta (80)

302. 14.04.1956   Home Championship
**SCOTLAND v ENGLAND  1-1**  (0-0)
*Hampden Park, Glasgow*
Referee: Leo Callaghan (Wales)    Attendance: 132,817

**SCOTLAND**: Thomas Younger, Alexander Hershaw Parker, John Davidson Hewie, Robert Evans, George Lewis Young (Cap), Archibald Glen, Graham Leggat, Robert Johnstone, Lawrence Reilly, John Livingstone McMillan, Gordon Smith.

**ENGLAND**: Reginald Derrick Matthews, Jeffrey James Hall, Roger William Byrne, James William Dickinson, William Ambrose Wright (Cap), Duncan Edwards, Thomas Finney, Thomas Taylor, Nathaniel Lofthouse, John Norman Haynes, William Perry.    Manager: Walter Winterbottom

**Goal**: Graham Leggat (60) / John Norman Haynes (89)

303. 09.05.1956
**ENGLAND v BRAZIL  4-2**  (2-0)
*Wembley, London*
Referee: Maurice Guigue (France)    Attendance: 97,000

**ENGLAND**: Reginald Derrick Matthews, Jeffrey James Hall, Roger William Byrne, Ronald Clayton, William Ambrose Wright (Cap), Duncan Edwards, Stanley Matthews, Peter John Walter Atyeo, Thomas Taylor, John Norman Haynes, Colin Grainger.    Manager: Walter Winterbottom

**BRAZIL**: GILMAR dos Santos Neves, Djalma Santos, Marcos Cortez "Pavão", ZÓZIMO Alves Calazans, NÍLTON Reís dos SANTOS, José Mendonça dos Santos "Dequinha", Waldir Pereira "Didi", Paulo de Almeida "Paulinho", ÁLVARO José Rodrigues Valente, GINO Orlando, José Ribamar de Oliveira "Canhoteiro".    Trainer: Flávio Costa

**Goals**: Thomas Taylor (3, 65), Colin Grainger (5, 83) / Paulo de Almeida "Paulinho" (53), Waldir Pereira "Didi" (55)

304. 16.05.1956
**SWEDEN v ENGLAND  0-0**
*Råsunda, Solna*
Referee: Leopold Sylvain Horn (Holland)    Att: 35,000

**SWEDEN**: Karl Svensson, Åke Johansson, Sven Axbom, Sven-Ove Svensson, Bengt Gustavsson (Cap), Sigvard Parling, Bengt Berndtsson, Gösta Löfgren, Jan Ekström, Bengt Lindskog, Gösta Sandberg.    Trainer: Rudolf Kock

**ENGLAND**: Reginald Derrick Matthews, Jeffrey James Hall, Roger William Byrne, Ronald Clayton, William Ambrose Wright (Cap), Duncan Edwards, John Reginald Berry, Peter John Walter Atyeo, Thomas Taylor, John Norman Haynes, Colin Grainger.    Manager: Walter Winterbottom

**305.  20.05.1956**
**FINLAND v ENGLAND  1-5**  (0-3)

*Olympia, Helsinki*

Referee: Karl Jørgensen (Denmark)    Attendance: 20,177

**FINLAND:** Keijo Hurri (40 Aarre Klinga), Väinö Pajunen, Aimo Sommarberg, Alpo Lintamo, Lauri Lehtinen (Cap), Reijo Jalava, Juhani Peltonen, Matti Hiltunen, Kai Pahlman, Olavi Lahtinen, Olli Forsgren.    Trainer: Kurt Weinreich

**ENGLAND:** Raymond Ernest Wood, Jeffrey James Hall, Roger William Byrne, Ronald Clayton, William Ambrose Wright (Cap), Duncan Edwards, Gordon Astall, John Norman Haynes, Thomas Taylor (43 Nathaniel Lofthouse), Dennis James Wilshaw, Colin Grainger.    Manager: Walter Winterbottom

**Goals:** Olli Forsgren (42) / Dennis James Wilshaw (20), John Norman Haynes (22), Gordon Astall (29), Nathaniel Lofthouse (63, 82)


**306.  26.05.1956**
**WEST GERMANY v ENGLAND  1-3**  (0-1)

*Olympia, West-Berlin*

Referee: István Zsolt (Hungary)    Attendance: 95,000

**WEST GERMANY:** Fritz Herkenrath, Erich Retter, Erich Juskowiak, Robert Schlienz, Heinz Wewers, Karl Mai, Erwin Waldner, Max Morlock (40 Alfred Pfaff), Ottmar Walter, Fritz Walter (Cap), Hans Schäfer.    Trainer: Josef Herberger

**ENGLAND:** Reginald Derrick Matthews, Jeffrey James Hall, Roger William Byrne, Ronald Clayton, William Ambrose Wright (Cap), Duncan Edwards, Gordon Astall, John Norman Haynes, Thomas Taylor, Dennis James Wilshaw, Colin Grainger.    Manager: Walter Winterbottom

**Goals:** Fritz Walter (85) / Duncan Edwards (26), Colin Grainger (63), John Norman Haynes (69)


**307.  06.10.1956    Home Championship**
**NORTHERN IRELAND v ENGLAND  1-1**  (1-1)

*Windsor Park, Belfast*

Referee: Hugh Phillips (Scotland)    Attendance: 58,420

**NORTHERN IRELAND:** Harry Gregg, William Edward Cunningham, Alfred McMichael, Robert Denis Blanchflower, John Blanchflower, Thomas Casey, William Bingham, James McIlroy, James Jones, William John McAdams, Peter James McParland.

**ENGLAND:** Reginald Derrick Matthews, Jeffrey James Hall, Roger William Byrne, Ronald Clayton, William Ambrose Wright (Cap), Duncan Edwards, Stanley Matthews, Donald George Revie, Thomas Taylor, Dennis James Wilshaw, Colin Grainger.    Manager: Walter Winterbottom

**Goal:** James McIlroy (10) / Stanley Matthews (3)


**308.  14.11.1956    Home Championship**
**ENGLAND v WALES  3-1**  (0-1)

*Wembley, London*

Referee: Hugh Phillips (Scotland)    Attendance: 93,796

**ENGLAND:** Edwin George Ditchburn, Jeffrey James Hall, Roger William Byrne, Ronald Clayton, William Ambrose Wright (Cap), James William Dickinson, Stanley Matthews, John Brooks, Thomas Finney, John Norman Haynes, Colin Grainger.    Manager: Walter Winterbottom

**WALES:** Alfred John Kelsey, Alfred Thomas Sherwood, Melvyn Hopkins, Alan Charles Harrington, William Raymond Daniel, Melvyn Charles, Derrick Sullivan, Terence Cameron Medwin, William John Charles, Ivor John Allchurch, Clifford William Jones.    Trainer: James Patrick Murphy

**Goals:** John Norman Haynes (52), John Brooks (54), Thomas Finney (75) / William John Charles (8)


**309.  28.11.1956**
**ENGLAND v YUGOSLAVIA  3-0**  (1-0)

*Wembley, London*

Referee: Edouard Harzic (France)    Attendance: 75,000

**ENGLAND:** Edwin George Ditchburn, Jeffrey James Hall, Roger William Byrne, Ronald Clayton, William Ambrose Wright (Cap), James William Dickinson, Stanley Matthews, John Brooks, Thomas Finney, John Norman Haynes (34 Thomas Taylor), Frank Blunstone.    Manager: Walter Winterbottom

**YUGOSLAVIA** Vladimir Beara, Bruno Belin, Branko Stanković, Lazar Tasić, Ivan Horvat (Cap), Vujadin Boškov, Zdravko Rajkov, Vladimir Čonč, Ivan Toplak, Bernard Vukas, Branko Zebec.    Trainer: Aleksandar Tirnanić

**Goals:** John Brooks (13), Thomas Taylor (65, 89)


**310.  05.12.1956    6th World Cup Qualifiers**
**ENGLAND v DENMARK  5-2**  (2-1)

*Molineux, Wolverhampton*

Referee: Maurice Guigue (France)    Attendance: 54,083

**ENGLAND:** Edwin George Ditchburn, Jeffrey James Hall, Roger William Byrne, Ronald Clayton, William Ambrose Wright (Cap), James William Dickinson, Stanley Matthews, John Brooks, Thomas Taylor, Duncan Edwards, Thomas Finney.    Manager: Walter Winterbottom

**DENMARK:** Theil Drengsgaard, Erling Linde Larsen, Verner Nielsen, Flemming Nielsen, Ove Hansen, Jørgen Olesen, Jørgen Hansen, Bent Petersen, Ove Bech Nielsen, Aage Rou Jensen (Cap), Jens Peder Hansen.    Trainer: Arne Sørensen

**Goals:** Thomas Taylor (18, 20, 48), Duncan Edwards (56, 77) / Ove Bech Nielsen (27, 52)

311. 06.04.1957    Home Championship
**ENGLAND v SCOTLAND  2-1**  (0-1)
*Wembley, London*

Referee: Pieter Roomer (Holland)    Attendance: 97,520

**ENGLAND**: Alan Hodgkinson, Jeffrey James Hall, Roger William Byrne, Ronald Clayton, William Ambrose Wright (Cap), Duncan Edwards, Stanley Matthews, Thomas Thompson, Thomas Finney, Derek Tennyson Kevan, Colin Grainger.    Manager: Walter Winterbottom

**SCOTLAND**: Thomas Younger, Eric Caldow, John Davidson Hewie, John Miller McColl, George Lewis Young (Cap), Thomas Henderson Docherty, Robert Young Collins, William Fernie, Lawrence Reilly, John Knight Mudie, Thomas Ring.

**Goals**: Derek Tennyson Kevan (63), Duncan Edwards (80) / Thomas Ring (1)


312. 08.05.1957    6th World Cup Qualifiers
**ENGLAND v REPUBLIC OF IRELAND  5-1**  (4-0)
*Wembley, London*

Referee: Hugh Phillips (Scotland)    Attendance: 52,000

**ENGLAND**: Alan Hodgkinson, Jeffrey James Hall, Roger William Byrne, Ronald Clayton, William Ambrose Wright (Cap), Duncan Edwards, Stanley Matthews, Peter John Walter Atyeo, Thomas Taylor, John Norman Haynes, Thomas Finney. Manager: Walter Winterbottom

**IRELAND**: Alan James Alexander Kelly, Daniel Christopher Donovan, Noel Eucharia Cantwell, Peter Desmond Farrell (Cap), Gerry Mackey, Patrick Saward, Alfred Ringstead, William Augustine Whelan, Dermot Patrick Curtis, Arthur Gerard Fitzsimons, Joseph Haverty.

**Goals**: Thomas Taylor (9, 18, 40), Peter Atyeo (38, 89) / Dermot Patrick Curtis (55)


313. 15.05.1957    6th World Cup Qualifiers
**DENMARK v ENGLAND  1-4**  (1-1)
*Idraetsparken, København*

Referee: Albert Dusch (West Germany)    Attendance: 35,000

**DENMARK**: Theil Drengsgaard, John Amdisen, Verner Nielsen, Flemming Nielsen, Ove Hansen, Jørgen Olesen, Jørgen Hansen, John Jensen, Erik Jensen, Aage Rou Jensen (Cap), Jens Peder Hansen.    Trainer: Arne Sørensen

**ENGLAND**: Alan Hodgkinson, Jeffrey James Hall, Roger William Byrne, Ronald Clayton, William Ambrose Wright (Cap), Duncan Edwards, Stanley Matthews, Peter John Walter Atyeo, Thomas Taylor, John Norman Haynes, Thomas Finney. Manager: Walter Winterbottom

**Goals**: John Jensen (27) / John Norman Haynes (29), Thomas Taylor (38, 89), Peter John Walter Atyeo (75)


314. 19.05.1957    6th World Cup Qualifiers
**REPUBLIC OF IRELAND v ENGLAND  1-1**  (1-0)
*Dalymount Park, Dublin*

Referee: Hugh Phillips (Scotland)    Attendance: 47,000

**IRELAND**: Thomas Fergus Godwin, Seamus Dunne, Noel Eucharia Cantwell (Cap), Patrick Saward, Ronald Nolan, Charles John Hurley, Alfred Ringstead, William Augustine Whelan, Dermot Patrick Curtis, Arthur Gerard Fitzsimons, Joseph Haverty.

**ENGLAND**: Alan Hodgkinson, Jeffrey James Hall, Roger William Byrne, Ronald Clayton, William Ambrose Wright (Cap), Duncan Edwards, Thomas Finney, Peter John Walter Atyeo, Thomas Taylor, John Norman Haynes, David Pegg. Manager: Walter Winterbottom

**Goals**: Alfred Ringstead (3) / Peter John Walter Atyeo (89)


315. 19.10.1957    Home Championship
**WALES v ENGLAND  0-4**  (0-2)
*Ninian Park, Cardiff*

Referee: Thomas Mitchell (Northern Ireland)    Att: 58,000

**WALES**: Alfred John Kelsey, Stuart Grenville Williams, Melvyn Hopkins, William Charles Harris, Melvyn Charles, David Lloyd Bowen, Terence Cameron Medwin, Ellis Reginald Davies, Desmond Frederick Palmer, Thomas Royston Vernon, Clifford William Jones.    Trainer: James Patrick Murphy

**ENGLAND**: Edward Hopkinson, Donald Howe, Roger William Byrne, Ronald Clayton, William Ambrose Wright (Cap), Duncan Edwards, Bryan Douglas, Derek Tennyson Kevan, Thomas Taylor, John Norman Haynes, Thomas Finney. Manager: Walter Winterbottom

**Goals**: Melvyn Hopkins (2 og), John Norman Haynes (44, 67), Thomas Finney (64)


316. 06.11.1957    Home Championship
**ENGLAND v NORTHERN IRELAND  2-3**  (0-1)
*Wembley, London*

Referee: Mervyn Griffiths (Wales)    Attendance: 40,000

**ENGLAND**: Edward Hopkinson, Donald Howe, Roger William Byrne, Ronald Clayton, William Ambrose Wright (Cap), Duncan Edwards, Bryan Douglas, Derek Tennyson Kevan, Thomas Taylor, John Norman Haynes, Alan A'Court. Manager: Walter Winterbottom

**NORTHERN IRELAND**: Harry Gregg, Richard Matthewson Keith, Alfred McMichael, Robert Denis Blanchflower, John Blanchflower, Robert Peacock, William Bingham, Samuel McKee McCrory, William Simpson, James McIlroy, Peter James McParland.

**Goals**: Alan A'Court (60), Duncan Edwards (80) / James McIlroy (30 pen), Samuel McKee McCrory (60), William J. Simpson (73)

**317. 27.11.1957**
**ENGLAND v FRANCE 4-0 (3-0)**
*Wembley, London*
Referee: Nikolai Latishev (USSR)    Attendance: 64,349
ENGLAND: Edward Hopkinson, Donald Howe, Roger William Byrne, Ronald Clayton, William Ambrose Wright (Cap), Duncan Edwards, Bryan Douglas, Robert William Robson, Thomas Taylor, John Norman Haynes, Thomas Finney.   Manager: Walter Winterbottom
FRANCE: Claude Abbes, Mustapha Zitouni, Richard Tylinski, Raymond Kaelbel, René Domingo, Bruno Bollini, Maryan Wisnieski, Joseph Ujlaki, Yvon Douis, Roger Piantoni (Cap), Jean Vincent.   Trainer: Albert Batteux
Goals: Thomas Taylor (3, 33), Robert Robson (24, 84)

**318. 19.04.1958    Home Championship**
**SCOTLAND v ENGLAND 0-4 (0-2)**
*Hampden Park, Glasgow*
Referee: Albert Dusch (West Germany)   Att: 127,874
SCOTLAND: Thomas Younger, Alexander Hershaw Parker, Harold Haddock, John Miller McColl, Robert Evans, Thomas Henderson Docherty (Cap), George Herd, James Murray, John Knight Mudie, James Forrest, Thomas Ewing.
ENGLAND: Edward Hopkinson, Donald Howe, Ernest James Langley, Ronald Clayton, William Ambrose Wright (Cap), William John Slater, Bryan Douglas, Robert Charlton, Derek Tennyson Kevan, John Norman Haynes, Thomas Finney. Manager: Walter Winterbottom
Goals: Bryan Douglas (20), Derek Tennyson Kevan (33, 75), Robert Charlton (67)

**319. 07.05.1958**
**ENGLAND v PORTUGAL 2-1 (1-0)**
*Wembley, London*
Referee: Albert Alsteen (Belgium)    Attendance: 72,000
ENGLAND: Edward Hopkinson, Donald Howe, Ernest James Langley, Ronald Clayton, William Ambrose Wright (Cap), William John Slater, Bryan Douglas, Robert Charlton, Derek Tennyson Kevan, John Norman Haynes, Thomas Finney. Manager: Walter Winterbottom
PORTUGAL: CARLOS António do Carmo Costa GOMES, VIRGÍLIO Marques Mendes (Cap), ÂNGELO Gaspar Martins, EMÍDIO da Silva GRAÇA, Miguel Arcanjo, Mário Torres, CARLOS Domingos DUARTE, Mário Esteves Coluna, JOSÉ AUGUSTO Pinto de Almeida (44 José António Barreto Travaços), Augusto Francisco Rocha, HERNÂNI Ferreira da Silva.   Trainer: José Maria Antunes
Goals: Robert Charlton (25, 68) / Carlos Duarte (51)

**320. 11.05.1958**
**YUGOSLAVIA v ENGLAND 5-0 (1-0)**
*JNA, Beograd*
Referee: István Zsolt (Hungary)    Attendance: 55,000
YUGOSLAVIA Vladimir Beara, Tomislav Crnković, Vasilije Šijaković, Dobrosav Krstić, Branko Zebec (Cap), Vujadin Boškov, Aleksandar Petaković, Todor Veselinović, Miloš Milutinović, Dragoslav Šekularac, Ilijaš Pašić.   Trainer: Aleksandar Tirnanić
ENGLAND: Edward Hopkinson, Donald Howe, Ernest James Langley, Ronald Clayton, William Ambrose Wright (Cap), William John Slater, Bryan Douglas, Robert Charlton, Derek Tennyson Kevan, John Norman Haynes, Thomas Finney. Manager: Walter Winterbottom
Goals: Miloš Milutinović (23), Aleksandar Petaković (56, 77, 83), Todor Veselinović (86)

**321. 18.05.1958**
**U.S.S.R. v ENGLAND 1-1 (0-1)**
*Lenin, Moskva*
Referee: Friedrich Seifert (Austria)    Attendance: 102,000
U.S.S.R.: Lev Yashin, Mikhail Ogonkov, Konstantin Krizhevskiy, Boris Kuznetzov, Yuriy Voynov, Igor Netto (Cap) (85 Viktor Tzarev), Gherman Apukhtin, Valentin Ivanov, Eduard Streltzov, Yuriy Falin, Anatoliy Ilyin.   Trainer: Gavril Kachalin
ENGLAND: Colin Agnew McDonald, Donald Howe, Thomas Banks, Harold Edwin Clamp, William Ambrose Wright (Cap), William John Slater, Bryan Douglas, Robert William Robson, Derek Tennyson Kevan, John Norman Haynes, Thomas Finney.   Manager: Walter Winterbottom
Goals: Valentin Ivanov (78) / Derek Tennyson Kevan (45)

**322. 08.06.1958    6th World Cup, 1st Round**
**ENGLAND v U.S.S.R. 2-2 (0-1)**
*Ullevi, Göteborg*
Referee: István Zsolt (Hungary)    Attendance: 49,348
ENGLAND: Colin Agnew McDonald, Donald Howe, Thomas Banks, Harold Edwin Clamp, William Ambrose Wright (Cap), William John Slater, Bryan Douglas, Robert William Robson, Derek Tennyson Kevan, John Norman Haynes, Thomas Finney. Manager: Walter Winterbottom
U.S.S.R.: Lev Yashin, Vladimir Kesarev, Konstantin Krizhevskiy, Boris Kuznetzov, Yuriy Voynov, Viktor Tzarev, Aleksandr Ivanov, Valentin Ivanov, Nikita Simonyan (Cap), Sergey Salnikov, Anatoliy Ilyin.   Trainer: Gavril Kachalin
Goals: Derek Tennyson Kevan (65), Thomas Finney (84 pen) / Nikita Simonyan (14), Aleksandr Ivanov (56)

323.  11.06.1958    6th World Cup, 1st Round
**BRAZIL v ENGLAND   0-0**

*Ullevi, Göteborg*

Referee:  Albert Dusch (West Germany)    Attendance: 40,895

**BRAZIL**:  GILMAR dos Santos Neves, Nílton De Sordi, Hideraldo Luiz Bellini (Cap), ORLANDO Peçanha de Carvalho, NÍLTON Reís dos SANTOS, Dino Sani, Waldir Pereira "Didi", JOEL Antônio Martins, José João Altafini "Mazzola", Edvaldo Izídio Neto "Vavá", Mário Jorge Lobo Zagallo.    Trainer:  Vicente Feola

**ENGLAND**:  Colin Agnew McDonald, Donald Howe, Thomas Banks, Harold Edwin Clamp, William Ambrose Wright (Cap), William John Slater, Bryan Douglas, Robert William Robson, Derek Tennyson Kevan, John Norman Haynes, Alan A'Court.    Manager:  Walter Winterbottom

324.  15.06.1958    6th World Cup, 1st Round
**ENGLAND v AUSTRIA   2-2**  (0-1)

*Ryavallen, Borås*

Referee:  Johannes Bronkhorst (Holland)    Att: 16,800

**ENGLAND**:  Colin Agnew McDonald, Donald Howe, Thomas Banks, Harold Edwin Clamp, William Ambrose Wright (Cap), William John Slater, Bryan Douglas, Robert William Robson, Derek Tennyson Kevan, John Norman Haynes, Alan A'Court.    Manager:  Walter Winterbottom

**AUSTRIA**:  Rudolf Szanwald, Walter Kollmann, Franz Swoboda, Gerhard Hanappi, Ernst Happel, Karl Koller, Ernst Kozlicek, Paul Kozlicek, Johann Buzek, Alfred Körner, Helmut Senekowitsch.    Trainer:  Josef Argauer

**Goals**:  Johnny Haynes (56), Derek Tennyson Kevan (74) / Karl Koller (15), Alfred Körner (71)

325.  17.06.1958    6th World Cup, 1st Round Play-off
**U.S.S.R. v ENGLAND   1-0**  (0-0)

*Ullevi, Göteborg*

Referee:  Albert Dusch (West Germany)    Attendance: 23,182

**U.S.S.R.**:  Lev Yashin, Vladimir Kesarev, Konstantin Krizhevskiy, Boris Kuznetzov, Yuriy Voynov, Viktor Tzarev, Gherman Apukhtin, Valentin Ivanov, Nikita Simonyan (Cap), Yuriy Falin, Anatoliy Ilyin.    Trainer:  Gavril Kachalin

**ENGLAND**:  Colin Agnew McDonald, Donald Howe, Thomas Banks, Ronald Clayton, William Ambrose Wright (Cap), William John Slater, Peter Brabrook, Peter Frank Broadbent, Derek Tennyson Kevan, John Norman Haynes, Alan A'Court.    Manager:  Walter Winterbottom

**Goal**:  Anatoliy Ilyin (68)

326.  04.10.1958    Home Championship
**NORTHERN IRELAND v ENGLAND   3-3**  (1-1)

*Windsor Park, Belfast*

Referee:  Robert Holley Davidson (Scotland)    Att: 58,000

**NORTHERN IRELAND**:  Harry Gregg, Richard Matthewson Keith, William George Leonard Graham, Robert Denis Blanchflower, William Edward Cunningham, Robert Peacock, William Bingham, Wilbur Cush, Thomas Casey, James McIlroy, Peter James McParland.

**ENGLAND**:  Colin Agnew McDonald, Donald Howe, Thomas Banks, Ronald Clayton, William Ambrose Wright (Cap), Wilfred McGuinness, Peter Brabrook, Peter Frank Broadbent, Robert Charlton, John Norman Haynes, Thomas Finney.    Manager:  Walter Winterbottom

**Goals**:  Wilbur W. Cush (33), Robert Peacock (57), Thomas Casey (70) / Robert Charlton (31, 77), Thomas Finney (61)

327.  22.10.1958
**ENGLAND v U.S.S.R.   5-0**  (1-0)

*Wembley, London*

Referee:  Maurice Guigue (France)    Attendance: 100,000

**ENGLAND**:  Colin Agnew McDonald, Donald Howe, Graham Laurence Shaw, Ronald Clayton, William Ambrose Wright (Cap), William John Slater, Bryan Douglas, Robert Charlton, Nathaniel Lofthouse, John Norman Haynes, Thomas Finney.    Manager:  Walter Winterbottom

**U.S.S.R.**:  Vladimir Beliayev, Vladimir Kesarev, Anatoliy Maslënkin, Boris Kuznetzov, Yuriy Voynov, Viktor Tzarev, Slava Metreveli, Valentin Ivanov, Nikita Simonyan (Cap), Alekper Mamedov, Anatoliy Ilyin.    Trainer:  Gavril Kachalin

**Goals**:  Johnny Haynes (45, 63, 80), Robert Charlton (84 pen), Nathaniel Lofthouse (89)

328.  26.11.1958    Home Championship
**ENGLAND v WALES   2-2**  (1-1)

*Villa Park, Birmingham*

Referee:  Albert Dusch (West Germany)    Attendance: 41,581

**ENGLAND**:  Colin Agnew McDonald, Donald Howe, Graham Laurence Shaw, Ronald Clayton, William Ambrose Wright (Cap), Ronald Flowers, Daniel Robert Clapton, Peter Frank Broadbent, Nathaniel Lofthouse, John Norman Haynes, Alan A'Court.    Manager:  Walter Winterbottom

**WALES**:  Alfred John Kelsey, Stuart Grenville Williams, Melvyn Hopkins, Victor Herbert Crowe, Melvyn Charles, David Lloyd Bowen, Terence Cameron Medwin, David Ward, Derek Robert Tapscott, Ivor John Allchurch, Philip Abraham Woosnam.    Trainer:  James Patrick Murphy

**Goals**:  Peter Frank Broadbent (42, 75) / Derek Robert Tapscott (15), Ivor John Allchurch (70)

### 329. 11.04.1959   Home Championship
**ENGLAND v SCOTLAND  1-0**  (0-0)

*Wembley, London*

Referee:  Joaquim de Campos (Portugal)    Att: 98,329

**ENGLAND**:  Edward Hopkinson, Donald Howe, Graham Laurence Shaw, Ronald Clayton, William Ambrose Wright (Cap), Ronald Flowers, Bryan Douglas, Peter Frank Broadbent, Robert Charlton, John Norman Haynes, Albert Douglas Holden.   Manager:  Walter Winterbottom

**SCOTLAND**:  William Dallas Fyfe Brown, Duncan Mackay, Eric Caldow, Thomas Henderson Docherty, Robert Evans (Cap), David Craig MacKay, Graham Leggat, Robert Young Collins, David George Herd, John Hart Dick, William Esplin Ormond.   Manager:  Andrew Beattie

**Goal**:  Robert Charlton (59)


### 330. 06.05.1959
**ENGLAND v ITALY  2-2**  (2-0)

*Wembley, London*

Referee:  Albert Dusch (West Germany)    Attendance: 92,000

**ENGLAND**:  Edward Hopkinson, Donald Howe, Graham Laurence Shaw, Ronald Clayton, William Ambrose Wright (Cap), Ronald Flowers, Warren Bradley, Peter Frank Broadbent, Robert Charlton, John Norman Haynes, Albert Douglas Holden.   Manager:  Walter Winterbottom

**ITALY**:  Lorenzo Buffon, Enzo Robotti, Sergio Castelletti, Franco Zaglio, Gaudenzio Bernasconi, Armando Segato (Cap), Amos Mariani, Guido Gratton, Sergio Brighenti, Carlo Galli, Gianfranco Petris.   Trainer:  Giovanni Ferrari

**Goals**:  Robert Charlton (26), Warren Bradley (38) / Sergio Brighenti (56), Amos Mariani (61)


### 331. 13.05.1959
**BRAZIL v ENGLAND  2-0**  (2-0)

*Maracana, Rio de Janeiro*

Referee:  Juan Brozzi (Argentina)   Attendance: 160,000

**BRAZIL**:  GILMAR dos Santos Neves, Djalma Santos, Hideraldo Luiz Bellini, ORLANDO Peçanha de Carvalho (32 Francisco Ferreira de Aguiar "Formiga"), NÍLTON Reís dos SANTOS, Dino Sani, Waldir Pereira "Didi", Júlio Botelho "Julinho", HENRIQUE Frade, Edson Arantes do Nascimento "Pelé", José Ribamar de Oliveira "Canhoteiro".   Trainer:  Vicente Feola

**ENGLAND**:  Edward Hopkinson, Donald Howe, James Christopher Armfield, Ronald Clayton, William Ambrose Wright (Cap), Ronald Flowers, Norman Victor Deeley, Peter Frank Broadbent, Robert Charlton, John Norman Haynes, Albert Douglas Holden.   Manager:  Walter Winterbottom

**Goals**:  Júlio Botelho "Julinho" (2), HENRIQUE Frade (28)


### 332. 17.05.1959
**PERU v ENGLAND  4-1**  (2-0)

*Nacional, Lima*

Referee:  Erwin Hiegger (Austria)    Attendance: 50,306

**PERU**:  Rafael Asca (Cap), Guillermo Fleming, José Fernández, Isaac Andrade, Juan De La Vega, Víctor Benítez, Oscar Montalvo, Miguel Loayza, Juan Joya, José Carrasco, Juan Seminario.   Trainer: György Orth

**ENGLAND**:  Edward Hopkinson, Donald Howe, James Christopher Armfield, Ronald Clayton, William Ambrose Wright (Cap), Ronald Flowers, Norman Victor Deeley, James Peter Greaves, Robert Charlton, John Norman Haynes, Albert Douglas Holden.   Manager:  Walter Winterbottom

**Goals**:  Juan Seminario (10, 40, 80), Juan Joya (70) / James Peter Greaves (58)


### 333. 24.05.1959
**MEXICO v ENGLAND  2-1**  (1-1)

*Olímpico de Centro Universitário, Ciudad de Mexico*

Referee:  Eunapio Gouveia Quiroz (Brazil)    Att: 83,000

**MEXICO**:  Antonio Carbajal, Juan Bosco, Jesús del Muro, Ignacio Jáuregui, Raúl Cárdenas, Francisco Flores, Alfredo del Aguila, Salvador Reyes, Carlos González (Héctor Hernández), Sabas Ponce (23 Antonio Jasso), Raúl Arellano.   Trainer:  Fernando Marcos

**ENGLAND**:  Edward Hopkinson, Donald Howe, James Christopher Armfield, Ronald Clayton, William Ambrose Wright (Cap), Wilfred McGuinness (68 Ronald Flowers), Albert Douglas Holden (68 Warren Bradley), James Peter Greaves, Derek Tennyson Kevan, John Norman Haynes, Robert Charlton.   Manager:  Walter Winterbottom

**Goals**:  Raúl Cárdenas (26), Salvador Reyes (67) / Derek Tennyson Kevan (14)


### 334. 28.05.1959
**U.S.A. v ENGLAND  1-8**  (1-1)

*Coliseum, Los Angeles*

Referee:  Ray Morgan (Canada)    Attendance: 14,000

**U.S.A.**:  Victor Ottoboni, Douglas Farquhar, Ben Cinowitz, Adolf Bachmeier (P. Kulitchenko), Bert Evans, John Peter Traina, Alfred Cameron, Edward Murphy (Cap), William Carson, William Looby, Albert Zerhusen.
Trainer:  James Reed

**ENGLAND**:  Edward Hopkinson, Donald Howe, James Christopher Armfield, Ronald Clayton, William Ambrose Wright (Cap), Ronald Flowers, W Bradley, James Peter Greaves, Derek Tennyson Kevan, John Norman Haynes, Robert Charlton.   Manager:  Walter Winterbottom

**Goals**:  Edward Murphy (9) / Warren Bradley (35), Ronald Flowers (52, 69), Robert Charlton (64, 82 pen, 85), Derek Tennyson Kevan (74), John Norman Haynes (87)

335. 17.10.1959   Home Championship
**WALES v ENGLAND  1-1**  (0-1)
*Ninian Park, Cardiff*

Referee: Thomas Mitchell (Northern Ireland)   Att: 62,000

**WALES**: Alfred John Kelsey, Stuart Grenville Williams, Melvyn Hopkins, Victor Herbert Crowe, Melvyn Tudor George Nurse, Derrick Sullivan, Terence Cameron Medwin, Philip Abraham Woosnam, Graham Moore, Ivor John Allchurch, Clifford William Jones.   Trainer: James Patrick Murphy

**ENGLAND**: Edward Hopkinson, Donald Howe, Anthony Allen, Ronald Clayton (Cap), Trevor Smith, Ronald Flowers, John Michael Connelly, James Peter Greaves, Brian Howard Clough, Robert Charlton, Edwin Holliday.
Manager: Walter Winterbottom

**Goal**: Graham Moore / James Peter Greaves (25)


336. 28.10.1959
**ENGLAND v SWEDEN  2-3**  (1-0)
*Wembley, London*

Referee: Robert Holley Davidson (Scotland)   Att: 80,000

**ENGLAND**: Edward Hopkinson, Donald Howe, Anthony Allen, Ronald Clayton (Cap), Trevor Smith, Ronald Flowers, John Michael Connelly, James Peter Greaves, Brian Howard Clough, Robert Charlton, Edwin Holliday.
Manager: Walter Winterbottom

**SWEDEN**: Bengt Nyholm, Orvar Bergmark (Cap), Sven Axbom, Torbjörn Jonsson, Åke Johansson, Sigvard Parling, Bengt Berndtsson, Henry Thillberg, Agne Simonsson, Rune Börjesson, Bengt Salomonsson.   Trainer: Eric Persson

**Goals**: John Michael Connelly (8), Robert Charlton (81) / Agne Simonsson (52, 55), Bengt Salomonsson (76)


337. 18.11.1959   Home Championship
**ENGLAND v NORTHERN IRELAND  2-1**  (1-0)
*Wembley, London*

Referee: Leo Callaghan (Wales)   Attendance: 60,000

**ENGLAND**: Ronald Derrick Springett, Donald Howe, Anthony Allen, Ronald Clayton (Cap), Kenneth Brown, Ronald Flowers, John Michael Connelly, John Norman Haynes, Joseph Henry Baker, Raymond Alan Parry, Edwin Holliday.
Manager: Walter Winterbottom

**NORTHERN IRELAND**: Harry Gregg, Richard Matthewson Keith, Alfred McMichael, Robert Denis Blanchflower, William Edward Cunningham, Robert Peacock, William Bingham, John Andrew Crossan, Wilbur W. Cush, James McIlroy, Peter James McParland.   Manager: Peter Doherty

**Goals**: Joseph Henry Baker (16), Raymond Alan Parry (89) / William Bingham


338. 09.04.1960   Home Championship
**SCOTLAND v ENGLAND  1-1**  (1-0)
*Hampden Park, Glasgow*

Referee: Jenö Sranko (Hungary)   Attendance: 129,193

**SCOTLAND**: Francis Haffey, Duncan Mackay, Eric Caldow, John Cumming, Robert Evans (Cap), Robert Johnston McCann, Graham Leggat, Alexander Young, Ian St. John, Denis Law, Andrew Best Weir.   Manager: Andrew Beattie

**ENGLAND**: Ronald Derrick Springett, James Christopher Armfield, Ramon Wilson, Ronald Clayton (Cap), William John Slater, Ronald Flowers, John Michael Connelly, Peter Frank Broadbent, Joseph Henry Baker, Raymond Alan Parry, Robert Charlton.   Manager: Walter Winterbottom

**Goal**: Graham Leggat (16) / Robert Charlton (50 pen)


339. 11.05.1960
**ENGLAND v YUGOSLAVIA  3-3**  (1-1)
*Wembley, London*

Referee: Robert Holey Davidson (Scotland)   Att: 60,000

**ENGLAND**: Ronald Derrick Springett, James Christopher Armfield, Ramon Wilson, Ronald Clayton (Cap), Peter Swan, Ronald Flowers, Bryan Douglas, John Norman Haynes, Joseph Henry Baker, James Peter Greaves, Robert Charlton.   Manager: Walter Winterbottom

**YUGOSLAVIA**: Milutin Šoškić, Vladimir Durković, Fahrudin Jusufi, Ante Žanetić, Branko Zebec, Željko Perušić, Luka Lipošinović (Cap), Dražen Jerković (46 Muhamed Mujić), Dragoslav Šekularac, Milan Galić, Borivoje Kostić.
Selection comittee: Dragomir Nikolić, Aleksandar Tirnanić, Ljubomir Lovrić

**Goals**: Bryan Douglas (43), James Peter Greaves (48), John Norman Haynes (85) / Milan Galić (27, 58), Borivoje Kostić (80)


340. 15.05.1960
**SPAIN v ENGLAND  3-0**  (1-0)
*Santiago Bernabéu, Madrid*

Referee: Albert Dusch (West Germany)   Attendance: 77,000

**SPAIN**: Antonio Ramallets, Enrique Pérez Díaz "Pachín", Jesús Garay, Sigfrido Gracia, Martín Vergés, Joan Segarra (Cap), Jesús María Pereda (44 Luis Del Sol), Eulogio Ramiro Martínez, Alfredo Di Stéfano, Joaquín Peiró, Francisco Gento.
Trainers: José Luis Costa, Ramón Gabilondo Alberdi, José Luis Lasplazas

**ENGLAND**: Ronald Derrick Springett, James Christopher Armfield, Ramon Wilson, Robert William Robson, Peter Swan, Ronald Flowers, Peter Brabrook, John Norman Haynes (Cap), Joseph Henry Baker, James Peter Greaves, Robert Charlton.   Manager: Walter Winterbottom

**Goals**: Joaquín Peiró (38), Eulogio Martínez (79, 85)

### 341. 22.05.1960
**HUNGARY v ENGLAND 2-0** (0-0)

*Népstadion, Budapest*

Referee: Concetto Lo Bello (Italy)    Attendance: 90,000

**HUNGARY**: Gyula Grosics, Sándor Mátrai, Ferenc Sipos, Jenő Dalnoki, Dezső Bundzsák, Antal Kotász, Károly Sándor, János Göröcs, Flórián Albert, János Dunai, Gyula Rákosi. Trainer: Lajos Baróti

**ENGLAND**: Ronald Derrick Springettt, James Christopher Armfield, Ramon Wilson, Robert William Robson, Peter Swan, Ronald Flowers, Bryan Douglas, John Norman Haynes (Cap), Joseph Henry Baker, Dennis Sydney Viollet, Robert Charlton. Manager: Walter Winterbottom

**Goals**: Flórián Albert (51, 76)

### 342. 08.10.1960    Home Championship
**NORTHERN IRELAND v ENGLAND 2-5** (1-2)

*Windsor Park, Belfast*

Referee: Hugh Phillips (Scotland)    Attendance: 60,000

**NORTHERN IRELAND**: Harry Gregg, Richard Matthewson Keith, Alexander Russell Elder, Robert Denis Blanchflower, John T. Forde, Robert Peacock, William Bingham, James McIlroy, William John McAdams, Alexander Derek Dougan, Peter James McParland.

**ENGLAND**: Ronald Derrick Springettt, James Christopher Armfield, Michael McNeil, Robert William Robson, Peter Swan, Ronald Flowers, Bryan Douglas, James Peter Greaves, Robert Alfred Smith, John Norman Haynes (Cap), Robert Charlton. Manager: Walter Winterbottom

**Goals**: William John McAdams (36, 53) / Robert Alfred Smith (15), James Peter Greaves (40, 47), Bryan Douglas (80), Robert Charlton (88)

### 343. 19.10.1960    7th World Cup Qualifiers
**LUXEMBOURG v ENGLAND 0-9** (0-4)

*Municipal, Luxembourg*

Referee: Johannes Martens (Holland)    Attendance: 5,500

**LUXEMBOURG** Théo Stendebach, Ernest Brenner (Cap), Nicolas Hoffmann, Ernest Jann, Fernand Brosius, Jean-Pierre Mertl, Adolphe Schmit, Henri Cirelli, Paul May, François Konter, Gaston Bauer.

**ENGLAND**: Ronald Derrick Springettt, James Christopher Armfield, Michael McNeil, Robert William Robson, Peter Swan, Ronald Flowers, Bryan Douglas, James Peter Greaves, Robert Alfred Smith, John Norman Haynes (Cap), Robert Charlton. Manager: Walter Winterbottom

**Goals**: Robert Charlton (3, 7, 66), Jimmy Greaves (16, 83, 85), Robert Alfred Smith (22, 46), John Norman Haynes (61)

### 344. 26.10.1960
**ENGLAND v SPAIN 4-2** (2-1)

*Wembley, London*

Referee: Maurice Guigue (France)    Attendance: 80,000

**ENGLAND**: Ronald Derrick Springettt, James Christopher Armfield, Michael McNeil, Robert William Robson, Peter Swan, Ronald Flowers, Bryan Douglas, James Peter Greaves, Robert Alfred Smith, John Norman Haynes (Cap), Robert Charlton. Manager: Walter Winterbottom

**SPAIN**: Antonio Ramallets, Marcos Alonso "Marquitos", Francisco Santamaría, Sigfrido Gracia, Martín Vergés, Manuel Ruiz Sosa, Enrique Mateos, Luis Del Sol, Alfredo Di Stéfano, Luis Suárez (Cap), Francisco Gento. Trainers: José Luis Costa, Ramón Gabilondo Alberdi, José Luis Lasplazas

**Goals**: James Peter Greaves (1), Bryan Douglas (42), Robert Alfred Smith (68, 82) / Luis Del Sol (12), Luis Suárez (51)

### 345. 23.11.1960    Home Championship
**ENGLAND v WALES 5-1** (3-0)

*Wembley, London*

Referee: Robert Holley Davidson (Scotland)    Att: 65,000

**ENGLAND**: Alan Hodgkinson, James Christopher Armfield, Michael McNeil, Robert William Robson, Peter Swan, Ronald Flowers, Bryan Douglas, James Peter Greaves, Robert Alfred Smith, John Norman Haynes (Cap), Robert Charlton. Manager: Walter Winterbottom

**WALES**: Alfred John Kelsey, Alan Charles Harrington, Graham Evan Williams, Victor Herbert Crowe, Melvyn Tudor George Nurse, Colin Walter Baker, Terence Cameron Medwin, Philip Abraham Woosnam, Kenneth Leek, Thomas Royston Vernon, Clifford William Jones.
Trainer: James Patrick Murphy

**Goals**: James Peter Greaves (2, 69), Robert Charlton (16), Robert Smith (22), John Haynes (61) / Kenneth Leek (75)

### 346. 15.04.1961    Home Championship
**ENGLAND v SCOTLAND 9-3** (3-0)

*Wembley, London*

Referee: Marcel Lequesne (France)    Attendance: 97,350

**ENGLAND**: Ronald Derrick Springettt, James Christopher Armfield, Michael McNeil, Robert William Robson, Peter Swan, Ronald Flowers, Bryan Douglas, James Peter Greaves, Robert Alfred Smith, John Norman Haynes (Cap), Robert Charlton. Manager: Walter Winterbottom

**SCOTLAND**: Francis Haffey, Robert Shearer, Eric Caldow (Cap), David Craig MacKay, William McNeill, Robert Johnston McCann, John Murdoch MacLeod, Denis Law, Ian St. John, Patrick Quinn, David Wilson.    Manager: John Miller McColl

**Goals**: Robert Robson (8), Jimmy Greaves (20, 29, 83), Bryan Douglas (55), Robert Alfred Smith (74, 85), John Norman Haynes (80, 82) / David Craig MacKay (49), David Wilson (53), Patrick Quinn (75)

### 347. 10.05.1961
**ENGLAND v MEXICO 8-0** (4-0)

*Wembley, London*

Referee: Robert Holley Davidson (Scotland)   Att: 77,000

**ENGLAND**: Ronald Derrick Springettt, James Christopher Armfield, Michael McNeil, Robert William Robson, Peter Swan, Ronald Flowers, Bryan Douglas, Derek Tennyson Kevan, Gerald Archibald Hitchens, John Norman Haynes (Cap), Robert Charlton.   Manager: Walter Winterbottom

**MEXICO**: Antonio Mota, Gustavo Peña, Guillermo Sepúlveda, Ignacio Jáuregui, Alfonso Portugal, Raúl Cárdenas, Alfredo del Aguila, Salvador Reyes, Carlos González, Francisco Flores (38 Tomás Reynoso), Sigifredo Mercado. Trainer: Ignacio Tréllez

**Goals**: Gerald Hitchens (2), Robert Charlton (12, 62, 76), Robert William Robson (22), Bryan Douglas (44, 89), Ronald Flowers (60 pen)

### 348. 21.05.1961   7th World Cup Qualifiers
**PORTUGAL v ENGLAND 1-1** (0-0)

*Nacional, Lisboa*

Referee: Pietro Bonetto (Italy)   Attendance: 65,000

**PORTUGAL**: Alberto da Costa Pereira, Mario Goulart Lino, HILÁRIO Rosário da Conceição, Fernando Mamede Mendes, GERMANO de Figueiredo, Fernando da Conceição Cruz, JOSÉ AUGUSTO Pinto de Almeida, Joaquim Santana, JOSÉ Carvalho Santos Pinto ÁGUAS (Cap), Mário Esteves Coluna, Domiciano Barrocal Gomes Cavém.
Trainer: Armando Ferreira

**ENGLAND**: Ronald Derrick Springett, James Christopher Armfield, Michael McNeil, Robert William Robson, Peter Swan, Ronald Flowers, Bryan Douglas, James Peter Greaves, Robert Alfred Smith, John Norman Haynes (Cap), Robert Charlton.   Manager: Walter Winterbottom

**Goals**: José Águas (59) / Ronald Flowers (82)

### 349. 24.05.1961
**ITALY v ENGLAND 2-3** (1-1)

*Olimpico, Roma*

Referee: Nikolai Latishev (USSR)   Attendance: 62,000

**ITALY**: Lorenzo Buffon (Cap) (56 Giuseppe Vavassori), Giacomo Losi, Sergio Castelletti, Bruno Bolchi, Sandro Salvadore, Giovanni Trapattoni, Bruno Mora, Francisco Ramon Lojacono, Sergio Brighenti, Omar Enrique Sivori, Mario Corso.   Trainer: Giovanni Ferrari

**ENGLAND**: Ronald Derrick Springettt, James Christopher Armfield, Michael McNeil, Robert William Robson, Peter Swan, Ronald Flowers, Bryan Douglas, James Peter Greaves, Gerald Archibald Hitchens, John Norman Haynes (Cap), Robert Charlton.   Manager: Walter Winterbottom

**Goals**: Omar Enrique Sivori (43), Sergio Brighenti (74) / Gerald Archibald Hitchens (39, 77), James Peter Greaves (86)

### 350. 27.05.1961
**AUSTRIA v ENGLAND 3-1** (2-1)

*Prater, Wien*

Referee: Karol Galba (Czechoslovakia)   Attendance: 90,000

**AUSTRIA**: Gernot Fraydl, Heribert Trubrig, Gerhard Hanappi, Erich Strobl, Karl Stotz, Karl Koller, Horst Nemec, Erich Hof, Johann Buzek, Helmut Senekowitsch, Friedrich Rafreider.   Trainer: Karl Decker

**ENGLAND**: Ronald Derrick Springettt, James Christopher Armfield, John Angus, Brian George Miller, Peter Swan, Ronald Flowers, Bryan Douglas, James Peter Greaves, Gerald Archibald Hitchens, John Norman Haynes (Cap), Robert Charlton.   Manager: Walter Winterbottom

**Goal**: Erich Hof (3), Horst Nemec (25), Helmut Senekowitsch (80) / James Peter Greaves (16)

### 351. 28.09.1961   7th World Cup Qualifiers
**ENGLAND v LUXEMBOURG 4-1** (3-0)

*Highbury, London*

Referee: Gerard Versyp (Belgium)   Attendance: 33,409

**ENGLAND**: Ronald Derrick Springettt, James Christopher Armfield (Cap), Michael McNeil, Robert William Robson, Peter Swan, Ronald Flowers, Bryan Douglas, John Fantham, Raymond Pointer, Dennis Sydney Viollet, Robert Charlton. Manager: Walter Winterbottom

**LUXEMBOURG** Paul Steffen, Ernest Brenner, Jeannot Hoffmann, Jules Zambon, Fernand Brosius, François Konter, Camille Dimmer (Cap), Henri Cirelli, Nicolas Hoffmann, René Schneider, Adolphe Schmit.

**Goals**: Raymond Pointer (35), Dennis Sydney Viollet (37), Robert Charlton (45, 76) / Camille Dimmer (69)

### 352. 14.10.1961   Home Championship
**WALES v ENGLAND 1-1** (1-1)

*Ninian Park, Cardiff*

Referee: Hugh Phillips (Scotland)   Attendance: 61,566

**WALES**: Alfred John Kelsey, Alan Charles Harrington, Stuart Grenville Williams, Melvyn Charles, William John Charles, Victor Herbert Crowe, Clifford William Jones, Philip Abraham Woosnam, David Ward, Ivor John Allchurch, George Graham Williams.   Trainer: James Patrick Murphy

**ENGLAND**: Ronald Derrick Springettt, James Christopher Armfield, Ramon Wilson, Robert William Robson, Peter Swan, Ronald Flowers, John Michael Connelly, Bryan Douglas, Raymond Pointer, John Norman Haynes (Cap), Robert Charlton.   Manager: Walter Winterbottom

**Goal**: George Graham Williams (30) / Bryan Douglas (44)

### 353. 25.10.1961    7th World Cup Qualifiers
### ENGLAND v PORTUGAL 2-0 (2-0)

*Wembley, London*

Referee: Marcel Bois (France)    Attendance: 100,000

**ENGLAND**: Ronald Derrick Springettt, James Christopher Armfield, Ramon Wilson, Robert William Robson, Peter Swan, Ronald Flowers, John Michael Connelly, Bryan Douglas, Raymond Pointer, John Norman Haynes (Cap), Robert Charlton.    Manager: Walter Winterbottom

**PORTUGAL**: Alberto da Costa Pereira, Mario Goulart Lino, HILÁRIO Rosário da Conceição, José Pérides, LÚCIO Soares, VICENTE Lucas, António Fernandes "Yaúca", EUSÉBIO da Silva Ferreira, JOSÉ Carvalho Santos Pinto ÁGUAS (Cap), Mário Esteves Coluna, Domiciano Barrocal Gomes Cavém. Trainer: Fernando Peyroteo

**Goals**: John Michael Connelly (5), Raymond Pointer (9)


### 354. 22.11.1961    Home Championship
### ENGLAND v NORTHERN IRELAND 1-1 (1-0)

*Wembley, London*

Referee: Leo Callaghan (Wales)    Attendance: 30,000

**ENGLAND**: Ronald Derrick Springettt, James Christopher Armfield, Ramon Wilson, Robert William Robson, Peter Swan, Ronald Flowers, Bryan Douglas, John Joseph Byrne, Raymond Crawford, John Norman Haynes (Cap), Robert Charlton. Manager: Walter Winterbottom

**NORTHERN IRELAND**: Victor Hunter, Edward James Magill, Alexander Russell Elder, Robert Denis Blanchflower, William John Terence Neill, James Joseph Nicholson, William Bingham, Hugh Henry Barr, William John McAdams, James McIlroy, James Christopher McLaughlin.

**Goal**: Robert Charlton (20) / James McIlroy (81)


### 355. 04.04.1962
### ENGLAND v AUSTRIA 3-1 (2-0)

*Wembley, London*

Referee: Pierre Schwinte (France)    Attendance: 50,000

**ENGLAND**: Ronald Derrick Springettt, James Christopher Armfield, Ramon Wilson, Stanley Anderson, Peter Swan, Ronald Flowers, John Michael Connelly, Roger Hunt, Raymond Crawford, John Norman Haynes (Cap), Robert Charlton.    Manager: Walter Winterbottom

**AUSTRIA**: Gernot Fraydl, Heribert Trubrig, Erich Hasenkopf, Rudolf Oslansky, Karl Stotz, Karl Koller, Adolf Knoll, Erich Hof, Johann Buzek, Ernst Fiala (40 Rudolf Flögel), Friedrich Rafreider.    Trainer: Karl Decker

**Goals**: Raymond Crawford (7), Ronald Flowers (38 pen), Roger Hunt (68) / Johann Buzek (76)


### 356. 14.04.1962    Home Championship
### SCOTLAND v ENGLAND 2-0 (1-0)

*Hampden Park, Glasgow*

Referee: Leopold Sylvain Horn (Holland)    Att: 132,431

**SCOTLAND**: William Dallas Fyfe Brown, Alexander William Hamilton, Eric Caldow (Cap), Patrick Timothy Crerand, William McNeill, James Curran Baxter, Alexander Silcock Scott, John Anderson White, Ian St. John, Denis Law, David Wilson.    Manager: John Miller McColl

**ENGLAND**: Ronald Derrick Springettt, James Christopher Armfield, Ramon Wilson, Stanley Anderson, Peter Swan, Ronald Flowers, Bryan Douglas, James Peter Greaves, Robert Alfred Smith, John Norman Haynes (Cap), Robert Charlton. Manager: Walter Winterbottom

**Goals**: David Wilson (13), Eric Caldow (88 pen)


### 357. 09.05.1962
### ENGLAND v SWITZERLAND 3-1 (3-1)

*Wembley, London*

Referee: D.Z. Izco (Spain)    Attendance: 35,000

**ENGLAND**: Ronald Derrick Springettt, James Christopher Armfield, Ramon Wilson, Robert William Robson, Peter Swan, Ronald Flowers, John Michael Connelly, James Peter Greaves, Gerald Archibald Hitchens, John Norman Haynes (Cap), Robert Charlton.    Manager: Walter Winterbottom

**SWITZERLAND**: Antonio Permunian (46 Kurt Stettler), Peter Rösch, Ely Tacchella, André Grobéty, Heinz Schneiter, Hans Weber, Charles Antenen, Roger Vonlanthen, Norbert Eschmann, Anton Allemann, Richard Dürr. Trainer: Karl Rappan

**Goals**: Ronald Flowers (20), Gerald Archibald Hitchens (25), John Michael Connelly (35) / Anton Allemann (32)


### 358. 20.05.1962
### PERU v ENGLAND 0-4 (0-4)

*Nacional, Lima*

Referee: Erwin Hiegger (Austria)    Attendance: 32,565

**PERU**: Rodolfo Bazán, Guillermo Fleming, Adolfo Donayre, Rodolfo Guzmán, Juan De La Vega (Cap) (59 Humberto Arguedas), Manuel Grimaldo, Nicolás Nieri, Víctor Zegarra (Nemesio Mosquera), Hugo Lobatón, Alejandro Zevallos, Oscar Montalvo. Trainer: Jaime De Almeyda

**ENGLAND**: Ronald Derrick Springettt, James Christopher Armfield, Ramon Wilson, Robert Frederick Moore, Maurice Norman, Ronald Flowers, Bryan Douglas, James Peter Greaves, Gerald Archibald Hitchens, John Norman Haynes (Cap), Robert Charlton.    Manager: Walter Winterbottom

**Sent off**: Manuel Grimaldo (89)

**Goals**: Ronald Flowers (15 pen), Jimmy Greaves (24, 37, 39)

359.   31.05.1962    7th World Cup, 1st Round
**HUNGARY v ENGLAND  2-1**  (1-0)

*Braden Kupar, Rancagua*

Referee: Leopold Sylvain Horn (Holland)    Att: 7,938

**HUNGARY:**  Gyula Grosics (Cap), Sándor Mátrai, Kálmán Mészöly, László Sárosi, Ernő Solymosi, Ferenc Sipos, Károly Sándor, Gyula Rákosi, Flórián Albert, Lajos Tichy, Máté Fenyvesi.   Trainer: Lajos Baróti

**ENGLAND:**  Ronald Derrick Springett, James Christopher Armfield, Ramon Wilson, Robert Frederick Moore, Maurice Norman, Ronald Flowers, Bryan Douglas, James Peter Greaves, Gerald Archibald Hitchens, John Norman Haynes (Cap), Robert Charlton.   Manager: Walter Winterbottom

**Goals:** Lajos Tichy (17), Flórián Albert (73) / Ronald Flowers (57 pen)

360.   02.06.1962    7th World Cup, 1st Round
**ENGLAND v ARGENTINA  3-1**  (2-0)

*Braden Kupar, Rancagua*

Referee: Nikolai Latishev (USSR)    Attendance: 9,794

**ENGLAND:**  Ronald Derrick Springett, James Christopher Armfield, Ramon Wilson, Robert Frederick Moore, Maurice Norman, Ronald Flowers, Bryan Douglas, James Peter Greaves, Alan Peacock, John Norman Haynes (Cap), Robert Charlton.   Manager: Walter Winterbottom

**ARGENTINA:**  Antonio Roma, Rubén Marino Navarro (Cap), Silvio Marzolini, Vladislao Wenceslao Cap, Raúl Alberto Páez, Federico Sacchi, Antonio Ubaldo Rattín, Juan Carlos Oleniak, Héctor Rubén Sosa, José Francisco Sanfilippo, Raúl Oscar Belén.   Trainer: Juan Carlos Lorenzo

**Goals:** Ronald Flowers (18 pen), Robert Charlton (42), James Peter Greaves (67) / José Francisco Sanfilippo (81)

361.   07.06.1962    7th World Cup, 1st Round
**BULGARIA v ENGLAND  0-0**

*Braden Kupar, Rancagua*

Referee: Arthur Blavier (Belgium)    Attendance: 4,000

**BULGARIA:**  Georgi Naidenov, Dimitar Dimov, Dobromir Jechev, Aleksandr D. Kostov, Dimitar Kostov, Ivan Dimitrov, Nikola Kovachev (Cap), Georgi Asparuhov, Petar Velichkov, Dinko Dermendjiev, Ivan Kolev.
Trainers: Georgi Pachedjiev & Krastiu Chakarov

**ENGLAND:**  Ronald Derrick Springett, James Christopher Armfield, Ramon Wilson, Robert Frederick Moore, Maurice Norman, Ronald Flowers, Bryan Douglas, James Peter Greaves, Alan Peacock, John Norman Haynes (Cap), Robert Charlton.   Manager: Walter Winterbottom

362.   10.06.1962    7th World Cup, 1st Round
**BRAZIL v ENGLAND  3-1**  (1-1)

*Sausalito, Viña del Mar*

Referee: Pierre Schwinte (France)    Attendance: 17,736

**BRAZIL:**  GILMAR dos Santos Neves, Djalma Santos, MAURO Ramos de Oliveira (Cap), ZÓZIMO Alves Calazans, NÍLTON Reís dos SANTOS, José Eli de Miranda "Zito", Waldir Pereira "Didi", Manoel Francisco dos Santos "Garrincha", Edvaldo Izídio Neto "Vavá", AMARILDO Tavares da Silveira, Mário Jorge Lobo Zagallo.   Trainer: Aymoré Moreira

**ENGLAND:**  Ronald Derrick Springett, James Christopher Armfield, Ramon Wilson, Robert Frederick Moore, Maurice Norman, Ronald Flowers, Bryan Douglas, James Peter Greaves, Gerald Archibald Hitchens, John Norman Haynes (Cap), Robert Charlton.   Manager: Walter Winterbottom

**Goal:** Garrincha (31, 59), Edvaldo Izídio Neto "Vavá" (53) / Gerald Archibald Hitchens (38)

363.   03.10.1962    2nd European Champs, 1st Round
**ENGLAND v FRANCE  1-1**  (0-1)

*Hillsborough, Sheffield*

Referee: Frede Hansen (Denmark)    Attendance: 35,380

**ENGLAND:**  Ronald Derrick Springett, James Christopher Armfield (Cap), Ramon Wilson, Robert Frederick Moore, Maurice Norman, Ronald Flowers, Michael Stephen Hellawell, Christopher Crowe, Raymond Ogden Charnley, James Peter Greaves, Alan Thomas Hinton.
Manager: Walter Winterbottom

**FRANCE:**  Pierre Bernard, Jean Wendling, André Lerond (Cap), André Chorda, Synakowski Maryan, René Ferrier, Laurent Robuschi, Joseph Bonnel, Raymond Kopa, Yvon Goujon, Paul Sauvage.   Trainer: Henri Guérin

**Goal:** Ronald Flowers (57 pen)

364.   20.10.1962    Home Championship
**NORTHERN IRELAND v ENGLAND  1-3**  (0-1)

*Windsor Park, Belfast*

Referee: James Barclay (Scotland)    Attendance: 55,000

**NORTHERN IRELAND:**  Robert James Irvine, Edward James Magill, Alexander Russell Elder, Robert Denis Blanchflower, William John Terence Neill, James Joseph Nicholson, William Humphries, Hugh Henry Barr, Samuel Thomas McMillan, James McIlroy, William Bingham.

**ENGLAND:**  Ronald Derrick Springett, James Christopher Armfield (Cap), Ramon Wilson, Robert Frederick Moore, Brian Leslie Labone, Ronald Flowers, Michael Stephen Hellawell, Frederick Hill, Alan Peacock, James Peter Greaves, Michael O'Grady.   Manager: Walter Winterbottom

**Goals:** Hugh Henry Barr (62) / James Peter Greaves (8), Michael O'Grady (71, 73)

365. 21.11.1962    Home Championship
**ENGLAND v WALES  4-0**  (2-0)
*Wembley, London*
Referee:  Samuel Carswell (Ireland)    Attendance:  27,500
**ENGLAND**:  Ronald Derrick Springettt, James Christopher Armfield (Cap), Graham Laurence Shaw, Robert Frederick Moore, Brian Leslie Labone, Ronald Flowers, John Michael Connelly, Frederick Hill, Alan Peacock, James Peter Greaves, Robert Victor Tambling.    Manager:  Walter Winterbottom
**WALES**:  Anthony Horace Millington, Stuart Grenville Williams, Reginald Clifford Sear, William Terence Hennessey, Melvyn Tudor George Nurse, Peter Malcolm Lucas, Barrie Spencer Jones, Ivor John Allchurch, Kenneth Leek, Thomas Royston Vernon, Terence Cameron Medwin.
Trainer:  James Patrick Murphy
**Goals**:  John Michael Connelly (10), Alan Peacock (35, 60), James Peter Greaves (88)

366. 27.02.1963    2nd European Champs, 1st Round
**FRANCE v ENGLAND  5-2**  (3-0)
*Parc des Princes, Paris*
Referee:  Josef Kandlbinder (Austria)    Attendance:  23,986
**FRANCE**:  Pierre Bernard, Jean Wendling, André Lerond (Cap), Bruno Rodzik, Synakowski Maryan, Robert Herbin, Maryan Wisnieski, Joseph Bonnel, Yvon Goujon, Yvon Douis, Lucien Cossou.    Trainer:  Henri Guérin
**ENGLAND**:  Ronald Derrick Springettt, James Christopher Armfield (Cap), Ronald Patrick Henry, Robert Frederick Moore, Brian Leslie Labone, Ronald Flowers, John Michael Connelly, Robert Victor Tambling, Robert Alfred Smith, James Peter Greaves, Robert Charlton.    Manager:  Alfred Ramsey
**Goals**:  Maryan Wisnieski (3, 75), Yvon Douis (32), Lucien Cossou (43, 82) /
Robert Alfred Smith (57), Robert Victor Tambling (74)

367. 06.04.1963    Home Championship
**ENGLAND v SCOTLAND  1-2**  (0-2)
*Wembley, London*
Referee:  Leopold Sylvain Horn (Holland)    Att:  98,606
**ENGLAND**:  Gordon Banks, James Christopher Armfield (Cap), Gerald Byrne, Robert Frederick Moore, Maurice Norman, Ronald Flowers, Bryan Douglas, James Peter Greaves, Robert Alfred Smith, James Melia, Robert Charlton.    Manager:  Alfred Ramsey
**SCOTLAND**:  William Dallas Fyfe Brown, Alexander William Hamilton, Eric Caldow (Cap), David Craig MacKay, John Francombe Ure, James Curran Baxter, William Henderson, John Anderson White, Ian St. John, Denis Law, David Wilson.
Manager:  John Miller McColl
**Goal**:  Bryan Douglas (79) / James Curran Baxter (29, 31 pen)

368. 08.05.1963
**ENGLAND v BRAZIL  1-1**  (0-1)
*Wembley, London*
Referee:  Leopold Sylvain Horn (Holland)    Att:  92,000
**ENGLAND**:  Gordon Banks, James Christopher Armfield (Cap), Ramon Wilson, Gordon Milne, Maurice Norman, Robert Frederick Moore, Bryan Douglas, James Peter Greaves, Robert Alfred Smith, George Edward Eastham, Robert Charlton.    Manager:  Alfred Ramsey
**BRAZIL**:  GILMAR dos Santos Neves, Antonio LIMA dos Santos, EDUARDO Barbosa Albuquerque, ROBERTO DIAS Branco, RILDO da Costa Menezes, José Ferreira Franco "Zequinha", MENGÁLVIO Pedro Figueiró, DORVAL Rodrigues, Antônio Wilson Honório "Coutinho", AMARILDO Tavares da Silveira (41 NEY de Oliveira), Pedro Rizetti "Pepe".
Trainer:  Aymoré Moreira
**Goal**:  Bryan Douglas (86) / Pedro Rizetti "Pepe" (18)

369. 29.05.1963
**CZECHOSLOVAKIA v ENGLAND  2-4**  (0-2)
*Tehelné pole, Bratislava*
Referee:  Bertil Lööw (Sweden)    Attendance:  50,000
**CZECHOSLOVAKIA**:  Viliam Schrojf, Jan Lála, Ladislav Novák (Cap), Svatopluk Pluskal, Ján Popluhár, Josef Masopust (43 Titus Buberník), Jozef Štibrányi, Adolf Scherer, Josef Kadraba, Andrej Kvašňák, Václav Mašek.
Trainer:  Rudolf Vytlačil
**ENGLAND**:  Gordon Banks, Kenneth John Shellito, Ramon Wilson, Gordon Milne, Maurice Norman, Robert Frederick Moore (Cap), Terence Lionel Paine, James Peter Greaves, Robert Alfred Smith, George Edward Eastham, Robert Charlton.    Manager:  Alfred Ramsey
**Goals**:  Adolf Scherer (52), Josef Kadraba (72) /
James Peter Greaves (18, 80), Robert Alfred Smith (44), Robert Charlton (71)

370. 02.06.1963
**EAST GERMANY v ENGLAND  1-2**  (1-1)
*Zentral, Leipzig*
Referee:  Konstantin Zecevic (Yugoslavia)    Att:  90,000
**EAST GERMANY**:  Harald Fritsche, Klaus Urbanczyk, Werner Heine (Cap), Hans-Dieter Krampe, Manfred Kaiser, Kurt Liebrecht, Rainer Nachtigall, Henning Frenzel, Peter Ducke, Jürgen Nöldner, Roland Ducke.    Trainer:  Károly Sós
**ENGLAND**:  Gordon Banks, James Christopher Armfield (Cap), Ramon Wilson, Gordon Milne, Maurice Norman, Robert Frederick Moore, Terence Lionel Paine, Roger Hunt, Robert Alfred Smith, George Edward Eastham, Robert Charlton.    Manager:  Alfred Ramsey
**Goals**:  Peter Ducke (24) /
Roger Hunt (45), Robert Charlton (70)

### 371. 05.06.1963
**SWITZERLAND v ENGLAND 1-8** (1-3)

*St. Jakob, Basel*

Referee: István Zsolt (Hungary)   Attendance: 49,800

**SWITZERLAND**: Kurt Stettler, André Grobéty, Heinz Schneiter, Ely Tacchella, Hans Weber (46 Rudolf Arn), Werner Leimgruber, Anton Allemann, Karl Odermatt, Jakob Kuhn, Heinz Bertschi, Philippe Pottier.   Trainer: Karl Rappan

**ENGLAND**: Ronald Derrick Springettt, James Christopher Armfield (Cap), Ramon Wilson, Anthony Herbert Kay, Robert Frederick Moore, Ronald Flowers, Bryan Douglas, James Peter Greaves, John Joseph Byrne, James Melia, Robert Charlton.   Manager: Alfred Ramsey

**Goals**: Heinz Bertschi (32) / Robert Charlton (19, 55, 83), John Joseph Byrne (30, 50), Bryan Douglas (42), Anthony Herbert Kay (69), James Melia (75)

### 372. 12.10.1963   Home Championship
**WALES v ENGLAND 0-4** (0-1)

*Ninian Park, Cardiff*

Referee: W. Brittle (Scotland)   Attendance: 48,350

**WALES**: David Michael Hollins, Stuart Grenville Williams, Graham Evan Williams, William Terence Hennessey, Harold Michael England, Alwyn Derek Burton, Leonard Allchurch, Thomas Royston Vernon, Ronald Wyn Davies, Ivor John Allchurch, Clifford William Jones.
Trainer: James Patrick Murphy

**ENGLAND**: Gordon Banks, James Christopher Armfield (Cap), Ramon Wilson, Gordon Milne, Maurice Norman, Robert Frederick Moore, Terence Lionel Paine, James Peter Greaves, Robert Alfred Smith, George Edward Eastham, Robert Charlton.   Manager: Alfred Ramsey

**Goals**: Robert Alfred Smith (5, 67), James Peter Greaves (65), Robert Charlton (86)

### 373. 23.10.1963
**ENGLAND v F.I.F.A. WORLD XI 2-1** (0-0)

*Wembley, London*

Referee: Robert Holley Davidson (Scotland)   Att: 100,000

**ENGLAND**: Gordon Banks, James Christopher Armfield (Cap), Ramon Wilson, Gordon Milne, Maurice Norman, Robert Frederick Moore, Terence Lionel Paine, James Peter Greaves, Robert Alfred Smith, George Edward Eastham, Robert Charlton.   Manager: Alfred Ramsey

**FIFA**: Lev Yashin (46 Milutin Soskic), Djalma Santos (46 Luis Eizaguirre), Karlheinz Schnellinger, Svatopluk Pluskal, Jan Popluhar, Josef Masopust (46 Jim Baxter), Raymond Kopa (59 Uwe Seeler), Denis Law, Alfredo Di Stefano, Eusebio (46 Ferenc Puskas), Francisco Gento.

**Goals**: Terence Lionel Paine (77), James Peter Greaves (86)

### 374. 20.11.1963   Home Championship
**ENGLAND v NORTHERN IRELAND 8-3** (4-1)

*Wembley, London*

Referee: Leo Callaghan (Wales)   Attendance: 55,000

**ENGLAND**: Gordon Banks, James Christopher Armfield (Cap), Robert Anthony Thomson, Gordon Milne, Maurice Norman, Robert Frederick Moore, Terence Lionel Paine, James Peter Greaves, Robert Alfred Smith, George Edward Eastham, Robert Charlton.   Manager: Alfred Ramsey

**NORTHERN IRELAND**: Harry Gregg, Edward James Magill, John Parke, Martin Harvey, William John Terence Neill, William James McCullough, William Bingham, William Humphries, Samuel J. Wilson, John Andrew Crossan, Matthew James Hill.   Manager: Robert Peacock

**Goals**: Terry Paine (2, 37, 61), Jimmy Greaves (20, 30, 60, 65), Robert Alfred Smith (46) /
John Andrew Crossan (44), Samuel J. Wilson (74, 85)

### 375. 11.04.1964   Home Championship
**SCOTLAND v ENGLAND 1-0** (0-0)

*Hampden Park, Glasgow*

Referee: Leopold Sylvain Horn (Holland)   Att: 133,245

**SCOTLAND**: Robert Campbell Forsyth, Alexander William Hamilton, James Kennedy, John Greig, William McNeill (Cap), James Curran Baxter, William Henderson, John Anderson White, Alan John Gilzean, Denis Law, David Wilson.   Manager: John Miller McColl

**ENGLAND**: Gordon Banks, James Christopher Armfield (Cap), Ramon Wilson, Gordon Milne, Maurice Norman, Robert Frederick Moore, Terence Lionel Paine, Roger Hunt, John Joseph Byrne, George Edward Eastham, Robert Charlton.   Manager: Alfred Ramsey

**Goal**: Alan John Gilzean (72)

### 376. 06.05.1964
**ENGLAND v URUGUAY 2-1** (1-0)

*Wembley, London*

Referee: István Zsolt (Hungary)   Attendance: 55,000

**ENGLAND**: Gordon Banks, George Reginald Cohen, Ramon Wilson, Gordon Milne, Maurice Norman, Robert Frederick Moore (Cap), Terence Lionel Paine, James Peter Greaves, John Joseph Byrne, George Edward Eastham, Robert Charlton.   Manager: Alfred Ramsey

**URUGUAY**: Walter Taibo, William Ruben Martínez, Nelson Díaz, Héctor Carlos Cincunegui, Darcy Pereira, Elbio Ricardo Pavoni, Nelson Flores, Julio César Cortés, Alberto Pedro Spencer, Roberto Gil, Juan Pintos.   Trainer: Rafael Milans

**Goals**: Johnny Byrne (43, 47) / Alberto Pedro Spencer (78)

377.  17.05.1964

**PORTUGAL v ENGLAND  3-4**  (1-2)

*Nacional, Lisboa*

Referee:  Juan Gardeazabal (Spain)    Attendance:  40,000

**PORTUGAL**:  Alberto Costa Pereira, Alberto Augusto Antunes Festa, GERMANO de Figueiredo, VICENTE Lucas, Fernando da Conceição Cruz, Mário Esteves Coluna (Cap), CUSTÓDIO João PINTO (43 HERNÂNI Ferreira da Silva), JOSÉ AUGUSTO Pinto de Almeida, EUSÉBIO da Silva Ferreira, José Augusto da Costa Sénica Torres, António SIMÕES da Costa.    Trainer:  José Maria Antunes

**ENGLAND**:  Gordon Banks, George Reginald Cohen, Ramon Wilson, Gordon Milne, Maurice Norman, Robert Frederick Moore (Cap), Peter Thompson, James Peter Greaves, John Joseph Byrne, George Edward Eastham, Robert Charlton.    Manager:  Alfred Ramsey

**Goals**:  Torres (18, 47), Eusébio (53) / Robert Charlton (18), John Joseph Byrne (44, 60, 88)


378.  24.05.1964

**REPUBLIC OF IRELAND v ENGLAND  1-3**  (1-2)

*Dalymount Park, Dublin*

Referee:  Robert Holley Davidson (Scotland)    Att:  45,000

**IRELAND**:  Noel Michael Dwyer, Anthony Peter Dunne, Noel Eucharia Cantwell (Cap), Frederick Strahan, William Browne, Michael McGrath, John Michael Giles, Matthew Andrew McEvoy, Edward Bailham, Patrick Ambrose, Joseph Haverty (5 Ronald Whelan).

**ENGLAND**:  Anthony Keith Waiters, George Reginald Cohen, Ramon Wilson, Gordon Milne, Ronald Flowers, Robert Frederick Moore (Cap), Peter Thompson, James Peter Greaves, John Joseph Byrne, George Edward Eastham, Robert Charlton.    Manager:  Alfred Ramsey

**Goals**:  Frederick Strahan (41) / George Edward Eastham (8), John Joseph Byrne (22), James Peter Greaves (55)


379.  27.05.1964

**U.S.A. v ENGLAND  0-10**  (0-4)

*Downing, New York*

Referee:  Ray Morgan (Canada)    Attendance:  5,000

**U.S.A.**:  Uwe Schwart, John Borodiak, Andrew Racz, Horst Rick, Justo Garcia, Charles Horvath, Walter Chyzowych, Mike Noha, Andrew Mate, Edward Murphy, Richard Wild.    Trainer:  John Herberger

**ENGLAND**:  Gordon Banks, George Reginald Cohen, Robert Anthony Thomson, Michael Alfred Bailey, Maurice Norman, Ronald Flowers (Cap), Terence Lionel Paine, Roger Hunt, Frederick Pickering, George Edward Eastham (33 Robert Charlton), Peter Thompson.    Manager:  Alfred Ramsey

**Goals**:  Roger Hunt (4, 22, 53, 64), Fred Pickering (6, 47, 74), Terence Lionel Paine (49, 69), Robert Charlton (68)


380.  30.05.1964    Brazil Jubilee

**BRAZIL v ENGLAND  5-1**  (1-0)

*Maracana, Rio de Janeiro*

Referee:  Pierre Schwinte (France)    Attendance:  77,000

**BRAZIL**:  GILMAR dos Santos Neves, CARLOS ALBERTO Tôrres, Hércules BRITO Ruas, Joel Camargo, RILDO da Costa Menezes, ROBERTO DIAS Branco, GÉRSON de Oliveira Nunes, Júlio Botelho "Julinho", Edvaldo Izídio Neto "Vavá", Edson Arantes do Nascimento "Pelé", RINALDO Luís Dias Amorim.    Trainer:  Vicente Feola

**ENGLAND**:  Anthony Keith Waiters, George Reginald Cohen, Ramon Wilson, Gordon Milne, Maurice Norman, Robert Frederick Moore (Cap), Peter Thompson, James Peter Greaves, John Joseph Byrne, George Edward Eastham, Robert Charlton.    Manager:  Alfred Ramsey

**Goal**:  RINALDO Luís Dias Amorim (35, 59), Edson Arantes do Nascimento "Pelé" (63), Júlio Botelho "Julinho" (68), ROBERTO DIAS Branco (88) / James Peter Greaves (47)


381.  04.06.1964    Brazil Jubilee

**ENGLAND v PORTUGAL  1-1**  (0-1)

*Pacaembu, Sao Paulo*

Referee:  Armando Marques (Brazil)    Attendance:  25,000

**ENGLAND**:  Gordon Banks, Robert Anthony Thomson, Ramon Wilson, Ronald Flowers, Maurice Norman, Robert Frederick Moore (Cap), Terence Lionel Paine, James Peter Greaves, John Joseph Byrne, Roger Hunt, Peter Thompson.    Manager:  Alfred Ramsey

**PORTUGAL**:  AMÉRICO Ferreira Lopes, Alberto Augusto Antunes Festa, JOSÉ ALEXANDRE da Silva BAPTISTA, JOSÉ CARLOS da Silva, Manuel Pedro Gomes, Fernando Mamede Mendes (30 VICENTE Lucas), Mário Esteves Coluna (Cap), JOSÉ AUGUSTO Pinto de Almeida, EUSÉBIO da Silva Ferreira, José Augusto da Costa Sénica Torres, Fernando PERES da Silva.    Trainer:  José Maria Antunes

**Sent off**:  José Augusto da Costa Sénica Torres (70)

**Goals**:  Roger Hunt (60) / Fernando PERES da Silva (42)

382. 06.06.1964    Brazil Jubilee
**ARGENTINA v ENGLAND  1-0**  (0-0)

*Maracana, Rio de Janeiro*

Referee: Leopold Sylvain Horn (Holland)    Att: 15,000

**ARGENTINA**: Amadeo Raúl Carrizo, José Manuel Ramos Delgado (Cap), Miguel Ángel Vidal, Carmelo Simeone, Antonio Ubaldo Rattín, Abel Omar Vieytez, Ermindo Ángel Onega, Alberto Rendo, Pedro Prospitti (40 Mario Norberto Chaldú), Alfredo Hugo Rojas, Roberto Marcelo Telch. Trainer: José María Minella

**ENGLAND**: Gordon Banks, Robert Anthony Thomson, Ramon Wilson, Gordon Milne, Maurice Norman, Robert Frederick Moore (Cap), Peter Thompson, James Peter Greaves, John Joseph Byrne, George Edward Eastham, Robert Charlton. Manager: Alfred Ramsey

**Goal**: Alfredo Hugo Rojas (66)


383. 03.10.1964    Home Championship
**NORTHERN IRELAND v ENGLAND  3-4**  (0-4)

*Windsor Park, Belfast*

Referee: W. Brittle (Scotland)    Attendance: 58,000

**NORTHERN IRELAND**: Patrick Anthony Jennings, Edward James Magill, Alexander Russell Elder, Martin Harvey, William John Terence Neill, William James McCullough, George Best, John Andrew Crossan, Samuel Wilson, James Christopher McLaughlin, Robert Munn Braithwaite.

**ENGLAND**: Gordon Banks, George Reginald Cohen, Robert Anthony Thomson, Gordon Milne, Maurice Norman, Robert Frederick Moore (Cap), Terence Lionel Paine, James Peter Greaves, Frederick Pickering, Robert Charlton, Peter Thompson.    Manager: Alfred Ramsey

**Goals**: Samuel Wilson (52), James C. McLaughlin (55, 75) / Frederick Pickering (3), James Peter Greaves (12, 16, 24)


384. 21.10.1964
**ENGLAND v BELGIUM  2-2**  (1-2)

*Wembley, London*

Referee: Concetto Lo Bello (Italia)    Attendance: 55,000

**ENGLAND**: Anthony Keith Waiters, George Reginald Cohen, Robert Anthony Thomson, Gordon Milne, Maurice Norman, Robert Frederick Moore (Cap), Peter Thompson, James Peter Greaves, Frederick Pickering, Terence Frederick Venables, Alan Thomas Hinton.    Manager: Alfred Ramsey

**BELGIUM**: Jean Nicolay, Georges Heylens, Laurent Verbiest, Jean Plaskie, Jean Cornelis, Gérard Sulon, Joseph Jurion (Cap), Frans Vermeyen, Paul Van Himst, Paul Vandenberg, Wilfried Puis.    Trainer: Arthur Ceeulers

**Goals**: Frederick Pickering (31), Alan Thomas Hinton (70) / Jean Cornelis (22), Paul Van Himst (42)


385. 18.11.1964    Home Championship
**ENGLAND v WALES  2-1**  (1-0)

*Wembley, London*

Referee: Thomas Mitchell (Northern Ireland)    Att: 40,000

**ENGLAND**: Anthony Keith Waiters, George Reginald Cohen, Robert Anthony Thomson, Michael Alfred Bailey, Ronald Flowers (Cap), Gerald Morton Young, Peter Thompson, Roger Hunt, Frank Wignall, John Joseph Byrne, Alan Thomas Hinton.    Manager: Alfred Ramsey

**WALES**: Anthony Horace Millington, Stuart Grenville Williams, Graham Evan Williams, William Terence Hennessey, Harold Michael England, Barrington Gerard Hole, Ronald Raymond Rees, Ronald Tudor Davies, Ronald Wyn Davies, Ivor John Allchurch, Clifford William Jones. Trainer: David Bowen

**Goals**: Frank Wignall (18, 60) / Clifford William Jones (75)


386. 09.12.1964
**HOLLAND v ENGLAND  1-1**  (0-0)

*Olympisch, Amsterdam*

Referee: Joseph Hannet (Belgium)    Attendance: 60,000

**HOLLAND**: Eddy Pieters Graafland, Frits Flinkevleugel, Rinus Israël, Daan Schrijvers (Cap), Cor Veldhoen, Bennie Muller, Piet Fransen, Klaas Nuninga, Hennie van Nee, Frans Bouwmeester, Coen Moulijn.    Trainer: Denis Neville

**ENGLAND**: Anthony Keith Waiters, George Reginald Cohen, Robert Anthony Thomson, Alan Patrick Mullery, Maurice Norman, Ronald Flowers (Cap), Peter Thompson, James Peter Greaves, Frank Wignall, Terence Frederick Venables, Robert Charlton.    Manager: Alfred Ramsey

**Goals**: Coen Moulijn (77) / James Peter Greaves (85)


387. 10.04.1965    Home Championship
**ENGLAND v SCOTLAND  2-2**  (2-1)

*Wembley, London*

Referee: István Zsolt (Hungary)    Attendance: 98,199

**ENGLAND**: Gordon Banks, George Reginald Cohen, Ramon Wilson, Norbert Peter Stiles, John "Jack" Charlton, Robert Frederick Moore (Cap), Peter Thompson, James Peter Greaves, Barry John Bridges, John Joseph Byrne, Robert Charlton. Manager: Alfred Ramsey

**SCOTLAND**: William Dallas Fyfe Brown, Alexander William Hamilton, Edward Graham McCreadie, Patrick Timothy Crerand, William McNeill (Cap), John Greig, William Henderson, Robert Young Collins, Ian St. John, Denis Law, David Wilson.    Manager: John Miller McColl

**Goals**: Robert Charlton (25), James Peter Greaves (35) / Denis Law (41), Ian St. John (59)

388. 05.05.1965
**ENGLAND v HUNGARY 1-0** (1-0)
*Wembley, London*
Referee: Pierre Schwinte (France)   Attendance: 70,000
**ENGLAND**: Gordon Banks, George Reginald Cohen, Ramon Wilson, Norbert Peter Stiles, John "Jack" Charlton, Robert Frederick Moore (Cap), Terence Lionel Paine, James Peter Greaves, Barry John Bridges, George Edward Eastham, John Michael Connelly.   Manager: Alfred Ramsey
**HUNGARY**: József Gelei, Sándor Mátrai, Kálmán Mészöly, László Sárosi, István Nagy, Ferenc Sipos, János Göröcs, Zoltán Varga, Ferenc Bene, Ferenc Nógrádi, Máté Fenyvesi dr. Trainer: Lajos Baróti
**Goal**: James Peter Greaves (17)

389. 09.05.1965
**YUGOSLAVIA v ENGLAND 1-1** (1-1)
*Crvena Zvezda, Beograd*
Referee: Gerö (Hungary)   Attendance: 70,000
**YUGOSLAVIA**: Zlatko Škorić, Vladimir Durković, Fahrudin Jusufi (Cap), Radoslav Bečejac, Velibor Vasović, Vladimir Popović, Vladimir Lukarić (46.Silvester Takač), Slaven Zambata, Vladimir Kovačević, Milan Galić, Dragan Džajić. Selection committee: Aleksandar Tirnanić, Milan Antolković, Abdulah Gegić, Miljan Miljanić
**ENGLAND**: Gordon Banks, George Reginald Cohen, Ramon Wilson, Norbert Peter Stiles, John "Jack" Charlton, Robert Frederick Moore (Cap), Terence Lionel Paine, James Peter Greaves, Barry John Bridges, Alan James Ball, John Michael Connelly.   Manager: Alfred Ramsey
**Goals**: Vladimir Kovačević (15) / Barry John Bridges (20)

390. 12.05.1965
**WEST GERMANY v ENGLAND 0-1** (0-1)
*Sachsenstadion, Nürnberg*
Referee: István Zsolt (Hungary)   Attendance: 65,000
**WEST GERMANY**: Hans Tilkowski, Josef Piontek, Horst-Dieter Höttges, Willi Schulz (Cap), Klaus-Dieter Sieloff, Max Lorenz (42 Heinz Steinmann), Karl-Heinz Thielen, Werner Krämer, Walter Rodekamp, Wolfgang Overath, Heinz Hornig. Trainer: Helmut Schön
**ENGLAND**: Gordon Banks, George Reginald Cohen, Ramon Wilson, Ronald Flowers, John "Jack" Charlton, Robert Frederick Moore (Cap), Terence Lionel Paine, Alan James Ball, Michael David Jones, George Edward Eastham, Derek William Temple.   Manager: Alfred Ramsey
**Goal**: Terence Lionel Paine (36)

391. 16.05.1965
**SWEDEN v ENGLAND 1-2** (1-1)
*Nya Ullevi, Göteborg*
Referee: Henri Faucheux (France)   Attendance: 18,975
**SWEDEN**: Arne Arvidsson, Hans Rosander, Lennart Wing, Hans Mild, Orvar Bergmark (Cap), Björn Nordqvist, Leif Eriksson, Henry Larsson, Agne Simonsson, Björn Carlsson, Örjan Persson.   Trainer: Lennart Nyman
**ENGLAND**: Gordon Banks, George Reginald Cohen, Ramon Wilson, Norbert Peter Stiles, John "Jack" Charlton, Robert Frederick Moore (Cap), Terence Lionel Paine, Alan James Ball, Michael David Jones, George Edward Eastham, John Michael Connelly.   Manager: Alfred Ramsey
**Goals**: Leif Eriksson (37) / Alan James Ball (19), John Michael Connelly (72)

392. 02.10.1965   Home Championship
**WALES v ENGLAND 0-0**
*Ninian Park, Cardiff*
Referee: Archibald F. Webster (Scotland)   Att: 30,000
**WALES**: Gareth Sprake, Peter Joseph Rodrigues, Colin Robert Green, William Terence Hennessey, Harold Michael England, Barrington Gerard Hole, Ronald Raymond Rees, Thomas Royston Vernon, Ronald Wyn Davies, Ivor John Allchurch, Gilbert Ivor Reece.
**ENGLAND**: Ronald Derrick Springettt, George Reginald Cohen, Ramon Wilson, Norbert Peter Stiles, John "Jack" Charlton, Robert Frederick Moore (Cap), Terence Lionel Paine, James Peter Greaves, Alan Peacock, Robert Charlton, John Michael Connelly.   Manager: Alfred Ramsey

393. 20.10.1965
**ENGLAND v AUSTRIA 2-3** (1-0)
*Wembley, London*
Referee: Pierre Schwinte (France)   Attendance: 65,000
**ENGLAND**: Ronald Derrick Springettt, George Reginald Cohen, Ramon Wilson, Norbert Peter Stiles, John "Jack" Charlton, Robert Frederick Moore (Cap), Terence Lionel Paine, James Peter Greaves, Barry John Bridges, Robert Charlton, John Michael Connelly.   Manager: Alfred Ramsey
**AUSTRIA**: Gernot Fraydl, Robert Sara, Johann Frank (29 Alfons Dirnberger), Walter Stamm, Walter Ludescher, Franz Hasil, Ewald Ullmann, Anton Fritsch, Johann Buzek, Rudolf Flögel, Adolf Macek.   Trainer: Eduard Frühwirth
**Goals**: Robert Charlton (3), John Michael Connelly (59) / Rudolf Flögel (53), Anton Fritsch (73, 80)

### 394. 10.11.1965   Home Championship
**ENGLAND v NORTHERN IRELAND 2-1** (1-1)

*Wembley, London*

Referee: Leo Callaghan (Wales)   Attendance: 70,000

**ENGLAND**: Gordon Banks, George Reginald Cohen, Ramon Wilson, Norbert Peter Stiles, John "Jack" Charlton, Robert Frederick Moore (Cap), Peter Thompson, Joseph Henry Baker, Alan Peacock, Robert Charlton, John Michael Connelly.   Manager: Alfred Ramsey

**NORTHERN IRELAND**: Patrick Anthony Jennings, Edward James Magill, Alexander Russell Elder, Martin Harvey, William John Terence Neill, James Joseph Nicholson, James McIlroy, John Andrew Crossan, William John Irvine, Alexander Derek Dougan, George Best.   Manager: Robert Peacock

**Goals**: Joseph Henry Baker (23), Alan Peacock (73) / William John Irvine (20)


### 395. 08.12.1965
**SPAIN v ENGLAND 0-2** (0-1)

*Santiago Bernabéu, Madrid*

Referee: Concetto Lo Bello (Italy)   Attendance: 30,000

**SPAIN**: José Angel Iribar, Severino Reija, Fernando Olivella (Cap), Manuel Sanchis, Jesús Glaría, Ignacio Zoco, José Armando Ufarte, ADELARDO Rodríguez Sánchez, Fernando Ansola, MARCELINO Martínez Cao, Carlos Lapetra (35 Nemesio Martín "Neme").   Trainer: José Villalonga

**ENGLAND**: Gordon Banks, George Reginald Cohen, Ramon Wilson, Norbert Peter Stiles, John "Jack" Charlton, Robert Frederick Moore (Cap), Alan James Ball, Roger Hunt, Joseph Henry Baker (35 Norman Hunter), George Edward Eastham, Robert Charlton.   Manager: Alfred Ramsey

**Goals**: Joseph Henry Baker (8), Roger Hunt (55)


### 396. 05.01.1966
**ENGLAND v POLAND 1-1** (0-1)

*Goodison Park, Liverpool*

Referee: Joseph Hannet (Belgium)   Attendance: 47,839

**ENGLAND**: Gordon Banks, George Reginald Cohen, Ramon Wilson, Norbert Peter Stiles, John "Jack" Charlton, Robert Frederick Moore (Cap), Alan James Ball, Roger Hunt, Joseph Henry Baker, George Edward Eastham, Gordon Harris.   Manager: Alfred Ramsey

**POLAND**: Marian Szeja, Jacek Gmoch, Henryk Brejza, Stanisław Oślizło (Cap), Andrzej Rewilak, Piotr Suski, Zygmunt Schmidt, Jan Wilim II (39 Jan Banaś), Józef Gałeczka, Jerzy Sadek, Janusz Kowalik.   Trainer: Ryszard Koncewicz

**Goals**: Robert Frederick Moore (74) / Jerzy Sadek (43)


### 397. 23.02.1966
**ENGLAND v WEST GERMANY 1-0** (1-0)

*Wembley, London*

Referee: Pieter Roomer (Holland)   Attendance: 75,000

**ENGLAND**: Gordon Banks, George Reginald Cohen, Keith Robert Newton (44 Ramon Wilson), Robert Frederick Moore (Cap), John "Jack" Charlton, Norman Hunter, Alan James Ball, Roger Hunt, Norbert Peter Stiles, Geoffrey Charles Hurst, Robert Charlton.   Manager: Alfred Ramsey

**WEST GERMANY**: Hans Tilkowski, Friedel Lutz, Max Lorenz, Willi Schulz, Wolfgang Weber, Horst Szymaniak (Cap), Werner Krämer, Franz Beckenbauer, Siegfried Held, Günter Netzer, Heinz Hornig (44 Alfred Heiß).   Trainer: Helmut Schön

**Goal**: Norbert Peter Stiles (41)


### 398. 02.04.1966   Home Championship
**SCOTLAND v ENGLAND 3-4** (1-2)

*Hampden Park, Glasgow*

Referee: Henri Faucheux (France)   Attendance: 123,052

**ENGLAND**: Gordon Banks, George Reginald Cohen, Keith Robert Newton, Norbert Peter Stiles, John "Jack" Charlton, Robert Frederick Moore (Cap), Alan James Ball, Roger Hunt, Robert Charlton, Geoffrey Charles Hurst, John Michael Connelly.   Manager: Alfred Ramsey

**SCOTLAND**: Robert Ferguson, John Greig (Cap), Thomas Gemmell, Robert White Murdoch, Ronald McKinnon, James Curran Baxter, James Connolly Johnstone, Denis Law, William Semple Brown Wallace, William John Bremner, William McClure Johnston.   Manager: John Prentice

**Goals**: Denis Law (42), James Connolly Johnstone (57, 82) / Geoff Hurst (18), Roger Hunt (34, 47), Robert Charlton (73)


### 399. 04.05.1966
**ENGLAND v YUGOSLAVIA 2-0** (2-0)

*Wembley, London*

Referee: Johannes Malka (East Germany)   Att: 55,000

**ENGLAND**: Gordon Banks, James Christopher Armfield (Cap), Ramon Wilson, Martin Stanford Peters, John "Jack" Charlton, Norman Hunter, Terence Lionel Paine, James Peter Greaves, Robert Charlton, Geoffrey Charles Hurst, Robert Victor Tambling.   Manager: Alfred Ramsey

**YUGOSLAVIA**: Milutin Šoškić, Vinko Kuci, Živorad Jevtić, Radoslav Bečejac, Branko Rašović, Velibor Vasović, Spasoje Samardžić, Vojislav Melić, Džemaludin Mušović, Josip Skoblar (Cap), Dragan Džajić.   Selection committee: Aleksandar Tirnanić, Milan Antolković, Miljan Miljanić

**Goals**: James Peter Greaves (10), Robert Charlton (35)

**400. 26.06.1966**
**FINLAND v ENGLAND 0-3** (0-2)
*Olympic, Helsinki*

Referee: Frede Hansen (Denmark)   Attendance: 12,899

**FINLAND:** Martti Halme, Pertti Mäkipää, Rainer Aho, Timo Kautonen, Reijo Kanerva, Seppo Kilponen, Markku Kumpulampi, Matti Mäkelä (Cap), Markku Hyvärinen, Aulis Laine, Antero Hyttinen.   Trainer: Olavi Laaksonen

**ENGLAND:** Gordon Banks, James Christopher Armfield (Cap), Ramon Wilson, Martin Stanford Peters, John "Jack" Charlton, Norman Hunter, Ian Robert Callaghan, Roger Hunt, Robert Charlton, Geoffrey Charles Hurst, Alan James Ball.   Manager: Alfred Ramsey

**Goals:** Martin Stanford Peters (42), Roger Hunt (44), John "Jack" Charlton (89)


**401. 29.06.1966**
**NORWAY v ENGLAND 1-6** (1-5)
*Ullevaal, Oslo*

Referee: Hans Carlsson (Sweden)   Attendance: 29,534

**NORWAY:** Sverre Andersen II (42 Kjell Kaspersen), Roar Johansen, Arild Mathisen, Arne Pedersen, Finn Thorsen, Edgar Stakset, Harald Sunde, Harald Berg, Ole Stavrum, Olav Nilsen, Erik Johansen.   Trainer: Ragnar Larsen

**ENGLAND:** Ronald Derrick Springettt, George Reginald Cohen, Gerald Byrne, Norbert Peter Stiles, Ronald Flowers, Robert Frederick Moore (Cap), Terence Lionel Paine, James Peter Greaves, Robert Charlton, Roger Hunt, John Michael Connelly.   Manager: Alfred Ramsey

**Goals:** Harald Sunde (4) / Jimmy Greaves (19, 21, 22, 37), Robert Frederick Moore (42), John Michael Connelly (74)


**402. 03.07.1966**
**DENMARK v ENGLAND 0-2** (0-1)
*Idraetsparken, København*

Referee: Ray Morgan (Canada)   Attendance: 32,000

**DENMARK:** Leif Nielsen, Johnny Hansen, Leif Hartwig (Cap), John Petersen, Henning Boel, Niels Møller, Bent Schmidt-Hansen, John Steen Olsen, Henning Enoksen, Tom Søndergaard, Ulrik Le Fevre.   Trainer: Poul Petersen

**ENGLAND:** Peter Phillip Bonetti, George Reginald Cohen, Ramon Wilson, Norbert Peter Stiles, John "Jack" Charlton, Robert Frederick Moore (Cap), Alan James Ball, James Peter Greaves, Geoffrey Charles Hurst, George Edward Eastham, John Michael Connelly.   Manager: Alfred Ramsey

**Goals:** John "Jack" Charlton (44), George Eastham (61)


**403. 05.07.1966**
**POLAND v ENGLAND 0-1** (0-1)
*Slaski, Chorzów*

Referee: István Zsolt (Hungary)   Attendance: 70,000

**POLAND:** Marian Szeja, Roman Strzałkowski, Henryk Brejza, Zygmunt Anczok, Walter Winkler, Jacek Gmoch, Piotr Suski, Józef Gałeczka, Włodzimierz Lubański (46 Jerzy Wilim I), Jan Liberda (Cap), Jerzy Kowalik.
Trainer: Antoni Brzeźańczyk

**ENGLAND:** Gordon Banks, George Reginald Cohen, Ramon Wilson, Norbert Peter Stiles, John "Jack" Charlton, Robert Frederick Moore (Cap), Alan James Balll, James Peter Greaves, Robert Charlton, Roger Hunt, Martin Stanford Peters.   Manager: Alfred Ramsey

**Goal:** Roger Hunt (14)


**404. 11.07.1966   8th World Cup, 1st Round**
**ENGLAND v URUGUAY 0-0**
*Wembley, London*

Referee: István Zsolt (Hungary)   Attendance: 87,148

**ENGLAND:** Gordon Banks, George Reginald Cohen, Ramon Wilson, Norbert Peter Stiles, John "Jack" Charlton, Robert Frederick Moore (Cap), Alan James Ball, James Peter Greaves, Robert Charlton, Roger Hunt, John Michael Connelly.   Manager: Alfred Ramsey

**URUGUAY:** Ladislao Mazurkiewicz, Florencio Horacio Troche (Cap), Jorge Carlos Manicera, Ignacio Luis Ubiña, Néstor Gonçalves, Omar Caetano, Julio César Cortés, Milton Viera, Héctor Jesús Silva, Pedro Virgilio Rocha, Domingo Salvador Pérez.   Trainer: Ondino Viera


**405. 16.07.1966   8th World Cup, 1st Round**
**ENGLAND v MEXICO 2-0** (1-0)
*Wembley, London*

Referee: Concetto Lo Bello (Italy)   Attendance: 92,570

**ENGLAND:** Gordon Banks, George Reginald Cohen, Ramon Wilson, Norbert Peter Stiles, John "Jack" Charlton, Robert Frederick Moore (Cap), Terence Lionel Paine, James Peter Greaves, Robert Charlton, Roger Hunt, Martin Stanford Peters.   Manager: Alfred Ramsey

**MEXICO:** Ignacio Calderón, Arturo Chaires, Gustavo Peña (Cap), Jesús del Muro, Gabriel Núñez, Guillermo Hernández, Ignacio Jáuregui, Isidoro Díaz, Salvador Reyes, Enrique Borja, Aarón Padilla.   Trainer: Ignacio Tréllez

**Goals:** Robert Charlton (38), Roger Hunt (75)

406.  20.07.1966    8th World Cup,  1st Round
**ENGLAND v FRANCE  2-0**  (1-0)
*Wembley, London*

Referee: Arturo Yamasaki (Peru)    Attendance: 98,720

**ENGLAND**:  Gordon Banks, George Reginald Cohen, Ramon Wilson, Norbert Peter Stiles, John "Jack" Charlton, Robert Frederick Moore (Cap), Ian Robert Callaghan, James Peter Greaves, Robert Charlton, Roger Hunt, Martin Stanford Peters.   Manager:  Alfred Ramsey

**FRANCE**:  Marcel Aubour, Jean Djorkaeff, Marcel Artelesa (Cap), Robert Budzinski, Bernard Bosquier, Joseph Bonnel, Robert Herbin, Jacques Simon, Yves Herbet, Philippe Gondet, Gérard Hausser.    Trainer: Henri Guérin

**Goals**:  Roger Hunt (38, 75)


407.  23.07.1966    8th World Cup,  Quarter-Finals
**ENGLAND v ARGENTINA  1-0**  (0-0)
*Wembley, London*

Referee: Rudolf Kreitlein (West Germany)    Att: 90,584

**ENGLAND**:  Gordon Banks, George Reginald Cohen, Ramon Wilson, Norbert Peter Stiles, John "Jack" Charlton, Robert Frederick Moore (Cap), Alan James Ball, Geoffrey Charles Hurst, Robert Charlton, Roger Hunt, Martin Stanford Peters.   Manager:  Alfred Ramsey

**ARGENTINA**:  Antonio Roma, Roberto Oscar Ferreiro, Roberto Alfredo Perfumo, José Rafael Albrecht, Silvio Marzolini, Jorge Raúl Solari, Antonio Ubaldo Rattín (Cap), Alberto Mario González, Ermindo Ángel Onega, Luis Alfredo Artime, Oscar Tomás Más.    Trainer: Juan Carlos Lorenzo

**Sent off**: Antonio Ubaldo Rattín (35)

**Goal**:  Geoffrey Charles Hurst (79)


408.  26.07.1966    8th World Cup,  Semi-Finals
**ENGLAND v PORTUGAL  2-1**  (1-0)
*Wembley, London*

Referee: Pierre Schwinte (France)    Attendance: 94,493

**ENGLAND**:  Gordon Banks, George Reginald Cohen, Ramon Wilson, Norbert Peter Stiles, John "Jack" Charlton, Robert Frederick Moore (Cap), Alan James Ball, Geoffrey Charles Hurst, Robert Charlton, Roger Hunt, Martin Stanford Peters.   Manager:  Alfred Ramsey

**PORTUGAL**:  José Pereira, Alberto Augusto Antunes Festa, José ALEXANDRE da Silva BAPTISTA, JOSÉ CARLOS da Silva, HILÁRIO Rosário da Conceição, Jaime da Silva Graça, Mário Esteves Coluna (Cap), JOSÉ AUGUSTO Pinto de Almeida, EUSÉBIO da Silva Ferreira, José Augusto da Costa Sénica Torres, António Simões.    Trainer: Otto Glória

**Goals**:  Robert Charlton (30, 79) / Eusébio (82 pen)


409.  30.07.1966    8th World Cup,  Final
**ENGLAND v WEST GERMANY  4-2**  (1-1, 2-2) (AET)
*Wembley, London*

Referee: Gottfried Dienst (Switzerland)    Attendance: 96,924

**ENGLAND**:  Gordon Banks, George Reginald Cohen, Ramon Wilson, Norbert Peter Stiles, John "Jack" Charlton, Robert Frederick Moore (Cap), Alan James Ball, Geoffrey Charles Hurst, Robert Charlton, Roger Hunt, Martin Stanford Peters.   Manager:  Alfred Ramsey

**WEST GERMANY**:  Hans Tilkowski, Horst-Dieter Höttges, Karl-Heinz Schnellinger, Franz Beckenbauer, Willi Schulz, Wolfgang Weber, Helmut Haller, Uwe Seeler (Cap), Siegfried Held, Wolfgang Overath, Lothar Emmerich.   Trainer: Helmut Schön

**Goals**:  Geoff Hurst (17, 100, 120), Martin Peters (78) / Helmut Haller (12), Wolfgang Weber (89)


410.  22.10.1966    3rd European Champs Qualifiers
**NORTHERN IRELAND v ENGLAND  0-2**  (0-1)
*Windsor Park, Belfast*

Referee: Robert Holley Davidson (Scotland)    Att: 48,600

**NORTHERN IRELAND**:  Patrick Anthony Jennings (46 William Stewart McFaul), John Parke, Alexander Russell Elder, Samuel John Todd, Martin Harvey, William James McCullough, William Ferguson, John Andrew Crossan, William John Irvine, Alexander Derek Dougan, George Best.

**ENGLAND**:  Gordon Banks, George Reginald Cohen, Ramon Wilson, Norbert Peter Stiles, John "Jack" Charlton, Robert Frederick Moore (Cap), Alan James Ball, Geoffrey Charles Hurst, Robert Charlton, Roger Hunt, Martin Stanford Peters.   Manager:  Alfred Ramsey

**Sent off**:  William Ferguson

**Goals**:  Roger Hunt (40), Martin Stanford Peters (59)


411.  02.11.1966
**ENGLAND v CZECHOSLOVAKIA  0-0**
*Wembley, London*

Referee: Pieter Roomer (Holland)    Attendance: 75,000

**CZECHOSLOVAKIA**:  Ivo Viktor, Jan Lála, Alexander Horváth, Ján Popluhár (Cap), Vladimír Táborský, Ján Geleta, Andrej Kvašňák, František Veselý, Juraj Szikora, Edmund Schmidt (42 Ladislav Kuna), Jozef Adamec.   Trainer: Josef Marko

**ENGLAND**:  Gordon Banks, George Reginald Cohen, Ramon Wilson, Norbert Peter Stiles, John "Jack" Charlton, Robert Frederick Moore (Cap), Alan James Ball, Geoffrey Charles Hurst, Robert Charlton, Roger Hunt, Martin Stanford Peters.   Manager:  Alfred Ramsey

412.  16.11.1966    3rd European Champs Qualifiers
**ENGLAND v WALES  5-1**  (3-1)
*Wembley, London*

Referee: Thomas Wharton (Scotland)    Attendance: 75,380

**ENGLAND**: Gordon Banks, George Reginald Cohen, Ramon Wilson, Norbert Peter Stiles, John "Jack" Charlton, Robert Frederick Moore (Cap), Alan James Ball, Geoffrey Charles Hurst, Robert Charlton, Roger Hunt, Martin Stanford Peters. Manager: Alfred Ramsey

**WALES**: Anthony Horace Millington, Colin Robert Green, Graham Evan Williams, William Terence Hennessey, Harold Michael England, Barrington Gerard Hole, Ronald Raymond Rees, Ronald Wyn Davies, Ronald Tudor Davies, Clifford William Jones, Alan Leslie Jarvis.   Trainer: David Bowen

**Goals**: Geoffrey Charles Hurst (30, 34), Robert Charlton (43), William Terrence Hennessey (65 og), "Jack" Charlton (84) / Ronald Wyn Davies (36)


413.  15.04.1967    3rd European Champs Qualifiers
**ENGLAND v SCOTLAND  2-3**  (0-1)
*Wembley, London*

Referee: Gerhard Schulenburg (West Germany)    Att: 99,063

**ENGLAND**: Gordon Banks, George Reginald Cohen, Ramon Wilson, Norbert Peter Stiles, John "Jack" Charlton, Robert Frederick Moore (Cap), Alan James Ball, James Peter Greaves, Robert Charlton, Geoffrey Charles Hurst, Martin Stanford Peters.   Manager: Alfred Ramsey

**SCOTLAND**: Ronald Campbell Simpson, Thomas Gemmell, Edward Graham McCreadie, John Greig (Cap), Ronald McKinnon, William John Bremner, James McCalliog, Denis Law, William Semple Brown Wallace, James Curran Baxter, Robert Lennox.   Manager: Robert Brown

**Goals**: John "Jack" Charlton (84), Geoff Hurst (88) / Denis Law (27), Robert Lennox (78), James McCalliog (87)


414.  24.05.1967
**ENGLAND v SPAIN  2-0**  (0-0)
*Wembley, London*

Referee: István Zsolt (Hungary)    Attendance: 97,500

**ENGLAND**: Peter Phillip Bonetti, George Reginald Cohen, Keith Robert Newton, Alan Patrick Mullery, Brian Leslie Labone, Robert Frederick Moore (Cap), Alan James Ball, James Peter Greaves, Geoffrey Charles Hurst, Roger Hunt, John William Hollins.   Manager: Alfred Ramsey

**SPAIN**: José Angel Iribar, Manuel Sanchis, Francisco Fernández Rodríguez "Gallego", Severino Reija, José Luis Violeta, José Martínez "Pirri", Jesús Glaría, JOSÉ MARÍA García, Amancio Amaro, Ramón Moreno Grosso, Francisco Gento (Cap).   Trainer: Domingo Balmanya

**Goals**: James Peter Greaves (70), Roger Hunt (75)


415.  27.05.1967
**AUSTRIA v ENGLAND  0-1**  (0-1)
*Prater, Wien*

Referee: Michel Kitabdjian (France)    Attendance: 50,000

**AUSTRIA**: Roman Pichler, Helmut Wartusch, Walter Glechner, Gerhard Sturmberger, Erich Fak, Roland Eschelmüller, Peter Schmidt, Helmut Köglberger, Franz Wolny, Helmut Siber, Thomas Parits.
Trainers: Erwin Alge & Johann Pesser

**ENGLAND**: Peter Phillip Bonetti, Keith Robert Newton, Ramon Wilson, Alan Patrick Mullery, Brian Leslie Labone, Robert Frederick Moore (Cap), Alan James Ball, James Peter Greaves, Geoffrey Charles Hurst, Roger Hunt, Norman Hunter. Manager: Alfred Ramsey

**Goal**: Alan James Ball (21)


416.  21.10.1967    3rd European Champs Qualifiers
**WALES v ENGLAND  0-3**  (0-1)
*Ninian Park, Cardiff*

Referee: John Robertson Gordon (Scotland)    Att: 44,960

**WALES**: Gareth Sprake, Peter Joseph Rodrigues, Colin Robert Green, William Terence Hennessey, Harold Michael England, Barrington Gerard Hole, Ronald Raymond Rees, William Alan Durban, John Francis Mahoney, Thomas Royston Vernon, Clifford William Jones.   Trainer: David Bowen

**ENGLAND**: Gordon Banks, George Reginald Cohen, Keith Robert Newton, Alan Patrick Mullery, John "Jack" Charlton, Robert Frederick Moore (Cap), Alan James Ball, Roger Hunt, Robert Charlton, Geoffrey Charles Hurst, Martin Stanford Peters.   Manager: Alfred Ramsey

**Goals**: Martin Stanford Peters (34), Robert Charlton (87), Alan James Ball (90 pen)


417.  22.11.1967    3rd European Champs Qualifiers
**ENGLAND v NORTHERN IRELAND  2-0**  (1-0)
*Wembley, London*

Referee: Leo Callaghan (Wales)    Attendance: 85,000

**ENGLAND**: Gordon Banks, George Reginald Cohen, Ramon Wilson, Alan Patrick Mullery, David Sadler, Robert Frederick Moore (Cap), Peter Thompson, Roger Hunt, Robert Charlton, Geoffrey Charles Hurst, Martin Stanford Peters. Manager: Alfred Ramsey

**NORTHERN IRELAND**: Patrick Anthony Jennings, John Parke, Alexander Russell Elder, Arthur Stewart, William John Terence Neill, Martin Harvey, William Gibson Campbell, William John Irvine, Samuel Wilson, James Joseph Nicholson, David Clements.

**Goals**: Geoffrey Charles Hurst (43), Robert Charlton (62)

418.  06.12.1967
**ENGLAND v U.S.S.R.  2-2**  (1-2)
*Wembley, London*
Referee: Rudolf Kreitlein (West Germany)   Att: 93,000
**ENGLAND**: Gordon Banks, Cyril Barry Knowles, Ramon Wilson, Alan Patrick Mullery, David Sadler, Robert Frederick Moore (Cap), Alan James Ball, Roger Hunt, Robert Charlton, Geoffrey Charles Hurst, Martin Stanford Peters.   Manager: Alfred Ramsey
**U.S.S.R.**: Yuriy Pshenichnikov, Viktor Anichkin, Albert Shesternev (Cap), Murtaz Khurtzilava, Yuriy Istomin, Valeriy Voronin, Igor Chislenko, József Sabo, Eduard Streltzov, Anatoliy Banishevskiy, Eduard Maloféev.   Trainer: Mikhail Yakushin
**Goals**: Alan James Ball (23), Martin Stanford Peters (72) / Igor Chislenko (42, 44)


419.  24.02.1968   3rd European Champs Qualifiers
**SCOTLAND v ENGLAND  1-1**  (1-1)
*Hampden Park, Glasgow*
Referee: Laurens van Ravens (Holland)   Att: 134,000
**SCOTLAND**: Ronald Campbell Simpson, Thomas Gemmell, Edward Graham McCreadie, William McNeill, Ronald McKinnon, John Greig (Cap), Charles Cooke, William John Bremner, John Hughes, William McClure Johnston, Robert Lennox.   Manager: Robert Brown
**ENGLAND**: Gordon Banks, Keith Robert Newton, Ramon Wilson, Alan Patrick Mullery, Brian Leslie Labone, Robert Frederick Moore (Cap), Alan James Ball, Geoffrey Charles Hurst, Michael George Summerbee, Robert Charlton, Martin Stanford Peters.   Manager: Alfred Ramsey
**Goal**: John Hughes (39) / Martin Stanford Peters (20)


420.  03.04.1968   3rd European Championships – Quarter-Finals
**ENGLAND v SPAIN  1-0**  (0-0)
*Wembley, London*
Referee: Gilbert Droz (Switzerland)   Attendance: 100,000
**ENGLAND**: Gordon Banks, Cyril Barry Knowles, Ramon Wilson, Alan Patrick Mullery, John "Jack" Charlton, Robert Frederick Moore (Cap), Alan James Ball, Roger Hunt, Michael George Summerbee, Robert Charlton, Martin Stanford Peters.   Manager: Alfred Ramsey
**SPAIN**: Salvador Sadurní, José Ignacio Sáez, Francisco Fernández Rodríguez "Gallego", Juan Manuel Canós, José Martínez "Pirri", Ignacio Zoco (Cap), Manuel Polinario "Poli", Amancio Amaro, Fernando Ansola, Ramón Moreno Grosso, José Claramunt.   Trainer: Domingo Balmanya
**Goal**: Robert Charlton (84)


421.  08.05.1968   3rd European Championships – Quarter-Finals
**SPAIN v ENGLAND  1-2**  (0-0)
*Santiago Bernabéu, Madrid*
Referee: Josef Krnavec (Czechoslovakia)   Att: 120,000
**SPAIN**: Salvador Sadurní, José Ignacio Sáez, Francisco Fernández Rodríguez "Gallego", Juan Manuel Canós, José Martínez "Pirri", Ignacio Zoco, Joaquin Rifé, Amancio Amaro, Ramón Moreno Grosso, Manuel Velázquez, Francisco Gento (Cap).   Trainer: Domingo Balmanya
**ENGLAND**: Peter Phillip Bonetti, Keith Robert Newton, Ramon Wilson, Alan Patrick Mullery, Brian Leslie Labone, Robert Frederick Moore (Cap), Alan James Ball, Martin Stanford Peters, Robert Charlton, Roger Hunt, Norman Hunter.   Manager: Alfred Ramsey
**Goals**: Amancio (48) / Martin Stanford Peters (55), Norman Hunter (82)


422.  22.05.1968
**ENGLAND v SWEDEN  3-1**  (2-0)
*Wembley, London*
Referee: Othmar Huber (Switzerland)   Attendance: 72,500
**ENGLAND**: Alex Cyril Stepney, Keith Robert Newton, Cyril Barry Knowles, Alan Patrick Mullery, Brian Leslie Labone, Robert Frederick Moore (Cap), Colin Bell, Martin Stanford Peters, Robert Charlton (70 Geoffrey Charles Hurst), Roger Hunt, Norman Hunter.   Manager: Alfred Ramsey
**SWEDEN**: Sven-Gunnar Larsson (85 Nils Hult), Jan Karlsson, Krister Kristensson, Björn Nordqvist (Cap), Roland Grip, Bo Göran Larsson, Sven Lindman, Leif Eriksson, Inge Ejderstedt (80 Rolf Andersson II), Thomas Nordahl, Örjan Persson.   Trainer: Orvar Bergmark
**Goals**: Martin Stanford Peters (36), Robert Charlton (38), Roger Hunt (73) / Rolf Andersson (90)


423.  01.06.1968
**WEST GERMANY v ENGLAND  1-0**  (0-0)
*Niedersachsen, Hannover*
Referee: Laurens van Ravens (Holland)   Attendance: 79,124
**WEST GERMANY**: Horst Wolter, Hans-Hubert Vogts, Max Lorenz, Ludwig Müller, Klaus Fichtel, Wolfgang Weber, Bernd Dörfel, Franz Beckenbauer, Johannes Löhr, Wolfgang Overath (Cap), Georg Volkert.   Trainer: Helmut Schön
**ENGLAND**: Gordon Banks, Keith Robert Newton, Cyril Barry Knowles, Norman Hunter, Brian Leslie Labone, Robert Frederick Moore (Cap), Alan James Ball, Colin Bell, Michael George Summerbee, Geoffrey Charles Hurst, Peter Thompson.   Manager: Alfred Ramsey
**Goal**: Franz Beckenbauer (82)

**424.  05.06.1968   3rd European Championships – Semi-Finals**
**ENGLAND v YUGOSLAVIA  0-1**  (0-0)
*Comunale, Firenze*
Referee:  José María Ortiz de Mendibil (Spain)    Att: 21,834
**ENGLAND**: Gordon Banks, Keith Robert Newton, Ramon Wilson, Alan Patrick Mullery, Brian Leslie Labone, Robert Frederick Moore (Cap), Alan James Ball, Martin Stanford Peters, Robert Charlton, Roger Hunt, Norman Hunter.  Manager: Alfred Ramsey
**YUGOSLAVIA** Ilija Pantelić, Mirsad Fazlagić (Cap), Milan Damjanović, Miroslav Pavlović, Blagoje Paunović, Dragan Holcer, Ilija Petković, Ivica Osim, Vahidin Musemić, Dobrivoje Trivić, Dragan Džajić.   Trainer: Rajko Mitić
**Sent off**: Mullery (86)
**Goal**: Dragan Džajić (86)

**425.  08.06.1968   3rd European Championships – Bronze Medal Play-off**
**ENGLAND v U.S.S.R.  2-0**  (1-0)
*Olimpico, Roma*
Referee:  István Zsolt (Hungary)    Attendance: 50,000
**ENGLAND**: Gordon Banks, Thomas James Wright, Ramon Wilson, Norbert Peter Stiles, Brian Leslie Labone, Robert Frederick Moore (Cap), Norman Hunter, Roger Hunt, Robert Charlton, Geoffrey Charles Hurst, Martin Stanford Peters.  Manager: Alfred Ramsey
**U.S.S.R.**: Yuriy Pshenichnikov, Yuriy Istomin, Albert Shesternev (Cap), Valentin Afonin, Vladimir Kaplichniy, Aleksandr Lenev, Eduard Malofeev, Gennadiy Logofet, Anatoliy Banishevskiy, Anatoliy Byshovets, Gennadiy Evryuzhikhin.   Trainer: Mikhail Yakushin
**Goals**: Robert Charlton (39), Geoffrey Charles Hurst (63)

**426.  06.11.1968**
**ROMANIA v ENGLAND  0-0**
*23 August, București*
Referee:  Radoslav Fiala (Czechoslovakia)    Att: 65,000
**ROMANIA**: Gheorghe Gornea, Lajos Sătmăreanu, Ion Barbu (Cap), Cornel Dinu, Mihai Mocanu, Vasile Gergely, Mircea Petescu (35 Radu Nunweiller VI), Ion Pîrcălab, Nicolae Dobrin (77 Flavius Domide), Florea Dumitrache, Mircea Lucescu.  Trainer: Angelo Niculescu
**ENGLAND**: Gordon Banks, Thomas James Wright (10 Robert McNab), Brian Leslie Labone, Robert Frederick Moore (Cap), Keith Robert Newton, Alan Patrick Mullery, Robert Charlton, Martin Stanford Peters, Alan James Ball, Geoffrey Charles Hurst, Roger Hunt.  Manager: Alfred Ramsey

**427.  11.12.1968**
**ENGLAND v BULGARIA  1-1**  (1-1)
*Wembley, London*
Referee:  Michel Kitabdjian (France)    Attendance: 80,000
**ENGLAND**: Gordon West, Keith Robert Newton (85 Paul Reaney), Robert McNab, Alan Patrick Mullery, Brian Leslie Labone, Robert Frederick Moore (Cap), Francis Henry Lee, Colin Bell, Robert Charlton, Geoffrey Charles Hurst, Martin Stanford Peters.  Manager: Alfred Ramsey
**BULGARIA**: Simeon Simeonov, Stoichko Peshev, Ivan Dimitrov, Boris Gaganelov (Cap), Dobromir Jechev, Dimitar Penev, Georgi Popov (46 Petar Jekov), Hristo Bonev, Georgi Asparuhov, Dimitar Yakimov, Dinko Dermendjiev.  Trainer: Stefan Bojkov
**Goals**: Geoffrey Charles Hurst (36) / Georgi Asparuhov (33)

**428.  15.01.1969**
**ENGLAND v ROMANIA  1-1**  (1-0)
*Wembley, London*
Referee:  John Callaghan (Scotland)    Attendance: 80,000
**ENGLAND**: Gordon Banks, Thomas James Wright, John "Jack" Charlton, Norman Hunter, Robert McNab, Norbert Peter Stiles, Robert Charlton (Cap), Alan James Ball, John Radford, Roger Hunt, Geoffrey Charles Hurst.  Manager: Alfred Ramsey
**ROMANIA**: Gheorghe Gornea, Lajos Sătmăreanu, Alexandru Boc, Cornel Dinu, Augustin Pax Deleanu, Dan Sabin Anca, Radu Nunweiller VI, Emerich Dembrovschi, Flavius Domide, Florea Dumitrache, Mircea Lucescu (Cap).  Trainer: Angelo Niculescu
**Goal**: John "Jack" Charlton (27) / Florea Dumitrache (74 pen)

**429.  12.03.1969**
**ENGLAND v FRANCE  5-0**  (1-0)
*Wembley, London*
Referee:  István Zsolt (Hungary)    Attendance: 85,000
**ENGLAND**: Gordon Banks, Keith Robert Newton, Terence Cooper, Alan Patrick Mullery, John "Jack" Charlton, Robert Frederick Moore (Cap), Francis Henry Lee, Colin Bell, Geoffrey Charles Hurst, Martin Stanford Peters, Michael O'Grady.  Manager: Alfred Ramsey
**FRANCE**: Georges Carnus, Jean Djorkaeff, Bernard Bosquier (Cap), Roger Lemerre, Jean-Paul Rostagni, Joseph Bonnel, Jacques Simon, Henri Michel, Yves Herbet, Charly Loubet, Georges Bereta.  Trainer: Georges Boulogne
**Goals**: Michael O'Grady (33), Geoffrey Charles Hurst (48 pen, 49, 80 pen), Francis Henry Lee (75)

430. 03.05.1969   Home Championship
**NORTHERN IRELAND v ENGLAND  1-3**  (0-1)
*Windsor Park, Belfast*
Referee: Joseph William Mullan (Scotland)   Att: 23,000
**NORTHERN IRELAND**: Patrick Anthony Jennings, David James Craig, Martin Harvey (Alexander Russell Elder), Samuel John Todd, William John Terence Neill, James Joseph Nicholson, Alexander S. McMordie, Thomas A. Jackson, Alexander Derek Dougan, William John Irvine, George Best.
**ENGLAND**: Gordon Banks, Keith Robert Newton, Robert McNab, Alan Patrick Mullery, Brian Leslie Labone, Robert Frederick Moore (Cap), Alan James Ball, Francis Henry Lee, Robert Charlton, Geoffrey Charles Hurst, Martin Stanford Peters.   Manager: Alfred Ramsey
**Goals**: Alexander S. McMordie (64) / Martin Peters (39), Francis Henry Lee (64), Geoffrey Charles Hurst (74 pen)


431. 07.05.1969   Home Championship
**ENGLAND v WALES  2-1**  (0-1)
*Wembley, London*
Referee: John Adair (Northern Ireland)   Attendance: 70,000
**ENGLAND**: Gordon West, Keith Robert Newton, Terence Cooper, Robert Frederick Moore (Cap), John "Jack" Charlton, Norman Hunter, Francis Henry Lee, Colin Bell, Jeffrey Astle, Robert Charlton, Alan James Ball.   Manager: Alfred Ramsey
**WALES**: Gareth Sprake, Peter Joseph Rodrigues, Roderick John Thomas, William Alan Durban, David Powell, Alwyn Derek Burton, Ronald Tudor Davies, John Benjamin Toshack, Ronald Wyn Davies, Graham Moore, Barrie Spencer Jones.   Trainer: David Bowen
**Goals**: Robert Charlton (58), Francis Henry Lee (72) / Ronald Tudor Davies (18)


432. 10.05.1969   Home Championship
**ENGLAND v SCOTLAND  4-1**  (2-1)
*Wembley, London*
Referee: Robert Héliès (France)   Attendance: 89,902
**ENGLAND**: Gordon Banks, Keith Robert Newton, Terence Cooper, Alan Patrick Mullery, Brian Leslie Labone, Robert Frederick Moore (Cap), Francis Henry Lee, Alan James Ball, Robert Charlton, Geoffrey Charles Hurst, Martin Stanford Peters.   Manager: Alfred Ramsey
**SCOTLAND**: James Herriot, Thomas Gemmell, Edward Graham McCreadie, Robert White Murdoch, William McNeill, John Greig, William Henderson, William John Bremner (Cap), Colin Anderson Stein, Alan John Gilzean (57 William Semple Brown Wallace), Edwin Gray.   Manager: Robert Brown
**Goals**: Martin Peters (16, 64), Geoffrey Hurst (20, 60 pen) / Colin Anderson Stein (43)


433. 01.06.1969
**MEXICO v ENGLAND  0-0**
*Azteca, Ciudad de Mexico*
Referee: Alberto Noriega Tejada (Peru)   Att: 105,000
**MEXICO**: Francisco Castrejón, Juan Manuel Alejandrez, Gustavo Peña, Gabriel Núñez, Mario Pérez, José Luis González, Antonio Munguía, Fernando Bustos, Enrique Borja, Luis Estrada, Cesáreo Victorino.   Trainer: Raúl Cárdenas
**ENGLAND**: Gordon West, Keith Robert Newton (87 Thomas James Wright), Terence Cooper, Alan Patrick Mullery, Brian Leslie Labone, Robert Frederick Moore (Cap), Francis Henry Lee, Alan James Ball, Robert Charlton, Geoffrey Charles Hurst, Martin Stanford Peters.   Manager: Alfred Ramsey


434. 08.06.1969
**URUGUAY v ENGLAND  1-2**  (0-1)
*Centenario, Montevideo*
Referee: Armando Marques (Brazil)   Attendance: 54,161
**URUGUAY**: Luis María Maidana, Arilio Genaro Ancheta, Juan Carlos Paz, Ignacio Luis Ubiña, Julio Walter Montero Castillo, Juan Martín Mujica, Luis Alberto Cubilla, Julio César Cortés, Héctor Jesús Silva, Roberto Matosas, Julio César Morales.   Trainer: Juan Eduardo Hohberg
**ENGLAND**: Gordon Banks, Thomas James Wright, Keith Robert Newton, Alan Patrick Mullery, Brian Leslie Labone, Robert Frederick Moore (Cap), Alan James Ball, Colin Bell, Robert Charlton (65 Francis Henry Lee), Geoffrey Charles Hurst, Martin Stanford Peters.   Manager: Alfred Ramsey
**Goals**: Luis Alberto Cubilla (53) / Francis Henry Lee (6), Geoffrey Charles Hurst (80)


435. 12.06.1969
**BRAZIL v ENGLAND  2-1**  (0-1)
*Maracana, Rio de Janeiro*
Referee: Ramon Barreto (Uruguay)   Attendance: 135,000
**BRAZIL**: GILMAR dos Santos Neves, CARLOS ALBERTO Tôrres, DJALMA Pereira DIAS Júnior, Joel Camargo, RILDO da Costa Menezes, CLODOALDO Tavares Santana, GÉRSON de Oliveira Nunes, Jair Ventura Filho "Jairzinho", Eduardo Gonçalves de Andrade "Tostão", Edson Arantes do Nascimento "Pelé", Jonas Eduardo Américo "Edu" (71 PAULO CÉSAR Lima).   Trainer: João Saldanha
**ENGLAND**: Gordon Banks, Thomas James Wright, Keith Robert Newton, Alan Patrick Mullery, Brian Leslie Labone, Robert Frederick Moore (Cap), Alan James Ball, Colin Bell, Robert Charlton, Geoffrey Charles Hurst, Martin Stanford Peters.   Manager: Alfred Ramsey
**Goal**: Eduardo Gonçalves de Andrade "Tostão" (79), Jair Ventura Filho "Jairzinho" (81) / Colin Bell (13)

**436. 05.11.1969**
**HOLLAND v ENGLAND 0-1** (0-0)
*Olympisch, Amsterdam*

Referee: Pavel Kazakov (USSR)   Attendance: 33,000

**HOLLAND:** Eddy Treijtel, Epi Drost, Rinus Israël, Hans Eijenbroek (Cap), Ruud Krol, Nico Rijnders, Wietze Veenstra (46 Gerrie Mühren), Johan Cruijff, Jan Mulder, Wim van Hanegem (46 Dick van Dijk), Robert Rensenbrink. Trainer: Georg Kessler

**ENGLAND:** Peter Phillip Bonetti, Thomas James Wright, Emlyn Walter Hughes, Alan Patrick Mullery, John "Jack" Charlton, Robert Frederick Moore (Cap), Francis Henry Lee (84 Peter Thompson), Colin Bell, Robert Charlton, Geoffrey Charles Hurst, Martin Stanford Peters. Manager: Alfred Ramsey

**Goal:** Colin Bell (69)


**437. 10.12.1969**
**ENGLAND v PORTUGAL 1-0** (1-0)
*Wembley, London*

Referee: M. Mouton (France)   Attendance: 100,000

**ENGLAND:** Peter Phillip Bonetti, Paul Reaney, Emlyn Walter Hughes, Alan Patrick Mullery, John "Jack" Charlton, Robert Frederick Moore (Cap), Francis Henry Lee, Colin Bell (70 Martin Stanford Peters), Jeffrey Astle, Robert Charlton, Alan James Ball. Manager: Alfred Ramsey

**PORTUGAL:** JOSÉ HENRIQUE de Rodrigues Marques, Joaquim Adriano José da Conceição, CARLOS Alberto Lourenço CARDOSO, JOSÉ CARLOS da Silva José (Cap), Alfredo Manuel Ferreira Silva Murça, Fernando Massano Tomé, António José da Conceiçao Oliveira "Toni", JAIME da Silva GRAÇA (72 MÁRIO Alberto Domingos CAMPOS), Félix Marques Guerreiro, MANUEL ANTÓNIO Leitão da Silva (72 Ernesto FIGUEIREDO Cordeiro), Jacinto João. Trainer: José Maria Antunes

**Goal:** John "Jack" Charlton (24)


**438. 14.01.1970**
**ENGLAND v HOLLAND 0-0**
*Wembley, London*

Referee: Heinz Siebert (West Germany)   Att: 75,000

**ENGLAND:** Gordon Banks, Keith Robert Newton, Terence Cooper, Martin Stanford Peters, John "Jack" Charlton, Norman Hunter, Francis Henry Lee (70 Alan Patrick Mullery), Colin Bell, Michael David Jones (70 Geoffrey Charles Hurst), Robert Charlton (Cap), Ian Storey-Moore. Manager: Alfred Ramsey

**HOLLAND:** Jan van Beveren, Epi Drost, Rinus Israël, Hans Eijenbroek (Cap), Ruud Krol, Nico Rijnders (65 Gerrie Mühren), Wim Jansen, Dick van Dijk, Johan Cruijff, Wim van Hanegem (70 Wietze Veenstra), Piet Keizer. Trainer: Georg Kessler


**439. 25.02.1970**
**BELGIUM v ENGLAND 1-3** (0-1)
*Parc Astrid, Bruxelles*

Referee: Antonio Sbardella (Italia)   Attendance: 20,594

**BELGIUM:** Jean Trappeniers, Georges Heylens, Nicolas Dewalque, Léon Jeck, Jean Thissen, Wilfried Van Moer, Jean-Baptiste Dockx, Odillon Polleunis (75 Jan Verheyen), Léon Semmeling, Johan Devrindt, Paul Van Himst (Cap). Trainer: Raymond Goethals

**ENGLAND:** Gordon Banks, Thomas James Wright, Terence Cooper, Robert Frederick Moore (Cap), Brian Leslie Labone, Emlyn Walter Hughes, Francis Henry Lee, Alan James Ball, Peter Leslie Osgood, Geoffrey Charles Hurst, Martin Stanford Peters. Manager: Alfred Ramsey

**Goals:** Jean-Baptiste Dockx (58) / Alan James Ball (27, 60), Geoffrey Charles Hurst (55)


**440. 18.04.1970   Home Championship**
**WALES v ENGLAND 1-1** (1-0)
*Ninian Park, Cardiff*

Referee: Thomas Wharton (Scotland)   Attendance: 50,000

**WALES:** Anthony Horace Millington, Peter Joseph Rodrigues, Roderick John Thomas, William Terence Hennessey, Harold Michael England, David Powell, Richard Lech Krzywicki, William Alan Durban, Ronald Tudor Davies, Graham Moore, Ronald Raymond Rees. Trainer: David Bowen

**ENGLAND:** Gordon Banks, Thomas James Wright, Emlyn Walter Hughes, Alan Patrick Mullery, Brian Leslie Labone, Robert Frederick Moore (Cap), Francis Henry Lee, Alan James Ball, Robert Charlton, Geoffrey Charles Hurst, Martin Stanford Peters. Manager: Alfred Ramsey

**Goals:** Richard Lech Krzywicki (40) / Francis Henry Lee (71)


**441. 21.04.1970   Home Championship**
**ENGLAND v NORTHERN IRELAND 3-1** (1-0)
*Wembley, London*

Referee: Gaspar Pintado Viu (Spain)   Attendance: 100,000

**ENGLAND:** Gordon Banks, Keith Robert Newton (82 Colin Bell), Emlyn Walter Hughes, Alan Patrick Mullery, Robert Frederick Moore, Norbert Peter Stiles, Ralph Coates, Brian Kidd, Robert Charlton (Cap), Geoffrey Charles Hurst, Martin Stanford Peters. Manager: Alfred Ramsey

**NORTHERN IRELAND:** Patrick Anthony Jennings, David James Craig, David Clements, William James O'Kane, William John Terence Neill (Cap), James Joseph Nicholson, Alexander S. McMordie, George Best, Alexander Derek Dougan, Anthony O'Doherty (Samuel Nelson), Robert John Lutton (John Cowan). Manager: William Bingham

**Goals:** Martin Peters (6), Geoffrey Charles Hurst (57), Robert Charlton (81) / George Best (50)

442.  25.04.1970   Home Championship
**SCOTLAND v ENGLAND  0-0**
*Hampden Park, Glasgow*

Ref:  Gerhard Schulenburg (West Germany)   Att:  137,438

**SCOTLAND**:  James Fergus Cruickshank, Thomas Gemmell, William Dickson, John Greig (Cap), Ronald McKinnon, Robert Moncur (82 Alan John Gilzean), James Connolly Johnstone, David Hay, Colin Anderson Stein, John O'Hare, William McInnany Carr.   Manager:  Robert Brown

**ENGLAND**:  Gordon Banks, Keith Robert Newton, Emlyn Walter Hughes, Norbert Peter Stiles, Brian Leslie Labone, Robert Frederick Moore (Cap), Peter Thompson (58 Alan Patrick Mullery), Alan James Ball, Jeffrey Astle, Geoffrey Charles Hurst, Martin Stanford Peters.   Manager:  Alfred Ramsey

443.  20.05.1970
**COLOMBIA v ENGLAND  0-4**  (0-2)
*Nemesio Camacho 'El Campín', Bogotá*

Referee:  Barrios (Venezuela)   Attendance:  36,000

**COLOMBIA**:  Otoniel Quintana, Arturo Rafael Segovia, Hermenegildo Segrera, Darío López, Gabriel Hernández, Alfonso Cañón, Oscar López, Oscar Francisco García, Luis Carlos Paz (Alfredo Arango), Alejandro Brand, Jorge Enrique Ramírez Gallego.   Trainer:  Cesar López Fretes

**ENGLAND**:  Gordon Banks, Keith Robert Newton, Terence Cooper, Alan Patrick Mullery, Brian Leslie Labone, Robert Frederick Moore (Cap), Francis Henry Lee, Alan James Ball, Robert Charlton, Geoffrey Charles Hurst, Martin Stanford Peters.   Manager:  Alfred Ramsey

**Goals**:  Martin Stanford Peters (3, 38), Robert Charlton (55), Alan James Ball (83)

444.  24.05.1970
**ECUADOR v ENGLAND  0-2**  (0-1)
*Olimpico Atahualpa, Quito*

Referee:  Alberto Noriega Tejada (Peru)   Attendance:  36,000

**ECUADOR**:  Edwin Roberto Mejía, Lincoln Utreras, Carlos German Campoverde, Enrique José Portilla, Atahúlfo Valencia, Jorge Washington Bolaños, Walter Cardeñas, Washington Muñoz (60 Marcelo Vicente Cabezas), Raúl Patricio Peñaherrera, Paúl Carrera (48 Tom Eugenio Rodríguez), Armando Tito Larrea.   Trainer:  Ernesto Guerra

**ENGLAND**:  Gordon Banks, Keith Robert Newton, Terence Cooper, Alan Patrick Mullery, Brian Leslie Labone, Robert Frederick Moore (Cap), Francis Henry Lee (46 Brian Kidd), Alan James Ball, Robert Charlton (70 David Sadler), Geoffrey Charles Hurst, Martin Stanford Peters.   Manager:  Alfred Ramsey

**Goals**:  Francis Henry Lee (4), Brian Kidd (75)

445.  02.06.1970   9th World Cup,  1st Round
**ENGLAND v ROMANIA  1-0**  (0-0)
*Jalisco, Guadalajara*

Referee:  Vital Loraux (Belgium)   Attendance:  50,000

**ENGLAND**:  Gordon Banks, Keith Robert Newton (50 Thomas James Wright), Brian Leslie Labone, Robert Frederick Moore (Cap), Terence Cooper, Alan Patrick Mullery, Robert Charlton, Alan James Ball, Francis Henry Lee (77 Peter Leslie Osgood), Geoffrey Charles Hurst, Martin Stanford Peters.   Manager:  Alfred Ramsey

**ROMANIA**:  Sterică Adamache, Lajos Sătmăreanu, Nicolae Lupescu, Cornel Dinu, Mihai Mocanu, Ion Dumitru, Radu Nunweiller VI, Emerich Dembrovschi, Gheorghe Tătaru II (74 Alexandru Neagu), Florea Dumitrache, Mircea Lucescu (Cap).   Trainer:  Angelo Niculescu

**Goal**:  Geoffrey Charles Hurst (64)

446.  07.06.1970   9th World Cup,  1st Round
**ENGLAND v BRAZIL  0-1**  (0-0)
*Jalisco, Guadalajara*

Referee:  Abraham Klein (Israel)   Attendance:  70,950

**ENGLAND**:  Gordon Banks, Thomas James Wright, Terence Cooper, Alan Patrick Mullery, Brian Leslie Labone, Robert Frederick Moore (Cap), Francis Henry Lee (64 Jeffrey Astle), Alan James Ball, Robert Charlton (64 Colin Bell), Geoffrey Charles Hurst, Martin Stanford Peters.   Manager:  Alfred Ramsey

**BRAZIL**:  FÉLIX Miélli Venerando, CARLOS ALBERTO Tôrres (Cap), Hercules BRITO Ruas, Wilson da Silva Piazza, EVERALDO Marques da Silva, CLODOALDO Tavares Santana, PAULO CÉSAR Lima, Jair Ventura Filho "Jairzinho", Eduardo Gonçalves de Andrade "Tostão (68 Roberto Lopes Miranda), Edson Arantes do Nascimento "Pelé", Roberto Rivelino.   Trainer:  Mário Jorge Lobo Zagallo

**Goal**:  Jair Ventura Filho "Jairzinho" (60)

447.  11.06.1970   9th World Cup,  1st Round
**ENGLAND v CZECHOSLOVAKIA  1-0**  (0-0)
*Jalisco, Guadalajara*

Referee:  Roger Machin (France)   Attendance:  49,000

**ENGLAND**:  Gordon Banks, Keith Robert Newton, John "Jack" Charlton, Robert Frederick Moore (Cap), Terence Cooper, Colin Bell, Robert Charlton (65 Alan James Ball), Alan Patrick Mullery, Martin Stanford Peters, Jeffrey Astle (65 Peter Leslie Osgood), Allan John Clarke.   Manager:  Alfred Ramsey

**CZECHOSLOVAKIA**:  Ivo Viktor (Cap), Karel Dobiaš, Václav Migas, Vladimír Hrivnák, Vladimír Hagara, Jaroslav Pollák, Ladislav Kuna, František Veselý, Ladislav Petráš, Jozef Adamec, Karol Jokl (71 Ján Čapkovič).   Trainer:  Josef Marko

**Goal**:  Allan John Clarke (49 pen)

448.  14.06.1970   9th World Cup, Quarter-Finals
**WEST GERMANY v ENGLAND  3-2**  (0-1, 2-2) (AET)
*Guanajuato, Léon*

Referee: Angel Norberto Coerezza (Argentina)   Att: 32,000

**WEST GERMANY**: Josef Maier, Horst-Dieter Höttges (46 Willi Schulz), Hans-Hubert Vogts, Franz Beckenbauer, Karl-Heinz Schnellinger, Klaus Fichtel, Reinhard Libuda (57 Jürgen Grabowski), Uwe Seeler (Cap), Gerhard Müller, Wolfgang Overath, Johannes Löhr.   Trainer: Helmut Schön

**ENGLAND**: Peter Phillip Bonetti, Keith Robert Newton, Terence Cooper, Alan Patrick Mullery, Brian Leslie Labone, Robert Frederick Moore (Cap), Francis Henry Lee, Alan James Ball, Robert Charlton (69 Colin Bell), Geoffrey Charles Hurst, Martin Stanford Peters (80 Norman Hunter). Manager: Alfred Ramsey

**Goals**: Franz Beckenbauer (69), Uwe Seeler (82), Gerhard Müller (108) / Alan Patrick Mullery (32), Martin Stanford Peters (50)


449.  25.11.1970
**ENGLAND v EAST GERMANY  3-1**  (2-1)
*Wembley, London*

Referee: Rudolf Scheurer (Switzerland)   Attendance: 93,000

**ENGLAND**: Peter Leslie Shilton, Emlyn Walter Hughes, Terence Cooper, Alan Patrick Mullery, David Sadler, Robert Frederick Moore (Cap), Francis Henry Lee, Alan James Ball, Geoffrey Charles Hurst, Allan John Clarke, Martin Stanford Peters.   Manager: Alfred Ramsey

**EAST GERMANY**: Jürgen Croy, Peter Rock, Lothar Kurbjuweit, Klaus Sammer, Michael Strempel (79 Henning Frenzel), Frank Ganzera, Harald Irmscher, Helmut Stein, Hans-Jürgen Kreische, Peter Ducke (Cap), Eberhard Vogel. Trainer: Georg Buschner

**Goals**: Francis Henry Lee (12), Martin Stanford Peters (21), Allan John Clarke (63) / Eberhard Vogel (27)


450.  03.02.1971 4th European Champs Qualifiers
**MALTA v ENGLAND  0-1**  (0-1)
*Empire, Gzira*

Referee: Ferdinand Marschall (Austria)   Attendance: 29,751

**MALTA**: Alfred Mizzi, Joe Grima, Alfred Mallia, Anton Camilleri, Emanuel 'Leli' Micallef, Edward Darmanin, Ronnie Cocks, William Vassallo, Joe Cini (Cap), Edward Theobald, Louis Arpa.   Trainer: Carm Borg

**ENGLAND**: Gordon Banks, Paul Reaney, Emlyn Walter Hughes, Alan Patrick Mullery (Cap), Roy Leslie McFarland, Norman Hunter, Alan James Ball, Martin Harcourt Chivers, Joseph Royle, James Colin Harvey, Martin Stanford Peters. Manager: Alfred Ramsey

**Goal**: Martin Stanford Peters (34)


451.  21.04.1971   4th European Champs Qualifiers
**ENGLAND v GREECE  3-0**  (1-0)
*Wembley, London*

Referee: Martti Hirviniemi (Finland)   Attendance: 55,123

**ENGLAND**: Gordon Banks, Peter Edwin Storey, Emlyn Walter Hughes, Alan Patrick Mullery, Roy Leslie McFarland, Robert Frederick Moore (Cap), Francis Henry Lee, Alan James Ball (78 Ralph Coates), Martin Harcourt Chivers, Geoffrey Charles Hurst, Martin Stanford Peters. Manager: Alfred Ramsey

**GREECE**: Nikolaos Hristidis, Giánnis Gaïtatzis, Aggelos Spíros, Apóstolos Toskas, Nikolaos Kampas (75 Efstáthios Haïtas), Nikolaos Stathopoulos, Dimítris Synetopoulos, Giórgos Koudas, Giórgos Dedes (88 Giórgos Delikaris), Dimítris Papaïoánnou (Cap), Mihális Kritikopoulos. Trainer: Lakis Petropoulos

**Goals**: Martin Chivers (23), Geoffrey Charles Hurst (68), Francis Henry Lee (87)


452.  12.05.1971   4th European Champs Qualifiers
**ENGLAND v MALTA  5-0**  (2-0)
*Wembley, London*

Referee: Einar Røed (Norway)   Attendance: 41,534

**ENGLAND**: Gordon Banks, Christopher Lawler, Terence Cooper, Robert Frederick Moore (Cap), Roy Leslie McFarland, Emlyn Walter Hughes, Francis Henry Lee, Ralph Coates, Martin Harcourt Chivers, Allan John Clarke, Martin Stanford Peters (75 Alan James Ball).   Manager: Alfred Ramsey

**MALTA**: Vincent Borg-Bonaci (46 Alfred Mizzi), Lewis Pace, Joe Grima, Anton Camilleri, Edward Darmanin, Alfred Delia, Ronnie Cocks (Cap), William Vassallo, John Bonett, Edward Theobald, Louis Arpa.   Trainer: Tony Formosa

**Goals**: Martin Chivers (30, 59), Francis Henry Lee (42), Allan John Clarke (46 pen), Christopher Lawler (75)


453.  15.05.1971   Home Championship
**NORTHERN IRELAND v ENGLAND  0-1**  (0-0)
*Windsor Park, Belfast*

Referee: Alistair McKenzie (Scotland)   Attendance: 33,000

**NORTHERN IRELAND**: Patrick Anthony Jennings, Patrick James Rice, Samuel Nelson, William James O'Kane, Alan Hunter, James Joseph Nicholson, Bryan Hamilton, Alexander S. McMordie (60 Thomas Cassidy), Alexander Derek Dougan (Cap), David Clements, George Best. Manager: William Bingham

**ENGLAND**: Gordon Banks, Paul Edward Madeley, Terence Cooper, Peter Edwin Storey, Roy Leslie McFarland, Robert Frederick Moore (Cap), Francis Henry Lee, Alan James Ball, Martin Harcourt Chivers, Allan John Clarke, Martin Stanford Peters.   Manager: Alfred Ramsey

**Goal**: Allan John Clarke (80)

454. 19.05.1971   Home Championship
**ENGLAND v WALES  0-0**

*Wembley, London*

Referee:  Malcolm Wright (Northern Ireland)    Att:  70,000

**ENGLAND**:  Peter Leslie Shilton, Christopher Lawler, Terence Cooper, Thomas Smith, Laurence Valentine Lloyd, Emlyn Walter Hughes, Francis Henry Lee, Ralph Coates, Geoffrey Charles Hurst, Anthony John Brown (72 Allan John Clarke), Martin Stanford Peters (Cap).    Manager:  Alfred Ramsey

**WALES**:  Gareth Sprake, Peter Joseph Rodrigues, Roderick John Thomas, Edward Glyn James, John Griffith Roberts, Terence Charles Yorath, Leighton Phillips, William Alan Durban, Ronald Tudor Davies, John Benjamin Toshack, Gilbert Ivor Reece (85 Ronald Raymond Rees).
Trainer:  David Bowen


455. 22.05.1971   Home Championship
**ENGLAND v SCOTLAND  3-1**  (3-1)

*Wembley, London*

Referee:  Jef Dorpmans (Holland)    Attendance:  91,469

**ENGLAND**:  Gordon Banks, Christopher Lawler, Terence Cooper, Peter Edwin Storey, Roy Leslie McFarland, Robert Frederick Moore (Cap), Francis Henry Lee (73 Allan John Clarke), Alan James Ball, Martin Harcourt Chivers, Geoffrey Charles Hurst, Martin Stanford Peters.
Manager:  Alfred Ramsey

**SCOTLAND**:  Robert Brown Clark, John Greig, James Andrew Brogan, William John Bremner, Francis McLintock, Robert Moncur (Cap), James Connolly Johnstone, Anthony Green (82 Andrew Jarvie), Peter Barr Cormack, David Thomson Robb, Hugh Patrick Curran (46 Francis Michael Munro).
Manager:  Robert Brown

**Goals**:  Martin Peters (9), Martin Harcourt Chivers (30, 40) / Hugh Patrick Curran (11)


456. 13.10.1971   4th European Champs Qualifiers
**SWITZERLAND v ENGLAND  2-3**  (2-2)

*St. Jakob, Basel*

Referee:  Vital Loraux (Belgium)    Attendance:  47,877

**SWITZERLAND**:  Marcel Kunz, Pierre-Albert Chapuisat (81 Georges Perroud), Peter Ramseier, Anton Weibel, Pirmin Stierli, Karl Odermatt, Jakob Kuhn, Rolf Blättler (75 Kurt Müller), Walter Balmer, Fritz Künzli, Daniel Jeandupeux.
Trainer:  Louis Maurer

**ENGLAND**:  Gordon Banks, Christopher Lawler, Terence Cooper, Alan Patrick Mullery, Roy Leslie McFarland, Robert Frederick Moore (Cap), Francis Henry Lee, Paul Edward Madeley, Martin Harcourt Chivers, Geoffrey Charles Hurst (85 John Radford), Martin Stanford Peters.
Manager:  Alfred Ramsey

**Goals**:  Daniel Jeandupeux (11), Fritz Künzli (42) / Geoffrey Hurst (1), Martin Chivers (12), A. Weibel (77 og)


457. 10.11.1971   4th European Champs Qualifiers
**ENGLAND v SWITZERLAND  1-1**  (1-1)

*Wembley, London*

Referee:  Constantin Bărbulescu (România)    Att:  90,423

**ENGLAND**:  Peter Leslie Shilton, Paul Edward Madeley, Terence Cooper, Peter Edwin Storey, Laurence Valentine Lloyd, Robert Frederick Moore (Cap), Michael George Summerbee (60 Martin Harcourt Chivers), Alan James Ball, Geoffrey Charles Hurst, Francis Henry Lee (83 Rodney William Marsh), Emlyn Walter Hughes.    Manager:  Alfred Ramsey

**SWITZERLAND**:  Mario Prosperi, Peter Ramseier, Pierre-Albert Chapuisat, Georges Perroud, Pirmin Stierli, Karl Odermatt, Rolf Blättler, Jakob Kuhn, Walter Balmer (69 Peter Meier), Fritz Künzli, Daniel Jeandupeux.
Trainer:  Louis Maurer

**Goal**:  Michael George Summerbee (8) / Karl Odermatt (26)


458. 01.12.1971   4th European Champs Qualifiers
**GREECE v ENGLAND  0-2**  (0-0)

*Karaiskaki, Athina*

Referee:  José María Ortiz de Mendibil (Spain)    Att:  34,014

**GREECE**:  Nikolaos Hristidis, Theódoros Pallas, Apóstolos Toskas, Anthimos Kapsis, Athanásios Aggelis, Konstantinos Eleftherakis, Dimítris Domazos (Cap), Konstantinos Nikolaïdis (73 Konstantinos Davourlis), Antónis Antoniadis, Dimítris Papaïoánnou, Giórgos Koudas (61 Mihális Kritikopoulos).    Trainer:  William Bingham

**ENGLAND**:  Gordon Banks, Paul Edward Madeley, Emlyn Walter Hughes, Colin Bell, Roy Leslie McFarland, Robert Frederick Moore (Cap), Francis Henry Lee, Alan James Ball, Martin Harcourt Chivers, Geoffrey Charles Hurst, Martin Stanford Peters.    Manager:  Alfred Ramsey

**Goals**:  Geoffrey Hurst (57), Martin Harcourt Chivers (90)


459. 29.04.1972   4th European Championships, Quarter-Finals
**ENGLAND v WEST GERMANY  1-3**  (0-1)

*Wembley, London*

Referee:  Robert Héliès (France)    Attendance:  100,000

**ENGLAND**:  Gordon Banks, Paul Edward Madeley, Emlyn Walter Hughes, Colin Bell, Robert Frederick Moore (Cap), Norman Hunter, Francis Henry Lee, Alan James Ball, Martin Harcourt Chivers, Geoffrey Charles Hurst (62 Rodney William Marsh), Martin Stanford Peters.    Manager:  Alfred Ramsey

**WEST GERMANY**:  Josef Maier, Horst-Dieter Höttges, Georg Schwarzenbeck, Franz Beckenbauer (Cap), Paul Breitner, Ulrich Hoeneß, Günter Netzer, Herbert Wimmer, Jürgen Grabowski, Gerhard Müller, Siegfried Held.
Trainer:  Helmut Schön

**Goal**:  Francis Henry Lee (77) / Ulrich Hoeneß (26), Günter Netzer (85 pen), Gerhard Müller (88)

460.  13.05.1972   4th European Championships – Quarter-Finals
**WEST GERMANY v ENGLAND  0-0**
*Olympia, West-Berlin*

Referee:  Milivoje Gugulovic (Yugoslavia)   Att: 76,200

**WEST GERMANY**: Josef Maier, Horst-Dieter Höttges, Georg Schwarzenbeck, Franz Beckenbauer (Cap), Paul Breitner, Heinz Flohe, Günter Netzer, Herbert Wimmer, Ulrich Hoeneß (70 Josef Heynckes), Gerhard Müller, Siegfried Held.   Trainer: Helmut Schön

**ENGLAND**: Gordon Banks, Paul Edward Madeley, Emlyn Walter Hughes, Peter Edwin Storey, Roy Leslie McFarland, Robert Frederick Moore (Cap), Alan James Ball, Colin Bell, Martin Harcourt Chivers, Rodney William Marsh (75 Michael George Summerbee), Norman Hunter (60 Martin Stanford Peters).   Manager: Alfred Ramsey


461.  20.05.1972   Home Championship
**WALES v ENGLAND  0-3**  (0-1)
*Ninian Park, Cardiff*

Referee:  William Joseph Mullan (Scotland)   Att: 34,000

**WALES**: Gareth Sprake, Peter Joseph Rodrigues, Roderick John Thomas, William Terence Hennessey, Harold Michael England, John Griffith Roberts (46 Gilbert Ivor Reece), Terence Charles Yorath, Ronald Tudor Davies, Ronald Wyn Davies, John Benjamin Toshack, William Alan Durban.   Trainer: David Bowen

**ENGLAND**: Gordon Banks, Paul Edward Madeley, Emlyn Walter Hughes, Peter Edwin Storey, Roy Leslie McFarland, Robert Frederick Moore (Cap), Michael George Summerbee, Colin Bell, Malcolm Ian Macdonald, Rodney William Marsh, Norman Hunter.   Manager: Alfred Ramsey

Goals: Emlyn Walter Hughes (25), Rodney Marsh (60), Colin Bell (61)


462.  23.05.1972   Home Championship
**ENGLAND v NORTHERN IRELAND  0-1**  (0-1)
*Wembley, London*

Referee:  William John Gow (Wales)   Attendance: 64,000

**ENGLAND**: Peter Leslie Shilton, Colin Todd, Emlyn Walter Hughes, Peter Edwin Storey, Laurence Valentine Lloyd, Norman Hunter, Michael George Summerbee, Colin Bell (Cap), Malcolm Ian Macdonald (69 Martin Harcourt Chivers), Rodney William Marsh, Anthony William Currie (58 Martin Stanford Peters).   Manager: Alfred Ramsey

**NORTHERN IRELAND**: Patrick Anthony Jennings, Patrick James Rice, Samuel Nelson, William John Terence Neill (Cap), Alan Hunter, David Clements, Daniel Hegan, Alexander S. McMordie, Alexander Derek Dougan, William John Irvine, Thomas A. Jackson.   Manager: Terence Neill

Goal: William John Terence Neill (33)


463.  27.05.1972   Home Championship
**SCOTLAND v ENGLAND  0-1**  (0-1)
*Hampden Park, Glasgow*

Referee:  Sergio Gonella (Italy)   Attendance: 119,325

**SCOTLAND**: Robert Brown Clark, John Jack Brownlie, William Donachie (74 Anthony Green), Robert Moncur, William McNeill, Peter Patrick Lorimer, William John Bremner (Cap), Archibald Gemmill (49 James Connolly Johnstone), Richard Asa Hartford, Luigi Macari, Denis Law.   Manager: Thomas Docherty

**ENGLAND**: Gordon Banks, Paul Edward Madeley, Emlyn Walter Hughes, Peter Edwin Storey, Roy Leslie McFarland, Robert Frederick Moore (Cap), Alan James Ball, Colin Bell, Martin Harcourt Chivers, Rodney William Marsh (84 Malcolm Ian Macdonald), Norman Hunter.   Manager: Alfred Ramsey

Goal: Alan James Ball (28)


464.  11.10.1972
**ENGLAND v YUGOSLAVIA  1-1**  (1-0)
*Wembley, London*

Referee:  Aurelio Angonese (Italy)   Attendance: 50,000

**ENGLAND**: Peter Leslie Shilton, Michael Dennis Mills, Frank Richard George Lampard, Peter Edwin Storey, Jeffrey Paul Blockley, Robert Frederick Moore (Cap), Alan James Ball, Michael Roger Channon, Joseph Royle, Colin Bell, Rodney William Marsh.   Manager: Alfred Ramsey

**YUGOSLAVIA** Enver Marić, Petar Krivokuća, Dragoslav Stepanović, Miroslav Pavlović (60 Ljubiša Rajković), Josip Katalinski (46 Dragan Holcer), Blagoje Paunović, Ilija Petković, Franjo Vladić, Dušan Bajević, Jovan Aćimović, Dragan Džajić (Cap).   Trainer: Vujadin Boškov

Goal: Joseph Royle (40) / Franjo Vladić (51)


465.  15.11.1972   10th World Cup Qualifiers
**WALES v ENGLAND  0-1**  (0-1)
*Ninian Park, Cardiff*

Referee:  William Joseph Mullan (Scotland)   Att: 36,384

**WALES**: Gareth Sprake, Peter Joseph Rodrigues (65 Gilbert Ivor Reece), Roderick John Thomas, William Terence Hennessey, Harold Michael England, Trevor Hockey, Leighton Phillips, John Francis Mahoney, Ronald Wyn Davies, John Benjamin Toshack, Leighton James.   Trainer: David Bowen

**ENGLAND**: Raymond Neal Clemence, Peter Edwin Storey, Emlyn Walter Hughes, Norman Hunter, Roy Leslie McFarland, Robert Frederick Moore (Cap), Kevin Joseph Keegan, Martin Harcourt Chivers, Rodney William Marsh, Colin Bell, Alan James Ball.   Manager: Alfred Ramsey

Goal: Colin Bell (35)

466. 24.01.1973    10th World Cup Qualifiers
**ENGLAND v WALES  1-1**  (1-1)

*Wembley, London*

Referee:  Malcolm Wright (Northern Ireland)    Att: 62,273

**ENGLAND**:  Raymond Neal Clemence, Peter Edwin Storey, Emlyn Walter Hughes, Norman Hunter, Roy Leslie McFarland, Robert Frederick Moore (Cap), Kevin Joseph Keegan, Colin Bell, Martin Harcourt Chivers, Rodney William Marsh, Alan James Ball.    Manager: Alfred Ramsey

**WALES**:  Gareth Sprake, Peter Joseph Rodrigues (80 Malcolm Edward Page), Roderick John Thomas, Trevor Hockey, Harold Michael England, John Griffith Roberts, Brian Clifford Evans, John Francis Mahoney, John Benjamin Toshack, Terence Charles Yorath, Leighton James.    Trainer: David Bowen

**Goal**:  Norman Hunter (41) / John Benjamin Toshack (23)


467. 14.02.1973
**SCOTLAND v ENGLAND  0-5**  (0-3)

*Hampden Park, Glasgow*

Referee:  Robert Wurtz (France)    Attendance: 48,470

**SCOTLAND**:  Robert Brown Clark, Alexander Forsyth, William Donachie, Martin McLean Buchan, Edmond Peter Skiruing Colquhoun, Peter Patrick Lorimer, William John Bremner (Cap), George Graham, William Morgan (19 Colin Anderson Stein), Luigi Macari, Kenneth Mathieson Dalglish.    Manager: William Esplin Ormond

**ENGLAND**:  Peter Leslie Shilton, Peter Edwin Storey, Emlyn Walter Hughes, Colin Bell, Paul Edward Madeley, Robert Frederick Moore (Cap), Alan James Ball, Michael Roger Channon, Martin Harcourt Chivers, Allan John Clarke, Martin Stanford Peters.    Manager: Alfred Ramsey

**Goals**:  Peter Lorimer (6 og), Allan John Clarke (12, 85), Michael Roger Channon (15), Martin Harcourt Chivers (76)


468. 12.05.1973    Home Championship
**ENGLAND v NORTHERN IRELAND  2-1**  (1-1)

*Goodison Park, Liverpool*

Referee:  Clive Thomas (Wales)    Attendance: 29,865

**ENGLAND**:  Peter Leslie Shilton, Peter Edwin Storey, David John Nish, Colin Bell, Roy Leslie McFarland, Robert Frederick Moore (Cap), Alan James Ball, Michael Roger Channon, Martin Harcourt Chivers, John Peter Richards, Martin Stanford Peters.    Manager: Alfred Ramsey

**NORTHERN IRELAND**:  Patrick Anthony Jennings, Patrick James Rice, David James Craig, William John Terence Neill (Cap), Alan Hunter, David Clements, Bryan Hamilton, Thomas A. Jackson, Samuel John Morgan, Martin Hugh Michael O'Neill, Trevor Anderson.    Manager: Terence Neill

**Goals**:  Martin Harcourt Chivers (9, 82) /
David Clements (22 pen)


469. 15.05.1973    Home Championship
**ENGLAND v WALES  3-0**  (2-0)

*Wembley, London*

Referee:  John Wright Paterson (Scotland)    Att: 38,000

**ENGLAND**:  Peter Leslie Shilton, Peter Edwin Storey, Emlyn Walter Hughes, Colin Bell, Roy Leslie McFarland, Robert Frederick Moore (Cap), Alan James Ball, Michael Roger Channon, Martin Harcourt Chivers, Allan John Clarke, Martin Stanford Peters.    Manager: Alfred Ramsey

**WALES**:  Thomas John Seymour Phillips, Peter Joseph Rodrigues, Roderick John Thomas, Trevor Hockey, Harold Michael England (David Frazer Roberts), John Griffith Roberts, John Francis Mahoney, John Benjamin Toshack, Malcolm Edward Page (William John Emanuel), Brian Clifford Evans, Leighton James.    Trainer: David Bowen

**Goals**:  Martin Chivers (23), Michael Roger Channon (30), Martin Stanford Peters (67)


470. 19.05.1973    Home Championship
**ENGLAND v SCOTLAND  1-0**  (0-0)

*Wembley, London*

Referee:  Kurt Tschenscher (West Germany)    Att: 95,950

**ENGLAND**:  Peter Leslie Shilton, Peter Edwin Storey, Emlyn Walter Hughes, Colin Bell, Roy Leslie McFarland, Robert Frederick Moore (Cap), Alan James Ball, Michael Roger Channon, Martin Harcourt Chivers, Allan John Clarke, Martin Stanford Peters.    Manager: Alfred Ramsey

**SCOTLAND**:  Alistair Robert Hunter, William Pullar Jardine, Daniel Fergus McGrain, James Allan Holton, Derek Joseph Johnstone, Peter Patrick Lorimer (80 Colin Anderson Stein), William John Bremner (Cap), David Hay, William Morgan, Luigi Macari (74 Joseph Jordan), Kenneth Mathieson Dalglish.    Manager: William Esplin Ormond

**Goal**:  Martin Stanford Peters (55)


471. 27.05.1973
**CZECHOSLOVAKIA v ENGLAND  1-1**  (0-0)

*Sparta, Praha*

Referee:  Rudolf Glöckner (East Germany)    Att: 25,000

**CZECHOSLOVAKIA**:  Ivo Viktor, Jan Pivarník, Ľudovít Zlocha, Václav Samek, Vladimír Hagara, Přemysl Bičovský, Ladislav Kuna (Cap), Igor Novák, Bohumil Veselý, Zdeněk Nehoda, Pavel Stratil.    Trainer: Václav Ježek

**ENGLAND**:  Peter Leslie Shilton, Paul Edward Madeley, Peter Edwin Storey, Colin Bell, Roy Leslie McFarland, Robert Frederick Moore (Cap), Alan James Ball, Michael Roger Channon, Martin Harcourt Chivers, Allan John Clarke, Martin Stanford Peters.    Manager: Alfred Ramsey

**Goal**:  Igor Novák (55) / Allan John Clarke (89)

### 472.  06.06.1973  10th World Cup Qualifiers
### POLAND v ENGLAND  2-0  (1-0)
*Slaski, Chorzów*

Referee: Paul Schiller (Austria)    Attendance: 73,714

**POLAND**: Jan Tomaszewski, Krzysztof Rześny, Mirosław Bulzacki, Jerzy Gorgoń, Adam Musiał, Jerzy Kraska, Lesław Ćmikiewicz, Kazimierz Deyna, Jan Banaś, Włodzimierz Lubański (Cap) (54 Jan Domarski), Robert Gadocha. Trainer: Kazimierz Górski

**ENGLAND**: Peter Leslie Shilton, Paul Edward Madeley, Emlyn Walter Hughes, Peter Edwin Storey, Roy Leslie McFarland, Robert Frederick Moore (Cap), Alan James Ball, Colin Bell, Martin Harcourt Chivers, Allan John Clarke, Martin Stanford Peters.    Manager: Alfred Ramsey

**Sent off**: Ball (79)

**Goals**: Robert Gadocha (7), Włodzimierz Lubański (47)

### 473.  10.06.1973
### U.S.S.R. v ENGLAND  1-2  (0-1)
*Lenin, Moskva*

Referee: Wolfgang Riedel (East Germany)    Att: 85,000

**U.S.S.R.**: Evgeniy Rudakov, Sergey Olshanskiy, Murtaz Khurtzilava (Cap), Evgeniy Lovchev, Vladimir Kaplichniy, Viktor Kuznetsov (46 Vladimir Fedotov), Vladimir Muntyan, Viktor Papaev (60 Yuriy Vasenin), Arkadiy Andreasyan (Vladimir Kozlov), Vladimir Onishchenko, Oleg Blokhin. Trainer: Evgeniy Goryanskiy

**ENGLAND**: Peter Leslie Shilton, Paul Edward Madeley, Emlyn Walter Hughes, Peter Edwin Storey, Roy Leslie McFarland, Robert Frederick Moore (Cap), Anthony William Currie, Michael Roger Channon (70 Michael George Summerbee), Martin Harcourt Chivers, Allan John Clarke (58 Malcolm Ian Macdonald), Martin Stanford Peters (58 Norman Hunter).    Manager: Alfred Ramsey

**Goals**: Vladimir Muntyan (66 pen) / Martin Chivers (10), Murtaz Khurtzilava (55 og)

### 474.  14.06.1973
### ITALY v ENGLAND  2-0  (1-0)
*Comunale, Torino*

Referee: Tsvetan Stanev (Bulgaria)    Attendance: 50,000

**ITALY**: Dino Zoff, Giuseppe Sabadini, Giacinto Facchetti (Cap), Romeo Benetti, Francesco Morini (46 Mauro Bellugi), Tarcisio Burgnich, Alessandro Mazzola, Fabio Capello, Pietro Anastasi, Gianni Rivera, Paolino Pulici (71 Franco Causio). Trainer: Ferruccio Valcareggi

**ENGLAND**: Peter Leslie Shilton, Paul Edward Madeley, Emlyn Walter Hughes, Peter Edwin Storey, Roy Leslie McFarland, Robert Frederick Moore (Cap), Anthony William Currie, Michael Roger Channon, Martin Harcourt Chivers, Allan John Clarke, Martin Stanford Peters.
Manager: Alfred Ramsey

**Goals**: Pietro Anastasi (38), Fabio Capello (52)

### 475.  26.09.1973
### ENGLAND v AUSTRIA  7-0  (3-0)
*Wembley, London*

Referee: Charles Corver (Holland)    Attendance: 48,000

**ENGLAND**: Peter Leslie Shilton, Paul Edward Madeley, Emlyn Walter Hughes, Colin Bell, Roy Leslie McFarland, Norman Hunter, Anthony William Currie, Michael Roger Channon, Martin Harcourt Chivers, Allan John Clarke, Martin Stanford Peters (Cap).    Manager: Alfred Ramsey

**AUSTRIA**: Friedrich Koncilia, Robert Sara, Johann Schmidradner, Eduard Krieger, Johann Eigenstiller (67 Werner Kriess), Roland Hattenberger (46 Manfred Gombasch), August Starek, Johann Ettmayer, Wilhelm Kreuz, Johann Krankl, Kurt Jara.    Trainer: Leopold Stastny

**Goals**: Michael Channon (9, 47), Allan John Clarke (28, 43), Martin Harcourt Chivers (61), Anthony William Currie (65), Colin Bell (89)

### 476.  17.10.1973    10th World Cup Qualifiers
### ENGLAND v POLAND  1-1  (0-0)
*Wembley, London*

Referee: Vital Loraux (Belgium)    Attendance: 90,587

**ENGLAND**: Peter Leslie Shilton, Paul Edward Madeley, Emlyn Walter Hughes, Colin Bell, Roy Leslie McFarland, Norman Hunter, Anthony William Currie, Michael Roger Channon, Martin Harcourt Chivers (88 Kevin James Hector), Allan John Clarke, Martin Stanford Peters (Cap). Manager: Alfred Ramsey

**POLAND**: Jan Tomaszewski, Antoni Szymanowski, Mirosław Bulzacki, Jerzy Gorgoń, Adam Musiał, Lesław Ćmikiewicz, Kazimierz Deyna (Cap), Henryk Kasperczak, Grzegorz Lato, Jan Domarski, Robert Gadocha.    Trainer: Kazimierz Górski

**Goal**: Allan John Clarke (63 pen) / Jan Domarski (57)

### 477.  14.11.1973
### ENGLAND v ITALY  0-1  (0-0)
*Wembley, London*

Referee: Francisco Marques Lobo (Portugal)    Att: 88,000

**ENGLAND**: Peter Leslie Shilton, Paul Edward Madeley, Emlyn Walter Hughes, Colin Bell, Roy Leslie McFarland, Robert Frederick Moore (Cap), Anthony William Currie, Michael Roger Channon, Peter Leslie Osgood, Allan John Clarke (74 Kevin James Hector), Martin Stanford Peters.    Manager: Alfred Ramsey

**ITALY**: Dino Zoff, Luciano Spinosi, Giacinto Facchetti (Cap), Romeo Benetti, Mauro Bellugi, Tarcisio Burgnich, Franco Causio, Fabio Capello, Giorgio Chinaglia, Gianni Rivera, Luigi Riva.    Trainer: Ferruccio Valcareggi

**Goal**: Fabio Capello (86)

478.  03.04.1974
**PORTUGAL v ENGLAND  0-0**
*da Luz, Lisboa*

Referee: Emilio Carlos Guruceta Muro (Spain)   Att: 10,000

**PORTUGAL**: Vítor Manuel Alfonso DAMAS de Oliveira, Francisco Moreira da Silva Rebelo, HUMBERTO Manuel de Jesus COELHO (Cap), JOSÉ de Jesus MENDES, ARTUR Manuel Soares CORREIA, OCTÁVIO Joaquim Coelho Machado, ARNALDO José da Silva (46 VÍTOR Manuel PEREIRA), António José da Conceiçao Oliveira "Toni" (46 VALTER Manuel Pereira da Costa), Rui Manuel Trindade Jordão, VÍTOR Manuel Ferreira BAPTISTA (65 ROMEU Fernando Fernandes da Silva), Jacinto João.
Trainer: José Maria Pedroto

**ENGLAND**: Phillip Benjamin Neil Frederick Parkes, David John Nish, Michael Pejic, Martin John Dobson, David Victor Watson, Colin Todd, Stanley Bowles, Michael Roger Channon, Malcolm Ian Macdonald (75 Alan James Ball), Trevor David Brooking, Martin Stanford Peters (Cap).
Manager: Alfred Ramsey

479.  11.05.1974   Home Championship
**WALES v ENGLAND  0-2**  (0-1)
*Ninian Park, Cardiff*

Ref: Redmond McFadden (Northern Ireland)   Att: 25,734

**WALES**: Thomas John Seymour Phillips, Philip Stanley Roberts (76 Leslie Cartwright), Roderick John Thomas, John Francis Mahoney, John Griffith Roberts (Cap), David Frazer Roberts, Gilbert Ivor Reece, Anthony Keith Villars, Ronald Tudor Davies (57 David Paul Smallman), Terence Charles Yorath, Leighton James.   Trainer: David Bowen

**ENGLAND**: Peter Leslie Shilton, David John Nish, Michael Pejic, Emlyn Walter Hughes (Cap), Roy Leslie McFarland, Colin Todd, Kevin Joseph Keegan, Colin Bell, Michael Roger Channon, Keith Weller, Stanley Bowles.
Manager: Joseph Mercer

**Goals**: Stanley Bowles (35), Kevin Joseph Keegan (47)

480.  15.05.1974   Home Championship
**ENGLAND v NORTHERN IRELAND  1-0**  (0-0)
*Wembley, London*

Referee: Robert Holley Davidson (Scotland)   Att: 45,500

**ENGLAND**: Peter Leslie Shilton, David John Nish, Michael Pejic, Emlyn Walter Hughes (Cap), Roy Leslie McFarland (36 Norman Hunter), Colin Todd, Kevin Joseph Keegan, Keith Weller, Michael Roger Channon, Colin Bell, Stanley Bowles (55 Frank Stewart Worthington).   Manager: Joseph Mercer

**NORTHERN IRELAND**: Patrick Anthony Jennings, Patrick James Rice, Samuel Nelson (82 Thomas A. Jackson), William James O'Kane, Alan Hunter, David Clements (Cap), Bryan Hamilton (73 Martin Hugh Michael O'Neill), Thomas Cassidy, Samuel John Morgan, Samuel Baxter McIlroy, Roland Christopher McGrath.   Manager: Terence Neill

**Goal**: Keith Weller (73)

481.  18.05.1974   Home Championship
**SCOTLAND v ENGLAND  2-0**  (2-0)
*Hampden Park, Glasgow*

Referee: Leonardus van der Kroft (Holland)   Att: 94,487

**SCOTLAND**: David Harvey, William Pullar Jardine, Daniel Fergus McGrain, John Henderson Blackley, James Allan Holton, James Connolly Johnstone, William John Bremner (Cap), David Hay, Peter Patrick Lorimer, Kenneth Mathieson Dalglish, Joseph Jordan.   Manager: William Esplin Ormond

**ENGLAND**: Peter Leslie Shilton, David John Nish, Michael Pejic, Emlyn Walter Hughes (Cap), Norman Hunter (46 David Victor Watson), Colin Todd, Michael Roger Channon, Colin Bell, Frank Stewart Worthington (70 Malcolm Ian Macdonald), Keith Weller, Martin Stanford Peters.
Manager: Joseph Mercer

**Goals**: Joseph Jordan (5), Colin Todd (31 og)

482.  22.05.1974
**ENGLAND v ARGENTINA  2-2**  (1-0)
*Wembley, London*

Referee: Arturo Andres Ithurralde (Argentina)   Att: 68,000

**ENGLAND**: Peter Leslie Shilton, Emlyn Walter Hughes (Cap), Alec Lindsay, Colin Todd, David Victor Watson, Colin Bell, Kevin Joseph Keegan, Michael Roger Channon, Frank Stewart Worthington, Keith Weller, Trevor David Brooking.
Manager: Joseph Mercer

**ARGENTINA**: Daniel Alberto Carnevali, Rubén Oscar Glariá (46 Enrique Ernesto Wolff), Ángel Hugo Bargas, Roberto Alberto Perfumo (Cap), Francisco Pedro Manuel Sá, Miguel Ángel Brindisi (67 René Orlando Houseman), Roberto Marcelo Telch, Carlos Vicente Squeo, Agustín Alberto Balbuena, Rubén Hugo Ayala, Mario Alberto Kempes.
Trainer: Vladislao Wenceslao Cap

**Goals**: Michael Channon (45), Frank Worthington (54) / Mario Alberto Kempes (58, 89 pen)

483.  29.05.1974
**EAST GERMANY v ENGLAND  1-1**  (0-1)
*Zentral, Leipzig*

Referee: György Müncz (Hungary)   Attendance: 95,000

**EAST GERMANY**: Jürgen Croy, Bernd Bransch (Cap), Joachim Fritsche, Konrad Weise, Siegmar Wätzlich, Harald Irmscher, Jürgen Sparwasser, Jürgen Pommerenke, Wolfram Löwe, Joachim Streich, Eberhard Vogel (60 Martin Hoffmann).
Trainer: Georg Buschner

**ENGLAND**: Raymond Neal Clemence, Emlyn Walter Hughes (Cap), Alec Lindsay, Colin Todd, David Victor Watson, Martin John Dobson, Kevin Joseph Keegan, Michael Roger Channon, Frank Stewart Worthington, Colin Bell, Trevor David Brooking.   Manager: Joseph Mercer

**Goal**: Joachim Streich (66) / Michael Roger Channon (68)

484. 01.06.1974
**BULGARIA v ENGLAND 0-1** (0-1)
*Vasil Levski, Sofia*
Referee: Rolf Nyhus (Nor)   Attendance: 70,000
**BULGARIA**: Rumiancho Goranov, Ivan Zafirov, Dobromir Jechev, Stefan Velichkov, Bojil Kolev, Dimitar Penev, Voin Voinov (78 Mladen Vasilev), Hristo Bonev (Cap), Atanas Mihailov, Krasimir Borisov, Georgi Denev (61 Pavel Panov). Trainer: Hristo Mladenov
**ENGLAND**: Raymond Neal Clemence, Emlyn Walter Hughes (Cap), Colin Todd, David Victor Watson, Alec Lindsay, Martin John Dobson, Trevor David Brooking, Colin Bell, Kevin Joseph Keegan, Michael Roger Channon, Frank Stewart Worthington. Manager: Joseph Mercer
**Goal**: Frank Stewart Worthington (44)

485. 05.06.1974
**YUGOSLAVIA v ENGLAND 2-2** (1-1)
*Crvena Zvezda, Beograd*
Referee: Sergio Gonella (Italy)   Attendance: 90,000
**YUGOSLAVIA**: Enver Marić, Ivan Buljan, Petar Krivokuća (20. Enver Hadžiabdić), Dražen Mužinić (46. Dušan Bajević), Josip Katalinski, Vladislav Bogićević, Ilija Petković, Branko Oblak, Ivan Šurjak, Jovan Aćimović, Dragan Džajić (Cap). Selection committee: Miljan Miljanić, Milan Ribar, Sulejman Rebac, Tomislav Ivić and Milovan Ćirić
**ENGLAND**: Raymond Neal Clemence, Emlyn Walter Hughes (Cap), Alec Lindsay, Colin Todd, David Victor Watson, Martin John Dobson, Kevin Joseph Keegan, Michael Roger Channon, Frank Stewart Worthington (67 Malcolm Ian Macdonald), Colin Bell, Trevor David Brooking.   Manager: Joseph Mercer
**Goals**: Ilija Petković (22), Branko Oblak (52) / Michael Roger Channon (6), Kevin Joseph Keegan (75)

486. 30.10.1974   5th European Champs Qualifiers
**ENGLAND v CZECHOSLOVAKIA 3-0** (0-0)
*Wembley, London*
Referee: Michel Kitabdjian (France)   Attendance: 83,858
**ENGLAND**: Raymond Neal Clemence, Paul Edward Madeley, Emlyn Walter Hughes (Cap), Martin John Dobson (65 Trevor David Brooking), David Victor Watson, Norman Hunter, Colin Bell, Gerald Charles James Francis, Frank Stewart Worthington (66 David Thomas), Michael Roger Channon, Kevin Joseph Keegan.   Manager: Donald Revie
**CZECHOSLOVAKIA**: Ivo Viktor, Jan Pivarník (Cap), Anton Ondruš, Jozef Čapkovič (64 Rostislav Vojáček), Vojtěch Varadín, Přemysl Bičovský (70 Ladislav Kuna), Ivan Pekárik, Miroslav Gajdůšek, Marián Masný, Ján Švehlík, Pavel Stratil. Trainer: Václav Ježek
**Goals**: Michael Roger Channon (72), Colin Bell (79, 82)

487. 20.11.1974   5th European Champs Qualifiers
**ENGLAND v PORTUGAL 0-0**
*Wembley, London*
Referee: Anton Bucheli (Switzerland)   Attendance: 84,461
**ENGLAND**: Raymond Neal Clemence, Paul Edward Madeley, David Victor Watson, Emlyn Walter Hughes (Cap), Terence Cooper (23 Colin Todd), Trevor David Brooking, Gerald Charles James Francis, Colin Bell, David Thomas, Michael Roger Channon, Allan John Clarke (70 Frank Stewart Worthington).   Manager: Donald Revie
**PORTUGAL**: Vítor Manuel Alfonso DAMAS de Oliveira, ARTUR Manuel Soares CORREIA, HUMBERTO Manuel de Jesus COELHO (Cap), Carlos Alexandre Fortes Alhinho, Firmino Baleizão de Graça Sardinha "Osvaldinho", Adelino de Jesus Teixeira, OCTÁVIO Joaquim Coelho Machado, VÍTOR Manuel Rosa MARTINS, João António Ferreira Resende Alves, Francisco "Chico" Delfim Dias Faria (85 ROMEU Fernando Fernandes da Silva), Tamagnini Manuel Gomes Baptista "Nené" (85 António Luís Alves Ribeiro Oliveira). Trainer: José Maria Pedroto

488. 12.03.1975
**ENGLAND v WEST GERMANY 2-0** (1-0)
*Wembley, London*
Referee: Robert Schaut (Belgium)   Attendance: 100,000
**ENGLAND**: Raymond Neal Clemence, Steven Whitworth, Ian Terry Gillard, Colin Bell (Cap), David Victor Watson, Colin Todd, Alan James Ball, Malcolm Ian Macdonald, Michael Roger Channon, Alan Anthony Hudson, Kevin Joseph Keegan. Manager: Donald Revie
**WEST GERMANY**: Josef Maier, Hans-Hubert Vogts, Karl-Heinz Körbel, Franz Beckenbauer (Cap), Rainer Bonhof, Bernhard Cullmann, Heinz Flohe, Herbert Wimmer (64 Helmut Kremers), Manfred Ritschel, Erwin Kostedde (75 Josef Heynckes), Bernd Hölzenbein.   Trainer: Helmut Schön
**Goals**: Colin Bell (26), Malcolm Ian Macdonald (66)

489. 16.04.1975 5th European Champs Qualifiers
**ENGLAND v CYPRUS 5-0** (2-0)
*Wembley, London*
Referee: Martti Hirviniemi (Finland)   Attendance: 68,245
**ENGLAND**: Peter Leslie Shilton, Paul Edward Madeley, David Victor Watson, Colin Todd, Kevin Thomas Beattie, Colin Bell, Alan James Ball (Cap), Alan Anthony Hudson, Michael Roger Channon (58 David Thomas), Malcolm Ian Macdonald, Kevin Joseph Keegan.   Manager: Donald Revie
**CYPRUS**: Makis Alkiviadis (58 Andreas Konstantínou II), Hristakis Kovis, Kyriakos Koureas, Stefanis Miháíl, Níkos Pantziaras, Dimitris Kyzas, Gregori Savva, Lakis Theodorou, Andreas Stylianou, Níkos Haralámpous (46 Andreas Konstantínou I), Markos Markou.
Trainer: Pampos Avraamides
**Goals**: Malcolm Ian Macdonald (3, 35, 48, 53, 87)

490.  11.05.1975    5th European Champs Qualifiers
**CYPRUS v ENGLAND  0-1**  (0-1)
*Tsirion, Limassol*

Referee: Tsvetan Stanev (Bulgaria)    Attendance: 16,200

**CYPRUS**: Andreas Konstantínou, Hristakis Kovis, Staúros Stylianou, Dimitris Kyzas, Níkos Pantziaras, Stefanis Mihaíl, Níkos Haralámpous, Antros Miamiliotis (78 Takis Papettas), Tassos Konstantínou, Gregori Savva, Andreas Kalogiros (57 Kokos Antoníou).    Trainer: Pampos Avraamides

**ENGLAND**: Raymond Neal Clemence, Steven Whitworth, Kevin Thomas Beattie (41 Emlyn Walter Hughes), David Victor Watson, Colin Todd, Colin Bell, David Thomas, Alan James Ball (Cap), Michael Roger Channon, Malcolm Ian Macdonald, Kevin Joseph Keegan (73 Dennis Tueart).    Manager: Donald Revie

**Goal**: Kevin Joseph Keegan (6)


491.  17.05.1975    Home Championship
**NORTHERN IRELAND v ENGLAND  0-0**
*Windsor Park, Belfast*

Referee: Thomas Reynolds (Wales)    Attendance: 36,500

**NORTHERN IRELAND**: Patrick Anthony Jennings, Patrick James Rice, William James O'Kane, Christopher James Nicholl, Alan Hunter, David Clements, Bryan Hamilton (Thomas Finney), Martin Hugh Michael O'Neill, Derek William Spence, Samuel Baxter McIlroy, Thomas Jackson.

**ENGLAND**: Raymond Neal Clemence, Steven Whithworth, Emlyn Walter Hughes, Colin Bell, David Victor Watson, Colin Todd, Alan James Ball (Cap), Colin Viljeon, Malcolm Ian Macdonald (70 Michael Roger Channon), Kevin Joseph Keegan, Dennis Tueart.    Manager: Donald Revie


492.  21.05.1975    Home Championship
**ENGLAND v WALES  2-2**  (1-0)
*Wembley, London*

Referee: John Wright Paterson (Scotland)    Att: 53,000

**ENGLAND**: Raymond Neal Clemence, Steven Whitworth, Ian Terry Gillard, Gerald Charles James Francis, David Victor Watson, Colin Todd, Alan James Ball (Cap), Michael Roger Channon (70 Brian Little), David Edward Johnson, Colin Viljeon, David Thomas.    Manager: Donald Revie

**WALES**: William David Davies, Roderick John Thomas, Malcolm Edward Page, John Francis Mahoney, John Griffith Roberts, Leighton Phillips, Arfon Trevor Griffiths, Brian Flynn, David Paul Smallman (56 Derek Showers), John Benjamin Toshack, Leighton James.    Trainer: Michael Smith

**Goals**: David Edward Johnson (10, 71) /
John Benjamin Toshack (55), Arfon Trevor Griffiths (56)


493.  24.05.1975    Home Championship
**ENGLAND v SCOTLAND  5-1**  (3-1)
*Wembley, London*

Referee: Rudolf Glöckner (East Germany)    Att: 98,241

**ENGLAND**: Raymond Neal Clemence, Steven Whitworth, Kevin Thomas Beattie, Colin Bell, David Victor Watson, Colin Todd, Alan James Ball (Cap), Michael Roger Channon, David Edward Johnson, Gerald Charles James Francis, Kevin Joseph Keegan (85 David Thomas).    Manager: Donald Revie

**SCOTLAND**: Stewart J. Kennedy, William Pullar Jardine (Cap), Daniel Fergus McGrain, Francis Michael Munro, Gordon McQueen, Alfred James Conn, Bruce David Rioch, Kenneth Mathieson Dalglish, Arthur Duncan (61 Thomas Hutchison), Derek James Parlane, Edward John MacDougall (71 Luigi Macari).    Manager: William Esplin Ormond

**Goals**: Gerald Francis (6, 65), Kevin Beattie (8), Colin Bell (40), David Johnson (75) / Bruce Rioch (41 pen)


494.  03.09.1975
**SWITZERLAND v ENGLAND  1-2**  (1-2)
*St. Jakob, Basel*

Referee: Werner Eschweiler (West Germany)    Att: 30,000

**SWITZERLAND**: Erich Burgener, Gilbert Guyot, Jörg Stohler, Serge Trinchero, Pius Fischbach, Hans-Peter Schild (63 Rudolf Elsener), René Hasler, René Botteron, Hans-Jörg Pfister, Kurt Müller, Daniel Jeandupeux.    Trainer: René Hüssy

**ENGLAND**: Raymond Neal Clemence, Steven Whitworth, Colin Todd, David Victor Watson, Kevin Thomas Beattie, Colin Bell, Anthony William Currie, Gerald Charles James Francis (Cap), Michael Roger Channon, David Edward Johnson (55 Malcolm Ian Macdonald), Kevin Joseph Keegan.    Manager: Donald Revie

**Goals**: Kurt Müller (30) /
Kevin Joseph Keegan (8), Michael Roger Channon (19)


495.  30.10.1975    5th European Champs Qualifiers
**CZECHOSLOVAKIA v ENGLAND  2-1**  (1-1)
*Tehelné pole, Bratislava*

Referee: Alberto Michelotti (Italy)    Attendance: 50,651

**CZECHOSLOVAKIA**: Ivo Viktor, Jan Pivarník (Cap), Anton Ondruš, Ladislav Jurkemik, Koloman Gögh (62 Karel Dobiaš), Jaroslav Pollák, Přemysl Bičovský, Ľubomír Knapp, Marián Masný, Peter Gallis, Zdeněk Nehoda.    Trainer: Václav Ježek

**ENGLAND**: Raymond Neal Clemence, Paul Edward Madeley, Ian Terry Gillard, Gerald Charles James Francis (Cap), Roy Leslie McFarland (46 David Victor Watson), Colin Todd, Kevin Joseph Keegan, Michael Roger Channon (74 David Thomas), Malcolm Ian Macdonald, Allan John Clarke, Colin Bell.    Manager: Donald Revie

**Goals**: Zdeněk Nehoda (45), Peter Gallis (47) /
Michael Roger Channon (26)

496.  19.11.1975    5th European Champs Qualifiers
**PORTUGAL v ENGLAND  1-1**  (1-1)

*José Alvalade, Lisboa*

Referee:  Erich Linemayr (Austria)    Attendance:  60,000

**PORTUGAL**:  Vítor Manuel Alfonso DAMAS de Oliveira, Francisco Moreira da Silva Rebelo (46 António Carlos de Sousa Laranjeira Lima "Taí"), Rui Gouveia Pinto Rodrigues (49 Álvaro CAROLINO do Nascimento), Fernando António José Freitas, ARTUR Manuel Soares CORREIA, OCTÁVIO Joaquim Coelho Machado, João António Ferreira Resende Alves, António José da Conceiçao Oliveira "Toni" (Cap), Tamagnini Manuel Gomes Baptista "Nené", VÍTOR Manuel Ferreira BAPTISTA, Mário Jorge MOINHOS de Matos.    Trainer:  José Maria Pedroto

**ENGLAND**:  Raymond Neal Clemence, Steven Whitworth, Kevin Thomas Beattie, Gerald Charles James Francis (Cap), David Victor Watson, Colin Todd, Kevin Joseph Keegan, Michael Roger Channon, Malcolm Ian Macdonald (74 David Thomas), Trevor David Brooking, Paul Edward Madeley (75 Allan John Clarke).    Manager:  Donald Revie

**Goal**:  Rui Rodrigues (16) / Michael Roger Channon (40)

497.  24.03.1976    Home Championship
**WALES v ENGLAND  1-2**  (0-0)

*Racecourse Ground, Wrexham*

Referee:  Foote (Scotland)    Attendance:  20,927

**WALES**:  Brian William Lloyd, Malcolm Edward Page, Joseph Patrick Jones, Leighton Phillips, Ian Peter Evans, Carl Stephen Harris, Terence Charles Yorath, Brian Flynn, Alan Thomas Curtis, John Griffith Roberts, Arfon Trevor Griffiths.    Trainer:  Michael Smith

**ENGLAND**:  Raymond Neal Clemence, Trevor John Cherry (46 David Thomas Clement), Michael Dennis Mills, Philip George Neal, Philip Brian Thompson, Michael Doyle, Kevin Joseph Keegan (Cap), Michael Roger Channon (46 Peter John Taylor), Philip John Boyer, Trevor David Brooking, Raymond Kennedy.    Manager:  Donald Revie

**Goals**:  Alan Thomas Curtis (90) / Raymond Kennedy (70), Peter John Taylor (80)

498.  08.05.1976    Home Championship
**WALES v ENGLAND  0-1**  (0-0)

*Ninian Park, Cardiff*

Referee:  Robert Holley Davidson (Scotland)    Att: 24,592

**WALES**:  William David Davies, Roderick John Thomas (David Edward Jones), Malcolm Edward Page, John Francis Mahoney, Leighton Phillips, Ian Peter Evans, Terence Charles Yorath, Brian Flynn, Alan Thomas Curtis (73 Arfon Trevor Griffiths), John Benjamin Toshack, Leighton James.    Trainer:  Michael Smith

**ENGLAND**:  Raymond Neal Clemence, David Thomas Clement, Michael Dennis Mills, Anthony Mark Towers, Brian Greenhoff, Philip Brian Thompson, Kevin Joseph Keegan, Gerald Charles James Francis (Cap), Stuart James Pearson, Raymond Kennedy, Peter John Taylor.    Manager:  Donald Revie

**Goal**:  Peter John Taylor (59)

499.  11.05.1976    Home Championship
**ENGLAND v NORTHERN IRELAND  4-0**  (2-0)

*Wembley, London*

Referee:  Clive Thomas (Wales)    Attendance:  48,000

**ENGLAND**:  Raymond Neal Clemence, Colin Todd, Michael Dennis Mills, Philip Brian Thompson, Brian Greenhoff, Raymond Kennedy, Kevin Joseph Keegan (65 Joseph Royle), Gerald Charles James Francis (Cap), Stuart James Pearson, Michael Roger Channon, Peter John Taylor (60 Anthony Mark Towers).    Manager:  Donald Revie

**NORTHERN IRELAND**:  Patrick Anthony Jennings, Patrick James Rice, Samuel Nelson (Peter William Scott), David Clements, Alan Hunter, Christopher James Nicholl, Bryan Hamilton, Thomas Cassidy, David McCreery, Derek William Spence, Samuel Baxter McIlroy.    Manager:  David Clements

**Goals**:  Gerald Charles James Francis (35), Michael Channon (36 pen, 77), Stuart James Pearson (60)

500.  15.05.1976    Home Championship
**SCOTLAND v ENGLAND  2-1**  (1-1)

*Hampden Park, Glasgow*

Referee:  Károly Palotai (Hungary)    Attendance:  85,165

**SCOTLAND**:  Alan Roderick Rough, Daniel Fergus McGrain, William Donachie, Thomas Forsyth, Colin MacDonald Jackson, Archibald Gemmill (Cap), Donald Sandison Masson, Bruce David Rioch, Edwin Gray (79 Derek Joseph Johnstone), Kenneth Mathieson Dalglish, Joseph Jordan.    Manager:  William Esplin Ormond

**ENGLAND**:  Raymond Neal Clemence, Colin Todd, Michael Dennis Mills, Philip Brian Thompson, Roy Leslie McFarland (70 Michael Doyle), Raymond Kennedy, Kevin Joseph Keegan, Gerald Charles James Francis (Cap), Stuart James Pearson (46 Trevor John Cherry), Michael Roger Channon, Peter John Taylor.    Manager:  Donald Revie

**Goal**:  Donald Masson (18), Kenneth Dalglish (49) / Michael Roger Channon (11)

**501. 23.05.1976   USA Bicentenary Cup**
**BRAZIL v ENGLAND  1-0**  (0-0)
*Coliseum, Los Angeles*
Ref:  Hans-Joachim Weyland (West Germany)    Att: 32,900
**BRAZIL**:  Emerson Leão, ORLANDO Pereira, MIGUEL Ferreira Pereira, Rigoberto Costa "Beto Fuscão", MARCO ANTÔNIO Feliciano (50 Francisco das Chagas Marinho), Paulo Roberto Falcão, Roberto Rivelino, Arthur Antunes Coimbra "Zico", Gilberto Alves "Gil", Antônio Rodrigues Filho "Neca" (Carlos ROBERTO de Oliveira "Dinamite"), Luís Ribeiro Pinto Neto "Lula".   Trainer: Osvaldo Brandão
**ENGLAND**:  Raymond Neal Clemence, Colin Todd, Michael Doyle, Philip Brian Thompson, Michael Dennis Mills, Gerald Charles James Francis (Cap), Trevor John Cherry, Trevor David Brooking, Kevin Joseph Keegan, Stuart James Pearson, Michael Roger Channon.   Manager: Donald Revie
**Goal**:  Roberto Dinamite (89)

**502. 28.05.1976**
**ENGLAND v ITALY  3-2**  (0-2)
*Yankee Stadium, New York*
Ref:  Hans-Joachim Weyland (West Germany)    Att: 46,650
**ENGLAND**:  John James Rimmer (46 Joseph Thomas Corrigan), David Thomas Clement, Philip George Neal (46 Michael Dennis Mills), Philip Brian Thompson, Michael Doyle, Anthony Mark Towers, Raymond Colin Wilkins, Trevor David Brooking, Joseph Royle, Michael Roger Channon (Cap), Gordon Alec Hill.   Manager: Donald Revie
**ITALY**:  Dino Zoff, Moreno Roggi (57 Aldo Maldera), Francesco Rocca, Romeo Benetti (57 Renato Zaccarelli), Mauro Bellugi, Giacinto Facchetti (Cap), Franco Causio (57 Claudio Sala), Fabio Capello, Francesco Graziani, Giancarlo Antognoni, Paolino Pulici.
Trainers: Fulvio Bernardini & Enzo Bearzot
**Goals**:  Michael Roger Channon (46, 53),
Philip Brian Thompson (48) / Francesco Graziani (15, 18)

**503. 13.06.1976   11th World Cup Qualifiers**
**FINLAND v ENGLAND  1-4**  (1-2)
*Olympia, Helsinki*
Referee:  Alfred Delcourt (Belgium)    Attendance: 24,336
**FINLAND**:  Göran Enckelman, Erkki Vihtilä, Arto Tolsa, Ari Mäkynen, Esko Ranta, Pertti Jantunen, Jouko Suomalainen (65 Seppo Pyykkö), Esa Heiskanen, Olavi Rissanen, Aki Heiskanen, Matti Paatelainen (Cap).   Trainer: Aulis Rytkönen
**ENGLAND**:  Raymond Neal Clemence, Colin Todd, Michael Dennis Mills, Philip Brian Thompson, Paul Edward Madeley, Trevor John Cherry, Kevin Joseph Keegan, Michael Roger Channon, Stuart James Pearson, Trevor David Brooking, Gerald Charles James Francis (Cap).   Manager: Donald Revie
**Goals**:  Matti Paatelainen (28) / Stuart James Pearson (14), Kevin Joseph Keegan (30, 60), Michael Roger Channon (56)

**504. 08.09.1976**
**ENGLAND v REPUBLIC OF IRELAND  1-1**  (1-0)
*Wembley, London*
Referee:  Hugh Alexander (Scotland)    Attendance: 51,000
**ENGLAND**:  Raymond Neal Clemence, Colin Todd, Paul Edward Madeley, Trevor John Cherry, Roy Leslie McFarland, Brian Greenhoff, Kevin Joseph Keegan (Cap), Raymond Colin Wilkins, Stuart James Pearson, Trevor David Brooking, Charles Frederick George (66 Gordon Alec Hill).   Manager: Donald Revie
**IRELAND**:  Michael Kearns, Patrick Martin Mulligan, James Paul Holmes, Michael Paul Martin, David Anthony O'Leary, William Brady, Gerard Anthony Daly, Gerard Anthony Francis Conroy, Stephen Derek Heighway, John Michael Giles (Cap), Daniel Joseph Givens.   Manager: John Michael Giles
**Goal**:  Stuart James Pearson (45) / Gerard Daly (52 pen)

**505. 13.10.1976   11th World Cup Qualifiers**
**ENGLAND v FINLAND  2-1**  (1-0)
*Wembley, London*
Referee:  Ulf Eriksson (Sweden)    Attendance: 92,000
**ENGLAND**:  Raymond Neal Clemence, Colin Todd, Kevin Thomas Beattie, Philip Brian Thompson, Brian Greenhoff, Raymond Colin Wilkins, Kevin Joseph Keegan (Cap), Michael Roger Channon, Joseph Royle, Trevor David Brooking (73 Michael Dennis Mills), Dennis Tueart (73 Gordon Alec Hill).   Manager: Donald Revie
**FINLAND**:  Göran Enckelman, Teppo Heikkinen, Erkki Vihtilä, Ari Mäkynen, Esko Ranta, Pertti Jantunen (61 Esa Heiskanen), Jouko Suomalainen (67 Seppo Pyykkö), Miikka Toivola, Jyrki Nieminen, Aki Heiskanen, Matti Paatelainen (Cap).   Trainer: Aulis Rytkönen
**Goals**:  Dennis Tueart (4), Joseph Royle (52) /
Jyrki Nieminen (48)

**506. 17.11.1976   11th World Cup Qualifiers**
**ITALY v ENGLAND  2-0**  (1-0)
*Olimpico, Roma*
Referee:  Abraham Klein (Israel)    Attendance: 70,718
**ITALY**:  Dino Zoff, Antonello Cuccureddu, Marco Tardelli, Romeo Benetti, Claudio Gentile, Giacinto Facchetti (Cap), Franco Causio, Fabio Capello, Francesco Graziani, Giancarlo Antognoni, Roberto Bettega.
Trainers: Fulvio Bernardini & Enzo Bearzot
**ENGLAND**:  Raymond Neal Clemence, David Thomas Clement (75 Kevin Thomas Beattie), Michael Dennis Mills, Brian Greenhoff, Roy Leslie McFarland, Emlyn Walter Hughes, Kevin Joseph Keegan (Cap), Michael Roger Channon, Stanley Bowles, Trevor John Cherry, Trevor David Brooking.   Manager: Donald Revie
**Goals**:  Giancarlo Antognoni (36), Roberto Bettega (77)

507. 09.02.1977
**ENGLAND v HOLLAND 0-2** (0-2)
*Wembley, London*

Referee: Werner Eschweiler (West Germany)   Att: 90,260

**ENGLAND**: Raymond Neal Clemence, David Thomas Clement, Kevin Thomas Beattie, Michael Doyle, David Victor Watson, Paul Edward Madeley (74 Stuart James Pearson), Kevin Joseph Keegan (Cap), Brian Greenhoff (40 Colin Todd), Trevor John Francis, Stanley Bowles, Trevor David Brooking. Manager: Donald Revie

**HOLLAND**: Piet Schrijvers, Wim Suurbier, Wim Rijsbergen, Ruud Krol, Hugo Hovenkamp, Willy van de Kerkhof, Jan Peters, Johan Neeskens, Johnny Rep (75 Kees Kist), Johan Cruijff (Cap), Robert Rensenbrink. Trainer: Johannes Zwartkruis

**Goals**: Jan Peters (28, 36)


508. 30.03.1977   11th World Cup Qualifiers
**ENGLAND v LUXEMBOURG 5-0** (1-0)
*Wembley, London*

Referee: Paul Bonett (Malta)   Attendance: 81,718

**ENGLAND**: Raymond Neal Clemence, John Gidman, Trevor John Cherry, Raymond Kennedy, David Victor Watson, Emlyn Walter Hughes, Kevin Joseph Keegan (Cap), Michael Roger Channon, Joseph Royle (46 Paul Mariner), Trevor John Francis, Gordon Alec Hill.   Manager: Donald Revie

**LUXEMBOURG** Raymond Zender, Jean-Louis Margue, Louis Pilot (Cap), Léon Mond, Jean Zuang, Roger Fandel, Marcel Di Domenico (76 Nibio Orioli), Gilbert Dresch, Nicolas Braun, Paul Philipp, Gilbert Dussier.   Trainer: Gilbert Legrand

**Goals**: Gilbert Dresch (86)

**Goals**: Kevin Joseph Keegan (10), Trevor John Francis (58), Raymond Kennedy (63), Michael Roger Channon (69, 81 pen)


509. 28.05.1977   Home Championship
**NORTHERN IRELAND v ENGLAND 1-2** (1-1)
*Windsor Park, Belfast*

Ref: Hans-Joachim Weyland (West Germany)   Att: 35,000

**NORTHERN IRELAND**: Patrick Anthony Jennings, James Michael Nicholl, Patrick James Rice, Thomas A. Jackson, Alan Hunter, Bryan Hamilton, Roland Christopher McGrath, Samuel Baxter McIlroy, Gerard Joseph Armstrong (49 Martin Hugh Michael O'Neill), David McCreery, Trevor Anderson (72 Derek William Spence).

**ENGLAND**: Peter Leslie Shilton, Trevor John Cherry, Michael Dennis Mills, Brian Greenhoff, David Victor Watson, Colin Todd, Raymond Colin Wilkins (65 Brian Ernest Talbot), Michael Roger Channon (Cap), Paul Mariner, Trevor David Brooking, Dennis Tueart.   Manager: Donald Revie

**Goals**: Roland Christopher McGrath (4) /
Michael Roger Channon (27), Dennis Tueart (86)


510. 31.05.1977   Home Championship
**ENGLAND v WALES 0-1** (0-1)
*Wembley, London*

Referee: John Robertson Gordon (Scotland)   Att: 48,000

**ENGLAND**: Peter Leslie Shilton, Philip George Neal, Michael Dennis Mills, Brian Greenhoff, David Victor Watson, Emlyn Walter Hughes, Kevin Joseph Keegan (Cap), Michael Roger Channon, Stuart James Pearson, Trevor David Brooking (79 Dennis Tueart), Raymond Kennedy.   Manager: Donald Revie

**WALES**: William David Davies, Roderick John Thomas, Joseph Patrick Jones, Leighton Phillips (46 David Frazer Roberts), Ian Peter Evans, John Francis Mahoney, Peter Anthony Sayer, Brian Flynn, Terence Charles Yorath, Nicholas Simon Deacy, Leighton James.   Trainer: Michael Smith

**Goal**: Leighton James (44 pen)


511. 04.06.1977   Home Championship
**ENGLAND v SCOTLAND 1-2** (0-1)
*Wembley, London*

Referee: Károly Palotai (Hungary)   Attendance: 98,103

**ENGLAND**: Raymond Neal Clemence, Philip George Neal, Michael Dennis Mills, Brian Greenhoff (57 Trevor John Cherry), David Victor Watson, Emlyn Walter Hughes (Cap), Trevor John Francis, Michael Roger Channon, Stuart James Pearson, Brian Ernest Talbot, Raymond Kennedy (67 Dennis Tueart).   Manager: Donald Revie

**SCOTLAND**: Alan Roderick Rough, Daniel Fergus McGrain, William Donachie, Thomas Forsyth, Gordon McQueen, Donald Sandison Masson (83 Archibald Gemmill), Bruce David Rioch (Cap), Richard Asa Hartford, William McClure Johnston, Kenneth Mathieson Dalglish, Joseph Jordan (43 Luigi Macari).   Manager: Alistair MacLeod

**Goal**: Michael Roger Channon (87 pen) /
Gordon McQueen (43), Kenneth Mathieson Dalglish (61)


512. 08.06.1977
**BRAZIL v ENGLAND 0-0**
*Maracana, Rio de Janeiro*

Referee: Alberto Ducatelli (Argentina)   Attendance: 77,000

**BRAZIL**: Emerson Leão, José Maria Rodrigues Alves "Zé Maria", João Justino Amaral dos Santos "Amaral", Édino Nazareth Filho "Edinho", José Rodrigues Neto, Antônio Carlos Cerezo "Toninho Cerezo", Arthur Antunes Coimbra "Zico", Roberto Rivelino, Gilberto Alves "Gil" (75 José Mário Donizeti Baroni "Zé Mário"), Carlos ROBERTO de Oliveira "Dinamite", PAULO CÉSAR Lima.   Trainer: Cláudio de Morais "Coutinho"

**ENGLAND**: Raymond Neal Clemence, Philip George Neal, Trevor John Cherry, Brian Greenhoff, David Victor Watson, Emlyn Walter Hughes, Kevin Joseph Keegan (Cap), Trevor John Francis, Stuart James Pearson (70 Michael Roger Channon), Raymond Colin Wilkins (70 Raymond Kennedy), Brian Ernest Talbot.   Manager: Donald Revie

513.  12.06.1977
**ARGENTINA v ENGLAND  1-1**  (1-1)
*Alberto Armando "La Bombonera", Buenos Aires*
Referee: Ramón Barreto Ruiz (Uruguay)   Att: 60,000
**ARGENTINA**: Héctor Rodolfo Baley, Vicente Alberto Pernía, Daniel Pedro Killer, Daniel Alberto Passarella, Alberto César Tarantini, Osvaldo César Ardiles, Américo Rubén Gallego, Ricardo Enrique Bochini (55 Omar Rubén Larrosa), Ricardo Daniel Bertoni, Leopoldo Jacinto Luque, Oscar Alberto Ortíz (55 Juan Ramón Rocha).   Trainer: César Luis Menotti
**ENGLAND**: Raymond Neal Clemence, Philip George Neal, Trevor John Cherry, Brian Greenhoff (46 Raymond Kennedy), David Victor Watson, Emlyn Walter Hughes, Kevin Joseph Keegan (Cap), Michael Roger Channon, Stuart James Pearson, Raymond Colin Wilkins, Brian Ernest Talbot.   Manager: Donald Revie
**Sent off**: Trevor Cherry (80), Ricardo Daniel Bertoni (82)
**Goals**: Ricardo Daniel Bertoni (15) / Stuart Pearson (3)


514.  15.06.1977
**URUGUAY v ENGLAND  0-0**
*Centenario, Montevideo*
Referee: Miguel Comesana (Argentina)   Attendance: 25,000
**URUGUAY**: Freddy Clavijo, Julio Rivadavia, Francisco Salomón, Alfredo de los Santos, Alfonso Darío Pereyra, Beethoven Javier, Rudy Rodríguez, Juan Ramón Carrasco, Alberto Raúl Santelli, Ildo Enrique Maneiro, Washington Olivera (73 Juan Muhlethaler).   Trainer: Omar Borrás
**ENGLAND**: Raymond Neal Clemence, Philip George Neal, Trevor John Cherry, Brian Greenhoff, David Victor Watson, Emlyn Walter Hughes, Kevin Joseph Keegan (Cap), Michael Roger Channon, Stuart James Pearson, Raymond Colin Wilkins, Brian Ernest Talbot.   Manager: Donald Revie


515.  07.09.1977
**ENGLAND v SWITZERLAND  0-0**
*Wembley, London*
Referee: Georges Konrath (France)   Attendance: 42,000
**ENGLAND**: Raymond Neal Clemence, Philip George Neal, Trevor John Cherry, Terence McDermott, David Victor Watson, Emlyn Walter Hughes (Cap), Kevin Joseph Keegan, Michael Roger Channon (46 Gordon Alec Hill), Trevor John Francis, Raymond Kennedy, Ian Robert Callaghan (80 Raymond Colin Wilkins).   Manager: Ronald Greenwood
**SWITZERLAND**: Erich Burgener, Pierre-Albert Chapuisat, Serge Trinchero, Lucio Bizzini, Pius Fischbach, Umberto Barberis, René Hasler (79 Jakob Brechbühl), René Botteron, Rudolf Elsener (85 Beat Rieder), Josef Küttel (58 Claudio Sulser), Otto Demarmels (46 Arthur von Wartburg).   Trainer: Roger Vonlanthen


516.  12.10.1977   11th World Cup Qualifiers
**LUXEMBOURG v ENGLAND  0-2**  (0-1)
*Municipal, Luxembourg*
Referee: Alojzy Jarguz (Poland)   Attendance: 10,621
**LUXEMBOURG** Jeannot Moes, Marcel Barthel, Roger Fandel (82 Joseph Zangerle), Léon Mond, Nicolas Rohmann, Paul Philipp (Cap), Romain Michaux, Jean Zuang, Gilbert Dussier, Nicolas Braun (80 Marcel Di Domenico), Vinicio Monacelli.   Trainer: Gilbert Legrand
**ENGLAND**: Raymond Neal Clemence, Trevor John Cherry, David Victor Watson (69 Kevin Thomas Beattie), Emlyn Walter Hughes (Cap), Raymond Kennedy, Ian Robert Callaghan, Terence McDermott (65 Trevor John Whymark), Raymond Colin Wilkins, Trevor John Francis, Paul Mariner, Gordon Alec Hill.   Manager: Ronald Greenwood
**Goals**: Raymond Kennedy (31), Paul Mariner (90)


517.  16.11.1977   11th World Cup Qualifiers
**ENGLAND v ITALY  2-0**  (1-0)
*Wembley, London*
Referee: Károly Palotai (Hungary)   Attendance: 92,500
**ENGLAND**: Raymond Neal Clemence, Philip George Neal, Trevor John Cherry, Raymond Colin Wilkins, David Victor Watson, Emlyn Walter Hughes (Cap), Kevin Joseph Keegan (83 Trevor John Francis), Steven James Coppell, Robert Dennis Latchford (75 Stuart James Pearson), Trevor David Brooking, Peter Simon Barnes.   Manager: Ronald Greenwood
**ITALY**: Dino Zoff, Marco Tardelli, Claudio Gentile, Romeo Benetti, Roberto Mozzini, Giacinto Facchetti (Cap) (83 Antonello Cuccureddu), Franco Causio, Renato Zaccarelli, Francesco Graziani (46 Claudio Sala), Giancarlo Antognoni, Roberto Bettega.   Trainer: Enzo Bearzot
**Goals**: Kevin Joseph Keegan (11), Trevor Brooking (80)


518.  22.02.1978
**WEST GERMANY v ENGLAND  2-1**  (0-1)
*Olympiastadion, München*
Referee: Franz Wöhrer (Austria)   Attendance: 77,850
**WEST GERMANY**: Josef Maier, Hans-Hubert Vogts (Cap), Rolf Rüssmann, Georg Schwarzenbeck, Herbert Zimmermann, Rainer Bonhof, Herbert Neumann (72 Bernhard Dietz), Heinz Flohe (33 Manfred Burgsmüller), Rudiger Abramczik, Bernd Hölzenbein (75 Ronald Worm), Karl-Heinz Rummenigge.   Trainer: Helmut Schön
**ENGLAND**: Raymond Neal Clemence, Philip George Neal, Michael Dennis Mills, Raymond Colin Wilkins, David Victor Watson, Emlyn Walter Hughes (Cap), Kevin Joseph Keegan (78 Trevor John Francis), Steven James Coppell, Stuart James Pearson, Trevor David Brooking, Peter Simon Barnes.   Manager: Ronald Greenwood
**Goal**: Ronald Worm (76), Rainer Bonhof (86) / Stuart James Pearson (44)

519.  19.04.1978
**ENGLAND v BRAZIL  1-1**  (0-1)
*Wembley, London*

Referee:  Charles Corver (Holland)    Attendance:  92,500

**ENGLAND**:  Joseph Thomas Corrigan, Michael Dennis Mills, Trevor John Cherry, Brian Greenhoff, David Victor Watson, Anthony William Currie, Kevin Joseph Keegan (Cap), Steven James Coppell, Robert Dennis Latchford, Trevor John Francis, Peter Simon Barnes.    Manager:  Ronald Greenwood

**BRAZIL**:  Emerson Leão, José Maria Rodrigues Alves "Zé Maria", ABEL Carlos da Silva Braga, João Justino Amaral dos Santos "Amaral", Édino Nazareth Filho "Edinho", Antônio Carlos Cerezo "Toninho Cerezo", Arthur Antunes Coimbra "Zico", Roberto Rivelino, Gilberto Alves "Gil", João Batista NUNES de Oliveira (60 João BATISTA da Silva), DIRCEU José Guimarães.    Trainer:  Cláudio de Morais "Coutinho"

**Goal**:  Kevin Joseph Keegan (70) / Gilberto Alves "Gil" (10)


520.  13.05.1978    Home Championship
**WALES v ENGLAND  1-3**  (0-1)
*Ninian Park, Cardiff*

Referee:  Malcolm Moffatt (Northern Ireland)    Att: 17,698

**WALES**:  William David Davies, Malcolm Edward Page, Joseph Patrick Jones, Leighton Phillips, David Edward Jones (70 Gareth Davies), Terence Charles Yorath (46 John Francis Mahoney), Brian Flynn, Carl Stephen Harris, Alan Thomas Curtis, Phillip John Dwyer, Michael Reginald Thomas.    Trainer:  Michael Smith

**ENGLAND**:  Peter Leslie Shilton, Michael Dennis Mills (Cap), Trevor John Cherry (16 Anthony William Currie), Brian Greenhoff, David Victor Watson, Raymond Colin Wilkins, Steven James Coppell, Trevor John Francis, Robert Dennis Latchford (32 Paul Mariner), Trevor David Brooking, Peter Simon Barnes.    Manager:  Ronald Greenwood

**Goals**:  Phillip John Dwyer (63) / Robert Latchford (8), Anthony William Currie (82), Peter Simon Barnes (89)


521.  16.05.1978    Home Championship
**ENGLAND v NORTHERN IRELAND  1-0**  (1-0)
*Wembley, London*

Referee:  John Robertson Gordon (Scotland)    Att: 55,000

**ENGLAND**:  Raymond Neal Clemence, Philip George Neal, Michael Dennis Mills, Raymond Colin Wilkins, David Victor Watson, Emlyn Walter Hughes (Cap), Anthony William Currie, Steven James Coppell, Stuart James Pearson, Anthony Stewart Woodcock, Brian Greenhoff.    Manager:  Ronald Greenwood

**NORTHERN IRELAND**:  James Archibald Platt, Bryan Hamilton, Peter William Scott, Christopher James Nicholl, James Michael Nicholl, Samuel Baxter McIlroy, David McCreery, Martin Hugh Michael O'Neill, Trevor Anderson, Gerard Joseph Armstrong, Roland Christopher McGrath (60 George Terence Cochrane).    Manager:  Robert Denis Blanchflower

**Goal**:  Philip George Neal (45)


522.  20.05.1978    Home Championship
**SCOTLAND v ENGLAND  0-1**  (0-0)
*Hampden Park, Glasgow*

Referee:  Georges Konrath (France)    Attendance:  88,319

**SCOTLAND**:  Alan Roderick Rough, Stuart Robert Kennedy, William Donachie, Thomas Forsyth, Kenneth Burns, Donald Sandison Masson (74 Archibald Gemmill), Bruce David Rioch (Cap) (74 Graeme James Souness), Richard Asa Hartford, William McClure Johnston, Kenneth Mathieson Dalglish, Joseph Jordan.    Manager:  Alistair MacLeod

**ENGLAND**:  Raymond Neal Clemence, Philip George Neal, Michael Dennis Mills, Anthony William Currie, David Victor Watson, Emlyn Walter Hughes (Cap) (73 Brian Greenhoff), Raymond Colin Wilkins, Steven James Coppell, Paul Mariner (76 Trevor David Brooking), Trevor John Francis, Peter Simon Barnes.    Manager:  Ronald Greenwood

**Goal**:  Steven James Coppell (83)


523.  24.05.1978
**ENGLAND v HUNGARY  4-1**  (3-0)
*Wembley, London*

Referee:  René Vigliani (France)    Attendance:  75,000

**ENGLAND**:  Peter Leslie Shilton, Philip George Neal, Michael Dennis Mills, Raymond Colin Wilkins, David Victor Watson (46 Brian Greenhoff), Emlyn Walter Hughes (Cap), Kevin Joseph Keegan, Steven James Coppell, Trevor John Francis, Trevor David Brooking (73 Anthony William Currie), Peter Simon Barnes.    Manager:  Ronald Greenwood

**HUNGARY**:  Sándor Gujdár, Péter Török, István Kocsis, Zoltán Kereki, József Tóth, Tibor Nyilasi, Sándor Pintér, Sándor Zombori, László Fazekas (46 Károly Csapó), András Törőcsik, László Nagy.    Trainer:  Lajos Baróti

**Goals**:  Peter Simon Barnes (11), Philip Neal (34 pen), Trevor John Francis (38), Anthony William Currie (82) / László Nagy (62)

**524. 20.09.1978   6th European Champs Qualifiers**
**DENMARK v ENGLAND  3-4**  (2-2)
*Idraetsparken, København*
Referee: Adolf Prokop (East Germany)   Attendance: 47,600
**DENMARK**: Birger Jensen, Flemming Nielsen, Henning Munk Jensen, Per Røntved (Cap), Søren Lerby, Carsten Nielsen, Flemming Lund, Frank Arnesen, Allan Rodenkam Simonsen, Benny Nielsen (46 Allan Hansen), Jørgen Kristensen. Trainer: Kurt Nielsen
**ENGLAND**: Raymond Neal Clemence, Philip George Neal, Michael Dennis Mills, Raymond Colin Wilkins, David Victor Watson, Emlyn Walter Hughes (Cap), Kevin Joseph Keegan, Steven James Coppell, Robert Dennis Latchford, Trevor David Brooking, Peter Simon Barnes.  Manager: Ronald Greenwood
**Goals**: Allan Simonsen (27 pen), Frank Arnesen (30), Per Røntved (86) / Kevin Joseph Keegan (17, 23), Robert Dennis Latchford (52), Philip George Neal (83)

**525. 25.10.1978   6th European Champs Qualifiers**
**REPUBLIC OF IRELAND v ENGLAND  1-1**  (1-1)
*Lansdowne Road, Dublin*
Referee: Heinz Aldinger (West Germany)   Att: 55,000
**IRELAND**: Michael Kearns, Patrick Martin Mulligan (Cap), Mark Thomas Lawrenson, David Anthony O'Leary (73 Eamonn Gregg), James Paul Holmes, Gerard Anthony Daly, William Brady, Anthony Patrick Grealish, Paul Gerard McGee (65 Francis Anthony Stapleton), Gerard Joseph Ryan, Daniel Joseph Givens.   Manager: John Michael Giles
**ENGLAND**: Raymond Neal Clemence, Philip George Neal, Michael Dennis Mills, Raymond Colin Wilkins, David Victor Watson (22 Philip Brian Thompson), Emlyn Walter Hughes (Cap), Kevin Joseph Keegan, Steven James Coppell, Robert Dennis Latchford, Trevor David Brooking, Peter Simon Barnes (81 Anthony Stewart Woodcock).
Manager: Ronald Greenwood
**Goals**: Gerard Anthony Daly (27) / Robert Latchford (8)

**526. 29.11.1978**
**ENGLAND v CZECHOSLOVAKIA  1-0**  (0-0)
*Wembley, London*
Referee: Erich Linemayr (Austria)   Attendance: 92,000
**ENGLAND**: Peter Leslie Shilton, Vivian Alexander Anderson, Philip Brian Thompson, David Victor Watson, Trevor John Cherry, Raymond Colin Wilkins, Anthony William Currie, Steven James Coppell, Anthony Stewart Woodcock (41 Robert Dennis Latchford), Kevin Joseph Keegan (Cap), Peter Simon Barnes.  Manager: Ronald Greenwood
**CZECHOSLOVAKIA**: Pavol Michalík, Jozef Barmoš, Rostislav Vojáček, Ladislav Jurkemik, Koloman Gögh, Ján Kozák, Karel Jarůšek (76 Antonín Panenka), František Štambachr, Marián Masný, Zdeněk Nehoda (Cap), Miroslav Gajdůšek.   Trainer: Jozef Vengloš
**Goal**: Steven James Coppell (69)

**527. 07.02.1979   6th European Champs Qualifiers**
**ENGLAND v NORTHERN IRELAND  4-0**  (1-0)
*Wembley, London*
Referee: Ulf Eriksson (Sweden)   Attendance: 91,244
**ENGLAND**: Raymond Neal Clemence, Philip George Neal, Michael Dennis Mills, Anthony William Currie, David Victor Watson, Emlyn Walter Hughes (Cap), Kevin Joseph Keegan, Steven James Coppell, Robert Dennis Latchford, Trevor David Brooking, Peter Simon Barnes.  Manager: Ronald Greenwood
**NORTHERN IRELAND**: Patrick Anthony Jennings (Cap), Patrick James Rice, Samuel Nelson, Christopher James Nicholl, James Michael Nicholl, David McCreery, Martin Hugh Michael O'Neill, Samuel Baxter McIlroy, Gerard Joseph Armstrong, William Thomas Caskey (50 Derek William Spence), George Terence Cochrane (81 Roland Christopher McGrath).   Manager: Robert Denis Blanchflower
**Goals**: Kevin Keegan (25), Robert Dennis Latchford (46, 64), David Victor Watson (50)

**528. 19.05.1979   Home Championship**
**NORTHERN IRELAND v ENGLAND  0-2**  (0-2)
*Windsor Park, Belfast*
Referee: Ian Foote (Scotland)   Attendance: 35,000
**NORTHERN IRELAND**: Patrick Anthony Jennings, Patrick James Rice, Samuel Nelson, Christopher James Nicholl, James Michael Nicholl, Victor Moreland (57 Roland Christopher McGrath), Bryan Hamilton, Samuel Baxter McIlroy, Gerard Joseph Armstrong, William Thomas Caskey, George Terence Cochrane (68 Derek William Spence).
**ENGLAND**: Raymond Neal Clemence, Philip George Neal, Michael Dennis Mills (Cap), Philip Brian Thompson, David Victor Watson, Raymond Colin Wilkins, Steven James Coppell, Terence McDermott, Robert Dennis Latchford, Anthony William Currie, Peter Simon Barnes.
Manager: Ronald Greenwood
**Goals**: David Victor Watson (11), Steven James Coppell (14)

**529. 23.05.1979   Home Championship**
**ENGLAND v WALES  0-0**
*Wembley, London*
Referee: Malcolm Moffatt (Northern Ireland)   Att: 70,220
**ENGLAND**: Joseph Thomas Corrigan, Trevor John Cherry, Kenneth Graham Sansom, Raymond Colin Wilkins (75 Trevor David Brooking), David Victor Watson, Emlyn Walter Hughes (Cap), Kevin Joseph Keegan (68 Steven James Coppell), Anthony William Currie, Robert Dennis Latchford, Terence McDermott, Laurence Paul Cunningham.
Manager: Ronald Greenwood
**WALES**: William David Davies, William Byron Stevenson, Joseph Patrick Jones, Leighton Phillips, Phillip John Dwyer, John Francis Mahoney, Terence Charles Yorath (Cap), Brian Flynn, Robert Mark James, John Benjamin Toshack (80 Carl Stephen Harris), Alan Thomas Curtis.
Manager: Michael Smith

**530. 26.05.1979   Home Championship**
**ENGLAND v SCOTLAND  3-1**  (1-1)
*Wembley, London*
Ref: António José da Silva Garrido (Portugal)   Att: 100,000
**ENGLAND**: Raymond Neal Clemence, Philip George Neal, Michael Dennis Mills, Philip Brian Thompson, David Victor Watson, Raymond Colin Wilkins, Kevin Joseph Keegan (Cap), Steven James Coppell, Robert Dennis Latchford, Trevor David Brooking, Peter Simon Barnes.   Manager: Ronald Greenwood
**SCOTLAND**: George Wood, George Elder Burley, Francis Tierney Gray, Paul Anthony Hegarty, Gordon McQueen, John Wark, Graeme James Souness, Richard Asa Hartford, Arthur Graham, Kenneth Mathieson Dalglish (Cap), Joseph Jordan.   Manager: John Stein
**Goals**: Peter Simon Barnes (44), Steven James Coppell (64), Kevin Joseph Keegan (70) / John Wark (20)

**531. 06.06.1979   6th European Champs Qualifiers**
**BULGARIA v ENGLAND  0-3**  (0-1)
*Vasil Levski, Sofia*
Referee: Ernst Dörflinger (Switzerland)   Attendance: 50,000
**BULGARIA**: Iordan Filipov, Nikolai Grancharov, Kiril Ivkov (Cap), Georgi Bonev, Ivan Iliev, Radoslav Zdravkov (61 Todor Barzov), Voin Voinov (46 Rusi Gochev), Krasimir Borisov, Andrei Jeliazkov, Pavel Panov, Chavdar Tsvetkov.   Trainer: Tsvetan Ilchev
**ENGLAND**: Raymond Neal Clemence, Philip George Neal, Michael Dennis Mills, Philip Brian Thompson, David Victor Watson, Raymond Colin Wilkins, Kevin Joseph Keegan (Cap), Steven James Coppell, Robert Dennis Latchford (65 Trevor John Francis), Trevor David Brooking, Peter Simon Barnes (79 Anthony Stewart Woodcock).   Manager: Ronald Greenwood
**Goals**: Kevin Joseph Keegan (33), David Victor Watson (54), Peter Simon Barnes (55)

**532. 10.06.1979**
**SWEDEN v ENGLAND  0-0**
*Råsunda, Solna*
Referee: Erich Linemayr (Austria)   Attendance: 35,691
**SWEDEN**: Jan Möller, Hans Borg, Håkan Arvidsson, Roland Åhman, Ingemar Erlandsson (46 Klas Johansson), Anders Linderoth, Mats Nordgren, Conny Torstensson, Anders Grönhagen, Tore Cervin, Sigvard Johansson (75 Peter Nilsson).   Trainer: Georg Ericsson
**ENGLAND**: Peter Leslie Shilton, Vivian Alexander Anderson, Trevor John Cherry, Terence McDermott (46 Raymond Colin Wilkins), David Victor Watson (46 Philip Brian Thompson), Emlyn Walter Hughes, Kevin Joseph Keegan (Cap), Anthony William Currie (67 Trevor David Brooking), Trevor John Francis, Anthony Stewart Woodcock, Laurence Paul Cunningham.   Manager: Ronald Greenwood

**533. 13.06.1979**
**AUSTRIA v ENGLAND  4-3**  (3-1)
*Prater, Wien*
Referee: Alexis Ponnet (Belgium)   Attendance: 60,000
**AUSTRIA**: Friedrich Koncilia, Robert Sara, Erich Obermayer, Bruno Pezzey, Ernst Baumeister, Roland Hattenberger, Wilhelm Kreuz, Kurt Jara, Kurt Welzl (55 Walter Schachner), Herbert Prohaska, Gernot Jurtin.   Trainer: Karl Stotz
**ENGLAND**: Peter Leslie Shilton (46 Raymond Neal Clemence), Philip George Neal, Michael Dennis Mills, Philip Brian Thompson, David Victor Watson, Raymond Colin Wilkins, Kevin Joseph Keegan (Cap), Steven James Coppell, Robert Dennis Latchford (46 Trevor John Francis), Trevor David Brooking, Peter Simon Barnes (70 Laurence Paul Cunningham).   Manager: Ronald Greenwood
**Goals**: Bruno Pezzey (19, 70), Kurt Welzl (26, 41) / Kevin Joseph Keegan (27), Steven James Coppell (47), Raymond Colin Wilkins (64)

**534. 12.09.1979   6th European Champs Qualifiers**
**ENGLAND v DENMARK  1-0**  (1-0)
*Wembley, London*
Referee: Cesar da Luz Dias Correia (Portugal)   Att: 88,660
**ENGLAND**: Raymond Neal Clemence, Philip George Neal, Michael Dennis Mills, Philip Brian Thompson, David Victor Watson, Raymond Colin Wilkins, Steven James Coppell, Terence McDermott, Kevin Joseph Keegan (Cap), Trevor David Brooking, Peter Simon Barnes.   Manager: Ronald Greenwood
**DENMARK**: Birger Jensen, Ole Højgaard, Sten Ziegler (Cap), Søren Busk, Morten Olsen, Søren Lerby, Frank Arnesen, Benny Nielsen (60 Jens Jørn Bertelsen), Henning Jensen, Allan Rodenkam Simonsen, Preben Elkjær-Larsen (80 Ove Flindt Bjerg).   Trainer: Josef Piontek
**Goal**: Kevin Joseph Keegan (17)

**535. 17.10.1979   6th European Champs Qualifiers**
**NORTHERN IRELAND v ENGLAND  1-5**  (0-2)
*Windsor Park, Belfast*
Referee: Alexis Ponnet (Belgium)   Attendance: 17,755
**NORTHERN IRELAND**: Patrick Anthony Jennings, Patrick James Rice, Samuel Nelson, James Michael Nicholl, Alan Hunter (46 Peter Rafferty), David McCreery, Thomas Cassidy, Samuel Baxter McIlroy, Gerard Joseph Armstrong, Thomas Finney (68 William Thomas Caskey), Victor Moreland.
**ENGLAND**: Peter Leslie Shilton, Philip George Neal, Michael Dennis Mills, Philip Brian Thompson, David Victor Watson, Raymond Colin Wilkins, Kevin Joseph Keegan (Cap), Steven James Coppell, Trevor John Francis, Trevor David Brooking (83 Terence McDermott), Anthony Stewart Woodcock.   Manager: Ronald Greenwood
**Goals**: Victor Moreland (pen) / Trevor John Francis (18, 62), Anthony Stewart Woodcock (34, 71), James Nicholl (74 og)

536. 22.11.1979   6th European Champs Qualifiers
**ENGLAND v BULGARIA   2-0**  (1-0)
*Wembley, London*
Referee:  Erik Fredriksson (Sweden)   Attendance: 71,491
ENGLAND:  Raymond Neal Clemence, Vivian Alexander Anderson, Kenneth Graham Sansom, Philip Brian Thompson (Cap), David Victor Watson, Raymond Colin Wilkins, Kevin Peter Reeves, Glenn Hoddle, Trevor John Francis, Raymond Kennedy, Anthony Stewart Woodcock.
Manager:  Ronald Greenwood
BULGARIA:  Hristo Hristov, Roman Karakolev, Borislav Dimitrov, Georgi Bonev, Ivan Iliev, Georgi Dimitrov, Todor Barzov, Plamen Markov, Boicho Velichkov (87 Krasimir Manolov), Andrei Jeliazkov (Cap), Chavdar Tsvetkov (29 Kostadin Kostadinov).   Trainer: Dobromir Tashkov
Goals:  David Victor Watson (9), Glenn Hoddle (69)


537. 06.02.1980   6th European Champs Qualifiers
**ENGLAND v REPUBLIC OF IRELAND   2-0**  (1-0)
*Wembley, London*
Referee:  Klaus Scheurell (East Germany)   Att: 90,299
ENGLAND:  Raymond Neal Clemence, Trevor John Cherry, Kenneth Graham Sansom, Philip Brian Thompson, David Victor Watson, Bryan Robson, Kevin Joseph Keegan (Cap), Terence McDermott, David Edward Johnson (60 Steven James Coppell), Anthony Stewart Woodcock, Laurence Paul Cunningham.   Manager: Ronald Greenwood
IRELAND:  Gerald Joseph Peyton (60 Ronald Healey), Christopher William Gerard Hughton, David Anthony O'Leary (68 Pierce O'Leary), Mark Thomas Lawrenson, Augustine Ashley Grimes, Gerard Anthony Daly, Anthony Patrick Grealish, William Brady (Cap), Frank O'Brien, Francis Anthony Stapleton, Stephen Derek Heighway.
Manager:  John Michael Giles
Goals:  Kevin Joseph Keegan (34, 74)


538. 26.03.1980
**SPAIN v ENGLAND   0-2**  (0-1)
*Nou Camp, Barcelona*
Referee: Volker Roth (West Germany)   Attendance: 50,000
SPAIN:  Luis Miguel Arkonada, Santiago Urquiaga, Miguel Bernardo Bianquetti "Migueli", José Ramón Alexanco (66 Antonio Olmo), Rafael Gordillo, Agustín Guisasola, Enrique Saura (46 José Diego), Francisco Javier Álvarez "Uría", Daniel Ruiz Bazan "Dani" (Cap), Jesús María Satrústegui, Juan Enrique Gómez "Juanito" (46 Francisco José Carrasco).
Trainer:  Ladislao Kubala

ENGLAND:  Peter Leslie Shilton, Philip George Neal (82 Emlyn Walter Hughes), Michael Dennis Mills, Philip Brian Thompson, David Victor Watson, Raymond Colin Wilkins, Kevin Joseph Keegan (Cap), Steven James Coppell, Trevor John Francis (77 Laurence Paul Cunningham), Raymond Kennedy, Anthony Stewart Woodcock.
Manager:  Ronald Greenwood
Goals:  Anthony Stewart Woodcock (16), Trevor Francis (65)


539. 13.05.1980
**ENGLAND v ARGENTINA   3-1**  (1-0)
*Wembley, London*
Referee:  Brian Robert McGinlay (Scotland)   Att: 92,000
ENGLAND:  Raymond Neal Clemence, Philip George Neal (76 Trevor John Cherry), Kenneth Graham Sansom, Philip Brian Thompson, David Victor Watson, Raymond Colin Wilkins, Kevin Joseph Keegan (Cap), Steven James Coppell, David Edward Johnson (76 Garry Birtles), Anthony Stewart Woodcock, Raymond Kennedy (72 Trevor David Brooking).
Manager:  Ronald Greenwood
ARGENTINA:  Ubaldo Matildo Fillol, Jorge Mario Olguín, José Daniel Van Tuyne, Daniel Alberto Passarella (Cap), Alberto César Tarantini, Juan Alberto Barbas (51 Carlos Luis Ischia), Américo Rubén Gallego, Diego Armando Maradona, Santiago Santamaría (63 Ramón Ángel Díaz), Leopoldo Jacinto Luque, José Daniel Valencia.
Trainer:  César Luis Menotti
Goals:  David Edward Johnson (41, 50), Kevin Keegan (68) / Daniel Alberto Passarella (55 pen)


540. 17.05.1980   Home Championship
**WALES v ENGLAND   4-1**  (2-1)
*Racecourse Ground, Wrexham*
Referee:  Ian Foote (Scotland)   Attendance: 24,386
WALES:  William David Davies, Peter Nicholas, Joseph Patrick Jones, David Edward Jones (46 Keith Pontin), Paul Terence Price, Terence Charles Yorath (Cap), David Charles Giles, Brian Flynn, Ian Patrick Walsh, Leighton James, Michael Reginald Thomas.   Trainer: Harold Michael England
ENGLAND:  Raymond Neal Clemence, Philip George Neal (20 Kenneth Graham Sansom), Trevor John Cherry, Philip Brian Thompson (Cap), Laurence Valentine Lloyd (80 Raymond Colin Wilkins), Raymond Kennedy, Steven James Coppell, Glenn Hoddle, Paul Mariner, Trevor David Brooking, Peter Simon Barnes.   Manager: Ronald Greenwood
Goal:  Michael Reginald Thomas (19), Ian Patrick Walsh (30), Leighton James (60), Philip Brian Thompson (66 og) / Paul Mariner (16)

**541. 20.05.1980   Home Championship**
**ENGLAND v NORTHERN IRELAND  1-1**  (0-0)
*Wembley, London*

Referee: Gwyn Pierce Owen (Wales)    Attendance: 33,676

**ENGLAND**: Joseph Thomas Corrigan, Trevor John Cherry, Kenneth Graham Sansom, Emlyn Walter Hughes (Cap), David Victor Watson, Raymond Colin Wilkins, Kevin Peter Reeves (70 Paul Mariner), Terence McDermott, David Edward Johnson, Trevor David Brooking, Alan Ernest Devonshire.    Manager: Ronald Greenwood

**NORTHERN IRELAND**: James Archibald Platt, James Michael Nicholl, Malachy Martin Donaghy, Christopher James Nicholl, John Patrick O'Neill, Thomas Cassidy (73 David McCreery), Samuel Baxter McIlroy, William Robert Hamilton (73 George Terence Cochrane), Gerard Joseph Armstrong, Thomas Finney, Noel Brotherston.    Manager: William Bingham

**Goal**: David Johnson (81) / George Terence Cochrane (83)

**542. 24.05.1980   Home Championship**
**SCOTLAND v ENGLAND  0-2**  (0-1)
*Hampden Park, Glasgow*

Ref: António José da Silva Garrido (Portugal)    Att: 85,000

**SCOTLAND**: Alan Roderick Rough, Daniel Fergus McGrain, Alexander Fordyce Munro (62 George Elder Burley), Paul Anthony Hegarty, Alexander McLeish, William Fergus Miller, Gordon David Strachan, Robert Sime Aitken (53 Andrew Mullen Gray), Archibald Gemmill (Cap), Kenneth Mathieson Dalglish, Joseph Jordan.    Manager: John Stein

**ENGLAND**: Raymond Neal Clemence, Trevor John Cherry, Kenneth Graham Sansom, Philip Brian Thompson (Cap), David Victor Watson, Raymond Colin Wilkins, Steven James Coppell, Terence McDermott, David Edward Johnson, Paul Mariner (71 Emlyn Walter Hughes), Trevor David Brooking.    Manager: Ronald Greenwood

**Goals**: Trevor David Brooking (8), Steven James Coppell (75)

**543. 31.05.1980**
**AUSTRALIA v ENGLAND  1-2**  (0-2)
*Cricket Ground, Sydney*

Referee: Tony Boskovic (Australia)    Attendance: 30,000

**AUSTRALIA**: Greg Woodhouse, Steve Perry, Jim Muir, Ivo Prskalo, Jim Tansey, Tony Henderson, John Yzendoorn, Jim Rooney (62 Theo Selemidis), Mark Jankovic, Gary Cole, Ken Boden (46 Peter Sharne).

**ENGLAND**: Joseph Thomas Corrigan, Trevor John Cherry (Cap), Frank Richard George Lampard, Brian Ernest Talbot, Russell Charles Osman, Terence Ian Butcher, Bryan Robson (88 Brian Greenhoff), Alan Sunderland (85 Peter David Ward), Paul Mariner, Glenn Hoddle, David Armstrong (70 Alan Ernest Devonshire).    Manager: Ronald Greenwood

**Goals**: Glenn Hoddle (10), Paul Mariner (25)

**544. 12.06.1980   6th European Champs, 1st Round**
**BELGIUM v ENGLAND  1-1**  (1-1)
*Comunale, Torino*

Referee: Heinz Aldinger (West Germany)    Att: 15,186

**BELGIUM**: Jean-Marie Pfaff, Eric Gerets, Luc Millecamps, Walter Meeuws, Michel Renquin, Wilfried Van Moer (88 Raymond Mommens), René Vandereycken, Julien Cools (Cap), François Vander Elst, Erwin Vandenbergh, Jan Ceulemans.    Trainer: Guy Thys

**ENGLAND**: Raymond Neal Clemence, Philip George Neal, Kenneth Graham Sansom, Philip Brian Thompson, David Victor Watson, Raymond Colin Wilkins, Kevin Joseph Keegan (Cap), Steven James Coppell (79 Terence McDermott), David Edward Johnson (68 Raymond Kennedy), Anthony Stewart Woodcock, Trevor David Brooking.    Manager: Ronald Greenwood

**Goal**: Jan Ceulemans (30) / Raymond Colin Wilkins (27)

**545. 15.06.1980   6th European Champs, 1st Round**
**ITALY v ENGLAND  1-0**  (0-0)
*Comunale, Torino*

Referee: Nicolae Rainea (România)    Attendance: 59,649

**ITALY**: Dino Zoff (Cap), Claudio Gentile, Gabriele Oriali, Romeo Benetti, Fulvio Collovatti, Gaetano Scirea, Franco Causio (88 Giuseppe Baresi), Marco Tardelli, Francesco Graziani, Giancarlo Antognoni, Roberto Bettega.    Trainer: Enzo Bearzot

**ENGLAND**: Peter Leslie Shilton, Philip George Neal, Kenneth Graham Sansom, Philip Brian Thompson, David Victor Watson, Raymond Colin Wilkins, Kevin Joseph Keegan (Cap), Steven James Coppell, Garry Birtles (75 Paul Mariner), Raymond Kennedy, Anthony Stewart Woodcock.    Manager: Ronald Greenwood

**Goal**: Marco Tardelli (78)

**546. 18.06.1980   6th European Champs, 1st Round**
**ENGLAND v SPAIN  2-1**  (1-0)
*San Paolo, Napoli*

Referee: Erich Linemayr (Austria)    Attendance: 14,440

**ENGLAND**: Raymond Neal Clemence, Vivian Alexander Anderson (83 Trevor John Cherry), Michael Dennis Mills, Philip Brian Thompson, David Victor Watson, Raymond Colin Wilkins, Terence McDermott, Glenn Hoddle (77 Paul Mariner), Kevin Joseph Keegan (Cap), Anthony Stewart Woodcock, Trevor David Brooking.    Manager: Ronald Greenwood

**SPAIN**: Luis Miguel Arkonada, Secundino Suárez "Cundi", Antonio Olmo, José Ramón Alexanco, Rafael Gordillo, Francisco Javier Álvarez "Uría", Jesús María Zamora, Julio Cardeñosa (46 Daniel Ruiz Bazan "Dani"), Juan Enrique Gómez "Juanito" (46 Francisco José Carrasco), Carlos Alonso González "Santillana" (Cap), Enrique Saura.
Trainer: Ladislao Kubala

**Goals**: Trevor Brooking (20), Anthony Woodcock (62) / Daniel Ruiz Bazan "Dani" (52 pen)

547.   10.09.1980   12th World Cup Qualifiers
**ENGLAND v NORWAY  4-0**  (1-0)
*Wembley, London*

Referee: Marcel van Langenhove (Belgium)   Att: 48,200

**ENGLAND**: Peter Leslie Shilton, Vivian Alexander Anderson, Kenneth Graham Sansom, Philip Brian Thompson (Cap), David Victor Watson, Bryan Robson, Eric Lazenby Gates, Terence McDermott, Paul Mariner, Anthony Stewart Woodcock, Graham Rix.   Manager: Ronald Greenwood

**NORWAY**: Tom Rüsz Jacobsen, Bjarne Berntsen, Tore Kordahl, Einar Jan Aas, Svein Grøndalen, Roger Albertsen, Åge Hareide, Arne Dokken, Arne Larsen Økland, Pål Jacobsen, Arne Erlandsen (83 Rune Ottesen).
Trainer: Tor Røste Fossen

**Goals**: Terence McDermott (37, 75 pen), Anthony Stewart Woodcock (66), Paul Mariner (85)

548.   15.10.1980   12th World Cup Qualifiers
**ROMANIA v ENGLAND  2-1**  (1-0)
*23 August, București*

Referee: Ulf Eriksson (Sweden)   Attendance: 75,000

**ROMANIA**: Vasile Iordache, Nicolae Negrilă, Ștefan Sameș, Costică Ștefănescu (Cap), Ion Munteanu, Aurel Țicleanu, Aurel Beldeanu (71 Ion Dumitru), Anghel Iordănescu, Zoltán Crișan, Rodion Gorun Cămătaru, Marcel Răducanu.
Trainer: Valentin Stănescu

**ENGLAND**: Raymond Neal Clemence, Philip George Neal, Kenneth Graham Sansom, Philip Brian Thompson (Cap), David Victor Watson, Bryan Robson, Graham Rix, Terence McDermott, Garry Birtles (65 Laurence Paul Cunningham), Anthony Stewart Woodcock, Eric Lazenby Gates (46 Steven James Coppell).   Manager: Ronald Greenwood

**Goals**: Marcel Răducanu (35), Anghel Iordănescu (75 pen) / Anthony Stewart Woodcock (64)

549.   19.11.1980   12th World Cup Qualifiers
**ENGLAND v SWITZERLAND  2-1**  (2-0)
*Wembley, London*

Referee: Johannes Nicolaas Ignatius Keizer (Holland)
Attendance: 70,000

**ENGLAND**: Peter Leslie Shilton, Philip George Neal, Kenneth Graham Sansom, Bryan Robson, David Victor Watson, Michael Dennis Mills (Cap), Steven James Coppell, Terence McDermott, Paul Mariner, Trevor David Brooking (82 Graham Rix), Anthony Stewart Woodcock.
Manager: Ronald Greenwood

**SWITZERLAND**: Erich Burgener, Alain Geiger, Heinz Hermann, Heinz Lüdi (46 André Egli), Roger Wehrli, Hans-Jörg Pfister, Umberto Barberis, René Botteron, Markus Tanner, Roland Schönenberger (37 Peter Marti), Rudolf Elsener.
Trainer: Léo Walker

**Goals**: Markus Tanner (22 og), Paul Mariner (36) / Hans-Jörg Pfister (76)

550.   25.03.1981
**ENGLAND v SPAIN  1-2**  (1-2)
*Wembley, London*

Referee: Werner Eschweiler (West Germany)   Att: 71,840

**ENGLAND**: Raymond Neal Clemence, Philip George Neal, Kenneth Graham Sansom, Bryan Robson, Terence Ian Butcher, Russell Charles Osman, Kevin Joseph Keegan (Cap), Trevor John Francis (81 Peter Simon Barnes), Paul Mariner, Trevor David Brooking (70 Raymond Colin Wilkins), Glenn Hoddle.
Manager: Ronald Greenwood

**SPAIN**: Luis Miguel Arkonada (Cap), José Antonio Camacho, Antonio Maceda, Miguel Tendillo, Rafael Gordillo, Joaquín Alonso, Jesús María Zamora, VÍCTOR Muñoz (68 Enrique Montero), Juan Enrique Gómez "Juanito" (84 Daniel Ruiz Bazan "Dani"), Jesús María Satrústegui, MARCOS Alonso Peña.   Trainer: José Emilio Santamaría Iglesias

**Goal**: Glenn Hoddle (26) / Jesús María Satrústegui (6), Jesús María Zamora (32)

551.   29.04.1981   12th World Cup Qualifiers
**ENGLAND v ROMANIA  0-0**
*Wembley, London*

Referee: Heinz Aldinger (West Germany)   Att: 62,500

**ENGLAND**: Peter Leslie Shilton, Vivian Alexander Anderson, Kenneth Graham Sansom, Bryan Robson, David Victor Watson (Cap), Russell Charles Osman, Raymond Colin Wilkins, Trevor David Brooking (70 Terence McDermott), Steven James Coppell, Trevor John Francis, Anthony Stewart Woodcock.   Manager: Ronald Greenwood

**ROMANIA**: Vasile Iordache, Nicolae Negrilă, Ștefan Sameș, Costică Ștefănescu (Cap), Ion Munteanu, Tudorel Stoica, Aurel Beldeanu, Anghel Iordănescu, Zoltán Crișan, Rodion Gorun Cămătaru, Ilie Balaci.   Trainer: Valentin Stănescu

**552. 12.05.1981**
**ENGLAND v BRAZIL  0-1**  (0-1)
*Wembley, London*

Referee: Erich Linemayr (Austria)    Attendance: 75,000

**ENGLAND**: Raymond Neal Clemence (Cap), Philip George Neal, Kenneth Graham Sansom, Bryan Robson, Alvin Edward Martin, Raymond Colin Wilkins, Steven James Coppell, Terence McDermott, Peter Withe, Graham Rix, Peter Simon Barnes.    Manager: Ronald Greenwood

**BRAZIL**: VALDIR de Arruda PERES, EDEVALDO de Freitas, José OSCAR Bernardi, Luiz Carlos Ferreira "Luisinho", Leovegildo Lins Gama Júnior, Antônio Carlos Cerezo "Toninho Cerezo", SÓCRATES Brasileiro Sampaio Vieira de Oliveira, Arthur Antunes Coimbra "Zico", PAULO ISIDORO de Jesus, José REINALDO da Lima, ÉDER Aleixo de Assis. Trainer: Telê Santana da Silva

**Goal**: Arthur Antunes Coimbra "Zico" (12)


**553. 20.05.1981    Home Championship**
**ENGLAND v WALES  0-0**
*Wembley, London*

Referee: Brian Robert McGinlay (Scotland)    Att: 34,280

**ENGLAND**: Joseph Thomas Corrigan, Vivian Alexander Anderson, Kenneth Graham Sansom, Bryan Robson, David Victor Watson (Cap), Raymond Colin Wilkins, Steven James Coppell, Glenn Hoddle, Peter Withe (82 Anthony Stewart Woodcock), Graham Rix, Peter Simon Barnes. Manager: Ronald Greenwood

**WALES**: William David Davies, Joseph Patrick Jones, Kevin Ratcliffe, Peter Nicholas, Leighton Phillips, Paul Terence Price, Carl Stephen Harris (60 David Charles Giles), Brian Flynn (Cap), Ian Patrick Walsh, Leighton James (65 Ian James Rush), Michael Reginald Thomas.
Trainer: Harold Michael England


**554. 23.05.1981    Home Championship**
**ENGLAND v SCOTLAND  0-1**  (0-0)
*Wembley, London*

Referee: Robert Wurtz (France)    Attendance: 90,000

**ENGLAND**: Joseph Thomas Corrigan, Vivian Alexander Anderson, Kenneth Graham Sansom, Raymond Colin Wilkins, David Victor Watson (Cap) (46 Alvin Edward Martin), Bryan Robson, Steven James Coppell, Glenn Hoddle, Peter Withe, Graham Rix, Anthony Stewart Woodcock (46 Trevor John Francis).    Manager: Ronald Greenwood

**SCOTLAND**: Alan Roderick Rough, Daniel Fergus McGrain (Cap), Francis Tierney Gray, William Fergus Miller, Alexander McLeish, David Alexander Provan (80 Paul Whitehead Sturrock), Raymond Strean McDonald Stewart, Richard Asa Hartford (27 David Narey), John Neilson Robertson, Steven Archibald, Joseph Jordan.    Manager: John Stein

**Goal**: John Neilson Robertson (64 pen)


**555. 30.05.1981    12th World Cup Qualifiers**
**SWITZERLAND v ENGLAND  2-1**  (2-0)
*St. Jakob, Basel*

Referee: Adolf Prokop (East Germany)    Attendance: 40,000

**SWITZERLAND**: Erich Burgener, Gian-Piero Zappa, Heinz Lüdi, Herbert Hermann (88 Martin Weber), André Egli, Roger Wehrli, René Botteron, Umberto Barberis, Alfred Scheiwiler, Claudio Sulser, Rudolf Elsener (85 Ernie Maissen).    Trainer: Paul Wolfisberg

**ENGLAND**: Raymond Neal Clemence, Michael Dennis Mills, Kenneth Graham Sansom, Raymond Colin Wilkins, David Victor Watson (80 Peter Simon Barnes), Russell Charles Osman, Steven James Coppell, Bryan Robson, Kevin Joseph Keegan (Cap), Paul Mariner, Trevor John Francis (36 Terence McDermott).    Manager: Ronald Greenwood

**Goals**: Alfred Scheiwiler (28), Claudio Sulser (30) / Terence McDermott (54)


**556. 06.06.1981    12th World Cup Qualifiers**
**HUNGARY v ENGLAND  1-3**  (1-1)
*Népstadion, Budapest*

Referee: Paolo Casarin (Italy)    Attendance: 68,000

**HUNGARY**: Béla Katzirz, Győző Martos, László Bálint, Imre Garaba, József Varga, Sándor Müller (55 András Komjáti), Tibor Nyilasi, József Mucha, László Fazekas (62 Béla Bodonyi), László Kiss, András Törőcsik.    Trainer: Kálmán Mészöly

**ENGLAND**: Raymond Neal Clemence, Philip George Neal, Michael Dennis Mills, Philip Brian Thompson, David Victor Watson, Bryan Robson, Steven James Coppell, Terence McDermott, Paul Mariner, Trevor David Brooking (72 Raymond Colin Wilkins), Kevin Joseph Keegan (Cap). Manager: Ronald Greenwood

**Goals**: Imre Garaba (45) / Trevor David Brooking (19, 60), Kevin Joseph Keegan (73 pen)


**557. 09.09.1981    12th World Cup Qualifiers**
**NORWAY v ENGLAND  2-1**  (2-1)
*Ullevaal, Oslo*

Referee: Jerzy Kacprzak (Poland)    Attendance: 28,500

**NORWAY**: Tore Antonsen, Bjarne Berntsen, Einar Jan Aas, Åge Hareide, Svein Grøndalen, Hallvar Thoresen, Roger Albertsen, Anders Giske, Tom Lund (75 Arne Dokken), Arne Larsen Økland (87 Trond Pedersen), Pål Jacobsen.    Trainer: Tor Røste Fossen

**ENGLAND**: Raymond Neal Clemence, Philip George Neal, Michael Dennis Mills, Philip Brian Thompson, Russell Charles Osman, Bryan Robson, Kevin Joseph Keegan (Cap), Terence McDermott, Paul Mariner (75 Peter Withe), Trevor John Francis, Glenn Hoddle (65 Peter Simon Barnes). Manager: Ronald Greenwood

**Goals**: Roger Albertsen (36), Hallvar Thoresen (41) / Bryan Robson (15)

**558. 18.11.1981   12th World Cup Qualifiers**
**ENGLAND v HUNGARY  1-0**  (1-0)
*Wembley, London*

Referee:  Georges Konrath (France)   Attendance:  92,000

**ENGLAND**:  Peter Leslie Shilton, Philip George Neal, Michael Dennis Mills, Philip Brian Thompson, Alvin Edward Martin, Bryan Robson, Kevin Joseph Keegan (Cap), Steven James Coppell (65 Anthony William Morley), Paul Mariner, Terence McDermott, Trevor David Brooking.
Manager:  Ronald Greenwood

**HUNGARY**:  Ferenc Mészáros, Győző Martos, László Bálint, Imre Garaba, József Tóth, Sándor Müller, Károly Csapó (76 Gábor Szántó), Sándor Sallai, László Fazekas (46 György Kerekes), András Törőcsik, László Kiss.
Trainer:  Kálmán Mészöly

**Goal**:  Paul Mariner (16)


**559. 23.02.1982   Home Championship**
**ENGLAND v NORTHERN IRELAND  4-0**  (1-0)
*Wembley, London*

Referee:  Gwyn Pierce Owen (Wales)   Attendance:  54,900

**ENGLAND**:  Raymond Neal Clemence, Vivian Alexander Anderson, Kenneth Graham Sansom, Raymond Colin Wilkins, David Victor Watson, Stephen Brian Foster, Kevin Joseph Keegan (Cap), Bryan Robson, Trevor John Francis (65 Cyrille Regis), Glenn Hoddle, Anthony William Morley (77 Anthony Stewart Woodcock).   Manager: Ronald Greenwood

**NORTHERN IRELAND**:  Patrick Anthony Jennings, James Michael Nicholl, Samuel Nelson, Malachy Martin Donaghy, Christopher James Nicholl, John Patrick O'Neill, Noel Brotherston (65 George Terence Cochrane), Martin Hugh Michael O'Neill (77 David McCreery), Gerard Joseph Armstrong, Samuel Baxter McIlroy, William Robert Hamilton.
Manager: William Bingham

**Goals**:  Bryan Robson (1), Kevin Joseph Keegan (56), Raymond Colin Wilkins (85), Glenn Hoddle (89)


**560. 27.04.1982   Home Championship**
**WALES v ENGLAND  0-1**  (0-0)
*Ninian Park, Cardiff*

Referee:  Oliver Donnelly (Northern Ireland)   Att: 25,000

**WALES**:  William David Davies, Christopher Marustik, Kevin Ratcliffe, Peter Nicholas, Nigel Charles Ashley Stevenson, Joseph Patrick Jones, Alan Thomas Curtis, Brian Flynn (Cap) (77 Carl Stephen Harris), Ian James Rush, Michael Reginald Thomas (46 Leighton James), Robert Mark James.
Trainer:  Harold Michael England

**ENGLAND**:  Joseph Thomas Corrigan, Philip George Neal, Kenneth Graham Sansom, Philip Brian Thompson (Cap), Terence Ian Butcher, Bryan Robson, Raymond Colin Wilkins, Trevor John Francis (80 Cyrille Regis), Peter Withe, Glenn Hoddle (52 Terence McDermott), Anthony William Morley.
Manager: Ronald Greenwood

**Goal**:  Trevor John Francis (74)


**561. 25.05.1982**
**ENGLAND v HOLLAND  2-0**  (0-0)
*Wembley, London*

Referee:  Paolo Bergamo (Italia)   Attendance:  69,000

**ENGLAND**:  Peter Leslie Shilton (Cap), Philip George Neal, Kenneth Graham Sansom, Philip Brian Thompson, Stephen Brian Foster, Bryan Robson, Raymond Colin Wilkins, Alan Ernest Devonshire (46 Graham Rix), Paul Mariner (72 Peter Simon Barnes), Terence McDermott, Anthony Stewart Woodcock.   Manager: Ronald Greenwood

**HOLLAND**:  Hans van Breukelen, Edo Ophof, Johnny Metgod (71 Frank Rijkaard), Michel van de Korput, Peter Boeve, Jan Peters (63 René van de Kerkhof), Ruud Krol (Cap), Arnold Mühren, Tschen La Ling (71 Kees van Kooten), Wim Kieft, Simon Tahamata.   Trainer: Kees Rijvers

**Goals**:  Anthony Stewart Woodcock (48), Paul Mariner (53)


**562. 29.05.1982   Home Championship**
**SCOTLAND v ENGLAND  0-1**  (0-1)
*Hampden Park, Glasgow*

Referee:  Jan Redelfs (West Germany)   Attendance:  80,529

**SCOTLAND**:  Alan Roderick Rough, George Elder Burley, Daniel Fergus McGrain (Cap), Allan James Evans, Alan David Hansen, David Narey, Graeme James Souness, Richard Asa Hartford (46 John Neilson Robertson), Kenneth Mathieson Dalglish, Alan Bernard Brazil, Joseph Jordan (63 Paul Whitehead Sturrock).   Manager: John Stein

**ENGLAND**:  Peter Leslie Shilton, Michael Dennis Mills, Kenneth Graham Sansom, Philip Brian Thompson, Terence Ian Butcher, Bryan Robson, Kevin Joseph Keegan (Cap) (56 Terence McDermott), Steven James Coppell, Paul Mariner (46 Trevor John Francis), Trevor David Brooking, Raymond Colin Wilkins.   Manager: Ronald Greenwood

**Goal**:  Paul Mariner (13)

563. 02.06.1982
**ICELAND v ENGLAND 1-1** (1-0)
*Laugardalsvøllur, Reykjavík*
Referee: Ib Nielsen (Denmark)   Attendance: 11,110
**ICELAND**: Guðmundur Baldursson, Trausti Haraldsson, Örn Óskarsson, Marteinn Geirsson (Cap), Sævar Jónsson, Karl Þórðarson, Janus Guðlaugsson, Atli Eðvaldsson, Teitur Þórðarson, Arnór Guðjohnsen (82 Pétur Ormslev), Lárus Guðmundsson.   Trainer: Jóhannes Atlason
**ENGLAND**: Joseph Thomas Corrigan, Vivian Alexander Anderson, David Victor Watson, Russell Charles Osman, Philip George Neal (Cap), Terence McDermott, Glenn Hoddle, Alan Ernest Devonshire (80 Steven John Perryman), Peter Withe, Cyrille Regis (40 Paul Goddard), Anthony William Morley.   Manager: Ronald Greenwood
**Goals**: Arnór Guðjohnsen (23) / Paul Goddard (69)

564. 03.06.1982
**FINLAND v ENGLAND 1-4** (0-2)
*Olympia, Helsinki*
Referee: Romualdas Jushka (USSR)   Att: 21,521
**FINLAND**: Pertti Alaja (68 Olavi Huttunen), Aki Lahtinen, Jukka Ikäläinen, Mikael Granskog, Esa Pekonen, Hannu Turunen (64 Pauno Kymäläinen), Kai Haaskivi, Pasi Rautiainen, Juhani Himanka, Atik Ismail, Jyrki Nieminen (55 Ari Valvee).   Trainer: Martti Kuusela
**ENGLAND**: Raymond Neal Clemence, Michael Dennis Mills, Philip Brian Thompson, Alvin Edward Martin, Kenneth Graham Sansom, Steven James Coppell (65 Trevor John Francis), Bryan Robson (58 Graham Rix), Raymond Colin Wilkins, Trevor David Brooking (68 Anthony Stewart Woodcock), Kevin Joseph Keegan (Cap), Paul Mariner. Manager: Ronald Greenwood
**Goals**: Kai Haaskivi (83 pen) /
Paul Mariner (13, 61), Bryan Robson (27, 58)

565. 16.06.1982   12th World Cup, 1st Round
**ENGLAND v FRANCE 3-1** (1-1)
*San Mames, Bilbao*
Ref: António José da Silva Garrido (Portugal)   Att: 44,172
**ENGLAND**: Peter Leslie Shilton, Michael Dennis Mills (Cap), Kenneth Graham Sansom (90 Philip George Neal), Philip Brian Thompson, Terence Ian Butcher, Bryan Robson, Steven James Coppell, Raymond Colin Wilkins, Paul Mariner, Trevor John Francis, Graham Rix.   Manager: Ronald Greenwood
**FRANCE**: Jean-Luc Ettori, Patrick Battiston, Christian Lopez, Marius Trésor, Maxime Bossis, René Girard, Jean-François Larios (74 Jean Amadou Tigana), Michel Platini (Cap), Alain Giresse, Dominique Rocheteau (71 Didier Six), Gérard Soler.   Trainer: Michel Hidalgo
**Goals**: Bryan Robson (1, 67), Paul Mariner (83) /
Gérard Soler (24)

566. 20.06.1982   12th World Cup, 1st Round
**ENGLAND v CZECHOSLOVAKIA 2-0** (2-0)
*San Mames, Bilbao*
Referee: Charles Corver (Holland)   Attendance: 42,000
**ENGLAND**: Peter Leslie Shilton, Michael Dennis Mills (Cap), Philip Brian Thompson, Terence Ian Butcher, Kenneth Graham Sansom, Steven James Coppell, Bryan Robson (46 Glenn Hoddle), Raymond Colin Wilkins, Trevor John Francis, Paul Mariner, Graham Rix.   Manager: Ronald Greenwood
**CZECHOSLOVAKIA**: Stanislav Seman (75 Karel Stromšik), Jozef Barmoš, Rostislav Vojáček, Libor Radimec, Jan Fiala, Pavel Chaloupka, Ladislav Jurkemik, Jan Berger, Petr Janečka (77 Marián Masný), Zdeněk Nehoda (Cap), Ladislav Vízek.   Trainer: Jozef Vengloš
**Goals**: Trevor John Francis (62), Jozef Barmoš (66 og)

567. 25.06.1982   12th World Cup, 1st Round
**ENGLAND v KUWAIT 1-0** (1-0)
*San Mames, Bilbao*
Ref: Gilberto Aristizabal Murcia (Colombia)   Att: 39,700
**ENGLAND**: Peter Leslie Shilton, Philip George Neal, Philip Brian Thompson, Stephen Brian Foster, Michael Dennis Mills (Cap), Steven James Coppell, Glenn Hoddle, Raymond Colin Wilkins, Graham Rix, Paul Mariner, Trevor John Francis.   Manager: Ronald Greenwood
**KUWAIT**: Ahmed Al Tarabolsi, Naeem Mubarak, Mahboub Mubarak, Walid Al Jasem Mubarak (75 Humoud Al Shemmari), Said Al Houti, Fatih Kamil Marzouq, Abdullah Al Buloushi, Abdul Aziz Al Anbari, Yousef Al Suwayed, Abdullah Mayoff, Faisal Al Dakheel.
**Goal**: Trevor John Francis (27)

568. 29.06.1982   12th World Cup, 2nd Round
**ENGLAND v WEST GERMANY 0-0**
*Santiago Bernabéu, Madrid*
Referee: Arnaldo David César Coelho (Brazil)   Att: 90,089
**ENGLAND**: Peter Leslie Shilton, Michael Dennis Mills (Cap), Philip Brian Thompson, Terence Ian Butcher, Kenneth Graham Sansom, Steven James Coppell, Raymond Colin Wilkins, Bryan Robson, Graham Rix, Trevor John Francis (77 Anthony Stewart Woodcock), Paul Mariner.
Manager: Ronald Greenwood
**WEST GERMANY**: Harald Schumacher, Manfred Kaltz, Ulrich Stielike, Karlheinz Förster, Hans-Peter Briegel, Bernd Förster, Wolfgang Dremmler, Paul Breitner, Hans Müller (73 Klaus Fischer), Uwe Reinders (62 Pierre Littbarski), Karl-Heinz Rummenigge (Cap).   Trainer: Josef Derwall

569.  05.07.1982    12th World Cup, 2nd Round
**SPAIN v ENGLAND  0-0**
*Santiago Bernabéu, Madrid*
Referee: Alexis Ponnet (Belgium)    Attendance: 60,000
**SPAIN**: Luis Miguel Arkonada (Cap), Santiago Urquiaga, Miguel Tendillo (72 Antonio Maceda), José Ramón Alexanco, Rafael Gordillo, Enrique Saura (67 Pedro Jesús Uralde), José Antonio Camacho, Miguel Angel "Perico" Alonso, Jesús María Zamora, Carlos Alonso González "Santillana", Jesús María Satrústegui.    Trainer: José Emilio Santamaría Iglesias
**ENGLAND**: Peter Leslie Shilton, Michael Dennis Mills (Cap), Philip Brian Thompson, Terence Ian Butcher, Kenneth Graham Sansom, Raymond Colin Wilkins, Bryan Robson, Graham Rix (63 Trevor David Brooking), Trevor John Francis, Paul Mariner, Anthony Stewart Woodcock (63 Kevin Joseph Keegan).    Manager: Ronald Greenwood

570.  22.09.1982    7th European Champs Qualifiers
**DENMARK v ENGLAND  2-2**  (0-1)
*Idraetsparken, København*
Referee: Charles Corver (Holland)    Attendance: 44,300
**DENMARK**: Troels Rasmussen, Ole Rasmussen, Søren Busk, Per Røntved (Cap), Søren Lerby, Jesper Olsen, Allan Hansen, Ivan Nielsen, Jens Jørn Bertelsen, Lars Bastrup, Preben Elkjær-Larsen.    Trainer: Josef Piontek
**ENGLAND**: Peter Leslie Shilton, Philip George Neal, Kenneth Graham Sansom, Raymond Colin Wilkins (Cap), Russell Charles Osman, Terence Ian Butcher, Anthony William Morley, Bryan Robson, Paul Mariner, Trevor John Francis, Graham Rix (83 Richard Anthony Hill).    Manager: Robert Robson
**Goals**: Allan Hansen (69 pen), Jesper Olsen (90) / Trevor John Francis (8, 81)

571.  13.10.1982
**ENGLAND v WEST GERMANY  1-2**  (0-0)
*Wembley, London*
Referee: Károly Palotai (Hungary)    Attendance: 68,000
**ENGLAND**: Peter Leslie Shilton, Gary Vincent Mabbutt, Kenneth Graham Sansom, Philip Brian Thompson, Terence Ian Butcher, Raymond Colin Wilkins (Cap), Richard Anthony Hill, Cyrille Regis (80 Luther Loide Blissett), Paul Mariner (80 Anthony Stewart Woodcock), David Armstrong (80 Graham Rix), Alan Ernest Devonshire.    Manager: Robert Robson
**WEST GERMANY**: Harald Schumacher, Manfred Kaltz, Gerhard Strack, Karlheinz Förster (5 Holger Hieronymus), Bernd Förster, Wolfgang Dremmler, Lothar Herbert Matthäus, Karl-Heinz Rummenigge (Cap), Hans-Peter Briegel, Norbert Meier (68 Pierre Littbarski), Klaus Allofs (88 Stephan Engels). Trainer: Josef Derwall
**Goal**: Anthony Stewart Woodcock (85) / Karl-Heinz Rummenigge (73, 82)

572.  17.11.1982    7th European Champs Qualifiers
**GREECE v ENGLAND  0-3**  (0-1)
*Kautatzógleio, Thessaloniki*
Referee: Adolf Prokop (East Germany)    Attendance: 41,534
**GREECE**: Nikolaos Sarganis, Giánnis Gounaris, Konstantinos Iosifidis, Anthimos Kapsis (Cap), Giórgos Foiros, Pétros Mihos, Spíros Livathinos, Hrístos Ardizoglou (40 Giórgos Kostikos), Anastásios Mitropoulos, Nikolaos Anastopoulos, Thomás Mavros (77 Sávvas Kofidis).
Trainer: Hrístos Arhontidis
**ENGLAND**: Peter Leslie Shilton, Philip George Neal, Kenneth Graham Sansom, Philip Brian Thompson, Alvin Edward Martin, Bryan Robson (Cap), Samuel Lee, Gary Vincent Mabbutt, Paul Mariner, Anthony Stewart Woodcock, Anthony William Morley.    Manager: Robert Robson
**Goals**: Anthony Stewart Woodcock (2, 62), Samuel Lee (68)

573.  15.12.1982    7th European Champs Qualifiers
**ENGLAND v LUXEMBOURG  9-0**  (4-0)
*Wembley, London*
Referee: Hreidar Jónsson (Iceland)    Attendance: 35,000
**ENGLAND**: Raymond Neal Clemence, Philip George Neal, Kenneth Graham Sansom, Samuel Lee, Terence Ian Butcher, Alvin Edward Martin, Bryan Robson (Cap), Gary Vincent Mabbutt (74 Glenn Hoddle), Luther Loide Blissett, Anthony Stewart Woodcock, Steven James Coppell (65 Mark Valentine Chamberlain).    Manager: Robert Robson
**LUXEMBOURG**: Jeannot Moes (Cap), Jean-Paul Girres, Nicolas Rohmann, Hubert Meunier, John Clemens, Marcel Bossi, Guy Hellers, Carlo Weis, Gilbert Dresch, Jeannot Reiter, Marcel Di Domenico (46 Alain Nurenberg).
Trainer: Louis Pilot
**Goals**: Marcel Bossi (18 og), Steven James Coppell (21), Anthony Stewart Woodcock (34), Luther Blissett (44, 53, 86), Mark Chamberlain (72), Glenn Hoddle (88), Philip Neal (90)

574.  23.02.1983    Home Championship
**ENGLAND v WALES  2-1**  (1-1)
*Wembley, London*
Referee: Robert Valentine (Scotland)    Attendance: 24,000
**ENGLAND**: Peter Leslie Shilton (Cap), Philip George Neal, Derek James Statham, Samuel Lee, Alvin Edward Martin, Terence Ian Butcher, Luther Loide Blissett, Gary Vincent Mabbutt, Paul Mariner, Gordon Sidney Cowans, Alan Ernest Devonshire.    Manager: Robert Robson
**WALES**: Neville Southall, Joseph Patrick Jones (44 George Frederick Berry), Kevin Ratcliffe, Paul Terence Price (Cap), Kenneth Francis Jackett, Brian Flynn, Gordon John Davies, Robert Mark James, Ian James Rush, Michael Reginald Thomas, John Francis Mahoney (80 Leighton James).
Trainer: Harold Michael England
**Goals**: Terence Butcher (39), Philip George Neal (78 pen) / Ian James Rush (14)

575. 30.03.1983    7th European Champs Qualifiers
**ENGLAND v GREECE  0-0**
*Wembley, London*

Referee: Dusan Krchnak (Czechoslovakia)    Att: 44,051

**ENGLAND**: Peter Leslie Shilton (Cap), Philip George Neal, Kenneth Graham Sansom, Samuel Lee, Alvin Edward Martin, Terence Ian Butcher, Steven James Coppell, Gary Vincent Mabbutt, Trevor John Francis, Anthony Stewart Woodcock (73 Luther Loide Blissett), Alan Ernest Devonshire (73 Graham Rix).    Manager: Robert Robson

**GREECE**: Nikolaos Sarganis, Giánnis Gounaris (Cap), Nikolaos Karoulias, Giánnis Galitsios, Pétros Mihos, Harálampos Xanthopoulos, Anastásios Mitropoulos (76 Giánnis Dontas), Konstantinos Kouis, Vaggélis Kousoulakis, Nikolaos Anastopoulos (85 Hrístos Ardizoglou), Giórgos Kostikos.    Trainer: Hrístos Arhontidis


576. 27.04.1983    7th European Champs Qualifiers
**ENGLAND v HUNGARY  2-0**  (1-0)
*Wembley, London*

Referee: Pietro d'Elia (Italy)    Attendance: 55,000

**ENGLAND**: Peter Leslie Shilton (Cap), Philip George Neal, Kenneth Graham Sansom, Samuel Lee, Alvin Edward Martin, Terence Ian Butcher, Gary Vincent Mabbutt, Trevor John Francis, Peter Withe, Luther Loide Blissett, Gordon Sidney Cowans.    Manager: Robert Robson

**HUNGARY**: Béla Katzirz, Győző Martos (69 Győző Burcsa), István Kocsis, Imre Garaba, József Tóth, Péter Hannich, Tibor Nyilasi, József Kardos, József Varga, László Kiss (69 András Törőcsik), Gyula Hajszán.    Trainer: Kálmán Mészöly

**Goals**: Trevor John Francis (32), Peter Withe (71)


577. 28.05.1983    Home Championship
**NORTHERN IRELAND v ENGLAND  0-0**
*Windsor Park, Belfast*

Referee: Howard King (Wales)    Attendance: 22,000

**NORTHERN IRELAND**: Patrick Anthony Jennings, James Michael Nicholl, Malachy Martin Donaghy, John McClelland, Christopher James Nicholl, Martin Hugh Michael O'Neill (Cap), Gerald Mullan (80 Noel Brotherston), Samuel Baxter McIlroy, Gerard Joseph Armstrong, William Robert Hamilton, Ian Edwin Stewart.    Manager: William Bingham

**ENGLAND**: Peter Leslie Shilton (Cap), Philip George Neal, Kenneth Graham Sansom, Glenn Hoddle, Terence Ian Butcher, Graham Paul Roberts, Gary Vincent Mabbutt, Luther Loide Blissett (69 John Charles Bryan Barnes), Peter Withe, Gordon Sidney Cowans, Trevor John Francis.    Manager: Robert Robson


578. 01.06.1983    Home Championship
**ENGLAND v SCOTLAND  2-0**  (1-0)
*Wembley, London*

Referee: Erik Fredriksson (Sweden)    Attendance: 84,000

**ENGLAND**: Peter Leslie Shilton (Cap), Philip George Neal, Kenneth Graham Sansom, Samuel Lee, Graham Paul Roberts, Terence Ian Butcher, Bryan Robson (25 Gary Vincent Mabbutt), Trevor John Francis, Peter Withe (46 Luther Loide Blissett), Glenn Hoddle, Gordon Sidney Cowans.    Manager: Robert Robson

**SCOTLAND**: James Leighton, Richard Charles Gough, Francis Tierney Gray, David Narey, Alexander McLeish, Gordon David Strachan, William Fergus Miller, Graeme James Souness (Cap), Eamonn John Peter Bannon (53 Alan Bernard Brazil), Andrew Mullen Gray, Charles Nicholas (67 John Wark).    Manager: John Stein

**Goals**: Bryan Robson (12), Gordon Sidney Cowans (52)


579. 12.06.1983
**AUSTRALIA v ENGLAND  0-0**
*Cricket Ground, Sydney*

Referee: Tony Boskovic (Australia)    Attendance: 28,000

**AUSTRALIA**: Terry Greedy, Alan Davidson, Charlie Yankos, David Ratcliffe, Steve O'Connor, Graham Jennings, Joe Watson, Jim Cant, Peter Katholos, John Kosmina, Phil O'Connor (65 David Mitchell).

**ENGLAND**: Peter Leslie Shilton (Cap), Daniel Joseph Thomas, Derek James Statham (69 John Charles Bryan Barnes), Steven Charles Williams, Russell Charles Osman, Terence Ian Butcher, Mark Francis Barham, John Charles Gregory, Luther Loide Blissett (59 Paul Anthony Walsh), Trevor John Francis, Gordon Sidney Cowans.    Manager: Robert Robson


580. 15.06.1983
**AUSTRALIA v ENGLAND  0-1**  (0-0)
*Lang Park, Brisbane*

Referee: Peter Rampley (Australia)    Attendance: 10,000

**AUSTRALIA**: Terry Greedy, Alan Davidson, Charlie Yankos, David Ratcliffe, Steve O'Connor, Graham Jennings, Joe Watson, Peter Katholos (69 Ken Murphy), Jim Cant, John Kosmina, Phil O'Connor (75 David Mitchell).

**ENGLAND**: Peter Leslie Shilton (Cap), Philip George Neal, Derek James Statham (21 Steven Charles Williams), Mark Francis Barham, Russell Charles Osman, Terence Ian Butcher, John Charles Gregory, Trevor John Francis, Paul Anthony Walsh, Gordon Sidney Cowans, John Charles Bryan Barnes.    Manager: Robert Robson

**Goal**: Paul Anthony Walsh (57)

### 581. 19.06.1983
**AUSTRALIA v ENGLAND 1-1 (1-1)**

*Olympic Park, Melbourne*

Referee: Jack Johnston (Australia)    Attendance: 20,000

**AUSTRALIA**: Terry Greedy, Charlie Yankos, Alan Davidson, David Ratcliffe, Steve O'Connor, Graham Jennings, Joe Watson, Jim Cant, Ken Murphy, John Kosima, Phil O'Connor.

**ENGLAND**: Peter Leslie Shilton (Cap) (46 Nigel Philip Spink), Philip George Neal (46 Daniel Joseph Thomas), Nicholas Pickering, Samuel Lee, Russell Charles Osman, Terence Ian Butcher, John Charles Gregory, Trevor John Francis, Paul Anthony Walsh (69 Luther Loide Blissett), Gordon Sidney Cowans, John Charles Bryan Barnes. Manager: Robert Robson

Goal: Philip Neal (27 og) / Trevor John Francis (25)

### 582. 21.09.1983    7th European Champs Qualifiers
**ENGLAND v DENMARK 0-1 (0-1)**

*Wembley, London*

Referee: Alexis Ponnet (Belgium)    Attendance: 82,500

**ENGLAND**: Peter Leslie Shilton, Philip George Neal, Kenneth Graham Sansom, Raymond Colin Wilkins (Cap), Russell Charles Osman, Terence Ian Butcher, Trevor John Francis, Samuel Lee (77 Luther Loide Blissett), Paul Mariner, John Charles Gregory, John Charles Bryan Barnes (70 Mark Valentine Chamberlain).    Manager: Robert Robson

**DENMARK**: Ole Kjær, Ole Rasmussen, Ivan Nielsen, Morten Olsen (Cap) (86 Jan Mølby), Søren Busk, Søren Lerby, Allan Rodenkam Simonsen, Jens Jørn Bertelsen, Jesper Olsen, Michael Laudrup (46 Preben Elkjær-Larsen), Klaus Berggreen. Trainer: Josef Piontek

Goal: Allan Rodenkam Simonsen (74)

### 583. 12.10.1983    7th European Champs Qualifiers
**HUNGARY v ENGLAND 0-3 (0-3)**

*Népstadion, Budapest*

Referee: Bruno Galler (Switzerland)    Attendance: 19,956

**HUNGARY**: Attila Kovács, Gyula Csonka, József Kardos, Imre Garaba, József Varga, Péter Hannich (65 László Szokolai), Ferenc Csongrádi, Tibor Nyilasi, Győző Burcsa (46 Antal Nagy), László Dajka, Gyula Hajszán.    Trainer: György Mezey

**ENGLAND**: Peter Leslie Shilton, John Charles Gregory, Kenneth Graham Sansom, Samuel Lee, Alvin Edward Martin, Terence Ian Butcher, Bryan Robson (Cap), Luther Loide Blissett (74 Peter Withe), Paul Mariner, Glenn Hoddle, Gary Vincent Mabbutt.    Manager: Robert Robson

Goals: Glenn Hoddle (14), Samuel Lee (20), Paul Mariner (43)

### 584. 16.11.1983    7th European Champs Qualifiers
**LUXEMBOURG v ENGLAND 0-4 (0-2)**

*Municipal, Luxembourg*

Referee: Cornelis Bakker (Holand)    Attendance: 5,410

**LUXEMBOURG** Jean-Paul Defrang, Romain Michaux, Marcel Bossi, Gilbert Dresch, Hubert Meunier, Robert Langers, Nico Wagner, Guy Hellers, Jean-Pierre Barboni (71 Gérard Jeitz), Jeannot Reiter, Théo Malget (56 Jean-Paul Girres). Trainer: Louis Pilot

**ENGLAND**: Raymond Neal Clemence, Michael Duxburyy, Kenneth Graham Sansom, Samuel Lee, Alvin Edward Martin, Terence Ian Butcher, Bryan Robson (Cap), Glenn Hoddle, Paul Mariner, Anthony Stewart Woodcock (24 John Charles Bryan Barnes), Alan Ernest Devonshire.    Manager: Robert Robson

Goals: Bryan Robson (11, 56), Paul Mariner (39) Terence Ian Butcher (50)

### 585. 29.02.1984
**FRANCE v ENGLAND 2-0 (0-0)**

*Parc des Princes, Paris*

Referee: Marcel van Langenhove (Belgium)    Att: 45,554

**FRANCE**: Joël Bats, Patrick Battiston (72 Thierry Tusseau), Yvon Le Roux, Maxime Bossis, Manuel Amoros, Jean Amadou Tigana, Alain Giresse, Michel Platini (Cap), Luis Fernandez, José Touré, Bruno Bellone (83 Dominique Rocheteau). Trainer: Michel Hidalgo

**ENGLAND**: Peter Leslie Shilton, Michael Duxburyy, Kenneth Graham Sansom, Samuel Lee (78 John Charles Bryan Barnes), Graham Paul Roberts, Terence Ian Butcher, Bryan Robson (Cap), Brian Stein (78 Anthony Stewart Woodcock), Paul Anthony Walsh, Glenn Hoddle, Steven Charles Williams. Manager: Robert Robson

Goals: Michel Platini (58, 71)

### 586. 04.04.1984    Home Championship
**ENGLAND v NORTHERN IRELAND 1-0 (0-0)**

*Wembley, London*

Referee: Ronald Bridges (Wales)    Attendance: 24,000

**ENGLAND**: Peter Leslie Shilton, Vivian Alexander Anderson, Graham Paul Roberts, Terence Ian Butcher, Alan Philip Kennedy, Samuel Lee, Raymond Colin Wilkins, Bryan Robson (Cap), Graham Rix, Trevor John Francis, Anthony Stewart Woodcock.    Manager: Robert Robson

**NORTHERN IRELAND**: James Archibald Platt, James Michael Nicholl, John McClelland, Gerard McElhinney, Malachy Martin Donaghy, Gerard Joseph Armstrong, Martin Hugh Michael O'Neill (Cap), William Robert Hamilton, Norman Whiteside, Samuel Baxter McIlroy, Ian Edwin Stewart.    Manager: William Bingham

Goal: Anthony Stewart Woodcock (49)

587. 02.05.1984   Home Championship
**WALES v ENGLAND  1-0**  (1-0)
*Racecourse Ground, Wrexham*

Referee: David Syme (Scotland)   Attendance: 14,250

**WALES**: Neville Southall, David Owen Phillips, Joseph Patrick Jones, Kevin Ratcliffe, Jeffrey Hopkins, Robert Mark James, Gordon John Davies, Alan Davies, Ian James Rush, Michael Reginald Thomas, Mark Leslie Hughes. Trainer: Harold Michael England

**ENGLAND**: Peter Leslie Shilton, Michael Duxburyy, Alan Philip Kennedy, Samuel Lee, Alvin Edward Martin (80 Terence William Fenwick), Mark Wright, Raymond Colin Wilkins (Cap), John Charles Gregory, Paul Anthony Walsh, Anthony Stewart Woodcock, David Armstrong (77 Luther Loide Blissett).   Manager: Robert Robson

**Goal**: Mark Leslie Hughes (17)

588. 26.05.1984   Home Championship
**SCOTLAND v ENGLAND  1-1**  (1-1)
*Hampden Park, Glasgow*

Referee: Paolo Casarin (Italy)   Attendance: 73,064

**SCOTLAND**: James Leighton, Richard Charles Gough, Arthur Richard Albiston, William Fergus Miller (Cap), Alexander McLeish, Gordon David Strachan (62 Paul Michael Lyons McStay), James Bett, John Wark, David Cooper, Steven Archibald, Mark Edward McGhee (62 Maurice Johnston). Manager: John Stein

**ENGLAND**: Peter Leslie Shilton, Michael Duxburyy, Kenneth Graham Sansom, Raymond Colin Wilkins, Graham Paul Roberts, Terence William Fenwick, Mark Valentine Chamberlain (74 Steven Kenneth Hunt), Bryan Robson (Cap), Anthony Stewart Woodcock (72 Gary Winston Lineker), Luther Loide Blissett, John Charles Bryan Barnes. Manager: Robert Robson

**Goal**: Mark Edward McGhee (13) / Anthony Woodcock (36)

589. 02.06.1984
**ENGLAND v U.S.S.R.  0-2**  (0-0)
*Wembley, London*

Referee: Michel Vautrot (France)   Attendance: 38,125

**ENGLAND**: Peter Leslie Shilton, Michael Duxburyy, Graham Paul Roberts, Terence William Fenwick, Kenneth Graham Sansom, Raymond Colin Wilkins, Bryan Robson (Cap), Mark Valentine Chamberlain, Trevor John Francis (70 Mark Wayne Hateley), Luther Loide Blissett, John Charles Bryan Barnes (66 Steven Kenneth Hunt).   Manager: Robert Robson

**U.S.S.R.**: Rinat Dasaev, Tengiz Sulakvelidze, Aleksandr Chivadze (Cap), Sergey Baltacha, Anatoliy Demyanenko, Sergey Aleynikov (86 Boris Pozdnyakov), Gennadiy Litovchenko, Khoren Oganesyan, Andrey Zygmantovich (20 Sergey Gotzmanov), Sergey Rodionov (87 Oleg Protasov), Oleg Blokhin.   Trainer: Eduard Malofeev

**Goals**: Sergey Gotzmanov (54), Oleg Protasov (89)

590. 10.06.1984
**BRAZIL v ENGLAND  0-2**  (0-1)
*Maracana, Rio de Janeiro*

Referee: Juan Cardellino (Uruguay)   Attendance: 56,126

**BRAZIL**: Roberto Costa, José LEANDRO de Souza Ferreira (68 WLADIMIR Rodrigues dos Santos), RICARDO GOMES Raymundo, José Carlos Nepomuceno Mozer, Leovegildo Lins Gama Júnior, José Sebastião Pires Neto, ZENON de Sousa Farias, Benedito ASSIS da Silva, Renato Portaluppi "Renato Gaúcho", Carlos ROBERTO de Oliveira "Dinamite" (66 José REINALDO da Lima), Carlos Alberto de Araújo Prestes "Tato". Trainer: Eduardo Antunes Coimbra "Edu Antunes"

**ENGLAND**: Peter Leslie Shilton, Michael Duxburyy, Kenneth Graham Sansom, Raymond Colin Wilkins, David Watson, Terence William Fenwick, Mark Valentine Chamberlain, Bryan Robson (Cap), Mark Wayne Hateley, Anthony Stewart Woodcock (76 Clive Darren Allen), John Charles Bryan Barnes.   Manager: Robert Robson

**Goals**: John Charles Bryan Barnes (43), Mark Hateley (65)

591. 13.06.1984
**URUGUAY v ENGLAND  2-0**  (1-0)
*Centenario, Montevideo*

Referee: L. Gonzales (Paraguay)   Attendance: 34,500

**URUGUAY**: Rodolfo Sergio Rodríguez, Nelson Daniel Gutiérrez, Eduardo Mario Acevedo, Néstor Montelongo (76 Carlos Eduardo Vázquez), Miguel Angel Bossio, Daniel Martínez, Carlos Alberto Aguilera, Ricardo Javier Perdomo, Wilmar Rubens Cabrera, Juan Ramón Carrasco (82 José Luis Zalazar), Luis Alberto Acosta (61 Rúben Sosa). Trainer: Omar Borrás

**ENGLAND**: Peter Leslie Shilton, Michael Duxburyy, Kenneth Graham Sansom, Raymond Colin Wilkins, David Watson, Terence William Fenwick, Bryan Robson (Cap), Mark Valentine Chamberlain, Mark Wayne Hateley, Clive Darren Allen (69 Anthony Stewart Woodcock), John Charles Bryan Barnes.   Manager: Robert Robson

**Goals**: Luis Acosta (8 pen), Wilmar Rubens Cabrera (68)

592.  17.06.1984
**CHILE v ENGLAND  0-0**
*Nacional, Santiago*
Referee:  Luís Carlos Félix Ferrara (Brazil)    Att: 9,876
**CHILE**:  Roberto Antonio Rojas, Hugo Tabilo, Eduardo Gómez, Manuel Araya, Luis Hormazábal, Alejandro Manuel Hisis Araya, Juan Soto Quintana (40 Luis Rodríguez), Claudio Toro (Eduardo Gino Cofré), Jorge Aravena, Luis Venegas, Juan Covarrubias (69 Héctor Eduardo Puebla).
Trainer: Luis Ibarra
**ENGLAND**:  Peter Leslie Shilton, Michael Duxburyy, Kenneth Graham Sansom, Raymond Colin Wilkins, David Watson, Terence William Fenwick, Bryan Robson (Cap), Mark Valentine Chamberlain (74 Samuel Lee), Mark Wayne Hateley, Clive Darren Allen, John Charles Bryan Barnes.
Manager: Robert Robson

593.  12.09.1984
**ENGLAND v EAST GERMANY  1-0**  (0-0)
*Wembley, London*
Referee:  Albert Thomas (Holland)    Attendance: 23,951
**ENGLAND**:  Peter Leslie Shilton, Michael Duxburyy, Kenneth Graham Sansom, Steven Charles Williams, Mark Wright, Terence Ian Butcher, Bryan Robson (Cap), Raymond Colin Wilkins, Paul Mariner (80 Trevor John Francis), Anthony Stewart Woodcock (80 Mark Wayne Hateley), John Charles Bryan Barnes.   Manager: Robert Robson
**EAST GERMANY**:  René Müller, Hans-Jürgen Dörner (Cap), Ronald Kreer, Dirk Stahmann, Uwe Zötzsche, Matthias Liebers, Rainer Troppa, Rainer Ernst (89 Jürgen Raab), Wolfgang Steinbach, Joachim Streich (76 Hans Richter), Ralf Minge.  Trainer: Bernd Stange
**Goal**:  Bryan Robson (82)

594.  17.10.1984    13th World Cup Qualifiers
**ENGLAND v FINLAND  5-0**  (2-0)
*Wembley, London*
Referee: Aleksander Suchanek (Poland)    Att: 47,234
**ENGLAND**:  Peter Leslie Shilton, Michael Duxburyy (46 Gary Andrew Stevens), Kenneth Graham Sansom, Steven Charles Williams, Mark Wright, Terence Ian Butcher, Bryan Robson (Cap) (75 Mark Valentine Chamberlain), Raymond Colin Wilkins, Mark Wayne Hateley, Anthony Stewart Woodcock, John Charles Bryan Barnes.   Manager: Robert Robson
**FINLAND**:  Olavi Huttunen, Esa Pekonen, Pauno Kymäläinen (Cap), Aki Lahtinen, Erkka Petäjä, Kai Haaskivi (46 Hannu Turunen), Leo Houtsonen, Kari Ukkonen, Jukka Ikäläinen, Pasi Rautiainen, Ari Valvee (70 Ari Hjelm).
Trainer: Martti Kuusela
**Goals**:  Mark Hateley (29, 49), Anthony Woodcock (40), Bryan Robson (70), Kenneth Graham Sansom (85)

595.  14.11.1984    13th World Cup Qualifiers
**TURKEY v ENGLAND  0-8**  (0-3)
*Inönü, Istanbul*
Referee:  Vojtech Christov (Czechoslovakia)    Att: 40,000
**TURKEY**:  Yaşar Duran, Ismail Kartal, Yusuf Altıntaş, Kemal Serdar, Cem Pamiroğlu, Raşit Çetiner, Müjdat Yetkiner, Ahmet Keloğlu, Ilyas Tüfekçi (46 Tuncay Soyak), Rıdvan Dilmen, Ali Erdal Keser.   Trainer:  Candan Tarhan
**ENGLAND**:  Peter Leslie Shilton, Vivian Alexander Anderson, Kenneth Graham Sansom, Steven Charles Williams (69 Gary Andrew Stevens), Mark Wright, Terence Ian Butcher, Bryan Robson (Cap), Raymond Colin Wilkins, Peter Withe, Anthony Stewart Woodcock (69 Trevor John Francis), John Charles Bryan Barnes.   Manager: Robert Robson
**Goals**:  Bryan Robson (13, 44, 58), Tony Woodcock (17, 61), John Barnes (48, 53), Vivian Anderson (87)

596.  27.02.1985    13th World Cup Qualifiers
**NORTHERN IRELAND v ENGLAND  0-1**  (0-0)
*Windsor Park, Belfast*
Referee:  Volker Roth (West Germany)    Attendance: 28,500
**NORTHERN IRELAND**:  Patrick Anthony Jennings, James Michael Nicholl, John McClelland, John Patrick O'Neill, Malachy Martin Donaghy, Samuel Baxter McIlroy (Cap), Paul Christopher Ramsey, Gerard Joseph Armstrong, Ian Edwin Stewart, James Martin Quinn, Norman Whiteside.
Manager: William Bingham
**ENGLAND**:  Peter Leslie Shilton, Vivian Alexander Anderson, Kenneth Graham Sansom, Alvin Edward Martin, Terence Ian Butcher, Trevor McGregor Steven, Raymond Colin Wilkins (Cap), Gary Andrew Stevens, Anthony Stewart Woodcock (78 Trevor John Francis), Mark Wayne Hateley, John Charles Bryan Barnes.   Manager: Robert Robson
**Goal**:  Mark Wayne Hateley (77)

597.  26.03.1985
**ENGLAND v REPUBLIC OF IRELAND  2-1**  (1-0)
*Wembley, London*
Referee:  George Brian Smith (Scotland)    Att: 34,793
**ENGLAND**:  Gary Richard Bailey, Vivian Alexander Anderson, Kenneth Graham Sansom, Trevor McGregor Steven, Mark Wright, Terence Ian Butcher, Bryan Robson (Cap) (82 Glenn Hoddle), Raymond Colin Wilkins, Mark Wayne Hateley (73 Peter Davenport), Gary Winston Lineker, Christopher Roland Waddle.   Manager: Robert Robson
**IRELAND**:  Patrick Bonner, Christopher William Gerard Hughton, Mark Thomas Lawrenson, Michael Joseph McCarthy, James Martin Beglin, Ronald Andrew Whelan (70 Kevin O'Callaghan), Gary Patrick Waddock, William Brady, Paul McGrath (46 David Anthony O'Leary), Eamonn Gerard O'Keefe (80 John Frederick Byrne), Francis Anthony Stapleton (Cap).   Manager: Eoin Hand
**Goals**:  Trevor Steven (45), Gary Lineker (76) / Liam Brady (88)

598. 01.05.1985    13th World Cup Qualifiers
**ROMANIA v ENGLAND  0-0**

*23 August, București*

Referee: Emilio Carlos Guruceta Muro (Spain)    Att: 60,000

ROMANIA: Silviu Lung, Nicolae Negrilă, Gino Iorgulescu (39 Ștefan Iovan), Costică Ștefănescu (Cap), Nicolae Ungureanu, Mircea Rednic, Ladislau Bölöni, Michael Klein, Gheorghe Hagi, Marcel Coraș (78 Marius Lăcătuș), Rodion Gorun Cămătaru.    Trainer: Mircea Lucescu

ENGLAND: Peter Leslie Shilton, Vivian Alexander Anderson, Kenneth Graham Sansom, Terence Ian Butcher, Mark Wright, Raymond Colin Wilkins, Bryan Robson (Cap), Trevor McGregor Steven, John Charles Bryan Barnes (72 Christopher Roland Waddle), Paul Mariner (85 Gary Winston Lineker), Trevor John Francis.    Manager: Robert Robson


599. 22.05.1985    13th World Cup Qualifiers
**FINLAND v ENGLAND  1-1**  (1-0)

*Olympia, Helsinki*

Referee: Siegfried Kirschen (East Germany)    Att: 30,311

FINLAND: Olavi Huttunen, Aki Lahtinen (84 Erkka Petäjä), Pauno Kymäläinen (Cap), Jukka Ikäläinen, Jyrki Nieminen, Hannu Turunen, Leo Houtsonen, Kari Ukkonen (78 Ari Hjelm), Mika Lipponen, Pasi Rautiainen, Jari Rantanen.    Trainer: Martti Kuusela

ENGLAND: Peter Leslie Shilton, Vivian Alexander Anderson, Kenneth Graham Sansom, Terence William Fenwick, Terence Ian Butcher, Trevor McGregor Steven (78 Christopher Roland Waddle), Raymond Colin Wilkins, Bryan Robson (Cap), Trevor John Francis, Mark Wayne Hateley, John Charles Bryan Barnes.    Manager: Robert Robson

Goals: Jari Rantanen (5) / Mark Wayne Hateley (50)


600. 25.05.1985    Rous Cup
**SCOTLAND v ENGLAND  1-0**  (0-0)

*Hampden Park, Glasgow*

Referee: Michel Vautrot (France)    Attendance: 66,489

SCOTLAND: James Leighton, Richard Charles Gough, Maurice Daniel Robert Malpas, William Fergus Miller, Alexander McLeish, Gordon David Strachan (71 Murdo Davidson MacLeod), Graeme James Souness (Cap), Robert Sime Aitken, James Bett, David Robert Speedie, Steven Archibald.    Manager: John Stein

ENGLAND: Peter Leslie Shilton, Vivian Alexander Anderson, Kenneth Graham Sansom, Terence William Fenwick, Terence Ian Butcher, Glenn Hoddle (80 Gary Winston Lineker), Raymond Colin Wilkins, Bryan Robson (Cap), Trevor John Francis, Mark Wayne Hateley, John Charles Bryan Barnes (63 Christopher Roland Waddle).    Manager: Robert Robson

Goal: Richard Charles Gough (68)


601. 06.06.1985
**ITALY v ENGLAND  2-1**  (0-0)

*Azteca, Ciudad de Mexico*

Referee: Antonio Marquez Ramirez (Mexico)    Att: 7,000

ITALY: Giovanni Galli (46 Franco Tancredi), Giuseppe Bergomi, Pietro Vierchowod, Giuseppe Baresi, Fulvio Collovatti (Cap) (46 Antonio Cabrini), Roberto Tricella, Bruno Conti (46 Pietro Fanna), Salvatore Bagni, Giuseppe Galderisi (84 Marco Tardelli), Antonio Di Gennaro, Alessandro Altobelli.
Trainer: Enzo Bearzot

ENGLAND: Peter Leslie Shilton, Gary Michael Stevens (63 Glenn Hoddle), Kenneth Graham Sansom, Trevor McGregor Steven, Mark Wright, Terence Ian Butcher, Bryan Robson (Cap), Raymond Colin Wilkins, Mark Wayne Hateley, Trevor John Francis (78 Gary Winston Lineker), Christopher Roland Waddle (69 John Charles Bryan Barnes).
Manager: Robert Robson

Goal: Salvatore Bagni (73), Alessandro Altobelli (89 pen) / Mark Wayne Hateley (74)


602. 09.06.1985
**MEXICO v ENGLAND  1-0**  (1-0)

*Azteca, Ciudad de Mexico*

Referee: Volker Roth (West Germany)    Attendance: 15,000

MEXICO: Pablo Larios, Mario Trejo, Félix Cruz Barbosa, Fernando Quirarte, Rafael Amador, Carlos Muñoz, Miguel España (85 Carlos de los Cobos), Manuel Negrete, Tomás Boy (58 Alejandro Domínguez), Javier Aguirre, Luis Flores (58 Carlos Manuel Hermosillo).    Trainer: Velibor Milutinović

ENGLAND: Gary Richard Bailey, Vivian Alexander Anderson, Kenneth Graham Sansom, Raymond Colin Wilkins (70 Peter Reid), David Watson, Terence William Fenwick, Bryan Robson (Cap), Trevor John Francis, Mark Wayne Hateley, Glenn Hoddle (80 Kerry Michael Dixon), John Charles Bryan Barnes (70 Christopher Roland Waddle).
Manager: Robert Robson

Goal: Luis Flores (20)


603. 12.06.1985
**ENGLAND v WEST GERMANY  3-0**  (1-0)

*Azteca, Ciudad de Mexico*

Referee: Jorge Leanza Sansone (Mexico)    Att: 10,000

ENGLAND: Peter Leslie Shilton, Gary Michael Stevens, Kenneth Graham Sansom, Glenn Hoddle, Mark Wright, Terence Ian Butcher, Bryan Robson (Cap) (73 Paul William Bracewell), Peter Reid, Kerry Michael Dixon, Gary Winston Lineker (59 John Charles Bryan Barnes), Christopher Roland Waddle.    Manager: Robert Robson

**WEST GERMANY**: Harald Schumacher (Cap), Thomas Berthold, Klaus Augenthaler, Ditmar Jakobs, Andreas Brehme, Matthias Herget, Lothar Herbert Matthäus, Felix Magath (59 Olaf Thon), Uwe Rahn, Pierre Littbarski (69 Herbert Waas), Frank Mill.    Trainer: Franz Beckenbauer

**Goals**: Bryan Robson (34), Kerry Michael Dixon (54, 67)

604.  16.06.1985
**U.S.A. v ENGLAND  0-5**  (0-2)
*Coliseum, Los Angeles*
Referee: Edgardo Codesal Mendez (Mexico)    Att: 10,145

**U.S.A.**: Arnold Mausser (46 Tim Harris), Kevin Troy Crow, Michael Windischmann, Dan Canter (54 Michael Brady), Paul David Caligiuri, Percival Joseph van der Beck, Edward Radwanski (79 Troy Snyder), Richard Dean Davis (Cap), Bruce Murray (46 Jacques Ladouceur), John Kerr (46 Jeffrey Scott Hooker), Hugo Pérez.    Trainer: Alketas Panagoulias

**ENGLAND**: Christopher Charles Eric Woods, Vivian Alexander Anderson, Kenneth Graham Sansom (46 David Watson), Glenn Hoddle (46 Trevor McGregor Steven), Terence William Fenwick, Terence Ian Butcher, Bryan Robson (Cap) (46 Peter Reid), Paul William Bracewell, Kerry Michael Dixon, Gary Winston Lineker, Christopher Roland Waddle (46 John Charles Bryan Barnes).    Manager: Robert Robson

**Goals**: Gary Winston Lineker (12, 47), Kerry Dixon (32, 73), Trevor McGregor Steven (80)

605.  11.09.1985    13th World Cup Qualifiers
**ENGLAND v ROMANIA  1-1**  (1-0)
*Wembley, London*
Referee: Karl-Heinz Tritschler (West Germany)    Att: 59,500

**ENGLAND**: Peter Leslie Shilton, Gary Michael Stevens, Mark Wright, Terence William Fenwick, Kenneth Graham Sansom, Glenn Hoddle, Bryan Robson (Cap), Peter Reid, Mark Wayne Hateley, Gary Winston Lineker (80 Anthony Stewart Woodcock), Christopher Roland Waddle (69 John Charles Bryan Barnes).    Manager: Robert Robson

**ROMANIA**: Silviu Lung, Nicolae Negrilă, Ştefan Iovan, Costică Ştefănescu (Cap), Nicolae Ungureanu, Mircea Rednic, Ladislau Bölöni, Michael Klein (87 Dorin Mateuţ), Gheorghe Hagi, Marcel Coraş (82 Romulus Gabor), Rodion Gorun Cămătaru.    Trainer: Mircea Lucescu

**Goals**: Glenn Hoddle (25) / Rodion Gorun Cămătaru (60)

606.  16.10.1985    13th World Cup Qualifiers
**ENGLAND v TURKEY  5-0**  (4-0)
*Wembley, London*
Referee: Anatoli Milchenko (USSR)    Attendance: 52,500

**ENGLAND**: Peter Leslie Shilton, Gary Michael Stevens, Mark Wright, Terence William Fenwick, Kenneth Graham Sansom, Glenn Hoddle, Raymond Colin Wilkins, Bryan Robson (Cap) (66 Trevor McGregor Steven), Gary Winston Lineker, Mark Wayne Hateley (84 Anthony Stewart Woodcock), Christopher Roland Waddle.    Manager: Robert Robson

**TURKEY**: Yaşar Duran, Ismail Demiriz, Yusuf Altintaş, Raşit Çetiner, Sedat III Özden, Abdülkerim Dürmaz, Müjdat Yetkiner, Şenol Çorlu (37 Hasan Şengün), Ünal Karaman, Hasan Vezir, Selçuk Yula.    Trainer: Coşkun Özarı

**Goals**: Christopher Waddle (14), Gary Lineker (18, 42, 53), Bryan Robson (35)

607.  13.11.1985    13th World Cup Qualifiers
**ENGLAND v NORTHERN IRELAND  0-0**
*Wembley, London*
Referee: Erik Fredriksson (Sweden)    Attendance: 70,500

**ENGLAND**: Peter Leslie Shilton, Gary Michael Stevens, Kenneth Graham Sansom, Glenn Hoddle, Mark Wright, Terence William Fenwick, Paul William Bracewell, Raymond Colin Wilkins (Cap), Kerry Michael Dixon, Gary Winston Lineker, Christopher Roland Waddle.    Manager: Robert Robson

**NORTHERN IRELAND**: Patrick Anthony Jennings, James Michael Nicholl, Malachy Martin Donaghy, John Patrick O'Neill, Alan McDonald, David McCreery, Stephen Alexander Penney (59 Gerard Joseph Armstrong), Samuel Baxter McIlroy (Cap), James Martin Quinn, Norman Whiteside, Ian Edwin Stewart (72 Nigel Worthington).    Manager: William Bingham

608.  29.01.1986
**EGYPT v ENGLAND  0-4**  (0-2)
*National, Cairo*
Referee: Antonios Vassaras (Greece)    Attendance: 20,000

**EGYPT**: Thabet El-Batal, Rabei Yassin, Hamada Sedki, Mahmoud Saleh, Mohamed Omar, Alaa Mayhoub, Magdi Abdel Ghani, Taher Abouzaid, Moustafa Abdou, Mohamed Hazem (80 Nasser El-Talees), Tarek Yehia (75 Gamel Abdel Hamid).

**ENGLAND**: Peter Leslie Shilton (75 Christopher Charles Eric Woods), Gary Michael Stevens, Mark Wright, Terence William Fenwick, Kenneth Graham Sansom, Trevor McGregor Steven (76 Richard Anthony Hill), Raymond Colin Wilkins (Cap), Gordon Sidney Cowans, David Lloyd Wallace, Mark Wayne Hateley, Gary Winston Lineker (50 Peter Andrew Beardsley).    Manager: Robert Robson

**Goals**: Trevor Steven (16), Mohamed Omar (41 og), David Wallace (55), Gordon Sidney Cowans (74)

609. 26.02.1986
**ISRAEL v ENGLAND 1-2** (1-0)
*Ramat Gan, Tel Aviv*
Referee: Philippe Mercier (Switzerland)   Att: 15,000

**ISRAEL**: Avi Ran, Eitan Aharoni, Menashe Shimonov, Avi Cohen, Efraim Davidi (42 Moshe Alu), Uri Malmilian, Moti Ivanir, Rifat Turk (62 Eli Cohen), Moshe Sinai, Zahi Armeli, Eli Ohana (62 Roni Rosenthal).   Trainer: Yosef Mirmovich

**ENGLAND**: Peter Leslie Shilton (81 Christopher Charles Eric Woods), Gary Michael Stevens, Alvin Edward Martin, Terence Ian Butcher, Kenneth Graham Sansom, Glenn Hoddle, Bryan Robson (Cap), Raymond Colin Wilkins, Peter Andrew Beardsley, Kerry Michael Dixon (54 Anthony Stewart Woodcock), Christopher Roland Waddle (81 John Charles Bryan Barnes).   Manager: Robert Robson

**Goals**: Eli Ohana (7) / Bryan Robson (52, 86 pen)

610. 26.03.1986
**U.S.S.R. v ENGLAND 0-1** (0-0)
*Dinamo, Tbilisi*
Referee: Velitchko Tsonchev (Bulgaria)   Attendance: 62,500

**U.S.S.R.**: Rinat Dasaev (Cap), Vladimir Bessonov (57 Gennadiy Litovchenko), Aleksandr Chivadze, Aleksandr Bubnov, Anatoliy Demyanenko, Oleg Kuznetsov, Sergey Gotzmanov, Aleksandr Zavarov (75 Igor Dobrovolskiy), Sergey Aleynikov, Georgiy Kondratiev, Sergey Rodionov (57 Oleg Blokhin).   Trainer: Eduard Malofeev

**ENGLAND**: Peter Leslie Shilton, Vivian Alexander Anderson, Kenneth Graham Sansom, Glenn Hoddle, Mark Wright, Terence Ian Butcher, Gordon Sidney Cowans (53 Stephen Brian Hodge), Raymond Colin Wilkins (Cap), Peter Andrew Beardsley, Gary Winston Lineker, Christopher Roland Waddle (75 Trevor McGregor Steven).   Manager: Robert Robson

**Goal**: Christopher Roland Waddle (67)

611. 23.04.1986   Rous Cup
**ENGLAND v SCOTLAND 2-1** (2-0)
*Wembley, London*
Referee: Michel Vautrot (France)   Attendance: 68,357

**ENGLAND**: Peter Leslie Shilton, Gary Michael Stevens, Kenneth Graham Sansom, Glenn Hoddle, David Watson, Terence Ian Butcher, Raymond Colin Wilkins (Cap) (46 Peter Reid), Trevor John Francis, Mark Wayne Hateley, Stephen Brian Hodge (75 Gary Andrew Stevens), Christopher Roland Waddle.   Manager: Robert Robson

**SCOTLAND**: Alan Roderick Rough, Richard Charles Gough, Maurice Daniel Robert Malpas, William Fergus Miller, Alexander McLeish, Stephen Nicol, Robert Sime Aitken, Graeme James Souness (Cap), Eamonn John Peter Bannon, David Robert Speedie, Charles Nicholas (58 Patrick Kevin Francis Michael Nevin).   Manager: Alexander Ferguson

**Goals**: Terence Ian Butcher (27), Glenn Hoddle (39) / Graeme James Souness (57 pen)

612. 17.05.1986
**ENGLAND v MEXICO 3-0** (3-0)
*Coliseum, Los Angeles*
Referee: Vincent Mauro (USA)   Attendance: 60,000

**ENGLAND**: Peter Leslie Shilton, Vivian Alexander Anderson, Kenneth Graham Sansom, Glenn Hoddle, Terence William Fenwick, Terence Ian Butcher, Bryan Robson (Cap) (71 Gary Andrew Stevens), Raymond Colin Wilkins (80 Trevor McGregor Steven), Mark Wayne Hateley (71 Kerry Michael Dixon), Peter Andrew Beardsley, Christopher Roland Waddle (71 John Charles Bryan Barnes).   Manager: Robert Robson

**MEXICO**: Pablo Larios, Mario Trejo, Félix Cruz Barbosa, Armando Manzo (46 Fernando Quirarte), Raúl Servín, Carlos Muñoz, Miguel España (75 Alejandro Domínguez), Manuel Negrete, Javier Aguirre, Carlos Manuel Hermosillo (46 Francisco Javier Cruz), Luis Flores.
Trainer: Velibor Milutinović

**Goals**: Mark Wayne Hateley (22, 31), Peter Beardsley (38)

613. 24.05.1986
**CANADA v ENGLAND 0-1** (0-0)
*Swanguard, Burnaby*
Referee: John Meachin (Canada)   Attendance: 8,050

**CANADA**: Paul Dolan, Robert Lenarduzzi, Terence Moore, Randolph Fitzgerald Samuel, Bruce Wilson, Paul James, Randy Ragan, Gerard Gray (80 Jamie Lowery), Mike Sweeney, Carl Valentine (76 Dale William Mitchell), Igor Vrablic.
Trainer: Anthony Keith Waiters

**ENGLAND**: Peter Leslie Shilton (46 Christopher Charles Eric Woods), Gary Michael Stevens, Kenneth Graham Sansom, Alvin Edward Martin, Terence Ian Butcher, Glenn Hoddle, Raymond Colin Wilkins (Cap) (73 Peter Reid), Stephen Brian Hodge, Mark Wayne Hateley, Gary Winston Lineker (66 Peter Andrew Beardsley), Christopher Roland Waddle (73 John Charles Bryan Barnes).   Manager: Robert Robson

**Goal**: Mark Wayne Hateley (58)

614. 03.06.1986   13th World Cup, 1st Round
**PORTUGAL v ENGLAND 1-0** (0-0)
*Tecnologico, Monterrey*
Referee: Volker Roth (West Germany)   Attendance: 19,998

**PORTUGAL**: Manuel Galrinho Bento (Cap), ÁLVARO Monteiro de MAGALHÃES, FREDERICO Nobre Rosa, António Henriques Fonseca Jesus Oliveira, Augusto Soares Inácio, António dos Santos Ferreira André, DIAMANTINO Manuel Fernandes Miranda (83 JOSÉ ANTÓNIO Prudêncio Conde Bargiela), CARLOS MANUEL Correia dos Santos, JAIME Moreira PACHECO, António Augusto Gomes de Silva "Sousa", Fernando Mendes Soares Gomes (71 Paulo Jorge dos Santos Futre).   Trainer: José Augusto da Costa Sénica Torres

ENGLAND: Peter Leslie Shilton, Gary Michael Stevens, Kenneth Graham Sansom, Glenn Hoddle, Terence William Fenwick, Terence Ian Butcher, Bryan Robson (Cap) (80 Stephen Brian Hodge), Raymond Colin Wilkins, Mark Wayne Hateley, Gary Winston Lineker, Christopher Roland Waddle (80 Peter Andrew Beardsley).   Manager: Robert Robson

Goal:  Carlos Manuel (74)


615.  06.06.1986     13th World Cup,  1st Round
ENGLAND v MOROCCO  0-0

*Tecnologico, Monterrey*

Referee:  Gabriel González (Paraguay)     Attendance:  24,600

ENGLAND: Peter Leslie Shilton, Gary Michael Stevens, Kenneth Graham Sansom, Glenn Hoddle, Terence William Fenwick, Terence Ian Butcher, Bryan Robson (Cap) (41 Stephen Brian Hodge), Raymond Colin Wilkins, Mark Wayne Hateley (75 Gary Andrew Stevens), Gary Winston Lineker, Christopher Roland Waddle.   Manager: Robert Robson

MOROCCO:  Badou Zaki, Labd Khalifa, Abdelmajid Lamris (74 Lahcen Ouadani), Moustapha El Biyaz, Noureddine Bouyahyaoui, Aldelmajid Dolmy, Adbelaziz Bouderbala, Moustapha Krimau, Mohammed Timoumi, Abdelkrim Merry (86 Abdelaziz Soulaimain), Moustapha Khairi.

Sent off:  Raymond Wilkins (43)


616.  11.06.1986     13th World Cup,  1st Round
ENGLAND v POLAND  3-0  (3-0)

*Universitario, Monterrey*

Referee:  André Daina (Switzerland)     Attendance:  20,460

ENGLAND: Peter Leslie Shilton (Cap), Gary Michael Stevens, Kenneth Graham Sansom, Glenn Hoddle, Terence William Fenwick, Terence Ian Butcher, Trevor McGregor Steven, Peter Reid, Gary Winston Lineker (80 Kerry Michael Dixon), Peter Andrew Beardsley (75 Christopher Roland Waddle), Stephen Brian Hodge.   Manager: Robert Robson

POLAND:  :  Józef Młynarczyk, Krzysztof Pawlak, Roman Wójcicki, Stefan Majewski, Marek Ostrowski, Dariusz Dziekanowski, Waldemar Matysik (46 Andrzej Buncol), Ryszard Komornicki (24 Jan Karaś), Jan Urban, Zbigniew Boniek (Cap), Włodzimierz Smolarek.
Trainer:  Antoni Piechniczek

Goals:  Gary Winston Lineker (8, 14, 36)


617.  18.06.1986     13th World Cup,  2nd Round
ENGLAND v PARAGUAY  3-0  (1-0)

*Azteca, Ciudad de Mexico*

Referee:  Jamal Al-Sharif (Syria)     Attendance:  98,728

ENGLAND: Peter Leslie Shilton (Cap), Gary Michael Stevens, Kenneth Graham Sansom, Glenn Hoddle, Alvin Edward Martin, Terence Ian Butcher, Trevor McGregor Steven, Peter Reid (57 Gary Andrew Stevens), Gary Winston Lineker, Peter Andrew Beardsley (80 Mark Wayne Hateley), Stephen Brian Hodge.   Manager: Robert Robson

PARAGUAY:  Roberto Fernández, Juan Bautista Torales (63 Jorge Alberto Guasch), César Zabala, Rogelio Wilfrido Delgado (Cap), Vladimiro Schettina Chepini, Jorge Amado Núñez, Buenaventura Ferreira, Julio César Romero, Roberto Cabañas, Adolfino Cañete, Alfredo Damián Mendoza.
Trainer:  Cayetano Ré Ramírez

Goals:  Gary Winston Lineker (32, 72), Peter Beardsley (56)


618.  22.06.1986     13th World Cup,  Quarter-Finals
ARGENTINA v ENGLAND  2-1  (0-0)

*Azteca, Ciudad de Mexico*

Referee:  Ali Ben Nasser (Tunisia)     Attendance:  114,580

ARGENTINA:  Nery Alberto Pumpido, José Luis Cuciuffo, José Luis Brown, Oscar Alfredo Ruggeri, Julio Jorge Olarticoechea, Ricardo Omar Giusti, Sergio Daniel Batista, Jorge Luis Burruchaga (76 Carlos Daniel Tapia), Héctor Adolfo Enrique, Diego Armando Maradona (Cap), Jorge Alberto Francisco Valdano.   Trainer:  Carlos Salvador Bilardo

ENGLAND: Peter Leslie Shilton (Cap), Gary Michael Stevens, Kenneth Graham Sansom, Glenn Hoddle, Terence Ian Butcher, Terence William Fenwick, Trevor McGregor Steven (73 John Charles Bryan Barnes), Peter Reid (63 Christopher Roland Waddle), Gary Winston Lineker, Peter Andrew Beardsley, Stephen Brian Hodge.   Manager: Robert Robson

Goals:  Diego Maradona (52, 56) / Gary Lineker (81)


619.  10.09.1986
SWEDEN v ENGLAND  1-0  (0-0)

*Råsunda, Solna*

Referee:  Werner Föckler (West Germany)     Att: 15,646

SWEDEN:  Jan Möller, Roland Nilsson, Glenn Ingvar Hysén (71 Torbjörn Persson), Peter Larsson, Stig Fredriksson (Cap), Ulf Eriksson, Robert Prytz, Glenn Peter Strömberg, Anders Palmér, Johnny Ekström, Björn Nilsson.   Trainer:  Olle Nordin

ENGLAND: Peter Leslie Shilton (Cap), Vivian Alexander Anderson, Alvin Edward Martin, Terence Ian Butcher, Kenneth Graham Sansom, Trevor McGregor Steven (80 Christopher Roland Waddle), Glenn Hoddle, Raymond Colin Wilkins, Stephen Brian Hodge, Kerry Michael Dixon, John Charles Bryan Barnes (58 Anthony Richard Cottee).   Manager:  Robert Robson

Goal:  Johnny Ekström (50)

620.  15.10.1986   8th European Champs Qualifiers
**ENGLAND v NORTHERN IRELAND  3-0**  (1-0)
*Wembley, London*
Referee:  Alphonse Constantin (Belgium)   Att: 35,300
**ENGLAND**:  Peter Leslie Shilton, Vivian Alexander Anderson, Kenneth Graham Sansom, Glenn Hoddle, David Watson, Terence Ian Butcher, Bryan Robson (Cap), Stephen Brian Hodge, Gary Winston Lineker, Peter Andrew Beardsley (84 Anthony Richard Cottee), Christopher Roland Waddle.  Manager:  Robert Robson
**NORTHERN IRELAND**:  Philip Anthony Hughes, Gary James Fleming, Alan McDonald, John McClelland (Cap), Nigel Worthington, Malachy Martin Donaghy, Norman Whiteside (84 Samuel Baxter McIlroy), Stephen Alexander Penney (74 James Martin Quinn), Colin John Clarke, David Anthony Campbell, Ian Edwin Stewart.   Manager:  William Bingham
**Goals**:  Gary Lineker (33, 80), Christopher Waddle (78)

621.  12.11.1986   8th European Champs Qualifiers
**ENGLAND v YUGOSLAVIA  2-0**  (1-0)
*Wembley, London*
Referee:  Franz Wöhrer (Austria)   Attendance: 60,000
**ENGLAND**:  Christopher Charles Eric Woods, Vivian Alexander Anderson, Mark Wright, Terence Ian Butcher (Cap), Kenneth Graham Sansom, Glenn Hoddle, Gary Vincent Mabbutt, Stephen Brian Hodge (82 Raymond Colin Wilkins), Gary Winston Lineker, Peter Andrew Beardsley, Christopher Roland Waddle (79 Trevor McGregor Steven).  Manager:  Robert Robson
**YUGOSLAVIA**  Mauro Ravnić, Zoran Vujović, Mirsad Baljić, Refik Šabanadžović, Marko Elsner, Faruk Hadžibegić, Haris Škoro (71 Semir Tuce; 79 Predrag Jurić), Srećko Katanec, Blaž Slišković, Milan Janković, Zlatko Vujović (Cap).
Trainer:  Ivan Osim
**Goals**:  Gary Mabbutt (21), Vivian Alexander Anderson (57)

622.  18.02.1987
**SPAIN v ENGLAND  2-4**  (1-2)
*Santiago Bernabéu, Madrid*
Referee:  Claudio Pieri (Italy)   Attendance: 35,000
**SPAIN**:  Andoni Zubizarreta, Miguel Porlán Noguera "Chendo" (63 Manuel Sanchís), José Antonio Camacho (Cap) (70 Genar Andrinúa), Juan Carlos Arteche, VÍCTOR Muñoz, Rafael Gordillo (63 Joaquín Alonso), José Miguel González "Míchel" (63 ROBERTO Fernández Bonillo), Ricardo Gallego, Francisco José Carrasco, Emilio Butragueño, Ramón Vázquez.
Trainer:  Miguel Muñoz Mozún

**ENGLAND**:  Peter Leslie Shilton (63 Christopher Charles Eric Woods), Vivian Alexander Anderson, Kenneth Graham Sansom, Glenn Hoddle, Anthony Alexander Adams, Terence Ian Butcher, Bryan Robson (Cap), Stephen Brian Hodge, Peter Andrew Beardsley, Gary Winston Lineker, Christopher Roland Waddle (70 Trevor McGregor Steven).
Manager:  Robert Robson
**Goals**:  Butragueño (14), Ramón (76) /
Gary Winston Lineker (23, 27, 47, 57)

623.  01.04.1987   8th European Champs Qualifiers
**NORTHERN IRELAND v ENGLAND  0-2**  (0-2)
*Windsor Park, Belfast*
Referee:  Emilio Soriano Aladren (Spain)   Att: 20,578
**NORTHERN IRELAND**:  George Dunlop, Gary James Fleming, Malachy Martin Donaghy, John McClelland (Cap), Alan McDonald, Paul Christopher Ramsey, David Anthony Campbell (59 Daniel Joseph Wilson), David McCreery, Kevin James Wilson, Norman Whiteside, Nigel Worthington.
Manager:  William Bingham
**ENGLAND**:  Peter Leslie Shilton (46 Christopher Charles Eric Woods), Vivian Alexander Anderson, Kenneth Graham Sansom, Gary Vincent Mabbutt, Mark Wright, Terence Ian Butcher, Bryan Robson (Cap), Stephen Brian Hodge, Peter Andrew Beardsley, Gary Winston Lineker, Christopher Roland Waddle.   Manager:  Robert Robson
**Goals**:  Bryan Robson (19), Christopher Roland Waddle (43)

624.  29.04.1987   8th European Champs Qualifiers
**TURKEY v ENGLAND  0-0**
*Atatürk, Izmir*
Referee:  Valeri Butenko (USSR)   Attendance: 25,000
**TURKEY**:  Fatih Uraz, Semih Yuvakuran, Ali Çoban, Erhan Önal, Ismail Demiriz, Riza Çalımbay, Savaş Demiral, Uğur Tütüneker, Hasan Vezir (87 Feyyaz Uçar), Ali Erdal Keser, Iskender Gönen (79 Ilyas Tüfekçi).   Trainer:  Mustafa Denizli
**ENGLAND**:  Christopher Charles Eric Woods, Vivian Alexander Anderson, Kenneth Graham Sansom, Gary Vincent Mabbutt, Anthony Alexander Adams, Glenn Hoddle, Bryan Robson (Cap), Clive Darren Allen (75 Mark Wayne Hateley), Gary Winston Lineker, Christopher Roland Waddle, Stephen Brian Hodge (75 John Charles Bryan Barnes).
Manager:  Robert Robson

625.  19.05.1987   Rous Cup
**ENGLAND v BRAZIL  1-1**  (1-1)
*Wembley, London*
Referee:  Michel Vautrot (France)     Attendance:  92,000
ENGLAND:  Peter Leslie Shilton, Gary Michael Stevens, Anthony Alexander Adams, Terence Ian Butcher, Stuart Pearce, Peter Reid, Bryan Robson (Cap), Christopher Roland Waddle, Gary Winston Lineker (76 Mark Wayne Hateley), Peter Andrew Beardsley, John Charles Bryan Barnes.
Manager:  Robert Robson

BRAZIL:  CARLOS Roberto Gallo, JOSIMAR Higino Pereira, Geraldo Dutra Pereira "Geraldão", RICARDO Roberto Barreto da ROCHA, Nélson Luís Kerschner "Nelsinho", William DOUGLAS Huminia Menezes, Paulo SILAS do Prado Pereira (82 Carlos Caetano Bledorn Verri "Dunga"), Carlos Eduardo "Edu" Marangon (82 RAÍ Souza Vieira de Oliveira), Luís Antônio Corrêa da Costa "Müller", Francisco Ernândi Lima da Silva "Mirandinha", VALDO Cāndido Filho.
Trainer:  Carlos Alberto Silva

Goal:  Gary Winston Lineker (34) / Francisco Ernândi Lima da Silva "Mirandinha" (35)


626.  23.05.1987   Rous Cup
**SCOTLAND v ENGLAND  0-0**
*Hampden Park, Glasgow*
Referee:  Dieter Pauly (West Germany)     Attendance:  64,713
SCOTLAND:  James Leighton, Richard Charles Gough, Murdo Davidson MacLeod, William Fergus Miller, Alexander McLeish, Paul Michael Lyons McStay, Neil Simpson, Robert Sime Aitken (Cap), Ian William Wilson, Brian John McClair (58 Charles Nicholas), Alistair Murdoch McCoist.
Manager:  Andrew Roxburgh

ENGLAND:  Christopher Charles Eric Woods, Gary Michael Stevens, Stuart Pearce, Glenn Hoddle, Mark Wright, Terence Ian Butcher, Bryan Robson (Cap), Stephen Brian Hodge, Mark Wayne Hateley, Peter Andrew Beardsley, Christopher Roland Waddle.   Manager:  Robert Robson


627.  09.09.1987
**WEST GERMANY v ENGLAND  3-1**  (2-1)
*Rheinstadion, Düsseldorf*
Referee:  Paolo Casarin (Italy)     Attendance:  50,000
WEST GERMANY:  Eike Immel, Matthias Herget, Andreas Brehme (61 Stefan Reuter), Jürgen Kohler, Guido Buchwald, Michael Frontzeck, Pierre Littbarski, Olaf Thon, Hans Dorfner, Rudolf Völler (78 Wolfram Wuttke), Klaus Allofs (Cap).
Trainer:  Franz Beckenbauer

ENGLAND:  Peter Leslie Shilton (Cap), Vivian Alexander Anderson (77 Stuart Pearce), Kenneth Graham Sansom, Glenn Hoddle (65 Neil John Webb), Anthony Alexander Adams, Gary Vincent Mabbutt, Peter Reid, John Charles Bryan Barnes, Peter Andrew Beardsley, Gary Winston Lineker, Christopher Roland Waddle (51 Mark Wayne Hateley).
Manager:  Robert Robson

Goal:  Pierre Littbarski (24, 33), Wolfram Wuttke (84) / Gary Winston Lineker (42)


628.  14.10.1987   8th European Champs Qualifiers
**ENGLAND v TURKEY  8-0**  (4-0)
*Wembley, London*
Referee:  Albert Thomas (Holland)     Attendance:  42,528
ENGLAND:  Peter Leslie Shilton, Gary Michael Stevens, Kenneth Graham Sansom, Trevor McGregor Steven (46 Glenn Hoddle), Anthony Alexander Adams, Terence Ian Butcher, Bryan Robson (Cap), Neil John Webb, Peter Andrew Beardsley (73 Cyrille Regis), Gary Winston Lineker, John Charles Bryan Barnes.   Manager:  Robert Robson

TURKEY:  Fatih Uraz, Riza Çalımbay, Semih Yuvakuran, Ali Çoban, Erhan Önal, Ali Gültiken (35 Savaş Demiral), Uğur Tütüneker, Muhammet Altıntaş, Ali Erdal Keser (35 Tanju Çolak), Kayhan Kaynak, Iskender Gönen.
Trainer:  Mustafa Denizli

Goals:  John Barnes (1, 28), Gary Lineker (8, 42, 71), Bryan Robson (59), Peter Beardsley (62), Neil John Webb (88)


629.  11.11.1987   8th European Champs Qualifiers
**YUGOSLAVIA v ENGLAND  1-4**  (0-4)
*JNA, Beograd*
Referee:  Michel Vautrot (France)     Attendance:  70,000
YUGOSLAVIA  Mauro Ravnic (46 Vladan Radača), Zoran Vujović, Mirsad Baljić, Srećko Katanec, Marko Elsner (27 Milan Janković), Faruk Hadžibegić, Dragan Stojković, Marko Mlinarić, Fadilj Vokri, Mehmed Baždarević, Zlatko Vujović (Cap).   Trainer:  Ivan Osim

ENGLAND:  Peter Leslie Shilton, Gary Michael Stevens, Kenneth Graham Sansom, Trevor McGregor Steven, Anthony Alexander Adams, Terence Ian Butcher, Bryan Robson (Cap) (75 Peter Reid), Neil John Webb (83 Glenn Hoddle), Peter Andrew Beardsley, Gary Winston Lineker, John Charles Bryan Barnes.   Manager:  Robert Robson

Goals:  Srećko Katanec (80) / Peter Andrew Beardsley (4), John Charles Bryan Barnes (17), Bryan Robson (20), Anthony Alexander Adams (25)

630.  17.02.1988
**ISRAEL v ENGLAND  0-0**
*Ramat Gan, Tel Aviv*
Referee: Alphonse Constantin (Belgium)   Att: 5,000
**ISRAEL**: Boni Ginzburg, Avi Cohen, Avi Cohen, Menashe Shimonov, Nir Alon, Eli Cohen, Uri Malmilian, Nir Klinger, Moti Ivanir (84 Avinoam Ovadia), Shalom Tikva (82 Daniel Brailovsky), Eli Driks (88 Moshe Eisenberg). Trainer: Miljenko Mihić
**ENGLAND**: Christopher Charles Eric Woods, Gary Michael Stevens, Stuart Pearce, Neil John Webb, David Watson, Mark Wright (74 Terence William Fenwick), Clive Darren Allen (67 Michael Gordon Harford), Stephen McMahon, Peter Andrew Beardsley (Cap), John Charles Bryan Barnes, Christopher Roland Waddle.  Manager: Robert Robson

631.  23.03.1988
**ENGLAND v HOLLAND  2-2**  (1-2)
*Wembley, London*
Referee: Adolf Prokop (East Germany)   Attendance: 74,590
**ENGLAND**: Peter Leslie Shilton, Gary Michael Stevens, Kenneth Graham Sansom, Trevor McGregor Steven, Anthony Alexander Adams, David Watson (72 Mark Wright), Bryan Robson (Cap), Neil John Webb (69 Glenn Hoddle), Peter Andrew Beardsley (35 Mark Wayne Hateley), Gary Winston Lineker, John Charles Bryan Barnes.
Manager: Robert Robson
**HOLLAND**: Hans van Breukelen, Sonny Silooy, Sjaak Troost, Ronald Koeman (Cap), Berry van Aerle, Jan Wouters, Arnold Mühren, Gerald Vanenburg, Johnny van't Schip (83 Addick Koot), Ruud Gullit (60 Hendrie Krüzen), Johnny Bosman. Trainer: Rinus Michels
**Goals**: Gary Winston Lineker (13), Anthony Adams (65) / Anthony Adams (20 og), Johnny Bosman (25)

632.  27.04.1988
**HUNGARY v ENGLAND  0-0**
*Népstadion, Budapest*
Referee: Karl-Heinz Tritschler (West Germany)   Att: 35,000
**HUNGARY**: József Szendrei, Tibor Balog, Attila Pintér, Antal Róth (65 István Varga), István Kozma, Imre Garaba, Lajos Détári, József Fitos, János Sass, József Kiprich (83 Kálmán Kovács), István Vincze.  Trainer: László Bálint
**ENGLAND**: Christopher Charles Eric Woods, Vivian Alexander Anderson, Stuart Pearce (46 Gary Michael Stevens), Trevor McGregor Steven, Anthony Alexander Adams, Gary Andrew Pallister, Bryan Robson (Cap), Stephen McMahon, Peter Andrew Beardsley (64 Mark Wayne Hateley), Gary Winston Lineker (83 Anthony Richard Cottee), Christopher Roland Waddle (64 Glenn Hoddle).
Manager: Robert Robson

633.  21.05.1988   Rous Cup
**ENGLAND v SCOTLAND  1-0**  (1-0)
*Wembley, London*
Referee: Joël Quiniou (France)   Attendance: 70,480
**ENGLAND**: Peter Leslie Shilton, Gary Michael Stevens, Kenneth Graham Sansom, Neil John Webb, David Watson, Anthony Alexander Adams, Bryan Robson (Cap), Trevor McGregor Steven (72 Christopher Roland Waddle), Peter Andrew Beardsley, Gary Winston Lineker, John Charles Bryan Barnes.  Manager: Robert Robson
**SCOTLAND**: James Leighton, Richard Charles Gough, Stephen Nicol, William Fergus Miller, Alexander McLeish, Murdo Davidson MacLeod, Neil Simpson (74 Thomas Burns), Paul Michael Lyons McStay, Robert Sime Aitken (Cap), Alistair Murdoch McCoist (77 Kevin William Gallacher), Maurice Johnston.  Manager: Andrew Roxburgh
**Goal**: Peter Andrew Beardsley (11)

634.  24.05.1988   Rous Cup
**ENGLAND v COLOMBIA  1-1**  (1-0)
*Wembley, London*
Ref: Karl-Josef Assenmacher (West Germany)   Att: 25,756
**ENGLAND**: Peter Leslie Shilton, Vivian Alexander Anderson, Kenneth Graham Sansom, Stephen McMahon, Mark Wright, Anthony Alexander Adams, Bryan Robson (Cap), Christopher Roland Waddle (73 Glenn Hoddle), Peter Andrew Beardsley (73 Mark Wayne Hateley), Gary Winston Lineker, John Charles Bryan Barnes.  Manager: Robert Robson
**COLOMBIA**: José René Higuita, Luis Fernando Herrera, Luis Carlos Perea, Andrés Escobar, Carlos Mario Hoyos, Bernardo Redín, Leonel de Jesús Álvarez, Alexis Enrique García, Carlos Alberto Valderrama, Arnoldo Alberto Iguarán (78 Alex "Didí" Valderrama), Jaime Arango (60 John Jairo Tréllez). Trainer: Francisco Maturana
**Goal**: Gary Winston Lineker (22) / Andrés Escobar (66)

635.  28.05.1988
**SWITZERLAND v ENGLAND  0-1**  (0-0)
*Olympique de la Pontaise, Lausanne*
Referee: Luigi Agnolin (Italy)   Attendance: 10,000
**SWITZERLAND**: Joël Corminboeuf, Marco Schällibaum, Alain Geiger, Thomas Tschuppert, Martin Weber, Thomas Bickel (82 Patrice Mottiez), Philippe Perret (46 Martin Andermatt), Heinz Hermann, Beat Sutter, Christophe Bonvin (67 Kubilay Türkyilmaz), Hanspeter Zwicker.
Trainer: Daniel Jeandupeux

**ENGLAND**: Peter Leslie Shilton (46 Christopher Charles Eric Woods), Gary Michael Stevens, Kenneth Graham Sansom, Neil John Webb, Mark Wright, Anthony Alexander Adams (46 David Watson), Bryan Robson (Cap) (79 Peter Reid), Trevor McGregor Steven (46 Christopher Roland Waddle), Peter Andrew Beardsley, Gary Winston Lineker, John Charles Bryan Barnes.   Manager: Robert Robson

**Goal**: Gary Winston Lineker (59)

636.   12.06.1988   8th European Champs, 1st Round
**REPUBLIC OF IRELAND v ENGLAND  1-0**  (1-0)
*Neckar, Stuttgart*
Referee: Siegfried Kirschen (East Germany)   Att: 53,000

**IRELAND**: Patrick Bonner, Christopher Barry Morris, Michael Joseph McCarthy, Kevin Bernard Moran, Christopher William Gerard Hughton, Raymond James Houghton, Paul McGrath, Ronald Andrew Whelan, Anthony Galvin (75 Kevin Mark Sheedy), John William Aldridge, Francis Anthony Stapleton (Cap) (62 Niall John Quinn).
Manager: John Charlton

**ENGLAND**: Peter Leslie Shilton, Gary Michael Stevens, Kenneth Graham Sansom, Neil John Webb (60 Glenn Hoddle), Mark Wright, Anthony Alexander Adams, Bryan Robson (Cap), John Charles Bryan Barnes, Peter Andrew Beardsley (82 Mark Wayne Hateley), Gary Winston Lineker, Christopher Roland Waddle.   Manager: Robert Robson

**Goal**: Raymond James Houghton (6)

637.   15.06.1988   8th European Champs, 1st Round
**HOLLAND v ENGLAND  3-1**  (1-0)
*Rheinstadion, Düsseldorf*
Referee: Paolo Casarin (Italy)   Attendance: 65,000

**HOLLAND**: Hans van Breukelen, Berry van Aerle, Ronald Koeman, Frank Rijkaard, Adri van Tiggelen, Jan Wouters, Arnold Mühren, Gerald Vanenburg (58 Wim Kieft), Erwin Koeman, Ruud Gullit (Cap), Marco van Basten (86 Wilbert Suvrijn).   Trainer: Rinus Michels

**ENGLAND**: Peter Leslie Shilton, Gary Michael Stevens, Kenneth Graham Sansom, Glenn Hoddle, Mark Wright, Anthony Alexander Adams, Bryan Robson (Cap), Trevor McGregor Steven (69 Christopher Roland Waddle), Peter Andrew Beardsley (72 Mark Wayne Hateley), Gary Winston Lineker, John Charles Bryan Barnes.
Manager: Robert Robson

**Goals**: Marco van Basten (43, 74, 76) / Bryan Robson (53)

638.   18.06.1988   8th European Champs, 1st Round
**U.S.S.R. v ENGLAND  3-1**  (2-1)
*Waldstadion, Frankfurt/Main*
Referee: José Rosa dos Santos (Portugal)   Att: 53,000

**U.S.S.R.**: Rinat Dasaev (Cap), Vladimir Bessonov, Vagiz Khidiyatullin, Oleg Kuznetzov, Gennadiy Litovchenko, Sergey Aleynikov, Aleksandr Zavarov (86 Sergey Gotzmanov), Aleksey Mikhaylichenko, Vasiliy Ratz, Igor Belanov (45 Viktor Pasulko), Oleg Protasov.   Trainer: Valeriy Lobanovskiy

**ENGLAND**: Christopher Charles Eric Woods, Gary Michael Stevens, Kenneth Graham Sansom, Glenn Hoddle, David Watson, Anthony Alexander Adams, Bryan Robson (Cap), Trevor McGregor Steven, Gary Winston Lineker (69 Mark Wayne Hateley), Stephen McMahon (53 Neil John Webb), John Charles Bryan Barnes.   Manager: Robert Robson

**Goals**: Sergey Aleynikov (3), Aleksey Mikhaylichenko (26), Viktor Pasulko (73) / Anthony Alexander Adams (16)

639.   14.09.1988
**ENGLAND v DENMARK  1-0**  (1-0)
*Wembley, London*
Referee: Alexis Ponnet (Belgium)   Attendance: 25,837

**ENGLAND**: Peter Leslie Shilton (46 Christopher Charles Eric Woods), Gary Michael Stevens, Stuart Pearce, David Carlyle Rocastle, Anthony Alexander Adams (65 Desmond Sinclair Walker), Terence Ian Butcher, Bryan Robson (Cap), Neil John Webb, Michael Gordon Harford (70 Anthony Richard Cottee), Peter Andrew Beardsley (85 Paul John Gascoigne), Stephen Brian Hodge.   Manager: Robert Robson

**DENMARK**: Troels Rasmussen, Bjarne Jensen (66 Jan Heintze), Kent Nielsen, Lars Olsen (Cap), Jan Bartram (85 Kurt Jørgensen), Jan Mølby, John Helt, Johnny Hansen, Kim Vilfort (85 Bjørn Kristensen), Lars Elstrup, Michael Laudrup.   Trainer: Josef Piontek

**Goal**: Neil John Webb (28)

640.   19.10.1988   14th World Cup Qualifiers
**ENGLAND v SWEDEN  0-0**
*Wembley, London*
Referee: Gérard Biguet (France)   Attendance: 65,628

**ENGLAND**: Peter Leslie Shilton, Gary Michael Stevens, Stuart Pearce, Neil John Webb, Anthony Alexander Adams (61 Desmond Sinclair Walker), Terence Ian Butcher, Bryan Robson (Cap), Peter Andrew Beardsley, Christopher Roland Waddle, Gary Winston Lineker, John Charles Bryan Barnes (79 Anthony Richard Cottee).   Manager: Robert Robson

**SWEDEN**: Thomas Ravelli, Roland Nilsson (77 Dennis Schiller), Glenn Ingvar Hysén, Peter Larsson, Roger Ljung, Jonas Thern, Glenn Peter Strömberg, Robert Prytz, Joakim Nilsson, Hans Holmqvist (63 Johnny Ekström), Stefan Pettersson.   Trainer: Olle Nordin

641. 16.11.1988
**SAUDI ARABIA v ENGLAND 1-1** (1-0)
*King Fahd, Riyadh*
Referee: Jasem Mandi (Bahrain)  Attendance: 8,000

**SAUDI ARABIA**: Abdullah Al-Deayea (44 Al-Subiani), Zaki Al-Saleh, Saleh Al-Nuaymah, Ahmad Jameel, Mohammed Abdul Jawad, Saleh Al-Mutlaq, Fahad Al-Mussaibeeh, Mohammed Al-Suwayed (75 Yousef Al-Thinnayan), Majid Abdullah, Saad Mubarak, Muhaisen Al-Jamaan (79 Masa'ad).

**ENGLAND**: David Andrew Seaman, Melwyn Sterland, Anthony Alexander Adams, Gary Andrew Pallister, Stuart Pearce, Michael Lauriston Thomas (80 Brian Marwood), Bryan Robson (Cap), David Carlyle Rocastle, Christopher Roland Waddle (80 Paul John Gascoigne), Gary Winston Lineker, Peter Andrew Beardsley (68 Alan Martin Smith). Manager: Robert Robson

**Goals**: Majid Abdullah (15) / Anthony Alexander Adams (54)

642. 08.02.1989
**GREECE v ENGLAND 1-2** (1-1)
*Olympiako, Athina*
Referee: Heinz Holzmann (Austria)  Attendance: 4,000

**GREECE**: Spíros Ikonomopoulos, Yákovos Hatziathanasiou (72 Stélios Manolas), Giórgos Koutoulas, Giánnis Kalitzakis, Konstantinos Mavridis, Panagiótis Tsalouhidis, Dimítris Saravakos (Cap), Konstantinos Lagonidis (39 Stéfanos Borbokis), Giánnis Samaras (46 Vaggelís Kalogeropoulos), Nikolaos Nioplias, Nikolaos Tsiantakis. Trainer: Alekos Sofianidis

**ENGLAND**: Peter Leslie Shilton, Gary Michael Stevens, Stuart Pearce, Neil John Webb, Desmond Sinclair Walker, Terence Ian Butcher, Bryan Robson (Cap), David Carlyle Rocastle, Alan Martin Smith (78 Peter Andrew Beardsley), Gary Winston Lineker, John Charles Bryan Barnes. Manager: Robert Robson

**Goals**: Dimítris Saravakos (1 pen) / John Charles Bryan Barnes (8), Bryan Robson (79)

643. 08.03.1989   14th World Cup Qualifiers
**ALBANIA v ENGLAND 0-2** (0-1)
*Qemal Stafa, Tiranë*
Referee: John Blankenstein (Holland)  Attendance: 25,000

**ALBANIA**: Halim Mersini, Hysen Zmijani, Mirel Josa, Skënder Hodja, Skënder Gega, Fatbardh Jera, Ylli Shehu, Artur Lekbello, Lefter Millo (75 Kujtim Majaçi), Arben Minga, Sulejman Demollari. Trainer: Shyqyri Rreli

**ENGLAND**: Peter Leslie Shilton, Gary Michael Stevens, Stuart Pearce, Neil John Webb, Desmond Sinclair Walker, Terence Ian Butcher, Bryan Robson (Cap), David Carlyle Rocastle, Christopher Roland Waddle (79 Peter Andrew Beardsley), Gary Winston Lineker (79 Alan Martin Smith), John Charles Bryan Barnes. Manager: Robert Robson

**Goals**: John Charles Bryan Barnes (17), Bryan Robson (62)

644. 26.04.1989   14th World Cup Qualifiers
**ENGLAND v ALBANIA 5-0** (2-0)
*Wembley, London*
Referee: Einar Halle (Norway)  Attendance: 60,602

**ENGLAND**: Peter Leslie Shilton, Gary Michael Stevens (77 Paul Andrew Parker), Stuart Pearce, Neil John Webb, Desmond Sinclair Walker, Terence Ian Butcher, Bryan Robson (Cap), David Carlyle Rocastle (67 Paul John Gascoigne), Peter Andrew Beardsley, Gary Winston Lineker, Christopher Roland Waddle. Manager: Robert Robson

**ALBANIA**: Blendi Nallbani, Hysen Zmijani, Agim Bubeqi, Skënder Hodja, Skënder Gega, Fatbardh Jera, Ylli Shehu, Artur Lekbello, Lefter Millo, Fatmir Hasanpapa (31 Pjerin Noga), Sulejman Demollari. Trainer: Shyqyri Rreli

**Goals**: Gary Lineker (7), Peter Andrew Beardsley (11, 62), Christopher Roland Waddle (70), Paul John Gascoigne (87)

645. 23.05.1989   Rous Cup
**ENGLAND v CHILE 0-0**
*Wembley, London*
Referee: Erik Fredriksson (Sweden)  Attendance: 15,628

**ENGLAND**: Peter Leslie Shilton, Paul Andrew Parker, Desmond Sinclair Walker, Terence Ian Butcher, Stuart Pearce, Neil John Webb, Bryan Robson (Cap), Paul John Gascoigne, Nigel Howard Clough, John Fashanu (70 Anthony Richard Cottee), Christopher Roland Waddle. Manager: Robert Robson

**CHILE**: Roberto Antonio Rojas, Leonel Contreras, Rubén Alberto Espinoza, Hugo Armando González, Fernando Astengo, Oscar Patricio Reyes, Elías Raúl Ormeño Pacheco, Jaime Augusto Pizarro, Osvaldo Heriberto Hurtado (55 Jaime Andrés Vera), Hugo Eduardo Rubio, Juan Covarrubias (46 Juan Carlos Letelier Pizarro). Trainer: Orlando Aravena

646. 27.05.1989   Rous Cup
**SCOTLAND v ENGLAND 0-2** (0-1)
*Hampden Park, Glasgow*
Referee: Michel Vautrot (France)  Attendance: 63,282

**SCOTLAND**: James Leighton, Stewart McKimmie, Maurice Daniel Robert Malpas, David McPherson, Alexander McLeish, Patrick Kevin Francis Michael Nevin, Paul Michael Lyons McStay, Robert Sime Aitken (Cap), Robert Connor (57 Peter Grant), Alistair Murdoch McCoist, Maurice Johnston. Manager: Andrew Roxburgh

**ENGLAND**: Peter Leslie Shilton, Gary Michael Stevens, Desmond Sinclair Walker, Terence Ian Butcher, Stuart Pearce, Trevor McGregor Steven, Neil John Webb, Bryan Robson (Cap), Christopher Roland Waddle, John Fashanu (31 Stephen George Bull), Anthony Richard Cottee (75 Paul John Gascoigne). Manager: Robert Robson

**Goals**: Christopher Roland Waddle (20), Stephen Bull (80)

647. 03.06.1989    14th World Cup Qualifiers
**ENGLAND v POLAND   3-0**  (1-0)
*Wembley, London*

Referee: Luigi Agnolin (Italy)    Attendance: 69,203

**ENGLAND**: Peter Leslie Shilton, Gary Michael Stevens, Desmond Sinclair Walker, Terence Ian Butcher, Stuart Pearce, Neil John Webb, Bryan Robson (Cap), Christopher Roland Waddle (77 Alan Martin Smith), Gary Winston Lineker, Peter Andrew Beardsley (77 David Carlyle Rocastle), John Charles Bryan Barnes.    Manager: Robert Robson

**POLAND**: Jarosław Bako, Waldemar Prusik (Cap), Roman Wójcicki, Damian Łukasik, Dariusz Wdowczyk, Krzysztof Warzycha, Waldemar Matysik, Jerzy Wijas, Jan Urban (70 Ryszard Tarasiewicz), Jan Furtok, Marek Leśniak (60 Roman Kosecki).    Trainer: Wojciech Łazarek

**Goals**: Gary Lineker (25), John Charles Bryan Barnes (70), Neil John Webb (83)


648. 07.06.1989
**DENMARK v ENGLAND   1-1**  (0-1)
*Idraetsparken, København*

Referee: Jacob Uilenberg (Holland)    Attendance: 18,400

**DENMARK**: Peter Schmeichel, Ivan Nielsen (69 John Larsen), Lars Olsen (Cap), Kent Nielsen, Henrik Risom, John Helt, Michael Laudrup, Jan Bartram, Henrik Andersen (63 Kim Vilfort), Brian Laudrup (87 Peter Rasmussen), Lars Elstrup.    Trainer: Josef Piontek

**ENGLAND**: Peter Leslie Shilton (64 David Andrew Seaman), Paul Andrew Parker, Desmond Sinclair Walker, Terence Ian Butcher, Stuart Pearce, David Carlyle Rocastle, Neil John Webb (46 Christopher Roland Waddle), Bryan Robson (Cap), John Charles Bryan Barnes (46 Stephen McMahon), Peter Andrew Beardsley (61 Stephen George Bull), Gary Winston Lineker.    Manager: Robert Robson

**Goals**: Lars Elstrup (56) / Gary Winston Lineker (26)


649. 06.09.1989    14th World Cup Qualifiers
**SWEDEN v ENGLAND   0-0**
*Råsunda, Solna*

Referee: Hubert Forstinger (Austria)    Attendance: 38,588

**SWEDEN**: Thomas Ravelli, Roland Nilsson, Glenn Ingvar Hysén (Cap), Peter Larsson, Roger Ljung, Leif Engqvist, Jonas Thern, Klas Ingesson (72 Glenn Peter Strömberg), Joakim Nilsson (77 Anders Erik Limpár), Johnny Ekström, Mats Magnusson.    Trainer: Olle Nordin

**ENGLAND**: Peter Leslie Shilton, Gary Michael Stevens, Desmond Sinclair Walker, Terence Ian Butcher (Cap), Stuart Pearce, Christopher Roland Waddle, Stephen McMahon, Neil John Webb (72 Paul John Gascoigne), John Charles Bryan Barnes (76 David Carlyle Rocastle), Peter Andrew Beardsley, Gary Winston Lineker.    Manager: Robert Robson


650. 11.10.1989    14th World Cup Qualifiers
**POLAND v ENGLAND   0-0**
*Slaski, Chorzów*

Referee: Emilio Soriano Aladren (Spain)    Att: 32,423

**POLAND**: Jarosław Bako, Piotr Czachowski, Zbigniew Kaczmarek, Dariusz Wdowczyk (Cap), Robert Warzycha, Ryszard Tarasiewicz, Janusz Nawrocki, Jacek Ziober, Krzysztof Warzycha (58 Jan Furtok), Dariusz Dziekanowski, Roman Kosecki.    Trainer: Andrzej Strejlau

**ENGLAND**: Peter Leslie Shilton, Gary Michael Stevens, Desmond Sinclair Walker, Terence Ian Butcher, Stuart Pearce, David Carlyle Rocastle, Stephen McMahon, Bryan Robson (Cap), Christopher Roland Waddle, Gary Winston Lineker, Peter Andrew Beardsley.    Manager: Robert Robson


651. 15.11.1989
**ENGLAND v ITALY   0-0**
*Wembley, London*

Referee: Hubert Forstinger (Austria)    Attendance: 67,500

**ENGLAND**: Peter Leslie Shilton (46 David John Beasant), Gary Michael Stevens, Stuart Pearce (66 Nigel Winterburn), Stephen McMahon (66 Stephen Brian Hodge), Desmond Sinclair Walker, Terence Ian Butcher, Bryan Robson (Cap) (46 Michael Christopher Phelan), Christopher Roland Waddle, Peter Andrew Beardsley (78 David Andrew Platt), Gary Winston Lineker, John Charles Bryan Barnes.    Manager: Robert Robson

**ITALY**: Walter Zenga, Giuseppe Bergomi (Cap), Paolo Maldini, Franco Baresi, Riccardo Ferri, Nicola Berti, Roberto Donadoni, Fernando De Napoli, Gianluca Vialli (82 Roberto Baggio), Giuseppe Giannini, Andrea Alessandro Carnevale (76 Aldo Serena).    Trainer: Azeglio Vicini


652. 13.12.1989
**ENGLAND v YUGOSLAVIA   2-1**  (1-1)
*Wembley, London*

Referee: Dieter Pauly (West Germany)    Attendance: 34,796

**ENGLAND**: Peter Leslie Shilton (46 David John Beasant), Paul Andrew Parker, Desmond Sinclair Walker, Terence Ian Butcher, Stuart Pearce (46 Anthony Robert Dorigo), Michael Lauriston Thomas (67 David Andrew Platt), David Carlyle Rocastle (67 Stephen Brian Hodge), Bryan Robson (Cap) (75 Stephen McMahon), Christopher Roland Waddle, Stephen George Bull, Gary Winston Lineker.
Manager: Robert Robson

**YUGOSLAVIA** Tomislav Ivković, Vujadin Stanojković, Predrag Spasić (83 Gordan Petrić), Zoran Vulić, Faruk Hadžibegić, Dragoljub Brnović (78 Andrej Panadić), Haris Škoro, Safet Sušić (Cap) (78 Robert Prosinečki), Radmilo Mihajlović, Dragan Stojković, Toni Savevski.
Trainer: Ivan Osim

**Goals**: Bryan Robson (1, 69) / Haris Škoro (17)

653. 28.03.1990
**ENGLAND v BRAZIL  1-0**  (1-0)
*Wembley, London*
Referee:  Klaus Peschel (East Germany)    Attendance:  80,000
**ENGLAND**:  Peter Leslie Shilton (11 Christopher Charles Eric Woods), Gary Michael Stevens, Desmond Sinclair Walker, Terence Ian Butcher (Cap), Stuart Pearce, Christopher Roland Waddle, Stephen McMahon, David Andrew Platt, John Charles Bryan Barnes, Peter Andrew Beardsley (78 Paul John Gascoigne), Gary Winston Lineker.
Manager:  Robert Robson
**BRAZIL**:  Cláudio André Mergen Taffarel, Jorge de Amorim Campos "Jorginho", José Carlos Nepomuceno Mozer (79 ALDAIR Nascimento Santos), MAURO Geraldo GALVÃO, RICARDO GOMES Raymundo, Paulo SILAS do Prado Pereira (46 Ricardo Rogério de Brito "Alemão"), Carlos Caetano Bledorn Verri "Dunga", VALDO Cândido Filho (79 BISMARCK Barreto Faria), Cláudio Ibrahim Vaz Leal "Branco", José Roberto Gama de Oliveira "Bebeto" (64 Luís Antônio Corrêa da Costa "Müller"), Antônio de Oliveira Filho "Careca".
Trainer:  Sebastião Lazaroni

**Goal**:  Gary Winston Lineker (36)

654. 25.04.1990
**ENGLAND v CZECHOSLOVAKIA  4-2**  (2-1)
*Wembley, London*
Referee:  Michel Girard (France)    Attendance:  21,342
**ENGLAND**:  Peter Leslie Shilton (46 David Andrew Seaman), Lee Michael Dixon, Stuart Pearce (46 Anthony Robert Dorigo), Trevor McGregor Steven, Desmond Sinclair Walker (46 Mark Wright), Terence Ian Butcher, Bryan Robson (Cap) (75 Stephen McMahon), Paul John Gascoigne, Stephen George Bull, Gary Winston Lineker, Stephen Brian Hodge.
Manager:  Robert Robson
**CZECHOSLOVAKIA**:  Luděk Mikloško, Julius Bielik, František Straka (68 Miroslav Kadlec), Ivan Hašek (Cap), Ján Kocian, Vladimír Kinier, Michal Bílek, Luboš Kubík, Ivo Knoflíček (60 Stanislav Griga), Tomáš Skuhravý (71 Vladimír Weiss), Ľubomír Moravčík.    Trainer: Jozef Vengloš

**Goals**:  Stephen George Bull (17, 55), Stuart Pearce (23), Paul John Gascoigne (89) /
Tomáš Skuhravý (11), Luboš Kubík (81)

655. 15.05.1990
**ENGLAND v DENMARK  1-0**  (0-0)
*Wembley, London*
Referee:  James McCluskey (Scotland)    Attendance:  27,463
**ENGLAND**:  Peter Leslie Shilton (45 Christopher Charles Eric Woods), Gary Michael Stevens, Stuart Pearce (45 Anthony Robert Dorigo), Stephen McMahon (77 David Andrew Platt), Desmond Sinclair Walker, Terence Ian Butcher (Cap), Stephen Brian Hodge, Paul John Gascoigne, Christopher Roland Waddle (70 David Carlyle Rocastle), Gary Winston Lineker (70 Stephen George Bull), John Charles Bryan Barnes.
Manager:  Robert Robson
**DENMARK**:  Peter Schmeichel, John Sivebæk, Kent Nielsen, Lars Olsen (Cap), Henrik Andersen, Jan Bartram, John Jensen, Kim Vilfort, Flemming Povlsen (70 Morten Bruun), Michael Laudrup (70 Lars Jakobsen), Brian Laudrup.
Trainer:  Richard Møller Nielsen

**Goal**:  Gary Winston Lineker (56)

656. 22.05.1990
**ENGLAND v URUGUAY  1-2**  (0-1)
*Wembley, London*
Referee:  Pietro D'Elia (Italy)    Attendance:  38,751
**ENGLAND**:  Peter Leslie Shilton, Paul Andrew Parker, Stuart Pearce, Stephen Brian Hodge (77 Peter Andrew Beardsley), Desmond Sinclair Walker, Terence Ian Butcher, Bryan Robson (Cap), Paul John Gascoigne, Christopher Roland Waddle, Gary Winston Lineker (77 Stephen George Bull), John Charles Bryan Barnes.    Manager: Robert Robson
**URUGUAY**:  Eduardo Pereira Martínez, Nelson Daniel Gutiérrez, Hugo Eduardo De León, José Oscar Herrera, José Batlle Perdomo, Alfonso Enrique Domínguez, Antonio Alzamendi, Santiago Javier Ostolaza, Enzo Francéscoli (Cap), Rúben Sosa (80 Sergio Daniel Martínez), Rúben Walter Paz.
Trainer:  Oscar Washington Tabárez

**Goal**:  John Charles Bryan Barnes (52) /
Santiago Javier Ostolaza (27), José Batlle Perdomo (61)

657. 02.06.1990
**TUNISIA v ENGLAND  1-1**  (1-0)
*Olympic El Menzah, Tunis*
Referee:  Rachid Medjiba (Algeria)    Attendance:  25,000
**TUNISIA**:  Boubakar Zitouni, Mohammed Madjebi, Taoufik Herichi, Ali Ben Neji, Mohamed Ali Mahjoubi, Sami Khemeri (82 Farah Rashid), Adel Sellimi, Abdelhamid Hergal (46 Dermech), Tarak Dhiab, Lotfi Rouissi, Khaled Ben Yahia.

**ENGLAND**: Peter Leslie Shilton, Gary Michael Stevens, Stuart Pearce, Stephen Brian Hodge (61 Peter Andrew Beardsley), Desmond Sinclair Walker, Terence Ian Butcher (61 Mark Wright), Bryan Robson (Cap), Paul John Gascoigne, Christopher Roland Waddle (78 David Andrew Platt), Gary Winston Lineker (78 Stephen George Bull), John Charles Bryan Barnes.   Manager: Robert Robson

**Goals**: Abdelhamid Hergal (26) / Stephen George Bull (90)

658.   11.06.1990      14th World Cup, 1st Round
**ENGLAND v REPUBLIC OF IRELAND   1-1**  (1-0)
*Sant'Elia, Cagliari*

Referee: Aron Schmidhuber (West Germany)    Att: 35,238

**ENGLAND**: Peter Leslie Shilton, Gary Michael Stevens, Stuart Pearce, Desmond Sinclair Walker, Terence Ian Butcher, Christopher Roland Waddle, Bryan Robson (Cap), Paul John Gascoigne, John Charles Bryan Barnes, Peter Andrew Beardsley (70 Stephen McMahon), Gary Winston Lineker (83 Stephen George Bull).   Manager: Robert Robson

**IRELAND**: Patrick Bonner, Christopher Barry Morris, Michael Joseph McCarthy (Cap), Kevin Bernard Moran, Stephen Staunton, Raymond James Houghton, Paul McGrath, Andrew David Townsend, Kevin Mark Sheedy, Anthony Guy Cascarino, John William Aldridge (64 Alan Francis McLoughlin).   Manager: John Charlton

**Goal**: Gary Winston Lineker (8) / Kevin Mark Sheedy (72)

659.   16.06.1990      14th World Cup, 1st Round
**ENGLAND v HOLLAND   0-0**
*Sant'Elia, Cagliari*

Referee: Zoran Petrovic (Yugoslavia)    Attendance: 35,267

**HOLLAND**: Hans van Breukelen, Berry van Aerle, Frank Rijkaard, Ronald Koeman, Adri van Tiggelen, Johnny van't Schip (74 Wim Kieft), Ruud Gullit (Cap), Jan Wouters, Richard Witschge, Hans Gillhaus, Marco van Basten.
Trainer: Leo Beenhakker

**ENGLAND**: Peter Leslie Shilton, Paul Andrew Parker, Desmond Sinclair Walker, Stuart Pearce, Mark Wright, Terence Ian Butcher, Bryan Robson (Cap) (65 David Andrew Platt), Paul John Gascoigne, Christopher Roland Waddle (59 Stephen George Bull), John Charles Bryan Barnes, Gary Winston Lineker.   Manager: Robert Robson

660.   21.06.1990      14th World Cup, 1st Round
**ENGLAND v EGYPT   1-0**  (0-0)
*Sant'Elia, Cagliari*

Referee: Kurt Röthlisberger (Switzerland)    Att: 34,959

**ENGLAND**: Peter Leslie Shilton (Cap), Paul Andrew Parker, Desmond Sinclair Walker, Mark Wright, Stuart Pearce, Christopher Roland Waddle (86 David Andrew Platt), Stephen McMahon, Paul John Gascoigne, John Charles Bryan Barnes, Stephen George Bull (84 Peter Andrew Beardsley), Gary Winston Lineker.   Manager: Robert Robson

**EGYPT**: Ahmed Shobeir, Ibrahim Hassan, Rabei Yasseen, Hany Ramzy, Hesham Yakan, Ismael Youssef, Magdi Abed El Ghani, Hossom Hassan, Gamal Abel El Hamid (77 Tarek Soliman), Adel Ramzy, Abdou (77 Abdelrahman).

**Goal**: Mark Wright (64)

661.   26.06.1990      14th World Cup, 2nd Round
**ENGLAND v BELGIUM   1-0**  (0-0, 0-0)  (AET)
*Renato Dall'Ara, Bologna*

Referee: Peter Mikkelsen (Denmark)    Attendance: 34,520

**ENGLAND**: Peter Leslie Shilton, Paul Andrew Parker, Desmond Sinclair Walker, Mark Wright, Terence Ian Butcher (Cap), Stuart Pearce, Christopher Roland Waddle, Stephen McMahon (71 David Andrew Platt), Paul John Gascoigne, Gary Winston Lineker, John Charles Bryan Barnes (74 Stephen George Bull).   Manager: Robert Robson

**BELGIUM**: Michel Preud'homme, Eric Gerets, Georges Grün, Stéphane Demol, Michel De Wolf, Léo Albert Clijsters, Bruno Versavel (106 Patrick Vervoort), Frank Richard Vander Elst, Vincenzo Scifo, Jan Ceulemans (Cap), Marc Degryse (64 Nicolaas Pieter Claesen).   Trainer: Guy Thys

**Goal**: David Andrew Platt (119)

662.   01.07.1990      14th World Cup, Quarter-Finals
**ENGLAND v CAMEROON   3-2**  (1-0, 2-2)  (AET)
*San Paolo, Napoli*

Referee: Edgardo Codesal Mendez (Mexico)    Att: 55,205

**ENGLAND**: Peter Leslie Shilton, Paul Andrew Parker, Mark Wright, Desmond Sinclair Walker, Stuart Pearce, Terence Ian Butcher (Cap) (74 Trevor McGregor Steven), Christopher Roland Waddle, Paul John Gascoigne, David Andrew Platt, Gary Winston Lineker, John Charles Bryan Barnes (46 Peter Andrew Beardsley).   Manager: Robert Robson

**CAMEROON**: Benjamin Massing, Bertin Ebwelle, Emmanuel Kunde, Francois Omam, Louis-Paul Mfede (62 Eugene Ekeke), Jean-Claude Pagal, Stephen Tataw, Thomas Libiih, Thomas N'kono, Cyrille Makanaky, Kessack Mabdean (46 Roger Milla).

**Goals**: David Platt (25), Gary Lineker (83 pen, 105 pen) / Emmanuel Kunde (61), Eugene Ekeke (65)

663.  04.07.1990    14th World Cup,  Semi-Finals
**WEST GERMANY v ENGLAND  1-1**  (0-0, 1-1) (AET)
*Delle Alpi, Torino*
Referee:  Jose Roberto Ramiz Wright (Brazil)    Att: 62,628
**WEST GERMANY**:  Bodo Illgner, Klaus Augenthaler, Thomas Berthold, Jürgen Kohler, Guido Buchwald, Andreas Brehme, Thomas Häßler (67 Stefan Reuter), Lothar Herbert Matthäus (Cap), Olaf Thon, Jürgen Klinsmann, Rudolf Völler (38 Karlheinz Riedle).    Trainer:  Franz Beckenbauer
**ENGLAND**:  Peter Leslie Shilton, Paul Andrew Parker, Stuart Pearce, Desmond Sinclair Walker, Mark Wright, Terence Ian Butcher (Cap) (70 Trevor McGregor Steven), Christopher Roland Waddle, David Andrew Platt, Paul John Gascoigne, Peter Andrew Beardsley, Gary Winston Lineker.    Manager:  Robert Robson
**Goal**:  Andreas Brehme (60) / Gary Winston Lineker (80)
**Penalties**:  0-1 Gary Lineker, 1-1 Andreas Brehme, 1-2 Peter Beardsley, 2-2 Lothar Matthäus, 2-3 David Platt, 3-3 Karlheinz Riedle, 3-3 Stuart Pearce (saved), 4-3 Olaf Thon, 4-3 Chris Waddle (missed)

664.  07.07.1990    14th World Cup,
Bronze Medal Play-off
**ITALY v ENGLAND  2-1**  (0-0)
*Comunale, Bari*
Referee:  Joël Quiniou (France)    Attendance: 51,426
**ITALY**:  Walter Zenga, Giuseppe Bergomi (Cap), Paolo Maldini, Franco Baresi, Pietro Vierchowod, Ciro Ferrara, Luigi De Agostini (64 Nicola Berti), Carlo Ancelotti, Salvatore Schillaci, Giuseppe Giannini (89 Riccardo Ferri), Roberto Baggio.    Trainer:  Azeglio Vicini
**ENGLAND**:  Peter Leslie Shilton (Cap), Gary Michael Stevens, Paul Andrew Parker, Desmond Sinclair Walker, Mark Wright (72 Christopher Roland Waddle), Anthony Robert Dorigo, Trevor McGregor Steven, David Andrew Platt, Stephen McMahon (72 Neil John Webb), Peter Andrew Beardsley, Gary Winston Lineker.    Manager:  Robert Robson
**Goal**:  Roberto Baggio (72), Salvatore Schillaci (86 pen) / David Andrew Platt (82)

665.  12.09.1990
**ENGLAND v HUNGARY  1-0**  (1-0)
*Wembley, London*
Referee:  Erik Fredriksson (Sweden)    Attendance: 51,459
**ENGLAND**:  Christopher Charles Eric Woods, Lee Michael Dixon, Stuart Pearce (46 Anthony Robert Dorigo), Paul Andrew Parker, Desmond Sinclair Walker, Mark Wright, David Andrew Platt, Paul John Gascoigne, Stephen George Bull (73 Christopher Roland Waddle), Gary Winston Lineker (Cap), John Charles Bryan Barnes.    Manager:  Graham Taylor

**HUNGARY**:  Zsolt Petry, László Disztl, Imre Garaba (73 Zoltán Aczél), Zsolt Limperger, Tamás Mónos (69 Tibor Simon), István Kozma, Zsolt Bücs (81 Tibor Balog II), Balázs Bérczy, József Keller, József Gregor, Kálmán Kovács.    Trainer:  Kálmán Mészöly
**Goal**:  Gary Winston Lineker (44)

666.  17.10.1990    9th European Champs Qualifiers
**ENGLAND v POLAND  2-0**  (1-0)
*Wembley, London*
Referee:  Tulio Lanese (Italy)    Attendance: 77,040
**ENGLAND**:  Christopher Charles Eric Woods, Lee Michael Dixon, Stuart Pearce, Paul Andrew Parker, Desmond Sinclair Walker, Mark Wright, David Andrew Platt, Paul John Gascoigne, Stephen George Bull (58 Peter Andrew Beardsley), Gary Winston Lineker (Cap) (58 Christopher Roland Waddle), John Charles Bryan Barnes.    Manager:  Graham Taylor
**POLAND**:  Józef Wandzik, Piotr Czachowski, Zbigniew Kaczmarek (Cap), Dariusz Wdowczyk, Robert Warzycha, Ryszard Tarasiewicz, Janusz Nawrocki, Roman Szewczyk, Jacek Ziober, Roman Kosecki (86 Dariusz Kubicki), Jan Furtok (76 Krzysztof Warzycha).    Trainer:  Andrzej Strejlau
**Goals**:  Gary Lineker (39 pen), Peter Andrew Beardsley (90)

667.  14.11.1990    9th European Champs Qualifiers
**REPUBLIC OF IRELAND v ENGLAND  1-1**  (0-1)
*Lansdowne Road, Dublin*
Referee:  Pietro D'Elia (Italy)    Attendance: 46,000
**IRELAND**:  Patrick Bonner, Christopher Barry Morris, Michael Joseph McCarthy (Cap), David Anthony O'Leary, Stephen Staunton, Ronald Andrew Whelan (74 Alan Francis McLoughlin), Paul McGrath, Raymond James Houghton, Niall John Quinn (61 Anthony Guy Cascarino), John William Aldridge, Andrew David Townsend.    Manager:  John Charlton
**ENGLAND**:  Christopher Charles Eric Woods, Lee Michael Dixon, Stuart Pearce, Anthony Alexander Adams, Desmond Sinclair Walker, Mark Wright, David Andrew Platt, Gordon Sidney Cowans, Peter Andrew Beardsley, Gary Winston Lineker (Cap), Stephen McMahon.    Manager:  Graham Taylor
**Goals**:  Anthony Cascarino (80) / David Andrew Platt (67)

**668. 06.02.1991**
**ENGLAND v CAMEROON 2-0** (1-0)
*Wembley, London*

Referee: John Blankenstein (Holland)   Attendance: 61,075

**ENGLAND**: David Andrew Seaman, Lee Michael Dixon, Stuart Pearce, Trevor McGregor Steven, Desmond Sinclair Walker, Mark Wright, Bryan Robson (Cap) (71 Gary Andrew Pallister), Paul John Gascoigne (66 Stephen Brian Hodge), Ian Edward Wright, Gary Winston Lineker, John Charles Bryan Barnes.   Manager: Graham Taylor

**CAMEROON**: Joseph-Antoine Bell, Ebwelle, Jules Onana, Emmanuel Kunde, Stephen Tataw, Louis-Paul M'Fede, Emile Mbouh-Mbouh, Jean-Claude Pagal, André Kana-Biyik (42 Thomas Libiih), Francois Omam-Biyik, Eugene Ekeke (78 Guy Tapoko).

**Goals**: Gary Winston Lineker (20 pen, 61)


**669. 27.03.1991    9th European Champs Qualifiers**
**ENGLAND v REPUBLIC OF IRELAND 1-1** (1-1)
*Wembley, London*

Referee: Kurt Röthlisberger (Switzerland)   Att: 77,753

**ENGLAND**: David Andrew Seaman, Lee Michael Dixon, Stuart Pearce, Anthony Alexander Adams (46 Lee Stuart Sharpe), Desmond Sinclair Walker, Mark Wright, Bryan Robson (Cap), David Andrew Platt, Peter Andrew Beardsley, Gary Winston Lineker (76 Ian Edward Wright), John Charles Bryan Barnes.   Manager: Graham Taylor

**IRELAND**: Patrick Bonner, Joseph Dennis Irwin, Kevin Bernard Moran (Cap), David Anthony O'Leary, Stephen Staunton, Andrew David Townsend, Paul McGrath, Raymond James Houghton, Niall John Quinn, John William Aldridge (71 Anthony Guy Cascarino), Kevin Mark Sheedy.
Manager: John Charlton

**Goal**: Lee Michael Dixon (9) / Niall John Quinn (27)


**670. 01.05.1991    9th European Champs Qualifiers**
**TURKEY v ENGLAND 0-1** (0-1)
*Atatürk, Izmir*

Referee: Wolf-Günter Wiesel (Germany)   Att: 25,000

**TURKEY**: Hayrettin Demirbaş, Riza Çalımbay, Recep Çetin, Ogün Temizkanoğlu, Gökhan Keskin, Ünal Karaman, Rıdvan Dilmen, Muhammet Altıntaş, Mehmet Özdilek, Tanju Çolak, Ali Gültiken (75 Feyyaz Uçar).   Trainer: Josef Piontek

**ENGLAND**: David Andrew Seaman, Lee Michael Dixon, Stuart Pearce, Dennis Frank Wise, Desmond Sinclair Walker, Gary Andrew Pallister, David Andrew Platt, Geoffrey Robert Thomas (46 Stephen Brian Hodge), Alan Martin Smith, Gary Winston Lineker (Cap), John Charles Bryan Barnes.
Manager: Graham Taylor

**Goal**: Dennis Frank Wise (32)


**671. 21.05.1991    Challenge Cup**
**ENGLAND v U.S.S.R. 3-1** (2-1)
*Wembley, London*

Referee: Emilio Soriano Aladren (Spain)   Att: 23,789

**ENGLAND**: Christopher Charles Eric Woods, Gary Michael Stevens, Anthony Robert Dorigo, Dennis Frank Wise (70 David Batty), Paul Andrew Parker, Mark Wright (Cap), David Andrew Platt, Geoffrey Robert Thomas, Alan Martin Smith, Ian Edward Wright (70 Peter Andrew Beardsley), John Charles Bryan Barnes.   Manager: Graham Taylor

**U.S.S.R.**: Aleksandr Uvarov, Andrey Chernyshev, Vasiliy Kulkov, Akhrik Tzveyba, Dmitry Galiamin, Igor Shalimov (67 Igor Korneev), Aleksey Mikhaylichenko, Andrey Kanchelskis, Vladimir Tatarchuk (50 Aleksandr Mostovoi), Dmitriy Kuznetzov, Igor Kolyvanov.   Trainer: Anatoliy Byshovetz

**Goals**: Alan Martin Smith (16), David Platt (43 pen, 89) / Vladimir Tatarchuk (9)


**672. 25.05.1991    Challenge Cup**
**ENGLAND v ARGENTINA 2-2** (1-0)
*Wembley, London*

Referee: Zoran Petrovic (Yugoslavia)   Attendance: 44,497

**ENGLAND**: David Andrew Seaman, Lee Michael Dixon, Stuart Pearce, David Batty, Desmond Sinclair Walker, Mark Wright, David Andrew Platt, Geoffrey Robert Thomas, Alan Martin Smith, Gary Winston Lineker (Cap), John Charles Bryan Barnes (63 Nigel Howard Clough).
Manager: Graham Taylor

**ARGENTINA**: Sergio Javier Goycochea, Sergio Fabián Vázquez, Fernando Andrés Gamboa, Oscar Alfredo Ruggeri, Carlos Alberto Enrique, Fabián Armando Basualdo, Claudio Omar García, Darío Javier Franco, Diego Pablo Simeone, Germán Ricardo Martellotto (59 Antonio Ricardo Mohamed), Ariel Eduardo Boldrini.   Trainer: Alfio Oscar Basile

**Goals**: Gary Winston Lineker (15), David Andrew Platt (50) / Claudio Omar García (65), Darío Javier Franco (70)


**673. 01.06.1991**
**AUSTRALIA v ENGLAND 0-1** (0-1)
*Sydney Football Ground, Sydney*

Referee: Barry Tasker (New Zealand)   Attendance: 35,472

**AUSTRALIA**: Robert Zabica, Ian Gray, Mehmet Durakovic, Ned Zelic, Alex Tobin, Tony Vidmar, Paul Wade, Mike Petersen, Aurelio Vidmar, Graham Arnold, Ernie Tapai (72 Greg Brown).

**ENGLAND**: Christopher Charles Eric Woods, Paul Andrew Parker, Mark Wright, Desmond Sinclair Walker, Stuart Pearce, David Andrew Platt, Geoffrey Robert Thomas, David Batty, Nigel Howard Clough, Gary Winston Lineker (Cap) (81 Dennis Frank Wise), David Eric Hirst (46 John Akin Salako).
Manager: Graham Taylor

**Goal**: Ian Gray (40 og)

674. 03.06.1991
**NEW ZEALAND v ENGLAND 0-1** (0-0)
*Mount Smart, Auckland*
Referee: Dennis Voutsinas (Australia)   Attendance: 17,520
**NEW ZEALAND**: Clint Gosling, Anthony Ferris, Rodger Gray, Malcolm Dunford, Ceri Evans, Michael Ridenton, Michael McGarry, Robert Ironside, Danny Halligan, Declan Edge, Fred de jong.
**ENGLAND**: Christopher Charles Eric Woods, Paul Andrew Parker, Stuart Pearce, David Batty (46 Brian Christopher Deane), Desmond Sinclair Walker, Earl Delisser Barrett, David Andrew Platt, Geoffrey Robert Thomas, Dennis Frank Wise, Gary Winston Lineker (Cap), Mark Everton Walters (70 John Akin Salako).   Manager: Graham Taylor
**Goal**: Gary Winston Lineker (90)

675. 08.06.1991
**NEW ZEALAND v ENGLAND 0-2** (0-1)
*Athletic Park, Wellington*
Referee: Richard Lorenc (Australia)   Attendance: 12,000
**NEW ZEALAND**: Grant Schofield, Anthony Ferris, Rodger Gray, Malcolm Dunford, Ceri Evans, Michael Ridenton, Michael McGarry, Robert Ironside, Danny Halligan, Declan Edge (62 Thomas Edge), Fred de Jong.
**ENGLAND**: Christopher Charles Eric Woods, Gary Andrew Charles, Stuart Pearce (Cap), Mark Wright, Desmond Sinclair Walker, David Andrew Platt, Geoffrey Robert Thomas, Dennis Frank Wise, Ian Edward Wright, Brian Christopher Deane (46 David Eric Hirst), John Akin Salako.
Manager: Graham Taylor
**Goals**: Stuart Pearce (12), David Eric Hirst (50)

676. 12.06.1991
**MALAYSIA v ENGLAND 2-4** (0-3)
*Merdeka, Kuala Lumpur*
Referee: R. Letchumanasamy (Malayisia)   Att: 45,000
**MALAYSIA**: Hassan, Sergebeth Singh, Lee Kin Hong, Mohammed Zaid Jamil (46 Abu Haniffa Azizol), Arumugam Jayakanthan, Chow Siew Yai, Ali Ahmad Yusof, Mohammed Nazri Nasir, Matian Marjan, Zainal Ab Hassan (66 Khairul Azman Mohammed), Dollah Salleh.
**ENGLAND**: Christopher Charles Eric Woods, Gary Andrew Charles, Stuart Pearce, David Batty, Desmond Sinclair Walker, Mark Wright, David Andrew Platt, Geoffrey Robert Thomas, Nigel Howard Clough, Gary Winston Lineker (Cap), John Akin Salako.   Manager: Graham Taylor
**Goals**: Gary Winston Lineker (1, 24, 31, 70)

677. 11.09.1991
**ENGLAND v GERMANY 0-1** (0-1)
*Wembley, London*
Referee: Aleksei Spirin (USSR)   Attendance: 59,493
**ENGLAND**: Christopher Charles Eric Woods, Lee Michael Dixon, Anthony Robert Dorigo, David Batty, Gary Andrew Pallister, Paul Andrew Parker, David Andrew Platt, Trevor McGregor Steven (66 Paul Andrew Stewart), Alan Martin Smith, Gary Winston Lineker (Cap), John Akin Salako (66 Paul Charles Merson).   Manager: Graham Taylor
**GERMANY**: Bodo Illgner, Manfred Binz, Stefan Effenberg, Jürgen Kohler, Guido Buchwald, Thomas Häßler, Lothar Herbert Matthäus (Cap), Andreas Möller, Andreas Brehme, Karlheinz Riedle, Thomas Doll (81 Jürgen Klinsmann).
Trainer: Hans-Hubert Vogts
**Goal**: Karlheinz Riedle (45)

678. 16.10.1991   9th European Champs Qualifiers
**ENGLAND v TURKEY 1-0** (1-0)
*Wembley, London*
Referee: António Martín Navarette (Spain)   Att: 50,896
**ENGLAND**: Christopher Charles Eric Woods, Lee Michael Dixon, Stuart Pearce, David Batty, Desmond Sinclair Walker, Gary Vincent Mabbutt, Bryan Robson, David Andrew Platt, Alan Martin Smith, Gary Winston Lineker (Cap), Christopher Roland Waddle.   Manager: Graham Taylor
**TURKEY**: Hayrettin Demirbaş, Recep Çetin, Ogün Temizkanoğlu, Gökhan Keskin, Tugay Kerimoğlu, Turhan Sofuoğlu, Feyyaz Uçar (76 Hami Mandıralı), Riza Çalımbay, Ünal Karaman, Oğuz Çetin, Orhan Çıkırıkçı.
Trainer: Josef Piontek
**Goal**: Alan Martin Smith (21)

679. 13.11.1991   9th European Champs Qualifiers
**POLAND v ENGLAND 1-1** (1-0)
*Lech, Poznań*
Referee: Hubert Forstinger (Austria)   Attendance: 22,000
**POLAND**: Jarosław Bako, Piotr Soczyński, Tomasz Wałdoch, Roman Szewczyk (77 Adam Fedoruk), Robert Warzycha, Piotr Czachowski, Dariusz Skrzypczak (79 Wojciech Kowalczyk), Jacek Ziober, Roman Kosecki, Jan Furtok, Jan Urban (Cap).
Trainer: Andrzej Strejlau
**ENGLAND**: Christopher Charles Eric Woods, Lee Michael Dixon, Stuart Pearce, Andrew Arthur Gray (46 Alan Martin Smith), Desmond Sinclair Walker, Gary Vincent Mabbutt, David Andrew Platt, Geoffrey Robert Thomas, David Carlyle Rocastle, Gary Winston Lineker (Cap), Andrew Sinton (70 Anthony Mark Daley).   Manager: Graham Taylor
**Goal**: Roman Szewczyk (32) / Gary Winston Lineker (76)

680. 19.02.1992

**ENGLAND v FRANCE 2-0** (1-0)

*Wembley, London*

Referee: Aron Schmidhuber (Germany)   Att: 58,723

**ENGLAND:** Christopher Charles Eric Woods, Robert Marc Jones, Stuart Pearce (Cap), Martin Raymond Keown, Desmond Sinclair Walker, Mark Wright, Neil John Webb, Geoffrey Robert Thomas, Nigel Howard Clough, Alan Shearer, David Eric Hirst (46 Gary Winston Lineker). Manager: Graham Taylor

**FRANCE:** Gilles Rousset, Manuel Amoros (Cap), Jocelyn Angloma, Basile Boli, Laurent Blanc, Bernard Casoni, Didier Deschamps, Luis Fernandez (71 Jean-Philippe Durand), Jean-Pierre Papin, Christian Perez (71 Amara Simba), Eric Cantona. Trainer: Michel Platini

**Goals:** Alan Shearer (44), Gary Winston Lineker (73)


681. 25.03.1992

**CZECHOSLOVAKIA v ENGLAND 2-2** (1-1)

*Strahov, Praha*

Referee: Gerhard Kapl (Austria)   Attendance: 3,300

**CZECHOSLOVAKIA:** Luděk Mikloško, Jozef Chovanec, Miloš Glonek, Miroslav Kadlec, Václav Němeček (Cap) (82 Jiří Němec), Karel Kula (86 Martin Frýdek), Pavel Hapal, Luboš Kubík, Michal Bílek, Tomáš Skuhravý, Ivo Knoflíček (89 Horst Siegl). Trainer: Milan Máčala

**ENGLAND:** David Andrew Seaman, Martin Raymond Keown, Stuart Pearce (Cap), David Carlyle Rocastle (46 Lee Michael Dixon), Desmond Sinclair Walker, Gary Vincent Mabbutt (72 Gary Winston Lineker), David Andrew Platt, Paul Charles Merson, Nigel Howard Clough (46 Paul Andrew Stewart), Mark Wayne Hateley, John Charles Bryan Barnes (51 Anthony Robert Dorigo). Manager: Graham Taylor

**Goals:** Tomáš Skuhravý (21), Jozef Chovanec (56) / Paul Charles Merson (27), Martin Raymond Keown (66)


682. 29.04.1992

**C.I.S. v ENGLAND 2-2** (1-1)

*Lenin, Moskva*

Referee: Piotr Werner (Poland)   Attendance: 25,000

**C.I.S.:** Dmitriy Kharin, Andrey Chernyshev, Kakhaber Tskhadadze, Akhrik Tzveyba, Igor Ledyakhov (46 Sergey Kiryakov), Igor Shalimov, Aleksey Mikhaylichenko, Andrey Kanchelskis (63 Valeriy Karpin), Igor Kolyvanov (46 Vladimir Lyuty), Aleksandr Mostovoi, Sergey Yuran (55 Viktor Onopko). Trainer: Anatoliy Byshovets

**ENGLAND:** Christopher Charles Eric Woods (80 Anthony Nigel Martyn), Gary Michael Stevens, Andrew Sinton (63 Keith Curle), Carlton Lloyd Palmer, Desmond Sinclair Walker, Martin Raymond Keown, David Andrew Platt, Trevor McGregor Steven (76 Paul Andrew Stewart), Alan Shearer (63 Nigel Howard Clough), Gary Winston Lineker (Cap), Anthony Mark Daley. Manager: Graham Taylor

**Goals:** Kakhaber Tskhadadze (44), Sergey Kiryakov (54) / Gary Winston Lineker (15), Trevor McGregor Steven (71)


683. 12.05.1992

**HUNGARY v ENGLAND 0-1** (0-0)

*Népstadion, Budapest*

Referee: Heinz Holzmann (Austria)   Attendance: 25,000

**HUNGARY:** István Brockhauser, András Telek, Emil Lőrincz, Zsolt Limperger, Tibor Simon, Ervin Kovács, István Pisont, Péter Lipcsei (64 Gábor Márton), József Szalma (42 Zoltán Kecskés), József Kiprich, István Vincze. Trainer: Imre Jenei

**ENGLAND:** Anthony Nigel Martyn (46 David Andrew Seaman), Gary Michael Stevens, Anthony Robert Dorigo, Keith Curle (46 Andrew Sinton), Desmond Sinclair Walker, Martin Raymond Keown, Neil John Webb (68 David Batty), Carlton Lloyd Palmer, Paul Charles Merson (46 Alan Martin Smith), Gary Winston Lineker (Cap) (70 Ian Edward Wright), Anthony Mark Daley. Manager: Graham Taylor

**Goal:** Neil John Webb (57)


684. 17.05.1992

**ENGLAND v BRAZIL 1-1** (0-1)

*Wembley, London*

Referee: James McCluskey (Scotland)   Attendance: 53,428

**ENGLAND:** Christopher Charles Eric Woods, Gary Michael Stevens, Anthony Robert Dorigo (72 Stuart Pearce), Carlton Lloyd Palmer, Desmond Sinclair Walker, Martin Raymond Keown, Anthony Mark Daley (72 Paul Charles Merson), Trevor McGregor Steven (46 Neil John Webb), David Andrew Platt, Gary Winston Lineker (Cap), Andrew Sinton (46 David Carlyle Rocastle). Manager: Graham Taylor

**BRAZIL:** CARLOS Roberto Gallo, LUÍS CARLOS Coelho WINCK (46 CHARLES Natali de Mendonça Ayres "Guerreiro"), José Carlos Nepomuceno Mozer, RICARDO GOMES Raymundo, Cláudio Ibrahim Vaz Leal "Branco", Mauro da Silva, LUÍS HENRIQUE Pereira dos Santos (74 VALDEIR Celso Moreira), RAÍ Souza Vieira de Oliveira, Renato Portaluppi "Renato Gaúcho" (78 Leovegildo Lins Gama Júnior), José Roberto Gama de Oliveira "Bebeto", VALDO Cândido Filho (72 PAULO SÉRGIO Silvestre do Nascimento). Trainer: Carlos Alberto Gomes Parreira

**Goal:** David Andrew Platt (49) / José Roberto Gama de Oliveira "Bebeto" (20)

685. 03.06.1992
**FINLAND v ENGLAND  1-2**  (1-1)

*Olympia, Helsinki*

Referee: Bo Karlsson (Sweden)    Attendance: 16,101

**FINLAND**: Olavi Huttunen, Jari Rinne (81 Jari Vanhala), Petri Järvinen, Erkka Petäjä, Erik Holmgren (46 Ari Heikkinen), Jari Kinnunen, Jari Litmanen (89 Jouko Vuorela), Marko Myyry, Ari Hjelm, Kimmo Tarkkio (70 Ari Tegelberg), Jyrki Huhtamäki.    Trainer: Jukka Vakkila

**ENGLAND**: Christopher Charles Eric Woods, Gary Michael Stevens (46 Carlton Lloyd Palmer), Stuart Pearce, Martin Raymond Keown, Desmond Sinclair Walker, Mark Wright, David Andrew Platt, Trevor McGregor Steven (82 Anthony Mark Daley), Neil John Webb, Gary Winston Lineker (Cap), John Charles Bryan Barnes (12 Paul Charles Merson).    Manager: Graham Taylor

**Goals**: Ari Hjelm (26) / David Andrew Platt (45, 62)


686. 11.06.1992    9th European Champs, 1st Round
**DENMARK v ENGLAND  0-0**

*Malmö Stadion*

Referee: John Blankenstein (Holland)    Attendance: 26,385

**DENMARK**: Peter Schmeichel, John Sivebæk, Kent Nielsen, Lars Olsen (Cap), Henrik Andersen, Kim Christofte, John Jensen, Kim Vilfort, Brian Laudrup, Flemming Povlsen, Bent Christensen.    Trainer: Richard Møller Nielsen

**ENGLAND**: Christopher Charles Eric Woods, Keith Curle (62 Anthony Mark Daley), Martin Raymond Keown, Desmond Sinclair Walker, Stuart Pearce, Trevor McGregor Steven, Carlton Lloyd Palmer, David Andrew Platt, Paul Charles Merson (71 Neil John Webb), Alan Martin Smith, Gary Winston Lineker (Cap).    Manager: Graham Taylor


687. 14.06.1992    9th European Champs, 1st Round
**FRANCE v ENGLAND  0-0**

*Malmö Stadion*

Referee: Sándor Puhl (Hungary)    Attendance: 26,535

**FRANCE**: Bruno Martini, Manuel Amoros (Cap), Laurent Blanc, Basile Boli, Bernard Casoni, Didier Deschamps, Frank Sauzée (46 Jocelyn Angloma), Luis Fernandez (74 Christian Perez), Jean-Philippe Durand, Eric Cantona, Jean-Pierre Papin.    Trainer: Michel Platini

**ENGLAND**: Christopher Charles Eric Woods, Stuart Pearce, Martin Raymond Keown, Desmond Sinclair Walker, David Andrew Platt, Trevor McGregor Steven, Carlton Lloyd Palmer, David Batty, Gary Winston Lineker (Cap), Andrew Sinton, Alan Shearer.    Manager: Graham Taylor


688. 17.06.1992    9th European Champs, 1st Round
**SWEDEN v ENGLAND  2-1**  (0-1)

*Råsunda, Solna*

Referee: José Rosa dos Santos (Portugal)    Att: 30,126

**SWEDEN**: Thomas Ravelli, Roland Nilsson, Jan Eriksson, Patrik Jonas Andersson, Joachim Björklund, Klas Ingesson, Stefan Schwarz, Jonas Thern (Cap), Anders Erik Limpár (46 Johnny Ekström), Tomas Brolin, Martin Dahlin.    Trainer: Tommy Svensson

**ENGLAND**: Christopher Charles Eric Woods, David Batty, Martin Raymond Keown, Desmond Sinclair Walker, Stuart Pearce, Anthony Mark Daley, Neil John Webb, Carlton Lloyd Palmer, Andrew Sinton (76 Paul Charles Merson), Gary Winston Lineker (Cap) (62 Alan Martin Smith), David Andrew Platt.    Manager: Graham Taylor

**Goals**: Jan Eriksson (52), Tomas Brolin (82) / David Platt (4)


689. 09.09.1992
**SPAIN v ENGLAND  1-0**  (1-0)

*El Sardinero, Santander*

Referee: José Alberto Veiga Trigo (Portugal)    Att: 22,000

**SPAIN**: Andoni Zubizarreta (Cap), Albert Ferrer, Roberto Solozábal, López, António Muñoz "Toni" (60 CRISTÓBAL Parralo Aguilera), José Miguel González "Míchel" (65 Jon Andoni Goikoetxea), Guillermo Amor, Juan Vizcaíno, Rafael Martín Vázquez (85 ALVARO Cervera Díaz), José María Bakero (71 ALFONSO Pérez), Gregorio Fonseca (50 FERNANDO Gómez).    Trainer: Javier Clemente Lazaro

**ENGLAND**: Christopher Charles Eric Woods, Lee Michael Dixon (46 David John Bardsley, 62 Carlton Lloyd Palmer), Stuart Pearce (Cap), Paul Emerson Ince, Desmond Sinclair Walker, Mark Wright, David White (78 Brian Christopher Deane), David Andrew Platt, Nigel Howard Clough, Alan Shearer, Andrew Sinton (78 Paul Charles Merson).    Manager: Graham Taylor

**Goal**: Fonseca (11)


690. 14.10.1992    15th World Cup Qualifiers
**ENGLAND v NORWAY  1-1**  (0-0)

*Wembley, London*

Referee: Arturo Brizio Carter (Mexico)    Attendance: 51,441

**ENGLAND**: Christopher Charles Eric Woods, Lee Michael Dixon (89 Carlton Lloyd Palmer), Stuart Pearce (Cap), David Batty, Desmond Sinclair Walker, Anthony Alexander Adams, David Andrew Platt, Paul John Gascoigne, Alan Shearer, Ian Edward Wright (69 Paul Charles Merson), Paul Emerson Ince.    Manager: Graham Taylor

**NORWAY**: Erik Thorstvedt, Tore Pedersen (24 Henning Berg), Rune Bratseth, Roger Nilsen, Stig Inge Bjørnebye, Kåre Ingebrigtsen, Gunnar Halle, Kjetil Rekdal, Erik Mykland (72 Jostein Flo), Jahn Ivar Jakobsen, Gøran Sørloth.    Trainer: Egil Olsen

**Goal**: David Andrew Platt (55) / Kjetil Rekdal (76)

691.  18.11.1992    15th World Cup Qualifiers
**ENGLAND v TURKEY  4-0**  (2-0)
*Wembley, London*

Referee:  Bo Karlsson (Sweden)    Attendance:  42,984

**ENGLAND**:  Christopher Charles Eric Woods, Lee Michael Dixon, Stuart Pearce (Cap), Carlton Lloyd Palmer, Desmond Sinclair Walker, Anthony Alexander Adams, David Andrew Platt, Paul John Gascoigne, Alan Shearer, Ian Edward Wright, Paul Emerson Ince.    Manager:  Graham Taylor

**TURKEY**:  Hayrettin Demirbaş, Recep Çetin, Bülent Korkmaz, Gökhan Keskin, Ogün Temizkanoğlu, Ünal Karaman, Mehmet Özdilek (46 Uğur Tütüneker), Oğuz Çetin, Orhan Çıkırıkçı, Hamı Mandıralı (69 Riza Çalımbay), Hakan Şükür.    Trainer:  Josef Piontek

**Goals**:  Paul John Gascoigne (16, 62), Alan Shearer (29), Stuart Pearce (60)


692.  17.02.1993    15th World Cup Qualifiers
**ENGLAND v SAN MARINO  6-0**  (2-0)
*Wembley, London*

Referee:  Roger Philippi (Luxembourg)    Attendance:  51,154

**ENGLAND**:  Christopher Charles Eric Woods, Lee Michael Dixon, Anthony Robert Dorigo, Carlton Lloyd Palmer, Desmond Sinclair Walker, Anthony Alexander Adams, David Andrew Platt (Cap), Paul John Gascoigne, Leslie Ferdinand, John Charles Bryan Barnes, David Batty.    Manager:  Graham Taylor

**SAN MARINO**:  Pier Luigi Benedettini, Bruno Muccioli, Mirco Gennari, Loris Zanotti, Claudio Canti, William Guerra, Pierangelo Manzaroli, Marco Mazza, Nicola Bacciocchi (64 Paolo Mazza), Massimo Bonini, Fabio Francini (81 Ivan Matteoni).    Trainer:  Giorgio Leoni

**Goals**:  David Platt (13, 24, 67, 83), Carlton Lloyd Palmer (78), Leslie Ferdinand (86)


693.  31.03.1993    15th World Cup Qualifiers
**TURKEY v ENGLAND  0-2**  (0-2)
*Atatürk, Izmir*

Referee:  Fabio Baldas (Italy)    Attendance:  60,000

**TURKEY**:  Engin Ipekoğlu (43 Hayrettin Demirbaş), Recep Çetin (69 Hamı Mandıralı), Bülent Korkmaz, Ogün Temizkanoğlu, Ali Günçar, Ünal Karaman, Mehmet Özdilek, Orhan Çıkırıkçı, Oğuz Çetin, Tugay Kerimoğlu, Feyyaz Uçar.    Trainer:  Josef Piontek

**ENGLAND**:  Christopher Charles Eric Woods, Lee Michael Dixon (46 Nigel Howard Clough), Andrew Sinton, Carlton Lloyd Palmer, Desmond Sinclair Walker, Anthony Alexander Adams, David Andrew Platt (Cap), Paul John Gascoigne, John Charles Bryan Barnes, Ian Edward Wright (85 Lee Stuart Sharpe), Paul Emerson Ince.    Manager:  Graham Taylor

**Goals**:  David Andrew Platt (7), Paul John Gascoigne (45)


694.  28.04.1993    15th World Cup Qualifiers
**ENGLAND v HOLLAND  2-2**  (2-1)
*Wembley, London*

Referee:  Peter Mikkelsen (Denmark)    Attendance:  73,163

**ENGLAND**:  Christopher Charles Eric Woods, Lee Michael Dixon, Desmond Sinclair Walker, Anthony Alexander Adams, Martin Raymond Keown, Carlton Lloyd Palmer, Paul Emerson Ince, Paul John Gascoigne (46 Paul Charles Merson), John Charles Bryan Barnes, Leslie Ferdinand, David Andrew Platt (Cap).    Manager:  Graham Taylor

**HOLLAND**:  Ed de Goey, Danny Blind, Frank de Boer, Frank Rijkaard, Jan Wouters (Cap), Aron Winter, Rob Witschge, Ruud Gullit (71 Peter van Vossen), Marc Overmars, Dennis Bergkamp, Johnny Bosman (46 John de Wolf).    Trainer:  Dick Advocaat

**Goals**:  John Charles Bryan Barnes (1), David Platt (24) / Dennis Bergkamp (35), Peter van Vossen (87 pen)


695.  29.05.1993    15th World Cup Qualifiers
**POLAND v ENGLAND  1-1**  (1-0)
*Slaski, Chorzów*

Referee:  Serge Muhmenthaler (Switzerland)    Att:  65,000

**POLAND**:  Jarosław Bako, Piotr Czachowski, Roman Szewczyk (Cap), Andrzej Lesiak, Dariusz Adamczuk, Roman Kosecki, Jerzy Brzęczek (84 Marcin Jałocha), Piotr Świerczewski, Marek Koźmiński, Marek Leśniak (73 Kazimierz Węgrzyn), Jan Furtok.    Trainer:  Andrzej Strejlau

**ENGLAND**:  Christopher Charles Eric Woods, Desmond Sinclair Walker, David John Bardsley, Anthony Alexander Adams, Anthony Robert Dorigo, Paul Emerson Ince, Carlton Lloyd Palmer (70 Ian Edward Wright), Paul John Gascoigne (79 Nigel Howard Clough), John Charles Bryan Barnes, David Andrew Platt (Cap), Edward Paul Sheringham.    Manager:  Graham Taylor

**Goals**:  Dariusz Adamczuk (35) / Ian Edward Wright (84)


696.  02.06.1993    15th World Cup Qualifiers
**NORWAY v ENGLAND  2-0**  (1-0)
*Ullevaal, Oslo*

Referee:  Sándor Puhl (Hungary)    Attendance:  22,250

**NORWAY**:  Erik Thorstvedt, Tore Pedersen, Rune Bratseth (82 Roger Nilsen), Stig Inge Bjørnebye, Gunnar Halle, Øyvind Leonhardsen, Kjetil Rekdal, Erik Mykland, Lars Bohinen, Jan Åge Fjørtoft (57 Göran Sørloth), Jostein Flo.    Trainer:  Egil Olsen

**ENGLAND**:  Christopher Charles Eric Woods, Lee Michael Dixon, Desmond Sinclair Walker (63 Nigel Howard Clough), Anthony Alexander Adams, Gary Andrew Pallister, Carlton Lloyd Palmer, David Andrew Platt (Cap), Paul John Gascoigne, Lee Stuart Sharpe, Leslie Ferdinand, Edward Paul Sheringham (46 Ian Edward Wright).    Manager:  Graham Taylor

**Goals**:  Øyvind Leonhardsen (42), Lars Bohinen (48)

697. 09.06.1993   U.S. Cup
**U.S.A. v ENGLAND   2-0**  (1-0)
*Foxboro, Boston*

Referee: Alfred Wieser (Austria)   Attendance: 37,652

**U.S.A.**: Anthony Michael Meola (Cap), Fernando Clavijo, John Joseph Doyle, Desmond Armstrong, Mike Lapper, Jeff Agoos, Thomas Dooley (67 Panayotis Alexi Lalas), John Andrew Harkes, Tabaré Ramos (82 Cobi Ngai Jones), Eric Wynalda (62 Earnest Stewart), Roy Wegerle.
Trainer: Velibor Milutinović

**ENGLAND**: Christopher Charles Eric Woods, Lee Michael Dixon, Carlton Lloyd Palmer (61 Desmond Sinclair Walker), Gary Andrew Pallister, Anthony Robert Dorigo, Paul Emerson Ince (Cap), Nigel Howard Clough, David Batty, Lee Stuart Sharpe, John Charles Bryan Barnes, Leslie Ferdinand (35 Ian Edward Wright).   Manager: Graham Taylor

**Goals**: Thomas Dooley (42), Panayotis Alexi Lalas (72)


698. 13.06.1993   U.S. Cup
**BRAZIL v ENGLAND   1-1**  (0-0)
*Robert F.Kennedy, Washington*

Referee: Helder Diaz (USA)   Attendance: 54,118

**BRAZIL**: Cláudio André Mergen Taffarel, Jorge de Amorim Campos "Jorginho", VÁLBER Roel de Oliveira, MÁRCIO Roberto dos SANTOS, Raimundo NONATO da Silva (5 Marcos Evangelista de Moraes "Cafu"), Carlos Caetano Bledorn Verri "Dunga", Luís Carlos Quintanilha "Luisinho" (57 Jorge Ferreira da Silva "Palhinha"), RAÍ Souza Vieira de Oliveira, VALDEIR Celso Moreira (67 ALMIR de Souza Fraga), Antônio de Oliveira Filho "Careca", ELIVÉLTON Alves Rufino.
Trainer: Carlos Alberto Gomes Parreira

**ENGLAND**: Timothy David Flowers, Earl Delisser Barrett, Desmond Sinclair Walker, Gary Andrew Pallister, Anthony Robert Dorigo, Paul Emerson Ince (Cap) (68 Carlton Lloyd Palmer), Andrew Sinton, David Batty (46 David Andrew Platt), Lee Stuart Sharpe, Nigel Howard Clough (83 Paul Charles Merson), Ian Edward Wright.   Manager: Graham Taylor

**Goal**: Márcio Santos (76) / David Andrew Platt (47)


699. 19.06.1993   U.S. Cup
**GERMANY v ENGLAND   2-1**  (1-1)
*Silverdome, Detroit*

Referee: Ernesto Filippi Cavani (Uruguay)   Att: 62,126

**GERMANY**: Bodo Illgner, Thomas Helmer, Guido Buchwald, Michael Schulz, Thomas Strunz, Christian Ziege, Stefan Effenberg (76 Michael Zorc), Lothar Herbert Matthäus (Cap), Andreas Möller (64 Matthias Sammer), Jürgen Klinsmann, Karlheinz Riedle.   Trainer: Hans-Hubert Vogts

**ENGLAND**: Anthony Nigel Martyn, Earl Delisser Barrett, Desmond Sinclair Walker, Gary Andrew Pallister (53 Martin Raymond Keown), David Andrew Platt (Cap), Paul Emerson Ince, Nigel Howard Clough (63 Ian Edward Wright), Andrew Sinton, Paul Charles Merson, John Charles Bryan Barnes, Lee Stuart Sharpe (46 Nigel Winterburn).
Manager: Graham Taylor

**Goal**: Stefan Effenberg (26), Jürgen Klinsmann (53) / David Andrew Platt (30)


700. 08.09.1993   15th World Cup Qualifiers
**ENGLAND v POLAND   3-0**  (1-0)
*Wembley, London*

Referee: Frans van den Wijngaert (Belgium)   Att: 71,220

**ENGLAND**: David Andrew Seaman, Robert Marc Jones, Anthony Alexander Adams, Gary Andrew Pallister, Stuart Pearce (Cap), David Andrew Platt, Paul Emerson Ince, Paul John Gascoigne, Lee Stuart Sharpe, Leslie Ferdinand, Ian Edward Wright.   Manager: Graham Taylor

**POLAND**: Jarosław Bako, Piotr Czachowski, Marek Koźmiński, Andrzej Lesiak, Dariusz Adamczuk (78 Jacek Bąk), Roman Kosecki (Cap), Jerzy Brzęczek, Robert Warzycha, Piotr Świerczewski, Jan Furtok (46 Jacek Ziober), Marek Leśniak.
Trainer: Andrzej Strejlau

**Goals**: Leslie Ferdinand (5), Paul John Gascoigne (49), Stuart Pearce (53)


701. 13.10.1993   15th World Cup Qualifiers
**HOLLAND v ENGLAND   2-0**  (0-0)
*Feyenoord, Rotterdam*

Referee: Karl-Josef Assenmacher (Germany)   Att: 48,000

**HOLLAND**: Ed de Goey, John de Wolf, Ronald Koeman (Cap), Frank de Boer, Frank Rijkaard, Jan Wouters, Erwin Koeman, Marc Overmars (74 Aron Winter), Dennis Bergkamp, Ronald de Boer (89 Ulrich van Gobbel), Bryan Roy.
Trainer: Dick Advocaat

**ENGLAND**: David Andrew Seaman, Paul Andrew Parker, Anthony Alexander Adams, Gary Andrew Pallister, Anthony Robert Dorigo, Carlton Lloyd Palmer (46 Andrew Sinton), David Andrew Platt (Cap), Paul Emerson Ince, Lee Stuart Sharpe, Paul Charles Merson (70 Ian Edward Wright), Alan Shearer.   Manager: Graham Taylor

**Goals**: Ronald Koeman (62), Dennis Bergkamp (68)

702. 17.11.1993    15th World Cup Qualifiers
**SAN MARINO v ENGLAND  1-7**  (1-3)
*Renato Dall'Ara, Bologna*
Referee:  Mohammad Nazri Abdullah (Malaysia)    Att: 2,378

**SAN MARINO**:  Pier Luigi Benedettini, Mauro Valentini (47 Luca Gobbi), Mirco Gennari, Loris Zanotti, Claudio Canti, William Guerra, Pierangelo Manzaroli, Pier Domenico Della Valle, Nicola Bacciocchi (62 Paolo Mazza), Massimo Bonini, Davide Gualtieri.    Trainer: Giorgio Leoni

**ENGLAND**:  David Andrew Seaman, Lee Michael Dixon, Desmond Sinclair Walker, Gary Andrew Pallister, Stuart Pearce (Cap), David Andrew Platt, Paul Emerson Ince, Andrew Sinton, Stuart Edward Ripley, Leslie Ferdinand, Ian Edward Wright.    Manager: Graham Taylor

**Goals**:  Davide Gualtieri (1) / Paul Emerson Ince (21, 73), Ian Edward Wright (34, 46, 78, 90), Leslie Ferdinand (38)

703. 09.03.1994
**ENGLAND v DENMARK  1-0**  (1-0)
*Wembley, London*
Referee:  Jacob Uilenberg (Holland)    Attendance: 71,970

**ENGLAND**:  David Andrew Seaman, Paul Andrew Parker, Anthony Alexander Adams, Gary Andrew Pallister, Graeme Pierre Le Saux, David Andrew Platt (Cap), Paul Emerson Ince (66 David Batty), Paul John Gascoigne (66 Matthew Paul Le Tissier), Darren Robert Anderton, Peter Andrew Beardsley, Alan Shearer.    Manager: Terry Venables

**DENMARK**:  Peter Schmeichel, Marc Rieper, Lars Olsen (Cap), Jakob Kjeldbjerg, Carsten Dethlefsen, John Jensen, Kim Vilfort (72 Jes Høgh), Michael Laudrup, Henrik Larsen, Brian Laudrup, Bent Christensen (72 Søren Frederiksen). Trainer:  Richard Møller Nielsen

**Goal**:  David Andrew Platt (16)

704. 17.05.1994
**ENGLAND v GREECE  5-0**  (3-0)
*Wembley, London*
Referee:  James McCluskey (Scotland)    Attendance: 23,659

**ENGLAND**:  Timothy David Flowers, Robert Marc Jones (82 Stuart Pearce), Anthony Alexander Adams, Stephen Andrew Bould, Graeme Pierre Le Saux, David Andrew Platt (Cap), Paul Charles Merson, Darren Robert Anderton (62 Matthew Paul Le Tissier), Peter Andrew Beardsley (69 Ian Edward Wright), Kevin Richardson, Alan Shearer.    Manager: Terry Venables

**GREECE**:  Hrístos Karkamanis, Efstratios Apostolakis, Giánnis Kalitzakis, Väïos Karagiánnis, Athanásios Kolitsidakis (46 Kiriákos Karataïdis), Nikolaos Tsiantakis, Nikolaos Nioplias, Panagiótis Tsalouhidis (Cap), Minás Hantzidis (46 Anastásios Mitropoulos), Sávvas Kofidis (70 Hrístos Kostis), Nikolaos Mahlas (46 Dimítris Saravakos).
Trainer: Alketas Panagoulias

**Goals**:  Darren Anderton (24), Peter Andrew Beardsley (37), David Andrew Platt (45 pen, 55), Alan Shearer (65)

705. 22.05.1994
**ENGLAND v NORWAY  0-0**
*Wembley, London*
Referee:  Kim Milton Nielsen (Denmark)    Att: 64,327

**ENGLAND**:  David Andrew Seaman, Robert Marc Jones, Anthony Alexander Adams, Stephen Andrew Bould, Graeme Pierre Le Saux, David Andrew Platt (Cap), Paul Emerson Ince (76 Ian Edward Wright), Darren Robert Anderton (76 Matthew Paul Le Tissier), Dennis Frank Wise, Peter Andrew Beardsley, Alan Shearer.    Manager:  Terry Venables

**NORWAY**:  Erik Thorstvedt (86 Ola By Rise), Erland Johnsen, Henning Berg, Rune Bratseth, Roger Nilsen (46 Alf Inge Håland), Ørjan Berg (67 Kåre Ingebrigtsen), Lars Bohinen, Jostein Flo, Kjetil Rekdal, Jahn Ivar Jakobsen, Jan Åge Fjørtoft (46 Gøran Sørloth).    Trainer:  Egil Olsen

706. 07.09.1994
**ENGLAND v U.S.A.  2-0**  (2-0)
*Wembley, London*
Referee:  Antonio Jesus Lopez Nieto (Spain)    Att: 38,629

**ENGLAND**:  David Andrew Seaman, Robert Marc Jones, Anthony Alexander Adams, Gary Andrew Pallister, Graeme Pierre Le Saux, Barry Venison, Darren Robert Anderton, David Andrew Platt (Cap), John Charles Bryan Barnes, Alan Shearer (80 Ian Edward Wright), Edward Paul Sheringham (80 Leslie Ferdinand).    Manager:  Terry Venables

**U.S.A.**:  Bradley Howard Friedel (81 Juergen Sommer), Jeff Agoos (70 Mike Lapper), Marcelo Luis Balboa, Panayotis Alexi Lalas, Paul David Caligiuri, Thomas Dooley (Cap), Mike Sorber, Claudio Reyna (81 Joseph-Max Moore), Cobi Ngai Jones, Earnest Stewart (81 Franklin Klopas), Hugo Pérez (46 Eric Wynalda).    Trainer:  Velibor Milutinović

**Goals**:  Alan Shearer (33, 40)

707. 12.10.1994
**ENGLAND v ROMANIA  1-1**  (1-1)
*Wembley, London*
Referee:  Joël Quiniou (France)    Attendance: 48,754

**ENGLAND**:  David Andrew Seaman, Robert Marc Jones (58 Stuart Pearce), Anthony Alexander Adams (Cap), Gary Andrew Pallister, Graeme Pierre Le Saux, Paul Emerson Ince, Robert Martin Lee (71 Dennis Frank Wise), Matthew Paul Le Tissier, John Charles Bryan Barnes, Alan Shearer, Ian Edward Wright (71 Edward Paul Sheringham).
Manager:  Terry Venables

**ROMANIA**:  Bogdan Stelea (87 Florian Prunea), Dan Petrescu, Daniel Claudiu Prodan, Miodrag Belodedici, Dorinel Munteanu, Ionuț Angelo Lupescu, Gheorghe Popescu, Gheorghe Hagi (Cap) (46 Tibor Selymes), Ilie Dumitrescu, Marius Lăcătuş (81 Florin Cârstea), Florin Răducioiu (78 Daniel Timofte).    Trainer:  Anghel Iordănescu

**Goal**:  Robert Martin Lee (45) / Ilie Dumitrescu (37)

708. 16.11.1994
**ENGLAND v NIGERIA  1-0**  (0-0)
*Wembley, London*
Referee: Leif Sundell (Sweden)    Attendance: 37,196
**ENGLAND**: Timothy David Flowers, Robert Marc Jones, Stephen Norman Howey, Neil Ruddock, Graeme Pierre Le Saux, Robert Martin Lee (26 Steve McManaman), David Andrew Platt (Cap), Dennis Frank Wise, John Charles Bryan Barnes, Peter Andrew Beardsley (78 Matthew Paul Le Tissier), Alan Shearer (48 Edward Paul Sheringham).
Manager: Terry Venables
**NIGERIA**: Peter Rufai, Uche Okafor, Augustine Eguavon, Uche Okechukwa, Benedict Iroha, Finidi George, Mutiu Adepoju (85 Nwankwo Kanu), Austin Okocha, Emmanuel Amunike, Daniel Amokachi (60 Viktor Ikpeba), Rashidi Yekini (60 Efan Ekoku).
**Goal**: David Andrew Platt (41)

709. 15.02.1995
**REPUBLIC OF IRELAND v ENGLAND  1-0**  (1-0)
*Lansdowne Road, Dublin*
Referee: Dick Jol (Holland)    Attendance: 46,000
**IRELAND**: Alan Thomas Kelly, Terence Michael Phelan, Joseph Dennis Irwin, Paul McGrath, Alan Nigel Kernaghan, Stephen Staunton, Edward John Paul McGoldrick, Andrew David Townsend (Cap), John Joseph Sheridan, Niall John Quinn, David Thomas Kelly.   Manager: John Charlton
**ENGLAND**: David Andrew Seaman, Warren Dean Barton, Anthony Alexander Adams, Gary Andrew Pallister, Graeme Pierre Le Saux, Darren Robert Anderton, David Andrew Platt (Cap), Paul Emerson Ince, Matthew Paul Le Tissier, Peter Andrew Beardsley, Alan Shearer.   Manager: Terry Venables
**Goal**: David Thomas Kelly (23)
The match was abandoned after 27 minutes due to crowd trouble. The F.A. decided to award caps for this match although the 1-0 scoreline would not stand in the records.

710. 29.03.1995
**ENGLAND v URUGUAY  0-0**
*Wembley, London*
Referee: Hellmut Krug (Germany)    Attendance: 34,894
**ENGLAND**: Timothy David Flowers, Robert Marc Jones, Anthony Alexander Adams, Gary Andrew Pallister, Graeme Pierre Le Saux (46 Steve McManaman), Barry Venison, Darren Robert Anderton, David Andrew Platt (Cap), John Charles Bryan Barnes, Peter Andrew Beardsley (66 Nicholas Jonathan Barmby), Edward Paul Sheringham (71 Andrew Alexander Cole).   Manager: Terry Venables
**URUGUAY**: Oscar Ferro, Luis Diego López, Oscar Aguirregaray Acosta, Álvaro Gutiérrez, Ronald Paolo Montero, Diego Martín Dorta, Pablo Javier Bengoechea (Cap), Gustavo Poyet, Néstor Gabriel Cedrés, Daniel Fonseca, Enzo Francéscoli (85 Debray Darío Silva).   Trainer: Héctor Núñez

711. 03.06.1995    Umbro Cup
**ENGLAND v JAPAN  2-1**  (0-0)
*Wembley, London*
Referee: Jacob Uilenberg (Holland)    Attendance: 21,142
**ENGLAND**: Timothy David Flowers, Gary Alexander Neville, John Robert Scales, David Gerald Unsworth, Stuart Pearce, Darren Robert Anderton, David Andrew Platt (Cap), David Batty (69 Paul John Gascoigne), Peter Andrew Beardsley (69 Steve McManaman), Alan Shearer, Stanley Victor Collymore (76 Edward Paul Sheringham).   Manager: Terry Venables
**JAPAN**: Kazuya Maekawa, Kazuaki Tasaka, Tesuji Hashiratani, Masami Ihara, Akira Narahashi, Hiroaki Morishima (81 Masahiro Fukuda), Motohiro Yamaguchi, Tsuyoshi Kitazawa, Noaki Soma (74 Hiroshige Yanagimoto), Kazuyoshi Miura, Masashi Nakayama (65 Masashi Nakayama).
**Goals**: Darren Robert Anderton (48), David Platt (88 pen)

712. 08.06.1995    Umbro Cup
**ENGLAND v SWEDEN  3-3**  (1-2)
*Elland Road, Leeds*
Referee: Leslie Mottram (Scotland)    Attendance: 32,008
**ENGLAND**: Timothy David Flowers, Warren Dean Barton, Colin Terence Cooper, Gary Andrew Pallister (80 John Robert Scales), Graeme Pierre Le Saux, Darren Robert Anderton, David Andrew Platt (Cap), John Charles Bryan Barnes (64 Nicholas Jonathan Barmby), Peter Andrew Beardsley (64 Paul John Gascoigne), Alan Shearer, Edward Paul Sheringham.
Manager: Terry Venables
**SWEDEN**: Thomas Ravelli, Gary Sundgren, Teddy Lucic, Joachim Björklund, Pontus Kåmark, Niclas Alexandersson, Håkan Mild, Magnus Erlingmark (85 Ola Andersson), Niklas Gudmundsson, Henrik Larsson, Kennet Andersson (85 Dick Lidman).   Trainer: Tommy Svensson
**Goals**: Edward Sheringham (44), David Andrew Platt (89), Darren Robert Anderton (90) /
Håkan Mild (11, 37), Kennet Andersson (46)

713. 11.06.1995    Umbro Cup
**ENGLAND v BRAZIL  1-3**  (1-0)
*Wembley, London*
Referee: Pierluigi Pairetto (Italy)    Attendance: 67,318
**ENGLAND**: Timothy David Flowers, Gary Alexander Neville, John Robert Scales (90 Warren Dean Barton), Colin Terence Cooper, Stuart Pearce, Darren Robert Anderton, David Andrew Platt (Cap), David Batty (78 Paul John Gascoigne), Graeme Pierre Le Saux, Alan Shearer, Edward Paul Sheringham (78 Stanley Victor Collymore).
Manager: Terry Venables

**BRAZIL**: Armelino Donizetti Quagliatto "Zetti", Jorge de Amorim Campos "Jorginho", ALDAIR Nascimento Santos (90 Ronaldo Rodrigues de Jesus "Ronaldão"), MÁRCIO Roberto dos SANTOS, ROBERTO CARLOS da Silva, Carlos Campos CÉSAR SAMPAIO, Carlos Caetano Bledorn Verri "Dunga" (Cap), Crizam César de Oliveira Filho "Zinho", Osvaldo Giroldo Júnior "Juninho Paulista" (84 LEONARDO Nascimento de Araújo), EDMUNDO Alves de Souza Neto, RONALDO Luís Nazário de Lima (76 GIOVANNI Silva de Oliveira).    Trainer:  Mário Jorge Lobo Zagallo

Goal:  Graeme Pierre Le Saux (38) / Osvaldo Giroldo Júnior "Juninho Paulista" (54), RONALDO Luís Nazário de Lima (61), EDMUNDO Alves de Souza Neto (76)

714.  06.09.1995
## ENGLAND v COLOMBIA  0-0
*Wembley, London*

Referee:  Marc Batta (France)     Attendance:  20,038

**ENGLAND**:  David Andrew Seaman, Gary Alexander Neville, Anthony Alexander Adams (Cap), Stephen Norman Howey, Graeme Pierre Le Saux, Steve McManaman, Jamie Frank Redknapp (74 John Charles Bryan Barnes), Paul John Gascoigne (74 Robert Martin Lee), Nicholas Jonathan Barmby, Dennis Frank Wise, Alan Shearer (74 Edward Paul Sheringham).    Manager:  Terry Venables

**COLOMBIA**:   José René Higuita, José Fernando Santa, Jorge Hernán Bermúdez, Alexis Antonio Mendoza, Wilmer Pérez, John Harold Lozano (46 Luis Quiñónez), Leonel de Jesús Álvarez, Faustino Hernán Asprilla, Iván René Valenciano, Freddy Eusebio Rincón, Carlos Alberto Valderrama.  Trainer:  Hernán Darío Gómez

715.  11.10.1995
## NORWAY v ENGLAND  0-0
*Ullevaal, Oslo*

Referee:  Karl-Erik Nilsson (Sweden)     Attendance:  21,006

**NORWAY**:  Erik Thorstvedt, Karl Petter Løken, Ronny Johnsen, Henning Berg, Stig Inge Bjørnebye, Tore André Flo, Lars Bohinen, Kjetil Rekdal, Øyvind Leonhardsen (63 Ståle Solbakken), Jahn Ivar Jakobsen, Jan Åge Fjørtoft (80 Harald Martin Brattbakk).    Trainer:  Egil Olsen

**ENGLAND**:  David Andrew Seaman, Gary Alexander Neville, Anthony Alexander Adams (Cap), Gary Andrew Pallister, Stuart Pearce, Steve McManaman, Jamie Frank Redknapp, Nicholas Jonathan Barmby (66 Edward Paul Sheringham), Dennis Frank Wise (66 Steven Brian Stone), Robert Martin Lee, Alan Shearer.    Manager:  Terry Venables

716.  15.11.1995
## ENGLAND v SWITZERLAND  3-1  (1-1)
*Wembley, London*

Referee:  Sándor Puhl (Hungary)     Attendance:  29,874

**ENGLAND**:  David Andrew Seaman, Gary Alexander Neville, Anthony Alexander Adams (Cap), Gary Andrew Pallister, Stuart Pearce, Steve McManaman, Jamie Frank Redknapp (7 Steven Brian Stone), Paul John Gascoigne, Robert Martin Lee, Alan Shearer, Edward Paul Sheringham.
Manager:  Terry Venables

**SWITZERLAND**:  Marco Pascolo, Marc Hottiger, Alain Geiger, Stéphane Henchoz, Yvan Quentin (82 Ramon Vega), Christophe Ohrel, Ciriaco Sforza, Sébastien Fournier (70 Stefan Wolf), Alain Sutter (80 Marco Grassi), Adrian Knup, Kubilay Türkyilmaz.    Trainer:  Roy Hodgson

**Goals**:  Stuart Pearce (45), Edward Paul Sheringham (56), Steven Brian Stone (78) / Adrian Knup (40)

717.  12.12.1995
## ENGLAND v PORTUGAL  1-1  (1-0)
*Wembley, London*

Referee:  Rune Pedersen (Norway)     Attendance:  28,592

**ENGLAND**:  David Andrew Seaman, Gary Alexander Neville, Anthony Alexander Adams (Cap), Stephen Norman Howey, Stuart Pearce (80 Graeme Pierre Le Saux), Nicholas Jonathan Barmby (80 Steve McManaman), Dennis Frank Wise (80 Gareth Southgate), Steven Brian Stone, Paul John Gascoigne, Leslie Ferdinand (68 Peter Andrew Beardsley), Alan Shearer.  Manager:  Terry Venables

**PORTUGAL**:  Adelino Augusto Graça Barbosa Barros "Neno", Carlos Alberto Oliveira "Secretário", JORGE Paulo COSTA Almeida, HÉLDER Marino Rodrigues Cristóvão, FERNANDO Manuel Silva COUTO (Cap), DIMAS Manuel Marques Teixeira, António José dos Santos Folha (69 PEDRO Alexandre Santos BARBOSA), PAULO Manuel Carvalho de SOUSA (46 PAULO Lourenço Martins ALVES), Luis Filipe Madeira Caeiro "Figo" (46 José Manuel Martins Dominguez), JOÃO Manuel VIEIRA PINTO (63 Daniel Cruz de Carvalho "Dani"), Ricardo Manuel Silva Sá Pinto.
Trainer:  António Luís Alves Ribeiro Oliveira

Goal:  Steven Brian Stone (44) / PAULO ALVES (58)

718.  27.03.1996
**ENGLAND v BULGARIA  1-0**  (1-0)
*Wembley, London*
Referee: Günther Benkö (Austria)   Attendance: 29708
**ENGLAND**: David Andrew Seaman, Gary Alexander Neville, Stephen Norman Howey, Gareth Southgate, Stuart Pearce (Cap), Steve McManaman, Paul John Gascoigne (76 David Andrew Platt), Paul Emerson Ince, Steven Brian Stone, Edward Paul Sheringham (76 Robert Martin Lee), Leslie Ferdinand (76 Robert Bernard Fowler).   Manager: Terry Venables
**BULGARIA**: Borislav Mihailov (46 Dimitar Popov), Emil Kremenliev (85 Radostin Kishishev), Petar Hubchev, Gosho Ginchev (46 Boncho Genchev), Trifon Ivanov, Zlatko Yankov, Ilian Kiriakov, Ivailo Iordanov (46 Daniel Borimirov), Iordan Lechkov, Emil Kostadinov, Liuboslav Penev (85 Nasko Sirakov).   Trainer: Dimitar Penev
**Goal**: Leslie Ferdinand (7)


719.  24.04.1996
**ENGLAND v CROATIA  0-0**
*Wembley, London*
Referee: Zbigniew Przesmycki (Poland)   Att: 33,650
**ENGLAND**: David Andrew Seaman, Gary Alexander Neville, Mark Wright, Stuart Pearce, Steve McManaman, Paul John Gascoigne, David Andrew Platt (Cap), Paul Emerson Ince, Steven Brian Stone, Edward Paul Sheringham, Robert Bernard Fowler.   Manager: Terry Venables
**CROATIA**: Marijan Mrmić, Dubravko Pavličić (75 Mladen Mladenović), Robert Jarni, Aljoša Asanović, Nikola Jerkan, Slaven Bilić, Robert Prosinečki, Alen Bokšić (71 Igor Pamić), Davor Šuker, Zvonimir Boban (46 Mario Stanić), Igor Štimac (58 Zvonimir Soldo).   Trainer: Miroslav Blažević


720.  18.05.1996
**ENGLAND v HUNGARY  3-0**  (1-0)
*Wembley, London*
Referee: Markus Merk (Germany)   Attendance: 34,184
**ENGLAND**: David Andrew Seaman (65 Ian Michael Walker), Gary Alexander Neville, Mark Wright (12 Gareth Southgate), Stuart Pearce, Robert Martin Lee, Paul Emerson Ince (65 Sol Campbell), David Andrew Platt (Cap) (65 Dennis Frank Wise), Darren Robert Anderton, Jason Malcolm Wilcox, Edward Paul Sheringham, Leslie Ferdinand (77 Alan Shearer). Manager: Terry Venables
**HUNGARY**: Zsolt Petry, János Bánfi, Vilmos Sebők, Attila Plókai, Mihály Mracskó (82 András Telek), Flórián Urbán, Tibor Balog II (62 Béla Illés), Árpád Hahn, Norbert Nagy (82 Imre Aranyos), Ferenc Horváth (82 Krisztián Lisztes), István Vincze (80 Gábor Egressy).   Trainer: János Csank
**Goals**: Darren Anderton (36, 62), David Andrew Platt (52)


721.  23.05.1996
**CHINA v ENGLAND  0-3**  (0-1)
*Worker's Stadium, Beijing*
Referee: Pierluigi Collina (Italy)   Attendance: 65,000
**CHINA**: Ou Chuliang, Xu Hong, Wei Qun, Fan Zyiyi, Li Hongjun, Xie Yuxin (46 Li Meng), Li Bing (46 Peng Weiguo), Jiang Feng (33 Gao Zhongxun), Ma Mingyn, Gao Feng, Hao Haidung.
**ENGLAND**: Timothy David Flowers (64 Ian Michael Walker), Gary Alexander Neville, Anthony Alexander Adams (Cap) (76 Ugochuku Ehiogu), Gareth Southgate, Philip John Neville, Steve McManaman (76 Steven Brian Stone), Jamie Frank Redknapp, Paul John Gascoigne, Darren Robert Anderton, Nicholas Jonathan Barmby (72 Peter Andrew Beardsley), Alan Shearer (72 Robert Bernard Fowler).
Manager: Terry Venables
**Goals**: Nicholas Barmby (30, 53), Paul John Gascoigne (64)


722.  08.06.1996   10th European Champs, 1st Round
**ENGLAND v SWITZERLAND  1-1**  (1-0)
*Wembley, London*
Referee: Manuel Diaz Vega (Spain)   Attendance: 76,567
**ENGLAND**: David Andrew Seaman, Gary Alexander Neville, Anthony Alexander Adams (Cap), Gareth Southgate, Stuart Pearce, Darren Robert Anderton, Paul Emerson Ince, Paul John Gascoigne (76 David Andrew Platt), Steve McManaman (69 Steven Brian Stone), Alan Shearer, Edward Paul Sheringham (68 Nicholas Jonathan Barmby).
Manager: Terry Venables
**SWITZERLAND**: Marco Pascolo, Sébastien Jeanneret, Ramon Vega, Stéphane Henchoz, Yvan Quentin, Johann Vogel, Alain Geiger (67 Marcel Koller), Ciriaco Sforza, Christophe Bonvin (69 Stéphane Chapuisat), Marco Grassi, Kubilay Türkyilmaz.   Trainer: Artur Jorge Braga Melo Teixeira
**Goals**: Alan Shearer (23) / Kubilay Türkyilmaz (82 pen)


723.  15.06.1996   10th European Champs, 1st Round
**ENGLAND v SCOTLAND  2-0**  (0-0)
*Wembley, London*
Referee: Pierluigi Pairetto (Italy)   Attendance: 76,864
**ENGLAND**: David Andrew Seaman, Gary Alexander Neville, Anthony Alexander Adams (Cap), Gareth Southgate, Stuart Pearce (46 Jamie Frank Redknapp, 84 Sol Campbell), Darren Robert Anderton, Paul Emerson Ince (79 Steven Brian Stone), Paul John Gascoigne, Steve McManaman, Alan Shearer, Edward Paul Sheringham.   Manager: Terry Venables
**SCOTLAND**: Andrew Lewis Goram, Stewart McKimmie, Thomas Boyd, Colin Calderwood, Edward Colin James Hendry, Stuart Murray McCall, Gary McAllister (Cap), John Angus Paul Collins, Thomas Valley McKinlay (81 Craig William Burley), John Spencer (66 Alistair Murdoch McCoist), Gordon Scott Durie (84 Eoin Jess).   Manager: Craig Brown
**Goals**: Alan Shearer (52), Paul John Gascoigne (78)

724. 18.06.1996  10th European Champs, 1st Round
**ENGLAND v HOLLAND  4-1**  (1-0)
*Wembley, London*

Referee: Gerd Grabher (Austria)   Attendance: 76,798

**ENGLAND**: David Andrew Seaman, Gary Alexander Neville, Anthony Alexander Adams (Cap), Gareth Southgate, Stuart Pearce, Darren Robert Anderton, Paul Emerson Ince (67 David Andrew Platt), Paul John Gascoigne, Steve McManaman, Alan Shearer (75 Robert Bernard Fowler), Edward Paul Sheringham (75 Nicholas Jonathan Barmby). Manager: Terry Venables

**HOLLAND**: Edwin van der Sar, Michael Reiziger, Danny Blind (Cap), Winston Bogarde, Aron Winter, Clarence Seedorf, Ronald de Boer (72 Patrick Kluivert), Richard Witschge (46 Johan de Kock), Jordi Cruijff, Dennis Bergkamp, Peter Hoekstra (72 Philip Cocu).   Trainer: Guus Hiddink

**Goals**: Alan Shearer (23 pen, 57), Edward Paul Sheringham (51, 62) / Patrick Kluivert (78)


725. 22.06.1996  10th European Champs, Quarter-Finals
**ENGLAND v SPAIN  0-0**  (AET)
*Wembley, London*

Referee: Marc Batta (France)   Attendance: 75,447

**ENGLAND**: David Andrew Seaman, Gary Alexander Neville, Gareth Southgate, Anthony Alexander Adams (Cap), Stuart Pearce, Darren Robert Anderton (108 Robert Bernard Fowler), David Andrew Platt, Paul John Gascoigne, Steve McManaman (108 Nicholas Jonathan Barmby), Alan Shearer, Edward Paul Sheringham (108 Steven Brian Stone). Manager: Terry Venables

**SPAIN**: Andoni Zubizarreta (Cap), Alberto Belsué, Rafael Alkorta (74 Juan Manuel López), ABELARDO Fernández, SERGI Barjuán, Jesús Manjarín (46 José Luis Pérez Caminero), Fernando Ruiz Hierro, Miguel Angel Nadal, Guillermo Amor, Francisco Narváez Machón "Kiko", Julio Salinas (46 Alfonso Pérez).   Trainer: Javier Clemente Lazaro

**Penalties**: 1-0 Alan Shearer, 1-0 Fernando Hierro (saved), 2-0 David Platt, 2-1 Guillermo Amor, 3-1 Stuart Pearce, 3-2 Alberto Belsué, 4-2 Paul Gascoigne, 4-2 Miguel Ángel Nadal (saved)


726. 26.06.1996  10th European Champs, Semi-Finals
**ENGLAND v GERMANY  1-1**  (1-1, 1-1) (AET)
*Wembley, London*

Referee: Sándor Puhl (Hungary)   Attendance: 75,862

**ENGLAND**: David Andrew Seaman, Gareth Southgate, Anthony Alexander Adams (Cap), Stuart Pearce, Darren Robert Anderton, David Andrew Platt, Paul Emerson Ince, Paul John Gascoigne, Steve McManaman, Alan Shearer, Edward Paul Sheringham.   Manager: Terry Venables

**GERMANY**: Andreas Köpke, Matthias Sammer, Markus Babbel, Thomas Helmer (110 Marco Bode), Stefan Reuter, Steffen Freund (119 Thomas Strunz), Dieter Eilts, Christian Ziege, Mehmet Scholl (77 Thomas Häßler), Andreas Möller (Cap), Stefan Kuntz.   Trainer: Hans-Hubert Vogts

**Goals**: Alan Shearer (3) / Stefan Kuntz (16)

**Penalties**: 0-1 Alan Shearer, 1-1 Thomas Häßler, 1-2 David Platt, 2-2 Thomas Strunz, 2-3 Stuart Pearce, 3-3 Stefan Reuter, 3-4 Paul Gascoigne, 4-4 Christian Ziege, 4-5 Teddy Sheringham, 5-5 Stefan Kuntz, 5-5 Gareth Southgate (saved), 5-6 Andreas Möller


727. 01.09.1996   16th World Cup Qualifiers
**MOLDOVA v ENGLAND  0-3**  (0-2)
*Republican, Chişinău*

Referee: Ilkka Koho (Finland)   Attendance: 9,500

**MOLDOVA**: Denis Romanenco, Serghei Secu, Ion Testimiţanu, Serghei Nani, Serghei Belous (58 Oleg Şişchin), Vladimir Gaidamaşciuc, Alexandru Curtianu, Serghei Epureanu, Iurie Miterev (62 Radu Rebeja), Alexandru Popovici, Serghei Cleşcenco.   Trainer: Ion Caras

**ENGLAND**: David Andrew Seaman, Gary Alexander Neville, Gary Andrew Pallister, Gareth Southgate, Stuart Pearce, Paul Emerson Ince, David Robert Beckham, Paul John Gascoigne (81 David Batty), Andrew George Hinchcliffe, Alan Shearer (Cap), Nicholas Jonathan Barmby (81 Matthew Paul Le Tissier).   Manager: Glenn Hoddle

**Goals**: Nicholas Jonathan Barmby (24), Paul Gascoigne (25), Alan Shearer (61)

728. 09.10.1996   16th World Cup Qualifiers
**ENGLAND v POLAND  2-1**  (2-1)
*Wembley, London*
Referee: Hellmut Krug (Germany)   Attendance: 74,663
**ENGLAND**: David Andrew Seaman, Gary Alexander Neville, Gareth Southgate (52 Gary Andrew Pallister), Andrew George Hinchcliffe, Stuart Pearce, Paul Emerson Ince, David Robert Beckham, Paul John Gascoigne, Steve McManaman, Alan Shearer (Cap), Leslie Ferdinand.   Manager: Glenn Hoddle
**POLAND**: Andrzej Woźniak, Paweł Wojtala, Jacek Zieliński, Marek Jóźwiak, Tomasz Hajto, Radosław Michalski, Piotr Nowak (Cap), Tomasz Wałdoch, Henryk Bałuszyński, Krzysztof Warzycha (76 Marek Saganowski), Marek Citko.
Trainer: Antoni Piechniczek
**Goals**: Alan Shearer (24, 38) / Marek Citko (7)


729. 09.11.1996   16th World Cup Qualifiers
**GEORGIA v ENGLAND  0-2**  (0-2)
*Boris Paichadze, Tbilisi*
Referee: Jorge Monteiro Coroado (Portugal)   Att: 48,000
**GEORGIA**: Irakli Zoidze, Nugzar Lobjanidze, Kakhaber Tskhadadze, Murtaz Shelia, Levan Kobiashvili, Kakhaber Gogichaishvili (78 Giorgi Gudushauri), Giorgi Nemsadze, Giorgi Kinkladze, Gocha Jamarauli, Temur Ketsbaia, Shota Arveladze (52 Gocha Gogrichiani).
Trainer: Aleksandr Chivadze
**ENGLAND**: David Andrew Seaman, Gareth Southgate, Sol Campbell, Anthony Alexander Adams (Cap), Paul Emerson Ince, David Robert Beckham, Paul John Gascoigne, Andrew George Hinchcliffe, David Batty, Leslie Ferdinand (81 Ian Edward Wright), Edward Paul Sheringham.
Manager: Glenn Hoddle
**Goals**: Edward Paul Sheringham (15), Leslie Ferdinand (37)


730. 12.02.1997   16th World Cup Qualifiers
**ENGLAND v ITALY  0-1**  (0-1)
*Wembley, London*
Referee: Sándor Puhl (Hungary)   Attendance: 75,055
**ENGLAND**: Ian Michael Walker, Gary Alexander Neville, Sol Campbell, Stuart Pearce, Paul Emerson Ince, David Robert Beckham, Matthew Paul Le Tissier (60 Leslie Ferdinand), David Batty (87 Ian Edward Wright), Steve McManaman (76 Paul Charles Merson), Graeme Pierre Le Saux, Alan Shearer (Cap).   Manager: Glenn Hoddle
**ITALY**: Angelo Peruzzi, Ciro Ferrara, Paolo Maldini (Cap), Demetrio Albertini, Fabio Cannavaro, Alessandro Costacurta, Angelo Di Livio, Roberto Di Matteo, Pier Luigi Casiraghi (76 Fabrizio Ravanelli), Dino Baggio, Gianfranco Zola (90 Diego Fuser).   Trainer: Cesare Maldini
**Goal**: Gianfranco Zola (19)


731. 29.03.1997
**ENGLAND v MEXICO  2-0**  (1-0)
*Wembley, London*
Referee: Vitor Manuel Melo Pereira (Portugal)   Att: 48,076
**ENGLAND**: David Benjamin James, Gareth Southgate, Martin Raymond Keown, Stuart Pearce, Paul Emerson Ince (Cap), David Batty (53 Jamie Frank Redknapp), Steve McManaman (68 Nicholas Butt), Robert Martin Lee, Graeme Pierre Le Saux, Edward Paul Sheringham (38 Ian Edward Wright), Robert Bernard Fowler.   Manager: Glenn Hoddle
**MEXICO**: Adolfo Ríos (58 Hugo Pineda), Pavel Pardo, Claudio Suárez, Duilio Davino, Jesús Ramón Ramírez, Alberto Coyote (46 Nicolás Ramírez), Luis García Postigo, Benjamín Galindo (55 Marcelino Bernal), Enrique Alfaro, Carlos Manuel Hermosillo (46 Ricardo Peláez), Luis Roberto Alves (46 Luis Hernández).   Trainer: Velibor Milutinović
**Goals**: Edward Sheringham (20 pen), Robert Fowler (55)


732. 30.04.1997   16th World Cup Qualifiers
**ENGLAND v GEORGIA  2-0**  (1-0)
*Wembley, London*
Referee: Rémi Harrel (France)   Attendance: 71,208
**ENGLAND**: David Andrew Seaman, Gary Alexander Neville, Anthony Alexander Adams (88 Gareth Southgate), Sol Campbell, Paul Emerson Ince (78 Jamie Frank Redknapp), David Robert Beckham, David Batty, Graeme Pierre Le Saux, Robert Martin Lee, Alan Shearer (Cap), Edward Paul Sheringham.   Manager: Glenn Hoddle
**GEORGIA**: Irakli Zoidze (55 Nikoloz Togonidze), Nugzar Lobjanidze, Kakhaber Tskhadadze, Murtaz Shelia (61 Gela Shekiladze), Giorgi Chikhradze (46 Kakhaber Gogichaishvili), Levan Kobiashvili, Giorgi Nemsadze, Gocha Jamarauli (46 Mikheil Kavelashvili), Giorgi Kinkladze (61 Giorgi Gakhokidze), Temur Ketsbaia (57 Archil Arveladze), Shota Arveladze (68 Amiran Mujiri).   Trainer: David Kipiani
**Goals**: Edward Paul Sheringham (43), Alan Shearer (90)


733. 24.05.1997
**ENGLAND v SOUTH AFRICA  2-1**  (1-1)
*Old Trafford, Manchester*
Referee: Anders Frisk (Sweden)   Attendance: 52,676
**ENGLAND**: Anthony Nigel Martyn, Philip John Neville, Gareth Southgate, Martin Raymond Keown, Stuart Pearce (Cap), Robert Martin Lee (80 Nicholas Butt), Paul John Gascoigne (90 Sol Campbell), Jamie Frank Redknapp (57 David Batty), Graeme Pierre Le Saux (68 David Robert Beckham), Ian Edward Wright, Edward Paul Sheringham (65 Paul Scholes).   Manager: Glenn Hoddle
**SOUTH AFRICA**: Andre Arendse, Sizwe Motaung, Mark Fish, Neil Torvey, Lucas Radebe, Theo Khumalo (77 Helman Mkhaele), Eric Tinkler (89 Shaun Bartlett), John Moshoeu, Phil Masinga (89 Lida Buthelezi), Brendan Augustine (55 Isaac Sikhosana), John Moeti.
**Goals**: Robert Lee (20), Ian Wright (76) / Phil Masinga (43)

734.   31.05.1997   16th World Cup Qualifiers
**POLAND v ENGLAND  0-2**  (0-1)

*Slaski, Chorzów*

Referee:  Urs Meier (Switzerland)   Attendance: 30,000

**POLAND**: Andrzej Woźniak, Marek Jóźwiak, Jacek Zieliński, Radosław Kałużny, Adam Ledwoń, Krzysztof Bukalski (46 Piotr Świerczewski), Tomasz Wałdoch, Piotr Nowak (Cap) (59 Cezary Kucharski), Sławomir Majak, Andrzej Juskowiak (52 Waldemar Adamczyk), Jacek Dembiński.
Trainer:  Antoni Piechniczek

**ENGLAND**: David Andrew Seaman, Gary Alexander Neville, Gareth Southgate, Sol Campbell, Paul Emerson Ince, David Robert Beckham (88 Philip John Neville), Paul John Gascoigne (16 David Batty), Graeme Pierre Le Saux, Robert Martin Lee, Alan Shearer (Cap), Edward Paul Sheringham.
Manager:  Glenn Hoddle

**Goals**: Alan Shearer (6), Edward Paul Sheringham (90)

735.  04.06.1997   Tournoi de France
**ENGLAND v ITALY  2-0**  (2-0)

*La Beaujoire, Nantes*

Referee:  Günther Benkö (Austria)   Attendance: 25,000

**ENGLAND**: Timothy David Flowers, Gareth Southgate, Martin Raymond Keown, Stuart Pearce, Philip John Neville, Paul Emerson Ince (Cap), David Robert Beckham, Paul Scholes, Graeme Pierre Le Saux (46 Gary Alexander Neville), Ian Edward Wright (77 Andrew Alexander Cole), Edward Paul Sheringham (79 Paul John Gascoigne).
Manager:  Glenn Hoddle

**ITALY**: Angelo Peruzzi, Ciro Ferrara (46 Alessandro Nesta), Antonio Benarrivo, Demetrio Albertini, Fabio Cannavaro, Alessandro Costacurta (Cap), Angelo Di Livio (46 Giampiero Maini), Roberto Di Matteo (17 Diego Fuser), Pier Luigi Casiraghi, Dino Baggio, Gianfranco Zola.
Trainer:  Cesare Maldini

**Goals**: Ian Edward Wright (26), Paul Scholes (43)

736.  07.06.1997   Tournoi de France
**FRANCE v ENGLAND  0-1**  (0-0)

*Le Mosson, Montpellier*

Referee:  Said Belqola (Morocco)   Attendance: 25,000

**FRANCE**: Fabien Barthez, Lilian Thuram, Laurent Blanc, Bruno Ngotty, Pierre Laigle (83 Bixente Lizarazu), Youri Djorkaeff, Patrick Vieira, Didier Deschamps (Cap), Christophe Dugarry (76 Zinedine Zidane), Nicolas Ouédec (63 Patrice Loko), Marc Keller.   Trainer:  Aimé Jacquet

**ENGLAND**: David Andrew Seaman, Gary Alexander Neville, Gareth Southgate, Sol Campbell, David Robert Beckham (73 Robert Martin Lee), Paul John Gascoigne, David Batty (46 Paul Emerson Ince), Philip John Neville, Graeme Pierre Le Saux, Alan Shearer (Cap), Ian Edward Wright (78 Edward Paul Sheringham).   Manager:  Glenn Hoddle

**Goal**: Alan Shearer (86)

737.  10.06.1997   Tournoi de France
**BRAZIL v ENGLAND  1-0**  (0-0)

*Parc des Princes, Paris*

Referee:  John Jairo Toro Rendon (Colombia)   Att: 33,000

**BRAZIL**: Cláudio André Mergen Taffarel, Marcos Evangelista de Moraes "Cafu", Vagno CÉLIO do Nascimento SILVA, ALDAIR Nascimento Santos, ROBERTO CARLOS da Silva, Carlos Caetano Bledorn Verri "Dunga", Flávio Conceição, LEONARDO Nascimento de Araújo (83 José Roberto da Silva Júnior "ZÉ ROBERTO"), DENÍLSON de Oliveira (22 Djalma Feitoza Dias "Djalminha"), ROMÁRIO de Souza Faria, RONALDO Luís Nazário de Lima.
Trainer:  Mário Jorge Lobo Zagallo

**ENGLAND**: David Andrew Seaman, Martin Raymond Keown (20 Gary Alexander Neville), Gareth Southgate, Sol Campbell, Philip John Neville, Paul Emerson Ince, Paul John Gascoigne, Paul Scholes (74 Robert Martin Lee), Graeme Pierre Le Saux, Alan Shearer (Cap), Edward Paul Sheringham (74 Ian Edward Wright).   Manager:  Glenn Hoddle

**Goal**: Romário (61)

738.  10.09.1997   16th World Cup Qualifiers
**ENGLAND v MOLDOVA  4-0**  (1-0)

*Wembley, London*

Referee:  Karl-Erik Nilsson (Sweden)   Attendance: 74,102

**ENGLAND**: David Andrew Seaman (Cap), Gary Alexander Neville, Gareth Southgate, Sol Campbell, Philip John Neville, David Robert Beckham (68 Stuart Edward Ripley, 76 Nicholas Butt), David Batty, Paul John Gascoigne, Paul Scholes, Leslie Ferdinand (83 Stanley Victor Collymore), Ian Edward Wright.
Manager:  Glenn Hoddle

**MOLDOVA**: Denis Romanenco, Oleg Fistican, Ion Testimițanu, Vitali Culibaba (52 Alexandru Suharev), Marin Spânu, Serghei Stroenco, Alexandru Curtianu (Cap), Oleg Șișchin (60 Alexandru Popovici), Iurie Miterev, Radu Rebeja, Serghei Rogaciov (74 Boris Cebotari).   Trainer:  Ion Caras

**Goals**: Paul Scholes (28), Ian Edward Wright (46, 89), Paul John Gascoigne (80)

739. 11.10.1997   16th World Cup Qualifiers
**ITALY v ENGLAND  0-0**
*Olimpico, Roma*

Referee: Mario van der Ende (Holland)   Attendance: 81,200

**ITALY**: Angelo Peruzzi, Alessandro Nesta, Paolo Maldini (Cap) (32 Antonio Benarrivo), Demetrio Albertini, Fabio Cannavaro, Alessandro Costacurta, Angelo Di Livio, Dino Baggio, Christian Vieri, Gianfranco Zola (64 Alessandro Del Piero), Filippo Inzaghi (46 Enrico Chiesa).
Trainer: Cesare Maldini

**ENGLAND**: David Andrew Seaman, Gareth Southgate, Anthony Alexander Adams, Sol Campbell, David Robert Beckham, David Batty, Paul John Gascoigne (88 Nicholas Butt), Paul Emerson Ince (Cap), Graeme Pierre Le Saux, Ian Edward Wright, Edward Paul Sheringham.
Manager: Glenn Hoddle

740. 15.11.1997
**ENGLAND v CAMEROON  2-0**  (2-0)
*Wembley, London*

Referee: Terje Hauge (Norway)   Attendance: 46,176

**ENGLAND**: Anthony Nigel Martyn, Gareth Southgate (39 Rio Gavin Ferdinand), Sol Campbell, Andrew George Hinchcliffe, Philip John Neville, David Robert Beckham, Paul John Gascoigne (73 Robert Martin Lee), Paul Scholes (79 Christopher Roy Sutton), Paul Emerson Ince (Cap), Steve McManaman, Robert Bernard Fowler.
Manager: Glenn Hoddle

**CAMEROON**: Vincent Ongandzi, Rigobert Song, Pierre Wome, Tobie Mimboe, Raymond Kalla, Job, Patrick Mboma (75 Geremi Njitap), Samuel Etchi, Etame (73 Solomon Olembe), Marc-Vivien Foe, Samuel Ipoua (46 Romarin Billong).

**Goals**: Paul Scholes (45), Robert Bernard Fowler (46)

741. 11.02.1998
**ENGLAND v CHILE  0-2**  (0-1)
*Wembley, London*

Referee: Ryszard Wojcik (Poland)   Attendance: 65,228

**ENGLAND**: Anthony Nigel Martyn, Gary Alexander Neville, Anthony Alexander Adams (Cap), Sol Campbell, Philip John Neville (46 Graeme Pierre Le Saux), David Batty (63 Paul Emerson Ince), Nicholas Butt, Robert Martin Lee, Dion Dublin, Michael James Owen, Edward Paul Sheringham (63 Alan Shearer).   Manager: Glenn Hoddle

**CHILE**: Nelson Antonio Tapia Rios, Pedro Reyes, Ronald Hugo Fuentes Núñez, Javier Luciano Margas Loyola, Moisés Fermín Villarroel Ayala, Nelson Rodrígo Parraguez Romero, Clarence Acuña Donoso, Francisco Ulises Rojas, José Luis Sierra Pando (88 Rodrígo Ignacio Valenzuela Avíles), Rodrígo Hernán Barrera Funes (77 Juan Enrique Carreño), José Marcelo Salas Melinao.   Trainer: Nelson Acosta López

**Goals**: José Marcelo Salas Melinao (45, 79 pen)

742. 25.03.1998
**SWITZERLAND v ENGLAND  1-1**  (1-0)
*Wankdorf, Bern*

Referee: Pascal Garibian (France)   Attendance: 17,100

**SWITZERLAND**: Joël Corminboeuf, Stéphane Henchoz, Murat Yakin, Ramon Vega, Raphaël Wicky (82 Johann Lonfat), Ciriaco Sforza, Johann Vogel, Sébastien Fournier, David Sesa (87 Adrian Kunz), Marco Grassi, Stéphane Chapuisat.
Trainer: Gilbert Gress

**ENGLAND**: Timothy David Flowers, Gareth Southgate, Rio Gavin Ferdinand, Martin Raymond Keown, Paul Emerson Ince, Andrew George Hinchcliffe, Robert Martin Lee, Paul Charles Merson (81 David Batty), Steve McManaman, Michael James Owen (68 Edward Paul Sheringham), Alan Shearer (Cap).   Manager: Glenn Hoddle

**Goal**: Ramon Vega (37) / Paul Charles Merson (69)

743. 22.04.1998
**ENGLAND v PORTUGAL  3-0**  (1-0)
*Wembley, London*

Referee: Manuel Diaz Vega (Spain)   Attendance: 63,463

**ENGLAND**: David Andrew Seaman, Gary Alexander Neville (81 Philip John Neville), Anthony Alexander Adams, Sol Campbell, David Robert Beckham (46 Paul Charles Merson), Paul Emerson Ince, Paul Scholes, David Batty, Graeme Pierre Le Saux, Edward Paul Sheringham (77 Michael James Owen), Alan Shearer (Cap).   Manager: Glenn Hoddle

**PORTUGAL**: VÍTOR Manuel Martins BAÍA (Cap), ABEL Luís Silva Costa XAVIER, Roberto Luís Gaspar Deus Severo "Beto", FERNANDO Manuel Silva COUTO, DIMAS Manuel Marques Teixeira (54 PEDRO Alexandre Santos BARBOSA), João Paulo Maio Santos "Paulinho Santos", Luis Filipe Madeira Caeiro "Figo", PAULO Manuel Carvalho de SOUSA (75 OCEANO Andrade da Cruz), José António CALADO da Silva, JOÃO Manuel VIEIRA PINTO (68 Nuno Fernando Gonçalves Rocha "Capucho"), Jorge Paulo CADETE Santos Reis.   Trainer: Humberto Manuel de Jesus Coelho

**Sent off**: Nuno Fernando Gonçalves Rocha "Capucho" (80)

**Goals**: Alan Shearer (5, 66), Edward Paul Sheringham (46)

744. 23.05.1998
**ENGLAND v SAUDI ARABIA  0-0**
*Wembley, London*

Referee:  Dick Jol (Holland)     Attendance:  63,733

**ENGLAND**:  David Andrew Seaman, Gary Alexander Neville, Anthony Alexander Adams, Gareth Southgate, David Robert Beckham (60 Paul John Gascoigne), Darren Robert Anderton, David Batty, Paul Scholes, Andrew George Hinchcliffe (74 Philip John Neville), Alan Shearer (Cap) (74 Leslie Ferdinand), Edward Paul Sheringham (60 Ian Edward Wright).
Manager:  Glenn Hoddle

**SAUDI ARABIA**: Mohammed Al-Daye, Mohammed Al-Jahni, Mohammed Al-Khlaiwi, Adbullah Zebramawi, Fuad Amin (78 Obeid Al-Dosary), Ibrahim Al-Shahrani, Sami Al-Jaber, Saeed Al-Owairan (75 Nawaf Al-Temiyat), Hussain Solaimani, Khaled Al-Muwalid, Khamis Al-Owairan.


745. 27.05.1998
**MOROCCO v ENGLAND  0-1**  (0-0)
*Mohammed V, Casablanca*

Referee:  Mourad Daami (Tunisia)     Attendance:  80,000

**MOROCCO**:  Driss Benzekri, Abdelilah Saber, Youssef Rossi, Rachid Negrouz, Abdelkrim El-Hadrioui, Said Chiba (63 Gharib Amzine), Taher El-Khalej, Youssef Chippo (79 Jamal Sellami), Salaheddine Bassir, Abderrahim Ouakili (73 Ahmed Reda Madouni), Rachid Robbi (63 Ali El-Khattabi).

**ENGLAND**:  Timothy David Flowers, Sol Campbell, Gareth Southgate, Martin Raymond Keown, Darren Robert Anderton, Paul Emerson Ince (Cap), Paul John Gascoigne, Steve McManaman, Graeme Pierre Le Saux, Dion Dublin (80 Leslie Ferdinand), Ian Edward Wright (25 Michael James Owen).
Manager:  Glenn Hoddle

**Goal**:  Michael James Owen (59)


746. 29.05.1998
**ENGLAND v BELGIUM  0-0**
*Mohammed V, Casablanca*

Referee:  Abderrahim El Arjoune (Morocco)     Att: 25,000

**ENGLAND**:  Anthony Nigel Martyn, Gary Alexander Neville (46 Rio Gavin Ferdinand), Sol Campbell (Cap) (76 Dion Dublin), Martin Raymond Keown, Philip John Neville (46 Michael James Owen), Robert Martin Lee, Paul John Gascoigne (46 David Robert Beckham), Nicholas Butt, Graeme Pierre Le Saux, Leslie Ferdinand, Paul Charles Merson.   Manager: Glenn Hoddle

**BELGIUM**:  Philippe Vande Walle, Eric Deflandre, Eric Van Meir, Glen De Boeck, Mike Verstraeten, Vital Borkelmans, Gert Verheyen (61 Gert Claessens), Vincenzo Scifo (Cap), Danny Boffin, Emile Lokonda Mpenza, Michaël Goossens (46 Mbo Jerôme Mpenza).    Trainer: Georges Leekens


747. 15.06.1998     16th World Cup,  1st Round
**ENGLAND v TUNISIA  2-0**  (1-0)
*Vélodrome, Marseille*

Referee:  Masayoshi Okada (Japan)     Attendance:  54,587

**ENGLAND**:  David Andrew Seaman, Gareth Southgate, Anthony Alexander Adams, Sol Campbell, Darren Robert Anderton, David Batty, Paul Scholes, Paul Emerson Ince, Graeme Pierre Le Saux, Alan Shearer (Cap), Edward Paul Sheringham (85 Michael James Owen).
Manager:  Glenn Hoddle

**TUNISIA**: Chokri El Ouaer, Hatem Trabelsi (79 Tarek Thabet), Sami Trabelsi, Khaled Badra, Mounir Boukadida, Jose Clayton, Khais Ghadhbane, Sirajeddine Chihi, Skander Souayah (46 Zoubeir Beya), Mehdi Ben Slimane (65 Imed Ben Younes), Adel Sellimi.    Trainer: Henryk Kasperczak

**Goals**:  Alan Shearer (43), Paul Scholes (89)

748. 22.06.1998     16th World Cup,  1st Round
**ROMANIA v ENGLAND  2-1**  (0-0)
*Municipal, Toulouse*

Referee:  Marc Batta (France)     Attendance:  35,000

**ENGLAND**:  David Andrew Seaman, Gary Alexander Neville, Anthony Alexander Adams, Sol Campbell, Darren Robert Anderton, Paul Emerson Ince (33 David Robert Beckham), Paul Scholes, David Batty, Graeme Pierre Le Saux, Alan Shearer (Cap), Edward Paul Sheringham (73 Michael James Owen).   Manager:  Glenn Hoddle

**ROMANIA**: Bogdan Stelea, Dan Petrescu, Gheorghe Popescu, Liviu Ciobotariu, Iulian Sebastian Filipescu, Constantin Gâlcă, Dorinel Munteanu, Gheorghe Hagi (Cap) (73 Ovidiu Stîngă, 84 Lucian Marinescu), Gabriel Popescu, Dinu Viorel Moldovan (87 Marius Lăcătuş), Adrian Bucurel Ilie.
Trainer: Anghel Iordănescu

**Goals**:  Dinu Viorel Moldovan (46), Dan Petrescu (88) / Michael James Owen (83)

749. 26.06.1998     16th World Cup,  1st Round
**ENGLAND v COLOMBIA  2-0**  (2-0)
*Felix-Bollaert, Lens*

Referee:  Arturo Brizio Carter (Mexico)     Attendance:  41,275

**ENGLAND**:  David Andrew Seaman, Gary Alexander Neville, Anthony Alexander Adams, Sol Campbell, Darren Robert Anderton (79 Robert Martin Lee), David Robert Beckham, Paul Emerson Ince (83 David Batty), Paul Scholes (73 Steve McManaman), Graeme Pierre Le Saux, Michael James Owen, Alan Shearer (Cap).     Manager: Glenn Hoddle

**COLOMBIA**:  Farid Camilo Mondragón, Wilmer Cabrera, Ever Antonio Palacios, Jorge Hernán Bermúdez, Luis Antonio Moreno, Mauricio Alberto Serna (46 Víctor Hugo Aristizábal), John Harold Lozano, Carlos Alberto Valderrama (Cap), Anthony William De Ávila (46 Hamilton Ricard), Freddy Eusebio Rincón, Léider Preciado (46 José Adolfo Valencia).
Trainer:  Hernán Darío Gómez

**Goals**:  Darren Robert Anderton (20), David Beckham (29)

750. 30.06.1998   16th World Cup,  2nd Round
**ARGENTINA v ENGLAND  2-2**  (2-2, 2-2)  (AET)
*Geoffroy-Guichard, Saint-Etienne*
Referee:  Kim Milton Nielsen (Denmark)    Att: 36,000
**ARGENTINA**:  Carlos Ángel Roa, Roberto Fabián Ayala, Matías Jesús Almeyda, José Antonio Chamot, Ariel Arnaldo Ortega, Nelson David Vivas, Diego Pablo Simeone (Cap) (91 Sergio Ángel Berti), Juan Sebastián Verón, Javier Adelmar Zanetti, Claudio Javier López (68 Marcelo Daniel Gallardo), Gabriel Omar Batistuta (68 Hernán Jorge Crespo).   Trainer:  Daniel Alberto Passarella
**ENGLAND**:  David Andrew Seaman, Gary Alexander Neville, Anthony Alexander Adams, Sol Campbell, Darren Robert Anderton (97 David Batty), David Robert Beckham, Paul Emerson Ince, Paul Scholes (78 Paul Charles Merson), Graeme Pierre Le Saux (71 Gareth Southgate), Michael James Owen, Alan Shearer (Cap).   Manager:  Glenn Hoddle
**Sent off**:  David Beckham (47)
**Goals**:  Gabriel Omar Batistuta (5 pen), Javier Zanetti (45) / Alan Shearer (10 pen), Michael James Owen (16)
**Penalties**:  1-0 Sergio Berti, 1-1 Alan Shearer, 1-1 Hernán Crespo (saved), 1-1 Paul Ince (saved), 2-1 Juan Sebastián Verón, 2-2 Paul Merson, 3-2 Marcelo Gallardo, 3-3 Michael Owen, 4-3 Roberto Ayala, 4-3 David Batty (saved)

751. 05.09.1998    11th European Champs Qualifiers
**SWEDEN v ENGLAND  2-1**  (2-1)
*Råsunda, Solna*
Referee:  Pierluigi Collina (Italy)    Attendance: 35,000
**SWEDEN**:  Magnus Hedman, Roland Nilsson, Patrik Jonas Andersson, Joachim Björklund, Pontus Kåmark (82 Teddy Lucic), Stefan Schwarz, Andreas Andersson (89 Daniel Andersson), Johan Mjällby, Fredrik Ljungberg, Henrik Larsson, Jörgen Pettersson.   Trainer: Tommy Söderberg
**ENGLAND**:  David Andrew Seaman, Gareth Southgate, Anthony Alexander Adams, Sol Campbell (75 Paul Charles Merson), Darren Robert Anderton (42 Robert Martin Lee), Paul Emerson Ince, Jamie Frank Redknapp, Paul Scholes (86 Edward Paul Sheringham), Graeme Pierre Le Saux, Michael James Owen, Alan Shearer (Cap).   Manager: Glenn Hoddle
**Sent off**:  Paul Ince (67)
**Goals**:  Andreas Andersson (30), Johan Mjällby (32) / Alan Shearer (2)

752. 10.10.1998    11th European Champs Qualifiers
**ENGLAND v BULGARIA  0-0**
*Wembley, London*
Referee:  László Vagner (Hungary)   Attendance: 72,974
**ENGLAND**:  David Andrew Seaman, Gary Alexander Neville, Gareth Southgate, Sol Campbell, Darren Robert Anderton (67 David Batty), Robert Martin Lee, Jamie Frank Redknapp, Paul Scholes (77 Edward Paul Sheringham), Andrew George Hinchcliffe (34 Graeme Pierre Le Saux), Michael James Owen, Alan Shearer (Cap).   Manager:  Glenn Hoddle
**BULGARIA**:  Zdravko Zdravkov, Radostin Kishishev, Valentin Naidenov, Ivailo Iordanov, Zlatko Yankov, Rosen Kirilov, Zlatomir Zagorcic, Ilian Iliev (62 Ilia Gruev), Milen Petkov, Hristo Stoichkov (60 Georgi Bachev), Marian Hristov (90 Georgi Ivanov).   Trainer:  Dimitar Dimitrov

753. 14.10.1998    11th European Champs Qualifiers
**LUXEMBOURG v ENGLAND  0-3**  (0-2)
*Josy Barthel, Luxembourg*
Referee:  Sotirios Vorgias (Greece)    Attendance: 8,200
**LUXEMBOURG**  Paul Koch, Ralph Ferron, Laurent Deville, Nico Funck, Frank Deville (84 Christian Alverdi), Daniel Theis (61 Luc Holtz), Jeff Strasser, Jeff Saibene, Patrick Posing, Manuel Cardoni, Marcel Christophe (78 Pablo Amodio).   Trainer:  Paul Philipp
**ENGLAND**:  David Andrew Seaman, Gareth Southgate, Rio Gavin Ferdinand, Sol Campbell, Philip John Neville, David Robert Beckham, Darren Robert Anderton (63 Robert Martin Lee), David Batty, Paul Scholes (76 Ian Edward Wright), Michael James Owen, Alan Shearer (Cap).   Manager: Glenn Hoddle
**Goals**:  Michael James Owen (19), Alan Shearer (40 pen), Gareth Southgate (90)

754. 18.11.1998
**ENGLAND v CZECH REPUBLIC  2-0**  (2-0)
*Wembley, London*
Referee:  Urs Meier (Switzerland)    Attendance: 33,535
**ENGLAND**:  Anthony Nigel Martyn, Martin Raymond Keown, Rio Gavin Ferdinand, Sol Campbell (Cap), Darren Robert Anderton, Paul Charles Merson (77 Lee Andrew Hendrie), David Robert Beckham, Nicholas Butt, Graeme Pierre Le Saux, Ian Edward Wright (71 Robert Bernard Fowler), Dion Dublin.   Manager: Glenn Hoddle
**CZECH REPUBLIC**:  Petr Kouba, Radoslav Látal (46 Martin Kotůlek), Tomáš Votava, Jiří Novotný (46 Roman Vonášek), Tomáš Řepka, Patrik Berger, Jiří Němec (Cap) (46 Miroslav Baranek), Radek Bejbl, Karel Poborský, Pavel Kuka (73 Radek Slončik), Vladimír Šmicer (46 Vratislav Lokvenc).   Trainer:  Jozef Chovanec
**Goals**:  Darren Robert Anderton (22), Paul Merson (40)

755. 10.02.1999
ENGLAND v FRANCE  0-2  (0-0)
*Wembley, London*
Referee: Hellmut Krug (Germany)    Attendance: 74,111
ENGLAND: David Andrew Seaman (46 Anthony Nigel Martyn), Lee Michael Dixon (72 Rio Gavin Ferdinand), Anthony Alexander Adams, Martin Raymond Keown (86 Jason Malcolm Wilcox), Graeme Pierre Le Saux, Darren Robert Anderton, Paul Emerson Ince, David Robert Beckham, Jamie Frank Redknapp (85 Paul Scholes), Michael James Owen (66 Andrew Alexander Cole), Alan Shearer (Cap). Caretaker Manager: Howard Wilkinson

FRANCE: Fabien Barthez, Lilian Thuram, Laurent Blanc (46 Frank Leboeuf), Marcel Desailly, Bixente Lizarazu, Didier Deschamps (Cap) (90 Vincent Candela), Zinedine Zidane, Youri Djorkaeff (83 Patrick Vieira), Emmanuel Petit, Robert Pires (46 Christophe Dugarry), Nicolas Anelka (83 Sylvain Wiltord).   Trainer: Roger Lemmere

Goals: Nicolas Anelka (69, 76)

756. 27.03.1999    11th European Champs Qualifiers
ENGLAND v POLAND  3-1  (2-1)
*Wembley, London*
Referee: Vitor Manuel Melo Pereira (Portugal)   Att: 73,836

ENGLAND: David Andrew Seaman, Gary Alexander Neville, Sol Campbell, Martin Raymond Keown, Graeme Pierre Le Saux, David Robert Beckham (78 Philip John Neville), Paul Scholes, Timothy Alan Sherwood, Steve McManaman (70 Raymond Parlour), Andrew Alexander Cole, Alan Shearer (Cap).   Manager: Kevin Keegan

POLAND: Adam Matysek, Tomasz Hajto, Tomasz Łapiński, Jacek Zieliński, Krzysztof Ratajczyk, Piotr Świerczewski (46 Tomasz Kłos), Jacek Bąk, Jerzy Brzęczek (Cap), Rafał Siadaczka (66 Wojciech Kowalczyk), Tomasz Iwan, Mirosław Trzeciak (83 Andrzej Juskowiak).   Trainer: Janusz Wójcik

Goals: Paul Scholes (11, 21, 70) / Jerzy Brzęczek (28)

757. 28.04.1999
HUNGARY v ENGLAND  1-1  (0-1)
*Népstadion, Budapest*
Referee: Lutz Michael Fröhlich (Germany)   Att: 40,000

HUNGARY: Gábor Király, Vilmos Sebők, György Korsós, János Hrutka, János Mátyus, Pál Dárdai, Gábor Halmai, István Pisont (46 József Somogyi), Tibor Dombi, Béla Illés, Attila Korsós (65 Norbert Tóth; 89 Miklós Herczeg). Trainer: Bertalan Bicskei

ENGLAND: David Andrew Seaman, Wesley Michael Brown (74 Michael Gray), Martin Raymond Keown, Rio Gavin Ferdinand (62 James Lee Carragher), Philip John Neville, David Batty, Nicholas Butt, Timothy Alan Sherwood, Steve McManaman (85 Jamie Frank Redknapp), Kevin Mark Phillips (83 Emile William Heskey), Alan Shearer (Cap). Manager: Kevin Keegan

Goal: János Hrutka (76) / Alan Shearer (22 pen)

758. 05.06.1999    11th European Champs Qualifiers
ENGLAND v SWEDEN  0-0
*Wembley, London*
Referee: José Maria Garcia-Aranda Encinar (Spain)
Attendance: 75,824

ENGLAND: David Andrew Seaman, Philip John Neville, Martin Raymond Keown (34 Rio Gavin Ferdinand), Sol Campbell, Graeme Pierre Le Saux (46 Michael Gray), David Robert Beckham (75 Raymond Parlour), Paul Scholes, David Batty, Timothy Alan Sherwood, Andrew Alexander Cole, Alan Shearer (Cap).   Manager: Kevin Keegan

SWEDEN: Magnus Hedman, Roland Nilsson, Pontus Kåmark, Patrik Jonas Andersson, Joachim Björklund, Stefan Schwarz, Håkan Mild (6 Niclas Alexandersson), Johan Mjällby (82 Daniel Andersson), Fredrik Ljungberg, Henrik Larsson (69 Magnus Svensson), Kennet Andersson.
Trainer: Tommy Söderberg

Sent off: Paul Scholes (51)

759. 09.06.1999    11th European Champs Qualifiers
BULGARIA v ENGLAND  1-1  (1-1)
*Balgarska Armia, Sofia*
Referee: Mario van der Ende (Holland)    Attendance: 25,000

BULGARIA: Dimitar Ivankov, Radostin Kishishev, Zlatomir Zagorcic, Stanimir Stoilov, Georgi Markov, Rosen Kirilov, Ilian Iliev (60 Daniel Borimirov), Milen Petkov, Stilian Petrov, Hristo Iovov (46 Martin Petrov), Hristo Stoichkov (73 Georgi Bachev).   Trainer: Dimitar Dimitrov

ENGLAND: David Andrew Seaman, Philip John Neville, Michael Gray, Gareth Southgate, Jonathan Woodgate (64 Raymond Parlour), Sol Campbell, David Batty, Jamie Frank Redknapp, Alan Shearer (Cap), Edward Paul Sheringham, Robert Bernard Fowler (81 Emile William Heskey).
Manager: Kevin Keegan

Sent off: Martin Petrov (58)

Goal: Georgi Markov (18) / Alan Shearer (13)

760. 04.09.1999    11th European Champs Qualifiers
**ENGLAND v LUXEMBOURG  6-0**  (5-0)
*Wembley, London*
Referee:  Sergei Shmolik (Belarus)    Attendance:  68,772
**ENGLAND**:  Anthony Nigel Martyn, Kieron Courtney Dyer (46 Gary Alexander Neville), Martin Raymond Keown, Anthony Alexander Adams (65 Philip John Neville), Stuart Pearce, Steve McManaman, David Robert Beckham (65 Michael James Owen), David Batty, Raymond Parlour, Alan Shearer (Cap), Robert Bernard Fowler.
Manager:  Kevin Keegan
**LUXEMBOURG**:  Philippe Felgen, Ralph Ferron, Manuel Schauls, Marc Birsens, Nico Funck, Jeff Saibene, Daniel Theis, Jean Vanek, Sacha Schneider (46 Christian Alverdi), Patrick Posing (82 Frank Deville), Marcel Christophe (62 Mikhail Zaritski).    Trainer:  Paul Philipp
**Goals**:  Alan Shearer (12 pen, 28, 34),
Steve McManaman (30, 44), Michael James Owen (90)

761. 08.09.1999    11th European Champs Qualifiers
**POLAND v ENGLAND  0-0**
*Wojska Polskiego, Warszawa*
Referee:  Günther Benkö (Austria)    Attendance:  15,000
**POLAND**:  Adam Matysek Tomasz Kłos (88 Jacek Bąk), Tomasz Wałdoch (Cap), Rafał Siadaczka, Jacek Zieliński, Tomasz Hajto, Radosław Michalski, Tomasz Iwan, Krzysztof Nowak, Radosław Gilewicz (63 Andrzej Juskowiak), Mirosław Trzeciak (58 Piotr Świerczewski).    Trainer:  Janusz Wójcik
**ENGLAND**:  Anthony Nigel Martyn, Gary Alexander Neville (13 Philip John Neville), Martin Raymond Keown, Anthony Alexander Adams, Stuart Pearce, Steve McManaman (79 Kieron Courtney Dyer), David Robert Beckham, Paul Scholes, David Batty, Alan Shearer (Cap), Robert Bernard Fowler (65 Michael James Owen).    Manager:  Kevin Keegan

762. 10.10.1999
**ENGLAND v BELGIUM  2-1**  (1-1)
*Stadium of Light, Sunderland*
Referee:  Anders Frisk (Sweden)    Attendance:  40,897
**ENGLAND**:  David Andrew Seaman (46 Anthony Nigel Martyn), Gareth Southgate, Anthony Alexander Adams, Martin Raymond Keown, Kieron Courtney Dyer (58 Philip John Neville), Paul Emerson Ince, Jamie Frank Redknapp, Frank James Lampard (76 Dennis Frank Wise), Stephen Andrew Guppy, Alan Shearer (Cap) (86 Emile William Heskey), Kevin Mark Phillips (58 Michael James Owen).
Manager:  Kevin Keegan
**BELGIUM**:  Geert De Vlieger (46 Ronald Gaspercic), Eric Deflandre, Jacky Peeters, Eric Van Meir, Davy Oyen, Yves Vanderhaeghe, Stefaan Tanghe (46 Johan Walem), Marc Wilmots (Cap), Nico Van Kerckhoven, Branko Strupar (74 Antonio Brogno), Gilles De Bilde.    Trainer:  Robert Waseige
**Goals**:  Alan Shearer (6), Jamie Frank Redknapp (67) /
Branko Strupar (14)

763. 13.11.1999    11th European Champs
– Qualification Play-Off
**SCOTLAND v ENGLAND  0-2**  (0-2)
*Hampden Park, Glasgow*
Referee:  Manuel Diaz Vega (Spain)    Attendance:  50,132
**SCOTLAND**:  Neil Sullivan, David Weir, Paul Ritchie, Christian Eduard Dailly, Edward Colin James Hendry (Cap), Craig William Burley, Barry Ferguson, Donald Hutchison, John Angus Paul Collins, William Dodds, Kevin William Gallacher (82 Mark Burchill).    Manager:  Craig Brown
**ENGLAND**:  David Andrew Seaman, Philip John Neville, Martin Raymond Keown, Anthony Alexander Adams, Sol Campbell, David Robert Beckham, Paul Scholes, Paul Emerson Ince, Jamie Frank Redknapp, Alan Shearer (Cap), Michael James Owen (67 Andrew Alexander Cole).
Manager:  Kevin Keegan
**Goals**:  Paul Scholes (21, 42)

764. 17.11.1999 11th European Champs,
Qualification Play-Off
**ENGLAND v SCOTLAND  0-1**  (0-1)
*Wembley, London*
Referee:  Pierluigi Collina (Italy)    Attendance:  76,848
**ENGLAND**:  David Andrew Seaman, Philip John Neville, Gareth Southgate, Anthony Alexander Adams, Sol Campbell, David Robert Beckham, Paul Scholes (90 Raymond Parlour), Paul Emerson Ince, Jamie Frank Redknapp, Alan Shearer (Cap), Michael James Owen (63 Emile William Heskey).
Manager:  Kevin Keegan
**SCOTLAND**:  Neil Sullivan, David Weir, Callum Iain Davidson, Christian Eduard Dailly, Edward Colin James Hendry (Cap), Craig William Burley, Barry Ferguson, John Angus Paul Collins, Neil McCann (74 Mark Burchill), Donald Hutchison, William Dodds.    Manager:  Craig Brown
**Goal**:  Donald Hutchison (38)

765. 23.02.2000
**ENGLAND v ARGENTINA  0-0**
*Wembley, London*
Referee:  Markus Merk (Germany)    Attendance:  74,008
**ENGLAND**:  David Andrew Seaman, Martin Raymond Keown (46 Rio Gavin Ferdinand), Gareth Southgate, Sol Campbell, Kieron Courtney Dyer (59 Philip John Neville), David Robert Beckham (73 Raymond Parlour), Paul Scholes, Jason Malcolm Wilcox, Dennis Frank Wise, Alan Shearer (Cap) (78 Kevin Mark Phillips), Emile William Heskey (79 Andrew Alexander Cole).    Manager:  Kevin Keegan

**ARGENTINA**: Pablo Oscar Cavallero, Roberto Fabián Ayala, Rodolfo Martín Arruabarrena (68 Nelson David Vivas), Roberto Néstor Sensini (35 Mauricio Roberto Pochettino), Diego Pablo Simeone, José Antonio Chamot, Cristián Alberto González, Javier Adelmar Zanetti, Juan Sebastián Verón, Gabriel Omar Batistuta (56 Hernán Jorge Crespo), Ariel Arnaldo Ortega (90 Gustavo Adrián López).
Trainer: Marcelo Alberto Bielsa

766. 27.05.2000
### ENGLAND v BRAZIL  1-1  (1-1)
*Wembley, London*

Referee: Ryszard Wojcik (Poland)     Attendance: 73,956

**ENGLAND**: David Andrew Seaman, Gary Alexander Neville, Martin Raymond Keown, Sol Campbell, Philip John Neville, David Robert Beckham, Paul Emerson Ince (59 Raymond Parlour, 90 Nicholas Jonathan Barmby), Paul Scholes, Dennis Frank Wise, Alan Shearer (Cap) (84 Robert Bernard Fowler), Michael James Owen (84 Kevin Mark Phillips).
Manager: Kevin Keegan

**BRAZIL**: Nélson de Jesus Silva "Dida", Marcos Evangelista de Moraes "Cafu", ANTÔNIO CARLOS Zago (81 ÉMERSON CARVALHO da Silva), ALDAIR Nascimento Santos, Sylvio Mendes Campos Júnior "Silvinho" (60 ROBERTO CARLOS da Silva), ÉMERSON Ferreira da Rosa, Carlos Campos CÉSAR SAMPAIO, José Roberto da Silva Júnior "Zé Roberto", RIVALDO Vitor Borba Ferreira, Márcio AMOROSO dos Santos (68 DENÍLSON de Oliveira), Francoaldo Sena de Souza "França".   Trainer: Wanderley Luxemburgo da Silva

**Goal**:  Michael James Owen (39) / "França" (45)

767. 31.05.2000
### ENGLAND v UKRAINE  2-0  (1-0)
*Wembley, London*

Referee: Lubos Michel (Slovakia)     Attendance: 55,965

**ENGLAND**: Anthony Nigel Martyn, Gareth Southgate, Anthony Alexander Adams, Sol Campbell, David Robert Beckham, Philip John Neville (73 Gareth Barry), Steve McManaman, Paul Scholes (73 Nicholas Jonathan Barmby), Steven Gerrard (81 Kieron Courtney Dyer), Alan Shearer (Cap), Robert Bernard Fowler (46 Emile William Heskey).
Manager: Kevin Keegan

**UKRAINE**: Vyacheslav Kernozenko (85 Maxim Levytskiy), Oleh Luzhniy, Yuriy Dmitrulin, Vladislav Vaschuk, Oleksandr Holovko, Serhiy Popov (71 Andriy Vorobei), Anatoliy Tymoschuk, Andriy Husyn, Serhiy Kandaurov (64 Hennadiy Moroz), Serhiy Rebrov, Andriy Shevchenko.
Trainer: Valeriy Lobanovskiy

**Goals**:  Robert Fowler (45), Anthony Alexander Adams (68)

768. 03.06.2000
### MALTA v ENGLAND  1-2  (1-1)
*National, Ta'Qali*

Referee: Stefano Braschi (Italy)     Attendance: 17,000

**MALTA**: Ernest Barry (90 Mario Muscat), Brian Said (77 Luke Dimech), Silvio Vella (41 Daniel Theuma), Darren Debono (33 David Camilleri), John Buttigieg (55 Jeffrey Chetcuti), Michael Spiteri (77 Ifeani Okonkwo), David Carabott (90 Adrian Ciantar), Carmel Busuttil (Cap) (46 Chucks Nwoko), Noel Turner (87 Nenad Veselji), Joseph Brincat (82 Jonathan Holland), Gilbert Agius (60 George Mallia).   Trainer: Josif Ilić

**ENGLAND**: Richard Ian Wright, Gary Alexander Neville, Martin Raymond Keown (59 Gareth Southgate), Sol Campbell, Philip John Neville, David Robert Beckham (80 Gareth Barry), Paul Scholes (69 Steve McManaman), Dennis Frank Wise (69 Paul Emerson Ince), Nicholas Jonathan Barmby, Alan Shearer (Cap) (51 Emile William Heskey), Kevin Mark Phillips (59 Robert Bernard Fowler).   Manager: Kevin Keegan

**Goals**:  David Carabott (27 pen) / Martin Raymond Keown (23), Emile William Heskey (75)

769. 12.06.2000     11th European Champs, 1st Round
### PORTUGAL v ENGLAND  3-2  (2-2)
*Philips, Eindhoven*

Referee: Anders Frisk (Sweden)     Attendance: 31,500

**PORTUGAL**: VÍTOR Manuel Martins BAÍA (Cap), ABEL Luís Silva Costa XAVIER, JORGE Paulo COSTA Almeida, FERNANDO Manuel Silva COUTO, DIMAS Manuel Marques Teixeira, PAULO Jorge Gomes BENTO, José Luís da Cruz Vidigal, Luis Filipe Madeira Caeiro "Figo", RUI Manuel César COSTA (84 Roberto Luís Gaspar Deus Severo "Beto"), JOÃO Manuel VIEIRA PINTO (75 SÉRGIO Paulo Marceneiro CONCEIÇÃO), Nuno Miguel Soares Pereira Ribeiro "Nuno Gomes" (90 Nuno Fernando Gonçalves Rocha "Capucho").
Trainer: Humberto Manuel de Jesus Coelho

**ENGLAND**: David Andrew Seaman, Gary Alexander Neville, Anthony Alexander Adams (82 Martin Raymond Keown), Sol Campbell, Philip John Neville, David Robert Beckham, Paul Emerson Ince, Paul Scholes, Steve McManaman (58 Dennis Frank Wise), Alan Shearer (Cap), Michael James Owen (46 Emile William Heskey).   Manager: Kevin Keegan

**Goals**:  Luis Filipe Madeira Caeiro "Figo" (22), JOÃO Manuel VIEIRA PINTO (38), Nuno Gomes (60) / Paul Scholes (3), Steve McManaman (18)

**770. 17.06.2000  11th European Champs, 1st Round**
**ENGLAND v GERMANY  1-0** (0-0)
*Communal, Charleroi*
Referee: Pierluigi Collina (Italy)    Attendance: 27,700

**ENGLAND**: David Andrew Seaman, Gary Alexander Neville, Martin Raymond Keown, Sol Campbell, Philip John Neville, David Robert Beckham, Paul Emerson Ince, Paul Scholes (72 Nicholas Jonathan Barmby), Dennis Frank Wise, Alan Shearer (Cap), Michael James Owen (61 Steven Gerrard). Manager: Kevin Keegan

**GERMANY**: Oliver Kahn (Cap), Markus Babbel, Lothar Herbert Matthäus, Jens Nowotny, Sebastian Deisler (72 Michael Ballack), Dietmar Hamann, Jens Jeremies (78 Marco Bode), Christian Ziege, Mehmet Scholl, Carsten Jancker, Ulf Kirsten (70 Paulo Roberto Rink).   Trainer: Erich Ribbeck

**Goal**: Alan Shearer (53)


**771. 20.06.2000  11th European Champs, 1st Round**
**ENGLAND v ROMANIA  2-3** (2-1)
*Du Pays, Charleroi*
Referee: Urs Meier (Switzerland)    Attendance: 27,000

**ENGLAND**: Anthony Nigel Martyn, Gary Alexander Neville, Martin Raymond Keown, Sol Campbell, Philip John Neville, David Robert Beckham, Paul Emerson Ince, Paul Scholes (81 Gareth Southgate), Dennis Frank Wise (75 Nicholas Jonathan Barmby), Alan Shearer (Cap), Michael James Owen (67 Emile William Heskey).   Manager: Kevin Keegan

**ROMANIA**: Bogdan Stelea, Cosmin Marius Contra, Gheorghe Popescu (Cap) (32 Miodrag Belodedici), Iulian Sebastian Filipescu, Cristian Eugen Chivu, Dan Petrescu, Constantin Gâlcă (68 Laurențiu Roşu), Dorinel Munteanu, Adrian Mutu, Dinu Viorel Moldovan, Adrian Bucurel Ilie (74 Ioan Viorel Ganea).   Trainer: Emerich Jenei

**Goals**: Alan Shearer (40 pen), Michael Owen (45) / Cristian Eugen Chivu (22), Dorinel Munteanu (48), Ioan Viorel Ganea (88 pen)


**772. 02.09.2000**
**FRANCE v ENGLAND  1-1** (0-0)
*Stade de France, Saint-Denis, Paris*
Referee: Juan Ansuategui Roca (Spain)    Attendance: 77,000

**FRANCE**: Bernard Lama, Lilian Thuram (80 Vincent Candela), Laurent Blanc (58 Frank Leboeuf), Marcel Desailly, Bixente Lizarazu, Didier Deschamps (Cap) (58 Patrick Vieira), Zinedine Zidane (65 Robert Pires), Youri Djorkaeff, Emmanuel Petit, Nicolas Anelka (46 Sylvain Wiltord), Thierry Henry (73 David Trézéguet).   Trainer: Roger Lemmere

**ENGLAND**: David Andrew Seaman, Sol Campbell, Anthony Alexander Adams (Cap) (46 Gareth Southgate), Martin Raymond Keown, Darren Robert Anderton (70 Kieron Courtney Dyer), David Robert Beckham, Gareth Barry, Dennis Frank Wise, Nicholas Jonathan Barmby (83 Steve McManaman), Paul Scholes (79 Michael James Owen), Andrew Alexander Cole. Manager: Kevin Keegan

**Goal**: Emmanuel Petit (64) / Michael James Owen (85)


**773. 07.10.2000  17th World Cup Qualifiers**
**ENGLAND v GERMANY  0-1** (0-1)
*Wembley, London*
Referee: Stefano Braschi (Italia)    Attendance: 76,377

**ENGLAND**: David Andrew Seaman, Gary Alexander Neville (46 Kieron Courtney Dyer), Anthony Alexander Adams (Cap), Martin Raymond Keown, Graeme Pierre Le Saux (77 Gareth Barry), Gareth Southgate, David Robert Beckham (83 Raymond Parlour), Paul Scholes, Nicholas Jonathan Barmby, Michael James Owen, Andrew Alexander Cole.  Manager: Kevin Keegan

**GERMANY**: Oliver Kahn, Marko Rehmer, Jens Nowotny, Thomas Linke, Carsten Ramelow, Dietmar Hamann, Marco Bode (87 Christian Ziege), Sebastian Deisler, Michael Ballack, Mehmet Scholl, Oliver Bierhoff (Cap).   Trainer: Rudolf Völler

**Goal**: Dietmar Hamann (14)


**774. 11.10.2000  17th World Cup Qualifiers**
**FINLAND v ENGLAND  0-0**
*Olympia, Helsinki*
Referee: Alain Sars (France)    Attendance: 36,210

**FINLAND**: Antti Niemi, Petri Helin (36 Juha Reini), Sami Hyypiä, Hannu Tihinen, Janne Saarinen (66 Janne Salli), Mika Nurmela, Jarkko Wiss, Simo Valakari, Jari Litmanen (Cap), Mikael Forssell (76 Shefki Kuqi), Jonatan Johansson.  Trainer: Antti Muurinen

**ENGLAND**: David Andrew Seaman, Philip John Neville, Gareth Southgate, Martin Raymond Keown (Cap), Gareth Barry (89 Wesley Michael Brown), Raymond Parlour, Paul Scholes, Dennis Frank Wise, Edward Paul Sheringham (69 Steve McManaman), Andrew Alexander Cole, Emile William Heskey.   Caretaker Manager: Howard Wilkinson

775. 15.11.2000
**ITALY v ENGLAND 1-0** (0-0)
*Delle Alpi, Torino*

Referee: Sándor Puhl (Hungary)   Attendance: 22,714

**ITALY**: Gianluigi Buffon, Fabio Cannavaro, Alessandro Nesta (67 Daniele Adani), Paolo Maldini (Cap) (74 Valerio Bertotto), Angelo Di Livio (52 Damiano Zenoni), Demetrio Albertini (52 Luigi Di Biagio), Gennaro Gattuso, Francesco Coco, Stefano Fiore, Filippo Inzaghi (72 Alessandro Del Piero), Marco Delvecchio (61 Simone Inzaghi).
Trainer: Giovanni Trapattoni

**ENGLAND**: David Benjamin James, Gary Alexander Neville, Rio Gavin Ferdinand, Gareth Southgate, Raymond Parlour (78 Darren Robert Anderton), Nicholas Butt (26 James Lee Carragher), David Robert Beckham (Cap), Kieron Courtney Dyer (83 Robert Bernard Fowler), Gareth Barry (83 Seth Art Maurice Johnson), Nicholas Jonathan Barmby, Emile William Heskey (73 Kevin Mark Phillips).
Caretaker Manager: Peter Taylor

**Goal**: Gennaro Gattuso (58)


776. 28.02.2001
**ENGLAND v SPAIN 3-0** (1-0)
*Villa Park, Birmingham*

Referee: Kyros Vassaras (Greece)   Attendance: 42,129

**ENGLAND**: David Benjamin James (46 Anthony Nigel Martyn), Philip John Neville (77 Gary Alexander Neville), Sol Campbell, Rio Gavin Ferdinand (46 Michael Ball), Chris Powell (46 Gavin McCann), David Robert Beckham (Cap) (46 Emile William Heskey), Nicholas Butt (46 Frank James Lampard), Nicholas Jonathan Barmby, Michael James Owen, Paul Scholes (46 Ugochuku Ehiogu), Andrew Alexander Cole.
Manager: Sven Göran Eriksson

**SPAIN**: Iker Casillas (64 José Santiago Cañizares), MANUEL PABLO García Díaz, Enrique Fernández Romero, ABELARDO Fernández Antuña (46 Francisco Jémez Martín "Paco"), UNAI Vergara Díez-Caballero, Iván Helguera, José Guardiola (81 Rubén Baraja), LUIS ENRIQUE Martínez García (Cap) (64 SERGI Barjuán), Gaizka Mendieta (64 Víctor Sánchez), RAÚL González Blanco (81 Joseba Etxeberría), Ismael Urzaiz (46 Javi Moreno).   Trainer: José Antonio Camacho

**Goals**: Nicholas Barmby (38), Emile Heskey (54), Ugochuku Ehiogu (70)


777. 24.03.2001   17th World Cup Qualifiers
**ENGLAND v FINLAND 2-1** (1-1)
*Anfield Road, Liverpool*

Referee: Valentin Ivanov (Russia)   Attendance: 44,262

**ENGLAND**: David Andrew Seaman, Gary Alexander Neville, Chris Powell, Steven Gerrard, Rio Gavin Ferdinand, Sol Campbell, David Robert Beckham (Cap), Paul Scholes, Andrew Alexander Cole (82 Robert Bernard Fowler), Michael James Owen (90 Nicholas Butt), Steve McManaman (72 Emile William Heskey).   Manager: Sven Göran Eriksson

**FINLAND**: Antti Niemi, Harri Ylönen (89 Petri Helin), Hannu Tihinen, Sami Hyypiä, Petri Pasanen, Joonas Kolkka (63 Shefki Kuqi), Mika Nurmela (63 Mikael Forssell), Jarkko Wiss, Aki Riihilahti, Jari Litmanen (Cap), Jonatan Johansson.
Trainer: Antti Muurinen

**Goals**: Michael Owen (44), David Beckham (50) /
Aki Riihilahti (26)


778. 28.03.2001   17th World Cup Qualifiers
**ALBANIA v ENGLAND 1-3** (0-0)
*Qemal Stafa Stadium, Tirana*

Referee: Alain Hamer (Luxembourg)   Attendance: 18,000

**ALBANIA**: Foto Strakosha, Ervin Fakaj, Geri Çipi, Arian Xhumba, Bledar Kola (82 Devi Muka), Altin Lala, Fatmir Vata (89 Altin Rraklli), Besnik Hasi, Arjan Bellai, Alban Bushi, Igli Tare (90 Ervin Skela).   Trainer: Medin Zhega

**ENGLAND**: David Andrew Seaman, Gary Alexander Neville, Ashley Cole, Nicholas Butt, Rio Gavin Ferdinand, Sol Campbell (29 Wesley Michael Brown), David Robert Beckham (Cap), Paul Scholes, Andrew Alexander Cole, Michael James Owen (84 Edward Paul Sheringham), Steve McManaman (46 Emile William Heskey).   Manager: Sven Göran Eriksson

**Goals**: Altin Rraklli (90) /
Michael Owen (73), Paul Scholes (85), Andrew Cole (90)

779. 25.05.2001
**ENGLAND v MEXICO  4-0**  (3-0)
*Pride Park, Derby*
Referee: Lucilio Cardoso Cortez Batista (Portugal)
Attendance: 33,697
**ENGLAND**: Anthony Nigel Martyn (46 David Benjamin James), Philip John Neville, Ashley Cole (46 Gareth Southgate), Rio Gavin Ferdinand (46 Joseph Cole), Martin Raymond Keown (46 Alan Smith), David Robert Beckham (Cap) (46 James Lee Carragher), Paul Scholes (46 Nicholas Butt), Steven Gerrard (46 Chris Powell), Michael James Owen (46 Michael Carrick), Emile William Heskey (67 Danny Mills), Robert Bernard Fowler (55 Edward Paul Sheringham). Manager: Sven Göran Eriksson
**MEXICO**: Oswaldo Sánchez, Claudio Suárez, Joaquín Beltrán (46 Duilio Davino), David Oteo, Hugo Chávez (46 Pavel Pardo), Marco Antonio Ruíz (58 Daniel Osorno), Alberto Coyote (78 David Rangel), Víctor Ruíz, Juan Pablo Rodríguez (83 Luis Ernesto Pérez Gómez), José Manuel Abundis, Antonio De Nigris.  Trainer: Enrique Meza
**Goals**: Paul Scholes (3), Robert Fowler (14), David Beckham (30), Edward Paul Sheringham (75).

781. 15.08.2001
**ENGLAND v HOLLAND  0-2**  (0-2)
*White Hart Lane, London*
Referee: Anders Frisk (Sweden)   Attendance: 35,238
**ENGLAND**: Anthony Nigel Martyn (46 David Benjamin James, 48 Richard Ian Wright), Gary Alexander Neville (46 Danny Mills), Ashley Cole (46 Chris Powell), James Lee Carragher, Wesley Michael Brown (46 Gareth Southgate), Martin Raymond Keown (49 Ugochuku Ehiogu), David Robert Beckham (Cap) (46 Michael Carrick), Paul Scholes (46 Frank James Lampard), Owen Hargreaves (46 Nicholas Jonathan Barmby), Robert Bernard Fowler (46 Michael James Owen), Andrew Alexander Cole (70 Alan Smith). Manager: Sven Göran Eriksson
**HOLLAND**: Edwin van der Sar (46 Ron Waterreus), Michael Reiziger, Jaap Stam (46 Mario Melchiot), Mark van Bommel (73 Denny Landzaat), Kevin Hofland, Giovanni van Bronckhorst, Boudewijn Zenden (46 Edgar Davids), Phillip Cocu (Cap) (80 Niels Oude Kamphuis), Marc Overmars (46 Roy Makaay), Patrick Kluivert (89 Pierre van Hooijdonk), Ruud van Nistelrooy (46 Jimmy Floyd Hasselbaink). Trainer: Louis van Gaal
**Goals**: Marc van Bommel (38), Ruud van Nistelrooy (39)

780. 06.06.2001    17th World Cup Qualifiers
**GREECE v ENGLAND  0-2**  (0-0)
*Olympiako Spyros Louis, Athina*
Referee: Rune Pedersen (Norway)   Attendance: 62,000
**GREECE**: Antónis Nikopolidis, Dimítris Mavrogenidis (70 Stélios Giannakópoulos), Panagiótis Fyssas, Giánnis Gkoúmas, Nikolaos Dabizas, Marínos Ouzounidis, Aggelos Basinás, Théodoros Zagorakis, Nikolaos Mahlas (65 Alexandros Alexandris), Giórgos Karagoúnis (24 Nikolaos Liberopoulos), Zísis Vrízas.  Trainer: Vasílis Daniíl
**ENGLAND**: David Andrew Seaman, Philip John Neville, Ashley Cole, Steven Gerrard, Rio Gavin Ferdinand, Martin Raymond Keown, David Robert Beckham (Cap), Paul Scholes (88 Nicholas Butt), Robert Bernard Fowler (80 Alan Smith), Michael James Owen, Emile William Heskey (75 Steve McManaman).  Manager: Sven Göran Eriksson
**Goals**: Paul Scholes (64), David Beckham (87).

782. 01.09.2001    17th World Cup Qualifiers
**GERMANY v ENGLAND  1-5**  (1-1)
*Olympiastadion, München*
Referee: Pierluigi Collina (Italy)   Attendance: 63,000
**GERMANY**: Oliver Kahn (Cap), Christian Wörns (46 Gerald Asamoah), Jens Nowotny, Thomas Linke, Marko Rehmer, Michael Ballack (67 Miroslav Klose), Dietmar Hamann, Jörg Böhme, Sebastian Deisler, Carsten Jancker, Olivier Neuville (78 Sebastian Kehl).  Trainer: Rudolf Völler
**ENGLAND**: David Andrew Seaman, Gary Alexander Neville, Ashley Cole, Steven Gerrard (78 Owen Hargreaves), Rio Gavin Ferdinand, Sol Campbell, David Robert Beckham (Cap), Paul Scholes (83 James Lee Carragher), Emile William Heskey, Michael James Owen, Nicholas Jonathan Barmby (65 Steve McManaman).  Manager: Sven Göran Eriksson
**Goals**: Carsten Jancker (6) / Michael Owen (12, 48, 65), Steven Gerrard (48), Emile Heskey (73)

783. 05.09.2001   17th World Cup Qualifiers
**ENGLAND v ALBANIA  2-0**  (1-0)
*St.James'Park, Newcastle*

Referee: Juan Antonio Fernández Marín (Spain)
Attendance: 51,046

**ENGLAND**: David Andrew Seaman, Gary Alexander Neville, Ashley Cole, Steven Gerrard (80 James Lee Carragher), Rio Gavin Ferdinand, Sol Campbell, David Robert Beckham (Cap), Paul Scholes, Emile William Heskey (54 Robert Bernard Fowler), Michael James Owen, Nicholas Jonathan Barmby (62 Steve McManaman).   Manager: Sven Göran Eriksson

**ALBANIA**: Foto Strakosha, Ervin Fakaj, Nevil Dede, Geri Çipi, Arian Xhumba, Arjan Bellai, Edvin Murati, Fatmir Vata, Besnik Hasi (46 Alban Bushi), Erion Bogdani (56 Igli Tare), Altin Rraklli (62 Devi Muka).   Trainer: Sulejman Demollari

**Goals**: Michael Owen (43), Robbie Fowler (88)


784. 06.10.2001   17th World Cup Qualifiers
**ENGLAND v GREECE  2-2**  (0-1)
*Old Trafford, Manchester*

Referee: Dick Jol (Holland)    Attendance: 66,000

**ENGLAND**: Anthony Nigel Martyn, Gary Alexander Neville, Ashley Cole (78 Steve McManaman), Steven Gerrard, Rio Gavin Ferdinand, Martin Raymond Keown, David Robert Beckham (Cap), Paul Scholes, Robert Bernard Fowler (67 Edward Paul Sheringham), Emile William Heskey, Nicholas Jonathan Barmby (46 Andrew Alexander Cole). Manager: Sven Göran Eriksson

**GREECE**: Antónis Nikopolidis, Hrístos Patsatzoglou, Panagiótis Fyssas, Nikolaos Dabizas, Leonídas Vokolos, Konstantinos Konstantinidis, Théodoros Zagorakis (56 Aggelos Basinás), Mihális Kasapis, Aggelos Harisatéas (73 Vasílis Lákis), Giórgos Karagoúnis, Thémistoklis Nikolaïdis (88 Nikolaos Mahlas).   Trainer: Otto Rehhagel

**Goals**: Edward Paul Sheringham (68), David Beckham (90) / Aggelos Harisatéas (36), Thémistoklis Nikolaïdis (70)


785. 10.11.2001
**ENGLAND v SWEDEN  1-1**  (1-1)
*Old Trafford, Manchester*

Referee: Claude Colombo (France)   Attendance: 64,413

**ENGLAND**: Anthony Nigel Martyn, Gary Alexander Neville (58 Danny Mills), James Lee Carragher (86 Philip John Neville), Rio Gavin Ferdinand, Gareth Southgate, Nicholas Butt (58 Daniel Murphy), Paul Scholes (86 Frank James Lampard), David Robert Beckham (Cap), Trevor Sinclair (58 Darren Robert Anderton), Emile William Heskey (58 Edward Paul Sheringham), Kevin Mark Phillips (58 Robert Bernard Fowler).   Manager: Sven Göran Eriksson

**SWEDEN**: Magnus Hedman (46 Magnus Kihlstedt), Johan Mjällby (62 Andreas Jakobsson), Michael Svensson, Christoffer Andersson, Erik Edman, Tobias Linderoth (46 Daniel Andersson), Niclas Alexandersson (84 Fredrik Söderström), Håkan Mild, Magnus Svensson (46 Anders Svensson), Marcus Allbäck, Zlatan Ibrahimovic (76 Yksel Osmanovski). Trainers: Tommy Söderberg & Lars Lagerbäck

**Goals**: David Beckham (28 pen) / Håkan Mild (44)


786. 13.02.2002
**HOLLAND v ENGLAND  1-1**  (1-0)
*Amsterdam ArenA*

Referee: Laurent Duhamel (France)   Attendance: 48,500

**HOLLAND**: Edwin van der Sar, Fernando Ricksen, Michael Reiziger, Frank de Boer (Cap) (67 Patrick Paauwe), Giovanni van Bronckhorst, Mark van Bommel (46 George Boateng), Ronald de Boer (59 Victor Sikora), Phillip Cocu (46 Edgar Davids), Marc Overmars (88 Roy Makaay), Ruud van Nistelrooy (64 Jimmy Floyd Hasselbaink), Patrick Kluivert. Trainer: Dick Advocaat

**ENGLAND**: Anthony Nigel Martyn (46 David Benjamin James), Gary Alexander Neville (77 Philip John Neville), Wayne Bridge (46 Chris Powell), Rio Gavin Ferdinand, Sol Campbell (46 Gareth Southgate), David Robert Beckham (Cap), Steven Gerrard (77 Frank James Lampard), Paul Scholes (77 Nicholas Butt), Darius Vassell (77 Joseph Cole), Emile William Heskey, Michael Ricketts (46 Kevin Mark Phillips).   Manager: Sven Göran Eriksson

**Goals**: Patrick Kluivert (26) / Darius Vassell (61)


787. 27.03.2002
**ENGLAND v ITALY  1-2**  (0-0)
*Elland Road, Leeds*

Referee: Herbert Fandel (Germany)   Attendance: 36,635

**ENGLAND**: Anthony Nigel Martyn (46 David Benjamin James), Danny Mills (46 Philip John Neville), Wayne Bridge (87 Gary Alexander Neville), Sol Campbell (46 Ledley King), Gareth Southgate (46 Ugochuku Ehiogu), David Robert Beckham (Cap) (46 Daniel Murphy), Nicholas Butt (46 Owen Hargreaves), Frank James Lampard (46 Joseph Cole), Trevor Sinclair (71 Edward Paul Sheringham), Emile William Heskey (46 Robert Bernard Fowler), Michael James Owen (46 Darius Vassell).   Manager: Sven Göran Eriksson

**ITALY**: Gianluigi Buffon, Christian Panucci (74 Francesco Coco), Marco Materazzi (57 Mark Iuliano), Alessandro Nesta (82 Daniele Adani), Fabio Cannavaro (Cap), Gianluca Zambrotta, Cristiano Doni (74 Damiano Tommasi), Luigi Di Biagio (57 Gennaro Gattuso), Cristiano Zanetti (57 Demetrio Albertini), Francesco Totti (46 Vincenzo Montella), Marco Delvecchio (74 Massimo Maccarone).
Trainer: Giovanni Trapattoni

**Goal**: Robert Fowler (68) / Vincenzo Montella (66, 90 pen)

**788. 17.04.2002**
**ENGLAND v PARAGUAY 4-0** (1-0)
*Anfield, Liverpool*
Referee: Cosimo Bolognino (Italy)    Attendance: 42,713
**ENGLAND**: David Andrew Seaman, Gary Alexander Neville (68 James Lee Carragher), Wayne Bridge (68 Philip John Neville), Steven Gerrard (46 Owen Hargreaves), Gareth Southgate (68 Edward Paul Sheringham), Martin Raymond Keown (46 Daniel Murphy), Nicholas Butt (46 Trevor Sinclair), Paul Scholes (46 Danny Mills), Darius Vassell (68 Frank James Lampard), Michael James Owen (Cap) (46 Joseph Cole), Kieron Courtney Dyer (46 Robert Bernard Fowler). Manager: Sven Göran Eriksson
**PARAGUAY**: Ricardo Javier Tavarelli Paiva, Denis Ramón Caniza, Celso Rafael Ayala, Carlos Alberto Gamarra Pavón (81 Julio César Cáceres), Francisco Javier Arce Rolón, Diego Antonio Gavilán Zárate (57 Pedro Alcides Sarabia Achucarro), Estanislao Struway Samaniego, Carlos Bonet Cáceres (82 Gustavo Eliseo Morínigo), Carlos Humberto Paredes, José Saturnino Cardozo (60 Richart Martín Báez), Roque Luis Santa Cruz Cantero.    Trainer: Cesare Maldini
**Goals**: Michael Owen (4), Daniel Murphy (47), Darius Vassell (55), Celso Ayala (78 og)

**789. 21.05.2002**
**SOUTH KOREA v ENGLAND 1-1** (0-1)
*World Cup 2002 Stadium, Seogwipo*
Referee: Ahmad Khalidi Supian (Malaysia)    Att: 39,231
**SOUTH KOREA**: Lee Woon-Jae, Song Chung-gug, Hong Myung, Choi Jin-Cheul, Kim Nam-II (90 Min-Sung Lee), Choi Tae-Uk (76 Cha), Lee Yong-Pyo, Yoo Sang-chul, Park Ji-sung, Seol Ki-hyeon (56 Ahn Hung-hwan), Lee Chun-Soo.
**ENGLAND**: Anthony Nigel Martyn (46 David Benjamin James), Danny Mills (68 Wesley Michael Brown), Ashley Cole (46 Wayne Bridge), Daniel Murphy (46 Joseph Cole), Rio Ferdinand (46 Martin Raymond Keown), Sol Campbell (46 Trevor Sinclair), Paul Scholes (46 Gareth Southgate), Emile William Heskey, Michael James Owen (Cap) (46 Edward Paul Sheringham), Owen Hargreaves, Darius Vassell. Manager: Sven Göran Eriksson
**Goal**: Park Ji-sung (52) / Michael Owen (25)

**790. 26.05.2002**
**CAMEROON v ENGLAND 2-2** (1-1)
*Kobe Wing Stadium, Kobe (Japan)*
Referee: Yoshitsugu Katayama (Japan)    Attendance: 36,424
**CAMEROON**: Boukar Alioum (78 Jacques Songo'o), Rigobert Song (69 Joseph Ndo), Raymond Kalla (56 Lucien Mettomo), Bill Tchato, Geremi Njitap (66 Nicolas Alnoudji), Pierre Wome (61 Pierre Njanka), Lauren Etame Mayer (60 Patrick Suffo), Vivien Foe (53 Eric Djemba-Djemba), Salomon Olembe (53 Daniel Ngom Kome), Samuel Eto'o (60 Joel Epalle), Patrick Mboma (66 Pius N'Diefe).
**ENGLAND**: Anthony Nigel Martyn (46 David Benjamin James), Rio Gavin Ferdinand (46 Martin Raymond Keown), Sol Campbell (46 Gareth Southgate), Wesley Michael Brown, Wayne Bridge, Paul Scholes (46 Danny Mills), Owen Hargreaves, Joseph Cole, Michael James Owen (Cap) (46 Edward Paul Sheringham), Emile William Heskey (46 Trevor Sinclair), Darius Vassell (77 Robert Bernard Fowler). Manager: Sven Göran Eriksson
**Goals**: Samuel Eto'o (5), Geremi Njitap (58) / Darius Vassell (12), Robert Fowler (90)

**791. 02.06.2002    17th World Cup, 1st Round**
**ENGLAND v SWEDEN 1-1** (1-0)
*Saitama Stadium 2002, Saitama (Japan)*
Referee: Carlos Simon (Brazil)    Attendance: 52,721
**ENGLAND**: David Andrew Seaman, Danny Mills, Ashley Cole, Rio Gavin Ferdinand, Sol Campbell, David Beckham (Cap) (63 Kieron Courtney Dyer), Paul Scholes, Michael James Owen, Emile William Heskey, Owen Hargreaves, Darius Vassell (74 Joseph Cole).    Manager: Sven Göran Eriksson
**SWEDEN**: Magnus Hedman, Olof Mellberg, Johan Mjällby (Cap), Tobias Linderoth, Niclas Alexandersson, Fredrik Ljungberg, Marcus Allbäck (80 Andreas Andersson), Henrik Larsson, Andreas Jakobsson, Teddy Lucic, Magnus Svensson (56 Anders Svensson).
Trainers: Tommy Söderberg & Lars Lagerbäck
**Goals**: Sol Campbell (24) / Niclas Alexandersson (59)

**792. 07.06.2002    17th World Cup, 1st Round**
**ENGLAND v ARGENTINA 1-0** (1-0)
*Sapporo Dome, Sapporo (Japan)*
Referee: Pierluigi Collina (Italy)    Attendance: 35,927
**ENGLAND**: David Andrew Seaman, Danny Mills, Ashley Cole, Rio Gavin Ferdinand, Sol Campbell, David Beckham (Cap), Paul Scholes, Michael James Owen (80 Wayne Bridge), Emile William Heskey (54 Edward Paul Sheringham), Owen Hargreaves (19 Trevor Sinclair), Nicholas Butt. Manager: Sven Göran Eriksson
**ARGENTINA**: Pablo Oscar Cavallero, Mauricio Roberto Pochettino, Walter Adrián Samuel, Juan Pablo Sorín, Javier Adelmar Zanetti, Diego Pablo Simeone, Juan Sebastián Verón (Cap) (46 Pablo César Aimar), Ariel Arnaldo Ortega, Diego Rodolfo Placente, Gabriel Omar Batistuta (60 Hernán Jorge Crespo), Cristián Alberto González (64 Claudio Javier López). Trainer: Marcelo Alberto Bielsa
**Goal**: David Beckham (44 pen)

793. 12.06.2002   17th World Cup,  1st Round
**NIGERIA v ENGLAND  0-0**

*Osaka Nagai Stadium, Osaka (Japan)*

Referee:  Brian Hall (USA)    Attendance: 44,864

**NIGERIA**: Vincent Enyeama, Joseph Yobo, Isaac Okoronkwo, Ifeanyi Udeze, Justice Christopher, Efe Sadje, Austin Okocha, Femi Opabunmi (86 Puis Ikedia), Benedict Akwuegbu, James Obiorah, Julius Aghahowa.

**ENGLAND**:  David Andrew Seaman, Danny Mills, Ashley Cole (85 Wayne Bridge), Trevor Sinclair, Rio Gavin Ferdinand, Sol Campbell, David Beckham (Cap), Paul Scholes, Michael James Owen (77 Darius Vassell), Emile William Heskey (69 Edward Paul Sheringham), Nicholas Butt.
Manager:  Sven Göran Eriksson

794. 15.06.2002 17th World Cup,  2nd Round
**ENGLAND v DENMARK  3-0**  (3-0)

*Big Swan Stadium, Niigata*

Referee:  Markus Merk (Germany)    Attendance: 40,582

**ENGLAND**:  David Andrew Seaman, Danny Mills, Ashley Cole, Trevor Sinclair, Rio Gavin Ferdinand, Sol Campbell, David Beckham (Cap), Paul Scholes (49 Kieron Courtney Dyer), Michael James Owen (46 Robert Bernard Fowler), Emile William Heskey (69 Edward Paul Sheringham), Nicholas Butt.   Manager: Sven Göran Eriksson

**DENMARK**:  Thomas Sørensen, Stig Tøfting (58 Claus Jensen), René Henriksen (Cap), Martin Laursen, Thomas Helveg (7 Kasper Bøgelund), Thomas Gravesen, Jesper Grønkjær, Jon Dahl Tomasson, Ebbe Sand, Niclas Jensen, Dennis Rommedahl.   Trainer: Morten Olsen

**Goals**:  Rio Ferdinand (5), Michael Owen (22), Emile Heskey (44)

795. 21.06.2002   17th World Cup,  Quarter-finals
**ENGLAND v BRAZIL  1-2**  (1-1)

*Shizuoka Stadium ECOPA, Shizuoka*

Referee:  Felipe Ramos Rizo (Mexico)    Attendance: 47,436

**ENGLAND**:  David Andrew Seaman, Danny Mills, Ashley Cole (80 Edward Paul Sheringham), Trevor Sinclair (56 Kieron Courtney Dyer), Rio Gavin Ferdinand, Sol Campbell, David Beckham (Cap), Paul Scholes, Michael James Owen (79 Darius Vassell), Emile William Heskey, Nicholas Butt.
Manager: Sven Göran Eriksson

**BRAZIL**: MARCOS Roberto Silveira Reis, Marcos Evangelista de Moraes "Cafu" (Cap), Lucimar da Silva Ferreira "Lúcio", José Vítor Roque Júnior, EDMÍLSON José Gomes de Moraes, ROBERTO CARLOS da Silva, GILBERTO Aparecido da SILVA, Ronaldo de Assis Moreira "Ronaldinho", José KLÉBERSON Pereira, RONALDO Luís Nazário de Lima (70 EDÍLSON da Silva Ferreira), RIVALDO Vitor Borba Ferreira.
Trainer:  Luiz Felipe Scolari

**Sent off**:  Ronaldo de Assis Moreira "Ronaldinho" (57)
**Goal**:  Michael Owen (23) / RIVALDO (45), "Ronaldinho" (50)

796. 07.09.2002
**ENGLAND v PORTUGAL  1-1**  (1-0)

*Villa Park, Birmingham*

Referee:  Tom Henning Ovrebo (Norway)    Att: 40,058

**ENGLAND**: David Benjamin James, Danny Mills (46 Wayne Bridge), Rio Gavin Ferdinand (46 Jonathan Woodgate), Gareth Southgate, Ashley Cole (46 Owen Hargreaves), Lee Bowyer (62 Trevor Sinclair), Steven Gerrard (46 David Dunn), Nicholas Butt (62 Daniel Murphy), Emile William Heskey, Alan Smith, Michael James Owen (Cap) (62 Joseph Cole).
Manager: Sven Göran Eriksson

**PORTUGAL**: VÍTOR Manuel Martins BAÍA (46 RICARDO Alexandre Martins Soares Pereira), Roberto Luís Gaspar Deus Severo "Beto" (46 Nuno Miguel Soares Pereira Ribeiro "Nuno Gomes"), Fernando José da Silva Freitas Meira (78 Luís JORGE Pinto da SILVA, FERNANDO Manuel Silva COUTO (Cap) (46 PAULO Renato Rebocho FERREIRA), SÉRGIO Paulo Marceneiro CONCEIÇÃO (46 NUNO Jorge Pereira Silva VALENTE), Armando Gonçalves Teixeira "Petit" (65 José Luís da Cruz Vidigal), RUI Manuel César COSTA (46 Luis BOA MORTE Pereira), RUI JORGE de Sousa Dias Macedo de Oliveira (46 Nuno Fernando Gonçalves Rocha "Capucho"), Luis Filipe Madeira Caeiro "Figo" (46 HUGO Miguel Ferreira VIANA), Pedro Miguel Carreiro Resendes "Pauleta" (46 JOÃO MANUEL PINTO Tomé Santos), "Simão" Pedro Fonseca Sabrosa (54 Francisco José Rodrigues Costa "Costinha").
Trainer: António Luís Alves Ribeiro Oliveira

**Goal**: Alan Smith (40) /
Francisco José Rodrigues Costa "Costinha" (79)

797. 12.10.2002   12th European Champs Qualifiers
**SLOVAKIA v ENGLAND  1-2**  (1-0)

*SK Slovan, Bratislava*

Referee:  Domenico Messina (Italy)    Attendance: 30,000

**SLOVAKIA**: Miroslav König, Marián Zeman, Peter Dzúrik, Peter Hlinka, Attila Pinte (89 Jozef Kožlej), Miroslav Karhan, Martin Petráš, Vladimír Janočko (89 Marek Mintál), Vladimír Leitner, Róbert Vittek (81 Ľubomir Reiter), Szilárd Németh.
Trainer: Ladislav Jurkemik

**ENGLAND**: David Andrew Seaman, Gary Alexander Neville, Ashley Cole, Steven Gerrard (77 Kieron Courtney Dyer), Jonathan Woodgate, Gareth Southgate, David Beckham (Cap), Paul Scholes, Emile William Heskey (90 Alan Smith), Michael James Owen (86 Owen Hargreaves), Nicholas Butt.
Manager: Sven-Göran Eriksson

**Goals**: Szilárd Németh (24) /
David Beckham (65), Michael Owen (82)

798. 16.10.2002    12th European Champs Qualifiers
**ENGLAND v MACEDONIA  2-2**  (2-2)
*Saint Marys, Southampton*
Referee: Arturo Dauden Ibáñez (Spain)    Attendance: 32,095

**ENGLAND**: David Andrew Seaman, Gary Alexander Neville, Ashley Cole, Steven Gerrard (55 Nicholas Butt), Jonathan Woodgate, Sol Campbell, David Beckham (Cap), Paul Scholes, Alan Smith, Michael James Owen, Wayne Bridge (58 Darius Vassell).    Manager: Sven-Göran Eriksson

**MACEDONIA**: Petar Miloševski, Robert Popov, Robert Petrov, Goce Sedloski, Aleksandar Vasoski, Veliče Šumulikovski, Vančo Trajanov (90 Milan Stojanoski), Aleksandar Mitreski, Goce Toleski (63 Goran Pandev), Artim Šakiri, Vlatko Grozdanovski.    Trainer: Nikola Džidži Ilievski

**Goals**: David Beckham (14), Steven Gerrard (36) /
Artim Šakiri (11), Vančo Trajanov (25)

799. 12.02.2003
**ENGLAND v AUSTRALIA  1-3**  (0-2)
*West Ham, London*
Referee: Manuel Enrique Mejuto González (Spain)
Attendance: 34,590

**ENGLAND**: David Benjamin James (46 Paul Robinson), Gary Alexander Neville (46 Danny Mills), Rio Gavin Ferdinand (46 Wesley Michael Brown), Sol Campbell (46 Ledley King), Ashley Cole (46 Paul Martyn Konchesky), David Beckham (Cap) (46 Owen Hargreaves), Frank James Lampard (46 Daniel Murphy), Paul Scholes (46 Jermaine Jenas), Kieron Courtney Dyer (46 Darius Vassell), James Beattie (46 Francis Jeffers), Michael James Owen (46 Wayne Rooney). Manager: Sven-Göran Eriksson

**AUSTRALIA**: Mark Schwarzer, Lucas Neill, Craig Moore, Tony Popovic (72 Tony Vidmar), Stan Lazaridis, Brett Emerton, Paul Okon (87 Kevin Muscat), Josip Skoko (46 Marco Bresciano), Scott Chipperfield (76 Vince Grella), Mark Viduka (85 Mile Sterjovski), Harry Kewell (56 John Aloisi).

**Goal**: Francis Jeffers (70) /
Tony Popovic (17), Harry Kewell (42), Brett Emerton (84)

800. 29.03.2003    12th European Champs Qualifiers
**LIECHTENSTEIN v ENGLAND  0-2**  (0-1)
*Rheinpark, Vaduz*
Referee: Giorgos Kasnaferis (Greece)    Attendance: 3548

**LIECHTENSTEIN**: Peter Jehle, Martin Telser, Fabio D'Elia, Daniel Hasler, Michael Stocklasa, Martin Stocklasa, Harry Zech (62 Franz Burgmeier), Ronny Büchel (86 Matthias Beck), Thomas Beck, Mario Frick (82 Thomas Nigg), Andreas Gerster. Trainer: Ralf Loose

**ENGLAND**: David Benjamin James, Gary Alexander Neville, Wayne Bridge, Steven Gerrard (66 Nicholas Butt), Rio Gavin Ferdinand, Gareth Southgate, David Beckham (Cap) (70 Daniel Murphy), Paul Scholes, Emile William Heskey (80 Wayne Rooney), Michael James Owen, Kieron Courtney Dyer. Manager: Sven-Göran Eriksson

**Goals**: Michael Owen (28), David Beckham (53)

801. 02.04.2003    12th European Champs Qualifiers
**ENGLAND v TURKEY  2-0**  (0-0)
*Stadium of Light, Sunderland*
Referee: Urs Meier (Switzerland)    Attendance: 47,667

**ENGLAND**: David Benjamin James, Gary Alexander Neville, Wayne Bridge, Steven Gerrard, Rio Gavin Ferdinand, Sol Campbell, David Beckham (Cap), Paul Scholes, Wayne Rooney (89 Kieron Courtney Dyer), Michael James Owen (58 Darius Vassell), Nicholas Butt.    Manager: Sven-Göran Eriksson

**TURKEY**: Rüştü Reçber, Fatih Akyel (78 Hakan Şükür), Bülent Korkmaz, Alpay Özalan, Ergün Penbe, Okan Buruk (59 Ümit Davala), Yıldıray Baştürk (70 Hasan Gökhan Şaş), Tugay Kerimoğlu, Emre Belözoğlu, Ilhan Mansız, Nıhat Kahvecı. Trainer: Şenol Güneş

**Goals**: Darius Vassell (75), David Beckham (90+2 pen)

802. 22.05.2003
**SOUTH AFRICA v ENGLAND  1-2**  (0-1)
*Durban*
Referee: Lim-Kee Chong (Mauritius)    Attendance: 48,000

**SOUTH AFRICA**: Brian Baloyi, Mbulelo Mabizela, Aaron Mokoena, Lucas Radebe, Thabang Molefe, Tebeho Mokoena (69 Jabulani Mendu), Macbeth Sibaya, Stanton Fredericks (77 Clement Mazibuko), Dleron Buckley, Benni McCarthy (67 Lesley Manyathela), Shaun Bartlett.

**ENGLAND**: David Benjamin James (46 Paul Robinson), Danny Mills, Rio Gavin Ferdinand (46 Matthew Upson), Gareth Southgate, Philip John Neville, David Beckham (Cap) (50 Jermaine Jenas), Steven Gerrard (82 Gareth Barry), Paul Scholes (75 Joseph Cole), Trevor Sinclair (58 Frank James Lampard), Emile William Heskey (65 Darius Vassell), Michael James Owen.    Manager: Sven-Göran Eriksson

**Goals**: Benni McCarthy (18) /
Gareth Southgate (1), Emile Heskey (64)

803. 03.06.2003
**ENGLAND v SERBIA & MONTENEGRO 2-1** (1-1)
*Leicester*
Referee: Paul Allaerts (Belgium)    Attendance: 30,900
**ENGLAND**: David Benjamin James, Danny Mills (62 James Lee Carragher), Matthew Upson (85 Gareth Barry), Gareth Southgate (46 John Terry), Ashley Cole (46 Wayne Bridge), Steven Gerrard (46 Jermaine Jenas), Paul Scholes (46 Owen Hargreaves), Philip John Neville (88 James Beattie), Frank James Lampard (62 Joseph Cole), Emile William Heskey (62 Darius Vassell), Michael James Owen (Cap) (46 Wayne Rooney).    Manager: Sven-Göran Eriksson

**SERBIA**: Dragoslav Jevrić (67 Dragan Žilić), Zoran Mirković (46 Nenad Brnović), Nemanja Vidić (82 Darko Kovačević), Dejan Stefanović (50 Mladen Krstajić), Slobodan Marković (68 Zoran Njeguš), Igor Duljaj (46 Branko Bošković), Nenad Kovačević (46 Nikola Malbaša), Boban Dmitrović (46 Goran Trobok), Saša Ilić (68 Predrag Mijatović), Zvonimir Vukić (46 Nenad Đorđević), Nenad Jestrović (74 Savo Milošević).
Trainer: Dejan Savičević

**Goals**: Steven Gerrard (35), Joseph Cole (83) / Nenad Jestrović (45)


804. 11.06.2003    12th European Champs Qualifiers
**ENGLAND v SLOVAKIA 2-1** (0-1)
*BT Cellnet Riverside, Middlesbrough*
Referee: Wolfgang Stark (Germany)    Attendance: 35,000
**ENGLAND**: David Benjamin James, Danny Mills (43 Owen Hargreaves), Ashley Cole, Steven Gerrard, Matthew Upson, Gareth Southgate, Frank James Lampard, Paul Scholes, Wayne Rooney (58 Darius Vassell), Michael James Owen (Cap), Philip John Neville.    Manager: Sven-Göran Eriksson

**SLOVAKIA**: Miroslav König, Michal Hanek, Marián Zeman, Martin Petráš, Vladimír Labant (38 Ondrej Debnár), Vladimír Janočko, Igor Demo (55 Marek Mintál), Radoslav Zabavník, Rastislav Michalík, Szilárd Németh (76 Ľubomir Reiter), Róbert Vittek.    Trainer: Ladislav Jurkemik

**Goals**: Michael Owen (62 pen, 73) / Vladimír Janočko (30)


805. 20.08.2003
**ENGLAND v CROATIA 3-1** (1-0)
*Portman Road, Ipswich*
Referee: Claus Bo Larsen (Denmark)    Attendance: 28,700
**ENGLAND**: David Benjamin James (46 Paul Robinson), Philip John Neville (81 Danny Mills), Rio Gavin Ferdinand (60 Matthew Upson), John Terry, Ashley Cole (60 Wayne Bridge), David Beckham (Cap) (60 Trevor Sinclair), Nicholas Butt (27 Frank James Lampard), Steven Gerrard (81 Daniel Murphy), Paul Scholes (60 Joseph Cole), Michael James Owen (60 Kieron Courtney Dyer), Emile William Heskey (76 James Beattie).    Manager: Sven-Göran Eriksson

**CROATIA**: Stipe Pletikosa (70 Tomislav Butina), Dario Šimić (46 Marko Babić), Stjepan Tomas, Robert Kovač, Josip Šimunić (72 Anthony Šerić), Boris Živković (71 Jasmin Agić), Jerko Leko (60 Đovani Rosso), Niko Kovač, Milan Rapaić (46 Darijo Srna), Marijo Marić (46 Ivica Mornar), Ivica Olić.
Trainer: Otto Barić

**Goals**: David Beckham (9 pen), Michael Owen (51), Frank Lampard (80) / Ivica Mornar (77)


806. 06.09.2003    12th European Champs Qualifiers
**MACEDONIA v ENGLAND 1-2** (1-0)
*Gradski, Skopje*
Referee: Frank de Bleeckere (Belgium)    Attendance: 20,500
**MACEDONIA**: Petar Miloševski, Goran Stavrevski, Vlatko Grozdanovski (56 Aguinaldo de Jesus Braga), Goran Pandev (47 Igor Gjuzelov), Igor Mitreski, Milan Stojanoski, Vančo Trajanov, Veliče Šumulikovski, Gjorgji Hristov (88 Dragan Dimitrovski), Artim Šakiri, Ilčo Naumovski.
Trainer: Dragan Kanatlarovski

**ENGLAND**: David Benjamin James, Gary Alexander Neville, Ashley Cole, Owen Hargreaves, John Terry, Sol Campbell, David Beckham (Cap), Frank James Lampard (46 Emile William Heskey), Wayne Rooney (74 Philip John Neville), Michael James Owen (84 Kieron Courtney Dyer), Nicholas Butt.    Manager: Sven-Göran Eriksson

**Goals**: Gjorgji Hristov (28) / Wayne Rooney (52), David Beckham (63)


807. 10.09.2003    12th European Champs Qualifiers
**ENGLAND v LIECHTENSTEIN 2-0** (0-0)
*Old Trafford, Manchester*
Referee: Knud Erik Fisker (Denmark)    Attendance: 64,931
**ENGLAND**: David Benjamin James, Gary Alexander Neville, Matthew Upson, John Terry, Wayne Bridge, David Beckham (Cap) (57 Owen Hargreaves), Steven Gerrard (57 Philip John Neville), Frank James Lampard, Wayne Rooney (67 Joseph Cole), James Beattie, Michael James Owen.
Manager: Sven-Göran Eriksson

**LIECHTENSTEIN**: Peter Jehle, Martin Telser, Michael Stocklasa (46 Sandro Maierhofer), Daniel Hasler, Christof Ritter, Martin Stocklasa, Roger Beck (56 Thomas Beck), Andreas Gerster, Fabio D'Elia (71 Ronny Büchel), Mario Frick, Franz Burgmeier.    Trainer: Walter Hörmann

**Goals**: Michael Owen (46), Wayne Rooney (50)

**808.  11.10.2003   12th European Champs Qualifiers**
**TURKEY v ENGLAND  0-0**
*Şükrü Saraçioglu, Istanbul*
Referee:  Pierluigi Collina (Italia)   Attendance: 45,000
**TURKEY**:  Rüştü Reçber, Ibrahim Üzülmez, Bülent Korkmaz, Fatih Akyel, Alpay Özalan, Emre Belözoğlu (80 Ergün Penbe), Okan Buruk (68 Ilhan Mansız), Tugay Kerimoğlu, Hakan Şükür, Nıhat Kahvecı, Sergen Yalçin (61 Tuncay Şanlı).
Trainer:  Şenol Güneş
**ENGLAND**:  David Benjamin James, Gary Alexander Neville, Ashley Cole, Steven Gerrard, John Terry, Sol Campbell, David Beckham (Cap), Paul Scholes (90+1 Frank James Lampard), Wayne Rooney (72 Kieron Courtney Dyer), Emile William Heskey (67 Darius Vassell), Nicholas Butt.
Manager:  Sven-Göran Eriksson

**809.  16.11.2003**
**ENGLAND v DENMARK  2-3**  (2-2)
*Old Trafford, Manchester*
Referee:  Vladimir Hrinak (Slovakia)   Attendance: 64159
**ENGLAND**:  David Benjamin James (46 Paul Robinson), Gary Alexander Neville (16 Glen Johnson), Matthew Upson, John Terry, Ashley Cole (46 Wayne Bridge), David Beckham (Cap) (66 Jermaine Jenas), Nicholas Butt (46 Philip John Neville), Frank James Lampard, Joseph Cole (76 Daniel Murphy), Wayne Rooney (66 Scott Parker), Emile William Heskey (46 James Beattie).   Manager: Sven-Göran Eriksson
**DENMARK**:  Thomas Sørensen, Thomas Helveg (46 Brian Priske), René Henriksen (Cap), Per Nielsen (71 Thomas Gaardsøe), Niclas Jensen, Morten Wieghorst (29 Daniel Jensen), Thomas Gravesen, Jesper Grønkjær (61 Peter Løvenkrands), Martin Jørgensen (84 Peter Madsen), Dennis Rommedahl (19 Kenneth Perez), Ebbe Sand (46 Jon Dahl Tomasson).   Trainer:  Morten Olsen
**Goals**:  Wayne Rooney (5), Joseph Cole (9) / Martin Jørgensen (8 pen, 30), Jon Dahl Tomasson (82)

**810.  18.02.2004**
**PORTUGAL v ENGLAND  1-1**  (0-0)
*Algarve, Faro*
Referee:  Viktor Kassai (Hungary)   Attendance: 28,000
**PORTUGAL**:  RICARDO Alexandre Martins Soares Pereira, PAULO Renato Rebocho FERREIRA (46 Luís MIGUEL Brito Garcia Monteiro), RUI JORGE de Sousa Dias Macedo de Oliveira (46 NUNO Jorge Pereira Silva VALENTE), JORGE Manuel Almeida Gomes de ANDRADE (75 RICARDO Alberto Silveira CARVALHO), FERNANDO Manuel Silva COUTO (83 Roberto Luís Gaspar Deus Severo "Beto"), Francisco José Rodrigues Costa "Costinha" (46 Anderson Luís de Souza "Deco"), Luis Filipe Madeira Caeiro "Figo" (Cap) (66 Luis BOA MORTE Pereira), Armando Gonçalves Teixeira "Petit" (83 HUGO Miguel Ferreira VIANA), Pedro Miguel Carreiro Resendes "Pauleta" (78 HUGO Miguel Pereira ALMEIDA), RUI Manuel César COSTA (61 TIAGO Cardoso Mendes), "Simão" Pedro Fonseca Sabrosa (46 Cristiano RONALDO Santos Aveiro).   Trainer: Luiz Felipe Scolari
**ENGLAND**:  David Benjamin James, Philip John Neville (46 Danny Mills), Gareth Southgate, Ledley King, Ashley Cole (17 Wayne Bridge, 86 Owen Hargreaves), David Beckham (Cap) (86 Jermaine Jenas), Nicholas Butt (86 James Lee Carragher), Paul Scholes (46 Kieron Courtney Dyer), Frank James Lampard (46 Joseph Cole), Michael James Owen (71 Emile William Heskey), Wayne Rooney (71 Alan Smith).
Manager:  Sven-Göran Eriksson
**Goals**:  Pauleta (71) / Ledley King (47)

**811.  31.03.2004   Swedish F.A. 100th Anniversary**
**SWEDEN v ENGLAND  1-0**  (0-0)
*Ullevi, Göteborg*
Referee:  Tom Henning Øvrebø (Norway)   Att: 40,464
**SWEDEN**:  Andreas Isaksson (46 Magnus Kihlstedt), Teddy Lucic, Olof Mellberg, Johan Mjällby (Cap) (46 Petter Hansson), Erik Edman, Mikael Nilsson, Anders Andersson (46 Tobias Linderoth), Anders Svensson (46 Kim Källström), Christian Wilhelmsson, Zlatan Ibrahimovic (90 Alexander Östlund), Johan Elmander (46 Mattias Jonson).
Trainers: Lars Lagerbäck and Tommy Söderberg
**ENGLAND**:  David Benjamin James, James Lee Carragher, Philip John Neville, John Terry (46 Anthony Gardner), Jonathan Woodgate (46 Gareth Southgate), Owen Hargreaves (60 Joseph Cole), Nicholas Butt (78 Scott Parker), Steven Gerrard (Cap) (60 Jermaine Jenas), Alan Thompson (60 Emile Heskey), Wayne Rooney (60 Alan Smith), Darius Vassell (12 Jermain Defoe).   Manager: Sven-Göran Eriksson
**Goal**:  Zlatan Ibrahimovic (54)

812.  01.06.2004    FA Summer Tournament
**ENGLAND v JAPAN  1-1**  (1-0)
*City of Manchester Stadium, Manchester*

Referee:  Roberto Rosetti (Italy)    Attendance:  38,581

**ENGLAND**:  David Benjamin James, Gary Alexander Neville (86 Philip John Neville), John Terry (88 Ledley King), Sol Campbell, Ashley Cole, David Beckham (82 Joseph Cole), Frank James Lampard (82 Nicholas Butt), Paul Scholes (77 Kieron Courtney Dyer), Steven Gerrard (82 Owen Hargreaves), Michael James Owen (77 Darius Vassell), Wayne Rooney (77 Emile Heskey).    Manager: Sven-Göran Eriksson

**JAPAN**:  Seigo Narazaki, Yuji Nakazawa, Tsuneyasu Miyamoto, Keisuke Tsuboi, Alessandro Santos, Shinji Ono, Junichi Inamoto (90 Fukunishi), Akira Kaji, Shunsuke Nakamura, Keiji Tamada (60 Takayuki Suzuki), Tatsuhiko Kubo (60 Atsushi Yanagisawa).

**Goal**:  Michael Owen (22) / Shinji Ono (53)


813.  05.06.2004    FA Summer Tournament
**ENGLAND v ICELAND  6-1**  (3-1)
*City of Manchester Stadium, Manchester*

Referee:  Jan Wegereef (Holland)    Attendance:  43,500

**ENGLAND**:  Paul Robinson (60 Ian Michael Walker), Gary Alexander Neville (46 Philip John Neville), Sol Campbell (46 Ledley King), James Lee Carragher (84 Jermain Defoe), Ashley Cole (46 Wayne Bridge), David Beckham (Cap) (46 Owen Hargreaves), Steven Gerrard(46 Kieron Courtney Dyer), Frank James Lampard (46 Nicholas Butt), Paul Scholes (46 Joseph Cole), Wayne Rooney (46 Emile Heskey), Michael James Owen (46 Darius Vassell).    Manager: Sven-Göran Eriksson

**ICELAND**:  Árni Gautur Arason, Ívar Ingimarsson, Indriði Sigurðsson (72 Jóhann Birnir Guðmundsson), Jóhannes Karl Guðjónsson (87 Auðun Helgason), Pétur Hafliði Marteinsson (46 Kristján Örn Sigurðsson), Heiðar Helguson (84 Tryggvi Guðmundsson), Hermann Hreiðarsson, Arnar Grétarsson, Eiður Smári Guðjohnsen (Cap), Þórður Guðjónsson (72 Hjálmar Jónsson), Helgi Sigurðsson (69 Bjarni Guðjónsson).    Trainer:  Ásgeir Sigurvinsson & Logi Ólafsson

**Goals**:  Frank James Lampard (25), Wayne Rooney (27, 38), Darius Vassell (57, 77), Wayne Bridge (68) / Heiðar Helguson (42)


814.  13.06.2004    12th European Champs, 1st Round
**FRANCE v ENGLAND  2-1**  (0-1)
*Estádio da Luz, Lisboa*

Referee:  Markus Merk (Germany)    Attendance:  62,487

**FRANCE**:  Fabien Barthez, William Gallas, Lilian Thuram, Mickael Silvestre (79 Willy Sagnol), Bixente Lizarazu, Robert Pires (75 Sylvain Wiltord), Claude Makélélé, Patrick Vieira, Zinedine Zidane (Cap), David Trézéguet, Thierry Henry.    Trainer:  Jacques Santini

**ENGLAND**:  David Benjamin James, Gary Alexander Neville, Ledley King, Sol Campbell, Ashley Cole, David Beckham (Cap), Frank James Lampard, Steven Gerrard, Paul Scholes (76 Owen Hargreaves), Wayne Rooney (76 Emile Heskey), Michael James Owen (69 Darius Vassell).    Manager:  Sven-Göran Eriksson

**Goal**:  Zinedine Zidane (90+1, 90+3pen) / Frank James Lampard (38)


815.  17.06.2004    12th European Champs, 1st Round
**ENGLAND v SWITZERLAND  3-0**  (1-0)
*Cidade de Coimbra, Coimbra*

Referee:  Valentin Ivanov (Russia)    Attendance:  28,214

**ENGLAND**:  David Benjamin James, Gary Alexander Neville, John Terry, Sol Campbell, Ashley Cole, David Beckham (Cap), Frank James Lampard, Steven Gerrard, Paul Scholes (70 Owen Hargreaves), Wayne Rooney (83 Kieron Courtney Dyer), Michael James Owen (72 Darius Vassell).    Manager:  Sven-Göran Eriksson

**SWITZERLAND**:  Jörg Stiel, Bernt Haas, Patrick Müller, Murat Yakin, Christoph Spycher, Raphaël Wicky, Fabio Celestini (53 Ricardo Cabanas), Benjamin Huggel, Hakan Yakin (83 Johan Vonlanthen), Stéphane Chapuisat (46 Daniel Gygax), Alexander Frei.    Trainer: Jakob Kühn

**Sent off**:  Bernt Haas (60)

**Goals**:  Wayne Rooney (23, 75), Steven Gerrard (82)


816.  21.06.2004    12th European Champs, 1st Round
**ENGLAND v CROATIA  4-2**  (2-1)
*da Luz, Lisboa*

Referee:  Pierluigi Collina (Italy)    Attendance:  57,047

**ENGLAND**:  David Benjamin James, Gary Alexander Neville, John Terry, Sol Campbell, Ashley Cole, David Beckham (Cap), Frank James Lampard (84 Philip John Neville), Steven Gerrard, Paul Scholes (70 Ledley King), Wayne Rooney (72 Darius Vassell), Michael James Owen.    Manager:  Sven-Göran Eriksson

**CROATIA**:  Tomislav Butina, Dario Šimić (67 Darijo Srna), Robert Kovač (46 Ivica Mornar), Boris Živković (Cap), Josip Šimunić, Đovani Rosso, Igor Tudor, Niko Kovač, Milan Rapaić (55 Ivica Olić), Dado Pršo, Tomislav Šokota.    Trainer: Otto Barić

**Goal**:  Paul Scholes (40), Wayne Rooney (45, 68), Frank James Lampard (79) / Niko Kovač (5), Igor Tudor (73)

817. 24.06.2004   12th European Championships – Quarter-Finals
**PORTUGAL v ENGLAND   2-2**  (0-1, 1-1)  (AET)
*da Luz, Lisboa*
Referee:  Urs Meier (Switzerland)   Attendance: 62,564
**PORTUGAL**:  RICARDO Alexandre Martins Soares Pereira, Luís MIGUEL Brito Garcia Monteiro (79 RUI Manuel César COSTA), RICARDO Alberto Silveira CARVALHO, JORGE Manuel Almeida Gomes de ANDRADE, NUNO Jorge Pereira Silva VALENTE, Francisco José Rodrigues Costa "Costinha" (63 "Simão" Pedro Fonseca Sabrosa), Nuno Ricardo de Oliveira Ribeiro "Maniche", Anderson Luís de Souza "Deco", Luis Filipe Madeira Caeiro "Figo" (Cap) (75 HÉLDER Manuel Marques POSTIGA), Cristiano RONALDO Santos Aveiro, Nuno Miguel Soares Pereira Ribeiro "Nuno Gomes".
Trainer:  Luiz Felipe Scolari
**ENGLAND**:  David Benjamin James, Gary Alexander Neville, John Terry, Sol Campbell, Ashley Cole, David Beckham (Cap), Frank James Lampard, Steven Gerrard (82 Owen Hargreaves), Paul Scholes (57 Philip John Neville), Wayne Rooney (27 Darius Vassell), Michael James Owen.
Manager:  Sven-Göran Eriksson
**Goals**:  Hélder Postiga (83), Rui Costa (110) / Michael Owen (3), Frank James Lampard (115)
**Penalties**:  0-0 David Beckham (missed), 1-0 Deco, 1-1 Michael Owen, 2-1 Simão Sabrosa, 2-2 Frank J. Lampard, 2-2 Rui Costa (missed), 2-3 John Terry 3-3 Cristiano Ronaldo, 3-4 Owen Hargreaves, 4-4 Maniche, 4-5 Ashley Cole, 5-5 Hélder Postiga, 5-5 Darius Vassell (saved), 6-5 Ricardo


818. 18.08.2004
**ENGLAND v UKRAINE   3-0**  (1-0)
*St. James' Park, Newcastle*
Referee:  Mike McCurry (Scotland)   Attendance: 35,387
**ENGLAND**:  David Benjamin James, Gary Alexander Neville (46 Glen Johnson), Ledley King, John Terry, Ashley Cole (60 James Lee Carragher), David Beckham (Cap), Frank James Lampard (73 Jermaine Jenas), Nicholas Butt (55 Shaun Wright-Phillips), Steven Gerrard (46 Kieron Courtney Dyer), Alan Smith (46 Jermain Defoe), Michael James Owen.
Manager:  Sven-Göran Eriksson
**UKRAINE**:  Oleksandr Shovkovskiy, Serhiy Fedorov, Andriy Rusol, Volodymyr Yezerskiy, Andriy Nesmachniy (64 Serhiy Kormiltsev), Anatoliy Tymoschuk, Oleh Shelayev, Andriy Vorobei, Ruslan Rotan (67 Serhiy Zakarlyuka), Oleh Husev (64 Oleksandr Radchenko), Andriy Shevchenko (Cap) (53 Andriy Voronin).   Trainer: Oleh Blokhin
**Goals**:  David Beckham (28), Michael James Owen (50), Shaun Wright-Phillips (72)

819. 04.09.2004    18th World Cup Qualifiers
**AUSTRIA v ENGLAND   2-2**  (0-1)
*Ernst-Happel-Stadion, Wien*
Referee:  Luboš Michel (Slovakia)   Attendance: 48,500
**AUSTRIA**:  Alexander Manninger, Joachim Standfest, Martin Stranzl, Martin Hiden, Emanuel Pogatetz, Gernot Sick, Dietmar Kühbauer, René Aufhauser (74 Markus Kiesenebner), Andreas Ivanschitz (Cap), Eduard Glieder (68 Roland Kollmann), Mario Haas (90 Mario Hieblinger).
Trainer:  Johann Krankl
**ENGLAND**:  David Benjamin James, Gary Alexander Neville, John Terry, Ledley King, Ashley Cole, David Beckham (Cap), Steven Gerrard (82 James Lee Carragher), Frank James Lampard, Wayne Bridge (84 Joseph Cole), Alan Smith (76 Jermain Defoe), Michael James Owen.
Manager:  Sven-Göran Eriksson
**Goals**:  Roland Kollmann (71), Andreas Ivanschitz (73) / Frank James Lampard (24), Steven Gerrard (64)


820. 08.09.2004    18th World Cup Qualifiers
**POLAND v ENGLAND   1-2**  (0-1)
*Śląski, Chorzów*
Referee:  Stefano Farina (Italy)   Attendance: 38,000
**POLAND**:  Jerzy Dudek, Michał Żewłakow, Jacek Bąk, Arkadiusz Głowacki, Tomasz Rząsa, Kamil Kosowski (80 Damian Gorawski), Mariusz Lewandowski, Sebastian Mila (63 Mariusz Kukiełka), Jacek Krzynówek, Maciej Żurawski, Grzegorz Rasiak (69 Andrzej Niedzielan).
Trainer:  Paweł Janas
**ENGLAND**:  Paul Robinson, Gary Alexander Neville (32 James Lee Carragher), John Terry, Ledley King, Ashley Cole, David Beckham (Cap) (89 Owen Hargreaves), Steven Gerrard, Frank James Lampard, Wayne Bridge, Jermain Defoe (87 Kieron Courtney Dyer), Michael James Owen.
Manager:  Sven-Göran Eriksson
**Goals**:  Maciej Żurawski (48) / Jermain Defoe (37), Arkadiusz Głowacki (58 og)


821. 09.10.2004    18th World Cup Qualifiers
**ENGLAND v WALES   2-0**  (1-0)
*Old Trafford, Manchester*
Referee:  Terje Hauge (Norway)   Attendance: 65,244
**ENGLAND**:  Paul Robinson, Gary Alexander Neville, Sol Campbell, Rio Gavin Ferdinand, Ashley Cole, David Beckham (Cap) (85 Owen Hargreaves), Nicholas Butt, Frank James Lampard, Wayne Rooney (87 Ledley King), Jermain Defoe (70 Alan Smith), Michael James Owen.
Manager:  Sven-Göran Eriksson

**WALES**: Paul Steven Jones, Mark Delaney, Daniel Gabbidon, Benjamin David Thatcher, Simon Davies, Jason Koumas (74 Robert Earnshaw), Craig Douglas Bellamy, Mark Anthony Pembridge (59 Carl Phillip Robinson), Gary Andrew Speed (Cap), Ryan Joseph Giggs, John Hartson.
Trainer: Mark Leslie Hughes
Goals: Frank James Lampard (4), David Beckham (76)

822.  13.10.2004   18th World Cup Qualifiers
**AZERBAIJAN v ENGLAND  0-1**  (0-1)
*Tofik Bahramov, Baku*
Referee: Alain Hamer (Luxembourg)   Attendance: 17,000
**AZERBAIJAN**: Dzhakhangir Hasanzade, Rafael Amirbekov, Avtandil Gadzhiev, Rashad Sadygov (Cap), Emin Guliyev, Kamal Guliyev (74 Ilgar Kurbanov), Mahir Shukuryov, Aslan Kerimov, Anatoli Ponomarev, Samir Aliyev (59 Kurban Kurbanov), Nadir Nabiyev (80 Rashad Abdullaev).
Trainer: Carlos Alberto Torres
**ENGLAND**: Paul Robinson, Gary Alexander Neville, Rio Gavin Ferdinand, Sol Campbell, Ashley Cole, Jermaine Jenas (72 Shaun Wright-Phillips), Nicholas Butt, Frank James Lampard, Michael James Owen (Cap), Wayne Rooney (85 Joseph Cole), Jermain Defoe (55 Alan Smith).
Manager: Sven-Göran Eriksson
Goal: Michael James Owen (22)

823.  17.11.2004
**SPAIN v ENGLAND  1-0**  (1-0)
*Santiago Bernabéu, Madrid*
Referee: Giórgos Kasnaferis (Greece)   Attendance: 48,000
**SPAIN**: Iker Casillas, Míguel Angel Salgado, Carlos Marchena (46 Pablo Ibáñez), Juan Gutiérrez "Juanito", Asier Del Horno, Joaquín Sánchez (78 Enrique Fernández Romero), Xavier Hernández "Xavi", Xabier "Xabi" Alonso (69 Pablo Orbáiz), José Antonio Reyes (57 Miguel Ángel Angulo), Fernando Torres (46 Albert Luque), RAÚL González Blanco (Cap) (46 José María Gutiérrez "Guti").   Trainer: Luis Aragones
**ENGLAND**: Paul Robinson, Gary Alexander Neville, Ashley Cole(76 Jermain Defoe), Rio Gavin Ferdinand (61 James Lee Carragher), John Terry (63 Matthew Upson), Nicholas Butt, David Beckham (Cap) (59 Shaun Wright-Phillips), Frank James Lampard (59 Jermaine Jenas), Wayne Bridge, Wayne Rooney (41 Alan Smith), Michael James Owen.
Manager: Sven-Göran Eriksson
Goal: Del Horno (9)

824.  09.02.2005
**ENGLAND v HOLLAND  0-0**
*Villa Park, Birmingham*
Referee: Peter Fröjdtfeldt (Sweden)   Attendance: 40,705
**ENGLAND**: Paul Robinson, Gary Alexander Neville, James Lee Carragher, Wesley Michael Brown, Ashley Cole, David Beckham (81 Kieron Courtney Dyer), Frank James Lampard (46 Owen Hargreaves), Stevan Gerrard (81 Jermaine Jenas), Wayne Rooney (60 Andrew Johnson), Michael James Owen, Shaun Wright-Phillips (60 Stewart Downing).
Manager: Sven-Göran Eriksson
**HOLLAND**: Edwin Van der Sar, Jan Kromkamp, Khalid Boulahrouz, Yoris Mathijsen, Giovanni van Bronckhorst, Denny Landzaat, Johnny Heitinga (62 Mark van Bommel), Rafael van der Vaart, Roy Makaay, Romeo Castelen (63 Ugur Yildirim), Dirk Kuijt.   Trainer: Marco van Basten

825.  26.03.2005   18th World Cup Qualifiers
**ENGLAND v NORTHERN IRELAND  4-0**  (0-0)
*Old Trafford, Manchester*
Referee: Wolfgang Stark (Germany)   Attendance: 65,239
**ENGLAND**: Paul Robinson, Gary Alexander Neville, John Terry, Rio Gavin Ferdinand, Ashley Cole, David Beckham (71 Kieron Courtney Dyer), Frank James Lampard, Steven Gerrard (71 Owen Hargreaves), Joseph Cole, Wayne Rooney (80 Jermain Defoe), Michael James Owen.
Manager: Sven-Göran Eriksson
**NORTHERN IRELAND**: Maik Stefan Taylor, Christopher Baird, Aaron William Hughes, Colin James Murdock, Anthony Capaldi, Tommy Doherty (58 Steven Davis), Keith Robert Gillespie, Damien Michael Johnson, Jeffrey Whitley (89 Andrew Kirk), Stuart Elliott, David Healy (89 Stephen Jones).
Manager: Lawrie Sanchez
Goals: Joseph Cole (47), Michael James Owen (51), Chris Baird (54 og), Frank James Lampard (62)

826.  30.03.2005   18th World Cup Qualifiers
**ENGLAND v AZERBAIJAN  2-0**  (0-0)
*St. James' Park, Newcastle*
Referee: Paulo Manuel Gomes Costa (Portugal)   Att: 49,046
**ENGLAND**: Paul Robinson, Gary Alexander Neville, Ashley Cole, John Terry, Rio Gavin Ferdinand (76 Ledley King), David Beckham (83 Jermain Defoe), Frank James Lampard, Joseph Cole, Steven Gerrard, Wayne Rooney (76 Kieron Courtney Dyer), Michael James Owen.   Manager: Sven-Göran Eriksson
**AZERBAIJAN**: Dmitriy Kramarenko, Rashad Sadygov, Aslan Kerimov, Rafael Amirbekov (46 Vugar Guliyev), Avtandil Gadzhiev, Ilgar Abdurahmanov, Zaur Gashimov, Rail Melikov, Elmar Bakhshiyev, Kurban Kurbanov (76 Anatoli Ponomarev), Nadir Nabiyev (76 Daniel Akhtiamov).
Trainer: Carlos Alberto Torres

Goals: Steven Gerrard (51), David Beckham (62)

827.  28.05.2005
**U.S.A. v ENGLAND  1-2**  (0-2)
*Soldier Field, Chicago*
Referee:  Benito Armando Archundia Tellez (Mexico)
Attendance:  47,637

U.S.A.:  Kasey Keller (Cap), Steven Cherundolo, George Edward Pope (73 Carlos Bocanegra), Cory Gibbs, Gregory Vanney, Steve Ralston (73 Robert Francis Convey), Kerry Zavagnin, Clinton Drew Dempsey (90 Clyde Simms), Landon Timothy Donovan, Joshua David Wolff, Brian John McBride (81 Conor Patrick Casey).   Trainer:  Bruce Arena

ENGLAND:  David Benjamin James, Glen Johnson, Wesley Michael Brown, Sol Campbell (46 Zat Knight), Ashley Cole (63 Jermain Defoe), Jermaine Jenas, Michael Carrick, Joseph Cole, Kieran Richardson (59 Philip John Neville), Alan Smith, Andrew Johnson (76 Luke Young).
Manager:  Sven-Göran Eriksson

Goals:  Clinton Dempsey (79) / Kieran Richardson (4, 44)


828.  31.05.2005
**COLOMBIA v ENGLAND  2-3**  (1-2)
*Giants, East Rutherford (USA)*
Referee:  Brian Hall (USA)    Attendance:  50,807

COLOMBIA:  Farid Camilo Mondragón, Hayder Palacios (72 Aldo Leao Ramírez), Luis Amaranto Perea, Mario Alberto Yepes (Cap) (81 Humberto Mendoza), Jair Benítez, Héctor Hugo Hurtado (46 Fabián Andrés Vargas), John Edwis Viáfara (60 Yulián Anchico), John Javier Restrepo (72 Oscar Díaz), Elkin Soto, Juan Pablo Ángel (60 Edixon Perea), Luis Gabriel Rey.   Trainer:  Reinaldo Rueda

ENGLAND:  David Benjamin James (46 Robert Green), Glen Johnson, Ashley Cole, Zat Knight, Philip John Neville, Michael Carrick, David Beckham (Cap) (72 Kieran Richardson), Jermaine Jenas, Peter Crouch (72 Jermain Defoe), Michael James Owen (72 Alan Smith), Joseph Cole (85 Luke Young).
Manager:  Sven-Göran Eriksson

Goals:  Mario Alberto Yepes (45), Aldo Leao Ramírez (78) / Michael Owen (36, 42, 58)


829.  17.08.2005
**DENMARK v ENGLAND  4-1**  (0-0)
*Parken, København*
Referee:  Tom Henning Ovrebo (Norway)     Att:  41,438

DENMARK:  Thomas Sørensen, Brian Priske, Per Nielsen (46 Michael Gravgaard), Daniel Agger, Niclas Jensen, Thomas Gravesen, Christian Poulsen (86 Daniel Jensen), Jesper Grønkjær (46 Dennis Rommedahl), Claus Jensen (72 Kenneth Perez), Martin Jørgensen (46 Thomas Kahlenberg), Jon Dahl Tomasson (64 Søren Larsen).   Trainer:  Morten Olsen

ENGLAND:  Paul Robinson (46 David Benjamin James), Gary Alexander Neville (46 Glen Johnson), Ashley Cole, John Terry (46 James Lee Carragher, Rio Gavin Ferdinand, Steven Gerrard, Jermaine Jenas, Frank James Lampard (64 Owen Hargreaves), David Beckham (Cap), Joseph Cole, Wayne Rooney, Jermain Defoe (46 Michael James Owen).
Manager:  Sven-Göran Eriksson

Goals:  Dennis Rommedahl (60), Jon Dahl Tomasson (63), Michael Gravgaard (67), Søren Larsen (90) / Wayne Rooney (87)


830.  03.09.2005     18th World Cup Qualifiers
**WALES v ENGLAND  0-1**  (0-0)
*Millenium, Cardiff*
Referee:  Brian Hall (USA)     Attendance:  70,795

WALES:  Danny Coyne, Richard Duffy, Robert Page (65 James Collins), Danny Gabbidon, Samuel Ricketts, David Partridge, Carl Fletcher, Carl Robinson (54 Jason Koumas), Simon Davis (70 Rob Earnshaw), Ryan Giggs (Cap), John Hartson.

ENGLAND:  Paul Robinson, Luke Young, Ashley Cole, James Lee Carragher, Rio Gavin Ferdinand, Steven Gerrard (85 Kieran Richardson), David Beckham (Cap), Frank James Lampard, Wayne Rooney, Shaun Wright-Phillips (68 Jermain Defoe), Joseph Cole (76 Owen Hargreaves).
Manager:  Sven-Göran Eriksson

Goal:  Joseph Cole (53)


831.  07.09.2005     18th World Cup Qualifiers
**NORTHERN IRELAND v ENGLAND  1-0**  (0-0)
*Windsor Park, Belfast*
Referee:  Brian Hall (USA)     Attendance:  14,000

NORTHERN IRELAND:  Maik Stefan Taylor, Christopher Baird, Anthony Capaldi, Stephen Craigan, Steven Davis, Keith Robert Gillespie, Damien Michael Johnson, David Healy (85 Ivan Sproule), Stephen James Quinn (78 Warren Feeney), Stuart Elliott (90 Michael Duff), Aaron Hughes (Cap).
Manager:  Lawrie Sanchez

ENGLAND:  Paul Robinson, Luke Young, Ashley Cole, Rio Gavin Ferdinand, James Lee Carragher, Steven Gerrard (76 Jermain Defoe), David Beckham (Cap), Frank James Lampard (81 Owen Hargreaves), Wayne Rooney, Michael James Owen, Shaun Wright-Phillips (54 Joseph Cole).
Manager:  Sven-Göran Eriksson

Goal:  David Healy (73)

832. 08.10.2005   18th World Cup Qualifiers
**ENGLAND v AUSTRIA  1-0** (1-0)
*Old Trafford, Manchester*

Referee: Luis Medina Cantalejo (Spain)

ENGLAND: Paul Robinson, Luke Young, James Lee Carragher, Steven Gerrard, John Terry, Sol Campbell (64 Rio Gavin Ferdinand), David Beckham (Cap), Frank James Lampard, Peter Crouch, Michael James Owen (81 Kieran Richardson), Joseph Cole (61 Ledley King).
Manager: Sven-Göran Eriksson

AUSTRIA: Jürgen Macho, Andreas Dober, Martin Stranzl, Paul Scharner, Andreas Ibertsberger (80 Andreas Lasnik), René Aufhauser, Markus Schopp (63 Saniel Kuljic), Markus Kiesenebner, Roland Linz, Andreas Ivanschitz, Markus Weissenberger (46 Yüksel Sariyar).
Trainer: Willibald Ruttensteiner

**Sent off:** David Beckham (58)

**Goal:** Frank Lampard (24 pen)


833. 12.10.2005   18th World Cup Qualifiers
**ENGLAND v POLAND  2-1** (1-1)
*Old Trafford, Manchester*

Referee: Kim Milton Nielsen (Denmark)

ENGLAND: Paul Robinson, Luke Young, James Lee Carragher, Ledley King, Rio Gavin Ferdinand, John Terry, Shaun Wright-Phillips (66 Peter Crouch), Frank James Lampard, Wayne Rooney, Michael James Owen (83 Jermaine Jenas), Joseph Cole (86 Alan Smith).
Manager: Sven-Göran Eriksson

POLAND: Artur Boruc, Marcin Baszczyński, Jacek Bąk (Cap), Mariusz Jop, Michał Żewłakow, Kamil Kosowski, Mariusz Lewandowski, Euzebiusz Smolarek (46 Jacek Krzynówek), Radosław Sobolewski (80 Arkadiusz Radomski), Grzegorz Rasiak, Maciej Żurawski (39 Tomasz Frankowski).
Trainer: Pawel Janas

**Goal:** Michael James Owen (44), Frank Lampard (80) / Tomasz Frankowski (45)


834. 12.11.2005
**ARGENTINA v ENGLAND  2-3** (1-1)
*Stade de Genève, Genève (Switzerland)*

Referee: Philippe Leuba (Switzerland)   Attendance: 29,000

ARGENTINA: Roberto Carlos Abbondanzieri, Javier Adelmar Zanetti, Roberto Fabián Ayala (74 Fabricio Coloccini), Walter Adrián Samuel, Juan Pablo Sorín, Martín Gastón Demichelis, Esteban Matías Cambiasso, Maximiliano Rubén Rodríguez, Juan Román Riquelme (84 Luis Oscar González), Carlos Alberto Tévez (86 Julio Ricardo Cruz), Hernán Jorge Crespo (70 Javier Pedro Saviola).
Trainer: José Néstor Pekerman

ENGLAND: Paul Robinson, Luke Young (82 Peter Crouch), John Terry, Rio Gavin Ferdinand, Wayne Bridge (46 Paul Martyn Konchesky), David Beckham, Ledley King (57 Joseph Cole), Steven Gerrard, Frank James Lampard, Wayne Rooney, Michael James Owen.   Manager: Sven-Göran Eriksson

**Goals:** Hernán Crespo (34), Walter Adrián Samuel (53) / Wayne Rooney (39), Michael James Owen (88, 90)


835. 01.03.2006
**ENGLAND v URUGUAY  2-1** (0-1)
*Anfield Road, Liverpool*

Referee: Stefano Farina (Italy)   Attendance: 40,013

ENGLAND: Paul Robinson, Gary Neville, Rio Gavin Ferdinand, John Terry (46 Ledley King), Wayne Bridge (28 Jamie Carragher), David Beckham (63 Shaun Wright-Phillips), Steven Gerrard (46 Jermaine Jenas), Michael Carrick, Joseph Cole, Wayne Rooney (63 Peter Crouch), Darren Bent.
Manager: Sven-Göran Eriksson

URUGUAY: Héctor Farbián Carini (46 Mario Sebastián Viera), Carlos Andrés Diogo, Diego Alfredo Lugano (Cap), Diego Roberto Godín, Pablo Martín Lima, Diego Fernando Pérez (88 Ignacio María González), Omar Heber Pouso, Gustavo Antonio Varela (90 Carlos Adrian Valdez), Gonzalo Vargas (76 Victorio Maximiliano Pereira), Diego Forlán (86 Alexander Jesús Medina), Mario Ignacio Regueiro (83 Jorge Andrés Martínez).   Trainer: Gustavo Ferrín

**Goals:** Peter Crouch (75), Joseph Cole (90) / Omar Heber Pouso (26)


836. 30.05.2006
**ENGLAND v HUNGARY  3-1** (0-0)
*Old Trafford, Manchester*

Referee: Pieter Vink (Holland)   Attendance: 56,323

ENGLAND: Paul Robinson, Gary Neville (46 Owen Hargreaves), Rio Ferdinand, John Terry (76 Sol Campbell), Ashley Cole, Jamie Carragher, David Beckham (Cap), Frank Lampard, Joseph Cole, Steven Gerrard (65 Peter Crouch), Michael Owen (65 Theo Walcott).
Manager: Sven-Göran Eriksson

HUNGARY: Gábor Király, Csaba Fehér, László Éger, Ádám Komlósi (9 Vilmos Vanczák), Péter Halmosi, Balázs Molnár (83 Krisztián Vadócz), Pál Dárdai (Cap), Balázs Tóth (62 Sándor Torghelle), Zoltán Gera, Szabolcs Huszti, Imre Szabics (73 Attila Polonkai).   Trainer: Péter Bozsik

**Goals:** Steven Gerrard (47), John Terry (51), Peter Crouch (84) / Pál Dárdai (55)

837. 30.05.2006
**ENGLAND v JAMAICA 6-0** (4-0)
*Old Trafford, Manchester*
Referee: Konrad Plautz (Austria)   Attendance: 56,323

**ENGLAND**: Paul Robinson (46 David Benjamin James), Jamie Carragher, Rio Ferdinand, John Terry (31 Sol Campbell), Ashley Cole (35 Wayne Bridge), David Beckham (68 Aaron Lennon), Frank Lampard (68 Michael Carrick), Steven Gerrard (78 Stewart Downing), Joseph Cole, Peter Crouch, Michael Owen.   Manager: Sven-Göran Eriksson

**JAMAICA**: Donovan Ricketts, Garfield Reid, Claude Davis, Damion Stewart, Omar Daley, Jermaine Hue (85 Jermaine Johnson), Jermaine Taylor (46 Shane Crawford), Jason Euell (79 Khari Stephenson), Jamal Campbell-Ryce, Luton Shelton (48 Deon Burton), Ricardo Fuller (76 Theodor Bennett). Trainer: Wendell Downswell

**Goals**: Frank Lampard (11), Jermaine Taylor (17 og), Peter Crouch (29, 65, 89), Michael Owen (32)


838. 10.06.2006   18th World Cup, 1st Round
**ENGLAND v PARAGUAY 1-0** (1-0)
*Frankenstadion, Frankfurt/Main*
Referee: Marco Antonio Rodríguez (Mexico)   Att: 48,000

**ENGLAND**: Paul Robinson, Gary Neville, Rio Ferdinand, John Terry, Ashley Cole, David Beckham (Cap), Frank Lampard, Steven Gerrard, Joseph Cole (83 Owen Hargreaves), Peter Crouch, Michael Owen (56 Stewart Downing). Manager: Sven-Göran Eriksson

**PARAGUAY**: Justo Wilmar Villar Viveros (8 Aldo Antonio Bobadilla), Denis Ramón Caniza, Julio César Cáceres, Carlos Alberto Gamarra Pavón (Cap), Delio César Toledo (82 Jorge Martín Núñez), Carlos Bonet Cáceres (68 Nelson Rafael Cuevas Amarilla), Roberto Miguel Acuña Cabello, Carlos Humberto Paredes, Cristián Miguel Riveros Núñez, Roque Luis Santa Cruz Cantero, Nelson Antonio Haedo Valdéz. Trainer: Aníbal Ruíz Leites


839. 15.06.2006   18th World Cup, 1st Round
**ENGLAND v TRINIDAD & TOBAGO 2-0** (0-0)
*Frankenstadion, Frankfurt/Main*
Referee: Toru Kamikawa (Japan)   Attendance: 41,000

**ENGLAND**: Paul Robinson, Jamie Carragher, Rio Ferdinand, John Terry, Ashley Cole, David Beckham (Cap), Frank Lampard, Steven Gerrard, Joseph Cole (75 Stewart Downing), Peter Crouch, Michael Owen (58 Wayne Rooney). Manager: Sven-Göran Eriksson

**TRINIDAD & TOBAGO**: Shaka Hislop, Cyd Gray, Dennis Lawrence, Brent Sancho, Christopher Birchall, Carlos Edwards, Densill Theobald (85 Evans Wise), Aurtis Whitley, Stern John, Kenwyne Jones (70 Cornell Glen), Dwight Yorke (Cap). Trainer: Leo Beenhakker

**Goals**: Peter Crouch (83), Steven Gerrard (90)


840. 20.06.2006   18th World Cup, 1st Round
**ENGLAND v SWEDEN 2-2** (1-0)
*RheinEnergieStadion, Köln*
Referee: Massimo Busacca (Switzerland)   Att: 45,000

**ENGLAND**: Paul Robinson, Jamie Carragher, Rio Ferdinand (56 Sol Campbell), John Terry, Ashley Cole, David Beckham (Cap), Owen Hargreaves, Frank Lampard, Joseph Cole; Wayne Rooney (69 Steven Gerrard), Michael Owen (4 Peter Crouch). Manager: Sven-Göran Eriksson

**SWEDEN**: Andreas Isaksson; Niclas Alexandersson, Olof Mellberg (Cap), Teddy Lucic, Erik Edman; Mattias Jonson (54 Christian Wilhelmsson), Tobias Linderoth (90 Daniel Andersson), Kim Källström, Fredrik Ljungberg, Marcus Allbäck (75 Johan Elmander), Henrik Larsson. Trainer: Lars Lagerbäck

**Goals**: Marcus Allbäck (51), Henrik Larsson (90) / Joseph Cole (34), Steven Gerrard (85)


841. 25.06.2006   18th World Cup, 2nd Round
**ENGLAND v ECUADOR 1-0** (0-0)
*Gottlieb-Daimler-Stadion, Stuttgart*
Referee: Frank De Bleeckere (Belgium)   Attendance: 52,000

**ENGLAND**: Paul Robinson, Owen Hargreaves, Rio Ferdinand, John Terry, Ashley Cole, David Beckham (Cap) (87 Aaron Lennon), Frank Lampard, Michael Carrick, Steven Gerrard (90 Stewart Downing), Joseph Cole (77 Jamie Carragher), Wayne Rooney.   Manager: Sven-Göran Eriksson

**ECUADOR**: Christian Rafael Mora, Ulises de la Cruz, Ivan Jacinto Hurtado (Cap), Giovanny Patricio Espinoza, Néicer Reasco, Edison Vicente Méndez, Edwin Rolando Tenorio (69 Cristian Rolando Lara), Segundo Alejandro Castillo, Luis Antonio Valencia, Agustín Javier Delgado, Carlos Tenorio (71 Iván Kaviedes).   Trainer: Luis Fernando Suárez

**Goal**: David Beckham (60)


842. 01.07.2006   18th World Cup, Quarter-Finals
**ENGLAND v PORTUGAL 0-0** (AET)
*Veltins-Arena, Gelsenkirchen*
Referee: Horacio Elizondo (Argentina)   Attendance: 52,000

**ENGLAND**: Paul Robinson, Gary Neville, Rio Ferdinand, John Terry, Ashley Cole, Owen Hargreaves; David Beckham (Cap) (52 Aaron Lennon, 119 Jamie Carragher), Frank Lampard, Steven Gerrard, Joseph Cole (65 Peter Crouch), Wayne Rooney.   Manager: Sven-Göran Eriksson

PORTUGAL: RICARDO Alexandre Martins Soares Pereira, Miguel Monteiro, Fernando José da Silva Freitas Meira, RICARDO Alberto Silveira CARVALHO, NUNO Jorge Pereira Silva VALENTE, Armando Teixeira 'Petit', Nuno Ribeiro de Oliveira Ribeiro "Maniche'", Cristiano RONALDO Santos Aveiro, Tiago Cardoso Mendes (74 HUGO Miguel Ferreira VIANA), Luís Filipe Madeira Caeiro "Figo" (Cap) (86 HÉLDER Manuel Marques POSTIGA), Pedro Resendes 'Pauleta' (63 "Simão" Pedro Fonseca Sabrosa).   Trainer:   Luiz Felipe Scolari

Penalties:  1-0 Simão Sabrosa, 1-0 Frank J. Lampard (saved), 1-0 Hugo Viana (missed), 1-1 Owen Hargreaves, 1-1 Armando Teixeira 'Petit' (miss), 1-1 Steven Gerrard (save), 2-1 Hélder Postiga, 2-1 Jamie Carragher (saved), 3-1 Cristiano Ronaldo Aveiro.

843.   16.08.2006
**ENGLAND v GREECE   4-0**  (4-0)
*Old Trafford, Manchester*

Referee:   Wolfgang Stark (Germany)      Attendance:   45,864

ENGLAND:   Paul Robinson (46 Christopher Kirkland), Gary Neville (78 Jamie Carragher), Rio Ferdinand, John Terry (Cap), Ashley Cole (81 Wayne Bridge), Steven Gerrard (79 Darren Bent), Owen Hargreaves, Frank Lampard, Stewart Downing (69 Aaron Lennon), Peter Crouch, Jermain Defoe (69 Kieran Richardson).    Manager:   Steve McClaren

GREECE:   Antónyis Nyikopolyídis, Loukás Víntra, Traianós Déllas (65 Yórgos Anatolákyis), Paraskevás Ántzas (46 Sotíris Kyiryákos), Tákyis Físsas (29 Panayótis Lagós), Theódoros Zagorákyis (Cap) (46 Ággyelos Basinás), Konstantínos Katsouránis, Yórgos Karangoúnyis, Stélyos Yannakópoulos (46 Dimítris Salpingyídis), Ággyelos Kharistéas, Yórgos Samarás (46 Yánnyis Amanatídis).

Goals:   John Terry (14), Frank Lampard (30), Peter Crouch (35, 42)

844.   02.09.2006      13th European Champs Qualifiers
**ENGLAND v ANDORRA   5-0**   (3-0)
*Old Trafford, Manchester*

Referee:   Bernhard Brugger (Austria)      Attendance:   56,290

ENGLAND:   Paul Robinson, Phil Neville (65 Aaron Lennon), Wesley Michael Brown, John Terry (Cap), Ashley Cole, Steven Gerrard, Owen Hargreaves, Frank Lampard, Stewart Downing (65 Kieran Richardson), Jermain Defoe (72 Andy Johnson), Peter Crouch.    Manager:   Steve McClaren

ANDORRA:   Jesús Álvarez 'Koldo', José García 'Txema', Oscar Sonejee, Toni Lima, Xavi Sánchez (46 Juli Sánchez), Márcio Vieira; Josep Ayala, Marc Pujol (48 Manolo Jiménez), Toni Sivera (78 Genís García), Justo Ruiz (Cap), Fernando Silva.    Trainer:   David Rodrigo

Goals:   Peter Crouch (5, 66), Steven Gerrard (13), Jermain Defoe (38, 47)

845.   06.09.2006      13th European Champs Qualifiers
**MACEDONIA v ENGLAND   0-1**   (0-0)
*Gradski, Skopje*

Referee:   Bertrand Layec (France)      Attendance:   16,500

MACEDONIA:   Jane Nikoloski; Goce Sedloski (Cap), Igor Mitreski, Nikolče Noveski, Vlade Lazarevski, Veliče Šumulikoski, Igor Jančevski (52 Darko Tasevski), Robert Petrov, Goran Pandev, Goran Maznov (56 Aco Stojkov), Ilčo Naumoski (74 Artim Šakiri).    Trainer:   Srečko Katanec

ENGLAND:   Paul Robinson; Phil Neville, Rio Ferdinand, John Terry (Cap), Ashley Cole, Steven Gerrard, Owen Hargreaves, Frank Lampard (84 Michael Carrick), Stewart Downing, Peter Crouch (87 Andy Johnson), Jermain Defoe (76 Aaron Lennon).    Manager:   Steve McClaren

Goal:   Peter Crouch (46)

846.   07.10.2006      13th European Champs Qualifiers
**ENGLAND v MACEDONIA   0-0**
*Old Trafford, Manchester*

Referee:   Markus Merk (Germany)      Attendance:   72,062

ENGLAND:   Paul Robinson, Gary Neville, John Terry (Cap), Ledley King, Ashley Cole, Steven Gerrard, Michael Carrick, Frank Lampard, Stewart Downing (70 Shaun Wright-Phillips), Wayne Rooney (74 Jermain Defoe), Peter Crouch.    Manager:   Steve McClaren

MACEDONIA:   Jane Nikoloski, Goce Sedloski (Cap), Igor Mitreski, Nikolče Noveski, Vlade Lazarevski, Veliče Šumulikoski, Aleksandar Mitreski, Robert Petrov, Goran Pandev (83 Darko Tasevski), Goran Maznov, Ilčo Naumoski (46 Aco Stojkov).    Trainer:   Srečko Katanec

847.   11.10.2006      13th European Champs Qualifiers
**CROATIA v ENGLAND   2-0**   (0-0)
*Maksimir, Zagreb*

Referee:   Roberto Rosetti (Italy)      Attendance:   38,000

CROATIA:   Stipe Pletikosa, Vedran Ćorluka, Robert Kovač, Dario Šimić, Josip Šimunić, Milan Rapaić (72 Ivica Olić), Niko Kovač (Cap), Luka Modrić, Niko Kranjčar (89 Marko Babić), Eduardo da Silva (82 Jerko Leko), Mladen Petrić. Trainer:   Slaven Bilić

ENGLAND:   Paul Robinson; Rio Ferdinand, John Terry (Cap), Jamie Carragher (72 Shaun Wright-Phillips), Gary Neville, Scott Parker (72 Kieran Richardson), Michael Carrick, Frank Lampard, Ashley Cole, Wayne Rooney, Peter Crouch (72 Jermain Defoe).    Manager:   Steve McClaren

Goals:   Eduardo da Silva (60), Gary Neville (68 og)

848. 15.11.2006
**HOLLAND v ENGLAND  1-1**  (0-1)

*Amsterdam ArenA*

Referee: Ľuboš Micheľ (Slovakia)   Attendance: 45,090

**HOLLAND**: Henk Timmer (46 Maarten Stekelenburg), Khalid Boulahrouz (61 Kew Jaliens), André Ooijer (Cap) (84 Jan Vennegoor of Hesselink), Joris Mathijsen, Urby Emanuelson, Denny Landzaat, Stijn Schaars, Clarence Seedorf, Rafael van der Vaart, Dirk Kuijt (61 Klaas-Jan Huntelaar), Arjen Robben.   Trainer: Marco van Basten

**ENGLAND**: Paul Robinson, Micah Richards, Rio Ferdinand, John Terry (Cap), Ashley Cole, Steven Gerrard, Michael Carrick, Frank Lampard, Andy Johnson (74 Shaun Wright-Phillips), Wayne Rooney, Joseph Cole (78 Kieran Richardson). Manager: Stephen McClaren

**Goals**: Rafael van der Vaart (86) / Wayne Rooney (37)


849. 07.02.2007
**ENGLAND v SPAIN  0-1**  (0-0)

*Old Trafford, Manchester*

Referee: Michael Weiner (Germany)   Attendance: 58242

**ENGLAND**: Benjamin Foster, Gary Neville (64 Micah Richards), Philip Neville (74 Stewart Downing), Michael Carrick, Rio Ferdinand, Jonathan Woodgate (64 Jamie Carragher), Shaun Wright-Phillips (70 Jermaine Defoe), Frank Lampard (78 Joey Barton), Peter Crouch, Kieron Dyer, Steven Gerrard (46 Gareth Barry).   Manager: Stephen McClaren

**SPAIN**: Iker Casillas, Sergio Ramos (46 López Angel), Joan Capdevila, Xavi Hernández, Carles Puyol (46 Francisco Javi Navarro), Pablo Ibañez, Miguel Angulo (56 Andres Iniesta), David Silva (65 Javier Arizmendi), David Albelda, David Villa (74 Francesc Fabregas), Fernando Morientes (46 Fernando Torres).   Trainer: Luis Aragones

**Goal**: Andres Iniesta (63)


850. 24.03.2007   13th European Champs Qualifiers
**ISRAEL v ENGLAND  0-0**

*Ramat Gan, Tel Aviv*

Referee: Tom Henning Ovrebo (Norway)   Att: 35,000

**ISRAEL**: Dudu Awat, Tal Ben Haim, Shimon Gershon, Yoav Ziv, Arik Benado, Yuval Shpungin, Walid Badir, Yossi Benayoun, Amit Ben Shushan (87 Gal Alberman), Toto Adurans Tamuz Temile (75 Elyaniv Barda), Pini Balali (69 Ben Sahar).   Trainer: Dror Kashtan

**ENGLAND**: Paul Robinson, Philip Neville (72 Micah Richards), Rio Ferdinand, John Terry, Jamie Carragher, Steven Gerrard, Frank Lampard, Owen Hargreaves, Aaron Lennon (83 Stewart Downing), Wayne Rooney, Andrew Johnson (80 Jermain Defoe).   Manager: Stephen McClaren


851. 28.03.2007   13th European Champs Qualifiers
**ANDORRA v ENGLAND  0-3**  (0-0)

*Olímpico de Montjuic, Barcelona*

Referee: Bruno Miguel Duarte Paixao (Portugal)
Attendance: 12,800

**ANDORRA**: Koldo Álvarez, Óscar Sonejee, Antoni Lima, José Manuel Ayala, Marc Bernaus, 6 Jordi Escura, Marcio Vieira, Genís García, Justo Ruíz (88 Juli Fernandez), Marc Pujol (69 Francisco Martinez), Juan Carlos Toscano Beltrán (90 Sergio Moreno).   Trainer: David Rodrigo

**ENGLAND**: Paul Robinson, Micah Richards (61 Kieron Dyer), John Terry, Rio Ferdinand, Ashley Cole, Aaron Lennon, Owen Hargreaves, Steven Gerrard, Stewart Downing, Andrew Johnson (79 David Nugent), Wayne Rooney (61 Jermain Defoe).   Manager: Stephen McClaren

**Goals**: Steven Gerrard (54, 76), David Nugent (90)


852. 01.06.2007
**ENGLAND v BRAZIL  1-1**  (0-0)

*Wembley, London*

Referee: Markus Merk (Germany)   Attendance: 88,745

**ENGLAND**: Paul Robinson, Jamie Carragher, Nicholas Shorey, Steven Gerrard, John Terry (72 Wesley Michael Brown), Ledley King, David Beckham (77 Jermaine Jenas), Frank Lampard (88 Michael Carrick), Alan Smith (62 Kieron Dyer), Michael Owen (83 Peter Crouch), Joseph Cole (62 Stewart Downing).   Manager: Stephen McClaren

**BRAZIL**: Da Silva Helton, Alves Daniel (65 Maicon), Gilberto, Silva, Naldo, Juan, Ronaldinho, Carlos Mineiro (63 Edmilson), Robinho (74 Diego), Kaka (71 Alves), Vagner Love.
Trainer: Carlos Dunga

**Goals**: John Terry (68) / Diego (90)


853. 06.06.2007   13th European Champs Qualifiers
**ESTONIA v ENGLAND  0-3**  (0-1)

*A Le Coq Arena, Tallinn*

Referee: Grzegorz Gilewski (Poland)   Attendance: 10,500

**ESTONIA**: Mart Poom, Enar Jääger, Andrei Stepanov, Dmitri Kruglov, Ragnar Klavan, Aleksandr Dmitrijev, Joel Lindpere, Konstantin Vassiljev, Oliver Konsa (46 Tarmo Neemelo), Vladimir Voskoboinikov, Sergei Terehhov (64 Tarmo Kink). Trainer: Jelle Goes

**ENGLAND**: Paul Robinson, Wesley Michael Brown, John Terry, Ledley King, Wayne Bridge, David Beckham (68 Kieron Dyer), Steven Gerrard, Frank Lampard, Joseph Cole (75 Stewart Downing), Peter Crouch, Michael Owen (88 Jermaine Jenas).   Manager: Stephen McClaren

**Goals**: Joseph Cole (37), Crouch (54), Owen (62)

854. 22.08.2007
**ENGLAND v GERMANY 1-2** (1-2)
*Wembley, London*

Referee: Massimo Puscaba (Switzerland)    Att: 86,133

**ENGLAND**: Paul Robinson (46 David Benjamin James), Micah Richards, Rio Ferdinand (46 Wesley Michael Brown), John Terry, Nicholas Shorey, David Beckham, Michael Carrick (55 Gareth Barry), Frank Lampard, Joseph Cole (70 Shaun Wright-Phillips), Alan Smith (57 Peter Crouch), Michael Owen (57 Kieron Dyer).    Manager: Stephen McClaren

**GERMANY**: Jens Lehmann, Arne Friedrich, Philip Lahm, Per Mertesacker, Christoph Metzelder, Christian Pander, Thomas Hitzlsperger, Bernd Schneider (90 Gonzalo Castro), Piotr Trochowski (72 Simon Rolfes), Kevin Kuranyi, David Odonkor (54 Roberto Hilbert).    Trainer: Joachim Löw

**Goals**: Frank Lampard (9) /
Kevin Kuranyi (26), Christian Pander (40)


855. 08.09.2007    13th European Champs Qualifiers
**ENGLAND v ISRAEL 3-0** (1-0)
*Wembley, London*

Referee: Pieter Vink (Holland)    Attendance: 85,400

**ENGLAND**: Paul Robinson, Micah Richards, Rio Ferdinand, John Terry, Ashley Cole, Shaun Wright-Phillips (83 David Bentley), Steven Gerrard (71 Philip Neville), Gareth Barry, Joseph Cole, Emile Heskey (71 Andrew Johnson), Michael Owen.    Manager: Stephen McClaren

**ISRAEL**: Dudu Awat, Yuval Shpungin, Tal Ben Haim, Shimon Gershon, Yoav Ziv, Yossi Benayoun, Walid Badir, Arik Benado (57 Omwer Golan), Idan Tal, Yaniv Katan, Barak Itzhaki (46 Toto Tamuz).    Trainer: Dror Kashtan

**Goals**: Shaun Wright-Phillips (20), Michael Owen (49), Micah Richards (66)


856. 12.09.2007    13th European Champs Qualifiers
**ENGLAND v RUSSIA 3-0** (2-0)
*Wembley, London*

Referee: Martin Hansson (Sweden)    Attendance: 86,100

**ENGLAND**: Paul Robinson, Micah Richards, Rio Ferdinand, John Terry, Ashley Cole, Shaun Wright-Phillips, Gareth Barry, Steven Gerrard, Joseph Cole (88 Philip Neville), Emile Heskey (80 Peter Crouch), Michael Owen (90 Stewart Downing).    Manager: Stephen McClaren

**RUSSIA**: Vyacheslav Malafeev, Vasili Berezutski, Sergei Ignashevich, Aleksei Berezutski, Aleksandr Anyukov (80 Aleksandr Kerzhakov), Diniyar Bilyaletdinov, Yuri Zhirkov, Igor Semshov (40 Vladimir Bystrov), Dmitri Sychev (63 Roman Pavlyuchenko), Andrei Arshavin, Konstantin Zyrianov. Trainer: Guus Hiddink

**Goals**: Michael Owen (7, 31), Rio Ferdinand (84)


857. 13.10.2007    13th European Champs Qualifiers
**ENGLAND v ESTONIA 3-0** (3-0)
*Wembley, London*

Referee: Nicolai Vollquartz (Denmark)    Attendance: 86,700

**ENGLAND**: Paul Robinson, Micah Richards, Sol Campbell, Rio Ferdinand (46 Jolean Lescott), Ashley Cole (49 Philip Neville), Shaun Wright-Phillips, Steven Gerrard, Gareth Barry, Joseph Cole, Wayne Rooney, Michael Owen (70 Frank Lampard).    Manager: Stephen McClaren

**ESTONIA**: Mart Poom, Dmitri Kruglov, Andrei Stepanov, Raio Piiroja, Enar Jääger, Taavi Rähn, Ragnar Klavan, Aleksandr Dmitrijev, Joel Lindpere, Tarmo Kink (62 Kristen Viikmae), Kaimar Saag.    Trainer: Viggo Jensen

**Goals**: Shaun Wright-Phillips (11), Wayne Rooney (32), Taavi Rahn (33 og)


858. 17.10.2007    13th European Champs Qualifiers
**RUSSIA v ENGLAND 2-1** (0-1)
*Luzhniki, Moskva*

Referee: Luis Medina Cantalejo (Spain)    Attendance: 80,000

**RUSSIA**: Vladimir Gabulov, Aleksei Berezutski, Sergei Ignashevich, Vasili Berezutski (46 Dmitri Torbinskiy), Aleksandr Anyukov, Konstantin Zyrianov, Igor Semshov, Diniyar Bilyaletdinov, Yuri Zhirkov, Andrei Arshavin (90 Denis Kolodin), Aleksandr Kerzhakov (58 Roman Pavlyuchenko). Trainer: Guus Hiddink

**ENGLAND**: Paul Robinson, Micah Richards, Rio Ferdinand, Sol Campbell, Jolean Lescott (79 Frank Lampard), Shaun Wright-Phillips (80 Stewart Downing), Steven Gerrard, Gareth Barry, Joseph Cole (80 Peter Crouch), Wayne Rooney, Michael Owen.    Manager: Stephen McClaren

**Goals**: Roman Pavlyuchenko (69 pen, 73) /
Wayne Rooney (29)


859. 16.11.2007
**AUSTRIA v ENGLAND 0-1** (0-1)
*Ernst-Happel, Wien*

Referee: Nicolai Vollquartz (Denmark)    Attendance: 39,432

**AUSTRIA**: Jurgen Macho (25 Alexander Manniger), Gyorgy Garics, Ronald Gercaliu, Franz Schiemer, Rene Aufhauser, Ivan Ivanschitz, Yuksel Sariyar (65 Martin Harnik), Joachim Standfest (78 Veli Kavlak), Martin Stranzl (86 Martin Hiden), Sanel Kuljic (46 Christoph Leitgeb), Marcus Weissenberger (46 Roman Kienast).    Trainer: Josef Hickersberger

**ENGLAND**: Scott Carson, Micah Richards, Sol Campbell (46 Wesley Michael Brown), Joleon Lescott, Wayne Bridge, David Beckham (62 David Bentley), Steven Gerrard (46 Gareth Barry), Frank Lampard, Joseph Cole (46 Ashley Young), Peter Crouch (73 Alan Smith), Michael Owen (34 Jermaine Defoe). Manager: Stephen McClaren

**Goal**: Peter Crouch (44)

860.  21.11.2007    13th European Champs Qualifiers
**ENGLAND v CROATIA  2-3**  (0-2)
*Wembley, London*

Referee:  Peter Fröjdfeldt (Sweden)    Attendance: 88,100

**ENGLAND**:  Scott Carson, Micah Richards, Sol Campbell, Joleon Lescott, Wayne Bridge, Shaun Wright-Phillips (46 David Beckham), Steven Gerrard, Gareth Barry (46 Jermain Defoe), Frank Lampard, Joseph Cole (80 Darren Bent), Peter Crouch.    Manager:  Stephen McClaren

**CROATIA**:  Stipe Pletikosa, Vedran Corluka, Dario Šimic, Robert Kovac, Josip Šimunic, Darijo Srna, Luka Modric, Niko Kovac, Niko Kranjcar (75 Danijel Pranjic), Ivica Olic (84 Ivan Rakitic), Eduardo da Silva (69 Mladen Petric).
Trainer:  Slaven Bilic

**Goals**:  Niko Kranjcar (8), Ivica Olic (14), Mladen Petric (77) / Frank Lampard (56 pen), Peter Crouch (65)


861.  06.02.2008
**ENGLAND v SWITZERLAND  2-1**  (1-0)
*Wembley, London*

Referee:  Felix Brych (Germany)    Attendance: 86,857

**ENGLAND**:  David Benjamin James, Wesley Michael Brown, Rio Ferdinand, Ashley Cole (74 Wayne Bridge), Matthew Upson, David Bentley, Steven Gerrard, Gareth Barry (73 Owen Hargreaves), Joseph Cole (57 Peter Crouch), Jermaine Jenas (57 Shaun Wright-Phillips), Wayne Rooney (87 Ashley Young).    Manager:  Fabio Capello

**SWITZERLAND**:  Diego Benaglio, Mario Eggimann, Stephan Lichtsteiner (46 Valon Behrami), Philippe Senderos (55 Stephane Grichting), Cristoph Spycher, Tranquillo Barnetta, Fernandes Gelson, Daniel Gygax (46 Johan Vonlanthen), Gokhan Inler, Hakan Yakin (63 Xavier Magairaz), Blaise Nkufo (46 Eren Derdiyok).    Trainer:  Köbi Kuhn

**Goals**:  Jermaine Jenas (40), Shaun Wright-Phillips (62) / Eren Derdiyok (58)


862.  26.03.2008
**FRANCE v ENGLAND  1-0**  (1-0)
*Stade de France, St. Denis*

Referee:  Florian Meyer (Germany)    Attendance: 78,500

**FRANCE**:  Gregory Coupet, William Gallas, Eric Abidal, Lilian Thuram, Francois Clerc, Claude Makelele, Jeremy Toulalan, Florent Malouda, Nicolas Anelka (80 Djibril Cisse), David Trezeguet (64 Sidney Govou), Frank Ribery.
Trainer:  Raymond Domenech

**ENGLAND**:  David Benjamin James, Wesley Michael Brown (63 Glen Johnson), John Terry (46 Joleon Lescott), Rio Ferdinand, Ashley Cole, David Beckham (63 David Bentley), Gareth Barry, Owen Hargreaves, Joseph Cole (46 Stewart Downing), Steven Gerrard (46 Michael Owen), Wayne Rooney (46 Peter Crouch).    Manager:  Fabio Capello

**Goal**:  Frank Ribery (32)


863.  28.05.2008
**ENGLAND v U.S.A.  2-0**  (1-0)
*Wembley, London*

Referee:  Kyros Vassaras (Greece)    Attendance: 71,233

**ENGLAND**:  David Benjamin James, Wesley Michael Brown (57 Glen Johnson), Rio Ferdinand, John Terry (Cap), Ashley Cole (82 Wayne Bridge), David Beckham (46 David Bentley), Owen Hargreaves, Frank Lampard (57 Gareth Barry), Steven Gerrard, Wayne Rooney (78 Joseph Cole), Jermain Defoe (68 Peter Crouch).    Manager:  Fabio Capello

**U.S.A.**:  Tim Howard (46 Brad Guzan), Steve Cherundolo (46 Frankie Hejduk), Oguchi Onyewu, Carlos Bocanegra, Heath Pearce, DaMarcus Beasley (68 Eddie Lewis), Michael Bradley, Ricardo Clark (78 Maurice Edu), Josh Wolff (68 Freddie Adu), Clint Dempsey, Eddie Johnson (89 Nate Jaqua).
Trainer:  Bob Bradley

**Goals**:  John Terry (38), Steven Gerrard (59)


864.  01.06.2008
**TRINIDAD & TOBAGO v ENGLAND  0-3**  (0-2)
*Hasely Crawford, Port of Spain*

Referee:  Enrico Wijngaarde (Surinam)    Attendance: 25,001

**TRINIDAD & TOBAGO**:  Clayton Ince, Dennis Lawrence, Ancil Farrier, Kern Cupid (46 Kareem Smith), Makan Hislop, Carlos Edwards, Aurtis Whitley, Keon Daniel (76 Kevaughn Connell), Khaleem Hyland (76 Dwight York), Stern John (74 Jerrol Forbes), Kenwyne Jones (11 Darryl Roberts, Osel Telesford).    Trainer:  Francisco Maturana

**ENGLAND**:  David Benjamin James (46 Joseph Hart), Glen Johnson, Wayne Bridge (84 Stephen Warnock), Gareth Barry, Rio Ferdinand (46 Phil Jagielka), Jonathan Woodgate, David Beckham (46 David Bentley), Stewart Downing (57 Ashley Young), Dean Ashton (46 Peter Crouch), Steven Gerrard, Jermain Defoe (69 Theo Walcott).    Manager:  Fabio Capello

**Goals**:  Gareth Barry (12), Jermaine Defoe (16, 49)


865.  20.08.2008
**ENGLAND v CZECH REPUBLIC  2-2**  (1-1)
*Wembley, London*

Referee:  Terje Hauge (Norway)    Attendance: 69,738

**ENGLAND**:  David Benjamin James, Wesley Michael Brown, Rio Ferdinand (58 Jonathan Woodgate), John Terry, Ashley Cole, David Beckham (79 Jermaine Jenas), Gareth Barry, Steven Gerrard (58 Joseph Cole), Frank Lampard (79 David Bentley), Jermain Defoe (46 Emile Heskey), Wayne Rooney (69 Stewart Downing).    Manager:  Fabio Capello

**CZECH REPUBLIC**:  Petr Cech, Zdenek Grygera (46 Zdenek Pospech), Tomas Ujfalusi, David Rozehnal, Marek Jankulovski, Stanislav Vlcek (46 David Jarolim), Radoslav Kovac (75 Jan Rajnoch), Jan Polak, Jaroslav Plasil (90 Michal Papadopulos), Radek Sirl (75 Michal Kadlec), Milan Baros (46 Vaclav Sverkos).    Trainer:  Petr Rada

**Goals**:  Wesley Michael Brown (45), Joseph Cole (90) / Milan Baros (22), Marek Jankulovski (48)

866.  06.09.2008    19th World Cup Qualifier
**ANDORRA v ENGLAND  0-2**  (0-0)

*Olímpico de Montjuic, Barcelona*

Referee: Cuneyt Cakir (Turkey)    Attendance: 17,500

**ANDORRA**:  Jesus Alvarez, Jose Txema, Oscar Sonejee (Cap), Antoni Lima (90 Juli Fernández), Ildefons Lima, Josep Ayala, Marc Pujol (90 Marc Vales), Manolo Jimenez, Xavier Andorra, Marcio Vieira, Fernando Silva (65 Juan Carlos Toscano).

**ENGLAND**:  David Benjamin James, Glen Johnson, Joleon Lescott, John Terry, Ashley Cole, Theo Walcott, Gareth Barry, Frank Lampard (79 David Beckham), Stewart Downing (46 Joseph Cole), Wayne Rooney, Jermain Defoe (46 Emile Heskey).    Manager: Fabio Capello

**Goals**:  Joseph Cole (49, 55)


867.  10.09.2008    19th World Cup Qualifier
**CROATIA v ENGLAND  1-4**  (0-1)

*Maksimir, Zagreb*

Referee: Lubos Michel (Slovakia)    Attendance: 35,000

**CROATIA**:  Stipe Pletikosa, Vedran Corluka, Robert Kovac, Josip Simunic, Niko Kovac (62 Nikola Pokrivac), Danijel Pranjic, Luka Modric, Darijo Srna, Ivan Rakitic, Mladen Petric (56 Dario Knezevic), Ivica Olic (73 Mario Mandzukic)

**ENGLAND**:  David James, Wesley Brown, Ashley Cole, Gareth Barry, Rio Ferdinand, John Terry (Cap) (88 Matthew Upson), Theo Walcott (84 David Beckham), Frank Lampard, Joseph Cole (52 Jermaine Jenas), Emile Heskey, Wayne Rooney. Manager: Fabio Capello

**Goals**:  Mario Mandzukic (78) /
Theo Walcott (26, 59, 63), Wayne Rooney (63)


868.  11.10.2008    19th World Cup Qualifier
**ENGLAND v KAZAKHSTAN  5-1**  (0-0)

*Wembley, London*

Referee: Paul Allaerts (Belgium)    Attendance: 89,107

**ENGLAND**:  David James, Wes Brown, Ashley Cole, Steven Gerrard, Rio Ferdinand, Matthew Upson, Theo Walcott (79 David Beckham), Frank Lampard, Emile Heskey, Wayne Rooney (87 Jermain Defoe), Gareth Barry (46 Shaun Wright-Phillips).    Manager: Fabio Capello

**KAZAKHSTAN**:  Alexandr Mokin, Alexandr Kirov (84 Talgat Sabalakov), Alexandr Kuchma, Alexandr Kislitsyn, Tanat Nusserbayev, Sergey Skorykh, Sergey Ostapenko (76 Gleb Maltsev), Rulsan Baltiyev, Sabrykhan Ibrayev, Zhambyl Kukeyev, Yuriy Logvinenko.    Trainer: Bernd Storck

**Goals**:  Zhambyl Kukeyev (68) /
Rio Ferdinand (52), Alexandr Kuchma (64 own goal), Wayne Rooney (76, 86), Jermain Defoe (90)


869.  15.10.2008    19th World Cup Qualifier
**BELARUS v ENGLAND  1-3**  (1-1)

*Dinamo, Minsk*

Referee: Terje Hauge (Norway)    Attendance: 32,000

**BELARUS**:  Yuri Zhevnov, Egor Filipenko, Aleksandr Kulchy, Sergei Omelyanchyuk, Dzmitry Verkhovtsov, Dmitry Molosh, Anton Putilo (67 Vitaly Rodionov), Pavel Sitko, Igor Stasevich (90 Vyacheslav Hleb), Vitaly Kutuzov (77 Oleg Strakhanovich), Vitaly Bulyga.    Trainer: Bernd Stange

**ENGLAND**:  David Benjamin James, Wesley Michael Brown, Rio Ferdinand (Cap), Wayne Bridge, Matthew Upson, Steven Gerrard, Frank Lampard, Gareth Barry, Theo Walcott (68 Shaun Wright-Phillips), Wayne Rooney (88 David Beckham), Emile Heskey (70 Peter Crouch).    Manager: Fabio Capello

**Goals**:  Pavel Sitko (28) /
Steven Gerrard (11), Wayne Rooney (50, 74)


870.  19.11.2008
**GERMANY v ENGLAND  1-2**  (0-1)

*Olympic, Berlin*

Referee: Massimo Busacca (Switzerland)    Att: 74,244

**GERMANY**:  Rene Adler (46 Tim Wiese), Arne Friedrich (68 Serdar Tasci), Simon Rolfes, Per Mertesacker, Heiko Westermann, Marvin Compper (77 Marcel Schafer), Bastian Schweinsteiger, Piotr Trochowski, Jermaine Jones (46 Marko Marin), Miroslav Klose (Cap) (46 Patrick Helmes), Mario Gomez (57 Lukas Podolski).    Trainer: Joachim Löw

**ENGLAND**:  David James (46 Scott Carson), Glen Johnson, Wayne Bridge, Matthew Upson, John Terry (Cap), Gareth Barry, Shaun Wright-Phillips (90 Peter Crouch), Michael Carrick, Stewart Downing, Jermain Defoe (46 Darren Bent), Gabriel Agbonlahor (77 Ashley Young).
Manager: Fabio Capello

**Goals**:  Patrick Helmes (63) /
Matthew Upson (23), John Terry (84)

871.  11.02.2009
**SPAIN v ENGLAND  2-0**  (1-0)
*Ramón Sánchez Pizjuán, Sevilla*
Referee: Stéphane Lannoy (France)    Attendance: 42,102
**SPAIN:** IKER CASILLAS Fernández (46 José Manuel "Pepe" REINA Páez), Joan CAPDEVILLA Méndez (46 Álvaro ARBELOA Coca), SERGIO RAMOS García, RAÚL ALBIOL Tortajada (75 Carlos MARCHENA López), Gerard PIQUÉ i Bernabéu, "Xavi" Xavier Hernández i Creus (84 Daniel González GÜIZA), Xabier "Xabi" ALONSO Olano, MARCOS Antonio SENNA Da Silva, Andrés INIESTA Luján, FERNANDO José TORRES Sanz (64 Fernando LLORENTE Torres), DAVID VILLA Sánchez (56 DAVID Jiménez SILVA). Manager: Vicente DEL BOSQUE González
**ENGLAND:** David Benjamin James (46 Robert Green), Ashley Cole, John Terry, Phil Jagielka (46 Matthew Upson), Glen Johnson, Michael Carrick, Shaun Wright-Phillips, Gareth Barry (46 Frank Lampard), Stewart Downing (46 David Beckham), Gabriel Agbonlahor (76 Carlton Cole), Emile Heskey (46 Peter Crouch).    Manager: Fabio Capello
**Goals:** DAVID VILLA Sánchez (36), Fernando LLORENTE Torres (82)

872.  28.03.2009
**ENGLAND v SLOVAKIA  4-0**  (1-0)
*Wembley, London*
Referee: Alain Hamer (Luxembourg)    Attendance: 85,512
**ENGLAND:** David Benjamin James (46 Ben Foster), Matthew Upson, John Terry, Ashley Cole, Glen Johnson, Gareth Barry, Steven Gerrard (46 Stewart Downing), Aaron Lennon (46 David Beckham), Frank Lampard, Emile Heskey (15 Carlton Cole, 34 Peter Crouch, 74 Michael Carrick), Wayne Rooney.    Manager: Fabio Capello
**SLOVAKIA:** Stefan Senecky, Peter Pekarík, Martin Skrtel, Marek Cech (46 Erik Jendrisek), Radoslav Zabavník, Jozef Valachovic, Ján Kozák (62 Marek Sapara), Marek Hamsík (79 Marek Mintál), Miroslav Karhan (82 Zdeno Strba), Róbert Vittek (46 Filip Holosko), Stanislav Sesták (71 Martin Jakubko).    Manager: Vladimir Weiss
**Goals:** Emile Heskey (7), Wayne Rooney (70, 90), Frank Lampard (82)

873.  01.04.2009    19th World Cup Qualifier
**ENGLAND v UKRAINE  2-1**  (1-0)
*Wembley, London*
Referee: Claus Bo Larsen (Denmark)    Attendance: 87,548
**ENGLAND:** David Benjamin James, John Terry, Ashley Cole, Glen Johnson, Rio Ferdinand (88 Phil Jagielka), Aaron Lennon (58 David Beckham), Frank Lampard, Steven Gerrard, Gareth Barry, Wayne Rooney, Peter Crouch (79 Shaun Wright-Phillips).    Manager: Fabio Capello

**UKRAINE:** Andriy Pyatov, Dmitro Chigrinskiy, Grigoriy Yarmash, Taras Mikhalik, Vyacheslav Shevchuk, Sergiy Valyaev (61 Sergiy Nazarenko), Valentin Slyusar (89 Maksim Kalinichenko), Aleksandr Aliyev, Anatoliy Tymoshchuk, Andriy Voronin (55 Andriy Shevchenko), Artem Milevskiy. Manager: Aleksey Mikhaylichenko
**Goals:** Peter Crouch (29), John Terry (85) / Andriy Shevchenko (74)

874.  06.06.2009    19th World Cup Qualifier
**KAZAKHSTAN v ENGLAND  0-4**  (0-2)
*Tsentralniy, Almaty*
Referee: Kristinn Jakobsson (Iceland)    Attendance: 24,000
**KAZAKHSTAN:** Aleksandr Mokin, Renat Abdulin, Aleksandr Kislitsyn, Aleksandr Kirov, Yuriy Logvinenko, Zhambyl Kukeev, Sergey Skorykh, Andrey Karpovich, Evgeniy Averchenko (74 Vyacheslav Erbes), Sergey Ostapenko (27 Sabyrkhan Ibraev), Tanat Nuserbaev.    Manager: Bernd Storck
**ENGLAND:** Robert Green, Matthew Upson, John Terry, Ashley Cole, Glen Johnson (76 David Beckham), Gareth Barry, Frank Lampard, Steven Gerrard, Emile Heskey (81 Jermain Defoe), Theo Walcott (46 Shaun Wright-Phillips), Wayne Rooney.    Manager: Fabio Capello
**Goals:** Gareth Barry (39), Emile Heskey (45+1), Wayne Rooney (72), Frank Lampard (78 pen)

875.  10.06.2009    19th World Cup Qualifier
**ENGLAND v ANDORRA  6-0**  (3-0)
*Wembley, London*
Referee: Bas Nijhuis (Netherlands)    Attendance: 57,897
**ENGLAND:** Robert Green, John Terry, Joleon Lescott, Ashley Cole (63 Wayne Bridge), Glen Johnson, David Beckham, Frank Lampard, Steven Gerrard (46 Ashley Young), Theo Walcott, Wayne Rooney (46 Jermain Defoe), Peter Crouch. Manager: Fabio Capello
**ANDORRA:** "Koldo" Jesús Luis Álvares de Eulate Güergue (89 JOSEP Antonio GÓMES Moreira), Antonio "Toni" LIMA Sola (47 MARC VALES González), José Manuel García Luema "Txema", ILDEFONS LIMA Solà, Josep Manel "Jose" AYALA Díaz, MÁRCIO VIEIRA de Vasconcelos, Xavier "Xavi" ANDORRÀ Julià, ÓSCAR Masand SONEJEE, Manolo "Manel" JIMÉNEZ Soria, FERNANDO José SILVA García (79 Julia "Juli" FERNÁNDEZ Ariza), Sergio "Sergi" MORENO Marín. Manager: DAVID RODRIGO Lo
**Goals:** Wayne Rooney (4, 38), Frank Lampard (29), Jermain Defoe (73, 75), Peter Crouch (80)

876.   12.08.2009
**NETHERLANDS v ENGLAND  2-2**  (2-0)
*Amsterdam ArenA, Amsterdam*
Referee:  Nicola Rizzoli (Italy)    Attendance:  48.000

**NETHERLANDS:**  Maarten Stekelenburg, André Ooijer, Joris Mathijsen, John Heitinga, Edson Braafheid, Rafael van der Vaart (46 Wesley Sneijder), Stijn Schaars (82 David Mendes da Silva), Nigel de Jong, Robin van Persie (46 Ryan Babel), Arjen Robben (55 Ibrahim Afellay), Dirk Kuyt (78 Klaas-Jan Huntelaar).    Manager:  Bert van Marwijk

**ENGLAND:**  Robert Green, John Terry, Ashley Cole (84 Wayne Bridge), Glen Johnson, Rio Ferdinand, Ashley Young (68 James Milner), David Beckham (46 Shaun Wright-Phillips), Gareth Barry (46 Michael Carrick), Frank Lampard, Emile Heskey (46 Jermain Defoe), Wayne Rooney (59 Carlton Cole).    Manager:  Fabio Capello

**Goals:**  Dirk Kuyt (10), Rafael van der Vaart (37) / Jermain Defoe (49, 76)


877.   05.09.2009
**ENGLAND v SLOVENIA  2-1**  (1-0)
*Wembley, London*
Referee:  Jonas Eriksson (Sweden)    Attendance: 67,232

**ENGLAND:**  Robert Green, John Terry, Ashley Cole, Matthew Upson (64 Joleon Lescott), Glen Johnson, Shaun Wright-Phillips (46 Aaron Lennon), Gareth Barry, Frank Lampard (46 Michael Carrick), Steven Gerrard (46 James Milner), Emile Heskey (46 Jermain Defoe), Wayne Rooney (80 Carlton Cole). Manager:  Fabio Capello

**SLOVENIA:**  Samir Handanovic, Marko Suler, Miso Brecko, Bostjan Cesar (34 Matej Mavric), Robert Koren, Bojan Jokic, Aleksander Radosavljevic (77 Rene Krhin), Andraz Kirm (78 Dalibor Stevanovic), Valter Birsa (65 Andrej Komac), Milivoje Novakovic (55 Zlatan Ljubijankic), Zlatko Dedic (71 Andrej Pecnik).    Manager:  Matjaz Kek

**Goals:**  Frank Lampard (31 pen), Jermain Defoe (63) / Zlatan Ljubijankic (85)


878.   09.09.2009   19th World Cup Qualifier
**ENGLAND v CROATIA  5-1**  (2-0)
*Wembley, London*
Referee:  Alberto Undiano Mallenco (Spain)    Att: 87,319

**ENGLAND:**  Robert Green, Matthew Upson, John Terry, Ashley Cole, Glen Johnson, Aaron Lennon (81 James Milner), Frank Lampard, Steven Gerrard (81 David Beckham), Gareth Barry, Emile Heskey (60 Jermain Defoe), Wayne Rooney.    Manager:  Fabio Capello

**CROATIA:**  Vedran Runje, Ivica Krizanac, Josip Simunic, Niko Kranjcar, Ognjen Vukovic, Darijo Srna, Danijel Pranjic, Nikola Pokrivac (46 Ivan Rakitic), Ivica Olic (46 Mladen Petric), Mario Mandzukic, Eduardo da Silva (73 Ivan Klasnic).    Manager:  Slaven Bilic

**Goals:**  Frank Lampard (7 pen, 59), Steven Gerrard (18, 66), Wayne Rooney (77) / Eduardo da Silva (71)


879.   10.10.2009   19th World Cup Qualifier
**UKRAINE v ENGLAND  1-0**  (1-0)
*Dnipro, Dnipropetrovsk*
Referee:  Damir Skomina (Slovenia)    Attendance:  31,000

**UKRAINE:**  Andriy Pyatov, Evgen Khacheridi, Oleksandr Kucher, Oleksiy Gay, Ruslan Rotan, Yaroslav Rakitskiy, Anatoliy Tymoshchuk, Sergiy Nazarenko (67 Andriy Yarmolenko), Vasiliy Kobin, Andriy Shevchenko (90+2 Oleg Gusev), Artem Milevskiy.  Manager:  Aleksey Mikhaylichenko

**ENGLAND:**  Robert Green, John Terry, Ashley Cole, Glen Johnson, Rio Ferdinand, Aaron Lennon (13 David Benjamin James goalkeeper), Frank Lampard, Steven Gerrard (46 James Milner), Michael Carrick, Emile Heskey (72 Carlton Cole), Wayne Rooney.    Manager:  Fabio Capello

**Sent off:**  Robert Green (12)

**Goal:**  Sergiy Nazarenko (30)

Andriy Shevchenko missed a penalty kick in the 14th minute.


880.   14.10.2009   19th World Cup Qualifier
**ENGLAND v BELARUS  3-0**  (1-0)
*Wembley, London*
Referee:  Lucílio CARDOSO CORTEZ BATISTA (Portugal)    Attendance: 76,897

**ENGLAND:**  Ben Foster, John Terry, Wayne Bridge (78 James Milner), Glen Johnson, Rio Ferdinand, Shaun Wright-Phillips, Aaron Lennon (58 David Beckham), Frank Lampard, Gareth Barry, Gabriel Agbonlahor (66 Carlton Cole), Peter Crouch.    Manager:  Fabio Capello

**BELARUS:**  Yuri Zhevnov, Aleksandr Yurevich, Sergey Sosnovskiy, Igor Shitov, Dmitriy Verkhovtsov, Sergey Omelyanchuk, Aleksandr Kulchiy, Maksim Bordachev (84 Nikolay Kashevski), Tsimafei Kalachev, Vitaliy Kutuzov (46 Vitaliy Rodionov), Sergey Kornilenko (77 Leonid Kovel).    Manager:  Bernd Stange

**Goals:**  Peter Crouch (3, 75), Shaun Wright-Phillips (60)

881.  14.11.2009
**BRAZIL v ENGLAND  1-0**  (0-0)
*Khalifa International Stadium, Doha*

Referee: Abdulrahman Abdou (Qatar)   Attendance: 50,000

**BRAZIL:** JÚLIO CÉSAR Soares Espíndola, THIAGO Emiliano SILVA, MAICON Douglas Sisenando, Lucimar da Silva Ferreira "Lúcio", MICHEL Fernandes BASTOS, GILBERTO Aparecido da SILVA, FELIPE MELO de Carvalho, ELANO Ralph Blumer (64 Daniel "Dani" ALVES da Silva), Ricardo Izecson dos Santos Leite "Kaká" (81 CARLOS EDUARDO Marques), NILMAR Honorato da Silva (81 JÚLIO César BAPTISTA), LUÍS FABIANO Clemente (67 Givanildo Vieira de Souza "Hulk").   Manager: Carlos Caetano Bledorn Verri "Dunga"

**ENGLAND:** Ben Foster, Wesley Michael Brown, Matthew Upson, Joleon Lescott, Wayne Bridge, Jermaine Jenas, Shaun Wright-Phillips (81 Peter Crouch), Gareth Barry (82 Tom Huddlestone), James Milner (87 Ashley Young), Darren Bent (55 Jermain Defoe), Wayne Rooney.   Manager: Fabio Capello

**Goal**: NILMAR Honorato da Silva (47)

LUÍS FABIANO Clemente missed a penalty kick in the 56th minute.

882.  03.03.2010
**ENGLAND v EGYPT  3-1**  (0-1)
*Wembley, London*

Referee: Carlos Manuel Torres (Paraguay)   Att: 80,602

**ENGLAND:** Robert Green, Matthew Upson, John Terry, Wesley Michael Brown, Leighton Baines, Gareth Barry, Frank Lampard (46 Michael Carrick), Steven Gerrard (73 James Milner), Theo Walcott (57 Shaun Wright-Phillips), Jermain Defoe (46 Peter Crouch), Wayne Rooney (86 Carlton Cole).   Manager: Fabio Capello

**EGYPT:** Essam El Hadary, Sayed Moawad (76 Mohamed Abdel-Shafy), Wael Gomaa, Ahmed Al-Muhammadi, Hosny Abd Rabo, Hany Saïd (86 Moatasem Salem), Ahmed Hassan (65 Gedo), Hossam Ghaly, Ahmed Fathy, Emad Moteab (65 Amr Zaki), Mohamed Zidan (76 Mohamed Abo Treka).   Manager: Hassan Shehata

**Goals**: Peter Crouch (57, 80), Shaun Wright-Phillips (75) / Mohamed Zidan (23)

883.  24.05.2010
**ENGLAND v MEXICO  3-1**  (2-1)
*Wembley, London*

Referee: Masaaki Toma (Japan)   Attendance: 88,638

**ENGLAND:** Robert Green (46 Joe Hart), Leighton Baines, Ledley King, Glenn Johnson, Rio Ferdinand (46 Jamie Carragher), Michael Carrick (62 Tom Huddlestone), James Milner (85 Adam Johnson), Steven Gerrard, Theo Walcott (77 Aaron Lennon), Peter Crouch (46 Jermain Defoe), Wayne Rooney.   Manager: Fabio Capello

**MEXICO:** ÓSCAR PÉREZ Rojas, PAUL Nicolás AGUILAR Rojas (52 PABLO Edson BARRERA Acosta), Francisco Javier Rodríguez Pinedo "Maza", RICARDO OSORIO Mendoza, CARLOS Arnoldo SALCIDO Flores, RAFAEL MÁRQUEZ Álvarez, GERARDO TORRADO Díez de Bonilla, EFRAIN JUÁREZ Valdez, GUILLERMO Luis FRANCO Farcuarson (46 JAVIER HERNÁNDEZ Balcazar), CARLOS Alberto VELA Garrido (62 José ANDRÉS GUARDADO Hernández), GIOVANI Alex DOS SANTOS Ramírez (72 CUAUHTÉMOC Bravo BLANCO).   Manager: JAVIER AGUIRRE Onandía

**Goals**: Ledley King (17), Peter Crouch (35), G. Johnson (47) / Guillermo Luis Franco Farcuarson (45)

884.  30.05.2010
**ENGLAND v JAPAN  2-1**  (0-1)
*UPC-Arena, Graz (Austria)*

Referee: Rene Eisner (Austria)   Attendance: 15,326

**ENGLAND:** David Benjamin James (46 Joe Hart), John Terry, Tom Huddlestone (46 Jamie Carragher), Ashley Cole, Glenn Johnson (46 Shaun Wright-Phillips), Rio Ferdinand, Aaron Lennon (77 Emile Heskey), Frank Lampard, Theo Walcott (46 Joe Cole), Darren Bent (46 Steven Gerrard), Wayne Rooney.   Manager: Fabio Capello

**JAPAN:** Eiji Kawashima, Marcus Tulio Tanaka, Yuji Nakazawa, Yuto Nagatomo, Makoto Hasebe, Yasuyuki Konno, Keisuke Honda, Yasuhito Endō (86 Keiji Tamada), Yuki Abe, Yoshito Ōkubo (71 Daisuke Matsui), Shinji Okazaki (65 Takayuki Morimoto).   Manager: Takeshi Okada

**Goals**: Marcus Tulio Tanaka (71 og), Yuji Nakazawa (83 og) / Marcus Tulio Tanaka (7)

Frank Lampard missed a penalty kick in the 56th minute.

885.  12.06.2010   19th World Cup Group C
**ENGLAND v USA  1-1**  (1-1)
*Royal Bafokeng, Rustenburg (South Africa)*
Referee: Carlos Eugênio SIMÓN (Brazil)   Att: 38,646
**ENGLAND:** Robert Green, Glenn Johnson, Ashley Cole, John Terry, Ledley King (46 Jamie Carragher), Steven Gerrard, Aaron Lennon, Frank Lampard, James Milner (30 Shaun Wright-Phillips), Wayne Rooney, Emile Heskey (79 Peter Crouch).   Manager: Fabio Capello
**USA:** Tim Howard, Carlos Bocanegra, Oguchi Onyewu, Steven Cherundolo, Jay DeMerit, Michael Bradley, Clint Dempsey, Landon Donovan, Ricardo Clark, Jozy Altidore (86 Stuart Holden), Robbie Findley (77 Edson Buddle).   Manager: Bob Bradley
**Goals**: Steven Gerrard (4) / Clint Dempsey (40)


886.  18.06.2010   19th World Cup Group C
**ENGLAND v ALGERIA  0-0**
*Cape Town Stadium, Cape Town (South Africa)*
Referee: Ravshan Irmatov (Uzbekistan)   Attendance: 64,100
**ENGLAND:** David Benjamin James, Glenn Johnson, Ashley Cole, John Terry, Jamie Carragher, Steven Gerrard, Aaron Lennon (63 Shaun Wright-Phillips), Frank Lampard, Gareth Barry (84 Peter Crouch), Wayne Rooney, Emile Heskey (74 Jermain Defoe).   Manager: Fabio Capello
**ALGERIA:** Raïs M'Bolhi, Madjid Bougherra, Nadir Belhadj, Anthar Yahia, Rafik Halliche, Ryad Boudebouz (74 Djamel Abdoun), Medhi Lacen, Karim Matmour, Karim Ziani (80 Adlène Guédioura), Hassan Yebda (88 Djamel Mesbah), Foued Kadir.   Manager: Rabah Saâdane


887.  23.06.2010   19th World Cup Group C
**SLOVENIA v ENGLAND  0-1**  (0-1)
*Nelson Mandela Bay, Port Elizabeth (South Africa)*
Referee: Wolfgang Stark (Germany)   Attendance: 36,893
**SLOVENIA:** Samir Handanovic, Miso Brecko, Marko Suler, Bostjan Cesar, Robert Koren, Bojan Jokic, Andraz Kirm (79 Tim Matavz), Aleksander Radosavljevic, Zlatan Ljubijankic (62 Zlatko Dedic), Valter Birsa, Milivoje Novakovic.   Manager: Matjaz Kek
**ENGLAND:** David Benjamin James, Glenn Johnson, Ashley Cole, John Terry, Matthew Upson, Steven Gerrard, Frank Lampard, Gareth Barry, James Milner, Wayne Rooney (72 Joe Cole), Jermain Defoe (85 Emile Heskey).   Manager: Fabio Capello
**Goal**: Jermain Defoe (22)


888.  27.06.2010   19th World Cup Round of 16
**GERMANY v ENGLAND  4-1**  (2-1)
*Free State Stadium, Bloemfontein (South Africa)*
Referee: Jorge Luis Larrionda Pietrafesa (Uruguay)   Attendance: 40,510
**GERMANY:** Manuel Neuer, Arne Friedrich, Philipp Lahm, Per Mertesacker, Jérôme Boateng, Sami Khedira, Bastian Schweinsteiger, Mesut Özil (83 Stefan Kießling), Lukas Podolski, Miroslav Klose (72 Mario Gómez), Thomas Müller (72 Piotr Trochowski).   Manager: Joachim Löw
**ENGLAND:** David Benjamin James, Glenn Johnson (87 Shaun Wright-Phillips), Ashley Cole, John Terry, Matthew Upson, Steven Gerrard, Frank Lampard, Gareth Barry, James Milner (64 Joe Cole), Wayne Rooney, Jermain Defoe (71 Emile Heskey).   Manager: Fabio Capello
**Goals**: Miroslav Klose (20), Lukas Podolski (32), Thomas Müller (67, 70) / Matthew Upson (37)


889.  11.08.2010
**ENGLAND v HUNGARY  2-1**  (0-0)
*Wembley, London*
Referee: Stéphane Lannoy (France)   Attendance: 72,024
**ENGLAND:** Joe Hart, John Terry (46 Michael Dawson), Ashley Cole (46 Kieran Gibbs), Phil Jagielka, Glenn Johnson, Adam Johnson, Gareth Barry, Frank Lampard (46 Bobby Zamora), Steven Gerrard (83 Jack Wilshere), Theo Walcott (46 Ashley Young), Wayne Rooney (67 James Milner).   Manager: Fabio Capello
**HUNGARY:** Gábor Király, Zoltán Lipták (55 Adám Komlósi), Vilmos Vanczák (46 Zsolt Laczkó), Roland Juhász, Zoltán Szélesi, Krisztián Vadócz, Szabolcs Huszti (46 Tamás Hajnal), Ákos Elek (60 Balasz Tóth), Zoltán Gera, Gergely Rudolf (85 Tamás Priskin), Balázs Dzsudzsák (46 Vladimir Koman).   Manager: Sándor Egervári
**Goals**: Steven Gerrard (69, 72) / Phil Jagielka (62 og)


890.  03.09.2010   14th European Champs Qualifier
**ENGLAND v BULGARIA  4-0**  (1-0)
*Wembley, London*
Referee: Viktor Kassai (Hungary)   Attendance: 73,426
**ENGLAND:** Joe Hart, Michael Dawson (57 Gary Cahill), Ashley Cole, Glenn Johnson, Phil Jagielka, Gareth Barry, Steven Gerrard, James Milner, Jermain Defoe (87 Ashley Young), Theo Walcott (74 Adam Johnson), Wayne Rooney.   Manager: Fabio Capello
**BULGARIA:** Nikolay Mihaylov, Zhivko Milanov, Stanislav Manolev (66 Veselin Minev), Ilian Stoyanov, Ivan Ivanov, Stanislav Angelov, Chavdar Yankov, Stilian Petrov, Martin Petrov, Valeri Bojinov (63 Dimitar Rangelov), Ivelin Popov (79 Georgi Peev).   Manager: Stanimir Stoilov
**Goals**: Jermain Defoe (3, 61, 86), Adam Johnson (83)

891.  07.09.2010    14th European Champs Qualifier
**SWITZERLAND v ENGLAND  1-3**  (0-1)
*St. Jakob-Park, Basel*
Referee:  Nicola Rizzoli (Italy)    Attendance: 37,500

SWITZERLAND:  Diego Benaglio, Stephan Lichtsteiner, Stéphane Grichting, Reto Ziegler, Steve von Bergen, Xavier Margairaz (46 Xherdan Shaqiri), Gökhan Inler, David Degen (64 Marco Streller), Pirmin Schwegler (83 Moreno Costanzo), Alexander Frei, Eren Derdiyok.  Manager: Ottmar Hitzfeld

ENGLAND:  Joe Hart, Ashley Cole, Joleon Lescott, Phil Jagielka, Glenn Johnson, Gareth Barry, Steven Gerrard, James Milner, Jermain Defoe (73 Darren Bent), Theo Walcott (13 Adam Johnson), Wayne Rooney (79 Shaun Wright-Phillips).  Manager: Fabio Capello

Sent off:  Stephan Lichtsteiner (65)

Goals:  Xherdan Shaqiri (71) /
Wayne Rooney (10), Adam Johnson (69), Darren Bent (88)


892.  12.10.2010    14th European Champs Qualifier
**ENGLAND v MONTENEGRO  0-0**
*Wembley, London*
Referee:  Manuel Gräfe (Germany)    Attendance: 73,451

ENGLAND:  Joe Hart, Joleon Lescott, Rio Ferdinand, Ashley Cole, Glenn Johnson, Ashley Young (74 Shaun Wright-Phillips), Adam Johnson, Gareth Barry, Steven Gerrard, Peter Crouch (70 Kevin Davies), Wayne Rooney.
Manager:  Fabio Capello

MONTENEGRO:  Mladen Bozovic, Elsad Zverotic, Stefan Savic, Milan Jovanovic, Marko Basa, Miodrag Dzudovic, Simon Vukcevic, Milorad Pekovic, Mitar Novakovic (62 Mladen Kascelan), Branko Boskovic (83 Fatos Beciraj), Radomir Djalovic (77 Andrija Delibasic).
Manager:  Zlatko Kranjcar


893.  17.11.2010
**ENGLAND v FRANCE  1-2**  (0-1)
*Wembley, London*
Referee:  Claus Bo Larsen (Denmark)    Attendance: 85,495

ENGLAND:  Ben Foster, Joleon Lescott, Phil Jagielka, Rio Ferdinand (46 Micah Richards), Gareth Barry (46 Adam Johnson), Jordan Henderson, Kieran Gibbs (72 Stephen Warnock), Steven Gerrard (85 Peter Crouch), James Milner, Andy Carroll (72 Jay Bothroyd), Theo Walcott (46 Ashley Young).  Manager: Fabio Capello

FRANCE:  Hugo Lloris, Adil Rami, Philippe Mexès (46 Mamadou Sakho), Éric Abidal, Bacary Sagna (87 Anthony Réveillère), Samir Nasri, Florent Malouda (77 Dimitri Payet), Yann M'Vila, Yoann Gourcuff (85 Guillaume Hoarau), Mathieu Valbuena (68 Alou Diarra), Karim Benzema (67 Loïc Rémy).  Manager: Laurent Blanc

Goals:  Peter Crouch (86) / K. Benzema (16), M. Valbuena (55)


894.  09.02.2011
**DENMARK v ENGLAND  1-2**  (1-1)
*Parken, København*
Referee:  Jonas Eriksson (Sweden)    Attendance: 21,523

DENMARK:  Thomas Sørensen, Mathias Jørgensen (46 Simon Kjær), Lars Jacobsen (60 Michael Silberbauer), Daniel Agger, Simon Poulsen (46 Daniel Wass), William Kvist (90 Martin Vingaard), Christian Eriksen, Christian Poulsen, Michael Krohn-Dehli (69 Nicklas Pedersen), Nicklas Bendtner, Dennis Rommedahl (81 Thomas Enevoldsen).
Manager:  Morten Olsen

ENGLAND:  Joe Hart, Michael Dawson (60 Gary Cahill), Ashley Cole (81 Leighton Baines), John Terry, Glen Johnson, James Milner, Frank Lampard (46 Scott Parker), Jack Wilshere (46 Gareth Barry), Darren Bent, Theo Walcott (68 Stewart Downing), Wayne Rooney (46 Ashley Young).
Manager:  Fabio Capello

Goals:  Daniel Agger (8) /
Darren Bent (10), Ashley Young (68)


895.  26.03.2011    14th European Champs Qualifier
**WALES v ENGLAND  0-2**  (0-2)
*Millennium, Cardiff*
Referee:  OLEGARIO Manuel Bartolo Faustino BENQUERENÇA (Portugal)    Attendance: 68,959

WALES:  Wayne Hennessey, Ashley Williams, Chris Gunter, Andrew Crofts, James Collins, Danny Collins, Aaron Ramsey, Joe Ledley, Andy King (65 David Vaughan), Steve Morison (65 Ched Evans), Craig Bellamy.  Manager: Gary Speed

ENGLAND:  Joe Hart, John Terry, Michael Dawson, Ashley Cole, Glen Johnson, Ashley Young, Scott Parker (88 Phil Jagielka), Jack Wilshere (82 Stewart Downing), Frank Lampard, Darren Bent, Wayne Rooney (70 James Milner).  Manager: Fabio Capello

Goals:  Frank Lampard (7 pen), Darren Bent (15)


896.  29.03.2011
**ENGLAND v GHANA  1-1**  (1-0)
*Wembley, London*
Referee:  Cüneyt Çakir (Turkey)    Attendance: 80,102

ENGLAND:  Joe Hart, Gary Cahill, Phil Jagielka, Glen Johnson (46 Joleon Lescott), Leighton Baines, Stewart Downing, Ashley Young (81 Danny Welbeck), Gareth Barry, Jack Wilshere (69 Matthew Jarvis), James Milner, Andy Carroll (59 Jermain Defoe).  Manager: Fabio Capello

GHANA:  Richard Kingson, John Mensah, Lee Addy (46 Dan Opare), John Paintsil, Isaac Vorsah (46 Jonathan Mensah), Anthony Annan (46 Derek Boateng), Sulley Ali Muntari (59 André Ayew), Kwadwo Asamoah (84 Samuel Inkoom), Emmanuel Agyemang-Badu, Dominic Adiyiah (69 Prince Tagoe), Asamoah Gyan.  Manager: Goran Stevanovic

Goals:  Andy Carroll (43) / Asamoah Gyan (90)

897.  04.06.2011   14th European Champs Qualifier
**ENGLAND v SWITZERLAND  2-2**  (1-2)

*Wembley, London*

Referee: Damir Skomina (Slovenia)   Attendance: 84,459

**ENGLAND:** Joe Hart, Ashley Cole (30 Leighton Baines), John Terry, Rio Ferdinand, Glenn Johnson, Scott Parker, Jack Wilshere, James Milner, Frank Lampard (46 Ashley Young), Darren Bent, Theo Walcott (78 Stewart Downing). Manager: Fabio Capello

**SWITZERLAND:** Diego Benaglio, Johan Djourou, Reto Ziegler, Philippe Senderos, Stephan Lichtsteiner, Granit Xhaka, Valon Behrami (58 Blerim Dzemaili), Tranquillo Barnetta (90 Innocent Emeghara), Xherdan Shaqiri, Gökhan Inler, Eren Derdiyok (74 Admir Mehmedi).   Manager: Ottmar Hitzfeld

**Goals**: Frank Lampard (37 pen), Ashley Young (51) / Tranquillo Barnetta (32, 35)


898.  02.09.2011   14th European Champs Qualifier
**BULGARIA v ENGLAND  0-3**  (0-3)

*Vasil Levski, Sofia*

Referee: Frank De Bleeckere (Belgium)   Attendance: 27,230

**BULGARIA:** Nikolay Mihaylov, Petar Zanev, Stanislav Manolev, Ivan Bandalovski (46 Georgi Sarmov), Ivan Ivanov, Nikolaj Bodurov, Stilian Petrov, Martin Petrov, Blagoy Georgiev, Ivelin Popov (81 Marcos Antônio Malachias Júnior "Marquinhos"), Tzvetan Genkov (61 Georgi Bozhilov).   Manager: Lothar Matthäus

**ENGLAND:** Joe Hart, John Terry, Ashley Cole, Chris Smalling, Gary Cahill, Ashley Young (61 James Milner), Scott Parker, Stewart Downing, Gareth Barry (80 Frank Lampard), Theo Walcott (83 Adam Johnson), Wayne Rooney.   Manager: Fabio Capello

**Goals**: Gary Cahill (13), Wayne Rooney (21, 45+1)


899.  06.09.2011   14th European Champs Qualifier
**ENGLAND v WALES  1-0**  (1-0)

*Wembley, London*

Referee: Robert Schörgenhofer (Austria)   Att: 77,128

**ENGLAND:** Joe Hart, Ashley Cole, John Terry, Gary Cahill, Chris Smalling, Stewart Downing (79 Adam Johnson), Gareth Barry, Ashley Young, James Milner, Frank Lampard (73 Scott Parker), Wayne Rooney (89 Andy Carroll). Manager: Fabio Capello

**WALES:** Wayne Hennessey, Chris Gunter, Andrew Crofts, Ashley Williams, Neil Taylor, Joe Ledley, Jack Collison (85 Andy King), Darcy Blake, Aaron Ramsey, Gareth Bale, Steve Morison (67 Robert Earnshaw).   Manager: Gary Speed

**Goal**: Ashley Young (35)


900.  07.10.2011   14th European Champs Qualifier
**MONTENEGRO v ENGLAND  2-2**  (1-2)

*Pod Goricom, Podgorica*

Referee: Wolfgang Stark (Germany)   Attendance: 11.340

**MONTENEGRO:** Mladen Bozovic, Elsad Zverotic, Stefan Savic, Miodrag Dzudovic, Simon Vukcevic, Milorad Pekovic, Mladen Kascelan (46 Milan Jovanovic), Vladimir Bozovic (79 Andrija Delibasic), Mirko Vucinic, Stevan Jovetic, Fatos Beciraj (64 Dejan Damjanovic).   Manager: Branko Brnovic

**ENGLAND:** Joe Hart, John Terry, Ashley Cole, Phil Jones, Gary Cahill, Ashley Young (60 Stewart Downing), Scott Parker, Gareth Barry, Theo Walcott (76 Danny Welbeck), Darren Bent (64 Frank Lampard), Wayne Rooney. Manager: Fabio Capello

**Sent off**: Wayne Rooney (74)

**Goals**: Elsad Zverotic (45), Andrija Delibasic (90+1) / Ashley Young (11), Darren Bent (31)


901.  12.11.2011
**ENGLAND v SPAIN  1-0**  (0-0)

*Wembley, London*

Referee: Frank De Bleeckere (Belgium)   Attendance: 87,189

**ENGLAND:** Joe Hart, Joleon Lescott, Ashley Cole, Glen Johnson, Phil Jagielka, Phil Jones (57 Jack Rodwell), Scott Parker (85 Kyle Walker), Frank Lampard (57 Gareth Barry), James Milner (76 Adam Johnson), Darren Bent (64 Danny Welbeck), Theo Walcott (46 Stewart Downing). Manager: Fabio Capello

**SPAIN:** IKER CASILLAS Fernández (46 José Manuel "Pepe" REINA Páez), Álvaro ARBELOA Coca, JORDI ALBA Ramos, SERGIO RAMOS García (75 Carles PUYOL Saforcada), Gerard PIQUÉ i Bernabéu, DAVID Jiménez SILVA (46 Juan Manuel MATA García), Sergio BUSQUETS Burgos (64 FERNANDO José TORRES Sanz), "Xavi" Xavier Hernández i Creus (46 Francesc "CESC" FÀBREGAS Soler), Xabier "Xabi" ALONSO Olano, Andrés INIESTA Luján (75 Santiago "Santi" CAZORLA González), DAVID VILLA Sánchez.
Manager: Vicente DEL BOSQUE González

**Goal**: Frank Lampard (49)

902.  15.11.2011
**ENGLAND v SWEDEN  1-0**  (1-0)
*Wembley, London*
Referee:  Pavel Královec (Czech Republic)   Att: 48,876
**ENGLAND:** Joe Hart (46 Scott Carson), John Terry, Phil Jones, Gary Cahill, Leighton Baines, Kyle Walker, Jack Rodwell (58 James Milner), Stewart Downing, Gareth Barry, Theo Walcott (58 Daniel Sturridge), Bobby Zamora (70 Darren Bent).   Manager: Fabio Capello
**SWEDEN:** Andreas Isaksson, Olof Mellberg (46 Jonas Olsson), Daniel Majstorovic, Mikael Lustig (55 Christian Wilhelmsson), Martin Olsson, Sebastian Larsson, Kim Källström (70 Anders Svensson), Rasmus Elm (87 Emir Bajrami), Pontus Wernbloom, Zlatan Ibrahimovic (46 Ola Toivonen), Johan Elmander.   Manager: Erik Hamrén
**Goal**: Gareth Barry (22)

903.  29.02.2012
**ENGLAND v NETHERLANDS  2-3**  (0-0)
*Wembley, London*
Referee:  Dr.Felix Brych (Germany)   Attendance: 76,283
**ENGLAND:** Joe Hart, Micah Richards, Gary Cahill, Leighton Baines, Chris Smalling (63 Phil Jones), Gareth Barry (46 James Milner), Ashley Young, Scott Parker, Adam Johnson (65 Stewart Downing), Steven Gerrard (33 Daniel Sturridge, 89 Theo Walcott), Danny Welbeck (80 Frazier Campbell). Manager: Stuart Pearce
**NETHERLANDS:** Maarten Stekelenburg, Erik Pieters (46 Stijn Schaars), Joris Mathijsen, Khalid Boulahrouz (82 Ron Vlaar), John Heitinga, Mark van Bommel, Wesley Sneijder (76 Urby Emanuelson), Nigel de Jong, Robin van Persie (46 Klaas-Jan Huntelaar, 62 Luuk de Jong), Arjen Robben, Dirk Kuyt.   Manager: Bert van Marwijk
**Goals**: Gary Cahill (85), Ashley Young (90+1) / Arjen Robben (58, 90+2), Klaas-Jan Huntelaar (58)

904.  26.05.2012
**NORWAY v ENGLAND  0-1**  (0-1)
*Ullevaal Stadion, Oslo*
Referee: Michael Weiner (Germany)   Attendance: 21,436
**NORWAY:** Rune Jarstein, Tom Høgli (39 Espen Ruud), Brede Hangeland, Vadim Demidov, John Arne Riise, Morten Pedersen (62 Christian Grindheim), Markus Henriksen (84 Valon Berisha), Alexander Tettey (90+1 Ruben Jenssen), Tarik Elyounoussi, Daniel Braaten (74 Erik Huseklepp), Mohammed Abdellaoue.   Manager: Egil Olsen
**ENGLAND:** Robert Green, Joleon Lescott, Phil Jones (87 Martin Kelly), Phil Jagielka, Leighton Baines, Stewart Downing (84 Adam Johnson), Ashley Young (73 Alex Oxlade-Chamberlain), Scott Parker (55 Theo Walcott), James Milner, Steven Gerrard (46 Gareth Barry, 73 Jordan Henderson), Andy Carroll.   Manager: Roy Hodgson
**Goal**: Ashley Young (9)

905.  02.06.2012
**ENGLAND v BELGIUM  1-0**  (1-0)
*Wembley, London*
Referee:  Peter Rasmussen (Denmark)   Attendance: 85,091
**ENGLAND:** Joe Hart, John Terry (70 Phil Jagielka), Ashley Cole, Glen Johnson, Gary Cahill (19 Joleon Lescott), Ashley Young (66 Jermain Defoe), Scott Parker, James Milner, Steven Gerrard (83 Jordan Henderson), Danny Welbeck (53 Wayne Rooney), Alex Oxlade-Chamberlain (66 Theo Walcott).   Manager: Roy Hodgson
**BELGIUM:** Simon Mignolet, Thomas Vermaelen, Timmy Simons, Axel Witsel, Jan Vertonghen, Kevin Mirallas (59 Nacer Chadli), Dries Mertens (72 Romelu Lukaku), Eden Hazard, Guillaume Gillet, Marouane Fellaini, Mousa Dembélé.   Manager: Marc Wilmots
**Goal**: Danny Welbeck (36)

906.  11.06.2012    14th European Champs Group D
**FRANCE v ENGLAND  1-1**  (1-1)
*Donbass Arena, Donetsk (Ukraine)*
Referee:  Nicola Rizzoli (Italy)   Attendance: 47,400
**FRANCE:** Hugo Lloris, Mathieu Debuchy, Patrice Evra, Adil Rami, Philippe Mexès, Yohan Cabaye (84 Hatem Ben Arfa), Franck Ribéry, Samir Nasri, Florent Malouda (85 Marvin Martin), Alou Diarra, Karim Benzema.   Manager: Laurent Blanc
**ENGLAND:** Joe Hart, Glen Johnson, Ashley Cole, John Terry, Joleon Lescott, Steven Gerrard, Ashley Young, James Milner, Scott Parker (78 Jordan Henderson), Alex Oxlade-Chamberlain (77 Jermain Defoe), Danny Welbeck (90+1 Theo Walcott).   Manager: Roy Hodgson
**Goals**: Samir Nasri (39) / Joleon Lescott (30)

907.  15.06.2012    14th European Champs Group D
**SWEDEN v ENGLAND  2-3**  (0-1)
*NSK Olimpiyskyi, Kiev (Ukraine)*
Referee: Damir Skomina (Slovenia)   Attendance: 64,640
**SWEDEN:** Andreas Isaksson, Olof Mellberg, Andreas Granqvist (66 Mikael Lustig), Martin Olsson, Jonas Olsson, Rasmus Elm (81 Christian Wilhelmsson), Sebastian Larsson, Anders Svensson, Kim Källström, Zlatan Ibrahimovic, Johan Elmander (79 Markus Rosenberg).   Manager: Erik Hamrén
**ENGLAND:** Joe Hart, Glen Johnson, Ashley Cole, John Terry, Joleon Lescott, Steven Gerrard, Ashley Young, James Milner (61 Theo Walcott), Scott Parker, Andy Carroll, Danny Welbeck (90 Alex Oxlade-Chamberlain).   Manager: Roy Hodgson
**Goals**: Glen Johnson (49 og), Olof Mellberg (59) / Andy Carroll (23), Theo Walcott (64), Danny Welbeck (78)

908.  19.06.2012  14th European Champs Group D
**ENGLAND v UKRAINE  1-0**  (0-0)
*Donbass Arena, Donetsk (Ukraine)*
Referee: Viktor Kassai (Hungary)  Attendance: 48,700

**ENGLAND:** Joe Hart, Glen Johnson, Ashley Cole, John Terry, Joleon Lescott, Steven Gerrard, Ashley Young, James Milner (70 Theo Walcott), Scott Parker, Wayne Rooney (87 Alex Oxlade-Chamberlain), Danny Welbeck (82 Andy Carroll).   Manager: Roy Hodgson

**UKRAINE:** Andriy Pyatov, Evgen Selin, Evgen Khacheridi, Yaroslav Rakitskiy, Anatoliy Tymoshchuk, Denys Garmash (78 Sergiy Nazarenko), Oleg Gusev, Andriy Yarmolenko, Artem Milevskiy (77 Bogdan Butko), Yevhen Konoplyanka, Marko Devic (70 Andriy Shevchenko).   Manager: Oleg Blokhin

**Goal:** Wayne Rooney (48)


909.  24.06.2012  14th Euro Champs Quarter Finals
**ENGLAND v ITALY  0-0**  (AET)
*NSK Olimpiyskyi, Kiev (Ukraine)*
Referee:  PEDRO PROENÇA Oliveira Alves Garcia (Portugal)
Attendance: 64,340

**ENGLAND:** Joe Hart, Glen Johnson, Ashley Cole, John Terry, Joleon Lescott, Steven Gerrard, Ashley Young, James Milner (61 Theo Walcott), Scott Parker (94 Jordan Henderson), Wayne Rooney, Danny Welbeck (61 Andy Carroll).
Manager: Roy Hodgson

**ITALY:** Gianluigi Buffon, Federico Balzaretti, Andrea Barzagli, Leonardo Bonucci, Ignazio Abate (90+1 Christian Maggio), Claudio Marchisio, Daniele De Rossi (80 Antonio Nocerino), Riccardo Montolivo, Andrea Pirlo, Mario Balotelli, Antonio Cassano (78 Alessandro Diamanti).
Manager: Cesare Prandelli

**Penalties:** 0-1 Mario Balotelli, 1-1 Steven Gerrard, Riccardo Montolivo (missed), 2-1 Wayne Rooney, 2-2 Andrea Pirlo, Ashley Young (missed), 2-3 Antonio Nocerino, Ashley Cole (saved), 2-4 Alessandro Diamanti


910.  15.08.2012
**ENGLAND v ITALY  2-1**  (1-1)
*Stade de Suisse, Bern (Switzerland)*
Referee: Sascha Kever (Switzerland)   Attendance: 15,000

**ENGLAND:** Jack Butland (46 John Ruddy), Kyle Walker, Phil Jagielka (62 Joleon Lescott), Gary Cahill, Leighton Baines (78 Ryan Bertrand), Adam Johnson, Ashley Young (62 James Milner), Tom Cleverley, Michael Carrick, Frank Lampard (69 Jake Livermore), Andy Carroll (46 Jermain Defoe).
Manager: Roy Hodgson

**ITALY:** Salvatore Sirigu, Angelo Ogbonna, Federico Balzaretti (46 Federico Peluso), Davide Astori, Antonio Nocerino, Stephan El Shaarawy (58 Manolo Gabbiadini), Daniele De Rossi, Alberto Aquilani (69 Andrea Poli), Ignazio Abate (86 Ezequiel Schelotto), Alessandro Diamanti (59 Marco Verratti), Mattia Destro (82 Diego Fabbrini).
Manager: Cesare Prandelli

**Goals:** Phil Jagielka (27), Jermain Defoe (80) / Daniele De Rossi (15)


911.  07.09.2012  20th World Cup Qualifier
**MOLDOVA v ENGLAND  0-5**  (0-3)
*Stadionul Zimbru, Chisinau*
Referee: Pol van Boekel (Netherlands)   Attendance: 10,500

**MOLDOVA:** Stanislav Namasco, Simeon Bulgaru, Victor Golovatenco, Alexandru Epureanu, Igor Armas, Alexandru Onica, Serghei Covalciuc, Alexandru Suvorov (46 Alexandru Dedov), Artur Patras, Alexandru Gatcan, Igor Picusceac (76 Eugeniu Sidorenco, 85 Georgi Ovsyannikov).
Manager: Ion Caras

**ENGLAND:** Joe Hart, John Terry, Joleon Lescott, Glen Johnson, Leighton Baines, Tom Cleverley, James Milner, Frank Lampard, Steven Gerrard (46 Michael Carrick), Jermain Defoe (68 Danny Welbeck), Alex Oxlade-Chamberlain (58 Theo Walcott).   Manager: Roy Hodgson

**Goals:** Frank Lampard (4 pen, 29), Jermain Defoe (32), James Milner (74), Leighton Baines (83)


912.  11.09.2012  20th World Cup Qualifier
**ENGLAND v UKRAINE  1-1**  (0-1)
*Wembley, London*
Referee: Cüneyt Çakir (Turkey)   Attendance: 68,102

**ENGLAND:** Joe Hart, Joleon Lescott, Leighton Baines (73 Ryan Bertrand), Glen Johnson, Phil Jagielka, Tom Cleverley (62 Danny Welbeck), Steven Gerrard, James Milner, Frank Lampard, Jermain Defoe, Alex Oxlade-Chamberlain (69 Daniel Sturridge).   Manager: Roy Hodgson

**UKRAINE:** Andriy Pyatov, Evgen Khacheridi, Evgen Selin (75 Vyacheslav Shevchuk), Yaroslav Rakitskiy, Oleg Gusev, Denys Garmash, Anatoliy Tymoshchuk, Ruslan Rotan (90+2 Sergiy Nazarenko), Yevhen Konoplyanka, Roman Zozulya (88 Marko Devic), Andriy Yarmolenko.   Manager: Oleg Blokhin

**Sent off:** Steven Gerrard (88)

**Goals:** Frank Lampard (87 pen) / Yevhen Konoplyanka (39)

913.  12.10.2012   20th World Cup Qualifier
**ENGLAND v SAN MARINO  5-0** (2-0)
*Wembley, London*

Referee: Gediminas Mazeika (Lithuania)   Att: 86,645

**ENGLAND:** Joe Hart, Phil Jagielka, Gary Cahill, Leighton Baines, Kyle Walker, Tom Cleverley, Michael Carrick (66 Jonjo Shelvey), Theo Walcott (10 Aaron Lennon), Wayne Rooney (73 Andy Carroll), Alex Oxlade-Chamberlain, Danny Welbeck.
Manager: Roy Hodgson

**SAN MARINO:** Aldo Simoncini, Alessandro Della Valle, Cristian Brolli, Fabio Vitaioli (84 Simone Bacciocchi), Davide Simoncini, Alex Gasperoni, Michele Cervellini, Mirko Palazzi, Matteo Coppini (75 Lorenzo Buscarini), Enrico Cibelli, Danilo Rinaldi (79 Andy Selva).   Manager: Giampaolo Mazza

**Goals:** Wayne Rooney (35 pen, 70), Danny Welbeck (37, 72), Alex Oxlade-Chamberlain (77)

914.  17.10.2012   20th World Cup Qualifier
**POLAND v ENGLAND  1-1** (0-1)
*Stadion Narodowy, Warszawa*

Referee: Gianluca Rocchi (Italy)   Attendance: 47,000

**POLAND:** Przemyslaw Tyton, Marcin Wasilewski, Lukasz Piszczek, Kamil Glik, Jakub Wawrzyniak, Eugen Polanski, Ludovic Obraniak (90 Ariel Borysiuk), Grzegorz Krychowiak, Kamil Grosicki (82 Arkadiusz Milik), Pawel Wszolek (63 Adrian Mierzejewski), Robert Lewandowski.
Manager: Waldemar Fornalik

**ENGLAND:** Joe Hart, Joleon Lescott, Ashley Cole, Glen Johnson, Phil Jagielka, Tom Cleverley, Michael Carrick, James Milner, Steven Gerrard, Jermain Defoe (67 Danny Welbeck), Wayne Rooney (72 Alex Oxlade-Chamberlain).
Manager: Roy Hodgson

**Goals:** Kamil Glik (70) / Wayne Rooney (31)

915.  14.11.2012
**SWEDEN v ENGLAND  4-2** (1-2)
*Friends Arena, Solna*

Referee: Svein Moen (Norway)   Attendance: 49,967

**SWEDEN:** Andreas Isaksson, Martin Olsson (46 Behrang Safari), Jonas Olsson, Mikael Lustig (74 Tobias Sana), Andreas Granqvist (73 Mikael Antonsson), Sebastian Larsson (86 Pontus Jansson), Kim Källström (61 Anders Svensson), Alexander Kacaniklic, Rasmus Elm, Mathias Ranégie (89 Pontus Wernbloom), Zlatan Ibrahimovic.
Manager: Erik Hamrén

**ENGLAND:** Joe Hart, Steven Caulker (74 Ryan Shawcross), Glen Johnson (75 Carl Jenkinson), Gary Cahill, Leighton Baines, Ashley Young (61 Daniel Sturridge), Leon Osman, Tom Cleverley (61 Jack Wilshere), Raheem Sterling (85 Wilfried Zaha), Steven Gerrard (75 Tom Huddlestone), Danny Welbeck.
Manager: Roy Hodgson

**Goals:** Zlatan Ibrahimovic (20, 78, 84, 90+1) / Danny Welbeck (35), Steven Caulker (38)

916.  06.02.2013
**ENGLAND v BRAZIL  2-1** (1-0)
*Wembley, London*

Referee: PEDRO PROENÇA Oliveira Alves Garcia (Portugal)
Attendance: 87,453

**ENGLAND:** Joe Hart, Glen Johnson, Ashley Cole (46 Leighton Baines), Gary Cahill, Chris Smalling, Steven Gerrard, Tom Cleverley (46 Frank Lampard), Jack Wilshere, Wayne Rooney, Danny Welbeck (61 James Milner), Theo Walcott (76 Aaron Lennon).   Manager: Roy Hodgson

**BRAZIL:** JÚLIO CÉSAR Soares Espíndola, DAVID LUIZ Moreira Marinho (79 João MIRANDA de Souza Filho), Bonfim Costa Santos DANTE, Daniel "DANI" ALVES da Silva, ADRIANO Correia Claro (70 FILIPE LUÍS Kasmirski), Ronaldo De Assis Moreira "RONALDINHO GAÚCHO" (46 LUCAS Rodrigues Moura da Silva), RAMIRES Santos do Nascimento (46 Marcos AROUCA da Silva), José Paulo Bezerra Maciel Júnior "PAULINHO" (62 JEAN Raphael Vanderlei Moreira), OSCAR dos Santos Emboaba Junior, NEYMAR da Silva Santos Júnior, LUÍS FABIANO Clemente (46 Frederico Chaves Guedes "FRED").
Manager: Luiz Felipe SCOLARI

**Goals:** Wayne Rooney (26), Frank Lampard (60) / Frederico Chaves Guedes "FRED" (48)

Ronaldo De Assis Moreira "RONALDINHO GAÚCHO" missed a penalty kick after 19 minutes.

917.  22.03.2013   20th World Cup Qualifier
**SAN MARINO v ENGLAND  0-8** (0-5)
*Stadio Olimpico di Serravalle, Serravalle*

Referee: Alain Bieri (Switzerland)   Attendance: 4,952

**SAN MARINO:** Aldo Simoncini, Alessandro Della Valle, Fabio Vitaioli, Davide Simoncini, Alex Gasperoni, Michele Cervellini, Fabio Bollini (81 Carlo Valentini), Mirko Palazzi, Enrico Cibelli (68 Lorenzo Buscarini), Andy Selva (74 Danilo Rinaldi), Matteo Vitaioli.   Manager: Giampaolo Mazza

**ENGLAND:** Joe Hart, Joleon Lescott, Leighton Baines, Kyle Walker, Chris Smalling, Tom Cleverley (56 Leon Osman), Ashley Young, Frank Lampard (66 Scott Parker), Jermain Defoe, Alex Oxlade-Chamberlain, Wayne Rooney (55 Daniel Sturridge).   Manager: Roy Hodgson

**Goals:** Alessandro Della Valle (12 og), Alex Oxlade-Chamberlain (29), Jermain Defoe (35, 77), Ashley Young (39), Frank Lampard (42), Wayne Rooney (54), Daniel Sturridge (70)

918.   22.03.2013   20th World Cup Qualifier
**MONTENEGRO v ENGLAND  1-1**  (0-1)
*Stadion Pod Goricom, Podgorica*
Referee: Jonas Eriksson (Sweden)   Attendance: 11,300
**MONTENEGRO:** Mladen Bozovic, Marko Basa, Elsad Zverotic, Stefan Savic, Vladimir Volkov, Miodrag Dzudovic, Simon Vukcevic (63 Milos Krkotic), Mitar Novakovic (46 Dejan Damjanovic), Vladimir Bozovic (75 Andrija Delibasic), Mirko Vucinic, Stevan Jovetic.   Manager: Branko Brnovic
**ENGLAND:** Joe Hart, Joleon Lescott, Ashley Cole, Chris Smalling, Glen Johnson, Tom Cleverley (76 Ashley Young), Michael Carrick, James Milner, Steven Gerrard, Danny Welbeck, Wayne Rooney.   Manager: Roy Hodgson
**Goals**: Dejan Damjanovic (76) / Wayne Rooney (6)


919.   29.05.2013
**ENGLAND v REPUBLIC OF IRELAND   1-1**  (1-1)
*Wembley, London*
Referee: William Collum (Scotland)   Attendance: 80,126
**ENGLAND:** Joe Hart (46 Ben Foster), Gary Cahill, Glen Johnson (46 Phil Jones), Phil Jagielka, Ashley Cole (53 Leighton Baines), Michael Carrick, Frank Lampard, Theo Walcott, Daniel Sturridge (33 Jermain Defoe), Wayne Rooney, Alex Oxlade-Chamberlain (87 James Milner).
Manager: Roy Hodgson
**REPUBLIC OF IRELAND:** David Forde, Séamus Coleman, John O'Shea, Stephen Kelly, Sean St Ledger, Glenn Whelan (73 Jeff Hendrick), Aiden McGeady (68 James McClean), James McCarthy, Jon Walters (81 Conor Sammon), Shane Long, Robbie Keane (65 Simon Cox).
Manager: Giovanni Trapattoni
**Goals**: Frank Lampard (23) / Shane Long (13)


920.   02.06.2013
**BRAZIL v ENGLAND 2-2**  (0-0)
*Maracaña, Rio de Janeiro*
Referee: WILMAR ROLDÁN Pérez (Colombia)   Att: 66,015
**BRAZIL:** JÚLIO CÉSAR Soares Espíndola, THIAGO Emiliano SILVA, FILIPE LUÍS Kasmirski (46 MARCELO Vieira da Silva Júnior), DAVID LUIZ Moreira Marinho, Daniel "DANI" ALVES da Silva, José Paulo Bezerra Maciel Júnior "PAULINHO" (83 BERNARD Anício Caldeira Duarte), OSCAR dos Santos Emboaba Junior (56 LUCAS Rodrigues Moura da Silva), LUIZ GUSTAVO Dias (46 Anderson HERNANES de Carvalho Andrade), NEYMAR da Silva Santos Júnior, Givanildo Vieira de Souza "HULK" (72 FERNANDO Lucas Martins), Frederico Chaves Guedes "FRED" (80 LEANDRO DAMIÃO da Silva dos Santos).
Manager: Luiz Felipe SCOLARI

**ENGLAND:** Joe Hart, Phil Jones, Glen Johnson (62 Alex Oxlade-Chamberlain), Phil Jagielka, Gary Cahill, Leighton Baines (32 Ashley Cole), James Milner, Frank Lampard, Michael Carrick, Theo Walcott (84 Jack Rodwell), Wayne Rooney.   Manager: Roy Hodgson
**Goals**: Frederico Chaves Guedes "FRED" (58), José Paulo Bezerra Maciel Júnior "PAULINHO" (83) / Alex Oxlade-Chamberlain (67), Wayne Rooney (79)


921.   14.08.2013
**ENGLAND v SCOTLAND 3-2**  (1-1)
*Wembley, London*
Referee: Dr. Felix Brych (Germany)   Attendance: 80,485
**ENGLAND:** Joe Hart, Phil Jagielka (84 Phil Jones), Gary Cahill, Leighton Baines, Kyle Walker, Steven Gerrard (62 Alex Oxlade-Chamberlain), Tom Cleverley (67 James Milner), Jack Wilshere (46 Frank Lampard), Wayne Rooney (67 Rickie Lambert), Danny Welbeck, Theo Walcott (75 Wilfried Zaha).
Manager: Roy Hodgson
**SCOTLAND:** Allan McGregor, Alan Hutton, Steven Whittaker, Grant Hanley, James Morrison (82 Jordan Rhodes), Russell Martin, Shaun Maloney (86 Steven Naismith), Scott Brown, Robert Snodgrass (68 Craig Conway), Kenny Miller (73 Leigh Griffiths), James Forrest (67 Charlie Mulgrew).
Manager: Gordon Strachan
**Goals**: T. Walcott (29), D. Welbeck (53), Rickie Lambert (70) / James Morrison (12), Kenny Miller (50)


922.   06.09.2013   20th World Cup Qualifier
**ENGLAND v MOLDOVA 4-0**  (3-0)
*Wembley, London*
Referee: Ivan Kruzliak (Slovakia)   Attendance: 61,607
**ENGLAND:** Joe Hart, Ashley Cole (46 Leighton Baines), Kyle Walker, Phil Jagielka, Gary Cahill, Jack Wilshere (60 Ross Barkley), Frank Lampard, Steven Gerrard, Theo Walcott, Danny Welbeck, Rickie Lambert (70 James Milner).
Manager: Roy Hodgson
**MOLDOVA:** Stanislav Namasco, Simeon Bulgaru (57 Alexandru Suvorov), Vitali Bordian, Victor Golovatenco, Alexandru Epureanu, Igor Armas, Eugeniu Sidorenco, Artur Ionita (19 Alexandru Onica), Serghei Gheorghiev (84 Aleksandr Pascenco), Alexandru Antoniuc, Alexandru Dedov.
Manager: Ion Caras
**Goals**: Steven Gerrard (12), Rickie Lambert (27), Danny Welbeck (45+1, 51)

923.  10.09.2013   20th World Cup Qualifier
**UKRAINE v ENGLAND  0-0**

*NSK Olimpiyskyi, Kiev*

Referee:  PEDRO PROENÇA Oliveira Alves Garcia (Portugal)   Attendance: 69,890

**UKRAINE:** Andriy Pyatov, Vyacheslav Shevchuk, Oleksandr Kucher, Evgen Khacheridi, Artem Fedetskiy, Taras Stepanenko, Oleg Gusev (68 Roman Bezus), EDMAR Golovski de Lacerda Aparecida, Roman Zozulya (90 Evgen Seleznyov), Andriy Yarmolenko (90+3 Dmytro Khomchenovsky), Yevhen Konoplyanka.   Manager: Mikhail Fomenko

**ENGLAND:** Joe Hart, Ashley Cole, Gary Cahill, Kyle Walker, Phil Jagielka, Jack Wilshere (66 Ashley Young), James Milner, Frank Lampard, Steven Gerrard, Theo Walcott (87 Tom Cleverley), Rickie Lambert.   Manager: Roy Hodgson


924.  11.10.2013   20th World Cup Qualifier
**ENGLAND v MONTENEGRO  4-1**  (0-0)

*Wembley, London*

Referee: Alberto Undiano Mallenco (Spain)   Att: 83,807

**ENGLAND:** Joe Hart, Phil Jagielka, Gary Cahill, Leighton Baines, Kyle Walker, Andros Townsend (80 Jack Wilshere), Frank Lampard (65 Michael Carrick), Steven Gerrard (87 James Milner), Wayne Rooney, Danny Welbeck, Daniel Sturridge.   Manager: Roy Hodgson

**MONTENEGRO:** Vukasin Poleksic, Savo Pavicevic (57 Fatos Beciraj), Milan Jovanovic, Elsad Zverotic, Stefan Savic, Vladimir Volkov (72 Simon Vukcevic), Ivan Kecojevic, Nikola Drincic, Branko Boskovic, Stevan Jovetic (81 Filip Kasalica), Dejan Damjanovic.   Manager: Branko Brnovic

**Goals**: Wayne Rooney (48), Branko Boskovic (62 og), Andros Townsend (78), Daniel Sturridge (90+3 pen) / Dejan Damjanovic (71)


925.  15.10.2013   20th World Cup Qualifier
**ENGLAND v POLAND  2-0**  (1-0)

*Wembley, London*

Referee: Damir Skomina (Slovenia)   Attendance: 85,186

**ENGLAND:** Joe Hart, Chris Smalling, Phil Jagielka, Gary Cahill, Leighton Baines, Andros Townsend (86 James Milner), Michael Carrick (71 Frank Lampard), Steven Gerrard, Danny Welbeck, Daniel Sturridge (82 Jack Wilshere), Wayne Rooney.   Manager: Roy Hodgson

**POLAND:** Wojciech Szczesny, Grzegorz Wojtkowiak, Piotr Celeban, Artur Jedrzejczyk, Kamil Glik, Waldemar Sobota (65 Slawomir Peszko), Adrian Mierzejewski (75 Piotr Zielinski), Mariusz Lewandowski (46 Mateusz Klich), Grzegorz Krychowiak, Jakub Blaszczykowski, Robert Lewandowski.   Manager: Waldemar Fornalik

**Goals**: Wayne Rooney (41), Steven Gerrard (88)


926.  15.11.2013
**ENGLAND v CHILE  0-2**  (0-1)

*Wembley, London*

Referee: Florian Meyer (Germany)   Attendance: 62,963

**ENGLAND:** Fraser Forster, Phil Jones (57 Chris Smalling), Glen Johnson, Gary Cahill, Leighton Baines, Jack Wilshere (71 Tom Cleverley), James Milner (66 Jermain Defoe), Frank Lampard (71 Jordan Henderson), Adam Lallana (77 Ross Barkley), Jay Rodrigues (57 Andros Townsend), Wayne Rooney.   Manager: Roy Hodgson

**CHILE:** CLAUDIO Andrés BRAVO Muñoz, MARCOS Andrés GONZÁLEZ Salazar, EUGENIO Estenan MENA Reveco, MAURICIO Anibal ISLA Isla (59 GONZALO Alejandro JARA Reyes), MARCELO Alfonso DÍAZ Rojas, Matías Ariel "MATI" FERNÁNDEZ Fernández (46 FELIPE Alejandro GUTIÉRREZ Leiva), GARY Alexis MEDEL Soto, JEAN André Eman BEUSEJOUR Coliquero (82 JOSÉ Pedro FUENZALIDA Gana), CHARLES Mariano ARÁNGUIZ Sandoval (46 CARLOS Emilio Tello CARMONA), EDUARDO Jesús VARGAS Rojas (72 CARLOS Andrés MUÑOZ Rojas), ALEXIS Alejandro SÁNCHEZ Sánchez.   Manager: JOSE Luis SAMPAOLI Moya

**Goals**: ALEXIS Alejandro SÁNCHEZ Sánchez (7, 90+4)


927.  19.11.2013
**ENGLAND v GERMANY  0-1**  (0-1)

*Wembley, London*

Referee: Stéphane Lannoy (France)   Attendance: 85,934

**ENGLAND:** Joe Hart, Kyle Walker, Chris Smalling, Phil Jagielka, Ashley Cole (53 Kieran Gibbs), Andros Townsend, Adam Lallana (76 Rickie Lambert), Steven Gerrard (56 Jordan Henderson), Tom Cleverley (64 Jack Wilshere), Daniel Sturridge, Wayne Rooney (71 Ross Barkley).
Manager: Roy Hodgson

**GERMANY:** Roman Weidenfeller, Heiko Westermann (67 Julian Draxler), Marcel Schmelzer (46 Marcell Jansen), Per Mertesacker, Jérôme Boateng (46 Mat Hummels, 65 Benedikt Höwedes), Marco Reus (82 André Schürrle), Toni Kroos, Mario Götze, Sven Bender, Lars Bender, Max Kruse (56 Sidney Sam).   Manager: Joachim Löw

**Goal**: Per Mertesacker (39)

**928.  05.03.2014**

**ENGLAND v DENMARK  1-0**  (0-0)

*Wembley, London*

Referee:  Kevin Blom (Netherlands)    Attendance:  68,573

**ENGLAND:**  Joe Hart, Ashley Cole (46 Luke Shaw), Chris Smalling, Glen Johnson, Gary Cahill, Jack Wilshere (59 Adam Lallana), Raheem Sterling (86 Andros Townsend), Jordan Henderson (77 Alex Oxlade-Chamberlain), Steven Gerrard, Daniel Sturridge (88 James Milner), Wayne Rooney (60 Danny Welbeck).    Manager: Roy Hodgson

**DENMARK:**  Kasper Schmeichel, Daniel Agger, Peter Ankersen, Simon Kjær (62 Andreas Bjelland), Lars Jacobsen (46 Jesper Juelsgård), Casper Sloth (62 Niki Zimling), Jakob Poulsen (81 Danny Olsen), Emil Larsen (46 Kasper Kusk), William Kvist, Michael Krohn-Dehli, Nicklas Bendtner (63 Morten Rasmussen).    Manager: Morten Olsen

**Goal:**  Daniel Sturridge (82)

**929.  30.05.2014**

**ENGLAND v PERU  3-0**  (1-0)

*Wembley, London*

Referee:  Viktor Kassai (Hungary)    Attendance:  83,578

**ENGLAND:**  Joe Hart, Phil Jagielka (73 Chris Smalling), Glen Johnson, Gary Cahill, Leighton Baines (75 John Stones), Adam Lallana (73 James Milner), Jordan Henderson, Steven Gerrard (64 Jack Wilshere), Danny Welbeck, Daniel Sturridge (82 Ross Barkley), Wayne Rooney (65 Raheem Sterling).
Manager: Roy Hodgson

**PERU:**  RAÚL Omar FERNÁNDEZ Valverde, ALBERTO Junior RODRÍGUEZ Valdelomar, CHRISTIAN Guillermo Martín RAMOS Garagay (68 HANSELL Argenis RIOJAS La Rosa), ALEXANDER Martín Marquinho CALLENS Asín, LUIS Alberto RAMÍREZ Lucay (60 Cristopher PAOLO César HURTADO Huertas), Paulo RINALDO CRUZADO Durand, ANDRÉ Martín CARRILLO Díaz (86 ÉDISON Michael FLORES Peralta), JOSEPMIR Aarón BALLÓN Villacorta, LUIS Jan Piers ADVÍNCULA Castrillón (78 MARIO Alfonso VELARDE Pinto), Victor YOSHIMAR YOTÚN Flores, JEAN Carlos Francisco DEZA Sánchez (65 RAÚL Mario RUIDÍAZ Misitich).    Manager: PABLO Javier BENGOECHEA Dutra

**Goals:**  Daniel Sturridge (32), Gary Cahill (65), Phil Jagielka (70)

**930.  04.06.2014**

**ECUADOR v ENGLAND  2-2**  (1-1)

*Dolphin Stadium, Miami (USA)*

Referee:  Jair Marrufo (USA)    Attendance:  21,534

**ECUADOR:**  MÁXIMO Orlando BANGUERA Valdivieso, JUAN Carlos PAREDES Reasco (90+1 GABRIEL Eduardo ACHILIER Zurita), JORGE Daniel GUAGUA Tamayo, FRICKSON Rafael ERAZO Vivero, WALTER Orlando AYOVÍ Corozo, ENNER Remberto VALENCIA Lastra (83 Alex RENATO IBARRA Mina), Luis ANTONIO VALENCIA Mosquera, CHRISTIAN Fernando NOBOA Tello (50 ÉDISON Vicente MÉNDEZ Méndez), JEFFERSON Antonio MONTERO Vite (68 MICHAEL Antonio ARROYO Mina), CARLOS Armando GRUEZO Arboleda (90 LUIS Fernando SARITAMA Padilla), FELIPE Salvador CAICEDO Corozo (46 JOAO Robin ROJAS Mendoza).    Manager: REINALDO RUEDA Rivera

**ENGLAND:**  Ben Foster, Phil Jones, Chris Smalling, Luke Shaw (74 John Stones), Jack Wilshere (87 Adam Lallana), Alex Oxlade-Chamberlain (63 Jon Flanagan), James Milner, Frank Lampard, Ross Barkley (84 Jordan Henderson), Wayne Rooney (65 Raheem Sterling), Rickie Lambert (84 Danny Welbeck).    Manager: Roy Hodgson

**Sent off**:  Luis ANTONIO VALENCIA Mosquera (79), Raheem Sterling (79)

**Goals**:  ENNER Remberto VALENCIA Lastra (8), MICHAEL Antonio ARROYO Mina (70) /
Wayne Rooney (29), Rickie Lambert (51)

**931.  07.06.2014**

**ENGLAND v HONDURAS  0-0**

*Dolphin Stadium, Miami (USA)*

Referee:  Ricardo Salazar (USA)    Attendance:  45,379

**ENGLAND:**  Joe Hart (75 Fraser Forster), Phil Jagielka, Glen Johnson, Gary Cahill, Leighton Baines, Jordan Henderson (83 Frank Lampard), Steven Gerrard (46 Jack Wilshere), Adam Lallana, Danny Welbeck (79 Rickie Lambert), Daniel Sturridge, Wayne Rooney (46 Ross Barkley).
Manager: Roy Hodgson

**HONDURAS:**  NOEL Eduardo VALLADARES Bonilla, MAYNOR Alexis FIGUEROA Róchez, VÍCTOR Salvador BERNÁRDEZ Blanco, BRAYAN Antonio BECKELES, EMILIO Arturo IZAGUIRRE Giron (90+1 MARIO Roberto MARTÍNEZ Hernández), ROGER Aníbal ESPINOZA Ramírez (87 JUAN Carlos GARCÍA), MARVIN Antonio CHÁVEZ (61 ANDY Aryel NAJAR Rodríguez), WILSON Roberto PALACIOS Suazo, LUIS Fernando GARRIDO (46 JORGE Aarón CLAROS Juárez), CARLOS Yaír COSTLY Molina (70 EDDER Gerardo DELGADO Zerón), JERRY Ricardo BENGTSON Bodden (74 JERRY Nelson PALACIOS Suazo).    Manager: LUIS Fernando SUÁREZ Guzman

**Sent off**:  BRAYAN Antonio BECKELES (65)

**932. 14.06.2014 20th World Cup Group D**
**ENGLAND v ITALY 1-2 (1-1)**
*Arena da Amazônia, Manaus (Brazil)*
Referee: Björn Kuipers (Netherlands)   Attendance: 39,800

**ENGLAND:** Joe Hart, Glen Johnson, Leighton Baines, Gary Cahill, Phil Jagielka, Steven Gerrard, Jordan Henderson (73 Jack Wilshere), Raheem Sterling, Daniel Sturridge (80 Adam Lallana), Wayne Rooney, Danny Welbeck (61 Ross Barkley). Manager: Roy Hodgson

**ITALY:** Salvatore Sirigu, Giorgio Chiellini, Matteo Darmian, Andrea Barzagli, Gabriel Paletta, Antonio Candreva (79 Marco Parolo), Claudio Marchisio, Daniele De Rossi, Andrea Pirlo, Marco Verratti (57 Thiago Motta), Mario Balotelli (73 Ciro Immobile). Manager: Cesare Prandelli

**Goals:** Daniel Sturridge (37) / Claudio Marchisio (35), Mario Balotelli (50)

**933. 19.06.2014 20th World Cup Group D**
**URUGUAY v ENGLAND 2-1 (1-0)**
*Arena Corinthians, São Paulo (Brazil)*
Referee: Carlos Velasco Carballo (Spain)   Att: 62,575

**URUGUAY:** Nestor FERNANDO MUSLERA, DIEGO Roberto GODÍN Leal, JOSÉ María GIMÉNEZ de Vargas, José MARTÍN CÁCERES Silva, ÁLVARO Daniel PEREIRA Barragán, CRISTIAN Gabriel RODRÍGUEZ Barrotti, Marcelo NICOLÁS LODEIRO Benítez (67 CHRISTIAN Ricardo STUANI Curbelo), EGIDIO Raúl ARÉVALO Ríos, ÁLVARO Rafael GONZÁLEZ Luengo (79 JORGE Ciro FUCILE Perdomo), LUIS Alberto SUÁREZ Díaz (88 SEBASTIÁN COATES Nion), EDINSON Roberto Gómez CAVANI. Manager: ÓSCAR Washington TABÁREZ Sclavo

**ENGLAND:** Joe Hart, Glen Johnson, Leighton Baines, Gary Cahill, Phil Jagielka, Steven Gerrard, Jordan Henderson (87 Rickie Lambert), Raheem Sterling (64 Ross Barkley), Daniel Sturridge, Wayne Rooney, Danny Welbeck (71 Adam Lallana). Manager: Roy Hodgson

**Goals:** LUIS Alberto SUÁREZ Díaz (39, 85) / Wayne Rooney (75)

**934. 24.06.2014 20th World Cup Group D**
**COSTA RICA v ENGLAND 0-0**
*Estádio Governador Magalhães Pinto, Belo Horizonte (Brazil)*
Referee: Jamel Haimoudi (Algeria)   Attendance: 57,823

**COSTA RICA:** KEYLOR Antonio NAVAS Gamboa, GIANCARLO GONZÁLEZ Castro, ÓSCAR Esau DUARTE Gaitan, JÚNIOR Enrique DÍAZ Campbell, CRISTIAN Esteban GAMBOA Luna, ROY MILLER Hernández, CELSO BORGES Mora (78 MICHAEL BARRANTES Rojas), YELTSIN Ignacio TEJEDA Valverde, JOEL Nathaniel CAMPBELL Samuels (65 MARCO Danilo UREÑA Porras), BRYAN Jafet RUIZ González, RANDALL BRENES Moya (59 CHRISTIÁN BOLAÑOS Navarro). Manager: JORGE Luis PINTO Afanador

**ENGLAND:** Ben Foster, Gary Cahill, Chris Smalling, Phil Jones, Luke Shaw, Jack Wilshere (73 Steven Gerrard), Frank Lampard, James Milner (76 Wayne Rooney), Adam Lallana (62 Raheem Sterling), Ross Barkley, Daniel Sturridge. Manager: Roy Hodgson

**935. 03.09.2014**
**ENGLAND v NORWAY 1-0 (0-0)**
*Wembley, London*
Referee: Manuel JORGE Neves Moreira de SOUSA (Portugal)
Attendance: 40,181

**ENGLAND:** Joe Hart, Phil Jones, John Stones (81 Calum Chambers), Gary Cahill (84 Phil Jagielka), Leighton Baines, Jack Wilshere (69 Fabian Delph), Raheem Sterling, Alex Oxlade-Chamberlain (69 James Milner), Jordan Henderson, Daniel Sturridge (89 Rickie Lambert), Wayne Rooney (69 Danny Welbeck). Manager: Roy Hodgson

**NORWAY:** Ørjan Nyland, Håvard Nordtveit, Vegard Forren, Omar Elabdellaoui, Per Skjelbred (69 Mohamed Elyounoussi), Ruben Jenssen (87 Morten Pedersen), Mats Møller Dæhli (57 Anders Konradsen), Martin Linnes (36 Per-Egil Flo), Stefan Johansen, Joshua King (76 Håvard Nielsen), Tarik Elyounoussi (79 Ola Kamara). Manager: Per-Mathias Høgmo

**Goal:** Wayne Rooney (68 pen)

**936. 08.09.2014 15th European Champs Qualifier**
**SWITZERLAND v ENGLAND 0-2 (0-0)**
*St. Jakob-Park, Basel*
Referee: Cüneyt Çakir (Turkey)   Attendance: 35,500

**SWITZERLAND:** Yann Sommer, Steve von Bergen, RICARDO Ivan RODRÍGUEZ Araya, Stephan Lichtsteiner, Johan Djourou, Xherdan Shaqiri, Gökhan Inler, Valon Behrami, Granit Xhaka (74 Blemir Dzemaili), Haris Seferovic, Admir Mehmedi (63 Josip Drmic). Manager: Vladimir Petkovic

**ENGLAND:** Joe Hart, Phil Jones (77 Phil Jagielka), Leighton Baines, John Stones, Gary Cahill, Fabian Delph, Jack Wilshere (73 James Milner), Raheem Sterling, Jordan Henderson, Danny Welbeck, Wayne Rooney (90 Rickie Lambert). Manager: Roy Hodgson

**Goals:** Danny Welbeck (58, 90+4)

937.  09.10.2014   15th European Champs Qualifier
**ENGLAND v SAN MARINO  5-0**  (2-0)
*Wembley, London*

Referee: Marcin Borski (Poland)   Attendance: 55,990

**ENGLAND:** Joe Hart, Phil Jagielka, Kieran Gibbs, Gary Cahill, Jack Wilshere, Raheem Sterling (46 Adam Lallana), James Milner, Jordan Henderson (46 Alex Oxlade-Chamberlain), Calum Chambers, Danny Welbeck (66 Andros Townsend), Wayne Rooney.   Manager: Roy Hodgson

**SAN MARINO:** Aldo Simoncini, Fabio Vitaioli, Nicola Chiaruzzi, Cristian Brolli, Alessandro Della Valle, Manuel Battistini, Luca Tosi (63 Lorenzo Gasperoni), Mirko Palazzi (73 Lorenzo Buscarini), Matteo Vitaioli, Andy Selva (87 Danilo Rinaldi), Adolfo José Hirsch.   Manager: Pierangelo Manzaroli

**Goals**: Phil Jagielka (25), Wayne Rooney (43 pen), Danny Welbeck (49), Andros Townsend (72), Alessandro Della Valle (78 og)

938.  12.10.2014   15th European Champs Qualifier
**ESTONIA v ENGLAND  0-1**  (0-0)
*A. Le Coq Arena, Tallinn*

Referee: Marijo Strahonja (Croatia)   Attendance: 10,195

**ESTONIA:** Sergei Pareiko, Artur Pikk, Igor Morozov, Ragnar Klavan, Enar Jääger, Martin Vunk (83 Dmitriy Kruglov), Konstantin Vassiljev (46 Joel Lindpere), Ilja Antonov, Karol Mets, Sergei Zenjov (80 Henrik Ojamaa), Henri Anier.   Manager: Magnus Pehrsson

**ENGLAND:** Joe Hart, Phil Jagielka, Leighton Baines, Gary Cahill, Fabian Delph (61 Alex Oxlade-Chamberlain), Jack Wilshere, Adam Lallana, Jordan Henderson (64 Raheem Sterling), Calum Chambers, Danny Welbeck (80 Rickie Lambert), Wayne Rooney.   Manager: Roy Hodgson

**Sent off**: Ragnar Klavan (48)

**Goal**: Wayne Rooney (74)

939.  15.11.2014   15th European Champs Qualifier
**ENGLAND v SLOVENIA  3-1**  (0-0)
*Wembley, London*

Referee: OLEGARIO Manuel Bartolo Faustino BENQUERENÇA (Portugal)   Attendance: 82,309

**ENGLAND:** Joe Hart, Phil Jagielka (89 Chris Smalling), Kieran Gibbs, Gary Cahill, Nathaniel Clyne, Jack Wilshere, Adam Lallana (80 James Milner), Jordan Henderson, Raheem Sterling (85 Alex Oxlade-Chamberlain), Danny Welbeck, Wayne Rooney.   Manager: Roy Hodgson

**SLOVENIA:** Samir Handanovic, Branko Ilic, Bostjan Cesar, Miso Brecko, Andraz Struna, Jasmin Kurtic (75 Rajko Rotman), Andraz Kirm (78 Zlatan Ljubijankic), Ales Mertelj, Valter Birsa (63 Dejan Lazarevic), Kevin Kampl, Milivoje Novakovic.   Manager: Srečko Katanec

**Goals**: Wayne Rooney (59 pen), Danny Welbeck (66, 72) / Jordan Henderson (57 og)

940.  18.11.2014
**SCOTLAND v ENGLAND  1-3**  (0-1)
*Celtic Park, Glasgow*

Referee: Jonas Eriksson (Sweden)   Attendance: 49,526

**SCOTLAND:** David Marshall (46 Craig Gordon), Steven Whittaker, Andrew Robertson, Charlie Mulgrew, Grant Hanley (66 Stevie May), Steven Naismith, Russell Martin, Shaun Maloney (81 Johnny Russell), Scott Brown (46 Darren Fletcher), Ikechi Anya (61 Barry Bannan), Chris Martin (46 James Morrison).   Manager: Gordon Strachan

**ENGLAND:** Fraser Forster, Chris Smalling, Luke Shaw (66 Kieran Gibbs), Nathaniel Clyne, Gary Cahill (46 Phil Jagielka), Stewart Downing (46 Adam Lallana), Jack Wilshere (87 Ross Barkley), Alex Oxlade-Chamberlain (80 Rickie Lambert), James Milner, Danny Welbeck (66 Raheem Sterling), Wayne Rooney.   Manager: Roy Hodgson

**Goals**: Andrew Robertson (83) / Alex Oxlade-Chamberlain (32), Wayne Rooney (47, 85)

941.  27.03.2015   15th European Champs Qualifier
**ENGLAND v LITHUANIA  4-0**  (2-0)
*Wembley, London*

Referee: Pavel Královec (Czech Republic)   Att: 83,671

**ENGLAND:** Joe Hart, Phil Jones, Leighton Baines, Nathaniel Clyne, Gary Cahill, Fabian Delph, Michael Carrick, Raheem Sterling, Jordan Henderson (71 Ross Barkley), Danny Welbeck (77 Theo Walcott), Wayne Rooney (71 Harry Kane).   Manager: Roy Hodgson

**LITHUANIA:** Giedrius Arlauskis, Marius Zaliūkas, Tomas Mikuckis (66 Simonas Stankevicius), Tadas Kijanskas, Georgas Freidgeimas, Vytautas Andriuskevicius (83 Vaidas Slavickas), Saulius Mikoliūnas (88 Donatas Kazlauskas), Karolis Chvedukas, Artūras Zulpa, Fiodor Cernych, Deivydas Matulevicius.   Manager: Igoris Pankratjevas

**Goals**: Wayne Rooney (6), Danny Welbeck (45), Raheem Sterling (58), Harry Kane (73)

942.  31.03.2015
**ITALY v ENGLAND  1-1**  (1-0)
*Juventus Stadium, Torino*
Referee:  Dr. Felix Brych (Germany)    Attendance: 31,138
**ITALY:**  Gianluigi Buffon, Andrea Ranocchia, Giorgio Chiellini (73 Emiliano Moretti), Leonardo Bonucci, Matteo Darmian (73 Luca Antonelli), Mirko Valdifiori (67 Marco Verratti), Roberto Soriano, Marco Parolo, Alessandro Florenzi (59 Ignazio Abate), Graziano Pellè (59 Ciro Immobile), ÉDER Citadin Martins (59 Franco Vázquez).
Manager:  Antonio Conte
**ENGLAND:**  Joe Hart, Phil Jones, Phil Jagielka, Kieran Gibbs (86 Ryan Bertrand), Chris Smalling (43 Michael Carrick), Nathaniel Clyne (46 Kyle Walker), Fabian Delph (71 Andros Townsend), Jordan Henderson (74 Ryan Mason), Theo Walcott (55 Ross Barkley), Wayne Rooney, Harry Kane.
Manager:  Roy Hodgson
**Goals**:  Graziano Pellè (29) / Andros Townsend (79)


943.  07.06.2015
**REPUBLIC OF IRELAND v ENGLAND  0-0**
*Aviva Stadium, Dublin*
Referee:  Arnold Hunter (Northern Ireland)    Att: 43.846
**REPUBLIC OF IRELAND:**  Keiren Westwood (61 Shay Given), Marc Wilson, John O'Shea (71 Paul McShane), Séamus Coleman, Robbie Brady, Glenn Whelan (63 Harry Arter), Aiden McGeady, James McCarthy (46 James McClean), Jeff Hendrick, Daryl Murphy (56 Jon Walters), David McGoldrick (46 Kevin Long).    Manager: Martin O'Neill
**ENGLAND:**  Joe Hart, Phil Jones, Chris Smalling, Gary Cahill (74 Phil Jagielka), Ryan Bertrand, Jack Wilshere (66 Ross Barkley), Raheem Sterling (66 Andros Townsend), James Milner, Adam Lallana (82 Theo Walcott), Jordan Henderson, Wayne Rooney (74 Jamie Vardy).    Manager: Roy Hodgson


944.  14.06.2015    15th European Champs Qualifier
**SLOVENIA v ENGLAND  2-3**  (1-0)
*Stozice Stadium, Ljubljana*
Referee:  Alberto Undiano Mallenco (Spain)    Att: 15,796
**SLOVENIA:**  Samir Handanovic, Bostjan Cesar, Miso Brecko, Bojan Jokic, Branko Ilic, Ales Mertelj, Jasmin Kurtic (79 Dejan Lazarevic), Andraz Kirm (72 Nejc Pecnik), Josip Ilicic (61 Valter Birsa), Kevin Kampl, Milivoje Novakovic.
Manager:  Srecko Katanec
**ENGLAND:**  Joe Hart, Kieran Gibbs, Phil Jones (46 Adam Lallana), Gary Cahill, Chris Smalling, Fabian Delph (85 Nathaniel Clyne), Andros Townsend (74 Theo Walcott), Jack Wilshere, Raheem Sterling, Jordan Henderson, Wayne Rooney.
Manager:  Roy Hodgson
**Goals**:  Milivoje Novakovic (37), Nejc Pecnik (84) / Jack Wilshere (57, 73), Wayne Rooney (86)


945.  05.09.2015    15th European Champs Qualifier
**SAN MARINO v ENGLAND  0-6**  (0-2)
*Stadio Olimpico di Serravalle, Serravalle*
Referee:  Leontios Trattou (Cyprus)    Attendance: 4.378
**SAN MARINO:**  Aldo Simoncini, Davide Simoncini (80 Alessandro Della Valle), Nicola Chiaruzzi, Cristian Brolli, Giovanni Bonini (72 Luca Tosi), Marco Berardi, Manuel Battistini, Mirko Palazzi, Matteo Vitaioli, Andy Selva (75 Danilo Rinaldi), Adolfo José Hirsch.
Manager:  Pierangelo Manzaroli
**ENGLAND:**  Joe Hart, Luke Shaw, Phil Jagielka, John Stones, Nathaniel Clyne, Jonjo Shelvey, James Milner (58 Fabian Delph), Ross Barkley, Alex Oxlade-Chamberlain (67 Theo Walcott), Jamie Vardy, Wayne Rooney (59 Harry Kane).
Manager:  Roy Hodgson
**Goals**:  Wayne Rooney (13 pen), Cristian Brolli (30 og), Ross Barkley (46), Theo Walcott (68, 78), Harry Kane (77)


946.  08.09.2015    15th European Champs Qualifier
**ENGLAND v SWITZERLAND  2-0**  (0-0)
*Wembley, London*
Referee:  Gianluca Rocchi (Italy)    Attendance: 75,751
**ENGLAND:**  Joe Hart, Luke Shaw, Chris Smalling, Nathaniel Clyne (69 John Stones), Gary Cahill, Jonjo Shelvey (58 Harry Kane), Fabian Delph (4 Ross Barkley), Raheem Sterling, James Milner, Alex Oxlade-Chamberlain, Wayne Rooney.
Manager:  Roy Hodgson
**SWITZERLAND:**  Yann Sommer, Fabian Schär, RICARDO Ivan RODRÍGUEZ Araya, Stephan Lichtsteiner, Timm Klose, Valentin Stocker (72 Haris Seferovic), Xherdan Shaqiri, Gökhan Inler, Valon Behrami (79 Blerim Dzemaili), Granit Xhaka, Josip Drmic (63 Breel Embolo).
Manager:  Vladimir Petkovic
**Goals**:  Harry Kane (67), Wayne Rooney (84 pen)


947.  09.10.2015    15th European Champs Qualifier
**ENGLAND v ESTONIA  2-0**  (1-0)
*Wembley, London*
Referee:  István Vad (Hungary)    Attendance: 75,427
**ENGLAND:**  Joe Hart, Chris Smalling, Nathaniel Clyne, Gary Cahill, Ryan Bertrand, Raheem Sterling, James Milner, Adam Lallana (73 Alex Oxlade-Chamberlain), Ross Barkley (87 Dele Alli), Theo Walcott (83 Jamie Vardy), Harry Kane.
Manager:  Roy Hodgson
**ESTONIA:**  Mihkel Aksalu, Artur Pikk, Ragnar Klavan, Ken Kallaste (88 Siim Luts), Enar Jääger, Taijo Teniste, Konstantin Vassiljev, Ats Purje (69 Sander Puri), Aleksandr Dmitrijev (70 Joel Lindpere), Karol Mets, Sergei Zenjov.
Manager:  Magnus Pehrsson
**Goals**:  Theo Walcott (45), Raheem Sterling (85)

948.　12.10.2015　15th European Champs Qualifier
**LITHUANIA v ENGLAND　0-3**　(0-2)
*Vilniaus LFF stadionas, Vilnius*
Referee: Kenn Hansen (Denmark)　Attendance: 5,051
**LITHUANIA:** Giedrius Arlauskis, Tomas Mikuckis, Linas Klimavicius, Georgas Freidgeimas, Vytautas Andriuskevicius (82 Egidijus Vaitkūnas), Artūras Zulpa, Vykintas Slivka, Mindaugas Panka, Arvydas Novikovas (64 Deimantas Petravicius), Fiodor Cernych, Lukas Spalvis (86 Deivydas Matulevicius).　Manager: Igoris Pankratjevas

**ENGLAND:** Jack Butland, Phil Jones, Phil Jagielka, Kieran Gibbs, Kyle Walker, Jonjo Shelvey, Adam Lallana (67 Dele Alli), Ross Barkley (73 Andros Townsend), Alex Oxlade-Chamberlain, Jamie Vardy, Harry Kane (59 Danny Ings).
Manager: Roy Hodgson

**Goals**: Ross Barkley (29), Giedierius Arlauskis 0-2 (35 og), Alex Oxlade-Chamberlain (62)


949.　13.11.2015
**SPAIN v ENGLAND　2-0**　(0-0)
*Estadio José Rico Pérez, Alicante*
Referee: Paolo Mazzoleni (Italy)　Attendance: 25,300
**SPAIN:** IKER CASILLAS Fernández, MARIO Gaspar Pérez Martínez, Gerard PIQUÉ í Bernabéu, JORDI ALBA Ramos, Marc BARTRA Aregall (82 César AZPILICUETA Tanco), THIAGO Alcântara do Nascimento (27 Santiago "SANTI" CAZORLA González), Andrés INIESTA Luján (46 Manuel Agudo Durán "NOLITO"), Francesc "CESC" FÀBREGAS Soler, Sergio BUSQUETS Burgos (78 Jorge Resurrección Merodio "KOKE"), Francisco "PACO" ALCÁCER García (74 PEDRO Eliezer Rodríguez Ledesma), DIEGO da Silva COSTA (64 Juan Manuel MATA García).
Manager: Vicente DEL BOSQUE González

**ENGLAND:** Joe Hart, Phil Jones, Kyle Walker, Chris Smalling (86 Gary Cahill), Ryan Bertrand, Fabian Delph (63 Dele Alli), Michael Carrick (90+1 Jonjo Shelvey), Raheem Sterling, Adam Lallana (63 Eric Dier), Ross Barkley (73 Wayne Rooney), Harry Kane.　Manager: Roy Hodgson

**Goals**: MARIO Gaspar Pérez Martínez (72), Santiago "SANTI" CAZORLA González (84)


950.　17.11.2015
**ENGLAND v FRANCE　2-0**　(1-0)
*Wembley, London*
Referee: Jonas Eriksson (Sweden)　Attendance: 71,223
**ENGLAND:** Joe Hart (46 Jack Butland), Kieran Gibbs, Eric Dier, Nathaniel Clyne, Gary Cahill, John Stones, Ross Barkley (79 Jonjo Shelvey), Dele Alli (88 Phil Jones), Raheem Sterling (68 Adam Lallana), Wayne Rooney, Harry Kane (80 Ryan Bertrand).　Manager: Roy Hodgson

**FRANCE:** Hugo Lloris, Laurent Koscielny, Lucas Digne, Raphaël Varane, Bacary Sagna, Yohan Cabaye (57 Lassana Diarra), Hatem Ben Arfa (46 Kingsley Coman), Morgan Schneiderlin (82 Moussa Sissoko), Blaise Matuidi (46 Paul Pogba), André-Pierre Gignac (57 Olivier Giroud), Anthony Martial (68 Antoine Griezmann).
Manager: Didier Deschamps

**Goals**: Dele Alli (39), Wayne Rooney (48)


951.　26.03.2016
**GERMANY v ENGLAND　2-3**　(1-0)
*Olympiastadion, Berlin*
Referee: Gianluca Rocchi (Italy)　Attendance: 71,413
**GERMANY:** Manuel Neuer, Mats Hummels (46 Jonathan Tah), Antonio Rüdiger, Jonas Hector, Emre Can, Marco Reus (64 André Schürrle), Mesut Özil, Toni Kroos, Sami Khedira, Mario Gómez (79 Mario Götze), Thomas Müller (75 Lukas Podolski).　Manager: Joachim Löw

**ENGLAND:** Jack Butland (45+1 Fraser Forster), Danny Rose, Chris Smalling, Nathaniel Clyne, Gary Cahill, Adam Lallana (71 Ross Barkley), Jordan Henderson, Eric Dier, Dele Alli, Danny Welbeck (71 Jamie Vardy), Harry Kane.
Manager: Roy Hodgson

**Goals**: Toni Kroos (43), Mario Gómez (57) / Harry Kane (61), Jamie Vardy (75), Eric Dier (90+1)


952.　29.03.2016
**ENGLAND v NETHERLANDS　1-2**　(1-0)
*Wembley, London*
Referee: Antonio Miguel Mateu Lahoz (Spain)　Att: 82,835
**ENGLAND:** Fraser Forster, John Stones, Chris Smalling (70 Phil Jagielka), Danny Rose (57 Nathaniel Clyne), Kyle Walker, Danny Drinkwater (84 Eric Dier), James Milner (81 Dele Alli), Adam Lallana (70 Harry Kane), Ross Barkley, Jamie Vardy, Daniel Sturridge (57 Theo Walcott).　Manager: Roy Hodgson

**NETHERLANDS:** Jeroen Zoet, Jetro Williams (81 Patrick van Aanholt), Jeffrey Bruma, Joël Veltman, Daley Blind, Georginio Wijnaldum, Riechedly Bazoer (78 Marco van Ginkel), Ibrahim Afellay, Quincy Promes (36 Luciano Narsingh), Vincent Janssen (90+2 Jordy Clasie), Memphis Depay.　Manager: Danny Blind

**Goals**: Jamie Vardy (41) / Vincent Janssen (51 pen), Luciano Narsingh (77)

**953.  22.05.2016**

**ENGLAND v TURKEY  2-1**  (1-1)

*Etihad Stadium, Manchester*

Referee:  Deniz Aytekin (Germany)     Attendance:  44,866

**ENGLAND:**  Joe Hart, Kyle Walker, John Stones, Danny Rose, Gary Cahill, Dele Alli, Eric Dier, Jack Wilshere (66 Jordan Henderson), Raheem Sterling (73 Danny Drinkwater), Harry Kane, Jamie Vardy.    Manager: Roy Hodgson

**TURKEY:**  Volkan Babacan, Gökhan Gönül, Hakan Balta, Caner Erkin (69 Ismail Köybasi), Mehmet Topal, Oguzhan Özyakup (69 Mahmut Tekdemir), Selçuk Inan, Hakan Çalhanoglu (78 Olcay Sahan), Ozan Tufan (87 Mevlüt Erdinç), Cenk Tosun, Volkan Sen (84 Yasin Öztekin).    Manager: Fatih Terim

**Goals**:  Harry Kane (3), Jamie Vardy (83) / Hakan Çalhanoglu (14)

Harry Kane missed a penalty kick after 72 minutes.

**954.  27.05.2016**

**ENGLAND v AUSTRALIA  2-1**  (1-0)

*Stadium of Light, Sunderland*

Referee:  Danny Makkelie (Netherlands)    Att: 46,595

**ENGLAND:**  Fraser Forster (87 Tom Heaton), John Stones, Chris Smalling (74 Eric Dier), Nathaniel Clyne, Ryan Bertrand, Danny Drinkwater, Jack Wilshere (46 James Milner), Raheem Sterling (76 Andros Townsend), Adam Lallana (46 Wayne Rooney), Jordan Henderson, Marcus Rashford (63 Ross Barkley).    Manager: Roy Hodgson

**AUSTRALIA:**  Mathew Ryan, Joshua Risdon (73 Milos Degenek), Brad Smith, Mark Milligan, Bailey Wright, Tom Rogic (74 Tomi Juric), Aaron Mooy (83 Jackson Irvine), Massimo Luongo (57 Chris Ikonomidis), Robbie Kruse (83 Craig Goodwin), Mile Jedinak, Jamie Maclaren (57 Matt McKay).    Manager: Ange Postecoglou

**Goals**:  Marcus Rashford (3), Wayne Rooney (55) / Eric Dier (75 og)

**955.  02.06.2016**

**ENGLAND v PORTUGAL  1-0**  (0-0)

*Wembley, London*

Referee:  Marco Guida (Italy)     Attendance:  82,503

**ENGLAND:**  Joe Hart, Danny Rose, Gary Cahill, Kyle Walker, Chris Smalling, James Milner (66 Jack Wilshere), Eric Dier, Dele Alli (90 Jordan Henderson), Wayne Rooney (78 Adam Lallana), Harry Kane (78 Daniel Sturridge), Jamie Vardy (66 Raheem Sterling).    Manager: Roy Hodgson

**PORTUGAL:**  RUI Pedro dos Santos PATRÍCIO, RICARDO Alberto Silveira CARVALHO (90 Éderzito António Macedo Lopes "ÉDER"), Adelino André Vieira de Freitas "VIEIRINHA", ELISEU Pereira dos Santos, BRUNO Eduardo Regufe ALVES, JOÃO MÁRIO Naval da Costa Eduardo (46 ANDRÉ Filipe Tavares GOMES), DANILO Luís Hélio Pereira, ADRIEN Sebastian Perruchet SILVA (72 RENATO Júnior Luz SANCHES), JOÃO Filipe Iria Santos MOUTINHO (73 WILLIAM Silva de CARVALHO), Rafael Alexandre Fernandes Ferreira "RAFA" da SILVA (38 JOSÉ Miguel da Rocha FONTE), Luís Carlos Almeida da Cunha "NANI" (61 RICARDO Andrade QUARESMA Bernardo).
Manager: FERNANDO Manuel Fernandes da Costa SANTOS

**Sent off**:  BRUNO Eduardo Regufe ALVES (35)

**Goal**:  Chris Smalling (86)

**956.  11.06.2016     15th European Champs Group B**

**ENGLAND v RUSSIA  1-1**  (0-0)

*Stade Vélodrome, Marseille (France)*

Referee:  Nicola Rizzoli (Italy)    Attendance:  62,343

**ENGLAND:**  Joe Hart, Kyle Walker, Danny Rose, Gary Cahill, Chris Smalling, Raheem Sterling (87 James Milner), Adam Lallana, Wayne Rooney (77 Jack Wilshere), Eric Dier, Dele Alli, Harry Kane.    Manager: Roy Hodgson

**RUSSIA:**  Igor Akinfeev, Igor Smolnikov, Sergey Ignashevich, Roman Neustädter (80 Denis Glushakov), Vasiliy Berezutskiy, Georgiy Shchennikov, Aleksandr Golovin (77 Roman Shirokov), Oleg Shatov, Aleksandr Kokorin, Fedor Smolov (85 Pavel Mamaev), Artem Dzyuba.    Manager: Leonid Slutskiy

**Goals**:  Eric Dier (73) / Vasiliy Berezutskiy (90+2)

**957.  16.06.2016     15th European Champs Group B**

**ENGLAND v WALES  2-1**  (0-1)

*Stade Bollaert-Delelis, Lens (France)*

Referee:  Dr. Felix Brych (Germany)     Attendance:  34,033

**ENGLAND:**  Joe Hart, Kyle Walker, Danny Rose, Gary Cahill, Chris Smalling, Raheem Sterling (46 Daniel Sturridge), Adam Lallana (73 Marcus Rashford), Wayne Rooney, Eric Dier, Dele Alli, Harry Kane (46 Jamie Vardy).    Manager: Roy Hodgson

**WALES:**  Wayne Hennessey, Chris Gunter, Neil Taylor, Ben Davies, James Chester, Ashley Williams, Joe Allen, Aaron Ramsey, Joe Ledley (67 Dave Edwards), Hal Robson-Kanu (72 Jonathan Williams), Gareth Bale.    Manager: Chris Coleman

**Goals**:  Jamie Vardy (56), Daniel Sturridge (90+1) / Gareth Bale (42)

958.   20.06.2016   15th European Champs Group B
**SLOVAKIA v ENGLAND   0-0**
*Stade Geoffroy-Guichard, Saint-Étienne (France)*
Referee:  Carlos Velasco Carvallo (Spain)   Att  39,051
**SLOVAKIA:**  Matús Kozácik, Peter Pekarík, Martin Skrtel, Ján Durica, Tomás Hubocan, Vladimír Weiss (78 Milan Skriniar), Ondrej Duda (57 Dusan Svento), Marek Hamsík, Juraj Kucka, Viktor Pecovsky (67 Norbert Gyömbér), Róbert Mak.
Manager:  Ján Kozák
**ENGLAND:**  Joe Hart, Gary Cahill, Chris Smalling, Nathaniel Clyne, Ryan Bertrand, Adam Lallana (60 Dele Alli), Jordan Henderson, Eric Dier, Jack Wilshere (56 Wayne Rooney), Jamie Vardy, Daniel Sturridge (76 Harry Kane).
Manager:  Roy Hodgson

959.   27.06.2016   15th Euro Champs Round of 16
**ENGLAND v ICELAND   1-2**  (1-2)
*Allianz Riviera, Nice (France)*
Referee:  Damir Skomina (Slovenia)   Attendance:  33,901
**ENGLAND:**  Joe Hart, Kyle Walker, Danny Rose, Gary Cahill, Chris Smalling, Raheem Sterling (60 Jamie Vardy), Wayne Rooney (87 Marcus Rashford), Eric Dier (46 Jack Wilshere), Dele Alli, Harry Kane, Daniel Sturridge.
Manager:  Roy Hodgson
**ICELAND:**  Hannes Halldórsson, Birkir Sævarsson, Ragnar Sigurdsson, Kári Árnason, Ari Skúlason, Jóhann Gudmundsson, Birkir Bjarnason, Gylfi Sigurdsson, Aron Gunnarsson, Kolbeinn Sigthorsson (76 Theódór Elmar Bjarnason), Jón Bödvarsson (89 Arnór Ingvi Traustason).
Managers:  Lars Lagerbäck & Heimir Hallgrímsson
**Goals**:  Wayne Rooney (4 pen) /
Ragnar Sigurdsson (6), Kolbeinn Sigthórsson (18)

960.   04.09.2016   21st World Cup Qualifier
**SLOVAKIA v ENGLAND   0-1**  (0-0)
*Stadión Antona Malatinského, Trnava*
Referee:  Milorad Mazic (Serbia)   Attendance:  18,111
**SLOVAKIA:**  Matús Kozácik, Dusan Svento (78 Filip Kiss), Martin Skrtel, Peter Pekarík, Tomás Hubocan, Ján Durica, Viktor Pecovsky (56 Norbert Gyömbér), Marek Hamsík, Ján Gregus, Michal Duris, Róbert Mak (72 Frantisek Kubík).
Manager:  Ján Kozák
**ENGLAND:**  Joe Hart, Gary Cahill, Kyle Walker, John Stones, Danny Rose, Raheem Sterling (71 Theo Walcott), Adam Lallana, Jordan Henderson (64 Dele Alli), Eric Dier, Wayne Rooney, Harry Kane (82 Daniel Sturridge).
Manager:  Sam Allardyce
**Sent off**:  Martin Skrtel (57)
**Goal**:  Adam Lallana (90+5)

961.   08.10.2016   21st World Cup Qualifier
**ENGLAND v MALTA   2-0**  (2-0)
*Wembley, London*
Referee:  Stefan Johannesson (Sweden)   Attendance:  81,718
**ENGLAND:**  Joe Hart, Kyle Walker, John Stones, Gary Cahill, Ryan Bertrand (19 Danny Rose), Jesse Lingard, Jordan Henderson, Dele Alli, Theo Walcott (68 Marcus Rashford), Daniel Sturridge (74 Jamie Vardy), Wayne Rooney.
Manager:  Gareth Southgate
**MALTA:**  Andrew Hogg, Alex Muscat, Ryan Camilleri, Steve Borg, Andrei Agius, Gareth Sciberras, Zach Muscat, Bjorn Kristensen, Paul Fenech, André Schembri (86 Rowen Muscat), Alfred Effiong (76 Michael Mifsud).
Manager:  Pietro Ghedin
**Goals**:  Daniel Sturridge (29), Dele Alli (38)

962.   11.10.2016   21st World Cup Qualifier
**SLOVENIA v ENGLAND   0-0**
*Stadion Stozice, Ljubljana*
Referee:  Deniz Aytekin (Germany)   Attendance:  13,274
**SLOVENIA:**  Jan Oblak, Bostjan Cesar (68 Miha Mevlja), Aljaz Struna, Miral Samardzic, Bojan Jokic, Valter Birsa (59 Rok Kronaveter), Jasmin Kurtic, Rene Krhin (84 Nik Omladic), Josip Ilicic, Roman Bezjak, Benjamin Verbic.
Manager:  Srecko Katanec
**ENGLAND:**  Joe Hart, Gary Cahill, Kyle Walker, John Stones, Danny Rose, Dele Alli (73 Wayne Rooney), Jesse Lingard, Jordan Henderson, Eric Dier, Theo Walcott (62 Andros Townsend), Daniel Sturridge (82 Marcus Rashford).
Manager:  Gareth Southgate

963.   11.11.2016   21st World Cup Qualifier
**ENGLAND v SCOTLAND   3-0**  (1-0)
*Wembley, London*
Referee:  Cüneyt Çakir (Turkey)   Attendance:  87,258
**ENGLAND:**  Joe Hart, Gary Cahill, Kyle Walker, John Stones, Danny Rose, Raheem Sterling, Adam Lallana, Jordan Henderson, Eric Dier, Daniel Sturridge (75 Jamie Vardy), Wayne Rooney.   Manager:  Gareth Southgate
**SCOTLAND:**  Craig Gordon, Christophe Berra, Lee Wallace, Grant Hanley, Ikechi Anya (79 Callum Paterson), Robert Snodgrass (82 Matt Ritchie), James Morrison (66 James McArthur), James Forrest, Darren Fletcher, Scott Brown, Leigh Griffiths.   Manager:  Gordon Strachan
**Goals**:  Daniel Sturridge (24), Adam Lallana (50), Gary Cahill (61)

964.  15.11.2016
**ENGLAND v SPAIN  2-2**  (1-0)
*Wembley, London*

Referee: Ovidiu Hategan (Romania)    Attendance: 83,716

**ENGLAND:** Joe Hart (46 Tom Heaton), John Stones, Danny Rose (79 Aaron Cresswell), Nathaniel Clyne, Gary Cahill (46 Phil Jagielka), Jesse Lingard, Raheem Sterling (65 Andros Townsend), Adam Lallana (27 Theo Walcott), Jordan Henderson, Eric Dier, Jamie Vardy (67 Marcus Rashford). Manager: Gareth Southgate

**SPAIN:** José Manuel "PEPE" REINA Páez, José Ignacio Fernández Iglesias "NACHO", Daniel "DANI" CARVAJAL Ramos, César AZPILICUETA Tanco, IÑIGO MARTÍNEZ Berridi, THIAGO Alcântara do Nascimento (56 ANDER HERRERA Agüera), Juan Manuel MATA García (46 IAGO ASPAS Juncal), DAVID Jiménez SILVA (64 Francisco Román Alarcón Suárez "ISCO"), Sergio BUSQUETS Burgos (78 Manuel Agudo Durán "NOLITO"), Víctor Machín Pérez "VITOLO" (46 Jorge Resurrección Merodio "KOKE"), Aritz ADURIZ Zubeldia (64 Álvaro Borja MORATA Martín). Manager: Julen LOPETEGUI Agote

**Goals:** Adam Lallana (9 pen), Jamie Vardy (48) / IAGO ASPAS Juncal (89), Francisco Román Alarcón Suárez "ISCO" (90+6)


965.  22.03.2017
**GERMANY v ENGLAND  1-0**  (0-0)
*Signal-Iduna-Park, Dortmund*

Referee: Damir Skomina (Slovenia)    Attendance: 60,109

**GERMANY:** Marc-André ter Stegen, Mats Hummels, Antonio Rüdiger, Joshua Kimmich, Jonas Hector, Julian Weigl (66 Emre Can), Toni Kroos, Leroy Sané, Julian Brandt (59 André Schürrle), Lukas Podolski (84 Sebastian Rudy), Timo Werner (77 Thomas Müller). Manager: Joachim Löw

**ENGLAND:** Joe Hart, Gary Cahill, Ryan Bertrand (83 Luke Shaw), Chris Smalling (84 John Stones), Michael Keane, Kyle Walker, Adam Lallana (65 Nathan Redmond), Dele Alli (71 Jesse Lingard), Eric Dier, Jake Livermore (83 James Ward-Prowse), Jamie Vardy (70 Marcus Rashford). Manager: Gareth Southgate

**Goal:** Lukas Podolski (69)


966.  26.03.2017    21st World Cup Qualifier
**ENGLAND v LITHUANIA  2-0**  (1-0)
*Wembley, London*

Referee: Ruddy Buquet (France)    Attendance: 77,690

**ENGLAND:** Joe Hart, Kyle Walker, John Stones, Michael Keane, Ryan Bertrand, Raheem Sterling (60 Marcus Rashford), Adam Lallana, Dele Alli, Eric Dier, Alex Oxlade-Chamberlain, Jermain Defoe (60 Jamie Vardy). Manager: Gareth Southgate

**LITHUANIA:** Ernestas Setkus, Egidijus Vaitkūnas, Linas Klimavicius, Tadas Kijanskas, Artūras Zulpa, Vykintas Slivka (87 Simonas Paulius), Vaidas Slavickas, Mantas Kuklys, Nerijus Valskis (73 Deivydas Matulevicius), Arvydas Novikovas (54 Mindaugas Grigaravicius), Fiodor Cernych. Manager: Edgaras Jankauskas

**Goals:** Jermain Defoe (21), Jamie Vardy (66)


967.  10.06.2017    21st World Cup Qualifier
**SCOTLAND v ENGLAND  2-2**  (0-0)
*Hampden Park, Glasgow*

Referee: Paolo Tagliavento (Italy)    Attendance: 48,520

**SCOTLAND:** Craig Gordon, Kieran Tierney, Andrew Robertson, Charlie Mulgrew, Christophe Berra, Robert Snodgrass (67 Ryan Fraser), James Morrison (46 James McArthur), Scott Brown, Stuart Armstrong, Ikechi Anya (81 Chris Martin), Leigh Griffiths. Manager: Gordon Strachan

**ENGLAND:** Joe Hart, Kyle Walker, Chris Smalling, Gary Cahill, Ryan Bertrand, Jake Livermore (90+2 Jermain Defoe), Adam Lallana, Dele Alli (84 Raheem Sterling), Eric Dier, Marcus Rashford (65 Alex Oxlade-Chamberlain), Harry Kane. Manager: Gareth Southgate

**Goals:** Leigh Griffiths (87, 90) / Alex Oxlade-Chamberlain (70), Harry Kane (90+3)


968.  13.06.2017
**FRANCE v ENGLAND  3-2**  (2-1)
*Stade de France, Paris – St. Denis*

Referee: Davide Massa (Italy)    Attendance: 79,000

**FRANCE:** Hugo Lloris, Raphaël Varane, Samuel Umtiti, Djibril Sidibé (89 Christophe Jallet), Benjamin Mendy (21 Lucas Digne), Paul Pogba, Thomas Lemar, N'Golo Kanté, Kylian Mbappé, Olivier Giroud (52 Laurent Koscielny), Ousmane Dembélé. Manager: Didier Deschamps

**ENGLAND:** Tom Heaton (46 Jack Butland), Kieran Trippier (76 Adam Lallana), John Stones, Phil Jones (82 Aaron Cresswell), Eric Dier, Gary Cahill, Ryan Bertrand (46 Kyle Walker), Raheem Sterling, Dele Alli, Alex Oxlade-Chamberlain, Harry Kane. Manager: Gareth Southgate

**Sent off:** Raphaël Varane (47)

**Goals:** Samuel Umtiti (22), Djibril Sidibé (43), Ousmane Dembélé (78) / Harry Kane (9, 48 pen)

969.  01.09.2017   21st World Cup Qualifier
**MALTA v ENGLAND  0-4**  (0-0)

*National Stadium, Ta'Qali*

Referee: Artur Manuel Ribeiro Soares Dias (Portugal)   Attendance: 16,994

**MALTA**: Andrew Hogg, Joseph Zefara (75 Ryan Camilleri), Samuel Magri, Steve Borg, Andrei Agius, Zach Muscat, Bjorn Kristensen, Ryan Fenech (83 Paul Fenech), André Schembri (86 Michael Mifsud), Stephen Pisani, Jean Farrugia. Manager: Pietro Ghedin

**ENGLAND**: Joe Hart, Kyle Walker, Phil Jones, Gary Cahill, Ryan Bertrand, Raheem Sterling (46 Marcus Rashford), Jake Livermore, Jordan Henderson, Dele Alli (70 Jamie Vardy), Alex Oxlade-Chamberlain (76 Danny Welbeck), Harry Kane. Manager: Gareth Southgate

**Goals**: Harry Kane (53, 90+2), Ryan Bertrand (86), Danny Welbeck (90+1),

970.  04.09.2017   21st World Cup Qualifier
**ENGLAND v SLOVAKIA  2-1**  (1-1)

*Wembley, London*

Referee: Clément Turpin (France)   Attendance: 67,823

**ENGLAND**: Joe Hart, Phil Jones, Gary Cahill, Ryan Bertrand, Kyle Walker, Jordan Henderson, Dele Alli (90+3 Jake Livermore), Eric Dier, Marcus Rashford (84 Danny Welbeck), Alex Oxlade-Chamberlain (83 Raheem Sterling), Harry Kane. Manager: Gareth Southgate

**SLOVAKIA**: Martin Dúbravka, Tomás Hubocan, Ján Durica, Martin Skrtel, Peter Pekarík, Stanislav Lobotka, Marek Hamsík (79 Ondrej Duda), Vladimír Weiss (68 Albert Rusnák), Milan Skriniar, Adam Nemec (69 Michal Duris), Róbert Mak. Manager: Ján Kozák

**Goals**: Eric Dier (37), Markus Rashford (59) / Stanislav Lobotka (3)

971.  05.10.2017   21st World Cup Qualifier
**ENGLAND v SLOVENIA  1-0**  (0-0)

*Wembley, London*

Referee: Felix Zwayer (Germany)   Attendance: 61,598

**ENGLAND**: Joe Hart, Gary Cahill, Ryan Bertrand, Kyle Walker, John Stones, Jordan Henderson, Raheem Sterling (85 Michael Keane), Eric Dier, Marcus Rashford, Alex Oxlade-Chamberlain (64 Jesse Lingard), Harry Kane. Manager: Gareth Southgate

**SLOVENIA**: Jan Oblak, Aljaz Struna, Miha Mevlja, Bojan Jokic, Bostjan Cesar, Rajko Rotman (79 Tim Matavz), Rene Krhin, Josip Ilicic, Benjamin Verbic, Andraz Sporar (55 Valter Birsa), Roman Bezjak (72 Jan Repas). Manager: Srecko Katanec

**Goal**: Harry Kane (90+4)

972.  08.10.2017   21st World Cup Qualifier
**LITHUANIA v ENGLAND  0-1**  (0-1)

*LFF Stadium, Vulnius*

Referee: Orel Grinfeeld (Israel)   Attendance: 5,400

**LITHUANIA**: Ernestas Setkus, Linas Klimavicius, Edvinas Girdvainis, Valdemars Borovskis, Vytautas Andriuskevicius, Artūras Zulpa, Ovidijus Verbickas, Vykintas Slivka (90+1 Karolis Chvedukas), Darvydas Sernas (76 Deivydas Matulevicius), Arvydas Novikovas, Fiodor Cernych. Manager: Edgaras Jankauskas

**ENGLAND**: Jack Butland, Kieran Trippier, John Stones, Harry Maguire, Michael Keane, Aaron Cresswell, Harry Winks, Jordan Henderson, Dele Alli (81 Jesse Lingard), Marcus Rashford (72 Daniel Sturridge), Harry Kane. Manager: Gareth Southgate

**Goal**: Harry Kane (27 pen)

973.  10.11.2017
**ENGLAND v GERMANY  0-0**

*Wembley, London*

Referee: Pawel Raczkowski (Poland)   Attendance: 81,382

**ENGLAND**: Jordan Pickford, Phil Jones (25 Joe Gomez), Eric Dier, Kieran Trippier (71 Kyle Walker), John Stones, Danny Rose (71 Ryan Bertrand), Harry Maguire, Ruben Loftus-Cheek, Jake Livermore (86 Jack Cork), Tammy Abraham (60 Marcus Rashford), Jamie Vardy (86 Jesse Lingard). Manager: Gareth Southgate

**GERMANY**: Marc-André ter Stegen, Mats Mummels, Marcel Halstenberg, Matthias Ginter, Antonio Rüdiger, Joshua Kimmich, Ilkay Gündogan (86 Sebastian Rudy), Mesut Özil, Julian Draxler (67 Emre Can), Leroy Sané (87 Julian Brandt), Timo Werner (73 Sandro Wagner).   Manager: Joachim Löw

974.  14.11.2017
**ENGLAND v BRAZIL  0-0**

*Wembley, London*

Referee: Artur Manuel Ribeiro Soares Dias (Portugal)   Attendance: 84,595

**ENGLAND**: Joe Hart, Ryan Bertrand (80 Ashley Young), Kyle Walker, John Stones, Harry Maguire, Joe Gomez, Eric Dier, Ruben Loftus-Cheek (35 Jesse Lingard), Jake Livermore (90 Danny Rose), Jamie Vardy (75 Dominic Solanke), Marcus Rashford (75 Tammy Abraham). Manager: Gareth Southgate

**BRAZIL**: ALISSON Ramses Becker, Daniel "DANI" ALVES da Silva, João MIRANDA de Souza Filho, Marcos Aoás Corrêa "MARQUINHOS", MARCELO Vieira da Silva Júnior, RENATO Soares de Oliveira AUGUSTO (68 Fernando Luis Roza "FERNANDINHO"), José Paulo Bezerra Maciel Júnior "PAULINHO", Philippe COUTINHO Correia (68 WILLIAN Borges da Silva), Carlos Henrique CASEMIRO, NEYMAR da Silva Santos Júnior, GABRIEL Fernando de JESUS (76 ROBERTO FIRMINO Barbosa de Oliveira). Manager: Adenor Léonardo Bachi "TITE"

975.  23.03.2018
**NETHERLANDS v ENGLAND  0-1**  (0-0)

*Amsterdam ArenA, Amsterdam*

Referee: JESÚS GIL Manzano (Spain)   Attendance: 51,500

NETHERLANDS:  Jeroen Zoet, Patrick van Aanholt, Stefan de Vrij (89 Wout Weghorst), Virgil van Dijk, Hans Hateboer, Matthijs de Ligt, Georginio Wijnaldum, Kevin Strootman (90 Donny van de Beek), Bas Dost (66 Ryan Babel), Memphis Depay, Quincy Promes (66 Davy Pröpper).

Manager: Ronald Koeman

ENGLAND:  Jordan Pickford, Danny Rose (71 Ashley Young), Kyle Walker, Kieran Trippier, John Stones, Joe Gomez (10 Harry Maguire, 89 Eric Dier), Jordan Henderson, Alex Oxlade-Chamberlain, Jesse Lingard (68 Dele Alli), Raheem Sterling (68 Danny Welbeck), Marcus Rashford (68 Jamie Vardy). Manager: Gareth Southgate

**Goal:** Jesse Lingard (59)


976.   27.03.2018
**ENGLAND v ITALY  1-1**  (1-0)

*Wembley Stadium, London*

Referee: Deniz Aytekin (Germany)   Attendance: 82,598

ENGLAND:  Jack Butland, Ashley Young (YC83), Kyle Walker (YC72), Kieran Trippier (60 Danny Rose), James Tarkowski, John Stones (73 Jordan Henderson), Alex Oxlade-Chamberlain (YC40) (60 Adam Lallana), Jesse Lingard (71 Lewis Cook), Eric Dier, Jamie Vardy (70 Marcus Rashford), Raheem Sterling.   Manager: Gareth Southgate

ITALY:  Gianluigi Donnarumma, Leonardo Bonucci, Mattia De Sciglio, Daniele Rugani, Davide Zappacosta, Antonio Candreva (56 Federico Chiesa), Marco Parolo, Jorge Luiz Frello Filho "JORGINHO", Lorenzo Pellegrini (79 Roberto Gagliardini), Ciro Immobile (64 Andrea Belotti), Lorenzo Insigne.   Manager: Luigi Di Biagio

**Goals:** Jamie Vardy (26) / Lorenzo Insigne (87 pen)


977.   02.06.2018
**ENGLAND v NIGERIA  2-1**  (2-0)

*Wembley Stadium, London*

Referee: Marco Guida (Italy)   Attendance: 70,025

ENGLAND:  Jordan Pickford, Ashley Young (68 Danny Rose), Gary Cahill, Kyle Walker, Kieran Trippier, John Stones, Dele Alli (82 Fabian Delph), Jesse Lingard (67 Ruben Loftus-Cheek), Eric Dier, Harry Kane (73 Danny Welbeck), Raheem Sterling (73 Marcus Rashford).   Manager: Gareth Southgate

NIGERIA: FRANCIS Odinaka UZOHO, LEON-Aderemi BALOGUN (46 KENNETH Josiah OMERUO), WILLIAM Paul TROOST-EKONG, BRIAN Oladapo IDOWU, Abdullahi Shehu (46 Tyronne Ebuehi), JOHN "MIKEL" Michael Nchekubu Obinna, Victor Moses (63 Ahmed Musa), JOEL Chukwuma OBI (46 JOHN Oguchukwu OGU), OGENYI Eddy ONAZI (46 Oghenekaro PETER ETEBO), Alexander Chuka "ALEX" IWOBI, ODION Jude IGHALO (77 KELECHI Promise IHEANACHO).   Manager: Gernot Rohr

**Goals:** Gary Cahill (7), Harry Kane (39) / Alexander Chuka "ALEX" IWOBI (47)


978.   07.06.2018
**ENGLAND v COSTA RICA  2-0**  (1-0)

*Elland Road, Leeds*

Referee: Hiroyuki Kimura (Japan)   Attendance: 36,104

ENGLAND:  Jack Butland (65 Nick Pope), Danny Rose, Phil Jones, Harry Maguire, John Stones (65 Gary Cahill), Trent Alexander-Arnold (64 Kieran Trippier), Jordan Henderson (64 Dele Alli), Fabian Delph, Ruben Loftus-Cheek (79 Jesse Lingard), Jamie Vardy (61 Danny Welbeck), Marcus Rashford.   Manager: Gareth Southgate

COSTA RICA:  KEYLOR Antonio NAVAS Gamboa, BRYAN Josué OVIEDO Jiménez (60 RONALD Alberto MATARRITA Ulate), CRISTIAN Esteban GAMBOA Luna (72 IAN Rey SMITH Quiros), GIANCARLO GONZÁLEZ Castro, KENDALL Jamaal WASTON Manley, FRANCISCO Javier CALVO Quesada, CELSO BORGES Mora, DAVID Alberto GUZMÁN Pérez (69 YELTSIN Ignacio TEJEDA Valverde), JOHAN Alberto VENEGAS Ulloa (61 CHRISTIÁN BOLAÑOS Navarro), MARCO Danilo UREÑA Porras, JOEL Nathaniel CAMPBELL Samuels.

Manager: ÓSCAR Antonio RAMÍREZ Hernández

**Goals:** Marcus Rashford (13), Danny Welbeck (76)

979.   18.06.2018   21st World Cup Group G
**TUNISIA v ENGLAND  1-2**  (1-1)
*Volgograd Arena, Volgograd (Russia)*
Referee:  WILMAR ROLDÁN Pérez (Colombia)
Attendance: 41,064
**TUNISIA**:  Mouez Hassen (15 Farouk Ben Mustapha), Syam Ben Youssef, Ali Maâloul, Yassine Meriah, Dylan Bronn, Naïm Sliti (74 Mohamed Ben Amor), Ferjani Sassi, Ellyes Skhiri, Wahbi Khazri (85 Saber Khalifa), Anice Badri, Fakhreddine Ben Youssef.   Manager:  Nabil Maâloul
**ENGLAND**:  Jordan Pickford, Ashley Young, Kyle Walker, Kieran Trippier, Harry Maguire, John Stones, Jordan Henderson, Dele Alli (80 Ruben Loftus-Cheek), Jesse Lingard (90+3 Eric Dier), Harry Kane, Raheem Sterling (68 Marcus Rashford).   Manager:  Gareth Southgate
**Goals**:  Ferjani Sassi (35 pen) / Harry Kane (11, 90+1)

980.   26.06.2018   21st World Cup Group G
**ENGLAND v PANAMA  6-1**  (5-0)
*Stadion Nizhny Novgorod, Nizhny Novgorod (Russia)*
Referee:  GHEAD Zaglol GRISHA (Egypt)
Attendance: 43,319
**ENGLAND**:  Jordan Pickford, Ashley Young, Kyle Walker, Kieran Trippier (70 Danny Rose), Harry Maguire, John Stones, Jordan Henderson, Jesse Lingard (63 Fabian Delph), Ruben Loftus-Cheek, Harry Kane (63 Jamie Vardy), Raheem Sterling.   Manager:  Gareth Southgate
**PANAMA**:  JAIME Manuel PENEDO Cano, ROMÁN Aureliano TORRES Morcillo, ÉRIC Javier DAVIS Grajales, FIDEL ESCOBAR Mendieta, MICHAEL Amir MURILLO Bermúdez, GABRIEL Enrique GÓMEZ Girón (69 FELIPE Abdiel BALOY Ramírez), ARMANDO Enrique COOPER Whitaker, ANÍBAL Casis GODOY Lemus (63 RICARDO Guardia ÁVILA), JOSÉ Luis RODRÍGUEZ Francis, BLAS Antonio Miguel PÉREZ Ortega, Édgar YOEL BÁRCENAS Herrera (69 ABDIEL ARROYO Molinar).   Manager:  HERNÁN Darío GÓMEZ Jaramillo
**Goals**:  John Stones (8, 40), H. Kane (22 pen, 45+1 pen, 62), Jesse Lingard (36) / FELIPE Abdiel BALOY Ramírez (78)

981.   28.06.2018   21st World Cup Group G
**ENGLAND v BELGIUM  0-1**  (0-0)
*Arena Baltika, Kaliningrad (Russia)*
Referee:  Damir Skomina (Slovenia)   Attendance: 33,973
**ENGLAND**:  Jordan Pickford, Gary Cahill, Danny Rose, Phil Jones, John Stones (46 Harry Maguire), Trent Alexander-Arnold (79 Danny Welbeck), Fabian Delph, Eric Dier, Ruben Loftus-Cheek, Jamie Vardy, Marcus Rashford.   Manager:  Gareth Southgate
**BELGIUM**:  Thibaut Courtois, Thomas Vermaelen (74 Vincent Kompany), Dedryck Boyata, Mousa Dembélé, Marouane Fellaini, Nacer Chadli, Leander Dendoncker, Adnan Januzaj (86' Dries Mertens), Youri Tielemans, Thorgan Hazard, Michy Batshuayi.   Manager:  ROBERTO MARTÍNEZ Montoliú
**Goal**:  Adnan Januzaj (51)

982.   03.07.2018   21st World Cup Round of 16
**COLOMBIA v ENGLAND  1-1**  (0-0, 1-1)  (AET)
*Otkrytiye Arena, Moscow (Russia)*
Referee:  Mark Geiger (USA)   Attendance: 44,190
**COLOMBIA**:  DAVID OSPINA Ramírez, SANTIAGO ARIAS Naranjo (116 CRISTIÁN Eduardo ZAPATA Valencia), JOHAN Andrés MOJICA Palacio, YERRY Fernando MINA González, DAVINSON SÁNCHEZ Mina, CARLOS Alberto SÁNCHEZ Moreno (79 Andrés MATEUS URIBE Villa), JUAN Guillermo CUADRADO Bello, JUAN Fernando QUINTERO Paniagua (88 LUIS Fernando MURIEL Fruto), WÍLMAR Enrique BARRIOS Terán, JEFFERSON Andrés LERMA Solís (62 CARLOS Arturo BACCA Ahumada), RADAMEL FALCAO García Zárate.   Manager:  José Néstor Pekerman
**ENGLAND**:  Jordan Pickford, Ashley Young (102 Danny Rose), Kyle Walker (113 Marcus Rashford), Kieran Trippier, Harry Maguire, John Stones, Jordan Henderson, Dele Alli (81' Eric Dier), Jesse Lingard, Harry Kane, Raheem Sterling (88 Jamie Vardy).   Manager:  Gareth Southgate
**Goals**:  YERRY Fernando MINA González (90+3) / Harry Kane (57 pen)
**Penalties**:  1-0 RADAMEL FALCAO García Zárate, 1-1 Harry Kane, 2-1 JUAN Guillermo CUADRADO Bello, 2-2 Marcus Rashford, 3-2 LUIS Fernando MURIEL Fruto, Jordan Henderson (missed), Andrés MATEUS URIBE Villa (missed), 3-3 Kieran Trippier, CARLOS Arturo BACCA Ahumada (missed), 3-4 Eric Dier

**983. 07.07.2018 21st World Cup Quarter-fiinals**
**SWEDEN v ENGLAND 0-2** (0-1)
*Cosmos Arena, Samara (Russia)*
Referee: Björn Kuipers (Netherlands)   Attendance: 39,991
**SWEDEN**: Robin Olsen, Andreas Granqvist, Victor Lindelöf, Ludwig Augustinsson, Emil Krafth (85 Pontus Jansson), Sebastian Larsson, Albin Ekdal, Emil Forsberg (65 Martin Olsson), Victor Claesson, Marcus Berg, Ola Toivonen (65 John Guidetti).   Manager: Janne Andersson
**ENGLAND**: Jordan Pickford, Ashley Young, Kyle Walker, Kieran Trippier, Harry Maguire, John Stones, Jordan Henderson (85 Eric Dier), Dele Alli (77 Fabian Delph), Jesse Lingard, Harry Kane, Raheem Sterling (90+1 Marcus Rashford).   Manager: Gareth Southgate
**Goals**: Harry Maguire (30), Dele Alli (58)

**984. 11.07.2018 21st World Cup Semi-finals**
**CROATIA v ENGLAND 2-1** (0-1, 1-1) (AET)
*Stadion Luzhniki, Moscow (Russia)*
Referee: Cüneyt Çakir (Turkey)   Attendance: 78,011
**CROATIA**: Danijel Subasic, Domagoj Vida, Ivan Strinic (95 Josip Pivaric), Dejan Lovren, Sime Vrsaljko, Luka Modric (119 Milan Badelj), Ivan Rakitic, Ivan Perisic, Marcelo Brozovic, Mario Mandzukic (115 Vedran Corluka), Ante Rebic (101 Andrej Kramaric).   Manager: Zlatko Dalic
**ENGLAND**: Jordan Pickford, Ashley Young (90 Danny Rose), Kyle Walker (112 Jamie Vardy), Kieran Trippier, Harry Maguire, John Stones, Jordan Henderson (97 Eric Dier), Dele Alli, Jesse Lingard, Harry Kane, Raheem Sterling (74 Marcus Rashford).   Manager: Gareth Southgate
**Goals**: Ivan Perisic (68), Mario Mandzukic (109) / Kieran Trippier (5)

**985. 14.07.2018 21st World Cup Third Place**
**BELGIUM v ENGLAND 2-0** (1-0)
*Krestovski Stadium, Saint-Petersburg (Russia)*
Referee: Alireza Faghani (Iran)   Attendance: 64,406
**BELGIUM**: Thibaut Courtois, Vincent Kompany, Jan Vertonghen, Toby Alderweireld, Thomas Meunier, Axel Witsel, Nacer Chadli (39 Thomas Vermaelen), Kevin De Bruyne, Youri Tielemans (78 Mousa Dembélé), Eden Hazard, Romelu Lukaku (60 Dries Mertens).
Manager: ROBERTO MARTÍNEZ Montoliú
**ENGLAND**: Jordan Pickford, Danny Rose (46 Jesse Lingard), Phil Jones, Kieran Trippier, Harry Maguire, John Stones, Fabian Delph, Eric Dier, Ruben Loftus-Cheek (84 Dele Alli), Harry Kane, Raheem Sterling (46 Marcus Rashford).   Manager: Gareth Southgate
**Goals**: Thomas Meunier (4'), Eden Hazard (82)

**986. 08.09.2018 UEFA Nations League Group 4**
**ENGLAND v SPAIN 1-2** (1-2)
*Wembley Stadium, London*
Referee: Danny Makkelie (Netherlands)   Attendance: 81,392
**ENGLAND**: Jordan Pickford, Kieran Trippier, Harry Maguire, John Stones, Luke Shaw (53 Danny Rose), Joe Gomez, Jordan Henderson (64 Eric Dier), Dele Alli, Jesse Lingard, Harry Kane, Marcus Rashford (90+4 Danny Welbeck).
Manager: Gareth Southgate
**SPAIN**: David DE GEA Quintana, SERGIO RAMOS García, MARCOS ALONSO Mendoza (87 IÑIGO MARTÍNEZ Berridi), José Ignacio Fernández Iglesias "NACHO", Daniel CARVAJAL Ramos, Sergio BUSQUETS i Burgos, THIAGO ALCÂNTARA do Nascimento (80 SERGI ROBERTO Carnicer), Francisco Román Alarcón Suárez "ISCO", SAÚL Ñíguez Esclapez, IAGO ASPAS Juncal (68 Marco ASENSIO Willemsen), RODRIGO Moreno Machado.
Manager: LUIS ENRIQUE Martínez García
**Goals**: Marcus Rashford (11) / SAÚL Ñíguez Esclapez (13), RODRIGO Moreno Machado (32)

**987. 11.09.2018**
**ENGLAND v SWITZERLAND 1-0** (0-0)
*King Power Stadium, Leicester*
Referee: Clément Turpin (France)   Attendance: 30,256
**ENGLAND**: Jack Butland, Danny Rose (79 Ben Chilwell), Kyle Walker, James Tarkowski (61 John Stones), Harry Maguire, Trent Alexander-Arnold (78 Kieran Trippier), Fabian Delph (68 Jordan Henderson), Eric Dier, Ruben Loftus-Cheek (61 Jesse Lingard), Danny Welbeck (61 Harry Kane), Marcus Rashford.   Manager: Gareth Southgate
**SWITZERLAND**: Yann Sommer, Johan Djourou, Stephan Lichtsteiner, Ricardo Rodríguez (46 François Moubandje), Fabian Schär, Manuel Akanji (46 Admir Mehmedi), Xherdan Shaqiri (80 Haris Seferovic), Granit Xhaka, Remo Freuler (66 Steven Zuber), Denis Zakaria (66 Edimilson Fernandes), Mario Gavranovic (66 Albian Ajeti).
Manager: Vladimir Petkovic
**Goal**: Marcus Rashford (54)

988.   12.10.2018   UEFA Nations League Group 4
**CROATIA v ENGLAND   0-0**

*Stadion HNK Rijeka, Rijeka*

Referee: Dr. Felix Brych (Germany)
Attendance: Behind closed doors.

**CROATIA**: Dominik Livakovic, Domagoj Vida, Dejan Lovren, Josip Pivaric, Tin Jedvaj, Luka Modric, Ivan Rakitic, Ivan Perisic (68 Marko Pjaca), Mateo Kovacic (73 Milan Badelj), Andrej Kramaric, Ante Rebic (80 Marko Livaja). Manager: Zlatko Dalic

**ENGLAND**: Jordan Pickford, Kyle Walker, Harry Maguire, John Stones, Ben Chilwell, Jordan Henderson, Ross Barkley, Eric Dier, Harry Kane, Raheem Sterling (78 Jadon Sancho), Marcus Rashford.   Manager: Gareth Southgate


989.   15.10.2018   UEFA Nations League Group 4
**SPAIN v ENGLAND   2-3**  (0-3)

*Estadio Benito Villamarín, Sevilla*

Referee: Szymon Marciniak (Poland)   Attendance: 50,355

**SPAIN**: David DE GEA Quintana, SERGIO RAMOS García, MARCOS ALONSO Mendoza, José Ignacio Fernández Iglesias "NACHO", Jonathan "JONNY" CASTRO Otto, Sergio BUSQUETS i Burgos, THIAGO ALCÁNTARA do Nascimento, SAÚL Ñíguez Esclapez (57 Francisco "PACO" ALCÁCER García), IAGO ASPAS Juncal (57 Daniel "DANI" CEBALLOS Fernández), RODRIGO Moreno Machado (72 Álvaro Borja MORATA Martín), Marco ASENSIO Willemsen. Manager: LUIS ENRIQUE Martínez García

**ENGLAND**: Jordan Pickford, Kieran Trippier (85' Trent Alexander-Arnold), Harry Maguire, Joe Gomez, Ben Chilwell, Ross Barkley (76 Kyle Walker), Eric Dier, Harry Winks (90+1 Nathaniel Chalobah), Harry Kane, Raheem Sterling, Marcus Rashford.   Manager: Gareth Southgate

**Goals**: Francisco "PACO" ALCÁCER García (58), SERGIO RAMOS García (90+7) /
Raheem Sterling (16, 38), Marcus Rashford (29)


990.   15.11.2018
**ENGLAND v UNITED STATES   3-0**  (2-0)

*Wembley Stadium, London*

Referee: JESÚS GIL Manzano (Spain)   Attendance: 68,155

**ENGLAND**: Jordan Pickford (46 Alex McCarthy), Lewis Dunk, Michael Keane, Trent Alexander-Arnold, Ben Chilwell (57 Eric Dier), Fabian Delph, Dele Alli (57 Jordan Henderson), Jesse Lingard (58 Wayne Rooney), Harry Winks (70 Ruben Loftus-Cheek), Jadon Sancho, Callum Wilson (79 Marcus Rashford).   Manager: Gareth Southgate

**UNITED STATES**: Brad Guzan, Jorge Villafaña (88 Shaq Moore), John Anthony Brooks, DeAndre Yedlin, Matt Miazga, Julian Green (62 Tyler Adams), Will Trapp (70 Kellyn Acosta), Christian Pulisic, Weston McKennie (76 Sebastian Lletget), Bobby Wood, Timothy Weah (76 Kenny Saief). Manager: Dave Sarachan

**Goals**: Jesse Lingard (25), Trent Alexander-Arnold (27), Callum Wilson (77)


991.   18.11.2018   UEFA Nations League Group 4
**ENGLAND v CROATIA   2-1**  (0-0)

*Wembley Stadium, London*

Referee: Anasthasios Sidiropoulos (Greece)
Attendance: 78,221

**ENGLAND**: Jordan Pickford, Kyle Walker, John Stones, Joe Gomez, Ben Chilwell, Fabian Delph (73 Jesse Lingard), Ross Barkley (63 Dele Alli), Eric Dier, Harry Kane, Raheem Sterling, Marcus Rashford (73 Jadon Sancho). Manager: Gareth Southgate

**CROATIA**: Lovre Kalinic, Domagoj Vida, Dejan Lovren, Sime Vrsaljko (26 Antonio Milic), Tin Jedvaj, Luka Modric, Ivan Perisic, Marcelo Brozovic, Nikola Vlasic (79 Marko Rog), Andrej Kramaric, Ante Rebic (46 Josip Brekalo). Manager: Zlatko Dalic

**Goals**: Jesse Lingard (78), Harry Kane (85) /
Andrej Kramaric (57)


992.   22.03.2019   16th European Champs Qualifiers
**ENGLAND v CZECH REPUBLIC   5-0**  (2-0)

*Wembley Stadium, London*

Referee: Artur Soares Dias (Portugal)   Attendance: 82,575

**ENGLAND**: Jordan Pickford, Kyle Walker, Harry Maguire, Michael Keane, Ben Chilwell, Jordan Henderson, Dele Alli (63 Declan Rice), Eric Dier (17 Ross Barkley), Jadon Sancho, Harry Kane, Raheem Sterling (70 Callum Hudson-Odoi). Manager: Gareth Southgate

**CZECH REPUBLIC**: Jirí Pavlenka, Ondrej Celustka, Theodor Gebre Selassie, Filip Novák, Pavel Kaderábek, Tomás Kalas, David Pavelka, Vladimír Darida (67 Lukás Masopust), Tomás Soucek, Jakub Jankto (46 Matej Vydra), Patrik Schick (82 Milan Skoda).   Manager: Jaroslav Silhavy

**Goals**: Raheem Sterling (24, 62, 68), Harry Kane (45+2 pen), Tomás Kalas (84 og)

**993.  25.03.2019   16th European Champs Qualifiers**
**MONTENEGRO v ENGLAND  1-5  (1-2)**
*Stadion Pod Goricom, Podgorica*
Referee:  Aleksey Kulbakov (Belarus)   Attendance:  8,329

**MONTENEGRO**:  Danijel Petkovic, Zarko Tomasevic, Stefan Savic, Marko Simic (74 Vladimir Jovovic), Filip Stojkovic, Adam Marusic, Marko Vesovic (70 Aleksandar Boljevic), Nikola Vukcevic, Mirko Ivanic, Fatos Beciraj (61 Marko Jankovic), Stefan Mugosa.   Manager:  Ljubisa Tumbakovic

**ENGLAND**:  Jordan Pickford, Danny Rose, Kyle Walker, Harry Maguire, Michael Keane, Ross Barkley (82 James Ward-Prowse), Dele Alli (64 Jordan Henderson), Declan Rice, Harry Kane (83 Callum Wilson), Raheem Sterling, Callum Hudson-Odoi.   Manager:  Gareth Southgate

**Goals**:  Marko Vesovic (17) / Michael Keane (30), Ross Barkley (38, 59), Harry Kane (71), Raheem Sterling (80)


**994.  06.06.2019   UEFA Nations League Semi-finals**
**NETHERLANDS**
     **v ENGLAND  3-1  (0-1, 1-1)  (AET)**
*Estádio Dom Afonso Henriques, Guimarães (Portugal)*
Referee:  Clément Turpin (France)   Attendance:  25,711

**NETHERLANDS**:  Jasper Cillessen, Daley Blind, Virgil van Dijk, Denzel Dumfries, Matthijs de Ligt, Georginio Wijnaldum, Marten de Roon (68 Donny van de Beek), Frenkie de Jong (114' Kevin Strootman), Ryan Babel (68 Quincy Promes), Memphis Depay, Steven Bergwijn (90 Davy Pröpper).   Manager:  Ronald Koeman

**ENGLAND**:  Jordan Pickford, Kyle Walker, Harry Maguire, John Stones, Ben Chilwell, Fabian Delph (77 Jordan Henderson), Ross Barkley, Declan Rice (105 Dele Alli), Jadon Sancho (61 Jesse Lingard), Raheem Sterling, Marcus Rashford (46 Harry Kane).   Manager:  Gareth Southgate

**Goals**:  Matthijs de Ligt (73), Kyle Walker (97 og), Quincy Promes (114) / Marcus Rashford (32 pen)


**995.  09.06.2019   UEFA Nations League Third place**
**SWITZERLAND v ENGLAND  0-0  (AET)**
*Estádio Dom Afonso Henriques, Guimarães (Portugal)*
Referee:  Ovidiu Hategan (Romania)   Attendance:  15,742

**SWITZERLAND**:  Yann Sommer, Ricardo Rodríguez (87 Josip Drmic), Fabian Schär, Kevin Mbabu, Nico Elvedi, Manuel Akanji, Xherdan Shaqiri (65 Steven Zuber), Granit Xhaka, Remo Freuler, Edimilson Fernandes (61 Denis Zakaria), Haris Seferovic (113 Noah Okafor).   Manager:  Vladimir Petkovic

**ENGLAND**:  Jordan Pickford, Danny Rose (70 Kyle Walker), Harry Maguire, Joe Gomez, Trent Alexander-Arnold, Fabian Delph (105 Ross Barkley), Dele Alli, Jesse Lingard (105 Jadon Sancho), Eric Dier, Harry Kane (75 Callum Wilson), Raheem Sterling.   Manager:  Gareth Southgate

**Penalties**:  0-1 Harry Maguire, 1-1 Steven Zuber, 1-2 Ross Barkley, 2-2 Granit Xhaka, 2-3 Jadon Sancho, 3-3 Manuel Akanji, 3-4 Raheem Sterling, 4-4 Kevin Mbabu, 4-5 Jordan Pickford, 5-5 Fabian Schär, 5-6 Eric Dier, Josip Drmic (missed).


**996.  07.09.2019   16th European Champs Qualifiers**
**ENGLAND v BULGARIA  4-0  (1-0)**
*Wembley Stadium, London*
Referee:  Marco Guida (Italy)   Attendance:  82,605

**ENGLAND**:  Jordan Pickford, Danny Rose, Kieran Trippier, Harry Maguire, Michael Keane, Jordan Henderson (67 Mason Mount), Ross Barkley, Declan Rice, Harry Kane (77 Alex Oxlade-Chamberlain), Raheem Sterling (71 Jadon Sancho), Marcus Rashford.   Manager:  Gareth Southgate

**BULGARIA**:  Plamen Iliev, Nikolaj Bodurov (65 Kristian Dimitrov), Strahil Popov, Vasil Bozhikov, Kristiyan Malinov, Anton Nedyalkov, Georgi Sarmov, Ivelin Popov, Galin Ivanov (82 Daniel Mladenov), WANDERSON Cristaldo Farias, Marcelo Nascimento da Costa "MARCELINHO" (67 Kiril Despodov).   Manager:  Krassimir Balakov

**Goals**:  Harry Kane (24, 49 pen, 73 pen), Raheem Sterling (55)


**997.  10.09.2019   16th European Champs Qualifiers**
**ENGLAND v KOSOVO  5-3  (5-1)**
*Saint Mary's Stadium, Southampton*
Referee:  Felix Zwayer (Germany)   Attendance:  30,155

**ENGLAND**:  Jordan Pickford, Harry Maguire, Michael Keane, Trent Alexander-Arnold, Ben Chilwell, Jordan Henderson, Ross Barkley (83 Mason Mount), Declan Rice, Jadon Sancho (85 Marcus Rashford), Harry Kane, Raheem Sterling.   Manager:  Gareth Southgate

**KOSOVO**:  Aro Muric, Fidan Aliti, Amir Rrahmani, Florent Hadërgjonaj, Mergim Vojvoda, Idriz Voca (59 Anel Rashkaj), Valon Berisha (85 Florent Hasani), Besar Halimi, Florent Muslija (46 Leart Paqarada), Bersant Celina, Vedat Muriqi.   Manager:  Bernard Challandes

**Goals**:  Raheem Sterling (8), Harry Kane (19), Mergim Vojvoda (38 og), Jadon Sancho (44, 45+1) / Valon Berisha (1, 49), Vedat Muriqi (55 pen)

Harry Kane missed a penalty kick (65)

**998. 11.10.2019 16th European Champs Qualifiers**
**CZECH REPUBLIC v ENGLAND 2-1** (1-1)
*Sinobo Stadium, Prague*
Referee: Damir Skomina (Slovenia)   Attendance: 18,651

**CZECH REPUBLIC**: Tomás Vaclík, Ondrej Celustka, Jakub Brabec, Jan Boríl, Vladimír Coufal, Vladimír Darida, Lukás Masopust (90 Jaromír Zmrhal), Tomás Soucek, Alex Král, Jakub Jankto (83 Jan Kopic), Patrik Schick (65 Zdenek Ondrásek).   Manager: Jaroslav Silhavy

**ENGLAND**: Jordan Pickford, Danny Rose, Kieran Trippier, Harry Maguire, Michael Keane, Jordan Henderson, Mason Mount (72 Ross Barkley), Declan Rice (88 Tammy Abraham), Jadon Sancho (73 Marcus Rashford), Harry Kane, Raheem Sterling.   Manager: Gareth Southgate

**Goals**: Jakub Brabec (9), Z. Ondrásek (85) / H. Kane (5 pen)


**999. 14.10.2019 16th European Champs Qualifiers**
**BULGARIA v ENGLAND 0-6** (0-4)
*Stadion Vasil Levski, Sofia*
Referee: Ivan Bebek (Croatia)   Attendance: 17,481

**BULGARIA**: Plamen Iliev, Petar Zanev, Georgi Terziev, Kamen Hadzhiev, Georgi Sarmov (46 Bozhidar Kraev), Ivelin Popov, Georgi Pashov, Georgi Kostadinov, WANDERSON Cristaldo Farias (76 Kristiyan Malinov), Ismail Isa (68 Galin Ivanov), Kiril Despodov.   Manager: Krassimir Balakov

**ENGLAND**: Jordan Pickford, Kieran Trippier, Harry Maguire, Tyrone Mings, Ben Chilwell, Jordan Henderson, Ross Barkley (73 Mason Mount), Harry Winks, Harry Kane, Raheem Sterling (73 Jadon Sancho), Marcus Rashford (76 Callum Wilson).   Manager: Gareth Southgate

**Goals**: Marcus Rashford (7), Ross Barkley (20, 32), Raheem Sterling (45+4, 69), Harry Kane (85)


**1000. 14.11.2019 16th European Champs Qualifiers**
**ENGLAND v MONTENEGRO 7-0** (5-0)
*Wembley Stadium, London*
Referee: ANTONIO MATEU Lahoz (Spain)   Att: 77,277

**ENGLAND**: Jordan Pickford, Harry Maguire, John Stones, Trent Alexander-Arnold, Ben Chilwell, Alex Oxlade-Chamberlain (56 James Maddison), Harry Winks, Mason Mount (70 Joe Gomez), Jadon Sancho, Harry Kane (57 Tammy Abraham), Marcus Rashford.   Manager: Gareth Southgate

**MONTENEGRO**: Milan Mijatovic, Risto Radunovic (46' Momcilo Raspopovic), Marko Simic, Aleksandar Sofranac, Marko Vesovic, Deni Hocko, Nikola Vukcevic, Dusan Lagator, Sead Haksabanovic (74' Aleksandar Boljevic), Fatos Beciraj, Vladimir Jovovic (65 Branislav Jankovic).
Manager: Faruk Hadzibegic

**Goals**: Alex Oxlade-Chamberlain (11), H. Kane (18, 24, 37), Marcus Rashford (30), Aleksandar Sofranac (66 og), Tammy Abraham (84)


**1001. 17.11.2019 16th European Champs Qualifiers**
**KOSOVO v ENGLAND 0-4** (0-1)
*Stadiumi Fadil Vokrri, Pristina*
Referee: Pawel Gil (Poland)   Attendance: 12,326

**KOSOVO**: Aro Muric, Fidan Aliti, Amir Rrahmani, Florent Hadërgjonaj (73 Edon Zhegrova), Mergim Vojvoda, Ibrahim Dresevic, Valon Berisha (65 Besar Halimi), Benjamin Kololli, Milot Rashica, Atdhe Nuhiu (82 Elbasan Rashani), Bersant Celina.   Manager: Bernard Challandes

**ENGLAND**: Nick Pope, Harry Maguire, Tyrone Mings, Trent Alexander-Arnold (84 Fikayo Tomori), Ben Chilwell, Alex Oxlade-Chamberlain (72 Mason Mount), Harry Winks, Declan Rice, Harry Kane, Raheem Sterling, Callum Hudson-Odoi (59 Marcus Rashford).   Manager: Gareth Southgate

**Goals**: Harry Winks (32), Harry Kane (79), M. Rashford (83), Mason Mount (90+1)


**1002. 05.09.2020 UEFA Nations League – Group A2**
**ICELAND v ENGLAND 0-1** (0-0)
*Laugardalsvöllur, Reykjavík*
Referee: Srdjan Jovanovic (Serbia)   Attendance: 0

**ICELAND**: Hannes Halldórsson, Kári Árnason, Hördur Magnússon, Sverrir Ingi Ingason, Hjörtur Hermannsson, Birkir Bjarnason, Victor Pálsson, Arnór Ingvi Traustason (76 Emil Hallfredsson), Jón Dagur Thorsteinsson (66 Arnór Sigurdsson), Albert Gudmundsson, Jón Bödvarsson (90+1 Hólmbert Fridjónsson).   Manager: Erik Hamrén

**ENGLAND**: Jordan Pickford, Kyle Walker, Kieran Trippier, Joe Gomez, James Ward-Prowse, Eric Dier, Declan Rice, Phil Foden (68 Danny Ings), Jadon Sancho (73 Trent Alexander-Arnold), Harry Kane (78 Mason Greenwood), Raheem Sterling.   Manager: Gareth Southgate

**Goal**: Raheem Sterling (90+2 pen)

Birkir Bjarnason missed a penalty kick (90)
Sent off: Kyle Walker (71), Sverrir Ingi Ingason (89)


**1003. 08.09.2020 UEFA Nations League – Group A2**
**DENMARK v ENGLAND 0-0**
*Telia Parken, København*
Referee: István Kovács (Romania)   Attendance: 0

**DENMARK**: Kasper Schmeichel, Andreas Christensen, Mathias Jørgensen "Zanka", Daniel Wass, Thomas Delaney, Yussuf Poulsen, Christian Eriksen, Christian Nørgaard (73 Pierre-Emile Højbjerg), Robert Skov, Martin Braithwaite (82 Simon Kjær), Kasper Dolberg (76 Rasmus Falk).   Manager: Kasper Hjulmand

**ENGLAND**: Jordan Pickford, Eric Dier, Kieran Trippier, Conor Coady, Joe Gomez, Declan Rice, Trent Alexander-Arnold (86 Ainsley Maitland-Niles), Kalvin Phillips (76 Jack Grealish), Jadon Sancho (60 Mason Mount), Harry Kane, Raheem Sterling.   Manager: Gareth Southgate

1004.  08.10.2020
**ENGLAND v WALES  3-0**  (1-0)
*Wembley Stadium, London*
Referee:  Robert Madden (Scotland)    Attendance: 0
**ENGLAND**:  Nick Pope, Kieran Trippier (58 Reece James), Conor Coady, Michael Keane, Joe Gomez (58 Tyrone Mings), Jack Grealish (76 Harvey Barnes), Harry Winks (75 James Ward-Prowse), Bukayo Saka (76 Ainsley Maitland-Niles), Danny Ings, Dominic Calvert-Lewin (58 Mason Mount), Kalvin Phillips.   Manager: Gareth Southgate
**WALES**:  Wayne Hennessey, Connor Roberts (73 Chris Gunter), Ben Davies, Joe Rodon (46 Ben Cabango), Ethan Ampadu (62 Will Vaulks), Chris Mepham, Joe Morrell (46 Dylan Levitt), Kieffer Moore (40 Neco Williams), Tyler Roberts, Rabbi Matondo, Jonathan Williams (73 Matthew Smith).   Manager: Ryan Giggs
**Goals**:  Dominic Calvert-Lewin (26), Conor Coady (53), Danny Ings (63)

1005.  11.10.2020    UEFA Nations League – Group A2
**ENGLAND v BELGIUM  2-1**  (1-1)
*Wembley Stadium, London*
Referee:  Tobias Stieler (Germany)    Attendance: 0
**ENGLAND**:  Jordan Pickford, Kyle Walker, Kieran Trippier, Harry Maguire, Trent Alexander-Arnold (79 Reece James), Jordan Henderson (65 Kalvin Phillips), Eric Dier, Declan Rice, Dominic Calvert-Lewin (65 Harry Kane), Marcus Rashford, Mason Mount (89 Jadon Sancho).   Manager: Gareth Southgate
**BELGIUM**:  Simon Mignolet, Toby Alderweireld, Dedryck Boyata, Timothy Castagne, Jason Denayer, Axel Witsel, Kevin De Bruyne (73 Yari Verschaeren), Thomas Meunier, Yannick Carrasco (83 Jérémy Doku), Youri Tielemans, Romelu Lukaku.   Manager: ROBERTO MARTÍNEZ Montoliú
**Goals**:  Marcus Rashford (39 pen), Mason Mount (65) / Romelu Lukaku (16 pen)

1006.  14.10.2020    UEFA Nations League – Group A2
**ENGLAND v DENMARK  0-1**  (0-1)
*Wembley Stadium, London*
Referee:  Jesús Gil Manzano (Spain)    Attendance: 0
**ENGLAND**:  Jordan Pickford, Kyle Walker, Conor Coady, Harry Maguire, Reece James, Ainsley Maitland-Niles (36 Tyrone Mings), Kalvin Phillips, Declan Rice (76 Jordan Henderson), Harry Kane, Mason Mount (73 Jadon Sancho), Marcus Rashford (72 Dominic Calvert-Lewin).   Manager: Gareth Southgate
**DENMARK**:  Kasper Schmeichel, Simon Kjær, Andreas Christensen (46 Mathias Jørgensen "Zanka"), Daniel Wass, Thomas Delaney, Christian Eriksen, Martin Braithwaite (73 Jannik Vestergaard), Yussuf Poulsen, Robert Skov (46 Joakim Mæhle), Pierre-Emile Højbjerg (88 Mathias Jensen), Kasper Dolberg (37 Pione Sisto).   Manager: Kasper Hjulmand
**Goals**:  Christian Eriksen (35 pen)
**Sent off**:  Harry Maguire (32), Reece James (90)

1007.  12.11.2020
**ENGLAND v REPUBLIC OF IRELAND  3-0**  (2-0)
*Wembley Stadium, London*
Referee:  Carlos del Cerro Grande (Spain)    Attendance: 0
**ENGLAND**:  Nick Pope (46 Dean Henderson), Harry Maguire, Michael Keane, Tyrone Mings (64 Ainsley Maitland-Niles), Reece James, Jack Grealish (62 Phil Foden), Harry Winks, Mason Mount (73 Jude Bellingham), Jadon Sancho, Bukayo Saka, Dominic Calvert-Lewin (63 Tammy Abraham).   Manager: Gareth Southgate
**REPUBLIC OF IRELAND**:  Darren Randolph, Shane Duffy, John Egan (14 Dara O'Shea), Cyrus Christie (61 Kevin Long), Matt Doherty, Daryl Horgan (61 Robbie Brady), Jeff Hendrick, Callum O'Dowda (61 James McClean), Alan Browne, Adam Idah (71 Ronan Curtis), Conor Hourihane (71 Jayson Molumby).   Manager: Stephen Kenny
**Goals**:  Harry Maguire (18), Jadon Sancho (31), Dominic Calvert-Lewin (56 pen)

1008.  15.11.2020    UEFA Nations League – Group A2
**BELGIUM v ENGLAND  2-0**  (2-0)
*King Power at Den Dreef, Leuven*
Referee:  Danny Makkelie (Netherlands)    Attendance: 0
**BELGIUM**:  Thibaut Courtois, Jan Vertonghen, Toby Alderweireld, Jason Denayer, Axel Witsel, Kevin De Bruyne, Thomas Meunier, Thorgan Hazard, Youri Tielemans, Dries Mertens (83 Dennis Praet), Romelu Lukaku.   Manager: ROBERTO MARTÍNEZ Montoliú
**ENGLAND**:  Jordan Pickford, Kyle Walker, Kieran Trippier (70 Jadon Sancho), Declan Rice, Tyrone Mings, Ben Chilwell (38 Bukayo Saka), Jordan Henderson (46 Harry Winks), Jack Grealish, Eric Dier, Mason Mount (69 Dominic Calvert-Lewin), Harry Kane.   Manager: Gareth Southgate
**Goals**:  Youri Tielemans (10), Dries Mertens (24)

1009.  18.11.2020   UEFA Nations League – Group A2
**ENGLAND v ICELAND  4-0**  (2-0)

*Wembley Stadium, London*

Referee:  Fábio José Costa Veríssimo (Portugal)
Attendance:  0

**ENGLAND**:  Jordan Pickford, Harry Maguire, Kyle Walker (64 Tyrone Mings), Kieran Trippier (85 Ainsley Maitland-Niles), Jack Grealish (76 Jadon Sancho), Eric Dier, Mason Mount (64 Harry Winks), Declan Rice, Phil Foden, Bukayo Saka, Harry Kane (76 Tammy Abraham).   Manager:  Gareth Southgate

**ICELAND**:  Ögmundur Kristinsson (46 Hannes Halldórsson), Birkir Sævarsson, Ari Skúlason, Kári Árnason, Sverrir Ingi Ingason, Hjörtur Hermannsson, Birkir Bjarnason (88 Ísak Bergmann Jóhannesson), Rúnar Sigurjónsson (62 Hólmar Eyjólfsson), Victor Pálsson, Albert Gudmundsson (73 Jón Dagur Thorsteinsson), Jón Bödvarsson (73' Kolbeinn Sigthórsson).   Manager:  Erik Hamrén

**Goals**:  Declan Rice (20), Mason Mount (24), Phil Foden (80, 84)

**Sent off**:  Birkir Sævarsson (54).